The Lincoln Record Society

VOLUME 27

THE

Registrum Antiquissimum

OF THE

Cathedral Church of Lincoln

Volume I

EDITED BY C. W. FOSTER

T0374700

1931

THE

PUBLICATIONS

OF THE

Lincoln Record Society

FOUNDED IN THE YEAR

1910

VOLUME 27

FOR THE YEAR ENDING 30TH SEPTEMBER, 1930

First published 1931
Unaltered reprint 2008

ISBN 9-780-90150-327-5

A Lincoln Record Society Publication
Published by The Boydell Press
an imprint of Boydell & Brewer Ltd
PO Box 9, Woodbridge, Suffolk IP12 3DF, UK
and of Boydell & Brewer Inc.
668 Mt Hope Avenue, Rochester, NY 14620, USA
web site: www.boydellandbrewer.com

A catalogue record for this book is available
from the British Library

THE

Registrum Antiquissimum

OF THE

Cathedral Church of Lincoln

Volume I

EDITED BY

C. W. FOSTER

CANON OF LINCOLN AND PREBENDARY OF LEICESTER SAINT MARGARET

PRINTED FOR

THE LINCOLN RECORD SOCIETY

BY

THE HEREFORD TIMES LIMITED, HEREFORD

1931

CATHEDRALIS ECCLESIE LINCOLNIENSIS
FIDELIBVS VNIVERSIS IOHANNES DE
SCHALBY CANONICVS EIVSDEM ECCLESIE
VITAM BONAM EXITVMQUE FELICEM.

Martilogivm Iohannis de Schalby.

PREFACE

The thanks of the Lincoln Record Society are due to the Dean and Chapter of Lincoln who have granted unlimited facilities of access to their archives, a privilege which may be emphasized, for, unhappily, in these days of increasing interest in historical research, students cannot always count on ready access to documents in ecclesiastical custody. Further, the Dean and Chapter have not only made a grant towards the cost of the present volume, but have also expressed the hope that they may be able to contribute to the expense of future volumes.

The Introduction explains the purpose and scope of this series of volumes, and makes acknowledgment of the debt which is owed by the present and future generations to those who in the past have laboured for the preservation of the archives of the church of Lincoln, amongst whom the most conspicuous are John of Schalby in the thirteenth and fourteenth, Bishop William Wake in the eighteenth, and Henry Bradshaw, Joseph Frederic Wickenden, and (Canon) Christopher Wordsworth in the nineteenth centuries. Of the scholars who, in 1925, when the plans were being laid for the present edition, wrote to express their appreciation of the importance of a critical edition of the Cathedral charters, five have already passed away, Professor Felix Liebermann, Sir Paul Vinogradoff, Dr J. H. Round, Dr T. F. Tout, and Mr J. P. Gilson : two are still living, Sir Henry Maxwell Lyte and Sir George F. Warner.

The present volume is the first-fruits of the work of indexing, dating, and copying the Cathedral charters extending over the last sixteen years, a task in which, for a short time, Mrs D. M. Stenton gave me valuable help. The original inspiration, however, was supplied in 1916 by her husband, Professor F. M. Stenton, on the occasion of an interview at Reading University College, which was the beginning of a delightful and inspiring friendship. It was he who taught me to appreciate the unique importance of the REGISTRUM ANTIQUISSIMUM and kindred documents at Lincoln for the history of the Danelaw, the part of England with regard to which he is the outstanding authority. Soon afterwards he paid me a visit in Lincolnshire, and it will be long before I shall forget his wonder and delight as I opened before his eyes box after box of the original charters. Each moment I expected to hear from his lips the famous ' Pro-di-gi-ous ' of the enthusiastic and simple-minded Dominie. According to the original plan, the volumes were to have been edited by Professor Stenton and myself, and an important part of his share of the work was to have been the writing of introductions to the several volumes. Soon, however, it became evident that it would be more convenient to have a comprehensive introduction in one of the later volumes ; and, further, that the great bulk of the work must necessarily be done by one who was living close to Lincoln. For these reasons Professor Stenton's name, at his express request, does not appear upon the title-page. He has, however, given me the most extensive and generous help in connection with the twelfth century royal charters, and more especially in regard to the English summaries which are printed at the head of the texts, and with the dating of the documents ; while he has with unfailing patience discussed many questions relating to the rest of the book. Moreover, to the first four texts he has contributed the important notes which are printed under his name. To these notes his direct responsibility is limited, though his scholarship has enriched the volume at innumerable points.

A distinguished German scholar, Dr Walther Holtzmann, until lately a lecturer in the University of Berlin, and now professor of modern history in the University of Halle, has placed me deeply in his debt by reading the proofs of the papal bulls and mandates. Out of his extensive knowledge of the mediæval papal chancery he has not only made many valuable suggestions, but has also supplied the notes which are printed under his name at the end of some of the bulls. Dr Holtzmann is now engaged in collecting the English material for a critical edition of the papal bulls and letters prior to the year 1198, which the Academy of Göttingen has had in hand since the year 1896.

Two classical scholars have read the proofs of the texts of the charters, and it may safely be assumed that the occasional breaches

ac regali auctoritate confirmo quieta ab omnibus consuetudinibus. Ad hec mat ecclie
Lincolieñ post genitorem meum huic honoris cumulum exaggero. uidelicet uo
lo ⁊ concedo sicut pat meus concessit. ut ipse mittat Remigiuj ⁊ constituat Abbatem
⁊ eccliam sce marie de Stou. tam ipse ⁊m successores sui ut pote in suo epali mane
rio. Quē uidelicet Abbatem ipse catholice elegit cum consilio Regis abbatisq; sue
dioceseos ⁊ monachoj ac cicoj suoj uel nõ ⁊ laicorum deum timentium. Mortuo
autē Abbate si in Abbatia idoneus aliquis reptri ualeat. consilio supdicto ab epo
eligat. constituat ⁊ ordinet. Sin autem. p abbatias suas epat uel p aliis alias
quesitum alium dignum in loco defuncti epc subroget. Ad usum u monachoj
concedo elemosinas qs Comes Leurie uxor ei Godeua dederunt ecclie de Stou.
uidelicet Newercham. Flatburch. Welleu apentac. excepto denario tcio coni
rat. Insup concedo sicut pat meus concessit Eglesham cum appendiciis suis ui
delicet auilettuna. Rollenduñ. ⁊ tretuna. Sufort. Et ecclia sce Abbe cum iacente
ei tetrula. ⁊ duob molendinis in Grineoort cum omnib consuetudinibz.
His aliisq; elemosinis Abbatia ut epali manerio constructa ⁊ dno ep̄o
phenniu maneat. Has au elemosinas omes concedo regali dono. tam eccleii
arum ⁊m tratum sub ordinatione ⁊ dispositione Remigii epi cui induentu
spicta mr ecclia cepit fundari ut ipe disponat ⁊ diuidat sicut s usui fu
erit ino matrem ecclesiam suamq; Abbatiam. Inqua uidelicet mre ecclia
canonici deo seruientes caste ⁊ catholice uiuant nulla q; inr eos pbenda
ematur uel uendat depulsa omni heresi symoniaca. Siquis au qd absit a
lir uoluerit uiuere. ⁊ canonicis peptis obedire noluerit fraterno amore pri
ma ⁊ secunda uice usq; ad ɜtiam a Decano ⁊ fratbz ceteris corrigatur. Si autē
adhuc rebellis ymanserit. ad noticiam epi puemat. Qui epo una cum
Decano ⁊ fratbz ceteris adiuncto ⁊ honum medicaminibz fratrem infir
mum sanare ⁊ corrige studeat. S uero ipe talir castigari noluerit. ⁊ p
po reatu pertinacis indulgere uoluerit omnibus reb; ecclie uacuus ut
accessit foras mittat. ⁊ alt moz sciente unto dignul ablbz; omi uiu
nere ut dictum est locum ⁊ tram occupantis optineat. His omnibus in
ɜmutabilir ita dispositis uero regali auctoritate phibeo. ut quislib;
euisq; ordinis sacratissimis locis supdictis uiolentiam aliqm faciat. uel de
reb; earunde aliquid minuat. Ch si ipe uel aliquis alius in futuru suadente
diabolo hoc uetitum facere temptauerit. depmat ⁊ compescat ei nequitiā
Rex qui tunc temporis inhac patriaqib; regnum ⁊ glam optinere ualeat in
secula seculoz Amen.

✠ Signu regis Willi.
✠ Signu dorobnensis Archiepi.
✠ S. Walchelini epi Winton.
✠ S. Mauricii epi Lundonie.
✠ S. Gundulfi epi rofensis.

✠ S. Osmundi epi saribetie.
✠ S. Roberti epi cestrensis.
✠ S. wlstani epi wigrecestre.
✠ S. hereberti epi thetfordensis.
✠ S. Radulfi epi cicestrensis.

of the rules of grammar that occur are not due to oversight in editing, but to lapses on the part of the original scribes, and not least of the scribes of the papal chancery. In this way Mr William Gilchrist Wilson, late vice-principal of King William's College in the Isle of Man, read the first half of the volume, and after his death, in 1930, Canon J. E. Standen read the remainder of the proofs. Mr Wilson's life was devoted to diligent and self-forgetful work for the successive generations of boys who came under his charge, many of whom, now in early or later manhood, acknowledge not only the benefit of his fine scholarship, but still more the permanence of his influence in the training of character.

There are others whose help I wish to acknowledge. Lord Monson has allowed access to the important manuscript collections of John Ross at Burton Hall relating to the history of the city and county of Lincoln. Mr J. W. F. Hill, of Lincoln, has supplied evidence about the topography of Lincoln, and especially about the long-forgotten district of Thorngate which is dealt with in Appendix II. For questions relating to ecclesiastical administration I have been able occasionally to turn to Professor A. Hamilton Thompson. The authorities of the British Museum kindly allowed a large number of the Cathedral charters to be deposited there, in order that they might be photographed for reproduction as illustrations by the Oxford University Press. The care which the " Hereford Times " Company and its readers have bestowed upon the proofs has materially lightened my labours. Mr R. Ingamells, of Timberland, has made the drawings for the various line blocks, including the facsimiles of the early Arabic numerals. Miss F. E. Thurlby, my secretary, has given me valuable assistance in innumerable matters of detail, and especially in making the index and correcting the proofs.

C. W. FOSTER

TIMBERLAND, LINCOLN,
3rd June, 1931

CONTENTS

DOCUMENTS

I. ROYAL

II. PAPAL

(vii)

ILLUSTRATIONS

ABBREVIATIONS AND NOTES

Abs.	Abstract.
Cl.	Clerk.
Con.	The continuator of the original scribe of the Registrum Antiquissimum (see below, p. xxvi)
Marg.	Margin.
O.	The original scribe of the Registrum Antiquissium (see below, pp. xxiv ff.).
Om.	Omit, omits.
Pd.	Printed.
Preb.	Prebend, prebendary.
Q	Quis, the redactor of the Registrum Antiquissimum (see below, pp. xxviii ff.).
Q2.	The redactor's scribes (see below, p. xxxiv n).
Rubric	A rubricated title in the Registrum Antiquissimum.
Texts	Under this head are specified the several MS texts used for each charter in this edition, the text from which a charter is printed having the first place assigned to it.
Var. R.	Various reading (or readings).
* † ‡	One or other of these signs is used to indicate the beginning of a new page of the Registrum Antiquissimum, when it comes in the middle of a charter.
Witn.	Witness.
2 ♃ φ	For these and other signs which occur under marginalia, see below, p. xxxviii.
1, 2, 3, etc.	Indicate the numbers of the charters in the Registrum Antiquissimum (see below, p. xiv).

MANUSCRIPTS

A. – – – – –	Registrum Antiquissimum (see below, p. xiii ff.).
Add. Chart. – – – –	Additional Charter (see below, p. xiv).
Add. (Extran.) Chart. – –	Additional (Extraneous) Charter (see below, p. xiv).
Bl. Bk. – – – –	Liber Niger or Black Book of the church of Lincoln, ed. by Henry Bradshaw, in *Lincoln Cathedral Statutes*, vol. i.
C. – – – – –	Cotton Cartulary (below, pp. xl, xli).
Ch. Roll – – –	Charter Roll (in Public Record Office).
D. – – – – –	Carte Decani (see below, p. xlii).
D. and C. – – – –	Muniments of the dean and chapter of Lincoln.
I. – – – – –	*Inspeximus.* For the several charters of *Inspeximus*, i–x, see below, pp. lvi–lxii.
Martilogium – – –	Liber Johannis de Schalby sive Martilogium (see below, pp. xxxi–iii).
Orig. – – – – –	Original charter in the muniment room of the dean and chapter of Lincoln.
P. – – – – –	Registrum Præantiquissimum (see below, pp. xxxix, xl).
R. – – – – –	Registrum (see below, pp. xli, xlii).
R.A., Reg. Ant. – – –	Registrum Antiquissimum.
S. – – – – –	Registrum Superantiquissimum (see below, p. xxxix).

PRINTED BOOKS

Berger – – – –	Berger, Élie, *Les Régistres d' Innocent IV*. Paris, 1897.
C.C.R. – – – –	*Calendar of the Charter Rolls* (Rolls Series).
Cal. Inq. – – –	*Calendar of Inquisitions post mortem* (Rolls Series).
Cal. Close Rolls – –	*Calendar of the Close Rolls* (Rolls Series).

Cal. Pat. Rolls – – –	*Calendar of the Patent Rolls* (Rolls Series).
D.B. – – – –	*Domesday Book* (Record Commission).
Delisle – – –	L. Delisle in Bibliothèque de L'Ecole des Chartres, vol. lxix.
E.H.R. – – – –	*The English Historical Review.*
Eyton – – – –	Eyton, R. W., *Court, Household, and Itinerary of King Henry II.* London and Dorchester, 1878.
Farrer, *Itin.* – – –	Farrer, W., *An Outline Itinerary of King Henry the First.* Oxford.
Giraldus Cambrensis –	*Giraldi Cambrensis Opera,* vol. vii, ed. by J. F. Dimock (Rolls Series).
Jaffé-Löwenfeld – –	Jaffé, Phillip, *Regesta Pontificum Romanorum,* 2nd ed. corr. ausp. G. Wattenbach curav. S. Löwenfeld, F. Kalterbrunner, P. Ewald, 1885–8.
L.R.S. – – – –	The Publications of the Lincoln Record Society.
Linc. Cath. Statutes –	*Statutes of Lincoln Cathedral,* ed. H. Bradshaw and Chr. Wordsworth. Cambridge, 1892–7.
The Lincolnshire Domesday –	*The Lincolnshire Domesday and the Lindsey Survey,* ed. C. W. Foster and T. Longley (Lincoln Record Society, vol. xix).
Mansi – – – –	Mansi, J. D., *Sacrorum Conciliorum nova et amplissima collectio.*
Migne – – –	Migne, J. P., *Patrologiæ cursus completus.* Paris, 1844–64.
Mon. – – – –	*Monasticon Anglicanum,* ed. Caley, Ellis, and Bandinel. London, 1817–30.
Potthast – – –	*Regesta pontificum Romanorum.*
Red Book – – –	*The Red Book of the Exchequer* (Rolls Series).
Regesta – – –	Davis, H. W. C., *Regesta Regum Anglo-Normannorum.* Oxford, 1913.
Wilkins – – –	Wilkins, David, *Concilia Magnæ Britanniæ et Hiberniæ.* London, 1737.

NOTES

The text of these volumes attempts to reproduce the documents letter for letter, with all marks of accentuation. Endorsements of original charters earlier than the seventeenth century have been printed, and also the marginalia of the cartularies. The abbreviated Latin forms have been extended, and where there might be any doubt in regard to the form intended italics have been used. The compendium which frequently occurs at the end of a name has been retained unless it has seemed likely that an extension was contemplated, and for such extensions italics have been used. Since the use of capitals in medieval texts is arbitrary, the modern use has been adopted, a course which may serve as a guide to the sense, and also help the student more readily to catch sight of names. The punctuation of the documents, though sometimes capricious, has been adhered to. Since print can never be a perfect substitute for an original document, facsimiles of thirty-four of the most important original charters are provided in this volume, and some facsimiles will be supplied in the volumes which are to follow.

The historical year, beginning 1st January, is used throughout this edition, except that in the texts of documents the original has been adhered to.

ADDENDUM

Page 3, before the second paragraph from the foot—insert

The facsimile opposite shews that the strip at the foot of the charter has been torn off while the ribband below it remains. At least as early as the thirteenth century, a membrane of the same shape, probably intended as a protection to the original, was attached to the charter. Some of the stitches by which it is attached are reproduced very faintly at the right hand end of the facsimile. The size of the document is $9\frac{5}{8}$ in. × $2\frac{5}{8}$ in.

INTRODUCTION

I

The REGISTRUM ANTIQUISSIMUM, which has supplied the title, as it has also furnished the framework, of the present series of volumes, is the earliest complete cartulary of the Cathedral Church of Saint Mary of Lincoln. It was written, apart from later additions, in the third decade of the thirteenth century, with ink which in the course of seven centuries has lost scarcely any of its original blackness. That its writer worked with meticulous care is proved by a collation of his work with the original texts, many of which are still preserved in the muniment room of the dean and chapter. He did not modernize the spelling of names, as the writer of the fourteenth century Registrum sometimes chose to do ; nor did he omit the witnesses. He copied with literal accuracy. As a consequence, his texts may be relied upon in the many instances where the original charters have been injured or lost.

The present work is intended to supply a critical edition of the texts of the charters, whether they be original documents or copies registered in cartularies in the muniment room of the dean and chapter, with a few texts from extraneous sources. The period proposed to be covered extends from the year 1061, the date of the only pre-Conquest document[1], to the death of bishop Hugh of Wells in 1235. It has, however, been found convenient, and indeed necessary, to print many documents which are later in date ; for this edition will include the whole of the REGISTRUM ANTIQUISSIMUM which contains additional matter of the thirteenth and three following centuries. Moreover, when dealing with documents which are not included in the cartulary, it has seemed desirable to avoid an arbitrary break at the year 1235 in a series of charters. The statement that the REGISTRUM ANTIQUISSIMUM has supplied the plan or framework for these volumes means

[1] Below, no. 247.

that the cartulary is printed consecutively, while charters which are not included in it are interpolated in the appropriate places. Each charter from the REGISTRUM ANTIQUISSIMUM is distinguished by having its serial number in the cartulary printed in Old English type in the middle of the page. The interpolated charters are marked by the words ADD. CHART. (Additional Charter), or, if they come from a source outside the muniment room of the dean and chapter, by the words ADD. (EXTRAN.) CHART. (Additional Extraneous Charter), printed in the middle of the page. The several sources will be described below, but here it may be explained that, if there is an original text, the document is printed from that text ; and that if there is no original document, the text of the REGISTRUM ANTIQUISSIMUM is preferred to any other. To the text which is printed in each instance is assigned the first place under the head of ' Texts ' ; and various readings in the other texts are given under the head of ' Var. R.'

The order of the REGISTRUM ANTIQUISSIMUM has been varied in two instances : (1) the charters of king Stephen have been printed in their proper place,[1] after those of Henry I, instead of being placed, as they are in the cartulary, after the charters of king John ; and (2) the papal bulls, and the episcopal grants of jurisdiction to the chapter, have been printed immediately after the royal charters.[2] As will appear below, when a new edition of the REGISTRUM ANTIQUISSIMUM was projected in the thirteenth century, directions were given that the bulls should come at the beginning of the new cartulary.

In the English note which precedes each document it has not been found convenient to aim at an over-strict uniformity. While most of the charters admit of a short summary of their contents, some, on account of their greater importance or difficulty, demand fuller treatment, and others, like the Forest Charter or the longer papal bulls, do not admit of any summary at all. In these English notes the names of places are given in their modern form and, where necessary, persons bearing the same name are distinguished, as for instance, bishop Robert I and

[1] Below, pages 48–64.
[2] Below, pages 186–265.

bishop Robert II, or the several Rannulfs who held the earldom of Chester. The nearest assignable date also has been added when a document is undated; and the historical year, or new style, has been adopted.

The documents include charters of the possessions not only of the common of the canons, and of the prebends, but also of the see of Lincoln; for the earliest gifts were made to the bishop or to the bishop and church of Lincoln, and the apportionment of the estates amongst the bishop, the dignitaries, the prebendaries, and the common fund was effected gradually during a considerable period. These possessions lay dispersed throughout the diocese of Lincoln which, as constituted by William the Conqueror, stretched, until the middle of the sixteenth century, from the Humber to the Thames. It comprised the counties of Lincoln, Leicester, Northampton, Rutland, Huntingdon, part of Hertford, Bedford, Buckingham, and Oxford. Cambridgeshire also was included until the foundation, in 1108, of the see of Ely, to which allusion is made in a bull of pope Innocent II.[1] The ancient diocese (and kingdom) of Lindsey, which comprised the northern and eastern parts of Lincolnshire was, in the eleventh century, claimed as their right by the archbishops of York, but the dispute was settled, by William Rufus, about 1093, in favour of the bishop of Lincoln.[2] Rutland did not become a fiscally independent shire until the twelfth century, and the fact that it is mentioned, seemingly as a county, in 1123–1133 is noteworthy.[3] Outside the diocese, the charters relate to land in London and in the counties of Berks, Derby, Hants, Kent, Nottingham, Surrey, and York. But it is for the history of the Northern Danelaw that the Lincoln charters are of first-rate importance. By far the greater number of them record grants of land in the county and city of Lincoln, while a majority of the rest relate to the counties of Nottingham, Derby, Leicester, and Rutland. These five shires, lying between the Welland and the Yorkshire border, formed the ancient territory of the Five Boroughs. In addition to the royal charters, the documents record the gifts of manors and churches by feudal

[1] Below, page 191.
[2] Below, no. 4.
[3] Below, no. 69.

magnates like the earls of Chester, Lincoln, Northampton, and Leicester ; and by powerful mesne tenants, like the Condets, the Amundavills, and the Kymes. But of even greater interest is the great stream of smaller gifts that flowed from the free peasants of Lincolnshire—the grants, for instance, ranging from one acre to nine acres of arable land, by Basing son of Osgot of Somercotes, Roger and Hugh the sons of Wigot son of Asger of Skidbrooke, Ketel Dumping of Saltfleetby, and Godric son of Alnad of Skidbrooke.[1] Sometimes it is stated that these gifts of land were placed upon the altar of Saint Mary.[2] These men's names proclaim their native descent, and in them may be seen the descendants of the rank and file of the Danish army which, in the second half of the ninth century, apportioned the county of Lincoln amongst its members. The native names persist, perhaps more especially in the city of Lincoln, until the fourteenth century ; but in the last quarter of the twelfth century it had become the fashion for a man who himself bore a native name to bestow Norman names upon his children.

The charters illustrate the history of an English secular cathedral church in respect of its organization and personnel, its endowments and its franchises ; and it may be noted that the present work seems to be the first attempt to provide a complete and critical edition of the texts of such a foundation.

The writ by which William the Conqueror transferred the see from Dorchester to Lincoln is still preserved in the cathedral[3] ; but the solemn charter of 1090 of William Rufus bestowing upon bishop Remigius authority to order and dispose of the churches and lands which had been given for the endowment of the see cannot be genuine in its present form, though it is probably founded on authentic documents.[4] The constitution which Remigius framed for his church, which was nearly identical with those of the churches of York and Salisbury, was derived from the cathedral of Bayeux, and the chapters of these three churches were established at about the same time.

[1] Reg. Ant., nos. 477, 505, 548, 549, 553.
[2] Ibid. nos. 242, 477.
[3] Below, no. 2.
[4] Below, no. 3.

The chapter of York is always said to have been established in 1090 by archbishop Thomas, who had been treasurer of Bayeux. Salisbury was certainly established by its bishop, Saint Osmund, for we have the text of the charter which he granted and the king confirmed, at Hastings, in 1091, and which was attested by the *signa* of, amongst others, archbishop Thomas of York and bishop Remigius.[1] The above-mentioned charter of William Rufus in favour of Remigius is attested by the *signum Dorobernensis archiepiscopi* and the *signum* of Osmund of Salisbury. *Dorobernensis* should indicate Canterbury, but at that time that see was vacant. Can it be that *Dorobernensis* is a mistake for *Eboracensis*, due to a misreading of the document on which the Lincoln text is based ?

The constitution which Remigius bestowed upon his church consisted of a chapter of secular canons with a dean as their permanent head.[2] A document which came to be incorporated in the charter of William Rufus provided that the canons should live *caste et catholice*, and that there should be no traffic among them in the buying and selling of prebends.[3] The chief members of the chapter, as at York and Salisbury, were the four principal personages, that is, the dean, precentor, chancellor, and treasurer, with the subdean and seven archdeacons. Some fifty years later an additional archdeacon had been provided for Stow. There were originally twenty-one canons ; but their number was increased to forty-two by bishop Bloet, and bishop Alexander added some more (*prebendas aliquot adiecit*), either two or four, as it is supposed.[4] Each canon was under obligation to say daily the psalms assigned to his stall, so that the whole psalter might be recited daily by the chapter on behalf of benefactors living and dead.[5] This fundamental customary duty of reciting the psalter has been observed from the beginning to the present day.

[1] *Regesta*, no. 319 ; *Mon.*viii, 1294–5.

[2] See Mr H. Bradshaw's account of the chapter in *Linc. Cath. Statutes* i, 30ff., edited, after his death, by Canon Christopher Wordsworth.

[3] Below, no. 3, the last part.

[4] Martilogium, ff. 1d, 2. *Giraldus Cambrensis* vii, 32, 195, 197.

[5] For the assignment of psalms when a new prebend was formed in 1290, see below, no. 278.

A series of episcopal grants shews how, in the middle of the twelfth century, the canons obtained almost complete immunity from episcopal and, its corollary, archidiaconal, control, not only in their church and chapter-house, but also in the lands and churches of the common and of the prebends.[1] The papal bulls tell the same story. From 1061 to 1163, with one exception in 1146,[2] the bulls are addressed to the bishop, and are confirmations of gifts of property.[3] After that date, they are almost always addressed to the canons or to the dean and chapter, and are mainly concerned with their rights and liberties.[4] So great, indeed, was the degree of independence which the canons obtained that in the early part of the thirteenth century the very right of the bishop to visit the chapter was disputed. By a papal sentence, however, it was established in 1245 that the bishop of Lincoln was to be admitted to visit and, failing correction by the chapter, to correct the dean and chapter, the inferior ministers of the church, and also the vicars, chaplains, and parishioners of the churches of the prebends and of the common ; but that the canons should render canonical obedience to the bishop, but should not be bound by oath thereto.[5] Thus the bishop of Lincoln had secured to him a position as *principale caput* of the chapter, and a pre-eminence that is more firmly established than that of the bishop at Salisbury and some other cathedral churches.[6]

The grant of jurisdiction was preceded by a gradual apportionment and division of the possessions of the church between the bishop and the canons. The portion which fell to the canons, consisting of manors, churches, lands, and other emoluments, was gradually divided into separate estates, to which new benefactions were sometimes made. Part was retained to be held by the chapter in common for the purpose of providing for the maintenance of the canons who resided and for the other expenses of the church. This was known as the ' common,' *communa, communia*, or *communio*. Another part provided

---

[1] Below, nos. 287–305. See especially, pages 250-1.
[2] Below, no. 252.
[3] Below, nos. 247–51, 254.
[4] Below, nos. 255–7, 260–1, 263, 266, 275–6.
[5] Below, no. 273.
[6] Below, p. 251.

separate incomes for the deanery and other dignities. The incomes of the archdeacons were derived mainly from the profits of their jurisdictions. The rest was divided up into separate prebendal estates, each prebend furnishing an income for a particular stall in the church. The prebend (*praebenda*) was the provender of a canon. Thus a canon of the church of Lincoln was also the prebendary of the prebend which provided his income. And it is important to remember that a dignity or a canonry bestowed no right to sit and vote in the chapter unless it was accompanied by the possession of a prebend.[1] A notification by the dean and chapter, *circa* 1150, states that bishop Robert Chesney, with their counsel and assent, had joined the prebend of the church of Langford to the archdeaconry of Oxford, so that every archdeacon of Oxford thenceforth might out of (*ex*) the same prebend be a canon of the church of Lincoln.[2] A bull of pope Eugenius III, addressed to the canons, in 1146, omits the possessions of the bishop, and distinguishes between the property of the prebends and that of the common.[3]

Many of the canons never resided at Lincoln. They might be king's clerks deeply engaged in public affairs, or foreigners who had been provided by the pope, and never perhaps set foot in England. Not only did these canons receive no share of the common, but they were required, in default of residing during a minimum period of four months in the year, to contribute a seventh part of the revenues of their prebends to the common for the support of the residentiaries. These payments were known as septisms.[4] The absent prebendaries were also required to provide vicars to serve in their place in the cathedral.[5] The number of canons who resided was small. About 1320–1330, the average number, including dignitaries, who performed the great residence (*fecerunt residenciam magnam*) was about thirteen.[6] In bishop Sutton's time the daily commons of the canons, which had been eightpence, was increased to twelvepence.[7]

[1] *Linc. Cath. Statutes* i, 32.
[2] D. and C., Dij/73/2/14.
[3] Below, no. 252, ll. 87–9. Cp. no. 255, ll. 117–18.
[4] Below, nos. 263–6.
[5] Below, no. 300.
[6] Audit of Accounts, D. and C., Bj/2/5, *passim*.
[7] Martilogium, f. 7.

These grants of separate jurisdictions and the division and appropriation of estates loosened the constant and intimate association of the bishop with his cathedral. The movement seems to have begun at Sens in 822, whence it spread to other churches. In England, the practice began, under Norman influence, soon after the Conquest, as at Salisbury under Saint Osmund.[1] At Lincoln, it was necessarily later; for the building of the cathedral was not finished until nearly the end of the eleventh century; endowments had to be accumulated, and the organization of the church completed. The reason given for the change is that the bishops, owing to their position of feudal magnates, with the obligation of giving counsel and military service, and discharging other feudal incidents, were often left without sufficient resources for the maintenance of their cathedrals.[2] The remedy adopted was the assignment of a large portion of the possessions to the chapters. Moreover, the bishop's frequent absences from his cathedral city rendered impossible the constant supervision which the services of a great church demanded.

This separation of functions and properties involved the establishing of separate registries. Hitherto, it would seem, the registry of the cathedral had served both the bishop and the canons. There is no conclusive evidence of the institution of a separate episcopal registry in the second half of the twelfth century, but it is inconceivable that no official record, however incomplete, was kept of the acts of such a bishop as Robert Chesney, and of the numerous charters which he granted and the frequent papal commissions which he received. It is not until the second decade of the thirteenth century, early in the episcopate of bishop Hugh of Wells, that the extant episcopal archives at Lincoln begin with rolls which are earlier than those of any other English diocese. Perhaps no systematic record was kept anywhere in the twelfth century. Even the extant papal registers are not a complete record, and some of the documents printed here are not to be found in them.

Only three of the bulls at Lincoln have hitherto been

[1] *The Cambridge Medieval History* vi, 540–9.

[2] *Ibid.*, pp. 540, 545, 549.

printed[1], and the value of these documents seems scarcely to have been appreciated. The earlier bulls, being precisely dated, help to determine the dates of some of the royal and private charters. They sometimes confirm a statement which, but for them, might rest on the authority of a single text. At times they establish the identification of a place that otherwise might remain unknown. Thus, four of the bulls jointly prove that Willingthorpe, a suburb of Lincoln, which has been only once met with elsewhere, is to be identified with the bishop's manor of Westgate, and with the little manor which bishop Remigius held in 1086.[2] Moreover, the bulls record gifts which otherwise might be unknown, or indicate the origin of grants of which mention is made only at a later date. Now and then, they make a significant addition to the evidence afforded by a royal or private grant. For instance, while Henry I grants to bishop Alexander licence to assign the third part of the service of the knights of the bishopric of Lincoln to the bishop's castle at Newark, in order that thenceforth they may perform castle-guard there,[3] a papal bull adds that it was at Lincoln castle that the bishop's predecessors had been wont to perform this service.[4] The notes on the papal documents contributed by Dr W. Holtzmann, of whose kindness and learning acknowledgment has been made in the Preface, are of special value. Amongst other things, he establishes the genuineness of the pre-Conquest bull of pope Nicholas II,[5] which, as he points out, supplies valuable evidence in regard to the ecclesiastical politics of Edward the Confessor. Out of his wide knowledge of papal history and archives, he is able to furnish information about papal chancellors, vice-chancellors, and cardinals, and with regard to itineraries of popes. Specially valuable are his notes upon the mandate of pope Innocent II,[6] commanding the legate, Henry bishop of Winchester, and archbishop Theobald and his suffragans to confirm bishop Alexander's sentence of excommunication against Robert earl of Leicester, who was withholding from the bishop his castle of Newark. In the struggle between king Stephen

[1] Below, nos. 248, 249, 273
[2] Below, nos. 248, 249, 250, 254. See especially pages 189–90.
[3] Below, no. 51.
[4] Below, no. 249, ll. 62–7, and pages 267–8.
[5] Below, no. 247.
[6] Below, no. 283.

and the bishops, it will be remembered, Alexander had been starved before the gate of the castle until it was surrendered by his men. The leaf of the cartulary on which the mandate is written has been very badly injured, but just enough remains to indicate the purport of the document, and to enable Dr Holtzmann with some confidence to reconstruct the injured text.

The church of Lincoln has the distinction of possessing an original copy of the Charter of Liberties granted by king John, at Runnymede, in 1215, commonly called Magna Carta.[1] This copy was chosen, in 1819, by the Public Records Commissioners for reproduction in facsimile and modern type ' because it was the handsomest extant of the four original copies.'[2] For this reason the charter has not been reprinted here. A registered copy of Henry III's reissue of Magna Carta in 1225,[3] of which the original is no longer extant at Lincoln, is however printed since only two copies remain, and the Lincoln text has a fair number of various readings. Of greater importance is an original copy of the first Forest Charter, in 1217, which, although it has not escaped injury, is more complete than the only other original copy that is known, namely, the one in Durham cathedral.[4] A facsimile of the Lincoln text will be found facing page 145. The reissue of the Forest Charter, in 1225, is also printed[5] since, of the three existing original texts, the Lincoln copy, although it has lost twenty-one words through injury to the foot, is more complete than the Durham cathedral text, though it is less perfect than the copy in the British Museum.

Two matters of interest, which involved a large amount of research, grew beyond the limits of a note, and have been embodied in appendixes. Appendix I[6] is concerned with the episcopal houses of residence at Lincoln. The wall of the king's *castellum* in which bishop Bloet obtained leave to make a gate in order that he might have a way out towards his house, is shewn to be, probably, the west wall of the castle near the Roman West gate of the city, and the new gate which the bishop made to be the still

[1] Below, no. 210.
[2] Below, page 137.
[3] Below, no. 221.
[4] Below, no. 219.
[5] Below, no. 220.
[6] Below, pages 267–76.

existing sallyport. The documents relating to the site and building of the Old Palace are then discussed, and the boundaries described in the charters are proved to correspond with the lines of the modern map. Appendix II[1] explains how Alice de Condet's mysterious castle of Thorngate, which king Stephen granted in pledge to bishop Alexander, proves to be a private castle in a forgotten suburb just outside the walls of the later Roman city of Lincoln. To this is added an account of the Condets who, though little known, were people of considerable importance.

Of the texts which are printed in the present volume the majority have previously appeared in print, though sometimes in an incomplete form—in Dugdale's *Monasticon*, the *Calendars of Charter Rolls, The English Historical Review, Lincoln Cathedral Statutes*, and elsewhere ; but it will be found convenient to have them collected together and indexed with a collation of the different texts. The documents however, which are now printed for the first time, are neither few nor unimportant. They include thirteen charters of king Stephen, and many papal documents. The remaining volumes of the series will consist of texts which, with comparatively few exceptions, have never been printed before.

Mr Bradshaw remarked that ' few Muniment-Rooms can boast of such an immense store of precious materials as Lincoln.'[2] The number of pre-Reformation original charters is about 4,200 ; in addition to which it is estimated that there are in cartularies 3,626 charters of which the original texts have disappeared :

Original charters	4,200
Charters of which the original texts are lost :	
In the Registrum Antiquissimum	680
In the Registrum (excluding the charters in the Reg. Ant.)	540
In Carte Decani[3]	250
In Liber de Ordinationibus Cantariarum[3] ...	960
In Chantries of John de Welburne and Henry duke of Lancaster[3]	300
In the Choristers' Cartulary[3]	36
In the Kniveton Leiger[3]	520
In the Cartulary of the Vicars Choral[3]	340
	7,826

[1] Below, pages 277–95.
[2] *Linc. Cath. Statutes* i, 85.
[3] Charters which are duplicated elsewhere are not included. All the numbers are approximate.

A majority of these documents is not later than the fourteenth century. In view of this wealth of materials, it has been decided to dispense with an elaborate apparatus of historical notes, such as would not only delay unduly the completion of the work, but would also increase its cost beyond the resources of the Lincoln Record Society. At the same time, the rule has not been adhered to pedantically where there are obscurities to be explained, questions of genuineness to be discussed, or identifications to be justified. Thus it has been possible to add to the value of this volume by including the notes of Professor F. M. Stenton on the first four charters, and of Dr W. Holtzmann on some of the papal bulls.

II

THE REGISTRUM ANTIQUISSIMUM

The Original Scribe and the Continuator

The REGISTRUM ANTIQUISSIMUM[1] is a volume of 250 vellum leaves, measuring 12½ inches in height, 8½ inches in breadth, and 2½ inches in thickness. An inscription written on a piece of paper which is fastened by wafers to the inside of the front cover, in the handwriting of Dr William Wake, bishop of Lincoln from 1705 to 1715, records that, whether by accident or guile, the book had been taken away from the church of Lincoln, and had been found and restored by the bishop himself :

REGISTRUM SEDIS LINCOLNIENSIS,

OMNIUM ANTIQUISSIMUM

FORTE ET UTILISSIMUM,

AB ECCLESIÂ ILLÂ SEU CASU SEU FRAUDE ABREPTUM,

COMPARAVIT, RESTITUIT

GUL :[2] EPISC : LINCOLN'

A.D : 1712.

When, however, Wake was translated to Canterbury, in 1716, it is evident that he took the volume with him ; for, after his death in 1737, it was found at Oxford amongst the manuscripts which he had bequeathed to Christ Church. In 1764, as appears from another note, similarly attached to the cover, the dean and canons of

[1] D. and C., A1/5.

[2] A modern hand has here inserted '[Wake]'.

that college, following the intention expressed by the bishop in the 'memorial note' printed above, returned the volume to the church of Lincoln :

HUNC LIBRUM INTER EOS MSS REPERTUM,
QUOS VIR REVERENDISS. EDI CHRISTI LEGAVIT,
LUBENTER ET ÆQUE,
QUOD ET TESTATOREM VOLUISSE
EX NOTA IPSIUS MEMORIALI COMPARET,
ECCLES : LINCOLN :
REDDIDERUNT DECANUS ET CANONICI
A.D 1764.

Since that time the REGISTRUM ANTIQUISSIMUM has remained in the muniment room as one of the most cherished possessions of the dean and chapter. To Wake is probably to be ascribed the numbering of the leaves of the book from 1 to 250, and the numbering, though not without some mistakes, of the documents which it contains from 1 to 1,073. The latter series of numerals is represented in the present edition by figures printed in Old English type.

The Table of Contents which is printed at the end of this Introduction shews that the REGISTRUM ANTIQUISSI-MUM is a composite volume, and indicates the dates of the several hands that wrote it. The date of the original scribe may be placed about 1225. The late Mr Henry Bradshaw, whose eminence as an authority on medieval handwriting it is unnecessary to emphasise, was inclined to place the date about 1216[1] ; but it would seem that some of the documents, though it is not possible to fix their exact year, must be dated about 1220 ; and two documents can be definitely assigned to the year 1219, and one to the year 1222.[2] As Mr Bradshaw remarks more than once, when giving his opinion about the dates of the Lincoln manuscripts, 'of course a closer examination would settle the point more accurately.'[3] The scribe was better at copying than at method, for he places the charters of Henry II immediately after those of Henry I, while those of Stephen have to be brought in after the texts of Richard and John. Moreover, after the charters of Henry II concerning the prebend of Asgarby, five

---

[1] *Linc. Cath. Statutes* i, 111.
[2] Reg. Ant., nos. 722, 724, 281.
[3] e.g. *Linc. Cath. Statutes* i, 9, 120.

charters of earls about the same prebend are drawn in, as it were, by attraction,[1] instead of being transcribed amongst the charters of the magnates on a later folio.

There are several indications that the original scribe never completed his work. Perhaps death intervened, for he seems to have stopped abruptly, leaving pages in several places seemingly unfinished. The last two charters of Henry II[2] and the last text of Stephen[3] have been supplied by a continuator whose date is probably about 1225–1235. The last of the charters of John also has been added by another hand. Had the original scribe not been interrupted, it seems unlikely that he would have omitted the copy of the Great Charter which had been received at Lincoln only a few years before, and some at least of the other texts of king John which are printed below; nor would he have been likely to ignore the Forest Charter issued in the second year of Henry III's reign. The charters of the West Riding of Lincolnshire and of the wapentakes of Wraggoe, Calcewath, and Candleshoe are left to be completed by other hands, and those of the wapentakes of Yarborough and Bradley are omitted altogether. For the Holland division of Lincolnshire there is but one charter, written in the middle of a page; and the texts of the Kesteven division and of the city of Lincoln have been finished by the continuator. At folio 182, the papal bulls come to a sudden stop in the middle of the series[4]; and the important series of charters concerning the jurisdiction of the chapter are not included.[5]

Something has been said already about the accuracy of the original scribe's work.[6] He followed a good tradition, for the fragments of the older cartularies which are described below set a very high standard of accuracy and completeness. To enable the reader to judge with what confidence he may depend on those of the scribe's texts for which the original charters no longer exist, a table is subjoined shewing the differences between the first fifteen original charters and the corresponding texts

[1] Below, nos. 129–133.
[2] Reg. Ant., nos. 153–4.
[3] *Ibid.*, no. 195.
[4] Below, page 230.
[5] Below, nos. 287–305.
[6] Above, page xiii.

in the cartulary. It may be added that where the original texts are now lost, the several royal charters of *inspeximus* supply a further proof of the accuracy of the cartulary.

		Original Charters	*Reg. Ant.*
No.	2, l. 3—	episcopatus	episcopatus Remigii
	l. 10—	Slaffordam	Slaffordiam
	l. 15—	exortatione	exhortatione
	l. 20—	Lestoniensem	Lectoniensem
			(*altered from* Lestoniensem)
	l. 21—	Buchingehamnensem	Buchingehanmensem[1]
		Eilesbiriensem	Eliesbiriensem
	l. 2 from foot—	pertualiter	perpetualiter
No.	42, ll. 5, 6—	Welingeham	Wellingeham
No.	52—nil		
No.	53, l. 2—	*omit*	baronibus
	l. 9—	tol	toll
		infangeneteof	Iinfangetheof
	l. 12—	obtinend'	optinend'
	l. 13—	umquam	unquam
	ll. 4, 17—	Alixandro	Alexandro
	l. 4 from foot —	Buh'	Buch'
	l. 2 from foot—	*omit*	Centesimo
No.	76, ll. 1, 2—	*omit*	comitibus
	last l.—	Oxen'	Oxeneford'
No.	77, l. 5—	Grenesbi	Greinsby
	l. 7—	Mathild'	Maltild'
No.	86, l. 9—	Angl'	Anglie
	l. 10—	Willelmo de Caisn'	W. de Caisnet'
	last l.—	Oxenef'	Oxeneford'
No.	97, last l.—	Will' Mart'	W. Mart'
No.	100, l. 3—	Anglie	Angl'
	l. 8—	in perpetuum	imperpetuum
	l. 10—	V*er*	Ver
No.	109—nil		
No.	116—nil		
No.	119, l. 5—	Ansgesbiam	Asgerbiam
	l. 11—	Weletona	Welletona
	l. 12—	Toma	Thoma
No.	124, l. 6—	Asgerbi	Asgerby
No.	135, l. 1 on p. 85—	Claindona	Claidona
	l. 3 on p. 85—	Almereio	Almerio
No.	136, l. 1—	Angl'	Anglie
	l. 5 on p. 86—	Andree	Andrréé
		Holeburn'	Holeburn

To these various readings should be added the name Lincoln', Lincol', Linc', which Reg. Ant. does not always

---

[1] The five minims of the eleventh and twelfth letters seem to be intended for *mn* in the one text and *nm* in the other, but these readings are not beyond doubt.

abbreviate in the same way as the original texts. Special mention also ought to be made of no. 137 which varies in so many places from the original charter that it may be concluded that the scribe of the cartulary followed another text. The charter has been so badly injured by damp as to be almost illegible in parts, and the injury may be as old as the twelfth century. Photography has now made it possible to read some words which formerly were illegible.

Additions about 1260

A quire[1] containing charters of bishop Hugh of Wells and bishop Grosseteste has been added by a hand of about 1260, and the same scribe has written a quire of documents of the time of bishop Lexington.[2] To the same hand also must be assigned the last charter of king John.[3] About the same date, perhaps, many of the titles of charters in red ink and the marginal titles in black ink were added, but this work was left unfinished. Ignoring the additions made after 1260, nos. 41–49, 85–102, 104–108, 161–163, 168–220, 472–473, 477–509, 514–553, 557–591, 596–599, 708–729, 739–760, 770–812, 816–832, 837–856, 861–886 have been left without rubricated or red ink titles ; but the spaces between the charters left by the original scribe shew that titles of some sort were a part of his plan.

The Redaction by Q

Towards the close of the thirteenth century, the manuscript was subjected to a careful and drastic redaction with a view to the making of a new cartulary. The redactor found not only that there was much to be added, but also that much rearrangement was needed. He therefore directed that the manuscript should be divided into two parts, which he subdivided under titles (tituli), as is shewn in the table of contents.[4] He also supplied much new material, and added many directions in various places. These directions, however, do not cover the whole of the ground, and it seems that the redactor, like the original scribe, never finished his work. When at length

---

[1] Reg. Ant., ff. 39–45.

[2] Ibid., ff. 234–238.

[3] Ibid., no. 164.

[4] Below, pages xlix–liii.

a new cartulary, the volume which is known as the REGISTRUM, was made *circa* 1320–30, its compiler did not follow the plan marked out by the redactor.

The occurrence of these directions on page after page of the cartulary inevitably raised the question of their author's identity: ' Quis esset ? ' ' Who was he ? ' and thus was the habit formed of calling him Q, a conveniently distinctive initial, which is used in the present edition. Fortunately, Q has, so to speak, left his finger-prints on many of the pages of the manuscript. He gives, in his own handwriting, a summary of the fees paid by Oliver Sutton at his consecration and enthronement, in 1280, as bishop of Lincoln, with the preface :

> ' Hec que secuntur vidi de facto fieri . [de domino Oliuero episcopo[1]] 7 ideo pro instructione futurorum in casu consimili hic ea annotaui'.[2]

Following the summary, he adds :

> ' Et ad exemplum futurorum quod vidi gestum circa funeracionem domini Oliueri episcopi Linc' hic duxi inserendum'.[3]

Preceding the summary of fees, Q caused a copy to be made of the ' Tractatus sive Summa de formis electionum Episcoporum,' which was composed, *circa* 1253, by Lawrence of Somercotes, papal subdeacon, canon of Chichester, and official of the diocese of Chichester.[4] The *Tractatus* describes, in much detail, the methods of election by inspiration, by scrutiny, and by compromise.

In these passages about the election and burial of bishop Sutton, and in the directions for copying referred to above, Q has left the evidence of his handwriting, which is large, bold, and firm. He must, usually, have written with a rather broad quill, and the first glance at a page will generally shew whether it contains any of his writing or not. When, however, lack of space demands compression, he can write with quite small letters. For the note about Sutton's funeral, he must have used a very

---

[1] Interlineated.
[2] Reg. Ant., no. 923.
[3] *Ibid.* Sutton died 13 November, 1299. See *Linc. Cath. Statutes* ii, p. cxxi.
[4] Reg. Ant., no. 922 ; printed in *Linc. Cath. Statutes* ii, pp. cxxv–xlii. Dr W. Holtzmann furnishes the information that there is an earlier German edition of the same treatise : *Der Traktat des Laurentius de Somercote über die Vornahme von Bischofswahlen entstanden im Yahre* 1254, herausgegeben und erlautert von A. von Wretschko (Weimar, 1907).

bad pen. Further, he used habitually a browner ink than is found elsewhere in the cartulary. This evidence suggests that Q may be identified with John of Schalby, who held several preferments in the diocese. On 26 February, 1290, Schalby was instituted to the church of Sutton le Marsh, in Lincolnshire (which he already held by commendation), on collation by the bishop.[1] This he vacated by institution to the church of Mumby, in the same county, on 4 December, 1294, on the presentation of the prior and convent of Markby.[2] He was still rector there in July, 1331,[3] and, no doubt, until his death in 1333. That he was a priest in 1298 is shewn by Sutton's roll of the archdeaconry of Lincoln.[4] On 11 October, 1299, he was instituted to the prebend of Bedford Major. This he vacated for the prebend of Welton Beckhall, 22 March, 1302,[5] which he exchanged 19 November, 1305, for the prebend of Dunham and Newport,[6] which he held till his death in 1333. The bishop was patron in all three instances. From about 1282–1299 he was registrar to bishop Sutton, and he tells us that for eight years he held a not unimportant place (*statu non infimo*) in bishop Dalderby's service.[7] It may be concluded that the post which he held was that of bishop's registrar from which he retired about 1308.[8]

On 8 November, 1308, Schalby protested in chapter that he was firmly purposed to reside at Lincoln within a short time, and prayed the chapter to lease to him some house suitable to his condition; and, if it could be done without prejudice to others of his brethren who by custom or of right had a preference in the choice of houses, he prayed that the house called Pollard's might be assigned to him at a reasonable valuation, adding that if any one of his brethren wished to have that house he would at once give it up, even if it had been granted to him.[9] The

---

[1] Sutton's roll of the archdeaconry of Lincoln, mem. 22.
[2] Sutton's Register, f. 227*d*.
[3] *Cal. Pat. Rolls*, 1330–1334, p. 149.
[4] Mem. 1.
[5] Episcopal Register ii, f. 276*d*.
[6] Chapter Acts, D. and C., A/2/22.
[7] Below, page xxxiii.
[8] Below, page xxxiv.
[9] Similarly, in 1315, Schalby in chapter prayed that other canons in residence who had no farms should be altogether preferred to him in the assignment of farms, and that he himself should await his turn of farms falling vacant (Chapter Acts, D. and C., A/2/22, f. 37).

chapter agreed to let sir John have the house, provided that it were not to the prejudice of any one who had a fuller right ; and although it was the custom for a canon, on receiving that house, to pay twenty marks, yet, since the house was utterly ruinated, and they ought to spend thirty pounds upon it, and seeing that they had not so many dwellings in the close as they used to have, they agreed that sir John should have it without the payment of the usual sum, in return for a yearly payment to the common of thirty-three shillings and fourpence, on condition that he should repair and maintain the house. Further, out of regard to him, and at the request and instance of certain of themselves, the chapter agreed that as an act of courtesy, three shillings and fourpence should be returned to him each year by the chapter-clerk during the tenancy.[1] Schalby continued his residence until his death. On 18 September, 1333, the chapter, at Schalby's request, on account of the defect of sight from which he was suffering, appointed Walter de Grenewyk, the chapter-clerk, to be his coadjutor and, for Schalby's solace, to provide for his person and the administration of his prebend. He did not live many weeks after this, for on 30th October his will with a codicil annexed was proved in chapter, and administration of his goods granted to his executors.[2] He must have been nearly eighty years old, for he can have been scarcely less than twenty-five when in 1282 he began to occupy the important office of bishop's registrar.

In the muniment room of the dean and chapter there is preserved the ' Liber Johannis de Schalby ecclesie Lincoln' canonici de Episcopis Lincolniensibus et gestis eorum.' A sixteenth century hand has added to this title ' qui et Martilogium olim vocitabatur,' by which name the Liber has since been always known.[3] He dedicates his work to all the faithful of the cathedral church of Lincoln, adding :

' Quoniam ob defectum scripture rerum bene gestarum memoria

---

[1] *Ibid.*, f. 14.

[2] D. and C., Chapter Acts, 1321–39, A/2/23. Unfortunately, the probate alone, and not the will itself, was registered.

[3] The book is described in *Linc. Cath. Statutes* i, 90–5, 241 ; J. F. Dimock printed the book from an incomplete copy in Matthew Hutton's transcripts in the Harleian collection in the British Museum (*Giraldus Cambrensis* vii, 193–216). Canon C. Wordsworth has printed the parts which Dimock omitted (*Linc. Cath. Statutes* ii, pp. lxiii–cxx).

sepe perit ; ego Johannes quedam contingencia statum ecclesie
Lincoln' predicte quorum aliqua scripta reperi in archiuis ecclesie
memorate aliqua a senioribus meis didici veritate fulciri et aliqua
fieri vidi censui redigere in scripturam ad certitudinem presencium
et memoriam futurorum.'[1]

The Martilogium (a shortened form of Martyrologium)
contains short memoirs of the bishops of Lincoln from
Remigius to Burghersh which, down to the time of Saint
Hugh, are evidently derived from the same source as the
lives in Giraldus ; but the greater part of Schalby's book
is chiefly concerned with a dispute between the dean,
Roger de Martivall, and the chapter in 1312. The dean
claimed the right of exercising an independent jurisdiction : the canons, amongst whom Schalby was the
protagonist, asserted that the jurisdiction should be exer-
cised jointly with the chapter. The controversy was
settled in favour of the chapter, in 1314, by the *laudum*
or award of bishop Dalderby. Schalby gives at full length
the Consuetudines of 1214, described in a marginal note
by his own hand as ' Registrum Vetus ',[2] on which he
and his fellow-canons took their stand ; and the Consuetudines of 1267, on which the dean relied. Against
the copy of the latter document, Schalby has added a
rubric : ' Registrum quod dicitur nouum, cuius auctor
ignoratur.'[3] The original copies of the two sets of *Consuetudines*, which are no longer extant, are believed to have
been contained in the Martyrology which was one of the
service-books in daily use, and this may account for the
title of ' Martilogium ' being given to Schalby's Liber.

The Martilogium was written towards the end of
Schalby's life. One entry is dated 1330,[4] but most of the
book was probably written some years earlier. The text
is the work of a rather careless scribe, but the rubricated
titles and marginal notes are evidently written by Schalby's
own hand, and that hand bears a close resemblance to Q̃'s
distinctive writing in the REGISTRUM ANTIQUISSIMUM.[5]
In both manuscripts arabic numerals, unusual at that
date, which are probably by the same hand, are used for

[1] Folio 1.
[2] Martilogium, f. 19.
[3] *Ibid.*, f. 12 (*Linc. Cath. Statutes* i, 54).
[4] Folio 34.
[5] Canon Christopher Wordsworth also noticed the likeness of the two hands
(*Linc. Cath. Statutes* ii, p. cxxin.).

numbering the leaves. On folio 30*d*, of the Martilogium, there is a collection of customs to which Schalby gives the title, ' De consuetudinibus non redactis in scripturam,' and prefaces it with the sentence,

' Svbscripta pro consuetudinibus obseruari vidi tempore quo resedi scilicet per annos[1] amplius et ea nullicubi reperi esse scripta.'

In the course of his memoir of bishop Sutton, he says :

' Et hec omnia noui qui ea de ipso scripsi quoniam in domo ipsius fui per annos octodecim registrator.'[2]

Again, when recording the death of bishop Dalderby, 12 January, 1320, he adds :

' Huic viro dei dum vitales carperet auras ille qui hec scripsit per octo annos in statu non infimo deseruiuit 7 condiciones eius sanctissimas bene nouit.'[3]

That both the Martilogium and the cartulary should manifest this passion for recording events for the benefit of posterity, and furnish this sort of personal notes, is worthy of remark : no parallel instance is known at Lincoln.

Another line of evidence may be now followed. As bishop's registrar, it was Schalby's duty to keep an official record of his master's official acts. At Lincoln this was at first written on rolls made up of membranes of vellum sewn end to end. For the first nine years of bishop Sutton's episcopate there are seven rolls, one for each archdeaconry (except Buckingham and Oxford which are lost), and a roll of commendations of churches to clerks, usually for six months. Bishop Gravesend's roll for the archdeaconry of Lincoln is sixty-six feet long, and much time, besides undue wear and tear, is consumed in turning from one part of the roll to another. In 1290 was begun the practice of making the entries on a separate set of quires of vellum for the institutions in each archdeaconry, for the ordinations, and for the memoranda of miscellaneous business. At the end of an episcopate, the quires were arranged in due order, and bound up in one or two volumes or registers. After Sutton's death, it is evident that someone went through the quires of institutions, writing at the head of

---

[1] Unfortunately, the scribe has omitted the number of the years.

[2] Folio 7.

[3] Folio 28.

the recto of most of the folios the year to which the page referred, and very often the name of the archdeaconry— e.g. ' Buk' anno xiiij,'—and numbering the leaves with Roman numerals. The same person, at a later date, supplied the years and archdeaconries for the first eight or nine years (1299–1308) of the institutions in bishop Dalderby's register, though the numbering of the leaves could not of course be done until the end of the episcopate. Now, an episcopal register is an official record in which no one may write except the registrar himself, or scribes deputed by him. At Sutton's death, a register had to be made up for the first time, and it may be concluded that Schalby himself as registrar supplied the necessary headings and numbers. It is significant in this connection that the notes by the same hand in bishop Dalderby's register cease about the time that Schalby resigned the registrarship. This hand is too large, bold, and uneven for that of a clerk, and it has a striking similarity to that of Q in the REGISTRUM ANTIQUISSIMUM. It is difficult to say quite confidently that the two hands are identical, for there is but little to compare. On the one hand all that the registers provide is the word ' anno ' repeated with the abbreviated name of one or other of the archdeaconries : on the other hand Q was much given to forming his capital letters in various ways : for instance, he used six different forms of the capital letter *D*. But the argument for identity is strengthened by the fact that the annotator and Q, who did their work at about the same date, both used ink of the same brown shade.

Although no single piece of the evidence may be regarded as conclusive, the cumulative effect is such as to leave no doubt that Q is to be identified with Schalby. This involves no chronological difficulty. Mr Bradshaw, indeed, thought that the redactor of the REGISTRUM ANTIQUISSIMUM and his scribes did their work ' early in Edward I's reign '[1] ; but a careful comparison of the hands of Q's scribes[2] with bishop Sutton's register which belongs to the last decade of the thirteenth century, reveals no appreciable difference of style between the two records. Further, a document of 1289[3] has been copied into the

---

[1] *Linc. Cath. Statutes* i, 111.

[2] ' Q2 ' is used below to indicate these scribes. There were probably two or, perhaps, three of them ; but it is impossible to distinguish their hands with certainty.

[3] *Reg. Ant.*, no. 993.

cartulary by one of Q's scribes, and Q himself obviously could not have written the account of the bishop's funeral before 1299. But, even if Q's work were put back to 1280, no chronological difficulty would arise, because Schalby was old enough in 1282 to be appointed bishop's registrar.

Q's work of redaction must be now described in detail :

(a) He directs that the cartulary shall fall into two parts (*partes*) and a number of subdivisions (*tituli*) ; but his directions, as will be shewn, were left incomplete :

PARS PRIMA

I.	De Priuilegiis [papal bulls] (f. 169)	A
[II.	Not indicated : perhaps intended for Carte Episcoporum]	B
III.	De Iurisdictione Capituli et Canonicorum (f. 183)	C
IV.	De Compositionibus (f. 186)	D
V.	De Appropriationibus Ecclesiarum (f. 195)	E
VI.	De Decimis (f. 203d.)	F
VII.	De Pensionibus (f. 209)	G
VIII.	De Patronatibus (f. 211d.)	H
IX.	De Vicariis Ecclesiarum de Communa (f. 205)	J
[X.	Not indicated : perhaps Carte Abbatum et Priorum (see R.A., no. 208 marg.)]	K
[XI.	Not indicated : perhaps De Electionibus (f. 189)]	M
[XII.	Not indicated : perhaps De Altaribus et Cantariis (see f. 211d.)]	L

PARS SECUNDA

XIII.	Carte Regum (f. 1)	N
[XIV.	Not indicated : perhaps Carte Comitum]	O
[XV.	Not indicated : perhaps Carte Commune (f. 130)]	P

(b) Q supplies much additional matter, chiefly by the hands of his scribes. This is written either where blank spaces were to be found in the cartulary or on fresh quires.[1] Sometimes he writes the first few words of a charter with his own hand, and leaves it to be finished by his scribe.[2] At the end of the work of the original scribe on folio 176d, Q adds no less than forty-five folios (folios 177–211) of new matter. Besides the documents which he has copied, he indicates others which are to be copied : besides *scripta* there are *scribenda*. Folio 211d supplies a clear indication that Q did not finish his task, for he has a

[1] e.g. ff. 67–73, ff. 130–133.
[2] e.g. Reg. Ant., nos. 356, 677, 902, 970, 987.

note 'De altaribus aliis intra ecclesiam . . . infra patet ad finem libri sub titulo de altaribus et cantariis,' whereas this *titulus*, which would have been of great interest, is nowhere to be found.

(*c*) He makes many notes that documents are (1) to be cancelled when they have been, or are to be, copied elsewhere in the cartulary, e.g. :

> 'Vacat quia supra scribitur in principio.' 'Scribitur alibi in proprio titulo.'

(2) to be removed to another position, e.g. :

> 'S*cribantur* inter cartas comitum.' 'Vacat hic quia in Jordeburg' (Reg. Ant., nos. 98, 433 ; Cp. nos. 227, 232, etc.)

(*d*) He has notes about the original texts of charters, e.g. :

> 'Hec carta est in cista domini decani cartarum' (Reg. Ant., no. 115 ; below, no. 146).*

Against charters of land in Corringham :

> 'Credo quod in cophino prebendarum sunt originalia de Coringham' (Reg. Ant., nos. 245–7).*

Against charters of land in Normanby :

> 'Originalia non patent adhuc' (Reg. Ant., nos. 249–50).*

Under Messingham :

> 'Originale non patet sciatur .S. de Wrth'' (Reg. Ant., no. 251).†

Under Glentham :

> '.iiij. carte plures sunt in cofino' (Reg. Ant., no. 256).

Under Ingham :

> 'Originalia de Ingham non comparent' (Reg. Ant., nos. 265–8).*

Under Bishop Norton :

> 'Originale non patet sed est inter cartas episcopi vt creditur et sic non ad communam' (Reg. Ant., no. 284).*

Under pope Adrian V :

> '[Apud A] Littere papales sunt in p[rimo ?] cofino longo sub predicto numero' (Below no. 277).*

At the head of the charters concerning the jurisdiction of the chapter and canons :

> 'Apud C. originalia sunt in vno cofino sub predicto signo' (Below, nos. 287–303).‡

The documents distinguished by an asterisk are now missing ; those marked with a dagger are extant ; of those marked with a double dagger some are extant.

(e) He specifies charters which are to be copied, e.g. :

' Scribantur hic Cotes et Stretton ' (Reg. Ant., f. 54).

' Hic debent sequi carte de Jordeburg et scribi ' (Reg. Ant., f. 55d.).

Four papal bulls (Reg. Ant., f. 182).

Under Compositions, ' Hic sunt continuande et scribende multe composiciones et diuerse ' (Reg. Ant., f. 187d.).

' De ecclesia sancti Bartholomei appropriacio . Instrumenta sunt penes pueros.'
' De appropriacio ecclesie de Hashebi similiter . 7 Hibaldstowe ' (Reg. Ant., f. 203).

(f) He numbered the folios from 1 to 177 with his own hand, using arabic figures. Facsimiles of these figures, which are unusual at so early a date, are given below :

He also numbered the papal bulls with Roman numerals, and it may have been he who supplied the same kind of numerals to the first fifty-eight texts in the cartulary.

Marginalia

The marginal notes supplied by Q have been mentioned already. A few comments by several hands at various dates have been made in the margin, but these, unlike Q's notes, generally have singularly little value. Most of them call attention to some special provision in the text. Sometimes a hand with a finger extended is drawn for this purpose. Two more important notes by a fourteenth century hand state that the houses which Robert de Stutevill gave *in prebendam* belonged to the prebend of Thorngate.[1] Another supplies an unflattering sketch of the subdean.[2] Against two charters a fourteenth century hand has written, ' Reperitur originale '[3] ; and against two

[1] Below, pages 201, 208, s.v. Marginalia.
[2] Below, page 210.
[3] Below, nos. 274, 275,

other texts the same hand has noted, 'Non reperitur originale,' and a later hand has altered the two notes in 1406, so that they read, 'Reperitur originale.'[1] All four charters, however, are missing now.

Against the first 195 texts, and a few later ones, in the cartulary many signs have been made :

2   ♃   φ   ·ŗ·   +   R'   pr   N   V

It has been found impossible to interpret the first six of these signs. They do not correspond with the endorsements of the original charters, nor do they indicate any intelligible classification. ' Pr ' stands for ' Prebenda,' and is placed against some of the documents which relate to prebendal estates. ' N ' means ' Nota.' ' V,' the initial of ' Vacat,' is written opposite many texts, but the reason for their being thus distinguished is not obvious. Although the signs appear to be of little value they have been printed under the head of ' Marginalia,' in so far as they are legible. Some of them are much faded, and some have probably become invisible.

The marginal titles of the texts in the REGISTRUM ANTIQUISSIMUM, which are generally the same as the rubricated titles when such titles have been supplied, are printed in this edition at the head of the texts to which they refer, followed by the word ' marg.' Distinctive marginalia in parallel texts have been noted.

The Make-up and Binding

In consequence of the manuscript having been left in so unfinished a condition by the original scribe and his continuator, it is probable that the quires remained unbound until Q arranged them in their present order and numbered the folios. Perhaps the book was not bound even after Q's redaction for, as has been said already, he too did not complete his task. Of the last thirty-eight folios, five leaves (234–238) were written about 1260 ; twenty-seven (212–233, 239–244) contain matter of the fourteenth and fifteenth centuries ; and six (245–250), documents of various dates written by sixteenth century hands. Therefore the volume did not assume its present form until late in the sixteenth century. The present

---

[1] Below, nos. 256, 257.

Item rex Angl. Sc. de illis brit. et R. buff. et I. de ven. et
Watton. et omnib. baron. et ministr. de notingsham. iam
fcm fal. Sc Watton at epi lnre. de invertella. defen-
der fe estas inc. p. dund' wapena. et pretep. qd in
summoneat' inde ad plac. mea. et conant. infra caruc
modo duob' vicec. et ill ibi summoneant. ubi summoneant' epc Rob. baresfor' fuis. et tam iustic debent
summon. et nolo et precipio qd epc habeat in wapi
car ille cum sibertas consuetud' suas et medimid'
fuas siem inrecessorif fui melt habuet et siem
iustic fulle debeat. et qo sic. clamc. ap. terit.

Item rex Angl. Off. vicecom. et omnib. baronib. fuis et
burgenfib. lmi. fal. Sciat me dedisse. do et Sca
marie lmi. et ipo Robro et a monsters unam mai
lmi. et qd et pane. de sol uruf. sposuf. Nos inde fintlar.
R. Nc emc. ap. stansfort. et s. R. baf. et v. de ab.

Item rex Angl. O. regine et omnib. baronib. de lnre
I. fcm fal. Sciant me concessisse. do et Sca o
iunoliensif ecclr. et Robro epo ecclam sci
roce. et ecclam de bareton. quas offer. v. uren

Item crassar. qui iurec. cedir humfrido i prebendal ecclam
Sci losti inretupec. vbi undm carrucaram tre que fuer omti seis. qd in
Sacceum abundat carrucaram tre que fuer omti seis. qd in
michi relduu siti crantrant i wenchesford. una m unsione
et in magno utuo iter fabros. ecclam de dunchi. vcroni
unam de dito nobis se buffet in bacam. sicade utida utila una
carrucaoa tre.

Inobr' digna fuauci epc omnib. Anisd' p. p̄ia laut offa
unat. Sal. Nouir in ueritas una nos ippetui absoluisse
omis canonicof fue eccle et subuectone qui de p̄benduf
eatuccar p̄sentef. cum infendr' qin i hoib. nominuad
ut p̄uocada. tam qbd offrienff. et autec thesauram.
ualfrida v. questone adiar. nob. iana. foutr. fuse p̄nesflo.
capitlo.

Rob. Angli lmre epc. Omnib. seis matris eccle filiis fal. Nouir
uniuersitat ura nos dedisse concessisse. p p̄sentemcra mea et
firmasse de medutn uiro antistatuocar I lmic. sol' annuos
sperauti somina. canonce resoluenti in unita lemet. sp. pa
up scandi. latirene sedl. I. qr. ap. pasch. vt. adfestu si michael.
Esse ille alte de kirchesl. p̄ud. alie de parm und. Robro eisdam
de parro und. suidiu a sepande. Will. de berling. Watto

binding of rough brown calf may belong to that time,
though the style rather suggests a date in the first half
of the seventeenth century.[1]   The two brass clasps which
are mounted on leather hinges are at least as old as the
binding. It may be added that the Registrum, the
Martilogium, the Carte Decani, the Liber de Ordinationibus
Cantariarum, as well as all the pre-Reformation Episcopal
Registers, were bound in the same style, with slight variations of line and ornament, and probably at about the
same date.

THE REGISTRUM SUPERANTIQUISSIMUM

This is the name which has been given to a fragment[2]
consisting of sixteen leaves of vellum which formed, or
were intended to form, part of a cartulary. The date of
the writing is about the end of the twelfth century, and
the pages measure 10¼ x 6½ inches. The marginal titles
of the charters are written in a very small hand a little
later than the text. A facsimile is given opposite. The
fragment contains fifty-nine charters or parts of charters,
all of which are found in the REGISTRUM ANTIQUISSIMUM
except the important mandate of pope Innocent II with
reference to the excommunication of the earl of Leicester
referred to above.[3] The texts run in the same order as
those of the REGISTRUM ANTIQUISSIMUM except that nos.
32, 137, 138, and 143 of that cartulary do not appear here.
The last document, no. 59 (= no. 259, below), is unfinished.

THE REGISTRUM PRÆANTIQUISSIMUM

This manuscript,[4] like the Superantiquissimum, is a
fragment, consisting of nine leaves of vellum which are
not always consecutive. There are lacunæ, after folios
2d, 3d, and 4d. Some of the leaves are badly injured so
that only parts of texts remain or are legible. The pages
measure 9¼ x 6¼ inches. The writing, which appears to
belong to the early years of the thirteenth century, is
rather smaller than that of the Superantiquissimum. The
initial letters of the first and twenty-first charters are

[1] Acknowledgment is due to Mr W. A. Marsden, Keeper of Printed Books
at the British Museum, for advice.
[2] D. and C., A1/4/1.
[3] Page xxi.
[4] D. and C., A1/4/2.

illuminated in green and red, and that of the second text in red. Marginal titles have been supplied by the person who wrote those in the Superantiquissimum. The charters generally do not follow the order of the REGISTRUM ANTI-QUISSIMUM. The differences between the Præantiquissi-mum and the Antiquissimum are not of much importance, except that in one charter the former supplies a clause of nine words which the latter, by an unusual lapse of the original scribe, omits.[1] The fragment supplies two interesting texts which are not found elsewhere.[2] A facsimile of the fragment faces page xxxix. The first four pages were pasted into the REGISTRUM ANTIQUISSIMUM, after folio 8, until Canon J. F. Wickenden removed them on 7 September, 1881, and placed them with the other five pages of the fragment.

THE COTTON CARTULARY

The title, written with red ink at the top of the first page of this cartulary,[3] is, ' Hic est liber Cartarum ecclesie beate Marie Lincol ' . quam transtulit Willelmus Rex primus.' It consists of twenty-five folios, measuring 8¾ x 6 inches, which are now bound up in one volume with other manuscripts. It may be presumed that the cartulary's real home is Lincoln, whence, like the REGIS-TRUM ANTIQUISSIMUM, it was carried away. Like the two earlier manuscripts, it is a fragment but, unlike them, it is in a perfect condition. It contains charters of William I, William II, Henry I, Henry II, and five papal bulls, but it ends suddenly in the middle of the fifth bull.[4] The order of the texts is more or less that of the REGISTRUM ANTIQUISSIMUM. A charter of Henry II is found here only.[5] On folio 13d two texts are written in a hand of the time of Henry III : the one is a copy of a charter of Henry I which also appears on folio 7d in the same hand as the rest of the manuscript[6] ; the other, which is dated 3 Henry III, and is concerned with the liberties of the dean and chapter in Asgarby and Fries-thorpe, will be printed in volume II of the present work.

---

[1] Below, page 203, ll. 3, 4.
[2] Below, nos. 306–7.
[3] Brit. Mus., Cotton MSS., Vesp. E xvi.
[4] No. 251, below.
[5] Below, no. 193.
[6] Below. no. 30.

III

Ncholaus. Epe. Seruus. Seruoz dei. Salomoni
venerabili. epo. horcacastrensi. suisq; successo
ribus ibiq; canonice pmouendis inppetuum. Cum mag
na nobis sollicitudine insistit cura pumusis dei ecclesiis
ac piis locis uigilandum ne aliquam necessitatis iacturam
sustineant. sed pprie utilitatis stipendia consequantur.
Ideo conuenit nos tota mentis integritate eisdem uenabi
libз locis. ut ea que sua sunt stabilita pmaneant puide.
Igitr quia petisti a nobis kme fili cum eadwardi regis
legatis atq; litteris nri uidelicet amici ut pori puilegii
pagina tue ecclie tibiq; nec non successoribз tuis omnia p
petualir confirmarem. que pfate ecclie iuste et legalirer
copetunt suggestioni tue gratant annuentes. phuius
nre constitucionis decreti et aplice sedis libale edictu
concedim et confirmam tibi. sicut sup legr tuisq;
successoribз ibidem canonice pmouendis inppetuum
queq; pfate ecclie prinent. tamque inpsentiarum
possidet uel possedit et maxime parochiam lindisi
ecclíamq; stou cu neuuerca et appendiciis quas inte
Aluric Archiepe eboracensis inuasit. iti plegatoz
nroz dicta ¬ partecessoz testimonia et scpta agno
uim. quamq; infuturo quocumq; modo diuinis ¬
humanis legibз adquirere poterit scilicet pnomina
ta ecclia cum omibз rebus et possessionibз suis ac
prinentiis mobilibз et inmobilibз seseq; mouentibз

The Cotton cartulary is written in a script of the early years of the thirteenth century, which is a little smaller than that of the Superantiquissimum or the Præantiquissimum ; and marginal titles have been added by a hand which is a little later than that of the text. The writing grows rather larger from folio 17d onwards. Each of the bulls[1] begin with a large initial illuminated in green and red like the initials in the Præantiquissimum. In the earlier part of the manuscript, red initials or rubrics occur on folios 1, 1d, 6, 14, and 17. A facsimile of folio 18 is given facing page xl.

THE REGISTRUM

This is[2] ' an enormous register of charters and privileges, compiled and written uniformly about 1330.'[3] The work may have been in hand ten or fifteen years earlier. The volume contains 272 leaves of vellum, measuring 16 x $9\frac{3}{4}$ inches. The documents have been numbered lately in pencil from 1 to 1942, and the folios from 1 to 272. Rubricated titles have been supplied to numbers 1–61. The handwriting is good and easy to read. The pages have been ruled to secure accurate alignment, and uniformity in ruling has been achieved by pricking the edges of the leaves. The work of the compiler is accurate, but the spelling of the names of persons and places has sometimes been modernized. Thus *ph* is often substituted for *f* in such a name as Radulfus, and *y* for *i* or *ia* in such an instance as Asgarbi or Asgarbia. Such substitutions should be taken into account, but they do not detract from the value of the record except for certain specialized studies. Present day copies of the Authorised Version of the Bible are a parallel instance : they are accurate, but the spelling has been modernized. Further, the cartulary is complete, including the names of witnesses and matters of common form. The Registrum is a valuable supplement to the REGISTRUM ANTIQUISSIMUM supplying not only documents of later date, but also many additional early charters of unimpeachable authenticity. The manuscript is made up of three parts :

    (*a*) ff. 1–76 (originally numbered with Arabic figures which suggest Q's hand), royal and other charters.

[1] ff. 18, 19, 20, 23, 25.
[2] D. and C., A1/6.
[3] Mr H. Bradshaw's note.

(b) ff. 78–152 (originally numbered i–lxxvj), 'Pars secunda. Registrum Cartarum contingentium Capitulum Lincoln' in Ciuitate et Suburbio Linc''.

(c) ff. 153–272 (formerly numbered, at various dates, 1–121), charters of places in the several wapentakes of Lincolnshire, and in Nottinghamshire and Oxfordshire, and later documents (ff. 264d–272).

There are no papal bulls and none of the charters with reference to the jurisdiction of the chapter that Q added to the REGISTRUM ANTIQUISSIMUM.

CARTE DECANI

At the head of folio 1 of this cartulary[1] the full title is given as, 'Carte tangentes Decanatum beate Marie Lincoln''. The volume consists of 94 folios of vellum, $14\frac{1}{2}$ x 9 inches. A hand, which is probably Q's, has numbered folios 7–41, and charters 1–114, with Arabic figures.[2] Later hands have continued the two series of numbers to the end of the book. A fourteenth century hand also has numbered the earliest folios from i to xxii. The manuscript may be dated about 1320, with various later additions. It is generally accurate, but is scarcely equal in that respect to the earlier cartularies. The documents, which are copied in full, are arranged under the heads of Chesterfield (nos. 1–60), Ashbourne (61–100), Wirksworth (101–125), Darley (126–164), Mansfield (165–173), Leverton (174–183), and Clayworth (184–275). The first four places are in Derbyshire, and the others in Nottinghamshire. Most of the documents are not found elsewhere, and a large part of the manuscript will be printed in the second volume of this series. The margins have been disfigured with inaccurate notes by hands of the fourteenth and fifteenth centuries, many of which ascribe documents to the wrong dean. There are also many elongated fingers pointing to clauses which happen to have interested the person who drew them.

THE LIBER DE ORDINATIONIBUS CANTARIARUM

This Liber[3] is a volume of 385 vellum leaves, measuring $12\frac{1}{2}$ x $8\frac{1}{4}$ inches. The folios have been numbered with

---

[1] D. and C., A1/7.

[2] It is significant that these series of the earliest Arabic figures in the several cartularies are always unfinished, and that they come to an end within the lifetime of Q.

[3] D. and C., A1/8.

several series of figures, both Roman and Arabic, and now a continuous numbering in pencil has been supplied. The writing is by various hands of the fourteenth and fifteenth centuries. A few of the charters are early enough to find a place in the present edition.

THE CHORISTERS' CARTULARY

This manuscript[1] consists of a single quarternion of twelve leaves of vellum, measuring 11½ x 8⅛ inches, with a limp vellum cover. It was written in the second half of the fourteenth century. The rubricated title at the head of the first folio is: *H[oc] est transcriptum cartarum 7 ceterorum scriptarum ad pueros . . . . . . Lincoln'* [query *pertinencium*]. The title on the cover is: *Liber ordinationis puerorum de Choro.* Two interesting charters (nos. 19 and 20), record that the abbot and convent of Selby, in 1295,

> 'attendentes atrium ecclesie Lincoln' tam angustum esse (quod propter frequentem 7 assiduam multitudinem moriencium illatorum comode non sufficit ad sepulcram (ob honorem dicte matrici ecclesie (7 pro merito participando (de huiusmodi pio opere caritatis ∴ concedimus (damus (7 assignamus (ac omnino quietum clamamus (7 presenti carta nostra confirmamus . . . decano 7 capitulo predicte ecclesie Linc' 7 successoribus suis aduocacionem (exilis ecclesie parochialis sancti Bartholomei retro castellum Linc' cum gleba ipsius ecclesie (necnon 7 cum pertinenciis suis in puram (liberam 7 perpetuam elemosinam ad sepulturam mortuorum specialiter inibi faciendam.'

OTHER CARTULARIES

It will be sufficient merely to mention the two remaining cartularies of the dean and chapter :

(*a*) The Chantries of John de Welburne (treasurer 1351–1381) and Henry duke of Lancaster (d. 1361)[2] ; and (*b*) The Knyveton Leiger.[3] These manuscripts are not to be drawn upon for this edition because the material in the former is too late, and the latter, since it is a family cartulary, demands separate treatment.

The cartulary of the Vicars Choral does not belong to the dean and chapter, although it is generally kept in their muniment room, but is the property of the Vicars,

---

[1] D. and C., A1/4/3.

[2] D. and C., A1/10.

[3] D. and C., A1/9.

who are a separate corporation. The documents which are registered in it are generally too late for inclusion under the present scheme.

ORIGINAL CHARTERS

In the dean and chapter's muniment room, the original pre-Reformation charters, to the number of about 4,200,[1] are in a generally good state of preservation, with the important exception that there is a woeful absence of seals. No royal charter has a seal earlier than the reign of Edward III, except the first Forest Charter of Henry III, of which the seal of the legate Gualo has survived in an imperfect state.[2] Even in the charters of Edward III the seals are few and much injured. But few specimens of the seals of bishops or of the chapter remain. The seals of humbler people, no doubt on account of their smaller size, have fared better, and there is a large number of seals of free peasants and of citizens of Lincoln. Often the seal tag also has disappeared; sometimes it has been neatly cut off; at other times torn away with consequent injury to the foot of the document.

The loss is not confined to seals. Many of the documents which were before the original scribe of the REGISTRUM ANTIQUISSIMUM and Q are no longer extant. Of the great papal bulls[3] confirming the possessions of the church of Lincoln, Q says that they are to be found ' apud [signum] A '; but none of them now exists. Against other papal bulls Q wrote, ' Littere papales sunt in [primo ?] cofino longo sub predicto numero ' [sc. A][4]; but they are not to be found. Again out of sixteen texts about jurisdiction no more than five survive. The evidence of the charters of *inspeximus* granted by Edward I and Edward III points to the same conclusion, for a large number of the documents that were inspected and confirmed in 1281, 1284, and 1330, have disappeared. Perhaps instead of regret over these losses, there should prevail a feeling of thankfulness that so much material of first-rate importance remains. The losses, however serious they be, seem almost negligible when compared with the almost wholesale disappearance of documents from the diocesan registry.

[1] Above, page xxiii.
[2] Below, page 148.
[3] Below, nos. 247–255.
[4] Below, page 230.

Since no copy, however exact it be, can tell as much as an original document, scholars will commend the decision of the Lincoln Record Society to supply facsimiles of some of the more important texts. In the present volume thirty-four charters are thus reproduced, and further facsimiles will be furnished in subsequent volumes.

CHARTERS OF INSPEXIMUS

The charters of *inspeximus* granted by Edward I and Edward III, which are described on pages lvi–lxii, below, have been collated with the texts that are printed here, and differences are noted under the head of ' Various Readings.' But the similar charters by the later kings have not been used for this edition, since each succeeding sovereign merely inspected, recited, and confirmed the charter of his predecessor, without examining afresh the charters of the chapter. A comparison of the charters of *inspeximus* of Edward I and Edward III with the original charters indicates a very high degree of accuracy, and they are of great value in confirming or correcting the other secondary texts.

THE RELATION OF THE REGISTRUM ANTIQUISSIMUM TO THE OTHER CARTULARIES

The Superantiquissimum : The order, as far as its fifty-eight charters extend, is generally the same as the order in A. Its agreement with the seven existing original texts is very close :

S agrees with Orig. against A[1]	8 times
S agrees with A against Orig.	8 times
S differs from Orig. and A which agree..	4 times
S differs from Orig. and A which differ..	3 times

S is more closely in agreement with A than with C. In no. 49, below, where S and C agree, A seems to have the better text, and is supported therein by an *inspeximus*. In no. 55, below, A has a clause which S and C omit. In no. 94, below, S and A read ' þig de Sai' where the *inspeximus* has ' Ing' de Sai.'

---

[1] For the abbreviations, see pages viii, ix, above.

The Præantiquissimum : The order of its twenty-one texts is very different from that of A. There are five original texts of charters which are common to A and P :

P agrees with A against Orig. ..   ..   5 times
P agrees with Orig. against A ..   ..   twice

In no. 252 below, P agrees generally with A against an *inspeximus.*

The Cotton MS. : The order of its seventy charters is generally the same as that in A. A collation of eleven of its texts which occur also in A and for which there are original charters shews that :

C agrees with Orig. against A ..   ..   18 times
C agrees with A against Orig. ..   ..   15 times
C differs from A and Orig. which agree..   *36 times
C, Orig. and A differ   ..   ..   ..   4 times

       * Twenty of these are in one charter.

This table excludes no. 137, below, which has been discussed above (page xxviii). In the texts common to C and A, for which there are no original charters, the reading of A is perhaps more often to be preferred. In no. 118, below, line 1, C has ' rex ' preceded by ' dei gracia ' which A omits, the date being before 1159. In the five bulls (nos. 247–251, below), the text of C is probably rather superior to A, especially in that it follows more closely the punctuation of the papal chancery ; and in that it has the form ' domni ' (gen.) when the reference is to the pope, whereas A has ' domini ' (no. 249, line 105, and no. 250, line 78). C also twice gives the correct date where A is a year behind (no. 249, line 104, and no. 250, line 77). In no. 250, line 57, both C and A read ' perturbat ' which is a mistake for ' perturbare.' In no. 251, line 28, C has ' manerium de Nortuna,' whereas A reads ' manerium de L   ,' leaving a blank as if the scribe could not read the name, which, however, is quite plain in C.

The weight of evidence is against A having been copied from S, P, or C. C never contained more than about a third of the royal charters in A. The instances of agreement between A on the one hand and S or P or C on the other perhaps point to the probability that the scribe of A was sometimes influenced by those texts. There is no evidence to shew that there was any earlier cartulary behind the extant texts, which might account in some measure for the differences of reading, though such a document might, perhaps, be suggested by such an example as no. 53, below, where S, C, and A omit the word ' Centesimo ' in the date, although the word appears in the original charter and also in an *inspeximus* of 1329. On the whole, the evidence seems to indicate that the original scribe of the REGISTRUM ANTIQUISSIMUM founded his work to a greater extent upon original documents than upon secondary texts. The Registrum also appears to be an independent work, based upon the original charters, which, in regard to minute differences, it not infrequently follows with even more fidelity than the REGISTRUM ANTIQUISSIMUM does.

No account, however brief, of the archives would be complete without some mention of the work of three scholars in the last quarter of the nineteenth century. Canon Joseph Frederic Wickenden, prebendary of Norton Episcopi, spent nearly eight years in cleaning, arranging, and docketing the documents, which he found to be in a state of dirt and disorder, though happily they had suffered scarcely at all from damp. He also placed the documents in the boxes and presses in which they are now preserved ; and he compiled a comprehensive list of the pre-Reformation charters, which has lately been bound in three volumes. He died on 23 October, 1883, and his work is commemorated on a brass tablet which the dean and chapter placed in the muniment-room.[1] The next name to be remembered is that of the eminent antiquary and scholar, Mr Henry Bradshaw, whose work has already been alluded to.[2] During the years 1879–1884 he devoted much time to a study of the contents of the muniment-room, and compiled a large part of the present manuscript catalogue in order, as he said, to make the result of Wickenden's labours available for others. Mr Bradshaw's chief work, however, was, with immense labour and ingenuity, to unravel the tangled skein of evidence for the history of the statutes of the church of Lincoln, a literary and historical quest which he followed with deep interest. He also prepared

[1] *Linc. Cath. Statutes* ii, pp. cclxxxiv–vii.
[2] See Index, *s.v.* Bradshaw.

for publication a critical edition of the *Liber Niger* or
Black Book of the church of Lincoln. His work was
cut short by his death on 10 February, 1886.[1] The third
name is that of Canon Christopher Wordsworth, formerly
prebendary of Lyddington, and now chancellor of Salisbury
cathedral, who edited what Mr Bradshaw had prepared
for publication. More than this, he gathered a great
body of additional material, and edited the whole in
three volumes, under the title of *Lincoln Cathedral Statutes*
(1892–1897). That monumental and learned work, a mine
in which the student continually finds unexpected treasure,
is indispensable to anyone who is concerned with the history
and constitution of the church of Lincoln. An earlier
benefactor who should not be forgotten is bishop Wake,
who found and restored, at what cost to himself we are
not told, the REGISTRUM ANTIQUISSIMUM which, whether
by accident or by fraud, had been taken away from the
church of Lincoln.[2]

The present writer is, however, fain to confess that his
thoughts are drawn especially to the canon, old and blind,
who six hundred years ago ' closed his latest day ' at
Lincoln—to John of Schalby, here shown to be identical
with Q the redactor of the REGISTRUM ANTIQUISSIMUM,
who classified, transcribed, and helped to preserve the
archives, and shewed an eager desire to record what he
had seen or had been able to discover. This, as Schalby
himself tells us, he did in order that those who were living,
as well as those who were to come, might have the certain
knowledge of the past which is needed for the wise
administration of the church of Lincoln.

[1] *Linc. Cath. Statutes*, vol. i, *passim*; vol. ii, p. cclxxxv.
[2] Above, pages xxiv–v.

TABLE OF CONTENTS

OF THE REGISTRUM ANTIQUISSIMUM

The numbered titles in italic type have been supplied by the editor.

The following abbreviations have been used:

O   The Original scribe, not later than 1225 (above, pages xxv–vi).
Con. The Continuator, probably 1225–35 (above, page xxvi).
Q   The Redactor, circa 1290–1300 (above, pages xxviii ff).
Q 2 The Redactor's scribes, circa 1290–1300 (above, pages xxxiv–v).

_____

O   nos. 168–194.

Con.   no. 195.

> These folios form a quire of which the leaves are half an inch narrower than the rest of the cartulary. At the foot of f. 34d, there is the note : ' Hic sunt .x. pecie.'

2. *Charters of Magnates—earls, bishops, etc.*

O   ff. 35–38d, nos. 196–220.

> Before nos. 206 and 207 (Concord between bishop Robert and the abbot and convent of Saint Albans) Q has written, ' Vacat hic quia inter composiciones '. Against no. 208 (Grant of the Old Temple) he has noted, ' Scribatur inter cartas abbatum priorum et uirorum religiosorum '.

3. *Charters of the times of bishop Hugh of Wells and bishop Grosseteste.*

c. 1260   ff. 39–45d, nos. 221–241. This quire seems to have been intended to form part of another volume. The bottom margins of the leaves, and the fore edges of ff. 43 and 44, have been barbarously cut off close to the text. The hand is small and neat. Folios 234–238 below are written by the same hand.

4. *Charters of the Common.* COMMUNA (Q).

ff. 46–55d. : West Riding

O   nos. 242–271, 273–275, 277–287.

Q 2   nos. 272, 276, 288, 289. Against the last two numbers Q has a note, ' De luminari altaris sancte Marie de prima . nec de communa.'

> At the foot of f. 55d, Q has written, ' Jordeburg ' . Hic debent sequi carte de Jordeburg' et scribi.'

ff. 56–66d : Walshcroft. COMMUNA (Q).

O   nos. 290–354.

Con.   nos. 355, 357, 358.

Q 2   no. 356.

ff. 67–81 : Wraggoe. COMMUNA (Q).

Q 2   nos. 359–388.

O   nos. 389–423.

Con.   nos. 424–426.

> Q 2 has copied the Croxby charters (nos. 373–377) here instead of under Walshcroft ; Q therefore writes, ' Vacat . Debet scribi in Walsecroft . sunt scripta et ideo vacant hic.'

ff. 82–105 : Louthesk. COMMUNA (Q).

O	nos. 427–473, 477–553.
Q 2	nos. 474, 476.
c. 1260	no. 475.
	ff. 106–112 : Calcewath. COMMUNA (Q).
O	nos. 554–591.
Q 2	nos. 592, 593.
14th cent.	nos. 594, 595 (concerning the appropriation of the churches of East Haddon, Haxey, and Owston).
	ff. 113–115d : Candleshoe. COMMUNA (Q).
O	nos. 596–609.
Q 2	nos. 610, 611.
O	ff. 116–118, nos. 612–625 : Candleshoe. Bolingbroke.
O	ff. 119–125d, nos. 626–659 : Hill. COMMUNA (Q).
O	ff. 126, 127, nos. 660–669 : Horncastle.
O	ff. 128, 129, nos. 670–676 : Gartree.
	ff. 129–133d. Holland. SECUNDA PARS (Q).
O	no. 681.
Q 2	nos. 677–680, 682–704.
O	ff. 134, 134d, nos. 705–707 : Shifford and Langford, co. Oxford. Q has written at the top of f. 134, ' Hoyland',' and ' Norhamtonsc' ' [sic].
	ff. 135–144d : Kesteven.
O	nos. 708–749, 760.
Q 2	nos. 750–759.
O	ff. 145d–147, nos. 761–769 : Nottinghamshire.
	ff. 148–168d. Lincoln. COMMUNA (Q).
O	nos. 770–826.
Con.	nos. 827–836.
O	nos. 837–860.
Con.	nos. 861–875.

5. *Papal Bulls*, ff. 169–182.   PRIMA PARS.   PRIMUS TITULUS. DE PRIUILEGIIS APUD A (Q).

O	nos. 876–886.
Q 2	nos. 887–904. After no. 904, Q has directed that four more bulls shall be copied.

   N.B.—Q's numbering of the folios with Arabic figures ends at f. 177.

Q 2	6. *Jurisdiction*, ff. 183–185, nos. 905–919 : .III. TITULUS. DE IURISDICCIONE CAPITULI ET CANONICORUM APUD C (Q).

   Against no. 918 Q has written, ' Scribatur cum dignitatibus . . .'

c. 1260   18. *Charters of the times of bishops Lexington and Gravesend,* ff. 234–238d, nos. 1053–1059, 1061, 1062 : pensions. This quire is by the same hand as ff. 39–45d above, but the margins here are intact.

16th cent.   no. 1060 : ordination of the vicarage of the churches of Castle Bytham and Holywell (see f. 18, above).

14th cent.   19. *Summary of gifts to the church of Lincoln, arranged under wapentakes,* ff. 239–244d, nos. 1063–1064.

16th cent.   20. *Ordinations of Vicarages,* ff. 245–250, nos. 1065–1073.

   21. A blank leaf, which may have been intended to serve as a cover.

ANALYSIS OF THE QUIRES
OF THE REGISTRUM ANTIQUISSIMUM

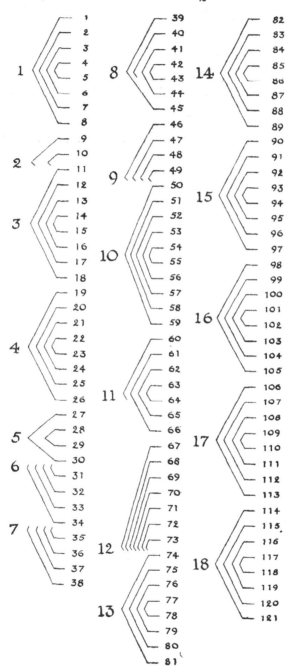

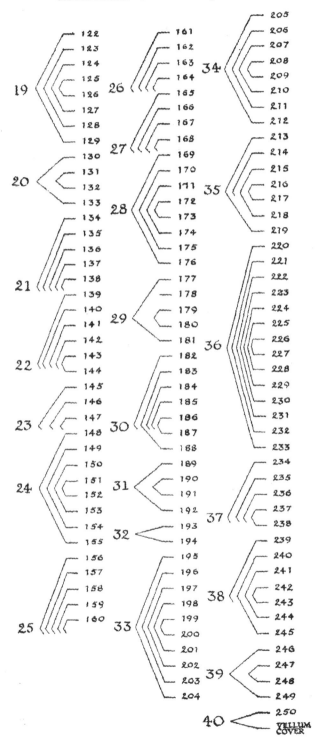

CHARTERS OF INSPEXIMUS

The following charters are used in this volume (see page xlv, above) :

Ii

Exemplification by Edward I of a solemn charter of William II, granted at the instance of bishop Oliver and the dean and chapter on account of injury to king William's charter. At Westminster. 20 May, 1281.

Edwardus dei gracia rex Angl*ie* (dominus Hibern*ie* 7 dux Aquitann*ie* archiepiscopis . episcopis . abbatibus . prioribus . comitibus . baronibus . iusticiariis . vicecomitibus . prepositis . ministris (7 omnibus balliuis 7 fidelibus suis salutem . Inspeximus : *No. 3, below, is recited.* Nos autem cartam predictam ad instantiam venerabilis patris Oliueri Lincoln' episcopi ac decani 7 capituli eiusdem loci propter rupturas 7 concissuras carte predicte duximus exemplificandam sub sigillo nostro . Hiis testibus venerabilibus patribus .R. Bathon*iensi* . 7 Wellensi . 7 .W. Norwycensi episcopis . Edmundo comite Cornub*ie* . Rogero le Bygot comite Norff*olcie* 7 marescallo Angl*ie* . Henrico de Laci comite Lincoln*ie* . Johanne de Warenna comite Surre*ie* . Johanne de Vesci . Ottone de Grandisono . Roberto de Tateshal' . Roberto Tybetot . Hugone filio Ottonis . Roberto filio Johannis 7 aliis . Dat' per manum nostram apud Westmonasterium vicesimo die Maii . anno regni nostri nono.

Endorsed : (i) In Orig. no. 4 : Exemplificacio domini regis E. de 7 super fundacione ecclesie Lincoln' impetrata tempore domini Oliueri episcopi (contemp.). (2) I. (3) Edwardus (14 cent.). (4) X vis' (14 cent.). (5) Tholstonne. (ii) In Orig. no. 5 : (1) Exemplificacio carte de fundacione ecclesie Lincoln' (14 cent.). (2) Tholstonne.
No. 4 : The seal has been torn away with some injury to the foot of the charter. Size 17¼ x 15¼ inches. No. 5 : Tag for seal. Size 13¼ x 13¼ inches.
Texts : MS—Orig. A1/3/4. Orig. A1/3/5 (a duplicate or contemporary copy). R61. Pd—See *C.C.R.*ii,251.

Iii

Inspeximus and exemplification by Edward I, confirming charters relating to the manor of Nettleham, co. Lincoln, granted at the instance of bishop Oliver on account of the seals of those charters having been broken. At Nettleham. 6 February, 1284.

[E]dwardus dei gracia rex Angl*ie* dominus Hibern*ie* 7 dux Aquitann*ie* archiepiscopis (episcopis (abbatibus prioribus (comitibus (baronibus iusticiariis (vicecomitibus (prepositis ministris 7 omnibus balliuis 7 fidelibus suis salutem . Inspeximus : *Nos. 61, 62, and 63, below, are recited.* Nos autem cartas predictas ad instanciam venerabilis patris .O. Lincoln' episcopi propter rupturas sigillorum cartarum illarum duximus exemplificandas sub sigillo nostro . Hiis testibus . venerabilibus patribus .R. Bathon*iensi* 7

Wellensi Thoma Meneuensi 7 .A. Dunolmensi episcopis . Henrico de Lascy comite Lincoln' . Thoma de Clare . Ottone de Grandisono . Rogero Extraneo . Roberto filio Johannis . Eustachio de Hacche 7 aliis . Dat' per manum nostram apud Nettelham . sexto die Februarij . anno regni nostri duodecimo.

Endorsed: (1) Edwardus pro Netelh' (14 cent.). (2) II. (3) Edwardus (14 cent.).
The seal has been torn away with some injury to the foot of the charter. Size: 10¼ x 9⅜ inches.
Texts: MS—Orig. A1/3/6. Pd—*C.C.R.*ii,271, nos. 1–3 (nos. 2 and 3 are printed in full).

Iiii

Inspeximus and confirmation of charters by Edward III in favour of Henry bishop of Lincoln and the dean and chapter ; and further grant that they shall not be impeded in their enjoyment of any of the liberties contained in the said charters by reason of any non-user in the past. At Westminster. 15 February, 1329.

[E]dwardus dei gracia rex Angl*ie* dominus Hibernie 7 dux Aquit*annie* archiepiscopis episcopis abbatibus prioribus comitibus baronibus iusticiariis vicecomitibus prepositis ministris 7 omnibus balliuis 7 fidelibus suis ꝰ salutem . Inspeximus cartam celebris memorie domini .W. quondam regis Angl*ie* progenitoris nostri in hec verba : *Thirty-six charters are recited :*

Inspex.	*Below*	*Inspex.*	*Below*
no. 1	no. 2	no. 19	no. 35
,, 2	,, 1	,, 20	,, 24
,, 3	,, 3	,, 21	,, 22
,, 4	,, 4	,, 22	,, 60
,, 5	,, 14	,, 23	,, 55
,, 6	,, 53	,, 24	,, 62
,, 7	,, 15	,, 25	,, 16
,, 8	,, 17	,, 26	,, 86
,, 9	,, 54a	,, 27	,, 102
,, 10	,, 54	,, 28	,, 92
,, 11	,, 48	,, 29	,, 87
,, 12	,, 46	,, 30	,, 94
,, 13	,, 21	,, 31	,, 85
,, 14	,, 49	,, 32	,, 146
,, 15	,, 34	,, 33	,, 140
,, 16	,, 41	,, 34	,, 142
,, 17	,, 33	,, 35	,, 186
,, 18	,, 67	,, 36	,, 179

Nos autem donaciones concessiones 7 confirmaciones predictas necnon omnia alia 7 singula in eisdem cartis 7 litteris contenta rata habentes 7 grata ea pro nobis 7 heredibus nostris quantum in nobis est venerabili patri Henrico episcopo Lincoln' cancellario nostro 7 successoribus suis episcopis eiusdem loci ac dilectis nobis in Christo decano 7 capitulo loci predicti 7 eorum successoribus concedimus 7 confirmamus sicut carte 7 littere predicte plenius testantur . Preterea ob specialem deuocionem quam ad dictam gloriosam Virginem Mariam dicte ecclesie Lincoln' patronam necnon ob affeccionem quam erga dictum episcopum suis exigentibus meritis intime gerimus 7 habemus (volentes eidem episcopo ac prefatis decano 7 capitulo graciam facere specialem ꞉ concessimus pro nobis 7 heredibus nostris 7 hac carta nostra confirmauimus prefato episcopo 7 predictis decano 7 capitulo quod licet idem episcopus vel predecessores sui aut prefati decanus 7 capitulum vel eorum predecessores libertatibus 7 quietanciis in eisdem cartis contentis vel earum aliqua casu aliquo emergente hactenus vsi non fuerint ꞉ idem tamen episcopus 7 successores sui in terris 7 feodis suis per se ac predicti decanus 7 capitulum 7 eorum successores in terris 7 feodis suis per se 7 eciam in communi (quociens opus fuerit libertatibus 7 quietanciis illis 7 earum qualibet tam pro se quam pro hominibus suis iuxta formam cartarum predictarum decetero sine occasione vel impedimento nostri . vel heredum nostrorum . iusticiariorum escaetorum vicecomitum aut aliorum balliuorum seu ministrorum nostrorum quorumcumque plene gaudeant 7 vtantur . Hiis testibus venerabilibus patribus .S. archiepiscopo Cantuariensi tocius Anglie primate .J. Eliensi 7 .W. Norwycensi episcopis . Edmundo comite Kancie auunculo nostro . Johanne de Warenna comite Surreie . Henrico de Percy . Johanne de Wysham senescallo hospicij nostri . 7 aliis . Dat' per manum nostram apud Westmonasterium quinto decimo die Februarij ꞉ anno regni nostre tercio .   Lek' . dupplicatur.

Seal torn away. Size : 26 x 32 inches.
Texts : MS—Orig. A1/3/7. Charter Roll, 9 Edward III, mem. 24. Pd—C.C.R. iv,101–5 (some of the texts are not printed in full).

liv

A similar *inspeximus* and confirmation of charters by Edward III in favour of Henry bishop of Lincoln and the dean and chapter ; with a similar further grant as to non-user in the past. At Westminster. 15 February, 1329.

Edwardus dei gracia rex, *etc. Thirty-one charters are recited :*

Inspex.	Below	Inspex.	Below
no. 1	no. 139	no. 4	no. 160
,, 2	,, 119	,, 5	,, 181
,, 3	,, 164	,, 6	,, 137

Inspex.		Below		Inspex.		Below	
no.	7	no.	180	no.	20	no.	161
,,	8	,,	184	,,	21	,,	197
,,	9	,,	136	,,	22	,,	213
,,	10	,,	149	,,	23	,,	205
,,	11	,,	115	,,	24	,,	211
,,	12	,,	112	,,	25	,,	230
,,	13	,,	109			Registrum	
,,	14	,,	308	,,	26	no.	109
,,	15	,,	172	,,	27	,,	114
,,	16	,,	183	,,	28	,,	245
,,	17	,,	148	,,	29	,,	65
,,	18	,,	145	,,	30	[see Note]	
,,	19	,,	170	,,	31	,,	67

The witnesses and date are the same as in Iiii above.

(1) Orig. no. 8: Seal torn away, with injury to the foot of the charter. Size: 22¼ x 31¼ inches. (2) Orig. no. 9: Seal torn away, with injury to the foot of the charter. Size: 23 x 33 inches.

Texts: MS—Orig. A1/3/8. Orig. A1/3/9. Charter Roll, 3 Edward III, mem. 22. Pd—*C.C.R.*iv,106–112 (some of the charters are not printed in full).

Note: Nos. 14 and 30 in the *inspeximus* are not found elsewhere at Lincoln. The latter document is calendared in *Cal. Patent Rolls*, 1317–1321, p. 257.

Iv

A similar *inspeximus* and confirmation of charters by Edward III in favour of Henry bishop of Lincoln and the dean and chapter; with a similar further grant as to non-user in the past. At Westminster. 15 February, 1329.

Edwardus dei gracia rex, *etc. Forty-nine charters are recited:*

Inspex.		Below		Inspex.		Below	
no.	1	no.	6	no.	11	no.	100
,,	2	,,	68	,,	12	,,	78
,,	3	,,	72	,,	13	,,	103
,,	4	,,	29	,,	14	,,	77
,,	5	,,	52	,,	15	,,	95
,,	6	,,	26	,,	16	,,	89
,,	7	,,	30	,,	17	,,	101
,,	8	,,	45	,,	18	,,	84
,,	9	,,	74	,,	19	,,	97
,,	10	,,	18	,,	20	,,	187

Inspex.	Below	Inspex.	Below
no. 21	no. 185	no. 36	no. 105
,, 22	,, 104	,, 37	,, 108
,, 23	,, 175	,, 38	,, 107
,, 24	,, 155	,, 39	,, 199
,, 25	,, 182	,, 40	,, 198
,, 26	,, 159	,, 41	,, 203
,, 27	,, 165	,, 42	,, 202
,, 28	,, 147	,, 43	,, 215
,, 29	,, 154	,, 44	,, 231
,, 30	,, 151	,, 45	,, 235
,, 31	,, 163	,, 46	,, 238
,, 32	,, 116	,, 47	,, 240
,, 33	,, 113	,, 48	,, 239
,, 34	,, 143	,, 49	,, 246
,, 35	,, 114		

The witnesses and date are the same as in Iiii, above.

Texts: MS—Charter Roll, 3 Edward III, mem. 4. The original document is not to be found at Lincoln; but it is recited in portions of charters of *inspeximus* of (probably) 2 Richard II and 2 Henry IV. Pd—*C.C.R.*iv,138–48 (some of the texts are not printed in full).

Note: Nos. 13, 43, 46 and 48 in the *inspeximus* are not found in any text at Lincoln.

Ivi

A similar *inspeximus* and confirmation of charters by Edward III in favour of Henry bishop of Lincoln and the dean and chapter; with a similar further grant as to non-user in the past. At Westminster. 15 February, 1329.

Edwardus dei gracia rex, *etc. Three charters are recited :*

Inspex.	Below.	Inspex.	Below.
no. 1	no. 25	no. 3	no. 110
,, 2	,, 95		

The witnesses and date are the same as in Iiii, above.

Texts: MS—Charter Roll, 3 Edward III, mem. 23. Pd—*C.C.R.*iv,105–6.

Ivii

Inspeximus and confirmation of charters by Edward III in favour of Henry bishop of Lincoln and the dean and chapter. At Westminster. 15 February, 1329.

[E]dwardus dei gracia rex Anglie dominus Hibernie 7 dux Aquit*annie* . archiepiscopis episcopis abbatibus prioribus comitibus baronibus iusticiariis vicecomitibus prepositis ministris 7 omnibus balliuis 7 fidelibus suis .' salutem . Inspeximus : *Five charters are recited :*

Inspex.	*Below*			*Inspex.*	*Below*	
no. 1	vol. ii.			no. 4	vol. ii, no. 341	
,, 2	,,	no. 318		,, 5	,,	
,, 3	,,	,, 306				

Nos autem donaciones (concessiones (reddicionem quietam clamanciam ac finem predictos necnon omnia alia 7 singula in eisdem carta litteris 7 fine contenta rata habentes 7 grata ea pro nobis 7 heredibus nostris quantum in nobis est venerabili patri Henrico episcopo Lincoln' cancellario nostro 7 successoribus suis episcopis eiusdem loci ac dilectis nobis in Christo . decano 7 capitulo loci predicti 7 eorum successoribus concedimus 7 confirmamus (sicut carta (littere 7 finis predicti (plenius testantur . Hiis testibus venerabilibus patribus .S. archiepiscopo Cantuar*iensi* tocius Anglie primate .J. Eliensi 7 .W. Norwicensi episcopis (Edmundo comite Kancie auunculo nostro (Johanne de Warenna comite Surre*ie* (Henrico de Percy (Johanne de Wysham senescallo hospicij nostri 7 aliis . Dat' per manum nostram apud Westmonasterium quinto decimo die Februarij anno regni nostri tercio . [Per] breue de priuato sigillo.

Endorsed : (1) xv vis' (14 cent.). (2) Copiatur (14 cent.). (3) Carta aduocationis ecclesie de Asshborne 7 pensionis quadragenta marcarum ecclesie de Gosberkirk (14 cent.). (4) Et de fine 7 concordia fact' in curia domini regis de 7 super dict' pensione 7 (sic ; 14 cent.).
The seal has been torn away, with injury to the foot of the charter. Size : 18 x 15¼ inches.
Texts : MS—Orig. A1/3/10. Charter Roll, 3 Edward III, mem. 2. Pd—*C.C.R.* iv, 149–50.

lviii

Inspeximus and confirmation of charters by Edward [*query* I *or* II].

Edwardus dei gracia rex, *etc.* *Eight charters are recited :*

Inspex.	*Below*	*Inspex.*	*Below*
no. 1	no. 2	no. 5	no. 41
,, 2	,, 1	,, 6	,, 67
,, 3	,, 3	,, 7	,, 87
,, 4	,, 4	,, 8	,, 49

The charter is unfinished, and lacks the usual clause confirming the charters inspected and the witnesses and date.

Text : MS—D163.

lix

Inspeximus and confirmation, with clause *licet*, in favour of master Thomas Southam, prebendary of Leighton manor, co. Huntingdon, of the following charters :

Inspex.	*Below*	*Inspex.*	*Below*
no. 1	vol. ii.	no. 3	vol. ii.
,, 2	no. 89		

At King's Langley. 14 March, 1384. By king's letter of the signet.

Texts : MS—Charter Roll, 7–8 Richard II, mem. 13. Pd—*C.C.R.*v,294.

lx

Exemplification by W[alter] archbishop of York of charters in favour of the dean and chapter of Lincoln (*circa* 1235).

Omnibus Christi fidelibus ad quos presens scriptum peruenerit .W. dei gracia Eboracensis archiepiscopus Anglie primas eternam in domino salutem . subscripta priuilegia Lincoln' ecclesie inspexisse in hec uerba : *Five charters are recited :*

Inspex.	*Below*	*Inspex.*	*Below*
no. 1	no. 287	no. 4	no. 256
,, 2	,, 289	,, 5	,, 257
,, 3	,, 288		

Text : MS—Part of a roll in the Lincoln Diocesan Registry, which formerly contained other charters.

LIST OF CHARTERS

PRINTED IN THIS VOLUME FROM ORIGINAL TEXTS AND THE
SEVERAL CARTULARIES

REG. ANT.	ORIG.	S	P	C	R	D	THIS VOL.
1	–	–	–	1	1	–	no. 1
2	A1/1/1	–	–	1d	1A	–	2
3	–	–	–	1d–3	2	–	3
4	–	–	–	–	3	–	4
5	–	–	–	–	–	–	5
6	–	–	–	3d	5	–	6
7	–	–	–	4	6	–	7
8	–	–	–	–	7	–	8
9	–	–	–	–	8	–	9
10	–	–	–	4	9	–	10
11	–	–	–	4	10	–	11
12	–	–	–	4	11	–	12
13	–	–	–	–	12	–	13
14	–	–	–	4	13, 196	1	14
15	–	–	–	6	–	–	15
16	–	–	–	–	–	–	16
17	–	–	–	6	–	–	17
18	–	–	–	6	–	–	18
19	–	–	–	6	–	–	19
20	–	–	–	–	–	201	20
21	–	–	–	6	–	–	21
22	–	1	–	6d	–	–	22
23	–	2	–	6d	800	–	23
24	–	3	–	7	–	–	24
25	–	4	–	7	–	–	25
26	–	5	–	7	–	–	26
27	–	6	–	7	17	–	27
28	–	7	–	7, 7d	–	–	28
29	–	8	–	7d	–	–	29
30	–	9	–	7d, 13d	15	–	30
31	–	10	–	7d	16	–	31
32	–	–	–	–	18	–	32
33	–	11	–	11d	–	–	33

A	Orig.	S	P	C	R	D	This vol.
34	–	12	–	8	–	–	no. 34
35	–	13	–	8	–	–	35
36	–	14	–	8	–	–	36
37	–	15	–	8, 8d	–	–	37
38	–.	–	–	8d	–	126	38
39	–	–	–	8d	–	–	39
40	–	–	–	–	19	–	40
41	–	–	–	8d	–	–	41
42	A1/1/4	–	–	8d	–	–	42
43	–	–	–	–	–	–	43
44	–	–	–	9	–	–	44
45	–	16	–	9	22	–	45
46	–	17	–	9	–	–	46
47=55	–	–	–	–	–	–	47
48	–	19	–	9d	–	–	48
49	–	20	–	9d	–	–	49
50	–	21	–	–	–	–	50
51	–	22	–	9d	–	–	51
52	A1/1/3	23	–	9d, 10	23	–	52
53	A1/1/2	24	–	10	–	–	53
54	–	25	–	10d	–	–	54
54a	–	26	–	10d	–	–	54a
55	–	18	–	9d	–	–	55
56	–	–	–	10d	–	–	56
57	–	–	–	–	–	–	57
58	–	–	–	10d	–	–	58
59	–	–	–	11	–	–	59
60	–	–	–	6d	–	–	60
61	–	–	–	–	–	–	61
62	–	–	–	–	–	–	62
63=1	–	–	–	–	–	–	63
64=3 (part)	–	–	–	–	–	–	64
65=905	–	–	–	–	–	–	65
66=884	–	–	–	–	–	–	66
66a=21	–	–	–	–	–	–	66a
67	–	–	–	–	–	–	67

A	Orig.	S	P	C	R	D	This vol.
68	–	–	–	–	–	–	no. 68
69	–	–	–	–	–	–	69
70	–	–	–	–	–	–	70
71	–	–	–	–	–	–	71
71a=26	–	–	–	–	–	–	71a
72	–	–	–	–	–	–	72
73	–	–	–	17, 17d	–	–	104
74	–	–	–	–	39	–	105
75	–	–	–	–	–	–	106
76	–	–	–	–	–	–	107
77	–	–	–	–	–	–	108
78	A1/1/11	–	–	–	–	–	109
79	–	–	–	–	–	–	110
80=54a	–	–	–	–	–	–	111
81	–	–	–	–	–	–	112
82	–	–	–	–	–	–	113
83	–	–	–	–	–	–	114
84	–	–	–	–	–	–	115
85	A1/1/14	–	–	–	–	–	116
86=56	–	–	–	–	–	–	117
87	–	–	–	12	–	–	118
88	A1/1/31	–	8	–	–	–	119
89	–	–	–	–	–	–	120
90	A1/1/34	–	–	–	–	–	121
91	A1/1/33	–	–	–	–	–	122
92	–	–	–	–	–	–	123
93	A1/1/32	–	–	–	–	–	124
94	–	–	–	–	–	–	125
95	–	–	–	–	–	–	126
96	–	–	9	–	–	–	127
97	–	–	–	–	–	–	128
98	–	–	–	–	–	–	129
99	–	–	–	–	–	–	130
100	Dij65/1/16	–	–	–	–	–	131
101	–	–	–	–	–	–	132
102	–	–	–	–	–	–	133

A	Orig.	S	P	C	R	D	This vol.
103	–	–	–	–	–		no. 134
104	A1/1/15	–	–	14, 14d	–	–	135
105	A1/1/26	–	–	14d	–	–	136
106	A1/1/13	–	–	15	38	–	137
107	A1/1/16	–	–	15, 15d	–	–	138
108	A1/1/35	–	–	15d	–	–	139
109	A1/1/23	–	–	15d, 16	–	–	140
110	–	–	–	–	–	–	141
111	–	–	–	16, 16d	–	–	142
112	A1/1/27	–	–	16d	36	–	143
113	–	–	–	–	–	–	144
114	A1/1/20	–	–	15	–	–	145
115	–	–	–	16d, 17	–	2, 127	146
116	A1/1/28	–	–	–	–	–	147
117	–	–	–	17	–	–	148
118	–	–	–	–	164	–	149
119	–	–	–	–	165	–	151
120	–	–	–	–	–	–	152
121	–	–	–	–	–	–	153
122	A1/1/12	–	15	–	–	–	154
123	A1/1/17	28	16	–	–	–	155
124	A1/1/22	29	–	–	46	–	156
125	–	30	17	–	47	–	157
126	–	31	18	–	42	–	158
127	A1/1/19	32	19	–	–	–	159
128	–	–	–	–	–	–	160
129	–	–	–	–	–	–	161
130	–	33	–	–	21	–	162
131	–	34	6	–	–	–	163
132	–	35	7	–	–	–	164
133	–	36	10	–	–	–	165
134	A1/1/38	37	11	–	35	–	166
135	–	38	–	–	37	–	167
136	A1/1/21	39	–	–	41	–	168
137	–	–	–	–	–	–	169
138	A1/1/29	–	–	–	–	–	170

A	ORIG.	S	P	C	R	D	THIS VOL.
139=856	–	40	–	–	801		no. 171
140	–	41	–	–	–	–	172
141	–	42	–	–	–	–	173
142	A1/1/24	43	–	–	40	–	174
143	–	–	–	–	–	–	175
144	–	44	–	–	33	–	176
145	–	45	–	–	34	–	177
146=133	–	–	–	–	–	–	178
147	A1/1/36	–	–	–	–	–	179
148	–	–	–	–	–	–	180
149	–	–	–	–	77	–	181
150	A1/1/18	–	–	–	–	–	182
151	–	–	–	–	–	–	183
152	–	–	–	–	–	–	184
153	–	–	–	–	–	60	185
154	A1/1/25	–	–	–	–	3	186
155	–	–	–	–	48A	–	196
156	A1/1/41	–	–	–	169	–	197
157	–	–	–	–	–	–	198
158	–	–	–	–	48	–	199
159	–	–	–	–	–	–	200
160	–	–	–	–	–	–	201
161	–	–	–	–	–	–	202
162	–	–	–	–	–	–	203
163	–	–	–	–	–	–	204
164	A1/1/44	–	–	–	–	–	205
165	–	–	–	–	–	–	216
166	–	–	–	–	–	–	217
167	–	–	–	–	–	–	218
168	–	–	–	–	29	–	75
169	A1/1/10	–	–	–	–	–	76
170	A1/1/9	–	–	–	–	–	77
171	–	–	–	–	–	–	78
172	–	–	–	–	–	–	79
173	–	–	–	–	–	–	80
174	–	–	–	–	26, 1093	–	81

A	Orig.	S	P	C	R	D	This vol.
175	–	–	–	–	31	–	no. 82
176	–	–	–	–	–	–	83
177	–	–	–	–	–	–	84
178	–	46	–	–	–	–	85
179	A1/1/8	47	–	–	–	–	86
180	–	48	–	–	–	–	87
181	–	49	–	–	30	–	88
182	–	50	–	–	25	–	89
183	–	51	–	–	–	–	90
184	–	52	–	–	–	–	91
185	–	53	–	–	–	–	92
186	–	54	–	–	–	–	93
187	–	55	–	–	–	–	94
188	–	56	–	–	–	–	95
189	–	57	–	–	28	–	96
190	A1/1/6	–	–	–	–	–	97
191	–	–	–	–	32	–	98
192	–	–	–	–	–	–	99
193	A1/1/7	–	–	–	27	–	100
194	–	–	–	–	–	–	101
195	–	–	–	–	–	–	102
876	–	–	–	18–19	–	–	247
877	–	–	–	19–20	–	–	248
878	–	–	–	20–3	–	–	249
879	–	–	–	23–5	–	–	250
880	–	–	–	25, 25d	–	–	251
881	Dij55/2/5	–	20	–	–	–	252
882	–	–	21	–	–	–	254
883	–	–	–	–	–	–	255
884	–	–	–	–	–	–	256
885	–	–	–	–	–	–	257
886	–	–	–	–	–	–	258
887	–	59	–	–	–	–	259
888	–	–	–	–	–	–	260
889	–	–	–	–	–	–	261
890	–	–	–	–	–	–	262

A	Orig.	S	P	C	R	D	This vol.
891	–	–	–	–	–		no. 263
892	–	–	–	–	–	–	264
893	–	–	–	–	–	–	265
894	–	–	–	–	–	–	266
895	–	–	–	–	–	–	267
896	Dij57/1/2	–	–	–	–	–	268
897	–	–	–	–	–	–	269
898	–	–	–	–	–	–	270
899	–	–	–	–	–	–	271
900	–	–	–	–	–	–	272
901	–	–	–	–	–	–	273
902	–	–	–	–	–	–	274
903	Dij57/1/3	–	–	–	–	–	275
904	–	–	–	–	–	–	276
904a	–	–	–	–	–	–	277
904b	Dij66/2/50, 51	–	–	–	–	–	278
904c	–	–	–	–	–	–	279
904d	–	–	–	–	–	–	280
904e	–	–	–	–	–	–	280d
905	–	–	–	–	–	–	287
906	–	–	–	–	–	–	288
907=909	Dij55/2/8	–	–	–	–	–	289
908	–	–	2	–	–	–	290
909	–	–	–	–	–	–	291
909a	–	–	–	–	–	–	292
910	–	–	–	–	–	–	293
911	–	–	–	–	–	–	294
912	Dij60/2/1	–	–	–	–	–	295
912a	–	–	–	–	–	–	296
913	–	–	–	–	–	–	297
914	–	–	–	–	–	–	298
915	–	–	–	–	–	–	299
916	–	–	–	–	–	–	300
917	–	–	–	–	–	–	301
918	Dij63/1/8	–	–	–	–	–	302
919	Dij63/1/9	–	–	–	–	–	303

LIST OF ADDITIONAL CHARTERS
PRINTED IN THIS VOLUME WHICH ARE NOT INCLUDED IN THE
Registrum Antiquissimum

Orig.	R.	Other texts at Lincoln	Extraneous texts	This vol.
A1/1/5	24	–	–	no. 73
	–	D131	Iv(9)	74
	–	–	Iv(13)	103
A1/1/40	166	–	–	150
	–	D130	Iv(20)	187
A1/1/37	637	–	–	188
	20	–	–	189
	43	–	–	190
	44	–	–	191
	45	–	–	192
	–	–	C,f.16	193
	–	–	Charter roll	194
A1/1/44a	–	–	–	206
A1/1/42	51	–	–	208
	50	–	–	209
A1/1/45	52	–	–	210
A1/1/43, 53	–	Iiv(24)	Charter rolls	211
	–	–	Charter roll	212
	–	Iiv(22)	,, ,,	213
	–	–	,, ,,	214
	–	–	Iv(43)	215
A1/1/46	–	–	–	219
A1/1/47	59	–	Durham Cath. MSS B.M., Add. Chart.	220
	58	–	–	221
A1/1/48	53	–	–	222
A1/1/51	53B	–	–	223
	53A	–	–	224
	54	–	–	225
	55	–	–	226
A1/1/54	–	–	Patent roll	227
A1/1/50, 60	–	–	Charter roll	228

Orig.	R.	Other texts at Lincoln	Extraneous texts	This vol.
A1/1/59	–	–	–	no. 229
	–	Iiv(25)	Charter roll	230
A1/1/49	–	–	Charter roll	231
	–	–	Iv(44), Charter roll	232
	–	–	Charter roll	233
	–	–	,,　　,,	234
A1/1/52	–	–	Iv(45)	235
	–	–	Charter roll	236
A1/1/53	–	–	,,　　,,	237
	–	–	Iv(46)	238
	–	–	Iv(48)	239
A1/1/55	–	–	Iv(47)	240
A1/1/56	–	–	–	241
	56	–	–	242
A1/1/57	–	–	–	243
	–	–	Patent roll	244
	57	–	–	245
	–	D4	Iv(49)	246
	–	Black Book, Schalby	–	281
Dij/57/1/7	–	–	–	282
	–	S58	–	283
Dij/57/1/5	–	–	–	284
Dij/57/1/6	–	–	–	285
	–	–	Rawlinson MSS	286
Dij/63/1/10	–	–	–	304
Dij/63/1/11	–	–	–	305
	–	P3	–	306
	–	P5	–	307
	–	Iiv(14)	–	308

[Registrum Antiquissimum]

Folio 1.

Hdl.   W<small>ILLELMI</small> R<small>EGIS</small> P<small>RIMI</small>.   .1.

Title by Q : .II. pars.   Primus titulus .ij. partis.   De cartis Regum (*see above, page* . . .).

.N.

1

1. Writ of William I, announcing to the earls and sheriffs, and to all the French and English in the bishopric of Remigius, that he enjoins that no bishop nor archdeacon shall henceforth hold pleas about ecclesiastical laws in the court of the hundred, or bring any cause which pertains to the government of souls to the judgement of secular men ; forbidding that any layman shall intermeddle in the matters which belong to the bishop ; and enjoining that judgement shall be done only in the bishop's seat, or in such place as the bishop shall appoint for the purpose. (1070–1076 ; query April, 1072.)

I.   De libertatibus ecclesiarum tocius Anglie (A marg.)[1].

.W.[2] gracia dei rex Anglo*rum*[3]. comitibus. vicecomitibus . 7 omnibus Francigenis 7 Anglis qui in episcopatu Remegii[4] episcopi terras habent salutem . Sciatis uos omnes 7 ceteri mei fideles qui in Anglia manent quod episcopales leges que non bene nec secundum sanctorum canonum precepta usque ad mea tempora in regno Anglorum fuerunt . communi concilio 7 consilio archiepiscoporum meorum 7 ceterorum episcoporum 7 abbatum 7 omnium principum regni mei emendandas[5] iudicaui . Propterea mando 7 regia auctoritate[6] precipio ut nullus episcopus uel archidiaconus de legibus episcopalibus amplius in hundret placita teneant[7] nec causam que ad regimen animarum pertinet ad iudicium secularium hominum adducant . Sed quicu*n*que secundum episcopales leges de quacu*n*que[8] causa uel culpa interpellatus fuerit ⫶ ad locum quem ad hoc episcopus elegerit ⫶ 7 nominauerit ⫶ ueniat . ibique de causa sua respondeat . 7 non secundum hundret sed secundum canones 7 episcopales leges rectum Deo 7 episcopo suo faciat . Si uero aliquis per superbiam

A

elatus ad iusticiam[9] episcopalem uenire noluerit ⁖ uocetur semel
7 secundo 7 tercio . quod si nec sic ad emendationem uenerit ⁖
excommunicetur . 7 si opus fuerit ad hoc uindicandum fortitudo
7 iusticia regis uel uicecomitis adhibeatur . Ille autem qui uocatus
ad iusticiam episcopi uenire noluit . pro unaquaque uocatione
legem episcopalem emendabit . Hoc etiam defendo 7 mea auctoritate
interdico . ne ullus uicecomes . aut prepositus . aut minister regis .
nec aliquis laicus homo [10]de legibus que ad episcopum pertinent
se intromittat . nec aliquis laicus homo[10] alium hominem sine
iusticia episcopi ad iuditium adducat . Iuditium uero in nullo loco
portetur nisi in episcopali sede aut in illo loco quem ad hoc episcopus
constituerit.

Marginalia : Item alia carta anglice scripta ⁖ continetur in eadem (contemporary).
Inferius folio ix sequente ad hoc signum o—o inferius de castitate (Q).
    Texts : MS—A1. A63. C,f.1. R1. Iiii(2). Iviii(2). Pd—Mon.viii,1270(3).
C.C.R. iv,101(2). Liebermann, *Gesetze der Angelsachsen* i, 485 (a critical edition
of the writ derived from the *Liber Pilosus* of Saint Paul's Cathedral and the present
text). Stubbs, *Select Charters illustrative of English Constitutional History* (9th
edition), p. 99 (from the London version). See *Regesta*, no. 94 (abs.).
    Var. R. : [1] The rubricated title is illegible. [2] Uuillelmus C. [3] Anglie A63.
[4] Remigii C Iviii. [5] emendandas C R. [6] posteste R. [7] om. teneant C. In A
' teneant ' is written on an erasure at the end of a line, and ' nec ' is pushed out into
the margin. [8] om. quacunque C. [9] instanciam R. [10]–[10] om. de legibus . . . . laicus
homo A63.
    Note by Professor F. M. Stenton : This famous document, generally known as
the Ordinance of William I separating the Spiritual and Temporal Courts, is preserved in two independent texts. In the present example the king addresses all
the sheriffs and all the Frenchmen and Englishmen holding land within Remigius'
bishopric. The second example, entered in the *Liber Pilosus* of Saint Paul's
Cathedral, is addressed to Ralf Bainard, Geoffrey de Mandeville, Peter de Valoignes,
and all the king's lieges of Essex, Hertfordshire, and Middlesex. These variant
addresses suggest that copies of the writ were sent in the first place to the principal
local agents of the Anglo-Norman administration, the sheriffs, and that an example
was kept in each cathedral church.
    (*The charter* De castitate *will be found at the end of no. 3, and at no. 64 below.*)

2

2. Notification by William I, addressed to T. the sheriff and
all the sheriffs in the bishopric of Remigius. By the authority and
advice of pope Alexander [II] and his legates, and of archbishop
Lanfranc and the other bishops of his kingdom, the king has transferred the see of Dorchester [co. Oxford], to the city of Lincoln.
He has also given land there, free of all customary payments, for
the building of the mother church of the whole bishopric ; and to
this church he has given the two manors of Welton by Lincoln
and Sleaford ; and also the churches of his three manors of Kirton
[in Lindsey], Caistor, and Wellingore [co. Lincoln], with their
lands and tithes ; and to this he has added the tithe of the renders
of those manors ; and also the churches of Saint Laurence and
Saint Martin in Lincoln. Further, he has granted to the said

church, at the request of bishop Remigius, the manor of Leighton [Bromswold, co. Huntingdon], formerly given to the bishop by earl Waltheof ; and the manor of Wooburn [co. Buckingham], which the king himself gave to Remigius with his episcopal staff. He also confirms the four churches of [Saint Mary] Bedford and Leighton [Buzzard, co. Bedford] and Buckingham and Aylesbury [co. Buckingham], which the bishop's predecessors had held, and which the king had already granted to him. (1070–1087.)

II. De translatione sedis episcopatus in Lin*colniam* 7 de munificentiis illustris regis .W. primi (A marg.).

.W. rex Anglorum .T. uicecomiti [omnibus[1]]que uicecomitibus [epis[1]]copatus Remigii episcopi[2] . salutem . Sciatis me transtulisse sedem episcopatus[3] Dorchacestrensis in Linconiam[4] ciuitatem . auctoritate [7 consilio[1]] Alexandri pap[e[1]] œ′ legatorum eius . necnon œ′ .L. archiepiscopi . œ′ aliorum episcoporum   [5] regni mei . ac ibidem terram ab omnibus consuetudinibus solutam œ′ quietam sufficienter ded[isse a[1]]d construendam matrem ęcclesiam totius episcopatus œ′ eiusdem officinas . Huic autem ęcclesię pro salute animę meę aliquid beneficii dare uolens . primum duo maneria concedo [Wel[1]]letonam uidelicœ′ 7 Slaffordam[6] cum apenditiis . ac deinde ęcclesias trium maneriorum meorum cum terris œ′ decimis . scilicœ′ Chirchetone[7] Castrę . atque[8] Wallingourę . Addo etiam omnem decimam totius redditus eorundem maneriorum ⁒ atque duas ęcclesias in Linconia[9] . scilicœ′ sancti Laurentii . 7 sancti Martini . Preterea ⁒ deprecatione œ′ exortatione[10] Remigii episcopi . concedo eidem ęcclesię manerium quoddam[11] quod uocatur Lestona[12] . quodque Waldeouus comes dudum per manum meam predicto episcopo dederat . œ′ quoddam alterum quod dicitur Waburna[13] . uidelicœ′ quod sibi olim cum episcopali baculo concesseram . Quattuor quoque ęcclesias . Bedefortensem[14] scilicœ′ atque Lestoniensem[15] . nec non [7[1]] Buchingehamnensem[16] . ac Eilesbiriensem[17] . quas predecessores sui tenuerant . quasque sibi de*deram perhenniter possidendas ⁒ ipsi[us c[1]]onsensu ac concessione . predictę ęcclesię cum omnibus apenditiis pertualiter[18] concedo . atque auctoritate regali confirmo . T*estibus* . [L.[1]] archiepiscopo . 7 E. uicecomite.

Facsimile opposite.

Endorsed : (1) Willelmi regis. (2) .W. r'. (3) Welt*ona*. (4) Willelmi regis de translatione sedis episcopatus 7 donis. (5) IIII. (6) V. (7) III⁰. (8) prima (all 13 cent.). Written on the attached membrane : (1) Translacio sedis Linc' a Dorkacestr*ia* tempore Willelmi conquestoris (13 cent.). (2) xvij carta visa (13 cent.). (3) A copy of the charter of Will'm Conqᵣ for translating the see (modern).

Texts : MS—Orig. A1/1/1. A2. C,f.1d. R1A. Iiii(1). Iviii(1). Pd—*Mon.* viii,1269–70(3). *Regesta*, no. 283 (abs.).

Var. R. : [1] The charter has been injured. The bracketed words are supplied from A. The rubricated title in A is illegible. [2] *om.* episcopi C. ; episcopi *interlineated* A. [3] *insert* Remigii A R. [4] Lincolniam A R. ; Lincoliam C. [5] A word has been erased in this space : *no erasure in* A C R. [6] Slaffordiam A C Iiii. [7] Chrchetone A C R. [8] ac R. [9] Lincolia A R. ; Lincollia C. [10] exhortatione A R Iiii Iviii. [11] *the first* d *is superscript.* [12] Lectona C R. [13] Woburna C. [14] Bedeford-

ensem Iiii.   [15] Lectoniensem A (*altered from* Lestoniensem) C R.   [16] Buchinge-
hanmsem A C; Buchingehamensem R.   [17] Eliesbiriensem A R.   [18] perpetualiter
A C R Iiii.

Note by Professor F. M. Stenton: Original charters of William I are extremely
rare, and while their rarity increases the value of any undoubted example, it means
that no definite rules exist by which the authenticity of individual documents can
be tested.   We possess hardly any examples of the chancery script of William's
later years, unless Domesday Book may be so regarded, and the formulas used
by the royal clerks can only be reconstructed by a comparison of charters preserved
in later copies.   It follows that the authenticity of the present charter must be
determined by historical rather than by palæographical or diplomatic considera-
tions.   Unfortunately, little help towards determining either the date of the charter
or its authenticity can be gathered from the names of addressees or witnesses.
T. the sheriff is presumably the obscure Thorald who is known to have been sheriff
of Lincolnshire between the years 1076–9 (Round, *Feudal England*, p. 329).   E. the
sheriff who attests in association with archbishop Lanfranc cannot be identified
with any assurance, but it is at least possible that the initial represents Erneis de
Burun, an important Lincolnshire baron, who is known to have acted as sheriff
of Yorkshire, and whose presence at court would be natural.   The abbreviation
of the few personal names which occur in the charter is really an argument in its
favour, for most forgers of the twelfth century bring personal names in considerable
number into their fabrications.

The strongest reason for believing that the charter comes from the time of
William I is the statement that the king had given the manor of Wooburn to bishop
Remigius *cum episcopali baculo*.   During the primacy of archbishop Anselm the
king's right to invest bishops with the symbols of their spiritual office was vehemently
contested by a strong, and ultimately successful, party in the church, and in 1107
Henry I was brought to agree that bishops should receive the ring and staff from
ecclesiastical hands.   It is really inconceivable that a clerk forging a charter at
any later time in the interest of Lincoln cathedral should have invented this explicit
admission that the founder of the church had received his staff from the king.   On
the other hand, William I, who claimed to fill in regard to the church the position
held by his English predecessors, might most naturally state that he had given a
manor to a bishop when he gave him his pastoral staff.   It is hard to believe that
so apposite a phrase can be an invention.   Medieval forgers were not subtle persons,
and none of them would have thrown himself back into the atmosphere of the
Conqueror's time in order to produce an incidental statement of this kind.   If
the charter is a forgery at all it must be earlier than 1107, and the improbability of
a fabrication of this kind at this time is so great that the charter can hardly be
regarded as other than a genuine product of William I's chancery.   The argument
against the authenticity of the charter which might be based on the narrowness
of the lost seal-strip is at most inconclusive.   The breadth of the strip at its base
must have been about seven-thirtieths of an inch.   Narrow as this is, the
strip on a grant by William I to Westminster abbey (Westminster charter no. xxiv)
of eight hides in the forest of Windsor bears the great seal, three inches in diameter,
on a strip which is no more than three-tenths of an inch wide; and the strip on
an original charter of William II, recently facsimilied by the Northamptonshire
Record Society (vol. iv, plate 1a), which still bears a portion of the great seal, is
but little stronger than the strip of William I's charter at Lincoln.   It is possible
that further investigation would shew a tendency to cut wider strips for the great
seal as the twelfth century went on.   However this may have been, it seems certain
that the narrowness of the strip in the present example is not abnormal for the
date of the charter.

Folio 1d.

Hdl.   CARTE REGIS *Willelmi Secundi.*

3

3.   Solemn charter of William II.   The king confirms his father's
gifts to the church of Lincoln which his father had ordered Remigius

to build, namely Welton [by Lincoln]; the churches of Saint Laurence and Saint Martin in Lincoln; the churches of the king's three manors of Wellingore, Kirton [in Lindsey], and Caistor, [co. Lincoln]; the church of Aylesbury with lands and tithes, namely, Stoke Mandeville, Walton [in Aylesbury], and Buckland, and the church of Buckingham with lands and tithes and one carucate in Gawcott, [co. Buckingham]; the church of Leighton [Buzzard, co. Bedford]; the church of Saint Mary, Bedford, and one hide and a mill; and another hide in Ford [see Note, page 10]; Sleaford with its appendages; Leighton [Bromswold, co. Huntingdon] with five carucates in Hougham, and one carucate in Redbourne [co. Lincoln]; which village (Leighton) earl Waltheof, at the request of Remigius, gave to the church of Lincoln; Wooburn [co. Buckingham], which the king's father gave to Remigius with his pastoral staff. The king also confirms the right of Remigius to appoint the abbot of Saint Mary of Stow, since it is in his episcopal manor. He also grants to the use of the monks the alms which earl Leofric and Godiva his wife gave to the church of Stow, namely Newark and Fledborough [co. Nottingham], and the wapentake of Well excepting the third penny of the shire. He also confirms his father's gift of Eynsham with its appendages, namely Milton [near Thame], Rollright, Yarnton, and Shifford [co. Oxford], and the church of Saint Ebbe with two mills in Oxford. In conclusion, provision is made that the canons of the church which Remigius has begun to found shall lead honest and chaste lives. (A.D. 1090.)

.III. De libertatibus 7 beneficiis . collatis Linc' ecclesie per .W. regem secundum (rubric).

In nomine Domini nostri Ihesu Christi anno ab incarnatione eiusdem Domini .M°xc°[1] . indictione .xiii.

Ego [2].W. rex Anglorum[2] .iii°. regni mei relabente anno ꝰ quod gratuito dono suo michi contulit qui sine penitentia munera largitur futurorum prescius deus . genitore meo Willelmo consenciente 7 me sui heredem faciente . qui muneris superni auxilio regnum idem succincte adquirendo habuit . 7 habitum celesti illustracione instructus prospere ac prudenter dum uixit exemplo cessante tractauit . Pro eiusdem inquam anime atque genitricis méé salute 7 ob meam temporalem maximeque protectionem perhennem[3] 7 ob meorum tam precessorum[4] quam successorum[5] remissionem peccatorum . necnon ad tocius regni mei salutem ꝰ ecclesiam sancte dei genitricis . quam predictus genitor meus Remigium pontificem uirum uenerabilem sacris uirtutibus pollentem . eiusdem antistitis[6] interuentu in Lincolia[7] ciuitate construere iussit tocius episcopatus

sedem consensu 7 auctoritate domini[8] Alexandri qui sancte Romane
ecclesie tunc uigili presidebat cura 7 legatorum eius quos ob hoc
stabiliendum huc precipue misit . necnon consilio Lanfrici[9] archiepiscopi uiri preclari . qui omnium ecclesiarum primatum tunc
citra mare[10] tenebat . aliorumque fidelium eius que uidelicet sedes
incompetenter ac satis obscure in Dorchacestra antiquitus posita
fuerat . ideoque antecessor meus prefatam ut supra docuimus
edificari precipiens ecclesiam ad eandem sufficienti spatio construendam necnon ad domus eidem seruientium officiis aptas .
prouiso quoque ac large ibi disposito mortuorum corporum cimiterio
terram in supradicte urbis sinu quietam . 7 ab omni garrulitatis
cuiuslibet strepitu liberam contulit ? insuper ad usum eidem ecclesie
sub canonica institucione Deo militantium hec stabiliter dedit .
dandoque permultis representationibus confirmauit Welletone cum
appendiciis suis . Et duas ecclesias in Lincolia[7] . sancti Laurencii
unam . sanctique Martini aliam . Et ecclesias trium maneriorum[11]
suorum cum terris 7 decimis que ad eas pertinent . 7 insuper omnem
decimam tocius redditus eorundem maneriorum[11] Walingoure .
Chirchetune[12] . 7 Castra . ecclesiam de Heilesberia[13] cum terris 7
decimis videlicet Stochas[14] . Waltona . Buchelant[15] . ecclesiam de
Buchingeham[16] cum terris 7 decimis 7 una karrucata[17] terre in
Gauecota[18] . ecclesiam de Lestuna[19] cum terris 7 decimis . ecclesiam
sancte Marie in Bedefort[20] . 7 unam hidam terre 7 unum molendinum
cum appendiciis suis . 7 alteram hidam terre in Fort cum una
uirgata . Eslafort[21] cum appendiciis suis . Lestunam[22] cum quinque
karrucatis[23] de terra in Acham[24] . et vna[25] in Ratburno quam
uillam comes Wallef intercessione 7 obsequio Remigii venerabilis
episcopi prefate ecclesie dedit . Watburno quam eidem episcopo
dedit cum pastorali baculo Willelmus pater meus rex egregius .
Ad supradictam inquam ecclesiam edificandam hec dona concedo
7 do post patrem meum* ac regali auctoritate confirmo quieta ab
omnibus consuetudinibus . Ad hec matri ecclesie Lincoliensi[25a] post
genitorem meum hunc honoris cumulum exaggero . uidelicet uolo
7 concedo sicut pater meus concessit . vt episcopus mittat Remigius[26]
7 constituat abbatem in ecclesiam sancte Marie de Stou[27] . tam
ipse quam successores sui . utpote in suo episcopali manerio . Quem
uidelicet abbatem ipse catholice elegerit cum consilio regis abba-
tumque sue dioceseos . 7 monachorum ac clericorum suorum necnon
7 laicorum[28] deum timentium . Mortuo autem abbate si in abbatia
idoneus aliquis reperiri[29] ualeat . consilio supradicto ab episcopo
eligatur . constituatur 7 ordinetur . Sin autem ? per abbatias sui
episcopatus uel per aliquas alias quesitum alium dignum in loco
defuncti episcopus[30] subroget . Ad usum uero monachorum concedo
elemosinas quas comes Leuricus 7 uxor eius Godeua dederunt
ecclesie de Stov[30a] . videlicet Newercham[31] . Flatburch[32] . Wellewapentac*um* . excepto denario tercio comitatus . Insuper concedo
sicut pater meus concessit Eglesham[33] cum appendiciis suis videlicet

Milcetuna[34] . Rollendriz . Erdentuna[35] . Sifort . Et ecclesia sancte Abbe cum adiacente[36] ei terrula . 7 duobus molendinis in Oxinefort cum omnibus consuetudinibus . Hiis[37] aliisque elemosinis abbatia in episcopali manerio constructa in dominio episcoporum perhenniter maneat . Has autem elemosinas omnes concedo regali dono . tam ecclesiarum quam terrarum sub ordinatione 7 dispositione Remigii episcopi cuius interuentu predicta mater ecclesia cepit fundari . ut ipse disponat 7 diuidat sicut sibi uisum fuerit inter matrem ecclesiam suamque abbatiam[38] . In qua uidelicet matre ecclesia canonici deo seruientes caste 7 catholice uiuant . nullaque inter eos prebenda ematur uel uendatur depulsa omni heresi symoniaca . Si quis autem quod absit aliter uoluerit uiuere . 7 canonicis preceptis obedire noluerit fraterno amore prima 7 secunda uice usque ad terciam a decano 7 fratribus ceteris[39] corrigatur[40] . Si autem adhuc rebellis permanserit ꞉ ad noticiam episcopi perueniat . Qui episcopus una cum decano 7 fratribus ceteris . adiunctis etiam orationum medicaminibus fratrem infirmum sanare 7 corrigere studeat . Si uero ipse taliter castigari noluerit ꞉ 7 proprio reatui pertinaciter indulgere uoluerit omnibus rebus ecclesie uacuus ut accessit foras[41] mittatur . 7 alter morum 7 scientie merito dignus absque omni munere ut dictum est locum eius terram occupantis optineat[41a] . Hiis omnibus incommutabiliter ita dispositis ueto 7 regali auctoritate prohibeo . ne[42] quislibet cuiusque ordinis sacratissimis locis supradictis uiolentiam aliquam faciat . uel de rebus eorumdem aliquid minuat . Quod si episcopus uel aliquis alius in futuro suadente diabolo hoc uetitum facere temptauerit ꞉ deprimat 7 compescat eius nequitiam . rex qui tunc temporis in hac patria regnauerit[43] ut regnum 7 gloriam optinere[43a] ualeat in secula seculorum Amen.[44]

[A C R[45]]	[Ii Iiii]
.✠ Signum regis Willelmi.	Signum regis Willelmi .✠.
.✠ Signum Dorobernensis archiepiscopi.	Signum Dorobernensis archiepiscopi .✠.
.✠ Signum Walchelini episcopi Wintoniensis.	Signum Mauricii Londoniensis episcopi .✠.
.✠ Signum Mauricii episcopi Lundonie.	Signum Gundulfi Rofensis episcopi .✠.
.✠ Signum Gundulfi episcopi Rofensis.	Signum Radulfi Cicestrensis episcopi .✠.
.✠ Signum Osmundi episcopi Sarisberie.[46]	Signum Alani comitis .✠.
.✠ Signum Roberti episcopi Cestrensis.	
.✠ Signum Wlstani episcopi Wigrecestre.[47]	Signum Walchelini episcopi Wintoniensis .✠.
	Signum Gilberti abbatis Westmonasterii .✠.
.✠ Signum Herberti episcopi Tedfordensis.[48]	Signum Herberti episcopi de Tetfort .✠.

[A C R⁴⁵]

☩ Signum Radulfi episcopi
Cicestrensis.

☩ Signum Roberti episcopi
Herefordensis.†

☩ Signum Gilleberti abbatis
Westmonast*erii*.

☩ Signum Baldewini abbatis
Sancti Eadmundi.⁴⁹

☩ Signum Pauli abbatis .
Sancti Albani.

☩ Signum Roberti cancellarii
ecclesie canonici.

☩ Signum Willelmi capellani
7 eiusdem.

☩ Signum Roberti comitis de
Moritonio.⁴⁹ᵃ

☩ Signum Rogeri comitis de
Monte gumeri.

☩ Signum Hugonis⁵⁰ comitis
Cestrensis.

☩ Signum Stephani comitis
de Albemarle.

☩ Signum Alani comitis.

☩ Signum Roberti comitis de
Mellent.

☩ Signum Symonis comitis.

☩ Signum Roberti comitis de
Nordanhumbre.

☩ Signum Eudonis⁵¹ dapiferi.

☩ Signum Hugonis de
Munfort.

☩ Signum Roberti filii
Hamonis.

☩ Signum Hamonis fratris
eius.

☩ Signum Roberti de Curci.

☩ Signum Iuonis Tailgebosc⁵²ᵃ.

☩ Signum Roberti de Oili.

☩ Signum Widonis fratris
eius.

☩ Signum Huberti de Rie.⁵³

☩ Signum Hugonis de Port.

☩ Signum Roberti de
Grentemaisnil.

[Ii Iiii]

Signum Osmundi Sarisberiensis
episcopi .☩.

Signum Rotberdi Cestrensis
episcopi .☩.

Signum Willelmi de Albeigni.☩.

Signum Balduini abbatis Sancti
Eadmundi .☩.

Signum Stephani de
Albamarl' .☩.

Signum Goisfridi de
Stoteuilla .☩.

Signum Roberti cancellarii .☩.

Signum Roberti episcopi de
Herfort .☩.

Signum Willelmi capellani 7
eiusdem ecclesie canonici.☩.

Signum Roberti comitis de
Moritania .☩.

Signum Rogeri comitis de ☩
Monte gomerico .☩.

Signum Hugonis comitis
Cestrensis .☩.

Signum Heudonis dapiferi .☩.

Signum Iuonis Talib*ois* .☩.

Signum Huberti de Ria .☩.

Signum Hugoni de Port .☩.

Signum Hugoni de Munfort .☩.

Signum Rotb*erti* de Olei⁵² .☩.

Signum Rotb*erti* filii Her-
moni .☩.

Signum Heremonis vicecomitis
de Cantua*ria* .☩.

Signum Rotb*erti* de Curcei .☩.

Signum Wid*onis* de Olei .☩.

Signum Rotb*erti* de
Grentemaisnil' .☩.

Signum Iuonis de
Grentem*aisnil'* .☩.

Signum Willelmi de P*er*ci .☩.

Signum Aluredi de Warh*am* .☩.

[A C R⁴⁵]   [Ii Iiii]

.⊠ Signum Iuonis fratris eius.   Signum Goisfridi de la Wirce .⊠.⁵⁴

.⊠ Signum Willelmi de Perci.

.⊠ Signum Alueredi de Warham.

.⊠ Signum Goisfridi de Wirce.

.⊠ Signum Goisfridi de Stoteuill'.

.⊠ Signum Willelmi de Albagni.

.⊠ Signum Rogeri.

Marginalia : See below, Var. R : 38, 40, 44.

Texts: MS—A3. A64 (for last part). C,ff.1d–3. R2. Ii (registered in R, no. 61). Iiii(3). Iviii(3). Pd—*Mon.*viii,1270(4). *Linc. Cath. Statutes* ii, 1–6. See *C.C.R.*iv,101(3).

There were seemingly two editions of this charter at Lincoln (1) represented by the texts A, C, and R, and (2) represented by Ii and Iiii. Of these, C, which dates from the beginning of the thirteenth century, is the oldest surviving text. Ii, which is an inspeximus dated 20 May, 1281, states that the king has exemplified the charter *propter rupturas et concissuras carte predicte*. Fire and earthquake and the fall of the central tower, unhappy incidents in the history of the cathedral, were not calculated to secure the preservation of muniments. It is evident that the document exemplified in Ii was considered the better text of the two, if indeed it was not the only surviving original text, in 1281, about which time Q was subjecting the cathedral charters to a critical inspection. Iiii is an inspeximus of numerous charters, dated 15 February, 1329–30.

The latter part of the present charter (see Var. R : ³⁸ below), as it appears in all the texts, seems to have been known by the title *De castitate*, and there was some degree of uncertainty with respect to its context. At the end of no. 1 above Q has written in the margin : *Inferius folio ix sequente ad hoc signum* o—o *inferius de castitate*. The place to which Q refers is part of an insertion into the body of the *Registrum Antiquissimum* consisting of two folios, written by a late twelfth century hand, which contain:

> no. 63, a duplicate of no. 1, against which Q has written : *Vacat hic quia supra scribitur in principio sed ibi non est adicio de castitate.*
>
> no. 64, *De honestate et castitate dictorum canonicorum*, a duplicate of the latter part of the present charter (no. 3), and against it is placed the sign o—o which corresponds with the same sign in the margin of no. 1 above.
>
> no. 65, a charter of bishop Robert II : *De iurisdiccione capituli et scribitur alibi in proprio titulo* (Q), a duplicate of no. 287 below.
>
> no. 66, a bull of pope Alexander III : *Confirmacio iurisdiccione scribitur alibi* (Q), a duplicate of no. 256 below.

It is to be noted that Q's notes either state or imply that nos. 63, 65, and 66 are to be cancelled, whereas it seems to be indicated that no. 64, *De castitate*, is to follow no. 1. Yet Q passes by without comment the incorporation of *De castitate* in the present text (no. 3). If he intended *De castitate* to be regarded as a separate document, he was embarrassed by the fact that, according to the best or, as is suggested above, the only existing original text it was incorporated in William II's charter (no. 3) which had been but lately confirmed by Edward I. It should, however, be borne in mind that, since Q never finished his revision of the Registrum Antiquissimum, his ultimate decision must remain uncertain.

Var. R : ¹ M⁰.L⁰xxxx⁰. C Ii Iiii. In C a new folio is begun at this point with the word ' Ego,' and the preceding words are repeated in its margin. ²⁻² Willelmus Anglorum rex Ii. ³ *perhennem added in* A marg. ⁴ *altered to* predecessorum *by interlineation* C. ⁵ *for* successorum *read* suorum R. ⁶ antistis C R. ⁷ *n interlineated to read* Lincolnia C. ⁸ domni C. ⁹ Lanfranci C Iiii Iviij. ¹⁰ matre R. ¹¹⁻¹¹ repeated A R. In A the repetition is cancelled by a line drawn through the words, probably by Q. ¹² Chirtetune Ii. ¹³ Helesberia Ii Iiii. ¹⁴ Stokas R. ¹⁵ Bochelant R. ¹⁶ Buchingheham Ii. ¹⁷ karucata Ii ; carrucata Iiii ; carucata R.

[18] Gauecote C.   [19] Lectuna C.   [20] Bedeford' R.   [21] Eslatfort C Ii.   [22] Lectunam C.
[23] karucatis Ii; carucatis R.   [24] Hacham C Iiii.   [25] vna *is added* in marg. by a later
hand; *om.* una C R.   [25a] Lincolniensi R Iiii.   [26] Remigius mittat Ii Iiii.   [27] Stowe R.
[28] laichorum Ii Iiii.   [29] repperiri C.   [30] *om.* episcopus R.   [30a] Stou C; Stowe R.   [31] New-
erkam Iiii.   [32] Flatburth R.; Fladburgh Iiii.   [33] *the* l *has been erased, and* n *written
above the* g, *to read* Engesham C.   [34] Miltuna Ii Iiii.   [35] Erdentona C; Erdenduna R.
[36] the first syllable has been interlineated A.   [37] His C.   [38] A marg. *has a note,*
hic . . . . . fundac' (14 cent.).   The rest of the charter is repeated, as a separate
document, in no. 64 below.   [39] ceteris fratribus Iiii.   [40] A marg. *has a note,* Nota.
Contra eos qui nolunt obedire preceptis decani et capituli post suam monicionem
amovendi sunt (14 cent.).   [41] foris R.   [41a] obtineat C.   [42] ne *is substituted for* ut *by
a marginal correction* A; ut A64 C Ii Iiii; ne R.   [43] regnauerit *interlineated* A.
[43a] obtinere C.   [44] R marg. *has a note,* Omnes excommunicati sunt ipso facto
cuiusque ordinis status vel condicionis sacratissimis locis supradictis qui violenciam
aliquam faciat [*sic*] vel de rebus eorundem aliquid minuat . 7 hec sub bullis plum-
beis Alexandri pape (14 cent.).   [45] The witnesses as given in Ii and Iiii are printed
above in the second column since they appear in a different order from that of
A C R.   Ii Iiii omit the bishop of Worcester, the abbot of Saint Paul's, the count
of Mellent, earl Simon, the earl of Northumberland, and Roger.   [46] Sarisbirie C R.
[47] Wigrescestrie R.   [48] Tedfortensis C.   [49] Edmundi R.   [49a] Moritonia C.   [50] *om.*
Hugonis R.   [51] Hugonis R.   [52] Oli Iiii.   [52a] Taillgebosc C.   [53] Rye R.   [54] *om.* ✠ Iiii.

Note : Ford was a district on the north side of the Ouse, in the western part
of the town of Bedford and the eastern part of the parish of Biddenham.   Ford
end Road in Bedford, which is a continuation of the present Midland Road (formerly Forthe Street), runs towards what was a ford of the river.   Dr G. H. Fowler,
who has supplied this information, is of the opinion that the one hide in Fort in the
present text is to be identified with the land of Saint Paul's church, Bedford, which,
in 1086, consisted of

(1) three virgates in Biddenham, which Osmund the canon of Saint Paul's,
Bedford, holds of the king.   Leuiet the priest held this land of king Edward
in alms, and afterwards of king William, which priest, when he was dying,
granted one virgate of this land to Saint Paul's church; and Ralf Tallgebosc
added the other two virgates to the same church in alms.

(2) one virgate in Biddenham which Ansfrid the canon holds [of the king].
Maruuen held it [T.R.E.], and could sell it to whom he willed.   Ralf Tallebosc
bestowed it in alms on the church of Saint Paul (*Domesday Book* (Record
Commission) i, f. 211a).

This hide was probably the land of the prebends of Bedford major and Bedford
minor in Lincoln cathedral, with which was associated the chapel of the Herne.

Note by Professor F. M. Stenton : If it could be accepted as a genuine document,
this charter would be an important piece of evidence as to the composition of the
court of William II.   The long list of witnesses is remarkable, and may well be
derived from authentic documents of this time which have now disappeared.   The
attestations of Robert de Curci, head of the French line of that house, of Robert
and Ivo de Grentemaisnil, and of Alfred of Wareham, cannot be mere inventions.
On the other hand, the objections to the charter in its present form are conclusive.
In the first place it is precisely dated 1090.   This date is disproved by the
attestation of Ralf Luffa bishop of Chichester, who according to the annals of his
own church was consecrated at Epiphany, 1091 (Annales Cicestrenses, ed. Liebermann, *Ungedruckte Anglo-Normannische Geschichtsquellen*, page 93).   Herbert
Losinga bishop of Thetford was consecrated in the same year and probably at the
same time.   As the charter is also dated in the third year of William II, which
ran from September, 1089, to September, 1090, the attestation of the bishop of
Chichester is fatal to its authenticity.   Moreover, it cannot be saved by assuming
that the date is wrong and that the charter really belongs to 1091 or some later
year.   Robert count of Mortain, who heads the witnesses of comital rank, had
rebelled against William II in 1088.   Even if he were subsequently reconciled to
the king, as a historian of the next generation asserts, he disappears from English
history in that year and the necrology of Grestain, his own foundation, states that
he died in 1090 (see Farrer, *Early Yorkshire Charters* ii, 326, for a discussion of
these events).   There is no mistaking the significance of these inconsistencies, and
on chronological grounds alone the authenticity of the charter must be abandoned.
In the second place, it would be hard to find any genuine document of the same
form.   Its inflated style would not alone condemn it, for allowance should be made

for abnormal phraseology in a solemn charter issued on a special occasion. The conclusive argument against its authenticity rests on its combination of secular and ecclesiastical matter. For the greater part of its length it is a confirmation of possessions to the church of Lincoln, but in the last twenty lines the character of the language changes, and a royal charter of confirmation passes into a series of ecclesiastical regulations relating to the discipline of the canons. Regulations like these might be issued by an ecclesiastical authority—a bishop for example, or a papal legate. But they are highly incongruous in a document which if genuine must come from a session of the king's court. It need not be assumed, however, that this charter is a mere fabrication. Its writer, whoever he may have been, must have had access to documents mentioning a considerable number of the Anglo-Norman barons of William II's time. He gives bishop Herbert of Thetford his correct style, and, to judge from the texts in A, C, and R, he knew how to arrange a long list of Anglo-Norman witnesses in a proper order of precedence. Probably the best explanation that can be given of this anomalous charter is to suggest that a genuine charter of confirmation issued by William II has been conflated with a set of precepts relating to canonical discipline issued by some ecclesiastical authority, and that witnesses derived from these and, perhaps, other documents now lost, have been run together. The separate existence of the final part of the charter is suggested by the history of the text as given above.

A good example of a similar combination of secular and ecclesiastical matter in a spurious document is given by the foundation charter of Reading abbey, printed from a poor copy in the *Monasticon* iv, 40 (1). Although this charter cannot be accepted as authentic, like the present Lincoln text it was composed before the end of the twelfth century.

*Folio 2.

Hdl.   *Carte Regis* WILLELMI SECUNDI   .2.

†Folio 2d.

Hdl.   WILLELMI REGIS *Secundi.*

4

4. Solemn charter of William II, son of king William, who by hereditary right succeeded king Edward. He has from his own possessions bought out the claim which the church of York and Thomas its archbishop had upon Lincoln and Lindsey, and upon the manors of Stow and Louth; and, instead of them, has given to the church of Saint Peter of York the abbey of Saint German, Selby, and the church of Saint Oswald, Gloucester, in such wise that archbishop Thomas and his successors shall hold the abbey as the archbishop of Canterbury has the bishopric of Rochester. In return for these gifts, archbishop Thomas has, with the consent of his clergy, in the presence of the king and the bishops and magnates, abandoned the aforesaid claim to the king and to Robert bishop of Lincoln and his successors. The king has done this in favour of bishop Robert because he was his chancellor. (Probably 1093.)

.IIII.[1] De liberacione calumpnie super Linc'. Lindes'. Stowe . 7 Luda (rubric).[2]

In nomine Patris 7 Filii 7[3] Spiritus Sancti Amen.
Summi Patris fuit consilium ut sanctam ciuitatem suam celestem
scilicet Ierosolym que superbia diaboli diuisa erat . morte dilectissimi
filii sui intercedente redintegraret . 7 per redemptionem generis
humani angelica dampna repararet . Hac consideratione ego
Willelmus Dei gratia rex Anglorum Willelmi regis filius qui Edwardo
regi hereditario iure successit[4] uidens ecclesiam Anglorum ex parte
diuisam 7 discordantem ? resarcire concupiui quod male scissum
fuerat 7 ad unitatem uere caritatis reuocare ? quod diu indiscussum
sub discordia manserat . Redemi igitur de meis propriis possessionibus calumpniam quam habebat Eburacensis ecclesia . 7 Thomas
eiusdem ecclesie archiepiscopus super Lincoliam[5] 7 super Lindissim .
7 super mansiones Stov[6] 7 Ludam . 7 dedi pro eis ecclesie sancti
Petri Eburacensis iure perpetuo possidendas abbatiam sancti
Germani de Saleby . 7 ecclesiam sancti Oswaldi de Gloecestra cum
omnibus ad eas iure pertinentibus . 7 ita dedi archiepiscopo . Thome .
7 successoribus eius abbatiam sancti Germani sicut archiepiscopus
Cantuariensis habet episcopatum Rofensem . Et propter hec predicta
beneficia benigne dimisit 7 gratanter . Thomas . archiepiscopus
in eternum consenciente clero eius predictam calumpniam in presentia
mea 7 episcoporum 7 procerum meorum michi 7 Roberto[7] episcopo
Lincoliensi[5] 7 successoribus eius . Huius autem calumpnie redemptionem feci[8] gratia eiusdem . Roberti[9] episcopi . quia cancellarius
meus extiterat.

.✠ Signum Willelmi regis.

.✠ Signum Anselmi Cantuariensis archiepiscopi[10].

.✠ Signum Thome Eboracensis
archiepiscopi.

.✠ Signum Walchelini Wen-
toniensis[11] episcopi.

.✠ Signum Gundulfi Rofensis
episcopi.

.✠ Signum Willelmi Dunel-
mensis episcopi.

Marginalia : 2.
Texts : MS—A. R3. Iiii(4). Iviii(4). Pd—*Mon.* viii, 1271(5). Raine, *Historians of the Church of York* iii, 21 (a poor text). Farrer, *Early Yorkshire Charters*
i, no. 126. *See* Davis, no. 341 = lxi.
Var. R : [1] written on an erasure. [2] Carta Willelmi regis secundi de . . . . . .
inter ecclesias Ebor' 7 Lincoln' super Lindissim 7 maneriis Stowe 7 Ludi R rubric.
[3] *insert* sancti R. [4] *the final* t *is nearly illegible in* A. [5] Lincoln' R. [6] Stowe R ;
Stou Iiii Iviii. [7] Rotberto Iii. [8] *insert* ego Iiii Iviii. [9] Rotberti Iiii. [10] Iiii
and Iviii place the bishops as follows : York, Winchester, Durham, Canterbury,
Rochester. [11] Winton' R Iiii.
Note by Professor F. M. Stenton : Apart from the slight uncertainty which
always hangs over solemn charters of the Anglo-Norman kings, in view of the rarity
of examples preserved in a contemporary form, this charter presents no grounds
for suspicion. A settlement such as is here recorded might naturally be expressed
in a solemn manner, and its ecclesiastical character may account for the absence
of any baronial witnesses. That an agreement was actually made between bishop
Robert of Lincoln and archbishop Thomas of York by the mediation of king
William II is certain. Hugh the Chantor, the historian of the first Norman archbishops of York, definitely states that the king made a *concordia* between these

prelates (*Historians of the Church of York and its Archbishops* (Rolls Series) ii, 106), although the archbishop was very unwilling to lose his authority over Lindsey and his possession of Stow, Louth, and Newark. Hugh adds that all England knew that bishop Robert gave the king three thousand pounds for this *concordia*. Reference to such a payment would be unseemly in a solemn instrument, and the statement in the charter that the king has made this *calumpniae redemptio* out of regard for bishop Robert, his chancellor, is a decent evasion of a somewhat unbecoming fact. As the dispute which was ended by the agreement broke out over archbishop Anselm's intention of consecrating bishop Robert, the present charter probably belongs to the year 1093.

Folio 3.

Hdl.   *Willelmi Regis* SECUNDI.   .3.

5

5. Writ of William II, notifying to O[sbert] the sheriff and the barons of Lincolnshire that he has given to Robert I bishop of Lincoln, as long as he lives, the third penny of the wapentake of Stow *ad firmam* for ten pounds a year by tale. (1093–1097.)

.V. De tercio denario de wapentach' Stowe (rubric and marg.).

.W. rex Anglorum .O. vicecomiti . 7 baronibus Lincolie . Francigenis . 7 Anglicis salutem . Sciatis me dedisse Roberto Lincoliensi episcopo tercium denarium del wapentac del Estou . ad firmam per .x. libras . numero quoque anno quamdiu uixerit ita illum habebit . Testibus . episcopo Dunelmensi . 7 Wach*elino* episcopo . 7 Rannulfo capellano.

Text : MS—A.
Note : The usual name of the wapentake is Well.

6

6. Writ of William II, notifying to P[eter] of Oxford [the sheriff] and his lieges of Oxfordshire, that bishop Robert I has, at his request, given back to Nigel brother of Guy de Oili the land which Guy held of the bishop and, during his life, gave back to God and Saint Mary. The bishop has done this on condition that Nigel shall hold the land for life and do service to him according to its value ; and that, after Nigel's death, the land, namely, six hides in Ascott [under Wychwood, co. Oxford], in the demesne of the church, shall revert [to the bishop] free from all claim on the part of any heir or any man who may have Nigel's land. (1093–1100.)

.VI. De terra de Escote (rubric and marg.).

.W.[1] rex Anglorum .P. de Oxineford[2] 7 fidelibus suis Francis 7 Anglis de Oxineford[2] scira salutem . Sciatis terram quam Wido de Oileio tenuit de Lincoliensi[3] episcopo . Roberto . 7 quam ipse Wido deo 7 sancte Marie 7 episcopo in uita sua reddidit . depreca-

tione mea predictum episcopum reddidisse Nigello fratri suo eo
tenore quod Nigellus eam in uita sua habeat . 7 deseruiat uersus
episcopum secundum valentiam[4] terre . Post uero decessum eius :
redeat ipsa terra . scilicet .vj. hidas[5] in Escota in dominio ecclesie
soluta 7 quieta sine clamora 7 querela alicuius heredis uel hominis .
qui predicti Nigelli terram habeat . Testibus . episcopo *Dunelmensi* .
7 Roberto Bigoto . 7 .W. [*blank*] 7 .G. fil' Rogeri[6] . 7 Gerardo Caluo .
7 H. de Bochlanda . 7 .N.[7] de Oili.

Texts :   MS—A.   C,f.3d.   R5.   Iv(1).   Pd—*Mon.*viii,1272(11).   *Regesta*,
no. 466 (abs.).   *Deputy Keeper's Report* xxix, app. p. 41 (abs.).   See *C.C.R.*iv,
138(1).
Var. R :   [1] Will' C, Iv.   [2] Oxeneford' Iv.   [3] Lincoln' R.   [4] ualentium C.   [5] *sic.*
[6] *for* .W. . . . . Rogeri *read* W. 7 G. fil*iis* Rogeri C ; *and read* W. Bakun 7 G. filio
Rogeri Iv.   [7] Nig' R.

7

7. Writ of William II, granting that Osbert of Lincoln may
give those eleven bovates which he holds of the king in Binbrook
[co. Lincoln] to the church of Lincoln *in prebenda* ; so that the
bishop may hold the land of the king, and keep the covenant which
he promised to Osbert. At Pont de l'Arche. (12 November,
1099.)

.VII. De .xi. bouatis terre in Bynnebroc (rubric and marg.) .
.W. rex Anglorum Roberto Lincolniensi[1] episcopo 7 omnibus
Francis 7 Anglis Lincolie . salutem . Sciatis me concessisse quod
Osbertus de Lincolia det illas .xi. bouatas terre quas tenet[2] in
Binnebroc de me ecclesie sancte Marie Lincolie in prebenda pro
amore dei . 7 pro patris 7 matris méé animabus ita quidem quod
ipse episcopus predictam terram de me teneat . 7 conuentionem
quam promisit Osberto teneat . Testibus . Rogero filio Giroldi . 7
Geroldo[3] de Calz . apud Pontem Arcars . pridie post festum sancti
Martini.

Marginalia : preb'.   Est in cofino cum ceteris cartis de prebenda (Q2).
Texts : MS—A.   C,f.4.   R6.   Pd—*Mon.* viii, 1272(12).   *Regesta*, no. 473 (abs.).
Var. R : [1] Lincoliensi C.   [2] quas tenet *written in marg.*   [3] Giroldo C.
Note : For the date, see *Facsimiles of Early Charters from Northamptonshire
Collections* (Northamptonshire Record Society iv, 9).

8

8. Writ of William II, commanding N. the sheriff to cause
bishop Remigius and his canons to have their church of Kirton
[in Lindsey] and that of Hibaldstow [co. Lincoln], with the tithes
belonging to them, as in the time of the king's father. (1087–1088.)

.VIII. De ecclesiis[1] de Kirketona 7 de Hibaldestowa (rubric
and marg.).

.W. rex Anglorum .N. vicecomiti salutem Mando tibi ut facias episcopo Remigio 7 canoncis suis habere ecclesiam suam de Chirchetona cum decimis que ad eam pertinent . 7 de Huboldestou[2] similiter . sicuti melius habuerunt tempore patris mei . Et uide ne pro penuria recti amplius inde clamorem audiam . Teste . episcopo Dunelmensi . per .W. de Werel*wast*.

Texts : MS—A. R7. Pd—*Regesta*, no. 305 (abs.).
Var. R : [1] ecclesia A marg. [2] Huboldestow R.

9

9. Writ of William II, addressed to Osbert the sheriff and the lieges of Lincolnshire, forbidding that bishop Robert I shall plead concerning any of the lands and churches of which bishop Remigius was seised on the day that he was alive and dead. (1093–1100.)

.IX. Quod episcopus Robertus non placitet de terris 7 ecclesiis (rubric and marg.).
.W. rex Anglorum . Osberto . vicecomiti . 7 fidelibus suis de Lincolia scira salutem . Sciatis quod nolo ut Robertus episcopus placitet de omnibus terris 7 ecclesiis de quibus Remigius episcopus saisitus fuit die qua uiuus 7 mortuus fuit . Teste . V*r*s*one* de Abe*tot*.

Texts : MS—A. R8. Pd—*Regesta*, nos. 467, lxxxvi.

10

10. Writ of William [query II], giving to the church of Lincoln and bishop R[obert] I the church of Saint Martin [in Lincoln] ; and commanding that if Norman shall justly claim any compensation the bishop shall supply it. (Query 1087–1100.)

.X. De ecclesia sancti Martini (rubric and marg.).
.W. rex Anglorum .T. vicecomiti . omnibusque fidelibus suis salutem . Sciatis me* dedisse sancte Marie ecclesie Lincolniensi[1] . 7 .R. episcopo ecclesiam sancti Martini cum omnibus appendiciis . Normando autem si iuste clamat de ecclesia aliquam misericordiam episcopus sibi faciat . Teste .E.[2] vicecomite.

Texts : MS—A. C,f.4. R9. Pd—*Mon*.viii,1272(13).
Var. R : [1] Lincoliensi C. [2] *om.* E C.
Note : The document is placed amongst the charters of William II in all the texts ; if, however, the sheriff to whom it is addressed is Thorold, an earlier date is indicated.

Folio 3d.

Hdl. WILLELMI REGIS SECUNDI.

11

11. Writ of William [query II], granting that the land of the canons of Lincoln shall be quit of all customary dues. (Query 1087–1100.)

.XI. De quietancia custumarum (rubric).

.W. rex .T. vicecomiti . salutem . Mando tibi quod ego terram canonicorum sancte Marie de Linc' de omnibus costumis[1] quietam esse concedo.

Marginalia : ·j· + φ (A). nota (C).
Texts : MS—A. C,f.4. R10. Pd—*Mon.*viii,1272(14).
Var. R : [1] custumis R.
Note : For the date see note to the preceding charter.

12

12. Writ of William II, addressed to Ivo Tailbois and Osbert the clerk, commanding that the canons of Saint Mary of Lincoln shall have their tithes and customary dues as they best had them in the time of the king's father. (1087–1100.)

.XII. De decimis 7 consuetudinibus bene habendis (rubric and marg.).

.W. rex Anglorum .I. Tailebois . 7 Osberto clerico salutem . Mando uobis 7 precipio ut canonici sancte Marie de Lincolia ita bene habeant decimas suas 7 consuetudines ∴ sicut eas melius habebant tempore patris mei . Teste R. episcopo.

Marginalia : ·j· + φ . . . In C : Nota.
Texts : MS—A. C,f.4. R11. Pd—*Mon.*viii,1272(15). *Regesta,* no. 406 (abs.)

13

13. Writ of William II, commanding O[sbert] the sheriff to reseise the canons of Lincoln in the lands of which they were dis-seised after the king fell sick, and to put by good pledges those who did the disseisin ; and especially is he to cause the canons to be reseised in the land of the church of Caistor [co. Lincoln]. (1093–1100.)

.XIII. Quod canonici resaisiantur . 7 ablata reddantur eisdem[1] (rubric and marg.).

W. rex Anglorum .O. vicecomiti Lincolie salutem . Precipio tibi vt canonicos sancte Marie Lincoliensis resaisias de terris suis unde dissaisiti sunt postquam ego in infirmitate cecidi . 7 **fac illis reddi**

quicquid inde postea ablatum est . Et illos qui eos dissaisierunt 7
sua post predictum terminum ceperunt ⁊ pone per bonos plegios .
Testibus . Roberto filio Hamonis . 7 . I. Taileb'² . Maxime resaisi
eos de terra ecclesie de Castra . T'. predictorum.

Texts : MS—A. R12. Pd—*Regesta*, nos. 407, lxvii.
Var. R : ¹ *for* Quod . . . eisdem *read* Carta quod canonici reseisiantur de terris
suis R rubric. ² Tailleb' R.

14

14. Writ of William II, addressed to archbishop Thomas [of
York], earl Roger, E. the sheriff, H[enry] de Ferrers, William
Peverel, and all his lieges of Nottinghamshire, notifying them that
he has given to the church of Lincoln and bishop Robert I and his
successors the church of Orston [co. Nottingham], and all that
belonged to it in king Edward's time ; and the churches of Chesterfield
and Ashbourne [co. Derby], and Mansfield [co. Nottingham], with
the chapels in the berewicks belonging to the four manors. This
gift was made on the morrow of the day on which archbishop
Anselm became the king's liege man. (1093, before 25 September.)

.XIIII. De ecclesiis de Oskinton'¹ . Cestrefeud² . Esseburn' .
Mamesfeld³ 7 de capellis (rubric and marg.).

.W. rex Anglorum Thome archiepiscopo 7 .R. episcopo de Cestra⁴ .
7 Rogero comiti . 7 .E. uicecomiti . 7 .H. de Ferrariis . 7 .W. Peuerel .
7 omnibus fidelibus suis Francigenis 7 Anglicis de Esnotingeham
scire⁵ 7 de Derbi scire⁶ salutem . Sciatis me dedisse ecclesie sancte
Marie de Lincolia . 7 Roberto⁷ episcopo eiusdem ecclesie 7 omnibus
successoribus suis in perpetuam possessionem pro anima patris
mei 7 matris méé 7 mea ecclesiam de Oschintona⁸ . 7 quicquid ad
eam⁹ pertinebat tempore regis Edwardi . 7 ecclesiam de Cestrefelt¹⁰ .
7 ecclesiam de Eseborna¹¹ . 7 ecclesiam de Mammesfelt¹² . 7 capellas
que sunt in berewicis que adiacent predictis . iiiior¹³ . maneriis .
Et uolo ut firmiter habeat eas cum terris 7 decimis 7 omnibus que
ad predictas ecclesias pertinebant tempore regis Edwardi . Hoc
donum factum est die crastina qua Anselmus archiepiscopus meus
ligius homo factus est . ¹⁴Testibus . Walchelino¹⁵ . episcopo Wen-
toniensi¹⁶ . 7 . W.¹⁷ episcopo Dunelmensi¹⁸ . 7 Ranulfo capellano .
7 Eudone dapifero . 7 Willelmo Peuerello . 7 Hamone¹⁹ dapifero .
7 Vrsone de Abetot²⁰ . 7 Rannulfo fratre Ilgeri.

Marginalia : *an illegible note.* In C : Nota.
Texts : MS—A. C,f.4. R13,196. D1. Iiii(5). Pd—*Mon.*viii,1271(6). *Regesta*,
no. 337 (abs.). See *C.C.R.*iv,101(5).
Var. R : ¹ Orskington' A marg. ; Oschintu . . C marg. ; Oskington' nunc
vocata Orston' R13 marg. ² Cesterfeld A marg. ³ Mammefeld A marg. ;
Mamesfeld C marg. ; Mannesfeld R13 marg. ⁴ Cestria R196 marg. ⁵ Noting-
hamschir' R196 D. ⁶ Derbyscire R13 ; Derebyschir' R196 ; Derbyscira
D. ⁷ Rotberto Iiii. ⁸ Hoskingtona R196 ; Oskyngtona D. ⁹ ad eam *written*

B

on an erasure A.   [10] Cestrefeld R13 and 196 D.   [11] Esseburna R196 ; Esborna D ; Eseburna Iiii.   [12] Mammesfeld C R13 D Iiii ;   Maunnesfeld R196.   [13] quatuor R196 D Iiii.   [14] *insert* Hiis R196.   [15] Walkelino R196.   [16] Wynton' R196.   [17] Will' D.   [18] Dunolnolm' R196 ; Dunolmens' D.   [19] Haymone D. Haimone Iiii.   [20] Habetot C.

Folio 4.

Hdl.   Carte Regis Henrici Primi.   .4.

15

15. Writ of Henry I, giving his manor of Nettleham [co. Lincoln], with the consent of his wife Maud, whose it was, to Saint Mary of Lincoln and bishop Robert I, who was the chancellor of his brother, king William. (Circa 1101.)

.XV. De manerio de Netelham' (rubric and marg.).

Henricus . rex Anglorum . Osberto vicecomiti Lincolie 7 Picoto filio Colsueni . et omnibus baronibus suis et fidelibus 7 Francis 7 Anglis de Lincole[1] scira ꞉ salutem . Sciatis me dedisse deo 7 sancte Marie de Lincolia 7 Roberto[2] episcopo qui fuit cancellarius .W. regis fratris mei manerium meum de Nethelham[3] . cum omnibus illis rebus que ad eum pertinent . Et uolo et precipio ut ipse eum ita teneat sicuti ego ipse in manu mea tenebam . Et concessu regine Matildis uxoris méé cuius erat . Testibus . Henrico comite de Warewic[4] . 7 Eudone dapifero . 7 Rogero . Bigoto . 7 Hamone[5] . dapifero . 7 Vrsone de Abetot[6] . apud[7].

Marginalia : ꞉i꞉ +. ·i· (beginning a series of numerals, cp. nos. 17–26).
Texts : MS—A. C,f.6. Iiii(7). Pd—*Mon.*viii,1271(8). See *C.C.R.*iv,101(7).
Var. R : [1] Lincolia C.   [2] Rotberto Iiii.   [3] Netelham C ; Netilham Iiii.   [4] Warwic Iiii.   [5] Honnoni Iiii.   [6] Habetot C.   [7] The place is omitted in all the texts.

16

16. Writ of queen Maud, granting the manor of Tixover [co. Rutland] to bishop Robert I. At Rockingham. (1104–6.)

.XVI. De Tychesouere 7 libertatibus (rubric and marg.).

.M. Anglorum regina abbati de Burch 7 comiti .S. 7 Roberto de Pauilli vicecomiti . 7 Michaeli de Hamesclape 7 omnibus baronibus Francis 7 Anglis de Norhamtone scira salutem . Sciatis me dedisse concessu regis domini mei Roberto episcopo Lincolie Tichesoure[1] 7 quicquid ad illud manerium pertinet cum soca . 7 saca . 7 tol . 7 theam[2] . 7 omnibus consuedinibus . Et uolo atque precipio ut ita bene 7 honorifice teneat de me sicuti ego[3] tenebam . Testibus . Waldrico cancellario . 7 Bernardo capellano . 7 Eudone dapifero . 7 Willelmo Peurello de Notingham . 7 Michaele de Hamesclape . apud Rochingeham[4].

Marginalia : +.
Texts : MS—A. Iiii(25). Pd—*C.C.R.*iv,102(25). Farrer *Itin.*, no. 147 (abs.).
Var. R : [1] Ticesoure Iiii.   [2] team Iiii.   [3] ego *follows* tenebam, *but is marked to precede it* A.   [4] Rochingham Iiii.

17

17. Writ of Henry I, granting, at the queen's request, to bishop Robert I the manor of Tixover. At Rockingham. (1104–1106.)

. XVII. De Tychouere[1] (*rubric* and *marg.*).

.H. rex Anglorum abbati de Borc.[2] comiti .S. Michaeli de Hames*lape* . 7 Roberto de Pauilli . 7 fidelibus suis Francis 7 Anglis de Norhamte[3] scira *:* salutem . Sciatis me concessisse Roberto episcopo Linc' terram de Tichesoura quam regina uxor mea ei dedit mea precatione . Et uolo ut bene 7 honorifice teneat cum soca . 7 saca . 7 toll . 7 team . 7 omnibus consuetudinibus . Testibus . W*alerico* canc*ellario* . 7 . E*udone* . dapifero . 7 W. Peuerel[4] . de Notingham . apud Rochingeham[5].

Marginalia : .ij. + .ij. In C : Istud non habetur.
Texts : MS—A. C,f.6. Iiii(8). Pd—*Mon.*viii,1271(9). Farrer, *Itin.*, no. 148 (abs.).
Var. R : [1] Tikesour' A marg. ; Tikesou. . C marg. [2] Burc C. [3] Norhantona C. [4] Peurello Iiii. [5] Rochinham C ; Rochingham Iiii.

18

18. Writ of Henry I, commanding R[obert] bishop of Chester, Robert de Ferrers, and Richard son of Gotse to reseise Robert I bishop of Lincoln and his churches of the Peak in lands, tithes, customs, etc., as they were seised on the day on which the king gave his lordship of the Peak to William Peverel. At Chute [co. Wiltshire]. (1106–1114.)

.XVIII. De ecclesiis de Pecco (rubric and marg.).

.H. rex Anglorum . R. episcopo de Cestra . 7 Roberto de Ferr*ariis* . 7 Ricardo filio Gotse salutem . Precipio uobis ut resaisiatis Robertum[1] episcopum 7 ecclesias suas de Pecco[2] de omnibus rebus in terris 7 decimis 7 consuetudinibus 7 pratis 7 siluis . sicut ipse 7 ecclesie saisiti erant ea die qua Willielmo Peurell'[3] dominium meum de Pecco dedi . Quia sibi non dedi nichil de hiis de quibus predicte ecclesie saisite erant . Teste comite de Mell*ent* . apud Ceat.

Marginalia : .iij. + Decani (Q).
Texts : MS—A. C,f.6. Iv(10). Pd—*Mon.*viii,1272(16). *C.C.R.* iv,139(10). Farrer, *Itin.*, no. 255 (abs.).
Var. R : [1] *add* Lincol' Iv. [2] C *inserts* et *superfluously*. [3] Peuerell' C.
Note : The north and south medieties of the church of Darley, in the wapentake and deanery of High Peak, were appropriated to the dean of Lincoln.

19

19. Writ of Henry I, giving to bishop Robert I the churches of three of the king's own manors, namely, Coxwold, Kirkby Moorside, and Hovingham [co. York]. At Woodstock. (1108–1115.)

.XIX. De ecclesiis de Cucwald[1] . Kirkeby[2] . 7 de Houingham' (rubric and marg.).

.H. rex Anglorum . Thome archiepiscopo . 7 Nigello de Albini . 7 Osberto vicecomiti . 7 omnibus baronibus . 7 fidelibus Francis 7 Anglicis de Euewicscira ꝛ salutem . Sciatis me dedisse Roberto Lincoliensi episcopo ecclesias scilicet de tribus maneriis meis . uidelicet de Cucuald . 7 de Chirchebi . 7 de Houingeham . 7 quicquid ad predictas ecclesias pertinet . Et uolo 7 firmiter precipio ut bene 7 honorifice teneat . Teste . Nigello de Albini apud Weodestocam.

Marginalia : iiij. +.
Texts : MS—A.   C,f.6.   Pd—*Mon.*viii,1272(17).   Farrer, *Itin.*, no. 245 (abs.).
Var. R : [1] Cucuwald C marg.   [2] Chirkebi A marg. ; Kirkebi C.
Note : These three churches are not found again in the possession of the bishop of Lincoln.

20

20. Writ of Henry I, commanding Thurstan the archbishop [of York] and Thurstan the archdeacon to cause the bishop of Lincoln and the church of Clayworth [co. Nottingham] to have the tithes, rights, and customs which belong to that church, especially from the king's men and from all other the parishioners. At Winchester. (1123–1133.)

.XX. De decimis de Claworth'[1] (rubric and marg.).

H[2]. rex Anglorum[3] Turstino archiepiscopo[4] 7 Turstino[5] archidiacono salutem . Precipio uobis quod faciatis iuste habere[6] episcopo Lincoln' 7 ecclesie de Claworth'[7] decimas 7 omnes rectitudines 7 consuetudines ipsi ecclesie pertinentes . 7 nominatim de hominibus meis 7 de omnibus parochianis aliis predicte ecclesie pertinentibus . Teste . Cancellario apud Wintoniam[8].

Marginalia : +. Eboracen' (Q). Decani (Q).
Texts : MS—A. The charter is written by a contemporary hand, with paler ink, in the bottom margin. D201. Pd—Farrer, *Itin.*, no. 598A (abs.).
Var. R : [1] Claworth' A marg.   [2] *insert* dei gracia D.   [3] *add* etc. D.   [4] *om.* Turstino archiepiscopo D.   [5] Turstano Eboraci D.   [6] habere iuste A, *but marked to be* transposed.   [7] Clawrth' D.   [8] Wynton' D.
Note : The church of Clayworth was appropriated to the deanery of Lincoln.

Folio 4d.

Hdl.   CARTE REGIS *Henrici Primi.*

21

21. Writ of Henry I, granting to bishop Robert I licence to make a door in the wall of the king's castle [of Lincoln], for the convenience of the bishop's house ; provided that the wall be not thereby weakened. At London. (1101–1115.)

.XXI. De faciendo exitu[1] in muro castelli[2] regis (rubric and marg.).

.H.[3] rex Anglie . Rannulfo Meschino . Os*berto* vicecomiti . 7 Picoto[4] filio Colsueni . 7 omnibus baronibus suis de Lincolia *:* salutem . Sciatis me concessisse Roberto episcopo Lincolie ut faciat exitus in muro castelli mei ad sua necessaria facienda ad domum suam . ita tamen ne murum propter hoc debilitetur . Testibus . Alano de Linc' . 7 Os*berto* vicecomite . apud Lund*onias*[5].

Marginalia : .v.
Texts : MS—A21.   A,f.11 (*struck out, and* va *cat written in marg.*).   C,f.6.   Iiii(13) Pd—*Mon.*viii,1272(18).   Farrer, *Itin.*, no. 308 (abs.).   See *C.C.R.*iv,101(13).
Var. R :   [1] exit*um* C.   [2] castellis C.   [3] Henr' A,f.11.   [4] Piccoto C.   [5] Lond' A,f.11 Iiii.

22

22. Writ of Henry I, addressed to W[illiam] d'Aubigny the Breton, R. Basset, Aubrey de Vere, the sheriff, and all the king's barons and officers of Nottinghamshire. If the bishop [Alexander] of Lincoln's wapentake of Newark is assessed to the king's geld as half a wapentake, they shall summon therefrom to the king's pleas and the shire no more than two men, as in the time of Robert, the bishop's predecessor. The bishop shall have in the wapentake all the franchises, customs, and rights which his predecessors had. At Fareham [co. Southampton]. (1123–1135.)

.XXII. De wapent*achio* de Newerk[1] (rubric and marg.).

.H. rex Angl*orum* W. de Alb*ini* Briton*i* . 7 . R. Bass*et* . 7 .A. de Ver . 7 vicecom*it'* . 7 omnibus baronibus 7 ministris de Notinghe- ham[2] scira salutem . Si wapentac episcopi Linc' de Niwercha[3] defendit se uersus me pro dimidio wapentac . tunc precipio quod non summoneatis inde ad placita mea . 7 comitatus . nisi tantummodo duos homines 7 illi ibi summoneantur . ubi summonebantur tempore Roberti antecessoris sui . 7 ubi iuste debent summoneri . Et uolo 7 precipio quod episcopus habeat in wapentac illo omnes libertates 7 consuetudines suas 7 rectitudines suas . sicut antecessores sui melius habuerunt . 7 sicut iuste habere debet . T*estibus* episcopo Sar*isbiriensis* . 7 cancellario . apud Fereh*am*.

Marginalia : vj. +. . . . . . . In S : De wapentac de Niwerc.
Texts : MS—A.   S1.   C,f.6d.   Iiii(21).   Pd—*Mon.*viii,1272(20).   See *C.C.R.* iv,102(21).
Var. R.   [1] Newerch' A marg.;   Niwewer. C marg.   [2] Notingeham S; Notin- ham C; Notingeh' Iiii.   [3] Niwerca Iiii.

23

23. Writ of Henry I, granting to Saint Mary and bishop Robert I and the canons his vineyard in Lincoln ; and commanding that John the reeve shall seise them therein. At Stamford. (1103– 1106.)

.XXIII.   De vinea Linc' (rubric and marg.).

.H. rex Angl*orum* Osberto[1] vicecomiti 7 omnibus baronibus suis et burgensibus Linc' salutem . Sciatis me dedisse deo 7 sancte Marie Linc' . 7 episcopo Roberto 7 canonicis vineam meam Linc' 7 quod ei pertinet . Et Iohauis[2] prepositus eos inde saisiat . Te*ste* . W*aldrico* cancellario . apud Stanford*iam* . 7 . Te*stibus* E[udone] dapifero . 7 . Vr*sone* de A*betot*.

Marginalia : vij. +. . . . . .
Texts : MS—A. S2.   C,f.6d.   R800.   Pd—*Mon*.viii,1272(21).   Farrer, *Itin.*, no. 151 (abs.).
Var. R. : ¹ *om.* Osberto R.   ² Johannes R.   *In* A S C u *is clearly distinguishable from* n *in this name.*

24

24. Writ of Henry I, granting to the church of Lincoln the churches of Saint Margaret [in Lincoln] and Haceby [co. Lincoln], which Osbert the sheriff gave. At Portsmouth. (1115.)

.XXIIII.   De ecclesiis sancte Margarete 7 de Hathseby (rubric). De ecclesia sancte Margarete 7 ecclesia de Hathsebi[1] (marg.).

.H. rex Angl*orum* . M. regine . 7 omnibus baronibus de Lincolia[2] scira salutem . Sciatis me concessisse deo 7 sancte Marie Linc'[3] ecclesie 7 Roberto[4] episcopo ecclesiam[5] sancte Margarete . 7 ecclesiam de Hatsebi[6] quas Osbertus vicecomes dedit 7 concessit eidem ecclesie . Teste episcopo Saresberie[7] apud Portesmundam.

Marginalia : viij. +.
Texts : MS—A. S3.   C,f.7.   Iiii(20).   Pd—*Mon*.viii,1275(46).   Farrer, *Itin.*, no. 339 (abs.).   See *C.C.R*.iv,102(20).
Var. R. : ¹ Harsebi S C, *the* s *in* C *being seemingly a correction.*   ² Lincola S Iiii. ³ Lincoliensis S C Iiii.   ⁴ Rotberto Iiii.   ⁵ *om.* ecclesiam C.   ⁶ Harsebi C.   *The charter roll has* Halsebi (*C.C.R*.iv,102(20)).   *Mon*.viii,1275(46), *by misreading* C, *has* Barsebi.   ⁷ Saresbirie C.

25

25. Writ of Henry I, giving to bishop Robert I the king's warren of Lincoln in so far as it lies in the soke of Newark [co. Nottingham] and Stow [co. Lincoln] ; and confirming the right of warren in the whole soke. At Wallingford [co. Berks]. (1101–1115.)

XXV.   De warenna Linc' quantum in soca de Newerk[1] . 7 Stowa[2] . erat (rubric and marg.).

.H. rex Angl*orum* . Rannulfo Mischino . 7 Osberto vicecomiti . 7 fidelibus suis de Lincolia[3] scira ? Francis 7 Anglis salutem . Sciatis me dedisse Roberto Lincoliensi episcopo warennam meam de Lincolia[4] quantum in soca de Niwerca[5] . 7 Stou[6] erat . Et concedo ei totam socam de Niwerca[5] 7 Stou[6] in warennam . Et si quis in

ea forifecerit ♪ precipio ut ipse episcopus habeat talem[7] forisfacturam
de ea qualem pater meus 7 frater habuisset . Teste . Hugone de
Euerm*u* . apud . Warengeford' [8].

Marginalia : ix. +.
Texts : MS—A. S4. C,f.7. Ivi(1). Pd—*Mon.*viii,1273(23). See *C.C.R.*iv,105(1).
Var. R. : [1] Newerc A marg.; Niwer . . S marg. C marg. [2] Stowe A marg.; Stou
S. marg.; Stow C marg. [3] Lincola S C Ivi. [4] Lincola Ivi. [5] Newerca Ivi.
[6] Stoue Ivi. [7] *om.* talem S C. [8] Warengefort C.

26

26. Writ of Henry I, granting to the bishop of Lincoln licence
to divert the king's highway through the bishop's town of Newark ;
and to make a causey for his vivary. At Woodstock [co. Oxford].
(1129–1133.) Cp. no. 46 below.

.XXVI. De strata de Newerk[1] diuertenda (rubric and marg.).

.H. rex Ang*lorum* . Ricardo Basset . 7 A. de Ver . 7 vicecom*it* . 7
baronibus de No*tinge[2] scira ♪ salutem . Concedo quod episcopus
Linc' diuertat regiam stratam que transibat per uillam suam de
Niwerca[3] per eandem uillam suam quacunque uoluerit . Et concedo
ipsi ut faciat calcetam uiuarii sui . Testibus G.[4] cancellario . 7
Willelmo de Alb*ini* Britone . apud Wdestoc[5].

Marginalia : x. +.
Texts : MS—A26. A71A. S5. C,f.7. Iv(6). Pd—*Mon.*viii,1273(24). Farrer,
Itin., no. 665 (abs.). See *C.C.R.*,iv,138(6).
Var. R. : [1] Newerc A26 marg.; Newerch' A71A marg.; Niwerc S marg. C marg.
[2] Notingeham A71A, Iv. [3] Niwercha A71A, Iv. [4] Gaufrido Iv. [5] Vdestoc' A71A ;
Wodestoc Iv.

*Folio 5.

Hdl.　　　　　　*Carte Regis* HENRICI PRIMI.　　　　　.5.

27

27. Writ of Henry I, commanding Osbert the sheriff of Lincoln
to cause bishop Robert I to have the churches of Caistor and Kirton
[in Lindsey], which the king's father gave in alms to Saint Mary
of Lincoln, according to the charter of the king's father, and as
bishop Remigius had them. At London. (1100–1115.)

XXVII. De ecclesiis de Castra . 7 Chirchetona[1] (rubric and
marg.).

.H. rex Ang*lorum* Osberto . vicecomiti Linc' salutem . Fac
habere Roberto episcopo Linc'[2] ecclesias de Castra[3] . 7 Chirchetona[4] .
7 decimas quas pater meus dedit in elemosinam deo 7 sancte Marie
Lincoliensi sicut carta quam fecit pater meus fieri ♪ dicit . 7 sicut

Remigius episcopus 7 ecclesia sancte Marie Lincolie eas unquam melius habuerunt . Et uide ne ei super hoc aliqua iniuria fiat . Teste Nigello de Oili . apud Lundon*ias*.

Marginalia: *scribatur* (query Q2). +
Texts: MS—A. S6. C,f.7. R17. Pd—*Mon*.viii,1273(25).
Var. R.: [1] Kirketon' S R.; *add* cum decimis A marg. [2] Lincolie S C R.
[3] Castre C. [4] Cherchetona R.

28

28. Writ of Henry I, commanding Rannulf Meschin, Osbert the sheriff, Picot son of Colsuen, and Wigot of Lincoln to go and view the boundary between the king's manor of Torksey and the bishop's manor of Stow ; and to cause the boundary to be defined by good men of the county, who may be required to confirm their testimony by oath. At Winchester. (1110–1114.)

.XXVIII. De diuisis faciendis inter Torkesi[1] 7 Stowe (rubric and marg.).

.H. rex Anglorum . Rannulfo Mischino[2] . 7 Osberto vicecomiti . 7 Picoto filio Colsueni . 7 Wigoto de Linc' ·: salutem . Ite 7 uidete diuisas inter manerium meum de Torchesi . 7 manerium de Estou . 7 facite recognoscere per probos homines de comitatu 7 diuidere predictas diuisas . Et si bene eis non credideritis sacramento confirment quod dixerint . Quia uolo ut episcopus bene 7 honorifice ibi habeat quod antecessores sui ibi habuerunt . Teste Wig*oto* Linc' . apud Wincestr*iam*.

Marginalia: +.
Texts: MS—A. S7. C,ff.7,7d. Pd—*Mon*.viii,1273(26). Farrer, *Itin*., no. 333 (abs.).
Var. R.: [1] Thorchesi S marg. C marg. [2] Meschino C.

29

29. Writ of Henry I, commanding Osbert the sheriff of Lincoln[shire] and Rannulf Meschin to cause bishop Robert I to hold all his lands, men, and possessions honourably. The king is unwilling that the bishop shall plead concerning the lands of which his predecessor was seised on the day that he was alive and dead, or concerning the churches which the bishop himself has held until now. At Lacock [co. Wilts]. (1100–1110.)

.XXIX. De terris 7 hominibus cum honore tenendis . 7 ne placitet de terris neque de ecclesiis (rubric and marg.).

.H. rex Angl*orum* Osberto . vicecomiti Lincol' . 7 Rannulfo Mischino ·: sal*utem* . Precipio ut faciatis Robertum Lincoliensem episcopum terras suas omnes 7 homines 7 omnia sua cum magno

honore tenere . Et nolo ut ullo modo placitet de terris de quibus
antecessor eius saisitus erat die qua uiuus 7 mortuus fuit . neque
de ecclesiis 7 quas ipse episcopus tenuit usque nunc . Teste . Vr*sone* .
de Abetot . apud La coc[1].

Marginalia: +.
Texts: MS—A. S8. C,f.7d. Iv(4). Pd—*Mon.*viii,1273(27). Farrer, *Itin.*, no.
30 (abs.). See *C.C.R.*iv,138(4).
Var. R.: [1] Lacoc S C.

30

30. Writ of Henry I, addressed to Osbert the sheriff of Lincoln-
[shire], Picot [son of Colsuen], and Alan [of Lincoln], commanding
that Welton [by Lincoln] shall be free from all gelds and customary
payments as in the time of the king's father and brother ; and free
especially from the aid that is now being collected ; because Welton
was given by the king's father and mother as alms [to the church
of Lincoln]. At Perry [Court, co. Huntingdon]. (1107–1115.)

.XXX. Quod Welleton' quieta sit de geldis . 7 consuetudinibus[1]
(rubric and marg.).

.H. rex Ang*lorum* Osberto . vicecomiti de Linc' 7 Picoto . 7 Alano
sal*utem* . Precipio quod Welletona cum apendiciis suis sit quieta
de omnibus geldis . 7 consuetudinibus sicut fuit tempore patris 7
fratris mei . Et nominatim de hoc auxilio . Quia elemosina patris
mei 7 matris fuit . Teste . Rannulfo cancellario . apud Peri.

Marginalia: *scribatur* (query Q2). +. ☞
Texts: MS—A. S9. C,f.7d. C,f.13d (a 13th century copy). R15. Iv(7).
Pd—*Mon.*viii,1273(28). *C.C.R.*iv,138(7); Farrer, *Itin.*, no. 259 (abs.).
Var. R.: [1] de libertatibus de Welleton' S marg.

31

31. Writ of Henry I, commanding that the church of Lincoln,
bishop Robert I, and the canons shall hold freely the manor of Welton
[by Lincoln], which the king's father gave *in prebenda* to Saint Mary.
At Newbury [co. Berks]. (Circa 1103–1107.)

.XXXI. Item de Welleton' quod quieta sit[1] (rubric). Item de
Welleton (marg.).

.H. rex Ang*lorum* Rannulfo Meschino . 7 Osberto . vicecomiti
Linc' . 7 omnibus fidelibus suis Francis 7 Anglis de Linc'[2] scira ⁊
salutem . Volo 7 precipio ut sancta Maria de Lincolia . 7 Robertus
episcopus . 7 canonici sancte Marie ita bene 7 ho*norifice habeant
7 quiete teneant manerium de Welletona quod pater meus dedit

sancte Marie in prebenda . 7 quicquid ibi pertinet sicut breuis
patris mei 7 fratris regis Willelmi precipiunt . Testibus Waldrico
cancellario . 7 . Vrsone de Abetot . apud Niweberiam³.

Marginalia in A: Scribatur (query Q2). In C: Nota.
Texts: MS—A. S10. C,f.7d. R16. Pd—Mon.viii,1273(29). Farrer, Itin.,
no. 95 (abs.).
Var. R.: ¹ De libertatibus manerii de Welleton' S marg. ² Lincole R. ³ add
post Epiphaniam domini R.

*Folio 5d.
Hdl.   Carte Regis Henrici Primi.

32

32. Writ of Henry I, addressed to the barons of the Exchequer,
commanding that the land of Saint Mary of Lincoln shall be quit
of the aid which he has received therefrom for his daughter's
business. At Westminster. (1110.)

.XXXII. Item quod tota terra beate Marie Linc' quieta sit
de omni consuetudine (rubric).

H. rex Anglorum ? baronibus de scaccario¹ salutem . Sciatis quod
nolo ut terra sancte Marie Linc'² sit in consuetudine propter
auxilium quod inde habui ad opus filie mee . sed sit ita quieta
sicut pater meus precepit . Testibus . Rogero episcopo Sarisbirie³ .
7 Ranulfo cancellario . apud Westmonasterium.

Marginalia: scribatur (query Q2).
Texts: MS—A; written in the margin at the foot of f. 5, by a contemporary
hand with ink of a paler colour, like A20. R18.
Var. R.: ¹ escecario R. ² de Lincolia R. ³ Salesberie R.

33

33. Writ of Henry I, granting to the church of Lincoln the
churches of [King's] Sutton [co. Northampton], and the land in
Horley [co. Oxford], which Ranulf bishop of Durham held of him
to increase the prebend which he and Elias his son had in the church
of Lincoln. The king wills that Elias shall have the prebend as
long as he lives ; and if he die before his father, the prebend shall
remain to his father. But after they are both dead, the prebend
shall remain to the church of Lincoln. At Hertford. (1110–1122.)

.XXXIII. De ecclesiis de Suttona¹ (rubric)².

.H. rex Anglorum Roberto episcopo Linc' . 7 canonicis sancte
Marie Linc' 7 omnibus baronibus Francis 7 Anglis de Lincolia
scira³ . 7 omnibus baronibus totius episcopatus Linc' salutem .
Sciatis me dedisse 7 concessisse deo 7 sancte Marie 7 ecclesie Linc'
ecclesias de Sutona 7 terras 7 consuetudines 7 decimas . 7 quicquid

ad eas pertinet . 7 terram de Horneleia . quam Rannulfus episcopus
Dunelmensis de me tenebat ad acrescens uidelicet prebende quam
ipse episcopus Rannulfus . 7 Elyas[4] filius suus in ecclesia sancte
Marie Linc' habebant . 7 uolo 7 concedo ut ipse Elyas[5] filius episcopi
Rannulfi prebendam illam totam cum acrescentibus[6] istis bene 7
honorifice quamdiu ipse uixerit : teneat . Quod si ille Elyas[4] prius
moriatur quam pater suus Rannulfus episcopus uolo 7 precipio ut
prebenda illa tota Rannulfo episcopo remaneat libera 7 quieta . Post
obitum uero utrorumque eorum prebenda illa tota deo 7 sancte
Marie 7 ecclesie Linc' 7 episcopo libera 7 quieta remaneat . Et hoc
idem Robertus[7] coram me Rannulfo episcopo 7 Elye[8] filio suo
concessit. Testibus Gaufrido archiepiscopo Rotomagi[9] . 7 Rannulfo
cancellario . apud Hertfort[10].

Marginalia in A: 2. Va cat. In C: Nota.
Texts: MS—A. S11. C,f.11d. Iiii(17). Pd—Mon.viii,1273(30). Farrer, Itin.,
no. 432 (abs.). See C.C.R.iv,102(17).
Var. R: [1] Sutona S. [2] De Sutton ecclesiis marg. [3] add 7 de Oxineford scira
S Iiii; add 7 de Oxineford scire C. Q has added in marg. 7 Oxenefordscir'. [4] Elias
Iiii. [5] Helyas C. [6] accrescentibus Iiii. [7] Rotbertus Iiii. [8] Elie Iiii. [9] Rotho-
magi S C Iiii. [10] Hertford Iiii.

34

34. Writ of Henry I, granting to Saint Mary of Lincoln and
bishop Robert I and his successors the church of Saint Benedict in
Wigford, at the request of Roger Bigod who gave it in alms to
Saint Mary. At Winchester. (Before 1107.)

.XXXIIII. De ecclesia sancti Benedicti in Wikefordia[1] (rubric
and marg.).

.H. rex Anglorum . Rannulfo Mischino . 7 Osberto vicecomiti . 7
omnibus baronibus suis Francis 7 Anglis de Lincolia[2] scira . salutem .
Sciatis me concessisse deo 7 sancte Marie de Lincolia 7 Roberto
episcopo 7 successoribus suis imperpetuum[3] habendam ecclesiam
sancti Benedicti de Wicheford[4] cum omnibus rebus ad ipsam
ecclesiam pertinentibus . 7 hoc precatu 7 voluntate Rogeri Bigot .
qui illam ecclesiam in elemosinam deo 7 sancte Marie dedit .
Testibus . Rogero episcopo . 7 Waldrico cancellario . 7 . Roberto
comite de Mellent . 7 . Henrico de Warewic . et ipso Rogero . 7 Hamone
dapifero . apud Wintoniam.

Texts: MS—A. S12. C,f.8. Iiii(15). Pd—Mon.viii,1273(31).
Var. R.: [1] Wicford marg. [2] Lincola S Iiii. [3] inperpetuum S C. [4] Wichefotl S;
Wichefort C; Wycheford Iiii.

35

35. Writ of Henry I, granting to the church of Lincoln the church
of Brand the priest of Corringham, and its land, namely two-and-a-
half carucates, *in prebenda*, provided that Brand, and his son after

him, shall hold of Saint Mary the said church and land *in prebenda* as long as they shall live. At Worcester. (1100–1115.)

.XXXV. De ecclesia de Coringham . 7 . ij . carucatis terre . 7 dimidiam (rubric and marg.).

.H. rex Anglie . Roberto Linc' episcopo . 7 Rannulfo Mischino . 7 Osberto vicecomiti . 7 baronibus suis 7 fidelibus Francis 7 Anglis de Lincolia[1] scira salutem . Sciatis me concessisse sancte Marie de Linc'[2] ecclesiam Brand presbiteri de Coringeham . 7 terram suam scilicet . ij . carrucatas 7 dimidiam in prebenda . ita tamen ut ipse Brand 7 filius eius post obitum patris ecclesiam predictam 7 terram in prebenda de sancta Maria teneant dum uixerint . T*este* . Rannulfo Mischino . apud Wirecestra*m*[3] . 7 . Testibus Osb*erto* vicecomite . 7 Romfara.

Marginalia : Va cat.
Texts : MS—A. S13 (damaged). C,f.8. Iiii(19). Pd—*Mon*.viii,1273(32). Farrer, *Itin.*, no. 189 (abs.). See *C.C.R.*iv,102(19).
Var. R. : [1] Lincola S C Iiii. [2] Lincola Iiii ; Lincol' C. [3] Wirecestram Iiii.

36

36. Writ of Henry I, granting to the church of Lincoln and bishop Robert I the church of Empingham [co. Rutland], and those three bovates of land which Gilbert of Ghent added in alms. [Henry] count of Eu has disseised the bishop. Aubrey [de Vere] the chamberlain is to reseise him therein. At Brampton [co. Huntingdon]. (1106–1110.)

.XXXVI. De ecclesia de Empingeham . 7 . iij . bouatis terre (rubric and marg.).

.H. rex Anglie . S. comiti . 7 Hugoni vicecomiti . 7 omnibus baronibus suis de Norhamtona[1] scira ? salutem . Sciatis me concessisse ecclesie sancte Marie Lincol' . 7 Roberto episcopo* Linc' ecclesiam de Empingeham[2] . 7 illas . iij . bovatas terre quas Gislebertus de Gant creuit in elemosina . Et uolo 7 precipio ut honorifice teneat cum omnibus consuetudinibus suis . Et si comes de Auco dissaisiuit eum ? tunc precipio . ut Alb*ericus*[3] camerarius eum[4] cito resaisiat . Teste . Osberto vicecomite . apud Brantonam.

Marginalia : Va cat. Alie carte sunt in pixide (Q).
Texts : MS—A. S14. C,f.8. Pd—*Mon*.viii,1273(33). Farrer, *Itin.*, no. 219 (abs.).
Var. R. : [1] Norhantona C. [2] Hempingeham C. [3] Abb' C. [4] *om.* eum S C.

*Folio 6.

Hdl.   *Carte Regis* HENRICI PRIMI.   .6.

37

37. Writ of Henry I, granting to Saint Mary and bishop Robert I and his successors the toll of the fairs of Stow ; to wit, on the feasts of Saint Mary in August [the Assumption, 15 August] and September [the Nativity, 8 September], and at Michaelmas and Pentecost. At Winchester. (1103–4, or 1107.)

.XXXVII. De theloneo in feriis de Stowe[1] (rubric and marg.).

H rex Anglie . A. archiepiscopo Cantuar*iensi* . 7 Ger*ardo* archiepiscopo Eboracensi . 7 episcopis suis 7 abbatibus . 7 omnibus baronibus suis 7 fidelibus Francis 7 Anglis tocius Anglie salutem . Sciatis me concessisse deo 7 sancte Marie 7 Roberto Linc' episcopo . 7 omnibus[2] successoribus suis imperpetuum habendum theloneum in feriis del Estou scilicet in festo sancte Marie Augusti . 7 in Septembris[3] . 7 illa feria que est in festiuitate sancti Michaelis . 7 in Pentecosten . Testibus . R. episcopo Salesb*erie*[4] . 7 comite de Mellent . 7 cancellario . 7 . R. Bigot . 7 Hamone dapifero . apud Winton*iam*.

Texts : MS—A. S15 (incomplete). C,ff.8,8d. Pd—*Mon.*viii,1274(34). Farrer, *Itin.*, no. 71 (abs.).
Var. R. : [1] del Estou S. [2] The rest is missing in S. [3] *sic.* [4] Saleberie C.

38

38. Writ of Henry I, granting to the church of Lincoln the churches of Derby and Wirksworth [co. Derby] *in prebendam.* (1100–1109.)

.XXXVIII. De ecclesiis de Derby[1] 7 de Wirkeswrthe[2] (rubric and marg.).

.H. dei gracia rex Angl*orum* . Roberto Couentreensi[3] episcopo . 7 Ricardo vicecomiti . 7 Rogero comiti . 7 Willelmo Peuerel . 7 Roberto de Ferariis . 7 omnibus fidelibus suis de Notingeham[4] scira[5] 7 de Derbere escira[6] . salutem . Sciatis me dedisse deo 7 sancte Marie Lincoliensis[7] ecclesie pro anima patris 7 matris méé 7 pro anima Willelmi regis fratris mei 7 mea . 7 Matildis regine vxoris méé ecclesias de Derbeia . 7 de Werchesorda in prebendam perpetuo iure possidendas ⁏ cum omnibus eis iure adiacentibus . Volo autem 7 precipio ut ita honorifice 7 quiete eas possideat ⁏ sicut melius fuerunt tempore regis Edwardi . 7 patris mei . Testibus . Matilde regina . 7 Roberto Haim*onis* filio . 7 Haim*one* dapifero . 7 Vrs*one* de Abetot[8] . 7 Osb*erto* vicecomite Lincol*ie*.

Marginalia : Va cat. + Derb' . . . . . . In C : Nota.
Texts : MS—A. C,f.8d. D126. Pd—*Mon.*viii,1274(35).
Var. R. : [1] Derbi A marg. ; Derebi C marg. [2] Wirkesworth' A marg. ; *om.* 7 de Wirkeswrthe C marg. [3] Couentrensi D. [4] Notinham C. [5] esscira D. [6] esscira C D. [7] Lincolliensis C. [8] Habetot C.
Note : The reason for marking this charter ' vacat ' is not evident, seeing that charters of other churches appropriated to the dean are not so marked, e.g. nos. 18 and 20.

39

39. Writ of Henry I, commanding Ralf de Rehart and his fellows to place the bishop of Lincoln in seisin of [the churches of]

Barkstone [co. Leicester] and Uffington [co. Lincoln]. At Southampton. (1114–1116.) (See no. 68 below.)

XXXIX. ¹De ecclesiis de Barkeston' 7 Offington'¹ (rubric and marg.).

.H. rex Anglie² . Radulfo de Rehart 7 sociis suis salutem . Saisite episcopum de Lincolia de Barchestona . 7 de Offintona . 7 de omnibus rebus que ad eam pertinent . 7 bene 7 honorifice teneat . Teste . Willelmo de Albinni . apud Hamtonam.

Marginalia: +. Va cat.
Texts: MS—A. C,f.8d. Pd—*Mon.*viii,274(36).
Var. R.: ¹⁻¹ De Barcheston' 7 Offinton' C marg. ² Angl' C.

40

40. Writ of Henry I, addressed to the sheriffs and officers in whose jurisdiction the canons of Lincoln have their prebends. The king commands that the canons shall hold those prebends as they held them best in the time of bishop Robert I. If any one shall do them any injury, the king's justice shall do them full right. At Portsmouth. (Probably 1123.)

.XL. Quod canonici Linc' honorifice 7 bene teneant prebendas 7 alia (rubric and marg.).

.H. rex Anglorum omnibus vicecomitibus . 7 ministris . in quorum ministeriis canonici Linc'¹ ecclesie² habent prebendas suas : salutem . Precipio quod omnes canonici Linc' ita bene 7 honorifice teneant prebendas suas . 7 in ecclesiis 7 decimis 7 domibus 7 terris 7 hominibus 7 denariis 7 consuetudinibus eisdem ubicumque aliquid inde habent sicut melius 7 honorificentius tenuerunt tempore Roberti episcopi Linc' . Et prohibeo ne aliquis faciat eis inde aliquam iniuriam . Et si aliquis eis iniuriam fecerit : iusticia mea faciat eis habere plenum rectum . Teste episcopo Sarisbirie . apud Portesmundam.³

Marginalia: *scribatur* (query Q2). iiij° +.
Texts: MS—A. R19.
Var. R.: ¹ Lincolie R. ² *om.* ecclesie R. ³ Portesmudam R.

Folio 6d.
Hdl.   CARTE REGIS *Henrici Primi.*

41

41. Writ of Henry I, granting to Saint Mary of Lincoln and bishop Robert I the churches of Nassington, Wood Newton, Tansor, and Southwick [co. Northampton], *in prebendam.* And the church and bishop shall hold them as at any time Leving, the king's scribe, best held them. At Westminster. (1110–1123.)

.XLI.　De ecclesiis de Nessing*ton*' Newenton' . Tanesour' . 7 Suthwic'[1] (marg.).

.H. rex Ang*lorum* . Symoni decano 7 toti capitulo sancte Marie Linc' . 7 Hugoni de Lere*cestra* . 7 omnibus baronibus Francis 7 Anglis de Norhamtescira[2] salutem . Sciatis me dedisse 7 concessisse deo 7 sancte Marie Lincol'. 7 Roberto episcopo pro anima patris 7 matris 7 fratris mei . 7 salute anime méé . 7 uxoris méé in prebendam . ecclesiam de Nessintona . 7 ecclesiam de Niwentona . 7 ecclesiam de Tanesoura . 7 ecclesiam de Sutwica[3] . cum terris 7 decimis 7 consuetudinibus que ad eas pertinent . Et uolo 7 firmiter precipio 7 concedo ut bene 7 honorifice teneant cum[4] quietudinibus 7 consuetudinibus . sicut Leuingus scriptor regis unquam melius 7 honorabilius tenuit . Testibus . Rogero episcopo Saresb*irie*[5] . 7 Rannulfo cancellario . 7 Johanne de Baic*is*[6] . apud Westmonast*erium*[7].

Marginalia : Ista carta est penes W. de Aualun (contemporary hand). A head with a fool's cap is drawn in marg. ユ. In C : De ecclesia de Nessiton'. Nota.

Texts : MS—A. C,f.8d. Iiii(16). Iviii(5). Pd—*Mon*.viii,1274(37). See *C.C.R.*iv, 101(16).

Var. R. : [1] *om.* Newenton' . . . Suthwic' C marg. [2] Norhantona scira C. [3] Sutwyca Iiii. [4] *insert* omnibus Iiii. [5] Sarebirie C. [6] Baioc*is* Iiii. [7] Westmonest' C.

Note : William of Avalun was prebendary of Nassington in 1222, when as prebendary he had 10s. a year in the name of a perpetual benefice from the rectory of Southwick (L.R.S.ii,112). In 1224 and 1232 he had an annual payment of two-and-a-half marks from either mediety of the church of Tansor (*ibid.*,123,165,216). In 1236 his name is placed first amongst the canons in two lists of witnesses (*ibid.*,xi,163,391).

42

42. Writ of Henry I, granting to the church and bishop Robert I of Lincoln twelve bovates which Ralf Basset proved by legal process to be in the king's demesne ; namely, six bovates in Burgh [on Bain] and six bovates in [South] Willingham [co. Lincoln]. At Guildford [co. Surrey]. (1121—January, 1122–3.)

.XLII.　[1]De .xij. bouatis terre in Burgo . 7 Wollingham'[1] (A marg.).

.H. rex Ang*lie* . comiti Ranulfo de Cestra[2] . 7 Hugoni de Legre*cestra* . 7 omnibus baronibus . de Linc'scira[3] ⫶ salutem . Sciatis me reddidisse deo 7 ęcclesię . 7 Roberto episcopo Lincol' .xij. bouatas terre quas Radulfus Basset disrationauit esse in dominio meo . videlicet . vj. bouatas in Burgo . 7 . vi. bouatas in Welingeham[4] . Et uolo 7 precipio quod bene . 7 honorifice . 7 libere teneat . cum saca . 7 soca . 7 toll . 7 theam . 7 infangen theof . 7 cum omnibus aliis consuetudinibus suis . sicut melius 7 honorificentius tenet alias terras suas . Testibus . Ranulfo cancellario . 7 Nigello de Albin*i* . 7 Willelmo de Tanc*ar*uilla . 7 Gaufrido de Glint*ona* . apud Geldeforda*m*.

Facsimile facing p. 36.

Endorsed : (1) de xij bouatis terre (12 cent.). (2) H. regis (13 cent.). (3) IЛI. H i. (13 cent.).

Part of the strip for the seal has been torn off, leaving only 1½ inches, and the ribband below it is missing. Size: 8½ x 3 inches.
Marginalia in A: + 2. In C: Nota pro Welingeh'.
Texts: MS—Orig. A1/1/4. A. C,f.8d. Pd—*Mon.*viii,1274(38). *E.H.R.*xxxiii,725. Farrer, *Itin.*, no. 464 (abs.).
Var. R.: ¹⁻¹sex bouat' terre in B*u*rgo [7 se]x in Welingeham C marg. ²de Cestre C. ³Lincoll' scira C. ⁴vi in Wellingeham A.
Note: Blore (*The History and Antiquities of the County of Rutland*, p. 136) wrongly identifies the places in the charter as Gainsborough and Willingham by Stow.

43

43. Writ of Henry I, restoring Kilsby [co. Northampton], with soke and sake, to Saint Mary of Lincoln and bishop Robert I, as in the time of king Edward and the king's father. At Westminster. (1100–1107.)

.XLIII.   De Kildesbi cum soca 7 sacha (marg.).

.H. rex Anglie . Symoni . comiti . 7 Willelmo de Cahaines . 7 omnibus fidelibus suis Francis 7 Anglicis salutem . Sciatis me reddidisse deo 7 sancte Marie Lincoliensi 7 Roberto episcopo Chilesbi cum soca 7 saca 7 omnibus consuetudinibus sicut unquam melius fuit tempore regis Edwardi 7 patris mei . Testibus . Rogero Big*ot* . 7 Haimone dapifero apud Westmonas*terium*.

Text: MS—A.
Note: William de Cahaines was sheriff of Northamptonshire in 1105.

44

44. Writ of Henry I, granting to Saint Mary of Lincoln all the houses which Robert de Stotvill gave to the said church *in prebenda*, to hold as Hugh son of Baldric best held them in the time of the king's father. At Windsor. (Circa 1107.)

.XLIIII.   De domibus que fuerunt Roberti de Stoteuilla (marg.).

.H. rex Anglorum . Roberto Legrecestrensi comiti . 7 Rannulpho le Mischin . 7 Osberto vicecomiti . 7 omnibus fidelibus suis Francis 7 Anglis de Lincol' scira . salutem. Volo ut sciatis me concessisse deo 7 sancte Marie de Lincolia pro anima patris mei 7 matris méé 7 fratris mei¹ 7 mea 7 vxoris méé Matildis . parentumque meorum omnes domos in prebenda quas Robertus de Stoteuilla dedit sancte Marie predicte ecclesie . Et uolo ut² ita bene 7 honorifice ipsa predicta ecclesia teneat domos illas sicut melius 7 quietius tenuit eas Hugo filius Baldrici tempore patris mei . Testibus . Matilde regina . 7 Roberto comite . de Legrecestr*ia* . 7 Henrico comite . 7 Rogero Bigot . 7 Willelmo de Albin*i* . apud Windesor*am*.

Marginalia: + 2 preb'. In C: De domibus que dedit .R. de . . . . uill' (C marg.).
Texts: MS—A. C,f.9. Pd—*Mon.*viii,1274(39).
Var. R.: ¹*om.* mei C. ²*om.* ut C.

45

45. Writ of Henry I, giving to Saint Mary of Lincoln and bishop Robert all the churches in the borough of Lincoln, within and without, which their priests held of the king. The king, however, retains any customary payments from these churches, which may belong to him. At Cirencester [co. Gloucester]. (1100–1107.)

.XLV. De omnibus ecclesiis Linc' (marg.).

.H. rex Anglorum Rannulfo Meschino . 7 Osberto vicecomiti Lincol' . 7 omnibus baro*nibus suis 7 Francis 7 Anglis salutem . Sciatis me dedisse deo 7 ecclesie sancte Marie Lincoliensi . 7 Roberto episcopo Linc' pro anima patris matrisque[1] méé . 7 . W. regis fratris mei . 7 antecessorum meorum . necnon 7 pro salute anime méé . 7 Matildis uxoris méé 7 omnium liberorum meorum . omnes ecclesias de burgo Lincolie intus 7 extra quas presbiteri earumdem ecclesiarum de me tenebant[2] . Et quicquid ipsis ecclesiis pertinet . Si quid uero consuetudinis michi de ipsis ecclesiis pertinet[3] ⁊ hoc in manu mea retineo . Testibus . Eudone dapifero . 7 Rogero Bigot[4] . 7 Haimone[5] dapifero . 7 Vrsone de Abetot . 7 Osberto vicecomiti apud Cirescestram[6].

Marginalia: vide plus in folio 23 (by a 16th century hand, directing attention to no. 158 below). Scribatur.
Texts: MS—A. S16 (defective). C,f.9. R22. Iv(8). Pd—Mon.viii,1274(40). See C.C.R.iv,138(8).
Var. R.: [1] for matrisque read 7 matris R. [2] teneant R. [3] up to this point the text of S is missing. [4] Big' R. [5] Haim' C; Ham' R. [6] Cirecestram C R.

*Folio 7.

Hdl.　　　　　Carte Regis . HENRICI . PRIMI.　　　　.7.

46

46. Writ of Henry I, granting to bishop Alexander licence to make a dike and causey for his vivary at Newark above the Foss Way; and to divert the Foss Way, as it passes through the town. At Woodstock [co. Oxford]. (1129–1135.)

.XLVI. De calceda de Newerch' (marg.).

.H. rex Anglorum . omnibus baronibus 7 vicecomit' 7 ministris suis 7 fidelibus de ¹Notingeham scira¹ ⁊ salutem . Sciatis me concessisse Alexandro episcopo Linc' quod faciat fossatum 7 calcedam[2] uiuarii sui de Niwerca[3] supra chiminum Fosse . 7 chiminum ipsum per eandem villam sicut uoluerit diuertat . Teste . W. de[4] Albini Britone . apud Wdestoc[5].

Marginalia: +. In C: De fossato 7 . . . uiuarii de Ni . . . .
Texts: MS—A. S17 (injured). C,f.9. Iiii(12). Pd—Mon.viii,1274(41). See C.C.R.iv,101(12).
Var. R.: ¹⁻¹ Notinghamsc'Iiii. [2] corrected from calcetam C. [3] Newerca Iiii. [4] om. de C. [5] Wdestock Iiii.

C

47

47. *A duplicate of no. 55 below. It is marked ' va cat' in marg., seemingly by* Q.

48

48. Writ of Henry I, granting to the bishop of Lincoln a fair lasting five days at the bishop's castle of Newark; namely, on the feast of Saint Mary Magdalene [22 July] and the four preceding days. The king directs that all who come thither to buy or to sell shall have the king's peace in coming and returning. At Fareham [co. Southampton]. (Query circa 1133.)

.XLVIII. De feria de Newerch'[1] (marg.).

.H. rex Angl*orum* . archiepiscopis . episcopis . abbatibus . comitibus . 7 omnibus baronibus . 7 fidelibus suis tocius Anglie ∴ salutem . Sciatis me concessisse episcopo Linc' feriam unam de . v. diebus ad castellum suum de Niwerca . scilicet die festi sancte Marie Magdalene . 7 . iiii. primis precedentibus diebus . Et omnes illi undecumque sint qui illuc uenerint causa emendi uel uendendi habeant meam firmam pacem illuc eundo 7 inde redeundo ne super hoc iniuste disturbentur . uel mercatum eorum unde in feria suas rectas dederint consuetudines super . x. libris . forisfacture . Teste . .E. filio Johannis apud Fereham.

Marginalia: *illegible.* + R.
Texts: MS—A. S19 (injured). C,f.9d. Iiii(11). Pd—*Mon.*viii,1272(10). See *C.C.R.*iv,101(11).
Var. R.: [1] Niwerc' C marg.

49

49. Writ of Henry I, giving to bishop Alexander the gate of Eastgate with the tower which is over it, in order that he may use it as a lodging. At Westbourne [co. Sussex]. (1130–1133.)

.XLIX. De porta de Estgate[1] (marg.).

.H. rex Angl*orum* . Willelmo de Albi*n*ni[2] . 7 Willelmo filio Haconis . vicecomiti . 7 omnibus baronibus 7 fidelibus suis Francis 7 Anglis[3] de Lincole scira salutem . Sciatis me dedisse 7 concessisse Alexandro episcopo Linc' portam de Estegata[4] cum turri[5] que supra ipsam est . ad se hospitandum . Et precipio quod illam honorifice teneat . Testibus . Rogero episcopo Sar*isbirie* . 7 Nigello episcopo de Ely . 7 Ricardo Basset . 7 A de[6] Ver de[7] Buneham[8].

Marginalia in Iviii: De carta de porta 7 terra de Estgate vbi quondam morabatur dominus Linc' episcopus.
Texts: MS—A. S20. C,f.9d. Iiii(14). Iviii(8). Pd—*Mon.*viii,1274(43). Farrer, *Itin.*, no. 708 (abs.). See *C.C.R.*iv,101(14).
Var. R.: [1] Estgata C marg., *which adds* cum terris. *and* Istud non habetur. [2] Albini S C. [3] Anglicis Iiii. [4] Estgata C. [5] *for* cum turri *read* cum terris S C. [6] A *and* de *are joined in* A. [7] apud S C Iiii. [8] Burnham Iiii.

Folio 7d.

Hdl. Carte Regis *Henrici Primi.*

50

50. Writ of Henry I, commanding Osbert the sheriff of Lincoln-[shire] to cause Hugh the canon to have the land of Hundon [in the parish of Caistor, co. Lincoln], which the men of Roger of Poitou hold, if it belongs to the alms of the king's father, namely to the church of Caistor. At Perry [Court, co. Huntingdon]. (1100–1115, probably 1110.)

.L. De terra de Hauedon*a* (rubric and marg.).

.H. rex Ang*lorum* . Osberto vicecomiti de Linc' . salutem . Precipio tibi ut iuste facias habere Hugonem canonicum terram de Hauendona quam homines Rogeri Pictau*ensis* tenent . si pertinet ad elemosinam patris mei videlicet ad ecclesiam de Castra . 7 ita ne pro penuria recti amplius inde clamorem audiam . Teste . Rannulfo cancellario . apud Peri.

Texts: MS—A. S21 (injured). Pd—Farrer, *Itin.*, p. 154, no. 259A (abs.).

51

51. Writ of Henry I, granting to bishop Alexander licence to assign the third part of the service of his knights of the bishopric of Lincoln to his castle of Newark, in order that they may henceforth perform castle-guard there, and their other services as the bishop shall dispose. At Blackmoor [co. Southampton]. (1123–1133.)

.LI. De tercia parte seruicii militum episcopi ponenda ad castellum de Newerk'[1] (rubric and marg.)[2].

.H. rex Ang*lorum* . omnibus iustic*iariis* . 7 baronibus . 7 vicecomitibus . 7 omnibus fidelibus suis tocius Anglie . salutem . Sciatis me concessisse Alexandro episcopo Linc' totam terciam partem de seruitio militum suorum de episcopatu Linc' ad ponend*um* eam ad castellum suum de Niwerca[3] ut ibi amodo faciant wardas . 7 alia seruitia sua que debent episcopo . sicut ipse episcopus hoc disposuerit . Testibus . [4] episcopo Sar*isbirie* . 7 .G. cancellario . 7 .W. de Pontearch' . apud Blachemoram.

Marginalia in C: De seruitio militum episcopi.
Texts: MS—A. S22. C,f.9d. Pd—*Mon.*viii,1274(44). Farrer, *Itin.*, no. 696 (abs.).
Var. R.: [1] Newerch' A marg.   [2] De seruicio militum episcopi S marg. C marg.
[3] Werca C.   [4] *insert* R. S C.

52

52. Writ of Henry I, recording that he has brought the abbot of Peterborough and the bishop of Lincoln into agreement in the plea that was between them touching the parish church of Peter-borough. The abbot, in the presence of the king and his court, has admitted the customs which the bishop claimed in that parish church ; in such wise that the bishop may hold therein his pleas, synod, and chapters, as in the other parish churches of the bishopric. The king also grants that the bishop may set the abbot a day to come into the chapter of Saint Mary of Lincoln, and do right to the bishop by the judgement of the chapter and of the abbot's peers. At Rouen. (1133–1135.)

.LII. De concordia facta inter episcopum Linc' 7 abbatem de Burgo (A rubric and marg.).

H. rex Anglorum . omnibus clericis . 7 laicis . in episcopatu Linc' constitutis ꞓ salutem.   Sciatis quia concordaui abbatem de Burgo cum episcopo Linc' . de placito controuersie que inter eos erat pro parrochiali[1] ecclesia de Burgo ita quod abbas ipse in presentia mea . 7 episcoporum . 7 baronum meorum 7 tocius curie mee pleniter recognouit consuetudines illas quas episcopus in ecclesia illa clama-bat . 7 eas ei in manu sua reddere uadiauit . ita quod . ecclesia illa consuetudinaria remansit episcopo Linc' ad tenendum in ea placita 7 sinodum 7 capitula sua . sicut alie parrochiales[1a] ecclesie episcopatus Linc' . in quibus hec fieri solita[2] sunt.   Concedo quoque 7 uolo quod episcopus diem conuenientem ponat abbati in capitulo sancte Marie Linc' . [3]7 uolo quod abbas illuc tunc ueniat . 7 rectum faciat episcopo Linc'[3] . per iudicium capituli sancte Marie 7 parium suorum abbatum . desicut res inter eos hucusque tractata est . Testibus . A. episcopo Carleolensi . 7 R. de Sigillo . 7 R. comite Gloecestrie . 7 Willelmo comite Warenne . 7 Brientio filio comitis . apud Rothomagum.

Facsimile opposite.
Marginalia : scribatur (Q).
Endorsed : (1) xxv carta visa (13 cent.).   (2) H. regis de controuersia contra abbatem Burgi (13 cent.).   (3) II .H. j. (? 13 cent.).   (4) ista carta posita inter cartas H.j. de priuilegiis (13–14 cent.).   (5) H'. prim' (Q).
There is a wide strip at the foot for the seal : the ribband below it has been torn off.   Size : 8⅜ x 5¼ inches.
Texts : MS—Orig. A1/1/3. A. S23. C,ff.9d,10. R23. Iv(5). Pd—Mon.viii, 1275(50). E.H.R.xxiii,726. Farrer, Itin., no. 721 (abs.). See C.C.R.iv,138(5).
Var. R. : [1] parochiali C. [1a] parochiales C. [2] solita is interlined above an erasure C. [3–3] added in marg. C.

53

53. Writ of Henry I, granting to the church of Lincoln and bishop Alexander and his successors the manor of Biggleswade [co. Bedford], to hold as the king best held it when it was in his hand. At Gillingham [co. Kent]. (1132.)

.LIII. De manerio de Bicleswath[1] cum soca . 7 saca[2] (A rubric and marg.).

H. rex Anglie Archiep[iscopi]s Ep[iscopi]s Abb[atibu]s Com[itibu]s Iustic[iariis] Baronib[us] Vic[ecomitibus] om[n]ib[us] fidelib[us] suis francis et anglicis Tot[ius] Anglie sal[ute]m.
Sciatis me reddidisse et co[n]cessisse deo et ecctie B[ea]te Marie Lincol[nie] et Alexandro Ep[iscop]o et om[n]ib[us] successorib[us] suis imp[er]petuu[m] Man[er]ium de Bichelefqu[ar]a cum t[er]ris et boscis et om[n]ib[us] ip[s]i Man[er]io p[er]tinentib[us] in bosco et plano in Ass[ar]to et in p[ra]tis. fa[...]
huius in Molend[inis] Ecctiis in via et Semit[is] i[n] p[ra]t[is] cu[m] soca et saca et tol et team et Infangenet[hef] cu[m] om[n]ib[us] libta[tibus]
et q[ui]etantiis et Consuetudinib[us] om[n]ib[us] reb[us] ad m[anerium] pertinentib[us] Ita b[e]n[e] in p[a]ce et honorifice et i[n]tegre sic[ut] ten[ui] Lanc[...] Ep[iscop]o et om[n]ib[us] successorib[us] et fec[i] ego ill[u]d maneriu[m] umq[uam] melius libe[r]ius tenu[i] du[m] fuit in m[an]u mea sic[ut] ali[quis]
aliis libe[r]ius ante me te[n]uisset. Hanc rogo reddition[em] et co[n]cession[em] meam sic[ut] sup[er]ius determinat[us] est firmam collaudo co[n]-
laudat[am] cōfirmo et illam p[er] p[re]t[er]em ecctie et Ep[iscop]o Alex[andr]o et successorib[us] ... imp[er]petuu[m] ... te[...]
res in co[n]cessa p[er]ostare confirmo et Rogo Ep[iscop]o Sar[...] et cancello[...] et pincerpo[...] D[omi]no Ap[...] Will[elm]o de P[...] Gilleb[er]to de [...]
de co[...] Co[n]stable et com[es] de Bus et ep[iscop]o et [...] Will[elm]o de Pont[...] D[omi]no Ap[...] Will[elm]o [...] Rob[er]to et Sigillo [...] R[...]
ANNO AB INCARNATIONE D[omi]ni M[illesi]mo C[entesimo] Trecesimo Secundo.

.H. rex Anglor*um*[3] . archiepiscopis . episcopis . abbatibus . comitibus . iusticiariis . baronibus[4] . vicecomitibus . 7 omnibus fidelibus
suis Francis 7 Anglis totius Anglię . salutem . Sciatis[4a] me reddidisse
7 concessisse . deo 7 ecclesię[5] beatę Marię Linc' . 7 Alixandro[6]
episcopo . 7 omnibus successoribus suis imperpetuum . manerium
de Bicheleswada . cum terris . 7 hominibus . 7 omnibus ipsi manerio
pertinentibus . in bosco . 7 plano . in aquis . 7 extra . in pratis . 7
pasturis . in molendinis . 7 ecclesia . in via 7 semitis . in piscariis .
cum soca . 7 saca . 7 tol[7] . 7 team . 7 infangeneteof[8] . cum omnibus
libertatibus 7 quietationibus 7 consuetudinibus . 7 omnibus rebus
eidem manerio pertinentibus . ita bene . 7 in pace 7 honorifice 7
quiete obtinend*um*[9] ecclesie Linc' . 7 pretaxato episcopo . 7 omnibus
successoribus eius . sicut ego illud manerium umquam[10] melius 7
liberius tenui dum fuit in manu mea . uel aliquis qui illud liberius
ante me tenuisset . Hanc itaque redditionem 7 concessionem meam .
sicut superius determi*natum est . factam ; collaudo . collaudatam
confirmo . 7 illam prefate ecclesię 7 episcopo Alixandro[11] . 7 successoribus eius . integre illibateque permansuram ; regia auctoritate .
7 á deo michi concessa potestate ; corroboro . Testibus . Rogero[12]
episcopo Sar*isbiriensi* . 7 G. cancellario . 7 Nigello nepote episcopi . 7
Roberto de Sigillo . 7 Roberto de Ver . conestabulario . 7 Vmfrido
de Buh*un*[13] dapifero . 7 Willelmo de Pontearch'[14] cam*era*rio . ap*ud*
Gillingeham.[15]

    ANNO AB INCARNATIONE DOMINI . Millesimo . Centesimo[16] .
Tricesimo Secundo ;

Facsimile opposite.
Endorsed : (1) de Bicleswada .H. reg*is* (12 cent.). (2) H. regis (12 cent.). (3) I. H. j.
(13 cent.). (4) H'. Regis Anglor*um* primi de Bikleswad' (13 cent.).
  The parchment is prolonged at the left hand end to form a tag (4⅞ inches long
by 2½ inches wide) for a seal; and there is a ribband at the foot. Size : 12½ x 6¼
inches.
  Marginalia : ✢ (A). In C : De manerio Bicleswad' (C).
  Texts : MS—Orig. A1/1/2. A. S24. C,f.10. Iiii(6). Pd—*Mon*.viii,1271(7).
*E.H.R.*xxiii,726. Farrer, *Itin.*, no. 678 (abs.). See *C.C.R.*iv,101(6).
  Var. R. : [1] Bickeleswath' A marg.   [2] sacha A marg. ; *om.* cum soca 7 saca S C.
[3] Anglorum S.   [4] *om.* baronibus A S C Iiii.   [4a] Scia C.   [5] *for* ecclesie *read* sancte C.
[6] Alexandro A S C Iiii.   [7] toll A S C.   [8] Iinfangetheof A ; Iinfangeteof S ; infangeteof
C.   [9] optinendum A Iiii.   [10] unquam A C Iiii.   [11] Alexandro A S C Iiii.   [12] *read*
R *for* Rogero C.   [13] Buch' A S C.   [14] Ponthearch' C.   [15] Gillingham Iiii.   [16] *om.*
Centesimo A S C.

Folio 8.

Hdl.   *Carte Regis* HENRICI PRIMI.   .8.

54

54. Writ of Henry I, granting to bishop Alexander licence to
have warren in all his land in Lincolnshire. At Arganchy. (1123–
1133.)

  .LIIII. De warenna[1] in Lincoln' syra[2] (rubric and marg.).

  .H. rex Anglie[3] vicecom*it*' . 7 baronibus . 7 omnibus ministris suis de Lincol' scira[4] ⁖ salutem . Sciatis quia concedo quod Alexander episcopus Linc'[5] habeat warennam in tota terra sua de Linc' scira[4] . Et prohibeo ne aliquis fuget in ea sine licentia ipsius episcopi . uel ministrorum suorum super .x. libris forifacture . Teste . Gaufrido[6] filio Pagani . apud Archenc'.[7]

Marginalia: ♃ +.
Texts: MS—A. S25. C,f.10d. Iiii(10). Pd—*Mon.*viii,1275(51), Farrer, *Itin.*, no. 717 (abs.). See *C.C.R.*iv,101(10).
Var. R.: [1] *add* episcopi S marg. [2] scira S marg.; De warenna Lincoln' C marg. [3] Angl' S C Iiii. [4] Lincolscire Iiii. [5] *om.* Linc' C. [6] *for* Gaufrido *read* G. C. [7] Identified as Argentan in *C.C.R.*iv,101(10).

54a

54a. Writ of Henry I, granting to bishop Alexander licence to have warren in all his land in Nottinghamshire. At Arganchy. (1123–1133.)

De warenna in Notingham[1] sira[2] (rubric and marg.).

.H. rex Anglorum . vicecomit' . ⁊ baronibus . ⁊ omnibus ministris suis de Notingeham[3] scira ⁖ salutem . Sciatis quia concedo quod Alexander episcopus Linc' habeat warennam in tota terra sua de Notingeham[4] scira . Et prohibeo ne aliquis fuget in ea sine licentia ipsius episcopi . uel ministrorum eius . super .x. libris forifacture . Teste . G.[5] filio Pagani . apud Archenc'.[6]

Marginalia in C: De warena Nothingeham scira.
Texts: MS—A54A. A80. S26. C,f.10d. Iiii(9). Pd—*Mon.*viii,1275(52). Farrer, *Itin.*, no. 717 (abs.). See *C.C.R.*iv,101(9).
Var. R.: [1] Nothingeham C marg. [2] syra A marg.; scira S. [3] Nothingeham Iiii. [4] Notinham C.; Nothingham Iiii. [5] *om.* G. A80. [6] Identified as Argentan in *C.C.R.*iv,101(9).

55

55. Writ of Henry I, granting to bishop Alexander licence to cause a bridge to be made over the water of Trent to his castle of Newark, provided that it be of no harm to the king's city of Lincoln or to his borough of Nottingham. At Fareham [co. Southampton]. (1129–1133.) See no. 47.

.LV. De ponte de Newerck'[1] (rubric and marg.).

.H. rex Anglorum . iusticiar' . ⁊ omnibus baronibus . ⁊ vice-comit'[2] . ⁊ fidelibus suis de Linc'[3] scira . ⁊ Notingeham scira[4] ⁖ salutem . Sciatis quod[5] concessi Alexandro episcopo Linc' . ut faciat fieri unum pontem super aquam Trente ad castellum suum de Niwerca ita quod non noceat ciuitati méé Linc' . neque burgo meo de Notingeham[6] . quod firma mea propter hoc non decidat[7] . Et si nocuerit ita[8] talem eum faciat qui non noceat . Testibus . episcopo Sar*isbiriensi* . 7 cancellario . 7 Eustacio filio Johannis apud Ferham.[9]

Marginalia: 2| +.
Texts: MS—A55. A47. S18. S27. C,f.9d. Iiii(23). Pd—*Mon*.viii,1274(42). Farrer, *Itin.*, no. 701 (abs.). See *C.C.R.*iv,102(23).
Var R.: [1] Newerch' A55 marg. A47 marg.; Niwerc' C marg.; Newerca S27. [2] *om.* 7 vicec' A47 S18 C. [3] Lincol' S18 S27 A47; Lincole Iiii. [4] *om.* 7 Notingeham scira A47. [5] quia S27. [6] Notingham A47. [7] quod . . . decidat *inserted by* A47 *in* marg.; *omitted by* S18 C Iiii. [8] ita *interlined* A47; *om.* ita C. [9] Ferrham S18 C Iiii.
Note: For the rebuilding of the bridge by John Russell, bishop of Lincoln, in 1486, after it had been destroyed ' bi gret rage [of] water flodes,' see *Lincoln Diocese Documents*, ed. Andrew Clark for the Early English Text Soc., pp. 256–9.

56

56. Writ of Henry I, granting to Saint Mary of Lincoln and Robert de Grainvill, the canon, the village of Asgarby [by Spilsby], which Roger son of Gerald gave to Saint Mary of Lincoln and the said Robert, *in prebendam*. At Westminster. (1121–1135.) See no. 117.

.LVI. De villa[1] de Asg*er*by[2] (rubric and marg.).

.H. rex Ang*lorum* . iustic' . vicecom*it* . baronibus . 7 ministris . omnibusque fidelibus suis Francis 7 Anglis . Lincol' schira[3] . salutem . Sciatis me concessisse 7 confirmasse deo 7 sancte Marie Linc' . 7 Roberto de Grainuill*a* canonico uillam Asgerbie[4] cum omnibus appendiciis suis . quam scilicet Rogerus filius Geroldi dedit deo 7 sancte Marie Linc' 7 predicto Roberto in prebendam 7 elemosinam . Quare uolo 7 firmiter precipio quatinus eandem villam in perpetuam possessionem bene 7 in pace 7 honorifice liberam 7 quietam de schira[5] 7 hundr*edo* 7 wap*entachio* teneant cum socca[6] 7 toll . 7 theam . 7 infangenethe*of*[7] . 7 cum omnibus consuetudinibus 7 libertatibus . sicut aliqua prebenda Linc'[8] ecclesie liberius 7 quietius tenet . Testibus . R. Sar*isbiriensi*[9] episcopo . 7 Roberto comite . Gleoc*estrie*[10] . apud Westmonasterium.[11]

Texts: MS—A56. A86. C,f.10d. Pd—*Mon*.viii,1275(53).
Var. R.: [1] *for* villa *read* prebenda C marg. [2] Asgerbi C marg. [3] scir' A86. [4] Asgherbie C. [5] scira A86 C. [6] cum sacca 7 socca A86. [7] infangheneth' A 86. [8] Lincol' A86. [9] S. ar' C. [10] Gloec' A86. [11] apud Wem' C.
Note: Robert the canon de Greinvilla was assessed at three carucates, which Wigot held under him, in the wapentake of Bolingbroke, A.D. 1115–1118 (*The Lincolnshire Domesday*, p. 252).

57

57. Writ of Henry I, commanding Osbert the sheriff to allow Robert de Grainvill to have his prebend of Lincoln as the king granted it to him by his writ. Before Arques. (1104–1106.)

.LVII. Item[1] de Asgerby[2] (rubric and marg.).

.H. rex Anglorum . Osberto vicecomiti . salutem . Precipio tibi ut permittas ita habere huic* Roberto de Grainuilla prebendam suam de Linc' sicut concessi ei per breue meum . Et amplius pro nulla noua consuetudine clamorem audiam . Teste . Hugone . de Euremov . ante Archas.

Texts: MS—A. Pd—Farrer, *Itin.*, p. 154, no. 105a (abs.).
Var. R.: [1] *om.* Item A marg. [2] Asgerbi A marg.

Folio 8d.

Hdl.   CARTE REGIS HENRICI PRIMI.

58

58. Writ of Henry I, notifying to bishop Robert I that he grants the alms of Roger son of Gerald, namely, the land of Asgarby, as he gave it to Saint Mary of Lincoln, to the behoof of Robert de Grainvill, canon of Lincoln, with the bishop's consent; and commanding the bishop to reseise him therein as he was seised in the time of the king's brother. At Winchester. (1100–1107.)

.LVIII. Item[1] de terra[2] de Asgerby[3] (rubric and marg.).

.H. rex Anglie[4] . R. episcopo Lincolniensi salutem . Scias[5] quod concedo elemosinam Rogeri filii Geroldi scilicet terram de Asgerbi[6] sicut ipse illam dedit sancte Marie Linc' . 7 sicut ipse posuit illam in prebendam ad opus Roberti de Grainuilla canonici Linc' tuo concessu . Quia nolo ut illam iniuste super hoc perdat . Et resaisi eum inde . sicut erat in tempore fratris mei . 7 die qua uiuus 7 mortuus fuit . Et quod inde postea captum est ꞏ fac ei reddi . Testibus . Roberto . filio Hamonis . 7 . G. filio . Ricardi . apud Wintoniam.

Texts: MS—A. C,f.10d.
Var. R.: [1] *om.* Item de terra A marg. [2] *for* terra *read* manerio C marg.
[3] Asgerb' A marg. [4] Angl' C. [5] Sciatis C. [6] Asgherbi C.

59

59. Writ of Henry I, addressed to earl Rannulf [of Chester], granting to Robert de Grainvill the land of Asgarby which the earl has proved against Walter of Ghent by legal process to be his possession, and has given to Robert in alms. At Woodstock [co. Oxford]. (1127–1130.)

Item de terra[1] de Asgerby (rubric and marg.).

.H. rex Anglorum . comiti . Rannulfo . salutem . Scias quod concedo Roberto de Grainuilla[2] terram . 7 omnes res de Asgerbi[3] quas dirrationasti contra Walterum de Gant . 7 quas ipsi Roberto in

elemosinam dedisti 7 concessisti . sicut tu ipse ei eas concessisti .
Et uolo ut ipse eas bene 7 in pace 7 honorifice teneat . Testibus .
Galfrido cancellario . 7 Nigello nepote episcopi . 7 Willelmo de
Tancaruilla . apud Odestocan.

Marginalia : The Roman numerals in the margin are discontinued after LVIII.
Texts: MS—A. C,f.11. Pd—Farrer, *Itin.*, no. 537 (abs.).
Var. R. : [1] *om.* Item de terra A marg. [2] Glanuill' C. [3] Asgherbi C.

60

60. Writ of Henry I, commanding the barons, vavasours, and
all the lords who hold lands within Well wapentake to come to
the pleas and wapentake of [Alexander] bishop of Lincoln, and to
do all that they owe to him at that wapentake in respect of their
lands, as they did to bishop Robert or any predecessor of the bishop's.
At Fareham [co. Southampton]. (1123–1133.)

Quod omnes ueniant ad Welle wapentachum[1] (rubric and marg.).
.H. rex Anglorum . omnibus baronibus 7 vauasoribus 7 omnibus
dominis qui terras tenent intra Welle wapentac ⫶ salutem . Precipio
quod omnes ueniatis ad placita . 7 wapentac . episcopi Linc' . quod
de me tenet . per summonitionem[2] . ministrorum suorum . 7 faciatis
ei omnes rectitudines . 7 consuetudines in omnibus rebus quas ei
debetis de terris uestris ad illud wapentac . ita bene 7 plenarie
sicut unquam plenius fecistis Roberto episcopo . uel alicui ante-
cessori suo . 7 quas iuste facere debetis . Et nisi feceritis ipse uos
iusticiet per pecuniam uestram . donec faciatis ne perdam pecuniam
meam quam episcopus michi inde reddere debet . Testibus . episcopo .
Sarisbirie . 7 . G. cancellario . apud Fereham.

Texts: MS—A. C,f.6d. Iiii(22). Pd—*Mon.*viii,1272(19). Farrer, *Itin.*, no. 702
(abs.).
Var. R. : [1] De forisfacturis non uenientium ad wapentachum episcopi C. [2] *corrected
from* soummonitionem C.

61

61. Writ of Henry I, giving to bishop Robert I the manor of
Nettleham, in accordance with the grant of the queen, whose land
it was. Dated at Winchester, on the feast of Saint German the
bishop, in the first year of the king's reign [31 July, 1101].

De manerio de Netelham[1] (rubric and marg.).
Henricus rex Anglorum . Osberto vicecomiti Lincolie . 7 Rannulfo
Meschino 7 omnibus baronibus de Lincole scira Francis 7 Anglis
salutem . Sciatis me dedisse deo 7 sancte Marie 7 Roberto[2] episcopo
Lincoliensi manerium de Netheneham[3] concessione regine cuius

erat . 7 volo 7 precipio ut ita bene 7 honorifice habeat sicuti illud
honorabilius 7 melius 7 quietius habebam in mea manu . Testibus .
M'. regina . 7 Rogero Big*ot* . apud Wincestram in die sancti Germani
episcopi in primo anno regni mei.[4]

Marginalia : ♃.
Texts: MS—A. Iii(1). Pd—In *C.C.R.*ii,271, it is stated that this charter is
printed in *Mon.*viii,1271 ; but the document printed there is no. 15 above. This
mistake has misled Farrer, and his abstract (*Itin.*, no. 100) is a conflation of no. 15
and no. 61 derived from the particulars given in *C.C.R.*ii,271, and *Mon.*viii,1271(8).
Var. R. : [1] Netelham' A marg. [2] Rotberto Iii. [3] Neteneham Iii. [4] mei *extends
into marg.*

62

62. Notification by queen Maud that king Henry, her lord,
at her grant and request, has given to bishop Robert I the manor
called Nettleham which is of her fee. At Winchester. (Probably
circa 1101.)

Item[1] de manerio de Netelham[2] (rubric and marg.).

.M. Ang*lorum* regina . O. vicecomiti Lincolie[3] 7 Ranulfo Meschino[4]
7 omnibus baronibus 7 fidelibus suis Francis 7 Anglis de Lincole
scira salutem . Sciatis quod rex Henricus dominus meus concessu
meo 7 precibus meis dedit Roberto[5] episcopo Lincolie manerium
quod uocatur Netelham quod de feudo meo est cum omnibus rebus
7 consuetudinibus que ad ipsum manerium pertinent . Testibus .
Hamone dapifero . 7 Vr*sone* de Abetot apud Vntoniam[6].

Marginalia : ♃.
Texts: MS—A. Iii(2). Iiii(24). Pd—*C.C.R.*ii,271(2). See *C.C.R.*iv,102(24).
Var. R. : [1] *om.* Item A marg. [2] Netelham' A marg. [3] Lincol' Iiii. [4] Mescino
Iiii. [5] Rotberto Iii Iiii. [6] Wintoniam Iii ; Wynton' Iiii.

Folio 9.
Hdl.   9.

63

63. Carta domini .W. dei gracia regis Anglie . ut predictum
est (rubric).

This charter is registered again at no. 1 *above.* Q *has written in the
left hand margin* Va cat, *and in the right hand margin* Vacat hic quia
supra scribitur in principio set ibi non est adicio de castitate (*see
no.* 64 *below*).

64

64. De honestate 7 castitate dictorum canonicorum (rubric).

This document forms the last part of no. 3 *above, beginning with the
words* : In qua uidelicet matre ecclesia canonici deo seruientes caste
7 catholice uiuant.

Marginalia : o—o (*the reference being to the corresponding sign in
no.* 1 *above*).

Folio 9d.

65

65. Carta Roberti dei gracia Linc' episcopi (rubric).

This charter is registered again at no. 287 *below.* Q *has written in the left hand margin :* De iurisdiccione capituli . 7 scribitur alibi in proprio titulo.

Folio 10.

Hdl.　　　　　　　　　　　　　　　　　　　　　　10.

66

66. Carta venerabilis Alexandri summi pontificis (rubric).

This charter is registered again at no. 256 *below.* Q *has written in the right hand margin :* Confirmacio iurisdiccionis scribitur alibi.

Folio 10d., blank.

Folio 11.

Hdl.　　　　CARTE REGIS HENRICI PRIMI.　　11.

66a

66a. De exitu in muro castelli faciendo (rubric and marg.).

This charter, which is registered again at no. 21 *above, has been crossed out, and* Q *has written in the left hand margin* Va cat *in pale ink, on the top of which another early hand has written the same two syllables in blacker ink.*

67

67. Writ of Henry I, committing to bishop Robert I the church of All Saints [in Hungate, Lincoln], and the churches of [Great] Grimsby, as Osbert the sheriff had them on the day that he was alive and dead. At Headington [co. Oxford]. The king commands Wigot to put the bishop in seisin thereof. (1114–1116.)

De ecclesia Omnium Sanctorum . 7 ecclesiis de Grimesby[1] (rubric and marg.).

.H. rex Ang*lorum* . Rannulfo Meschino . 7 Wig*oto* vicecomiti . 7 Roberto de la Haia . 7 Radulfo de Haiencurt[2] . 7 omnibus fidelibus suis Francis 7 Anglis de Lincolia scira salutem . Sciatis me commendasse Roberto episcopo Lincolie ecclesiam Omnium Sanctorum . 7 quicquid ad eam pertinet infra burgum 7 ẹxtra . 7 ecclesias de Grimesbia . 7 quicquid ad eas pertinet . sicut Osbertus vicecomes eas melius habuit die qua uiuus 7 mortuus fuit . Teste . Rannulfo cancellario . apud Heddendonam . Et tu Wig*ote* eum inde saisias . Te*ste* eodem.

Marginalia : 2 +. *An illegible note.*
Texts : MS—A. Iiii(18). Iviii(6). Pd—*Mon*.viii,1275(45). Farrer, *Itin.*, no. 357 (abs.). See *C.C.R.*iv,102(18).
Var. R. : [1] Grimesbi A marg. [2] Bencurt Iiii Iviii.

68

68. Writ of Henry I, granting to bishop Robert I the churches of Uffington [co. Lincoln] and Barkstone [co. Leicester], as Theodoric best held them. At Southampton, when the king crossed the sea [into Normandy]. (1114–1116.)

De ecclesiis de Offinton'[1] . 7 Barkeston' (rubric and marg.).

.H. rex Anglor*um*[2] . Radulfo de Watneuilla . 7 Radulfo de Bosco Rohari . 7 Hugoni de Hottot salutem . Sciatis me concessisse Roberto Linc'[3] episcopo ecclesiam de Offintona . 7 quicquid ad eam pertinet . in decimis . 7 in pratis 7 in terris . 7 in omnibus redditibus que ad illam ecclesiam iuste pertinent . 7 ecclesiam de Barchestona cum omnibus rebus 7 ecclesiis que ad eam pertinent . sicut unquam Teoderic*us* melius 7 quietius eas habuit . Testibus . Mat*illide*[4] regina . 7 .W. de Tanc*aruilla* . 7 Willelmo de Albini . apud Hamtonam in transitu regis.

Marginalia : + Offington' 7 Barkeston' . . . + . . (query Q).
Texts : MS—A. Iv(2). Pd—*C.C.R.*iv,138(2). Farrer, *Itin.*, no. 375 (abs.).
Var. R. : [1] Offington' A marg. [2] Anglorum Iv. [3] Lincolniensi Iv. [4] Mathillide Iv.
Note : In 1086 Robert de Todeni held land both in Barkstone and in Uffington (*D.B.* i, p. 233b, col. 2 ; *The Lincolnshire Domesday*, 18/11) ; and later the church of Barkstone was appropriated to Belvoir priory, which also had a pension from the church of Uffington (*Valor Eccles.* iv, 116).

69

69. Writ of Henry I, pardoning bishop Alexander and quit-claiming him in respect of three hundred marks of silver which the king claimed that the bishop owed him as the pledge of Holme. At Blackmoor [co. Southampton]. (1123–1133.)

De .ccc. marcis . condonatis[1] . Alexandro episcopo Linc*oliensi* (rubric and marg.).

.H. rex Anglor*um* . omnibus baronibus 7 fidelibus suis Francis 7 Anglis de Lincole scira 7 Rotelanda 7 Norhamtone scira salutem . Sciatis me perdonasse Alexandro episcopo Linc*oliensi* . 7 me eum

quietum clamasse de .ccc. marcis argenti . quas clamabam me
debere habere pro vadio de Holma . Et uolo quod inde quietus
sit . Testibus . episcopo Sar*isbirie* . 7 .G. cancellario . apud
Blachemoram.

Marginalia: + + ♃. *An illegible note, query by* Q.
Text: MS—A. Pd—Farrar, *Itin.*, no. 696A (abs.).
Var R.: ¹ perdonatis A marg.
Note: The nature of the transaction to which the present text relates must
remain conjectural. Professor F. M. Stenton suggests that (1) X owes 300 marks
to the king ; (2) X gives *Holma* to the bishop on the understanding that the bishop
pays the debt to the king ; (3) the king pardons the debt to the bishop out of favour
to him ; (4) the bishop will go on holding the land till X has paid 300 marks to
him, the king's ' pardon ' being personal to the bishop, and not affecting the original
understanding between the bishop and X ; (5) X pays the bishop 300 marks, and
gets *Holma* back again.
  Therefore *Holma* may have been anybody's land in the three named counties.
From the size of the sum it must have been a considerable estate, and yet no place
of the name is known in Northamptonshire and Rutland. Of the places of the
name in Lincolnshire the most probable is Holme Spinney, an important manor
which included the adjoining villages of Beckingham, Sutton, Fenton, and Stragglethorpe. The place has long been extinct, though its site may plainly be seen
near Sutton. In 1086 this manor, which was assessed at twenty-four carucates,
was held in chief by Gilbert de Gant, who had been succeeded by his son Walter
de Gant, at the date of the present charter (*The Lincolnshire Domesday*, 24/78 ;
Final Concords (Lincoln Record Society xix), pp. lx, lxi). Moreover, the de Gants
were tenants in chief in the other two named counties. In Domesday Book, under
Northamptonshire, Gilbert de Gant is entered not only as the tenant of land in
that county, but also as holding eleven and a half hides and one bovate in Empingham [in Rutland], of which all but four hides were of the king's soke of ' Roteland '
(*Domesday Book* i, p. 227b, col. 1). This manor passed in the twelfth century,
through his marriage with Alice de Gant, to Roger de Mowbray (Blore, *Rutland*,
p. 113), who granted the church of Empingham, with the lands and tithes and all
the other things and customs which belonged to it, to Lincoln cathedral, to hold
it as it was best held by his predecessors, namely, Gilbert de Gant and Walter his
son and Gilbert de Gant the son of Walter (see Registrum Antiquissimum, no. 203,
printed below in volume ii of the present series). Gilbert de Gant also held two
carucates in Burley on the Hill, in Rutland, in 1086 (*The Lincolnshire Domesday*,
24/80). The mention of Rutland as a county at the date of the text is noteworthy.
For another instance of a *uadium* see no. 99 below.

70

70. Writ of Henry I, granting to bishop Alexander licence to
give to Richard de Vernon an exchange to the value of the land
of Richard's which the bishop requires for the enlargement of his
park at Thame. At Rouen. (*Circa* 1130.)

De escambio terre dato Ricardo de Vernon' pro parco de Thame
augmentando (rubric and marg.).

.H. rex Ang*lorum* . episcopo Sar*isbirie* . 7 vicecomit' . 7 omnibus
baronibus 7 fidelibus suis Francis 7 Anglis de Oxenefort sira salutem .
Sciatis quod concedo ut episcopus Alexander Linc' det Ricardo de
Vernon escambium ad ualens terre Ricardi quam episcopus requirit
de eo ad augmentum parci sui de Tama . T*estibus* . Nigello nepote
episcopi . 7 . G. filio Pagani . apud Rothom*agum*.

Marginalia: +. *An illegible note, query by* Q.
Text: MS—A. Pd—Farrer, *Itin.*, no. 621A (abs.).

71

71. Writ of Henry I, commanding Geoffrey the steward of Stephen the count of [Brittany] to reseise bishop Robert I in the church of Hough on the Hill, as the count gave it to him, and to allow him to hold it till the count returns. At Windsor. (1100–1115.)

De ecclesia de Hag (rubric and marg.).

.H. rex Anglorum . Goisfrido dapifero comitis Stephani . 7 ministris suis salutem . Mando uobis 7 precipio ut resaisiatis Robertum episcopum Linc' de ecclesia de Hac sicut Stephanus comes ei dedit . 7 in pace teneat quousque comes redeat . Et si quid inde captum est ? cito reddatur . Quod nisi feceritis ? Osbertus vice-comes Linc' hec cito faciat . Teste Nigello de Oili apud Windresores.

Marginalia : 2|. *An illegible note, query by* Q.
Texts : MS—A. Pd—Farrer, *Itin.*, no. 322A (abs.).

Folio 11d.
Hdl.   HENRICI PRIMI.

71a

71a. De strata de Newerk diuertenda (rubric and marg.).

Marginalia : 2|.

This charter, which is registered again at no. 26 above, has been crossed out, and Va cat hic *has been written in the right hand margin, query by* Q2.

72

72. Writ of Henry I, giving to bishop Robert I all the land which Gladwin held of the king, and all his service, *per tres parmenos* which the king gave to the bishop. At Trumpington [co. Cambridge]. (*Circa* 1109.)

De terra Gladewini . quam de rege tenebat (rubric and marg.).

.H. rex Anglorum . Thome archiepiscopo . 7 Osberto vicecomiti . 7 Roberto de Lacei . 7 Nigello de Albinneio . 7 omnibus baronibus suis Francis 7 Anglis de Euerwic scira 7 de Notingeham scira salutem . Sciatis me dedisse Roberto Linc' episcopo totam terram Gladwini quam de me tenebat 7 totum seruitium suum . Et uolo ut bene 7 honorifice teneat cum ¹saca 7 soca¹ 7 toll . 7 team . 7 infangentheof² . 7 omnibus consuetudinibus . *Testibus* . *Rannulfo Dunelmensi* episcopo . 7 cancellario . 7 Gisleberto de Aquila . per tres parmenos quos ego ei dedi apud Tromplintonam³.

Marginalia : 2.
Texts : MS—A. Iv(3). Pd—*C.C.R.*iv,138(3). Farrer, *Itin.*, no. 244 (abs.).
Var R. : ¹⁻¹ soca 7 saca I. ² infangenteof I. ³ Tromphintonam I.

Folio 12, *blank.*

Hdl.　　　　　　　　　　　　　　　　　　　12

Folio 12d, blank.

ADD. CHART.

73. Writ of Henry I, addressed to bishop Robert I, Ranulf Meschin, Osbert the sheriff, Picot son of Colswain, and the men of Lincolnshire, confirming the laws, rights, and customs that he granted to them when he first received the crown ; and desiring them to assure him by oath that they will defend his realm against all men, and especially against Robert count of Normandy, his brother, until Christmas ; and commanding them to take this security from the men of his demesnes, both French and English ; and the king's barons are to cause their men to give the same security to them [i.e. in the shire-moot] as the barons themselves have granted to the king. At Winchester. (June–July, 1101.)

De legibus rectitudinibus 7 consuetudinibus concessis (R. rubric).

Henr*icus* . rex Angl*orum* . Roberto . Lincol' . episcopo . 7 Ranulfo . Mischino . 7 Osb*erto* . uicecomiti . 7 Picot[1] filio Colsuen . *œ'* omnibus hominibus Francis 7 Anglis . de Lincole scira *.·* salutem . Sciatis quod ego uobis concedo tales lagas[2] . 7 rectitudines . 7 consuetudines . quales ego uobis dedi 7 concessi . quando imprimis coronam recepi . *œ'* uolo . ut assecuretis michi sacramento terram meam Anglie . ad tenendum 7 ad defendendum contra omnes homines . 7 nominatim contra Rotb*ertum*[3] comitem Normannie . fratrem meum usque ad natal*em*[4] Domini . 7 vobis predictis precipio . ut hanc securitatem recipiatis de meis dominicis hominibus Francigenis . 7 Anglis . 7 barones mei faciant uobis habere hanc eandem securitatem de omnibus suis hominibus sicut michi concesserunt . Testibus . Ansello[5] [archiepiscop[6]]o . 7 Rotb*erto*[7] comite . de Mellend . 7 . R. filio Haim*onis* . 7 Eudone . dapifero . apud [Wicestram[6]].

Facsimile facing p. 36.
Endorsed : (1) H. j. (13 cent.). (2) Carta H. regis primi de libertatibus (15 cent.). (3) xxvij carta visa (? 13 cent.).
Strip for seal torn off. Size : 5⅜ x 2 inches.
Texts : MS—Orig. A1/1/5. R24. Pd—*E.H.R.*xxi,505. Delisle, p. 573. Farrer, *Itin.*, no. 24 (abs.).
Var. R. : [1] Picoto R. [2] leges R. [3] Robertum R. [4] natale R. [5] Anselm' R. [6] *supplied from R, the left hand corner of the charter having been torn off.* [7] Roberto R.
Note : Mr W. H. Stevenson has a valuable note on this charter in *E.H.R.*xxi, 505–9, in which he shews that it must be dated June–July, 1101. The ink of the charter is faded, and the text is in parts difficult to read. A close inspection shews that a few corrections should be made in the text which Mr Stevenson printed (*op. cit.*, p. 506) : l. 3 (above) *for* Picoto *read* Picot ; l. 3 *for* ac omnibus *read œ'* omnibus ; l. 7 *for* Quare uolo *read œ'* uolo ; l. 10 *for* natale *read* natalem. The place from which the charter was issued has now been supplied from the copy in R, which Mr Stevenson did not notice on his visit to Lincoln. A facsimile of the charter, from a photograph by the Reverend H. E. Salter, is given in *E.H.R.*xxvi,488.

74. Writ of Henry I, commanding Robert bishop of Chester and Godfrey archdeacon of Chester to cause the king's church of Darley [co. Derby] to have the tithes and customs of Winster [co. Derby], as it best had them in the time of kings Edward and William I. At Nottingham. (1121–1126.)

H rex Angl*orum* Roberto episcopo de Cestra 7 Godfrido[1] archidiacono salutem Precipio uobis . vt faciatis habere ecclesie mee de Derleia decimas 7 consuetudines de Winesterna[2] ita sicut[3] melius habuit tempore regis Edwardi regis 7 patris mei Et si homines in predicta villa manentes decimas reddere noluerint ⁊ facite idem[4] quod vestro ministerio pertinet 7 vicecomites de Notingham inde forisfacturam meam accipiant Teste Rogero episcopo Salesb*iriensi* apud Notingham.

Marginalia: Confirm' de nouo per Edwardum.
Texts: MS—D131. Iv(9). Pd—*C.C.R.*iv,138-9(9).
Var. R.: [1] Godefrido Iv. [2] Vinesterna Iv. [3] sicuti Iv. [4] *for* idem *read* ind* Iv.

Folio 31.

Hdl.   Carte Stephani Regis.   .3.1.

168

75. Writ of Stephen, confirming the gift which his uncle, king Henry, made to the church of Lincoln and to bishop Robert Bloet of all the churches in the borough of Lincoln which their priests held of the said king Henry. At Oxford. (1135–1154, probably late in the period.)

De ecclesiis Linc'[1] (marg.).

Steph*anus* rex Anglorum . archiepiscopis 7 episcopis 7 iusticiar*iis* . 7 vicecomitibus . 7 baronibus 7 ministris 7 omnibus fidelibus suis tocius Anglie salutem . Sciatis me concessisse donationem illam quam rex Henricus auunculus meus fecit ecclesie sancte Marie de Linc' . 7 episcopo eiusdem ecclesie Roberto Blouet[2] de ecclesiis omnibus de burgo Linc' quas presbiteri earundem ecclesiarum de eodem rege .H. tenebant infra burgum 7 extra . Quare precipio quod predicta ecclesia Linc' . 7 episcopus ecclesias illas bene 7 in pace 7 quiete teneant cum omnibus pertinenciis earum 7 libertatibus sicut rex Henricus eas illis dedit . 7 concessit 7 carta sua confirmauit . Testibus . W. Mart*ello* . 7 Ricardo de Luci . 7 Willelmo de Caisneto[3] . apud Oxeneford*iam*.

Marginalia: .i. 2_.
Texts: MS—A. R29.
Var. R. [1] De ecclesiis infra burgum Lincoln' R rubric. [2] Bluet R. [3] Caisnet R.

VII

169

76. Writ of Stephen, granting the church of Langford [co. Oxford] *in prebendam* to the church of Lincoln. At Oxford. (1135–1146.)

De ecclesia de Langeford' (A marg.).

S'. rex Ang*lorum* . archiepiscopis . episcopis . abbatibus . comitibus[1] . iustic*iariis* . vicecomitibus . baronibus . ministris 7 omnibus fidelibus suis totius Anglie *:* salutem . Sciatis me dedisse 7 concessisse deo 7 ecclesie sancte Marie Lincol' ecclesiam de Langeford' in prebendam *:* cum omnibus terris 7 decimis 7 aliis rebus ad ecclesiam predictam pertinentibus . Quare volo 7 firmiter precipio quod ecclesia sancte Marie Lincol' teneat hec omnia predicta in perpetuam elemosinam 7 in prebendam bene 7 in pace 7 libere 7 quiete ab omni seculari exactione . Testibus . Willelmo de Ipra . 7 Willelmo Mart*ello* . 7 Ricardo de Luci . apud Oxen*efordiam.*[2]

Facsimile opposite.
Marginalia in A : .ii.
Endorsed : Langeford ecclesia (13–14 cent.).
A strip at the foot for seal, and below it a ribband. Size : 5¾ x 3½ inches.
Texts : MS—Orig. A1/1/10. A. Pd—*E.H.R.*xxiii,727.
Var. R. : [1] *om.* comitibus A. [2] Oxeneford' A.

170

77. Writ of Stephen, commanding that bishop Alexander shall have the knights whom the king gave to him from the fee of Roger of Poitou ; namely, Ralf son of Hacon and Eudo of Grainsby, as he had them on the day on which the king first came to the siege of Lincoln. At Lincoln. (1140–1147 : probably Christmas, 1146.)

De seruitio Radulfi filii Haconis 7 Eudonis de Greinesbi (A marg.).

S'. rex Ang*lorum* . iustic' . 7 vice*comit*'[1] . 7 ministris suis 7 omnibus fidelibus suis Francis 7 Ang*lis* de Linc' scira salutem . Precipio quod Alexander episcopus Linc' teneat 7 habeat milites suos quos ei dedi de feodo Rogeri Pictau*ensis* . scilicet Radulfum filium Haconis . 7 Eudon*em* de Grenesbi[2] . ita bene 7 in pace 7 libere 7 quiete sicut illos tenuit die qua primum ueni ad obsidionem Linc' . ne super hoc inde ab aliquo infestetur . Teste . Mathilde[3] regina . apud Lincol'.

Facsimile opposite.
Marginalia in A : iii. 2.
Endorsed : (1) S' regis de feodo Radulfi 7 Eudonis (12 cent.). (2) III. S. (12 cent.).
The strip at the foot for the seal, and the ribband, have been torn off. Size : 6⅛ x 1½ inches.
Texts : MS—Orig. A1/1/9. A. Iv(14). Pd—*E.H.R.*xxiii,727. *C.C.R.*iv,139(14).
Var. R. : [1] vicecomitibus Iv. [2] Greinsby A ; Grenesby Iv. [3] Maltild' A.

171

78. Writ of Stephen, giving to bishop Alexander the service which Ralf son of Hacon and Eudo of Grainsby were wont to do to Geoffrey son of Payn. At Oxford. (1135–1147.)

De seruicio eorundem (marg.).

.S. rex Anglo*rum* . omnibus baronibus suis 7 fidelibus suis Linc' scira salutem . Sciatis me dedisse 7 concessisse Alexandro[1] episcopo Linc' seruicium Radulfi filii Haconis . 7 seruicium Eudonis[2] de Greinesby quod faciebant Galfrido filio Pagani . Testibus . episcopo Sari*sbiriensi* . 7 episcopo Wint*oniensi* . episcopo Cicestre*nsi* . cancellario apud Oxen*efordiam*.

Marginalia: 2 .
Texts: MS—A. Iv(12). Pd—*C.C.R*.iv,139(12).
Var. R.: [1] Alixandro Iv. [2] Eidonis Iv.

172

79. Writ of Stephen, commanding that Ralf the canon of Asgarby [by Spilsby] shall hold the land, which the men of Lusby used to hold in the prebend of Asgarby, as Robert de Grainvill best held it, and as Ralf has proved his claim to it before the king's justiciar. At Rockingham [co. Northampton]. (1140–1144.)

De prebenda de Asgerb*ia* (marg.).

.S. rex Anglo*rum* episcopo Linc' . 7 vice*comit'* . 7 omnibus ministris suis de Lincol' scira : salutem . Precipio quod Radulfus canonicus de Ansgerbi teneat terram suam quam homines de Lucebi tenebant in prebenda de Angerby cum omnibus appenditiis suis . ita bene 7 in pace 7 iuste 7 libere 7 honorifice sicut Robertus de Grainuill*a* unquam melius uel liberius eam tenuit . 7 sicut eam disrationauit coram iustic*ia* mea . ne super hoc ponatur inde in placitum nisi nominatim precepero . neque clamorem* inde audiam . Teste . Rogero cancellario apud Rochingeham.

Text: MS—A.

**Folio 31d.*
Hdl.   CARTE REGIS *Stephani*.

173

80. Writ of Stephen, commanding that the prebend of Asgarby, belonging to Ralf the canon, shall have soke and sake and toll and team and infangenethef as any prebend of Lincoln best has them; and that Ralf shall hold the prebend as Robert de Grainvill, his predecessor, best held it. At Stamford [co. Lincoln]. (1135–1147.)

De libertatibus de Asgerbi (marg.).

.S. rex Anglorum . episcopo Linc' . 7 iustic' . 7 vicecomit' . 7 baronibus . 7 omnibus fidelibus suis de Linc' scira salutem . Precipio quod prebenda Radulfi canonici sancte Marie Linc' de Ansgerby habeat socham 7 sacham 7 tol 7 theam 7 infangenetheof . 7 omnes alias libertates 7 consuetudines suas ita bene 7 plene sicut aliqua prebenda Lincol' melius 7 liberius habet . Et sit quieta de placitis 7 querelis 7 scira 7 hundredo 7 wapentaco . 7 omnibus rebus excepto murdro . 7 latrocinio . Et Radulfus sic libere 7 honorifice teneat eam sicut Robertus de Grainuilla canonicus predecessor suus unquam melius tenuit 7 quietius . Teste . A. episcopo Linc' . 7 cancellario . apud Stanfordiam.

Text: MS—A.

174

81. Writ of Stephen, giving to the church of Lincoln, in perpetual alms and *in prebendam*, half a carucate which William *nepos* of Martell de Tanea held of him in chief in Canwick, for a yearly render to the king of fourteen pence. At London. (1147–1152.)

De dimidia carucata terre in Kanewich' (marg.).

.S.[1] rex Anglorum . archiepiscopis . episcopis . abbatibus . comitibus . iustic' . vicecomit' . baronibus . 7 omnibus ministris 7 fidelibus suis Francis 7 Anglis de Lincol' scira[2] . 7 tocius Anglie salutem . Sciatis me dedisse 7 concessisse deo 7 ecclesie beate Marie Linc' in perpetuam elemosinam 7 prebendam . dimidiam carrucatam terre quam Willelmus nepos[3] Martelli de Tanea[4] tenebat in Canewic[5] de me in capite per . xiiii. denarios reddendos inde michi per annum de seruitio . Quare uolo 7 firmiter precipio quod ecclesia beate Marie prefata habeat 7 teneat illam dimidiam carrucatam terre in prebendam cum prefato seruitio pertinenti . bene . 7 in pace . 7 libere[6] . 7 honorifice . 7 ab omni seculari exactione quiete sicut melius uel liberius tenet alias tenuras[7] 7 prebendas . Testibus . Matilde regina . 7 comite Gisleberto[8] . 7 Gwillelmo[9] de Ipra . 7 Willelmo Martello . 7 Ricardo de Luci . 7 Ricardo de Canuilla[10] . apud Lundoniam.[11]

Marginalia : 2.
Texts: MS—A. R26. R1093.
Var. R.: [1] [S]tephanus R1093. [2] Lincolsc' R26; Lincolneschir' R1093. [3] nepos *interlineated in paler ink, probably by* Q A. [4] Taner R26; Tane R1093. [5] Canewyk R1093. [6] *om.* 7 libere R26. [7] *insert* suas R26. [8] Gilberto R26. [9] Will' R26 R1093. [10] Cauilla R26 R1093. [11] Lond' R26 R1093.

175

82. Writ of Stephen, giving to the church of Lincoln the tithe of his *firma* of the city of Lincoln in perpetual alms and *in prebendam*. And the king gives similarly to the same church the church of North Kelsey *in prebendam*. At London. (1136–1147.)

De decima firme ciuitatis Linc' . De ecclesia de North Keleseia (marg.).

.S. rex Anglorum . archiepiscopis . episcopis . abbatibus . comitibus . baronibus . iusticiariis . vicecomitibus . ministris . 7 omnibus fidelibus suis Francis 7 Anglis[1] ·: salutem . Sciatis me dedisse 7 concessisse deo 7 ecclesie beate Marie Linc' [2]decimam firme méé ciuitatis Linc'[2] in perpetuam elemosinam 7 in prebendam . Quare uolo 7 firmiter precipio quod predicta ecclesia beate Marie habeat prefatam decimam meam . 7 in perpetuum possideat illam bene 7 in pace . 7 libere . 7 quiete sicut elemosinam meam . Preterea concedo 7 do ecclesie beate Marie predicte ecclesiam de Nordchelesi[3] in perpetuam elemosinam 7 prebendam possidendam cum omnibus eidem ecclesie adiacentibus . Testibus . M. regina . 7 comite Willelmo de Warena . 7 Willelmo de Ipra . 7 Ricardo de Luci . 7 Willelmo Martello . apud Londoniam.

Marginalia: 2.
Texts: MS—A. R31.
Var. R.: [1] insert tocius Anglie R.   [2]–[2] decimam . . . ciuitatis Linc' written in marg., and marked for inclusion in text A.   [3] Nortchelesi R.

176

83. Writ of Stephen, giving to the church of Lincoln and the canons thereof the eighteen pounds in land, and the sokemen, formerly given by him *in prebendas*, in exchange for the tithe of Kirton [in Lindsey] and Caistor. The king commands that those sokemen shall in all things obey the said church and canons. At Nottingham. (1135–1154.)

De .xviii. libris 7 sochemannis (marg.).

.S. rex Anglorum . episcopo Linc' . 7 iustic' . 7 vicecomit' . 7 ministris suis omnibus de Lincol' scira ·: salutem . Sciatis me dedisse 7 concessisse ecclesie sancte Marie Linc' 7 canonicis* eiusdem ecclesie illas .xviii. libras terre 7 sochemannos quas eis in prebendas dedi in escambium decime sue de Cherchetona 7 de Castra cum omnibus consuetudinibus 7 rectitudinibus . 7 libertatibus quas in illis habebam . 7 quas rex Henricus inde habebat . Et ideo precipio quod illi sochemanni plenarie eis in omnibus intendant . Teste . Willelmo de Albini pincerna . apud Notingham'.

Marginalia: 2.
Text: MS—A.

*Folio 32.

Hdl.   *Carte Regis* STEPHANI.   .3.2.

177

84. Writ of Stephen, releasing bishop Alexander from the payment of ten pounds which he and bishop Robert I his predecessor were wont to render yearly by way of *firma* for the wapentake of Well. At Oxford. (1135–1139.)

De .x. libris perdonatis episcopo Alexandro de Welle wapentac (marg.).

.S. rex Ang*lorum* . iustic' . vice*comit'* . baronibus . 7 omnibus fidelibus suis Francis 7 Anglis de Lincol' scir*a*[1] ; salutem . Sciatis me dedisse 7 finaliter perdonasse Alexandro[2] episcopo Linc' . illas .x.[3] libras . quas ipse 7 Robertus episcopus antecessor suus reddere solebant de firma per annum pro Welle wapentac . Quare uolo 7 firmiter precipio quod idem episcopus Alexander[4] teneat illud wapentac bene 7 in pace libere 7 quiete cum omnibus illis libertatibus 7 quietationibus cum quibus ipse 7 Robertus episcopus melius tenuerunt quando illas .x.[3] libras reddebant . Testibus . Willelmo[5] Mart*ello* . 7 . A. de Ver . 7 Hugone . Bigoto . 7 Willelmo[5] de Alb*ini* . pincerna . apud Oxene*fordiam*.[6]

Texts : MS—A. Iv(18). Pd—*C.C.R.*iv,140(18).
Var. R. : [1] Lincolescira Iv. [2] Alixandro Iv. [3] decem Iv. [4] Alixander Iv. [5] *for* Willelmo *read* W. *in* R. [6] Oxen' Iv.

178

85. Writ of Stephen, confirming the gift of half a hide in Quarrendon [co. Buckingham] which Robert de Tinchebrai made to the church of Saint Mary of Aylesbury in return for leave to make a burial ground at Quarrendon. At Nottingham. (1135–1147.)

De dimidia hida terre in Querendon*a*[1] (marg.).

.S. rex Ang*lorum* episcopo Lincol' 7 iustic' 7 vice*comit'* 7 baronibus 7 ministris 7 omnibus fidelibus suis Francis 7 Anglis de Buchingeham[2] scir*a* salutem . Sciatis quia concedo 7 confirmo illam donationem quam Robertus de Tenarchebrai fecit deo 7 ecclesie beate Marie Aile*sberie* de dimidia hida terre de Querendona pro concessu cimiterii de Querendona habendum 7 construendum in eadem uilla . Quare uolo 7 firmiter precipio quod ecclesia predicta hanc dimidiam hidam terre teneat . 7 in perpetuam elemosinam possideat bene 7 in pace 7 libere 7 quiete sicut tenet aliam possessionem suam . Testibus . comite Symone . 7 Ricardo de Canuill*a* . 7 Ricardo de Walb*eri*[3] apud Notingeham.[4]

Marginalia : 2..
Texts : MS—A. S46. Iiii(31). Pd—*C.C.R.*iv,103(31).
Var. R. : [1] De ecclesia de Aillesb*eria* (13 cent.). Eylisbury (15 cent.) S marg. [2] Bucchingeham Iiii. [3] Wall'i Iiii. [4] North't' Iiii.

179

86. Writ of Stephen, giving the church of Brampton [co. Huntingdon] to the church of Lincoln *in prebendam*. At Oxford. (1146–1149.)

De ecclesia de Bramton' (A marg.).

.S'. rex Ang*lorum* . archiepiscopis . 7 episcopis . 7 iustic*iariis* . 7 vice*comitibus* . 7 baronibus . 7 ministris . 7 omnibus fidelibus suis totius Anglie . salutem . Sciatis me dedisse 7 concessisse deo 7 ecclesie sancte Marie Linc' in prebendam ecclesiam de Bramtona cum terris 7 decimis 7 omnibus aliis pertinentiis eius . Quare uolo 7 firmiter precipio quod ecclesia sancte Marie ecclesiam illam de Bramtona bene 7 in pace 7 libere 7 quiete 7 honorifice teneat 7 habeat in perpetuum ⫶ sicut melius tenet alias ecclesias quas .W. auus meus 7 auunculi mei reges Anglorum[1] eidem ecclesie in prebendas dederunt . Testibus . Ricardo de Luci . 7 Willelmo de Caisn*eto*[2] . 7 Ricardo de Canuill*a* . apud Oxenef*ordiam*.[3]

Facsimile facing page 49.
Marginalia : 2..
Endorsed : (1) S (12 cent.). (2) de ecclesia Brantone (12 cent.). (3) xxx (13 cent.).
Strip at the foot for seal, with a ribband below it. Size : 6½ x 4⅛ inches.
Texts : MS—Orig. A1/1/8. A. S47. Iiii(26). Pd—*Mon.*viii,1275(48) in part.
*E.H.R.*xxiii,728.
Var. R. : [1] Anglie A. [2] W. de Caisnet' A S. [3] Oxeneford' A ; Oxenefor' S.

180

87. Writ of Stephen, giving to bishop Alexander the land which is between Saint Michael's church [in Lincoln] and the ditch, as the ditch reaches to the city wall, and twenty shillings in land of the king's demesne adjacent to the church. If the bishop shall build a house upon it for his own dwelling, the king grants the land as a perpetual possession to the church of Lincoln and to the bishop, quit of all customary payments. He also grants to the bishop the actual ditch and city wall at that place that the bishop may make a way of ingress, and do what is convenient for his building. At Rouen. (Probably 1137.)

De terra inter ecclesiam sancti Michaelis 7 fossatum .A. episcopo data . 7 .xx. solidatas terre[1] (marg.).

.S. rex Ang*lorum* iustic' . 7 baronibus . 7 vice*comit'* . 7 ministris . 7 omnibus fidelibus suis Francis 7 Anglis de Lincol' scira ⫶ salutem . Sciatis me dedisse 7 concessisse Alexandro episcopo Linc' terram que est inter ecclesiam sancti Michaelis 7 fossatum . desicut fossatum* se extendat[2] in murum ciuitatis . Et in proximo loco circa ecclesiam predictam .xx. solidatas terre de dominio meo . Quare uolo 7 firmiter precipio quod in pace eam[3] teneat . 7 libere . 7 honorifice 7 quiete cum soca 7 sacha 7 toll . 7 theam . 7 infangene-theof[4] . 7 cum omnibus libertatibus 7 quietacionibus . cum quibus erat dum in dominio meo erat . Et si idem episcopus in ea domum sibi edificauerit ad propriam sui mansionem ⫶ tunc concedo ecclesie Linc' 7 sibi 7 successoribus suis episcopis in eternam possessionem predictam terram quietam de omni consuetudine . Et eodem loco concedo eidem episcopo ipsum fossatum 7 murum ciuitatis ad introitus suos faciendum . 7 utilia sui edificii faciendum . Testibus . ⁵cancellario . Rogero⁵ . 7 Hugone Big' . apud Roth*omagum*.

Marginalia in Iviii : Nota pro manerio episcopi Linc'.
Texts : MS—A. S48. Iiii(29). Iviii(7). Pd—*C.C.R.*iv,103(29).
Var. R.: ¹ De terra iuxta sanctum Michaelem S marg. ² extendit Iiii. ³ eam in pace S Iiii. ⁴ infangeneteof Iiii. ⁵⁻⁵ cancellario regis Iiii.

*Folio 32d.

181

88. Letter of Stephen, addressed to bishop Alexander. At the request of Baldric de Sigillo, his clerk, the king has given to the church of Lincoln, in perpetual alms, fourteen pounds a year by way of tithe of the *firma* of the city of Lincoln *in prebendam* for the use of the said Baldric. He commands and earnestly requests that the bishop should add the same amount to the prebend from his own property, for the honour and profit of the church, that honour may arise therefrom to the king and the bishop and to Baldric who has served the king well. For this the king will give the bishop many thanks ; and he bids him send one of his canons to receive investiture in the prebend at his hand, and to bring back seisin to the church by the king's ring, together with his charter, and to invest Baldric in the prebend on behalf of the bishop and chapter ; and the canon is to come to the king at Oxford, because he will find him there. At Oxford. (1140–1147.)

De .xiiii. libris . datis Baldrico de Sigillo de firma ciuitatis Linc' in prebendam¹ (marg.).

.S. rex Ang*lorum* .A. episcopo Linc'² salutem . Scias quia per requisitionem Baldrici de Sigillo clerici mei dedi 7 concessi deo 7 ecclesie sancte Marie Linc' in perpetuam elemosinam .xiiii. libras . singulis annis de decima de firma mea ciuitatis Linc' in prebendam ad opus ipsius Baldrici . Ego autem ex mea parte tibi mando 7 obnixe te requiro quatinus tantum ex tuo addas eidem prebende prefate ad honorem 7 utilitatem ecclesie quod honor etiam³ inde sit michi 7 tibi 7 illi qui multum michi seruiuit . 7 grates multiplices inde tibi sciam⁴ . Et mittas michi unum ex canonicis tuis de eadem⁵ ecclesia qui de manu mea inuestituram eiusdem prebende recipiat . 7 saisinam per anulum meum ecclesie deferat . simul cum carta mea . 7 qui ex tua parte 7 capituli tui ipsum Baldricum de predictis inuestiat . Et canonicus ueniat ad me circa Oxenefordi*am* quia⁶ ibidem me inueniet . Testibus . M'. regina . 7 Willelmo de Ipra . 7 Ricardo de Luci . apud Oxenefordi*am*.⁷

Marginalia : 2.
Texts: MS—A. S49. R30.
Var. R.: ¹ De xiiij libris in ciuitate Li'c'l' S marg. ² *om.* Linc' R. ³ 7 R. ⁴ *query for* faciam. ⁵ eade S. ⁶ *for* Oxenefordi*am* quia *read* mensem R. ⁷ Oxenef' S ; Oxen' R.

182

89. Writ of Stephen, confirming to the church of Lincoln the manors and churches which were given by William I (see no. 2 above). At Lincoln. (1135–1153.)

¹De maneriis de Welleton' Slaford . Lecton' . Woborna 7 ecclesiis pluribus (marg.).¹

.S. rex Anglo*rum* . archiepiscopis . episcopis . abbatibus . iustic*iariis* . comitibus . baronibus . vicecomitibus . ministris . 7 omnibus fidelibus suis tocius Angl*ie*² salutem . Sciatis quod concedo ecclesie sancte Marie de Linc'³ manerium Welletone . 7 manerium de Slafordi*a*⁴ cum appendiciis suis⁵ . 7 tres ecclesias de tribus maneriis meis scilicet de Cherchetona⁶ . 7 de Castra . 7 de Wellingoura cum terris 7 decimis earum . 7 preter hoc omnem decimam eorundem maneriorum de redditibus meis . 7 concedo eidem ecclesie duas ecclesias in Linc'⁷ . scilicet ecclesiam sancti Laurentii . 7 ecclesiam sancti Martini . 7 manerium de Lectona⁸ . 7 manerium de Woburna . 7 .iiii⁰ʳ⁹ . ecclesias scilicet de Bedefordi*a*¹⁰ . 7 de Lechtona¹¹ . 7 de Buchingham¹² . 7 de Ailesber*ia* in perpetuam elemosinam . Quare precipio quod ipsa ecclesia sancte Marie Linc'⁷ bene 7 in pace 7 libere 7 quiete 7 honorifice teneat 7 habeat omnes supradictas tenuras¹³ in maneriis . 7 ecclesiis . 7 decimis in libera 7 quieta elemosina . sicut rex .W.¹⁴ auus meus illas ei dedit 7 concessit . 7 carta sua confirmauit . quam testificor me uidisse coram baronibus meis in Linc'¹⁵ . Testibus . comite Eustaci*o* . 7 Radulfo de Haia . 7 Ricardo de Canuil*la* . 7 Waltero de Aiencurt . 7 Raina*ldo* de Creuequer¹⁶ . apud Linc'.

Marginalia : 2̣ Hic Buckyngh' (query Q).
Texts : MS—A. S50. R25. Iv(16). Iix(2). Pd—*C.C.R.*iv,140(16). *C.C.R.* v,294(2).
Var. R. : ¹⁻¹ Leghton manerium R marg. ² Anglie R. ³ Lincoln' Iix. ⁴ Slaford S Iix ; Slafford' R. ⁵ eius R Iv. ⁶ Chircheton' R. ⁷ Lincoln' Iix. ⁸ Lechtona S ; Lehtona R Iv ; Leghtona Iix. ⁹ quatuor Iv Iix. ¹⁰ Bedeford S Iv. ¹¹ Lehton' R ; Leghton' Iv Iix. ¹² Buchingeh' R Iv Iix. ¹³ teneuras R Iv Iix. ¹⁴ Will*elmus* R Iix. ¹⁵ Lincol' R. ¹⁶ Creuec*ur* R Iv Iix.

Folio 33.

Hdl.　　　　　　　　　　　　　　　　　　　　　　　　　　.3.3.

183

90. Writ of Stephen, giving to bishop Alexander the church of the king's manor of Torksey [co. Lincoln]. At Woodstock. (1135–1147.)

De ecclesia de Torkeseia (marg.).

.S. rex Anglo*rum* . episcopo Linc' . 7 baronibus . 7 iustic' . 7 vice*comit*' . 7 omnibus fidelibus suis de Linc'¹ scira ⸳ salutem . Sciatis me dedisse 7 concessisse Alexandro episcopo Linc' in elemosinam ecclesiam manerii mei de Torcheseia cum terris 7 decimis

7 elemosinis 7 omnibus rebus eidem ecclesie pertinentibus . Quare
uolo 7 precipio quod bene 7 in pace 7 libere 7 quiete teneat . Testibus .
episcopo de Ely . 7 cancellario . 7 Rogero de Fiscanno[2] . 7 R. de
Ver . apud Wdestoch.[3]

Marginalia : Hic +.
Texts : MS—A. S51.
Var. R. : [1] Lincol' S. [2] *The initial letter should be f, though it is indistinguishable
from* s *in* A *and* S. [3] Wdestoc' S.

184

91. Writ of Stephen, giving to bishop Alexander his manor
of Eagle [co. Lincoln]. At Oxford. (1135–1147.)

De manerio de Eicla ꞏ cum soca 7 saca (marg.).

.S. rex Anglorum . iustic' . 7 baronibus . 7 vicecomit' .
7 ministris . 7 omnibus fidelibus suis Francis 7 Anglis de Linc' scira
salutem . Sciatis me dedisse 7 concessisse Alexandro episcopo Linc'
manerium meum de Eicla[1] cum omnibus adiacentiis suis in bosco
7 plano 7 in aliis rebus sicut erat dum esset in manu Henrici regis
7 mea . Et uolo 7 firmiter precipio quod illud bene 7 in pace 7
honorifice 7 libere 7 quiete teneat de me in capite cum toll 7 theam
7 infangenetheof . 7 cum saca 7 soca . 7 cum omnibus aliis libertatibus cum quibus rex Henricus illud melius 7 liberius tenuit .
7 ego post illum in bosco 7 plano 7 pratis 7 pasturis 7 aquis 7
molendinis . 7 in uia . 7 in[2] semitis . 7 in omnibus aliis locis . Testibus .
episcopo Wintoniensi . 7 episcopo Sarisbiriensi . 7 cancellario . apud
Oxenefordiam.

Marginalia : 2 Hic.
Texts : MS—A. S52.
Var. R. : [1] Eiccla S. [2] *om.* in S.

185

92. Writ of Stephen, giving to bishop Alexander licence to have
a fair in the bishop's manor of Sleaford, beginning on the day
before the feast of Saint Denis [9 October], and continuing on the
morrow and the day after the feast. At Odiham [co. Southampton].
(1135–1148.)

De feria in Laffordia[1] (marg.).

.S. rex Anglorum . iusticiariis . vicecomitibus . 7 baronibus . 7
omnibus fidelibus suis tocius Anglie ꞏ salutem . Sciatis me dedisse
7 concessisse . A.[2] episcopo Linc' 7 successoribus suis post eum
quod habeat unam feriam in manerio suo de Eslaford[3] . que incipiat
die proxima ante festum sancti Dionisii . 7 duret in crastino . 7
die sequente post festum . Quare uolo 7 precipio quod omnes illuc
euntes 7 ibi morantes 7 inde redeuntes habeant meam firmam pacem
cum omnibus suis . dando ibi suas rectas consuetudines . ne super

hoc ab aliquo iniuste disturbentur alicubi super .x. libras forifacture .
Testibus . R. cancellario . 7 . W. Martello . 7 . A. de Ver . 7 R. de
Ver . 7 Radulfo filio Walteri apud Odiham.

Marginalia : 2 Hic +.
Texts: MS—A. S53. Iiii(28). Pd—*C.C.R.*iv,102–3(28).
Var. R. : ¹ Eslaford S. ² Alex' Iiii. ³ Esladford Iiii.

186

93. Writ of Stephen, granting to the church of Lincoln and
Robert Chesney, bishop thereof, one die for coining money in
the bishop's town of Newark. At Lincoln. (1148–1154.)

¹De uno cunco in Newerch'¹ (marg.).

.S. rex Anglorum . archiepiscopis . episcopis abbatibus . iusticiariis .
comitibus . baronibus . ministris . 7 omnibus fidelibus suis Anglie .
salutem . Sciatis me concessisse ecclesie sancte Marie de Linc' . 7
Roberto de Caisneto eiusdem ecclesie episcopo habere in perpetuum
unum cuncum² ad operandam monetam in uilla sua de Newerca .
Quare uolo 7 firmiter precipio quod ecclesia Lincoliensis 7 predictus
Robertus episcopus cuncum² illum bene 7 in pace 7 libere 7 quiete
7 honorifice habeant 7 successores eiusdem Roberti Lincoliensis
ecclesie episcopi inperpetuum possideant . Testibus . Hugone
episcopo Dunelmensi . 7 Roberto de Gant cancellario . 7 Baldrico
de Sigillo . 7 Ricardo de Luci . 7 Ricardo de Canuilla apud Linc'.³

Marginalia : R'.
Texts: MS—A. S54.
Var. R. : ¹⁻¹ De prato iuxta Lincol' S (*this title properly belongs to* no. 96 *below*).
² *sic for* cuneum. ³ Lincol' S.

187

94. Writ of Stephen, giving to the church of Lincoln and the
canons eighteen pounds in land *in prebendam* in the wapentake of
Corringham [co. Lincoln] in exchange for eighteen pounds which
they were wont to have in Kirton [in Lindsey] and Caistor [co.
Lincoln] for tithes, namely, three carucates and three bovates in
Northorpe, five carucates and seven bovates in Blyton and Wharton,
two carucates and five bovates and two-thirds of a bovate in Pilham, seven bovates in Gilby and Wharton, and nine and a half
bovates by the Trent. At Oxford. (1138–1139.)

De .xviii. libratis terre in Coringham wapentac in escambium
.xviii. libris de Castre 7 Kirketona (marg.).

.S. rex Anglorum . iustic' . 7 baronibus . 7 vicecomit' . 7
ministris . 7 omnibus fidelibus suis Francis* 7 Anglis de Lincol'¹
scira ? salutem . Sciatis me dedisse 7 concessisse ecclesie sancte
Marie Lincol' 7 canonicis .xviii. libratas terre in Coringeham

wapentac in escambium .xviii. libr*atarum* quas solebant habere in Cherchetona 7 Castre[2] pro decimis in prebenda scilicet . in Torp .iii. carrucatas terre . 7 .iii. bouatas in Blitona . 7 Wartona .v. carrucatas terre . 7 .vii. bouatas in Phileh*am*[3] .ii. carrucatas . 7 .v. bouatas . 7 .ii. partes unius bouate in Gillebi . 7 Wartona . vii. bouatas . ad Trentam .ix. bouatas . 7 dimidiam . Quare uolo 7 firmiter precipio quod bene 7 in pace 7 libere 7 quiete 7 honorifice teneant in bosco 7 plano 7 pratis 7 pasturis 7 in omnibus locis 7 rebus omnibus cum socha 7 sacha 7 toll 7 theam 7 infangenethef[4] 7 cum omnibus illis libertatibus 7 rectitudinibus 7 consuetudinibus quas ego ipse in terris predictis habui dum in manu mea essent . 7 cum illis consuetudinibus quas rex Henricus inde habebat . Testibus . R. episcopo Sar*isbiriensi* . 7 R. episcopo Excestr*ensi*[5] . 7 Symone episcopo Wigrecestr*ensi*[6] . 7 . A. episcopo Lincol'[7] . 7 R. cancellario . 7 R. comite Legrecestr*ie*[8] . 7 Symone comite . 7 . R. comite Warewic[9] . 7 Milone Gloecestr*ie*[10] . 7 R. de Oilli . 7 . W. Mart*ello* . 7 þig'[11] de Sai . 7 H. de Traci . apud Oxeneford*iam*.

Marginalia : 2..
Texts : MS—A. S55. Iiii(30). Pd—*C.C.R.*iv,103(30).
Var. R. : [1] Lincole Iiii. [2] Castra Iiii. [3] Pileh' S ; Piriham Iiii. [4] infangenetef Iiii. [5] Exon' Iiii. [6] Wygorn' Iiii. [7] Linc' Iiii. [8] Legr' Iiii. [9] Warwic' Iiii. [10] Gloec' Iiii. [11] Ingel*ramo* Iiii.

Folio 33d.

188

95. Writ of Stephen, addressed to the barons and lieges of the honour of Dover and of Kent, giving to bishop Alexander the fee of Adam de Hedfelda ; and enjoining that the castle-guard which Adam used to do at Dover, he may do where it pleases the bishop, either at the bishop's castle of Newark or elsewhere. At Durham. (1136–1138.)

[1]De feoda Ade de Hedfeld 7 warda facienda apud Newerch'[1] (marg.).

.S. rex Angl*orum* . baronibus . 7 omnibus fidelibus suis Francis 7 Anglis de honore Doure 7 de comitatu de Chent salutem . Sciatis me dedisse 7 concessisse .A. episcopo Lincol'[2] feodum Ade de Hedfelda . Et uolo 7 precipio quod wardam quam faciebat apud Douram ꝰ faciat ubi episcopo placuerit . aut ad castellum suum de Niwerca[3] aut alibi . Testibus . cancellario . 7 Hugone Big*ot*[4] . apud Dunelm*um*.

Marginalia : 2..
Texts : MS—A. S56. Iv(15). Ivi(2). Pd—*C.C.R.*iv,105–6(2),140(15).
Var. R. : [1-1] De warda de Niwerca S marg. [2] Linc. S Iv. [3] Newercha Iv ; Newerca Ivi. [4] Byg' Ivi.

189

96. Writ of Stephen, commanding that the church of Lincoln shall be seised of its meadow near Lincoln as it was seised on the day on which king Henry was alive and dead [1 December, 1135], and afterwards in the king's own time ; and that if any part thereof has been taken, it is to be restored ; otherwise, the king's justice, earl William, will do it. At Oxford. (1141–1154.)

De prato iuxta Linc'[1] (marg.).

.S. rex Ang*lorum* . prepositis . ꝡ burgensibus Lincol'[2] salutem . Precipio quod ecclesia sancte Marie Lincol'[2] sit saisita ꝡ tenens de prato suo iuxta Lincol'[2] . ita bene ꝡ plene ꝡ libere ꝡ quiete sicut melius uel plenius saisita fuit die qua rex Henricus fuit uiuus ꝡ mortuus ꝡ meo tempore postea . Et si quid super hoc inde captum est ꝉ reddatur . Et nisi feceris ꝉ iusti*ci*a mea comes Willemus faciat ne super hoc amplius audiam inde clamorem pro penuria pleni recti . uel iusticie . Teste . R.[3] cancellario . apud Oxeneford*iam*[4].

Marginalia : 2⟂. Nota (Q).
Texts : MS—A. S57 (*the text ends with the words* inde clamorem). R28.
Var. R. : [1] Lincolniam R. [2] Linc' S. [3] Rob' R. [4] Oxen' R.

190

97. Writ of Stephen, commanding that bishop Robert II shall hold his lands and tenements within the city of Lincoln and without as his predecessors best held them in the time of king Henry. At Saint Albans. (1148–1154.)

De terris episcopi infra Linc' ꝡ extra (A marg.).

.S'. rex Ang*lorum* . iustic' . ꝡ vic*ecomit*' . ꝡ prepositis . ꝡ ciuibus suis Linc' ꝉ salutem . Precipio quod Robertus episcopus Linc'[1] teneat omnes terras ꝡ teneuras suas infra ciuitatem Linc' ꝡ extra . ita [bene ꝡ[2]] quiete ꝡ in pace ꝡ honorifice sicut predecessores sui episcopi Linc'[1] eas melius ꝡ liberius tenuerunt tempore Henrici regis auunculi mei . ne super hoc aliquis eas infestet ullo modo . Et idem episcopus omnes libertates ꝡ liberas consuetudines suas ita bene ꝡ plenarie habeat ꝉ sicut predecessores sui eas melius habuerunt . Teste . Willelmo[3] Mart*ello* . apud Sanctum Albanu*m*.

Facsimile opposite.
Endorsed : (1) S. regis de teneuris infra Linc' ꝡ extra (12 cent.). (2) VI .s. (13 cent.).
The strip at foot for seal and a ribband below it have both been torn off. Size : 6 x 4 inches.
Marginalia : 2⟂. Nota (Q).
Texts : MS—Orig. ᴀ1/1/6. A. Iv(19). Pd—*E.H.R.*xxiii,728. *C.C.R.*iv, 140–1(19).
Var. R. : [1] Lincol' A. [2] *supplied from* A, *the original charter having been injured.* [3] W. *in* A.

VIII

Et id. Cc...

Teste Henrico Archiepiscopo, Capellano... Comes... Elias de Wintonia... Omnibus fidelibus suis... Sciatis me dedisse et... concessisse Deo et Ecclesie Beate Marie sitam in prebenda Capellanie de Blida... cum Ecclesiis et Capellis et decimis... et omnibus aliis... eidem Capellanie pertinentibus. Quare volo et firmiter precipio quod Ecclesia Beate Marie... teneat omnia predicta... in pace et honorifice et libere et quiete in perpetuum... ab omni seculari exactione... et... teneat alias prebendas suas... testibus Petro de N... et Willelmo de Lima... et Ricardo... et... de Essexa et Adam de Belt...

Folio 34.

Hdl.   .3.4.

191

98. Writ of Stephen, commanding the justice, reeves, and citizens of Lincoln to cause Baldric, the king's chaplain, to have the tithe of the *firma* of the city of Lincoln, which the king gave to the church of Saint Mary and to Baldric *in prebendam*. At Lincoln. (1140–1154.) (See no. 88 above.)

De eadem decima firme ciuitatis Lincoln' (Rrubric).
.S. rex Anglorum . iustic' . 7 prepositis 7 ciuibus suis Linc' salutem . Precipio uobis quod faciatis habere Baldrico capellano meo decimam firme méé ciuitatis Lincol' quam dedi ecclesie beate Marie 7 ei in prebendam . 7 ita ne inde fallat quin illam ei reddatis ad illos terminos statutos quibus reddi solet 7 debet firma ciuitatis . Teste . Willelmo de Ipra apud Lincol'.[1]

Marginalia : 2̣ φ.
Texts : MS—A. R32.
Var. R. : [1] Linc' R.

192

99. Writ of Stephen, granting to bishop Alexander the pledge which Adelidis de Condet gave him of her castle of Thorngate, and of her lands, namely, Wickhambreux in Kent, Grimston in Nottinghamshire, and [South] Carlton, Thurlby [near Lincoln], Eagle, and Skellingthorpe in Lincolnshire. The king has also granted to the bishop the wardship of Adelidis' son. And the king commands that the bishop shall hold the premises until her son is of such an age that he can hold the land and be made a knight. At Lincoln. (Probably 1141.)

.S. rex Anglorum . iusticiariis . 7 vicecomitibus . 7 baronibus . 7 ministris . 7 omnibus fidelibus suis Francis 7 Anglis Lincolie scira 7 de Chent ⁊ salutem . Sciatis quia concedo Alexandro episcopo Linc' vadium quod Adelidis de Condet fecit ei de castello suo de Tornegat 7 de terris suis . scilicet de Wicham in Chent cum appendiciis suis . 7 in Notingeham scira de Grimeston cum appenditiis suis . 7 in Lincol' scira de Carletona . 7 de Torlebi . 7 de Eicla cum appenditiis suis . 7 de Scheldinghop cum appendiciis suis . 7 custodiam filii sui . Quare uolo 7 firmiter precipio quod idem .A. episcopus teneat omnia hec supradicta bene 7 in pace 7 libere 7 quiete 7 honorifice . nec ponatur inde in placitum donec filius ipsius Adelidis de Condet talis etatis sit quod possit terram tenere 7 miles fieri . Testibus . comite Symone . 7 Roberto de Stuteuilla . 7 Radulfo de Haia apud Lincol'.

Marginalia: 2 Hic φ.
Text: MS—A.
Note: For Thorngate see pages 277 ff.
The identification above of Wickhambreux is proved by the fact that the manor of that place was held by Walter de Clifford who married Agnes daughter and heir of Roger de Cundy. The manor afterwards passed to the Braose family from whom the second element of its name was derived (Hasted, *The History of Kent* iii, 658). For another instance of a *uadium* see no. 69 above and page 284 below.

193

100. Writ of Stephen, giving to the church of Lincoln *in prebendam* the chapelry of Blyth [co. Nottingham] with its churches, chapels, tithes, lands, etc. At Oxford. (1145.)

De capellaria de Blida (A marg.).

S'. rex Anglorum . archiepiscopis . episcopis . abbatibus . comitibus . iusticiariis . vicecomitibus . baronibus . ministris . 7 omnibus fidelibus suis totius Anglie[1] ·' salutem . Sciatis me dedisse 7 concessisse deo 7 ecclesie beate Marie Lincol'[2] in prebendam capellariam de Blida . cum ecclesiis 7 capellis 7 decimis 7 terris 7 omnibus aliis rebus eidem capellarie pertinentibus . Quare volo 7 firmiter precipio quod ecclesia beate Marie Linc' hec omnia predicta bene 7 in pace 7 honorifice 7 libere 7 quiete in perpetuum[3] teneat ab omni seculari exactione . sicut melius 7 liberius tenet alias prebendas suas . Testibus . Roberto de Ver[4] . 7 Willelmo de Ipra . 7 Ricardo de Luci[5] . 7 Henrico de Essexa . 7 Adam[6] de Belun[7] . apud Oxenefordiam.

Facsimile facing page 60.
Endorsed: (1) .S. pot· inter cartas de prebendis (13 cent.). (2) X carta visa (13 cent.). (3) Carta S regis de capellaria de Blida (? 15 cent.).
Strip at foot for seal, ribband below it. Size: 6¼ x 4½ inches.
Marginalia in A: 2.
Texts: MS—Orig. A1/1/7. A. R27. Iv(11). Pd—*E.H.R.*xxiii,727. *C.C.R.*iv, 139(11).
Var. R.: [1] Angl' A. [2] Linc' A R. [3] imperpetuum A. [4] Ver A. [5] Lucy Iv. [6] Ad' R. [7] Bel'n Iv.

194

101. Writ of Stephen, giving to bishop Alexander the house which was William Turniant's at Lincoln, with the whole messuage, and commanding that the tenant of the house shall hold it of the bishop as he was wont to hold it of the king. At Rouen. (1135–1147. Query circa 1139.)

De domo que fuit Willelmi Torniant (marg.).

.S. rex Anglorum . iustic' . 7 baronibus . 7 vicecomit' . 7 ministris suis . 7 omnibus fidelibus suis Francis 7 Anglis Lincol' scira[1] salutem . Sciatis me dedisse 7 concessisse Alexandro[2] episcopo Linc' domum

que fuit Willelmi *Turniant*[3] in Linc' . cum tota mansura . Et
uolo 7 firmiter precipio quod qui eam tenuerit *:* eam de predicto
episcopo teneat sicut de me ipso eam tenere solebat . Et idem
episcopus eam teneat cum omnibus consuetudinibus 7 libertatibus
cum quibus tenet aliam terram suam quam quietius tenet .
Teste . cancellario Rogero apud Rotho*magum*.[4]

Marginalia: 2. Hic V.
Texts: MS—A. Iv(17). Pd—*C.C.R.*iv,140(17).
Var. R.: [1] Lincolescir' Iv. [2] Alixandro Iv. [3] Turniantd Iv. [4] *The initial* R
seems to be a correction from P.

Folio 34d.

195

102. Writ of Stephen, giving the church of North Kelsey *in
prebendam* to the church of Lincoln. At London. (Circa 1141.)

De ecclesia de Northkelesi*a* (marg.).

.S. rex Anglo*rum* . archiepiscopis . episcopis . abbatibus . comitibus .
iustic*iariis* . vicecomitibus . baronibus . 7 omnibus ministris . 7
fidelibus suis Francis . 7 Anglis tocius Anglie *:* salutem . Sciatis
me dedisse . 7 concessisse inperpetuam elemosinam pro anima
regis . Henrici . 7 pro salute anime mee deo 7 ecclesie beate Marie
Linc' . in prebendam ecclesiam de Norhtchelesia[1] . cum omnibus
appendiciis suis . Quare uolo . 7 firmiter precipio quod ipsa ecclesia
Linc' . eam teneat . 7 habeat bene 7 in pace . 7 libere . 7 quiete .
7 honorifice . 7 absolute ab omni seculari exactione inperpetuam
elemosinam . Et ut hec donacio mea rata illibataque[2] teneatur .
7 conseruetur *:* presentis sigilli mei impressione confirmo . 7 subscriptorum attestacione corroboro . Matill' . regina . comite Gilleberto[3] . 7 comite Herueyo[4] . 7 . Willelmo de Ipra . 7 Roberto de
V*er* . 7 Willelmo Mart*ello* . 7 Ricardo de Luci . 7 Rogero de Fraxino .
apud Lond*oniam*.

Marginalia: 2.
Texts: MS—A (*probably written by* Q2). Iiii(27). Pd—*Mon.*viii,1275(49) in
part. *C.C.R.*iv,102(27).
Var. R.: [1] Northcheleseia Iiii. [2] *insert* imperpetuum Iiii. [3] Gisl' Iiii. [4] Herueio
Iiii.
At the foot of the page: Hec sunt x pecie.

ADD. (Extran.) Chart.

103. Writ of Stephen, granting to bishop Robert [Chesney]
the king's justice of Lincoln and Lincolnshire, as bishop Robert
Bloet and bishop Alexander best had it. At Drax [co. York].
(1153–1154.)

S. rex Anglorum comitibus baronibus abbatibus vicecomitibus
ministris et civibus Linc' et omnibus fidelibus suis Linc' et Linc'
scira salutem . Sciatis me concessisse Roberto episcopo Linc'
iustitiam meam de Linc' et de Linc' scira . Quare volo et firmiter

precipio quod idem Robertus episcopus iustitiam meam ita bene
et in pace et honorifice et plenarie habeat sicut Robertus Bloet
vel Alexander episcopi Linc' predecessores eius illam melius
habuerunt . Et precipio vobis quod per summonicionem ministrorum
suorum veniatis ad placita mea tenenda et iudicia mea facienda
sicut melius et plenius faciebatis tempore regis Henrici avunculi
mei . Et nisi feceritis ipse iustitiet vos per catalla vestra quod
faciatis . Testibus Hugone episcopo Dunelmensi et Ricardo de
Luci et Ricardo de Canvill' apud Dracas.

Text: MS—Iv(13). Pd—*C.C.R.*iv,139(13).

Folio 13.

Hdl.   CARTE .H. REGIS SECUNDI.   .1.3.

73

104. Notification by Henry II that the suit which has been
long carried on between Robert II bishop of Lincoln and Robert abbot
of Saint Albans and their churches touching the subjection of the
abbot and monastery of Saint Albans and the fifteen churches
formerly privileged, has been ended before the king and the magnates of his kingdom in this manner : The bishop, with the assent
of his chapter, has renounced the claim which he had preferred
against the abbot and his brethren that the monastery itself and
the fifteen privileged churches which they have in their territory
should be subject to the church of Lincoln, and to himself as bishop ;
and that, with the consent of the king and by the advice of the
bishops, and with the assent of the chapter of Lincoln, the bishop
has received from the abbot and his brethren the village called
Fingest [co. Buckingham] with its church for ten pounds' worth
of land. Wherefore it is the king's pleasure that henceforth the
monastery and the fifteen churches shall be free to receive chrism
for themselves and oil and benediction for their abbot and the
rest of the sacraments of the church from what bishop they please ;
and that the abbey shall remain free as the king's demesne church
in his hand for ever ; and that the tithe of Wakerley [co Northamp-
ton], which the abbot and brethren had given to the church of
Lincoln, shall remain in their own possession for ever ; but that
the rest of the monastery's churches established throughout the
bishopric of Lincoln shall render the obedience and subjection that
other churches are wont to render to the bishop of Lincoln and
his archdeacons. At Westminster. (8 March, 1163.)

De concordia . inter abbatem sancti Albani . 7 Robertum . Linc'
episcopum[1] (rubric and marg.).

.H.[2] rex Anglorum 7 dux Normannorum 7 Aquitanorum . 7 comes
Andegauorum . archiepiscopis . episcopis . abbatibus . comitibus
7 omnibus baronibus 7 fidelibus suis tocius Anglie Francis 7 Anglis
salutem . Sciatis quod controuersia que diu fuerat agitata inter
Robertum episcopum Linc'[3] . 7 Robertum abbatem sancti Albani
7 eorum ecclesias de subiectione abbatis 7 monasterii sancti Albani .
7 .xv.[4] ecclesiarum iamdudum priuilegiatarum coram me 7 Thoma
archiepiscopo Cantuariensi . 7 Rogero archiepiscopo Eboracensi . 7
aliis episcopis 7 baronibus regni mei hoc modo terminata est . Robertus
episcopus Linc' assensu capituli sui imperpetuum renunciauit illi
controuersie quam aduersus Robertum abbatem sancti Albani 7
fratres eius mouerat . quia monasterium ipsum Sancti Albani .
7 .xv.[4] illas ecclesias quas in territorio suo priuilegiatas habent
Lincon'[3] ecclesie 7 sibi ut ipsius episcopo in subiectionem petebat .
Et ut ab ea imperpetuum conquiesceret de manu ipsius abbatis
7 fratrum eius villam que dicitur Tingeherst cum ecclesia 7 omnibus
pertinenciis eiusdem pro .x.[5] libratis terre libere 7 quiete ecclesie
Linc'[3] imperpetuum decetero possidendam assensu meo 7 episcoporum consilio capitulo Linc'[3] [6]assensum prebente recepit . 7 ius
quod in iamdicta abbatia sancti Albani 7 in persona Roberti abbatis
7 successorum suorum . 7 iamdictis .xv.[4] ecclesiis ecclesie sue 7
sibi 7 successoribus suis uendicabat ⫽ in manu mea pro se 7 suis
successoribus assensu capituli sui imperpetuum refutauit . Quare
uolo quod decetero liberum sit monasterio beati[7] Albani . 7 .xv.[4]
iamdictis ecclesiis crisma sibi 7 oleum 7 benedictionem abbati suo.7
cetera omnia sacramenta ecclesie absque reclamatione Linc'[8] ecclesie
a quo uoluerint episcopo accipere . 7 abbatia sicut mea dominica
ecclesia in manu mea in perpetuum libera remanebit[9] . decima de
Wacherleia quam primo Linc'[3] ecclesie dederant penes eam imperpetuum remanente . Relique uero eiusdem monasterii ecclesie
passim per episcopatum Linc'[3] constitute obedientiam 7 subiectionem quam cetere ecclesie debent episcopo Linc'[3] 7 archidiaconis
suis exhibebunt . Et si quid conceptum est in priuilegiis monachorum
super illis ecclesiis uel cellis uel personis in eis commorantibus
tam clericis . monachis . quam laicis nullum robur aduersus hanc
conuentionem obtinebit[10] . Quare uolo 7 firmiter precipio quod
ista compositio firma sit . 7 stabilis imperpetuum . 7 eam hac mea
carta[11] confirmo . Testibus . Thoma archiepiscopo Cantuariensi .
Rogero archiepiscopo Eboracensi . Henrico Wintoniensi . Nigello
Eliensi . Willelmo Norwicensi . Hilario Cicestrenensi . Jocelino
Sarisbiriensi . Waltero Rofensi . Hugone Dunelmensi . Gileberto
Herefordensi . Bartholomeo Exoniensi . Ricardo Couentrensi .
episcopis . Laurencio Westmonasterii . Willelmo Ramesie . Gregorio
Malmesbirie . Reginaldo[12] Perscon'[13] . Clemente Eboraci . Ailrico
Riuallis abbatibus . Roberto comite Legrecestrie[14] . comite .H.

E

Big*ot* . comite Willelmo de Arunde*l'* . Ricardo de Luc*i*[15] . Ricardo de Humez conestable[16] . Henrico filio Ge*raldi* apud Westm*onas-terium*.

Marginalia: ♃. De concordia o—|—o Wakerley (Q).
Texts: MS—A.   C,ff.17,17d.   Iv(22).   Pd—*Mon*.viii,1276(63)   in   part. *C.C.R*.iv,141-2(22).
Var. R.: [1] *add* 7 ecclesiam Linc' A marg.   [2] Henr' C.   [3] Lincol' C.   [4] quindecim Iv.   [5] decem Iv.   [6] *insert* in hoc C Iv.   [7] sancti C.   [8] Lincol' C; Lincon' Iv.   [9] *corrected from* permanebit C.   [10] optinebit Iv.   [11] *om.* carta C.   [12] Rog' C.   [13] *representing some form of* Pershore   (*In* A206 *below, the form is* Persorensi).   [14] Legrec' C.   [15] Luci C.   [16] *sic in* A Iv; conest' C.

74

105. Writ of Henry II, commanding that the bishop of Lincoln shall hold his tenements within the borough and without as freely as any of his predecessors held them in the time of king Henry, the king's grandfather; and that the clerks and servants of Saint Mary of Lincoln shall have the lands, customs, and franchises which they were wont to have at that time; and that no new customs shall be demanded from the bishop or his men.   At Woodstock.   (Before 1156.)

De libertatibus episcopi . clericorum . 7 seruientum ecclesie Linc' (rubric and marg.).

.H. rex Ang*lorum* 7 dux Norm*annorum* 7 Aquit*anorum* 7 comes Andeg*auorum* . prepositis 7 ciuibus Linc' salutem . Precipio quod episcopus Linc' habeat 7 teneat omnia tenementa sua infra burgum 7 extra ita bene 7 in pace 7 libere 7 integre 7 honorifice sicut aliquis predecessorum episcoporum Linc' melius tenuit 7 liberius tempore regis .H. aui mei . Et clerici Linc' 7 seruientes sancte Marie Linc' habeant omnes illas rectas consuetudines 7 libertates quas habere solebant tempore regis .H.[1] aui mei . Et prohibeo uobis ne super hoc de terris predicti episcopi uel hominibus eius aliquas nouas exigatis consuetudines quas facere non debeant . quia ipse episcopus 7 omnes* homines sui 7 tenure 7 possessiones eius sunt in mea manu 7 custodia 7 protectione . Teste . magistro Johanne de Oxen-*fordia* . apud Wodesto*cham*.

Marginalia: ♃ ·j· φ .N. V Nota (Q).   In R: De libertatibus concessis episcopo clericis 7 seruientibus ecclesie Linc' (R rubric).
Texts: MS—A.   R39.   Iv(36).   Pd—*C.C.R*.iv,145(36).
Var. R.: [1] *om.* .H. R.

*Folio 13d.

75

106. Writ of Henry II, notifying that his chaplain Geoffrey Dominicus and his men and possessions are in the king's hand and protection; and commanding that Geoffrey shall hold the prebend which he has within the city of Lincoln, which bishop Robert gave him, namely, the church of Saint Martin with its cemetery and men and stalls as freely as any canon held that prebend in the time of the king's grandfather. At Caen. (1154–1165.)

De prebenda domini Galfridi capellani domini regis (rubric).

.H. rex Angl*orum* . 7 dux Norm*annorum* 7 Aquit*anorum* . 7 comes And*egauorum* . vi*cecomit'* . 7 prepositis 7 ministris suis Linc' salutem . Sciatis quod Gaufridus dominicus capellanus meus 7 homines 7 omnes res sue sunt in mea manu 7 custodia 7 protectione . Et ideo uolo 7 firmiter precipio quod teneat prebendam suam quam habet infra ciuitatem Linc' . quam Robertus Linc' episcopus ei dedit . videlicet ecclesiam Sancti Martini cum cimiterio 7 hominibus 7 stallis 7 aliis pertinentiis suis bene . 7 in pace . libere . quiete . integre . 7 plenarie . 7 honorifice . sicut unquam aliquis canonicus illam prebendam melius 7 liberius 7 integrius tenuit tempore regis .H. aui mei . Et prohibeo quod nullus ei uel hominibus uel rebus suis aliquam iniuriam uel contumeliam faciat . Et si quis ei uel hominibus uel rebus suis forisfecerit ⁖ uos eis sine dilatione plenariam iusticiam faciatis . Testibus . Rotr*odo* episcopo Ebor*oicensi*[1] . Philippo episcopo Baioc*ensi* . Ern*ulfo* episcopo Lexou*ensi* . Ricardo de Hum*et* constabulario apud Cadom*um*.

Marginalia: + φ va cat V. De prebenda sancti Martini (Q).
Text: MS—A.
Var. R.: [1] *written* Eboȝ, *as if* Eboracensi *were intended.*

76

107. Writ of Henry II, commanding that his land in Torksey [co. Lincoln] shall henceforth be in warren, and remain in the custody of bishop Robert II. At Woodstock. (1155–1158.)

De warenna de Torkeseya[1] (rubric and marg.).

.H. rex Angl*orum* . 7 dux Norm*annorum* 7 Aquit*anorum* . 7 comes And*egauorum* . comitibus . iustic' . baronibus . vice*comit'* . ministris . 7 omnibus fidelibus suis de Lincol' sir*a*[2] ⁖ salutem . Volo 7 precipio quod tota terra mea de Torcheseia amodo sit in warenna . 7 remaneat in custodia Roberti Linc' episcopi . Et nullus in ea fuget super .x. libras forisfacture . Teste . Thoma[3] cancellario . apud Wodestocam.

Marginalia: ♃ φ.
Texts: MS—A. Iv(38). Pd—*C.C.R.*iv,146(38).
Var. R.: [1] Torkeseia marg. [2] Lincolscir' Iv. [3] Toma Iv.

77

108. Writ of Henry II, commanding the justices and sheriffs of Lincolnshire and Nottinghamshire to cause a recognition to be made by the oath of lawful men as to what rights of justice the predecessors of bishop Robert II had in the time of Henry I over those who without their licence chased or took hares in their warren ; and to cause the bishop to have such rights as shall be recognized. At Rouen.   (1155–1164.)

De iusticia inquirenda de warenna (rubric).

.H. rex Anglorum . 7 dux Normannorum . 7 Aquitanorum . 7 comes Andegauorum . iusticiariis 7 vicecomitibus Linc' sire 7 Notingeham sire[1] salutem . Precipio quod faciatis recognosci per sacramentum legalium hominum quam iusticiam habuerunt episcopi predecessores Roberti Lincol' episcopi tempore .H. regis aui mei . super illos qui sine eorum licentia fugabant uel leporem capiebant in warenna sua . 7 sicut recognita fuerit faciatis habere integre 7 plenarie eidem .R. Linc' episcopo . Teste Rotrodo Ebroicensi episcopo apud Rothomagum.

Marginalia : De warenna. R'.
Texts : MS—A. Iv(37). Pd—C.C.R.iv,145–6(37).
Var. R. : ¹ Notinquehanscir' Iv.

78

109. Writ of Henry II, granting to bishop Robert II warren in his towns of Newark, Stow, and Louth as his predecessors had in the time of Henry I ; and forbidding that any one shall chase or take hares without his licence, under forfeiture of ten pounds. At Dover.   (1154–1166.)

De warenna de Newerck'[1] de Stowa 7 Luda (A rubric and marg.).

.H' rex Anglorum dux Normannorum 7 Aquitanorum 7 comes Andegauorum . iustic' . vicecomit' . 7 omnibus ministris suis de Notinghamsira . 7 de Linc' sira : salutem . Concedo quod Robertus episcopus Linc' habeat warennam in uilla sua de Newerca . 7 de Stowa 7 de Luda . sicut aliquis predecessorum suorum eas melius liberius 7 honorificencius habuit . tempore regis Henrici aui mei . Et prohibeo quod nullus sine licencia ipsius fugat[2] in eis uel capiat leporem : super .x. libras forisfacture . Teste . Ricardo de Humet' constabulario apud Doueram.

Facsimile opposite.
Endorsed : (1) De warenna episcopi (12 cent.). (2) XIII H. ij. (13 cent.).
Strip for seal : the ribband below it has been torn off. Size 6 x 3¼ inches.
Marginalia in A : ♃ N φ.
Texts : MS—Orig. A1/1/11. A. Iiv(13). Pd—E.H.R.xxiv,305. C.C.R.iv,109(13).
Delisle, p. 160 (abs.).
Var. R. : ¹ Newerch' A marg. ² fuget Iiv.

Folio 14.
Hdl.   14

79

110. A similar grant to bishop Robert II of warren between Newark and Stow, to whomsoever the land may belong.   At Rouen (1158–1163.)

IX

H. Rex Angl' Dux Norm' [...] Com' Andeg' [...] bned [...] Comit[...]
[...] ministris suis de [...] Salutem [...] Concedo q[uod]
[...] Epo lined [...] in uilla sua de [...] et [...]
[...] sicut [...] predecessor[...] sua ea [...] [...]
[...] Regis [...] dni mei [...] [...]
[...] super [...] ut q[...] leporem [...] sup [...] [...]
[...] de [...] de Dou[...]

H. Rex Angl' [...] Dux Norm' [...] Aquit' [...] Com' Andeg' Omnib[us] Baronib[us]
[...] de Incoltsir' [...] Salutem. Sciatis me comendasse Rb[er]to Epo lined [...]
[...] mea [...] Incolt' [...] Hereuic' [...] Quare pro[hibeo] q[uod] nullus in ea fu-
git ut capiat leporem [...] sup forisfactura mea'. S[ed] in ea pace sit
qua fuit [...] huius [...] Regis [...] dni mei. T[este] Theobaldo Archiepo
Cant'. [...] Reginald [...] [...] apud Clarend'.

H. Rex Angl' [...] Dux Norm' [...] Aquit' [...] Com' Andeg' Iust[iciariis] [...] Baron[ibus] [...] Omnib[us] fidelib[us] suis de
lined' scir' [...] Salutem. Sciatis me concessisse [...] confirmasse D[e]o [...] Sc[t]e Marie lined' [...] Rad[ulfo] de Cadomo canonico lined' [...] Successorib[us] eius Canonicis uillam [...] cu[m] Omnib[us] p[er]tinentiis suis in p[er]petu[am]
[...] liberam elemosina[m] [...] nolo [...] firmit[er] p[er]cipio q[uod] eand[em] uillam in p[er]petua possessione b[e]n[e] [...] in
pace [...] honorifice libere [...] quieta de Comitatib[us] [...] sc[...] [...] hundr[edis]. [...] q[uod] ip[s]a[m] teneant cu[m] socca [...]
sacca [...] thol [...] them [...] Infangeth' [...] cu[m] Omnib[us] Consuetudinib[us] [...] libertatib[us] sicut aliq[ua] p[re]benda
lined' [...] quieti [...] liberi tenet. Teste Rob[er]to Epo lined' [...] Philippo Baioc' Epo apud lund'.

De warenna inter Newerk'[1] 7 Stowa cuiuscumque sit terra (rubric and marg.).

.H. rex Anglorum . 7 dux Normannorum . 7 Aquitanorum . 7 comes Andegauorum . iusticiariis . vicecomitibus . 7 omnibus ministris suis Lincolie sire . 7 Notingueham sire[2] salutem . Precipio quod episcopus Linc' .R. habeat warennam suam inter Newerc[3] 7 Stowam cuiuscumque sit terra . sicut predecessores sui melius 7 liberius habuerunt tempore .H. regis aui mei . Et prohibeo ne quis in ea fuget uel leporem capiat super .x. libras[4] forifacture . Teste . Rotrodo Ebroicensi[5] episcopo Rothomagum.

Marginalia: φ R'.
Texts: MS—A. Ivi(3). Pd—C.C.R.iv,106(3).
Var. R.: [1] Newerch' marg. [2] Not' scir' Ivi. [3] Newerc' Ivi. [4] libris Ivi.
[5] Roberto Ebor' Ivi (see no. 106 above).

80

111. De warenna in Notingham (rubric and marg.).

A duplicate of no. 54a above.

Marginalia: φ R' . . .

81

112. Writ of Henry II, granting to bishop Robert II warren in his land of Thame [co. Oxford] as his predecessors had it in the time of Henry I. At Brill [co. Buckingham]. (Probably 1157.)

De warenna de Thama (rubric and marg.).

.H. rex Anglorum . dux Normannorum . 7 Aquitanorum . 7 comes Andegauorum . iustic' . vicecomit' . 7 omnibus ministris suis de Oxeneford' sira[1] salutem . Concedo quod Robertus episcopus Linc' habeat warennam in terra sua de Thama sicut antecessores sui eam melius 7 honorabilius habuerunt tempore Henrici regis aui mei . Et prohibeo ne quis in ea fuget uel capiat leporem sine licentia eius . super .x. libras forisfacture . Teste . Thoma cancellario apud Bruhullam.

Marginalia: φ R'.
Texts: MS—A. Iiv(12). Pd—C.C.R.iv,109(12).
Var. R.: [1] Oxenfordsir' Iiv.

82

113. Writ of Henry II, granting to bishop Robert II warren between Lincoln and Newark, as bishops Robert I and Alexander had it in the time of Henry I. At Rouen. (1154–1167.)

De warenna inter Lincolniam . 7 Newerck'[1] (rubric and marg.).

.H. rex Anglorum . dux Normannorum . 7 Aquitanorum . 7 comes Andegauorum . iusticiariis . vicecomitibus . 7 omnibus ministris suis tocius Anglie salutem . Sciatis me concessisse 7 confirmasse Roberto episcopo Linc' quod habeat warenam inter Lincol'[2] 7 Newerc[3] . sicut Robertus episcopus uel Alexander episcopus eam melius 7 liberius tenuerunt tempore regis Henrici aui mei . Et

prohibeo ne quis in ea fuget uel capiat leporem super .x.[4] libra*s*
forisfacture sine eius licentia . Testibus . episcopo Cicestren*si* . 7
Jocelino de Bail*ol* apud Rotoma*gum*.

Marginalia: 2 φ.
Texts: MS—A. Iv(33). Pd—*C.C.R.*iv,145(33).
Var. R.: [1] Newerch' marg. [2] Lincoll' Iv. [3] Newerc' Iv. [4] decem Iv.

83

114. Writ of Henry II, commanding that the bishop of Lincoln
shall have warren in all his land in Lincolnshire.   At Woodstock.
(1154–1180.)

De warenna in Linc' syra (rubric and marg.).

.H. rex Angl*orum* . 7 dux Norma*nnorum* 7 Aquit*anorum* . 7
comes Ande*gauorum* . iustic'[1] . vicecomit' . baronibus . 7
omnibus ministris suis de Linc' scira salutem . Precipio quod
episcopus Linc' habeat warennam in tota terra sua de Linc' scira .
Et prohibeo ne quis in ea fuget uel leporem capiat sine licentia eius
super .x.[2] libra*s* forisfacture . Teste Ricardo de Hum*ez* constabulario
apud Wdestoch*am*.[3]

Marginalia: φ +.
Texts: MS—A. Iv(35). Pd—*C.C.R.*iv,145(35).
Var. R.: [1] iustitiis Iv. [2] decem Iv. [3] Wudestoch' Iv.

84

115. Writ of Henry II, granting to bishop Robert II warren in
his land of Banbury as his predecessors had it in the time of Henry I.
At Brill [co. Buckingham].   (Probably 1157.)

De warenna de Banneburi*a*[1] (rubric and marg.).

.H. rex Angl*orum* . dux Norma*nnorum* . 7 Aquit*anorum* . 7 comes
Ande*gauorum* . iustic' . vicecomit' . 7 omnibus ministris
suis Oxeneford' sire[2] salutem . Concedo quod Robertus episcopus
Linc' habeat warennam in terra sua de Banneb*ir*a[3] . sicut antecessores sui eam melius 7 honorabilius habuerunt tempore Henrici
regis aui mei . Et prohibeo ne quis* in ea fuget . uel capiat leporem
sine licentia eius super .x. libras forisfacture . Testibus . Thoma
cancellario apud Bruhullam.

Marginalia: 2 φ +.
Texts: MS—A. Iiv(11). Pd—*C.C.R.*iv,109(11).
Var. R.: [1] Bannebir' marg. [2] Oxeneforsira Iiv. [3] Bannebury Iiv.

*Folio 14d.

Hdl.   H. REGIS SECUNDI.

85

116. Writ of Henry II, commending to bishop Robert II the
king's warren between Lincoln and Newark.   At York.   (1154–
1160.)

De warenna inter Linc' 7 Newerch' (A marg.).

H'. rex Anglorum . 7 dux Normannorum 7 Aquitanorum . 7 comes Andegauorum . omnibus[1] baronibus suis de Lincoll'sira ꞓ salutem Sciatis me commendasse Roberto episcopo Linc' warennam meam inter Lincoll' ꞓ 7 Newercam . Quare pr[ecipio] quod nullus in ea fuget uel capiat leporem ꞓ super forisfacturam meam . set in ea pace sit ꞓ qua fuit tempore Henrici regis aui mei ·. Testibus . Theobaldo archiepiscopo Cantuariensi . 7 comite Reginaldo Cornubie . apud Eboracum ;

Facsimile facing page 68.
Endorsed : XXII .H. ij. (13 cent.).
A wide strip for seal, and probably a ribband also, have been torn off. Size : 5½ x 3 inches.
Marginalia in A : 2| R'.
Texts : MS—Orig. A1/1/14. A. Iv(32). Pd—*C.C.R.*iv,144(32). *E.H.R.*xxiv, 306.
See Delisle, p. 550.
Var. R. : [1] *om.* omnibus Iv.

Folio 15.

Hdl.　　　　　　Carte .H. Regis . Secundi.　　.1.5.

86

117.　De villa de Asgerb' (marg.).

A duplicate of no. 56 *above.*

Marginalia : lib' + D'.

87

118.　Writ of Henry II, addressed generally, confirming Asgarby [by Spilsby] *in prebendam,* to master Ralf of Caen, the canon, and his successors, to hold as freely as Welton or any other prebend is held. At Westminster. (1155–1158.)

De Asgarbi . 7 libertatibus eiusdem (marg.).

.H.[1] rex[2] Anglorum . 7 dux Normannorum . 7 Aquitanorum . 7 comes Andegauorum[3] . archiepiscopis . episcopis . abbatibus . comitibus . baronibus . iusticiariis . vicecomitibus . 7 omnibus ministris suis 7 omnibus fidelibus suis Francis 7 Anglis tocius Anglie . salutem . Sciatis me concessisse 7 hac mea presenti carta confirmasse deo 7 ecclesie sancte Marie Linc' 7 magistro Radulfo de Cadomo canonico 7 successoribus suis Ansgerbiam cum omnibus pertinenciis suis in liberam 7 perpetuam prebendam 7 elemosinam . Quare uolo 7 firmiter precipio quod predictus Radulfus 7 successores sui eandem prebendam habeant 7 teneant bene . 7 in pace . libere . quiete . integre . plenarie . 7 honorifice . in bosco . 7 plano . in pratis . 7 paschuis[4] . in uiis . 7 semitis . in aquis . 7 molendinis . in stagnis . 7 uiuariis . 7 in omnibus aliis locis . cum soca . 7 saca . 7 theol . 7 teham 7 infangenetheph' . Et concedo quod sit quieta de sciris . 7 hundretis . placitis . 7 querelis . 7 wapentacis . 7 omnibus aliis

occasionibus . asisis . Danegeld' . 7 murdr*is* . sicut prebende de
Welletona uel alique alie quietiores sunt . Testibus . Roberto Linc'
episcopo . 7 Thoma cancellario . Ricardo de Hum*ez* constabulario .
War*ino* filio Ger*aldi* camerario . apud Westmonasterium.

Marginalia : lib' + N.
Texts : MS—A. C,f.12.
Var. R. : *¹ insert* dei gracia C.   *² secundus interlineated by* Q *in* A.   *³* Andegauie C.
⁴ pascuis C.

88

119. A similar writ of confirmation, addressed to the king's
justices, barons, sheriff, and officers of Lincolnshire. At Westminster. (1155–1158.)

De Asgarb*i* . 7 libertatibus (A marg.).

H. rex Angl*orum* 7 dux Norm*annorum* 7 Aquit*anorum* . 7 comes
And*egauorum* . episcopo Linc' . 7 justic' . 7 baronibus . 7
vic*ecomit'* . 7 omnibus ministris s[uis de¹] Linc' scyra *:* salutem .
Sciatis me concessisse 7 confirmasse deo 7 sancte Marie de² Linc'
[7¹] Radulfo canonico 7 successoribus suis Ansgesbiam³ cum omnibus
pertinentiis suis in liberam 7 perpetuam [preben¹] dam 7 elemosinam .
Quare volo 7 firmiter precipio quod eandem prebendam teneant
bene 7 in pace 7⁴ libere 7 [quiete cum¹] soca 7 saca 7 toll 7 team⁵
7 infangenetheof⁶ . et sit quieta de scyris⁷ 7 hundr*edis* . 7
wa[pentacs⁸ . 7¹] comitatibus . 7 omnibus assisis 7 Danegeldis . 7
murdris⁹ sicut prebend*ę* de Weletona¹⁰ uel aliqua alia quietiores
sunt . Testibus . R. episcopo Linc' . 7 . Toma¹¹ cancellario . 7
Ricardo de Hum*ez* constabulario . 7 Warino filio Ger*aldi* camerario .
apud Westmonast*erium*.

Endorsed : (1) de Askerbi (13 cent.). (2) H.ij. bona . murdr' (14 cent.).
Tag for seal, and written on it is ' Confirmacio Asgerbi ut est Welleton' libera.'
Marginalia : De prebenda de Asg*er*bi P.
Texts : MS—Orig.ᴀ1/1/31. A. P8. Iiv(2). Pd—*E.H.R.*xxiv,311. *C.C.R.*iv,
106(2). See Delisle, pp. 152–3.
Var. R. : *¹ supplied from* A, *the charter having been injured.* *² om.* de *in* P. *³* Asger-
biam A P. *⁴ om.* 7 P. *⁵* them P. *⁶* infangenth' P. *⁷* siris P. *⁸ sic in* A ; wap' P ;
wapentac' Iiv. *⁹* murdr' P. *¹⁰* Welletona A P. *¹¹* Thom' A Iiv ; T' P.

Folio 15d.
Hdl.   H*enrici* R*egis* *Secundi.*

89

120. Notification that, in 8 Henry II, Asgarby, the prebend of
Ralf the subdean of Lincoln, was quit of Danegeld, namely six shillings
and three pence in respect of three carucates, in Lent, at the
Treasury, at London; and the quittance is written on the roll.
(Lent, 1162.)

De quietancia de Danegeld (marg.).

Sciant presentes 7 futuri quod in octauo anno Henrici secundi regis Anglie fuit quieta prebenda Radulfi subdecani sancte Marie Linc' . scilicet Asgerbi de Danegeldo . scilicet de .vi. solidis . 7 .iii. denariis . pro .iii. carrucatis in quadragesima ad scacarium apud Lundoniam . 7 scripta fuit quitantia in rollo . Testibus . domino Nigello Elyensi episcopo . Roberto comite Lecestrie . Henrico filio Giroldi . 7 aliis baronibus . 7 Hugone canonico clerico Walteri de Amundeuilla dapiferi . 7 Rannulfi [sic] de Chent.

Text: MS—A.
Note: On the pipe roll of 8 Henry II, A.D. 1161–2, ' In perdona per breue regis Radulfo de Cadomo .vi. s.' (Pipe Roll Soc. v, 19).

90

121. Writ of Henry II, commanding that master Ralf of Caen, the king's clerk, shall have his prebend of Asgarby with all its franchises, as the charters of the lords of the fee witness, and as the king has confirmed it to the church of Lincoln by his charter; and forbidding that any one shall do him damage, since he and his possessions are in the king's protection. At Le Mans. (1154–1172.)

De prebenda de Asgerbi (A marg.).

.H. rex Anglorum 7 dux Normannorum 7 Aquitanorum 7 comes Andegauorum . vicecomit' . Linc' sire . 7 ministris suis ꞉ salutem ; Precipio quod magister Radulfus de Cadomo clericus meus . habeat 7 teneat bene 7 in pace libere quiete integre plenarie honorifice prebendam suam de Asgerbi[1] cum pertinentiis suis 7 cum omnibus libertatibus suis . sicut carte dominorum feodi testantur . et sicut illam confirmaui ecclesie Linc' . per cartam meam . Et prohibeo quod nullus ei inde aliquam iniuriam uel contumeliam faciat . quia ipse 7 omnes res sue sunt in [mea[2]] manu 7 custodia 7 protectione . Teste . cancellario apud Cenomum.

Endorsed: (1) de Askerbi (13 cent.). (2) de libertate Asgerbi (13 cent.). (3) .H.ij. (13 cent.).
There is a wide strip at the foot for a seal, and a ribband below it.
Texts: MS—Orig. A1/1/34. A. Pd—E.H.R.xxiv,312. Delisle, p. 556 (abs.).
Var. R.: [1] Asgerby A. [2] supplied from A, the charter having been injured.

91

122. Writ of Henry II, confirming to the church of Lincoln and to Ralf of Caen, canon of Lincoln, and his successors, the village of Asgarby in prebendam. At London. (1154–1163.)

De villa de Asgerbi (A marg.).

.H'. rex Anglorum 7 dux Normannorum 7 Aquitanorum 7 comes Andegauorum . iustic' . vicecomit' . baronibus 7 omnibus

fidelibus suis de Linc' scira ⁖ salutem . Sciatis me concessisse 7
confirmasse deo 7 sancte Marie Linc' 7 Radulfo de Cadomo canonico
Linc' . 7 successoribus eius canonicis villam Asgerbi cum omnibus
pertinentiis suis in prebendam 7 liberam elemosinam . Quare uolo
7 firmiter precipio . quod eandem uillam in perpetuam possessionem
bene 7 in pace 7 honorifice liberam 7 quietam de comitatibus 7
sciris 7 hundretis . 7 wapentacis teneant . cum socca 7 sacca¹ 7
thol 7 them² 7 infangetheof³ . 7 cum omnibus consuetudinibus 7
libertatibus sicut aliqua prebenda Linc' ecclesie quietius 7 liberius
tenet . Teste Roberto episcopo Linc' 7 Philippo Baiocensi episcopo
apud Lundoniam.

Facsimile facing page 68.
Endorsed : (1) H. secundi de Askerbi (13 cent.). (2) bona (14 cent.). (3) . . .
libertat' sine . . . (13 cent.).
Strip for seal : the ribband below it has been torn off. Size : 7 x 2¾ inches.
Texts : MS—Orig. A1/1/33. A. Pd—*E.H.R.*xxiv,311. Delisle, p. 558 (abs).
Var. R. : ¹ soca 7 saca A. ² toll 7 team A. ³ infangenetheof A.

92

123. Writ of Henry II, commanding bishop R[obert] II to cause
Ralf of Caen to hold his prebend of Asgarby with its appurtenances
as in the time of Henry I ; and to suffer no one to do him damage,
because the king does not wish the church of Lincoln to lose any
of its rights anywhere in his time. At Rouen. (1155–1166.)

De prebenda . de Asgerbi (marg.).

.H. rex Anglorum 7 dux Normannorum . 7 Aquitanorum . 7
comes Andegauorum .R. Linc' episcopo salutem . Precipio tibi
quod facias Radulfum de Cadomo tenere bene 7 in pace 7 iuste
prebendam suam de Asgerbi cum omnibus pertinenciis suis in boscho
7 in plano 7 in pasturis sicut ea prebenda solet eas habere tempore
.H. regis aui mei . 7 non patiaris quod aliquis ei faciat iniuriam aut
contumeliam . Nolo enim quod ecclesia sancte Marie aliquid de
iure suo perdat alicubi tempore meo . Teste . cancellario . apud
Rothomagum.

Text : MS—A.

93

124. Writ of Henry II, confirming to the church of Lincoln
and to Robert of Caen, canon of Lincoln, and his successors, the
village of Asgarby, with the same franchises as any other prebend
of Lincoln holds, and as Henry I granted by his charter. At
Lincoln. (1154–1163.)

De villa de Asgarbi (A marg.).

.H'. re[x Anglorum 7 dux Normannorum 7¹] Aquitanorum .
7 comes Andegauorum . iustic' . vicecomit' . 7 baronibus .
7 omnibus fidelibus suis [de Lincolnesira¹] ⁖ salutem . Sciatis me

concessisse 7 confirmasse deo 7 sancte Marię Lincoln' 7 Radulfo
de Kadamo canonico* Linc'[2] 7 successoribus eius canonicis . villam
Asgerbi[3] . cum omnibus pertinentiis suis . in prebendam 7 liberam
elemosinam . Quare uolo 7 firmiter precipio . quatenus eandem
uillam . in perpetuam possessionem . bene . 7 in pace . 7 honorifice
teneant . liberam 7 quietam . de siris 7 hundretis 7 wap*entaciis* .
cum socca 7 sacca[4] 7 tol 7 tem[5] . 7 infangenethef[6] . 7 cum omnibus
consuetudinibus . 7 libertatibus . sicut aliqua prebenda Lincoln'[7]
ecclesie quietius 7 liberius tenet . 7 sicut . Henricus rex auus meus
concessit per cartam suam . Testibus . Roberto . episcopo Lincoln*iensi* . 7 Philippo Baioc*ensi* episcopo . apud Lincoln*iam*.

Facsimile facing page 89.
Endorsed : (1) villa de Askerbi (13 cent.).   (2) bona . (14 cent.).   (3) T. Harrys,
and notary's mark (? 16 cent.).   (4) Henry 2nd.   Grant of the Town of Asgarby
(modern).
A wide strip at the foot for the seal and the ribband below it have been torn off.
Size : 6¾ x 4⅞ inches.
Marginalia in A : quod . teneant.
Texts : MS—Orig. A1/1/32.   A.   Pd—*E.H.R.*xxiv,311.   Delisle, p. 557 (abs.).
Var. R. : ¹ *supplied from* A, *the charter having been injured.*   ² Lincol' A.   ³ Asgerby
A.   ⁴ soca 7 saca A.   ⁵ theam A.   ⁶ infangenetheof A.   ⁷ Linc' A.

Folio 16.
Hdl.   *Henrici Regis* SECUNDI.   .1 6.

94

125. Writ of Henry II, addressed to Richard de Camvill, and
his officers of the wapentake of Bolingbroke, and to all lords and
neighbours of the prebend of Asgarby, commanding that the
prebend shall have its revenue and common as it best had them
in the time of Henry I. At Westminster. (Query circa 1164.)

De prebenda de Asgerb*i* (marg.).

.H. rex Angl*orum* . 7 dux Norman*norum* . 7 Aquit*anorum* . 7
comes And*egauorum* . Ricardo de Camuill*a* 7 ministris suis de
Bulimbroc wap*entac* 7 omnibus dominis 7 vicinis prebende Asgerbi
salutem . Precipio quod prebenda sancte Marie Linc' de Asgerbi
habeat libere 7 plenarie 7 iuste exitum suum in boschum . 7 planum .
7 mariscum . 7 mercatum . 7 communem pasturam sicut melius
7 liberius habuit tempore regis .H. aui mei . Et prohibeo ne aliquis
super hoc ei iniuriam faciat . Quod nisi feceritis ꞉ vicecomes Linc'
sire fieri faciat . Teste . Petro de Mara apud Westmonasterium.

Marginalia : + ...
Text : MS—A.

95

126. Writ of Henry II, addressed to William de Roumara,
earl of Lincoln, and the neighbours, both clerks and laymen, of
the prebend of Asgarby, commanding that Ralf of Caen the canon,
and his men of Asgarby and their possessions shall have their

revenue and common as they best had them in the time of Henry I.
At London.   (1154–1162.)

De Asgerbi (marg.).

.H. rex Anglorum . 7 dux Normannorum . 7 Aquitanorum . 7
comes Andegauorum . Willelmo de Roumara comiti Linc' . 7 clericis
7 laicis uicinis prebende Asgerby . omnibus que fidelibus suis de
Lincoliescir' salutem . Precipio quod Radulfus de Cadomo canonicus
7 homines illius de Asgerby . 7 omnes res eorum bene 7 in pace 7
iuste 7 libere 7 quiete 7 honorifice habeant exitum suum 7 communam suam in paschuis 7 mariscis in uiis 7 semitis 7 in boscho
7 in plano 7 in mercatis 7 in omnibus locis sicut melius 7 honorabilius ipsi uel predecessores eorum habere solebant tempore .H.
regis aui mei . Et prohibeo ne aliquis super hoc eos iniuste disturbet .
Quod si quis fecerit justicia mea de Lincol' scira plenariam iusticiam
inde faciat . ne pro penuria recti uel plenarie iusticie clamorem inde
amplius audiam . Teste Ricardo episcopo Lundoniensi . 7 Roberto
comite Legrecestrie . apud Lundoniam.

Marginalia : ecclesie Linc' 7 prebend' Asgerbi (16 cent. *A cross in the text
indicates that these words are to be inserted after* canonicus, *or are a note upon*
canonicus, *in line* 4 *of the text ; but their late date does not justify their inclusion in
the text*).   + . . .
Text : MS—A.

96

127. Writ of Henry II, granting that Ralf of Caen shall have
his warren in his prebend of Asgarby, as William de Roumara best
had it, and confirmed it by his charter.   At Bridgnorth [co. Salop].
(Query 1155.)

De warenna de Asgerbi (marg.).

.H. rex Anglorum . 7 dux Normannorum . 7 Aquitanorum . 7
comes . Andegauorum . iustic' . 7 vicecomit' . 7 ministris .
7 omnibus fidelibus suis de Linc' sira salutem . Concedo quod
Radulfus de Cadomo habeat warennam suam in prebenda sua de
Asgerbi . sicut Willelmus de Rumara illam plenius 7 melius habuit
7 ei concessit 7 per cartam suam confirmauit . Et prohibeo ne quis
in ea fuget uel leporem capiat sine eius licentia[1] super .x. libras
forisfacture . Teste . Ricardo de Humez constabulario apud
Brugiam.

Texts : MS—A. P9.
Var. R. : [1] sine eius licentia *written in marg. by a contemporary hand, and marked
for insertion in the text.*

Folio 16d.
Hdl.   CARTA .H. REGIS SECUNDI.

97

128. Writ of Henry II, commanding that master Ralf, canon
of Lincoln, shall hold all the lands and tenements which the men

of Hareby and of Bolingbroke, who were his tenants in the prebend of Asgarby, sold or quitclaimed or abjured in his court.   At Westminster. (1154–1160.)

De terris quas homines de Harebi 7 de Bolingbroc ꞓ uendiderunt Radulfo de Cadomo (marg.).

.H. rex Anglie . 7 dux Normannie . 7 Aquitanie . 7 comes Andegauie . R. episcopo Linc' . 7 iustic' . 7 vicecomit' . 7 ministris . 7 fidelibus suis de Linc' scira . salutem . Precipio quod magister Radulfus canonicus sancte Marie Linc' teneat in pace 7 libere 7 iuste 7 honorifice omnes terras 7 7 [sic] teneuras quas homines de Harebi 7 de Bulincbroc qui de prebenda de Asgerbi de ipso tenebant ei uendiderunt uel quietas clamauerunt uel in curia sua abiurauerunt . Et prohibeo ne quis ei inde iniuriam uel contumeliam faciat . Teste .H. de Essexia constabulario . apud Westmonasterium.

Text: MS—A.

98

129. Charter of Gilbert [of Ghent] earl of Lincoln, confirming to bishop Robert II, A[delmus] the dean, and the chapter of Lincoln half a carucate which Saier de Arcellis claimed that he had in the territory of Asgarby, but, at the end of his days, quitclaimed to Saint Mary and Ralf the canon of Lincoln and his successors. (1154–1156.)

De dimidia carucata terre in Asgerbi (marg.).

Roberto Dei gratia Linc' episcopo .A. decano totique capitulo sancte Marie Linc' . omnibus amicis 7 fidelibus suis Francis 7 Anglis Gislebertus comes Linc' ꞓ salutem . Sciatis quod Saherus de Arcellis in fine dierum suorum pro salute anime sue 7 predecessorum suorum remisit deo 7 sancte Marie 7 Radulfo canonico 7 successoribus suis canonicis Linc' . 7 quietam clamauit in presencia mea 7 assensu meo totam calumpniam quam dicebat se habere in dimidia carrucata terre infra territorium Asgerbi . 7 eandem terram cum omnibus appendiciis suis bene 7 in pace 7 libere . 7 quietam ab omni exactione 7 terreno seruitio in perpetuam elemosinam possidendam eis concessit . 7 carta sua confirmauit . Ego uero Gislebertus comes ex parte mea illud idem concedo 7 confirmo . 7 hanc donationem pro salute anime illius firmam 7 stabilem inperpetuum esse uolo 7 concedo . 7 inpressione sigilli mei communio . Testibus . abbate Croilandie . Waltero abbate Bardeneia [sic] . Hereberto priore Spalling' . Raginaldo de Wincebi . Alueredo presbiteris . Willelmo clerico Lucebi . Lamberto de Moltona . Leone de Arcellis . Raginaldo de Cornubia . Baldewino de Gant . Imero de Lucebi . Willelmo capellano . Waltero Flandrense.

Marginalia: +   + scribantur inter cartas comitum. Q's note refers to nos. 129–133.
Text: MS—A.

99

130. Charter of William of Roumare, confirming to bishop A[lexander] and the chapter of Lincoln the gift which, as he had ascertained from his barons and ancient men of the wapentake of Bolingbroke, was made to the church of Lincoln by Roger son of Gerold, his father, and Lucy his mother, namely, Asgarby and all that is contained within the boundaries of that village, *in prebendam.* (1123–1147.)

De prebenda de Asgerb*i* (marg.).

.A. Lincoln' episcopo totique capitulo sancte Marie Linc' . omnibus que amicis suis 7 hominibus suis 7 ministris suis Francis 7 Anglis Willelmus de Roumara salutem . Inquisiui a baronibus 7 antiquis hominibus meis de Bulincbroc wapentac 7 aperte cognoui 7 scio quod Rogerus filius Geroldi pater meus 7 Lucia mater mea dederunt deo 7 sancte Marie Linc' pro salute animarum suarum 7 ante-cessorum suorum Asgerbiam in prebendam 7 in elemosinam liberam 7 quietam 7 in perpetuam possessionem . Et ego Willelmus pro salute mea 7 eorum 7 omnium amicorum meorum ex parte mea illud idem uolo 7 concedo 7 confirmo carta mea ad opus Dei 7 sancte Marie Linc' in prebendam 7 elemosinam videlicet Asgerbiam 7 quicquid infra terminos 7 diuisas eiusdem uille continetur . cum omnibus libertatibus 7 consuetudinibus quas habet aliqua alia prebenda de liberioribus prebendis sancte Marie Linc' . Volo itaque 7 concedo illam omnino esse liberam 7 quietam ab omni exactione 7 laico domino 7 seculari seruici [*sic*] in quantum ego 7 heredes mei eam possumus facere liberam 7 nichil in ea requirimus preter ecclesiasticum beneficium quod pro nobis fit ob hanc donationem in ecclesia sancte Marie 7 parrochia Linc' episcopatus . Testes inde sunt huius donationis . Robertus de Cantelu . Ricardus de Bolonia . Herbertus de Calz . Rogerus le Calceis . Wido de Ver . Hamo pre-positus . Henricus* frater eius . Hugo de Turs . Willelmus de Broi . 7 alii multi milites . 7 homines de wa*pentacio* Bolingbroc . Et clerici . G. Mal' . Haco . Bereng*er* . Willelmus de Raebi . Willelmus Bochart . Stephanus capellanus . 7 Robertus . 7 plures alii clerici 7 laici de soca 7 villate Asgerbi magna pars . valete.

Text: MS—A.

Folio 17.

Hdl.   .1 7.

100

131. A similar charter of confirmation, in which it is stated that the original gift was made to the church of Lincoln and Robert de Grainvill, the canon. (1123–1147.)

De eadem prebenda (A marg.).

.A. Linc'[1] episcopo 7 decano totique capitulo sancte Marie Linc'[1] .
omnibus que dei fidelibus 7 amicis 7 hominibus suis Francis 7 Anglis
Willelmus de Romara ? salutem . Sciant qui modo sunt 7 qui futuri
sunt quod ego Willelmus[2] de Roumara uolens scire ueritatem
de prebenda Asgerbi[3] inquisiui eam a melioribus 7 antiquioribus
hominibus meis de honore meo 7 aperte cognoui 7 didici ab eis
quod Rogerus filius Geroldi pater meus 7 Lucia mater mea dederunt
deo 7 sancte Marie Linc' 7 Roberto de Grainuilla[4] canonico pro
salute animarum suarum 7 antecessorum suorum Asgerbiam[5] cum
omnibus appendiciis suis in prebendam 7 puram elemosinam .
liberam . quietam . 7 in perpetuam possessionem . Et ego Willelmus
pro salute mea 7 eorum 7 omnium amicorum meorum ex parte
mea illud concedo 7 confirmo per cartam meam ad opus dei 7 sancte
Marie Linc'[1] in prebendam 7 elemosinam scilicet Asgerbiam[5]
predictam 7 quicquid infra terminos 7 diuisas eiusdem uille continetur . volo itaque 7 firmiter concedo illam omnino esse liberam
7 quietam ab omni exactione 7 terreno seruitio . 7 perpetuam possessionem esse ecclesie sancte Marie Linc'[1] [6] cum omnibus libertatibus
7 consuetudinibus sicut aliqua alia prebenda Linc'[1] ecclesie liberius
tenet . Et sciatis quod nichil terreni seruitii uel consuetudinis in
ea retinui . neque tempore meo uel heredum meorum . uel in aliquo
tempore . preter participationem beneficiorum 7 orationum que
pro nobis 7 antecessoribus nostris fiunt[7] propter hanc donationem in ecclesia sancte Marie 7 in parrochia Linc'[1] episcopatus .
Testibus . Roberto de Cantelupo . Ricardo de Bolonia . Hereberto[8]
de Salz . Rogero le Calceis . Widone de Ver[9] . Hamone preposito .
Henrico fratre eius . Hugo[10] de Turs . Will*elmo* de Broe . Rad*ulfo*
de sancto Albino . 7 multis aliis militibus . 7 Waltero de Bening-
word' . Baldrico de Calis . 7 multis de wap*entacio*[11] Bolimbroc .
Et clericis . Gaufrido Malebissa . Hacone . Berengero . Willelmo
de Raebi[12] . Willelmo de Andreby[13] . Baldrico . Stephano capellano .
7 Roberto 7 Ricardo de Calis . Dauid . Waltero de Asgerbi[14] .
Dauid . Vlfo . Osmundo . Achi . Louone . 7 multis aliis de Asgherb*i* .
7 de patria illa . valete.

Marginalia: + ...
Texts: MS—A. Dij,65/1/16 (a 14 cent. copy).
Var. R.: [1] Lincoln' Dij. [2] .W. Dij. [3] de Asgerby Dij. [4] Graumuill' Dij.
[5] Asgerbyam Dij. [6] *insert superfluously* ecclesie Dij. [7] fiunt A marg., *marked
for inclusion in text.* [8] Herberto Dij. [9] Wydone de Veer Dij. [10] Hugone Dij.
[11] wapentag' Dij. [12] Raeby Dij. [13] Andrebi. [14] Asgerby Dij.

101

132. Charter of young William of Roumare, son of earl William
[of Roumare], confirming the same gift to bishop Alexander and
the chapter of Lincoln and Ralf the canon of Asgarby ; and giving
to the said Ralf his warren and his pursuit of hares within the
boundaries of the village of Asgarby. (1140–1147.)

De eadem prebenda 7 warenna (marg.).

.A. episcopo Linc' 7 capitulo sancte Marie . 7 dapifero . 7 constabulario . 7 ministris suis de Bulinbroc wapen*tacio* . omnibus que
fidelibus sancte dei ecclesie Willelmus iuuenis de Rumara filius
Willelmi comitis salutem . Notum sit uobis me concessisse 7 confirmasse elemosinam Rogeri filii Geroldi aui mei 7 Willelmi patris
mei . 7 eam finaliter 7 imperpetuum dedisse ecclesie sancte Marie
Linc' 7 Radulfo canonico scilicet As*g*erby cum omnibus appenditiis
suis . 7 hiis omnibus que infra metas eiusdem uille continentur .
Volo itaque 7 concedo ut eandem uillam teneant bene 7 in pace
7 honorifice in prebendam 7 elemosinam cum* omnibus consuetudinibus 7 libertatibus suis solutam 7 liberam 7 quietam ab
omni seculari seruitio 7 exactione . 7 concedo 7 dono eidem Radulfo
canonico warennam suam 7 deductum suum plenarie de leporibus
capiendis infra diuisas As*g*erby uille prenominate absque repulsa
7 causatione . Omnibus que amicis meis mando 7 hominibus meis
omnibus precipio ut eum 7 omnia sua manuteneant ne fiat illi iniuria
uel contumelia . Teste Johanne abbate de Bardenai . 7 Waltero
monacho . 7 Willelmo archidiacono . 7 Sampsone canonico . 7
Waltero de Bardenai . 7 Hacone decano . 7 Ricardo de Calis . 7
Rainaldo de Wincebi . 7 Alueredo . 7 Herberto de Calz . 7 Roberto
de Bolonia . 7 Widone . 7 Alexandro de Otteby . 7 Henrico de
Maletot . 7 Adam de Bulimbroc.

Text: MS—A.

Folio 17d.

102

133. Charter of William [of Roumare] earl of Lincoln, giving
to Saint Mary of Lincoln and Ralf the canon of Asgarby and his
successors warren in the prebend of Asgarby, within the whole
territory of that village ; with the right of pursuing game into the
earl's warren. (1152–1155.)

De warenna de Asgerb*i* (marg.).

Willelmus comes Linc' omnibus ministris 7 hominibus suis Francis
Anglis salutem . Notum sit uobis 7 omnibus presentibus 7 futuris
me dedisse 7 concessisse 7 carta mea confirmasse deo 7 sancte
Marie Linc' warennam in prebenda As*g*erby infra totum territorium
eiusdem uille . Quare uolo 7 firmiter concedo quod predicta ecclesia
Linc' . 7 Radulfus canonicus Asgerbi 7 successores eius canonici
eiusdem prebende libere 7 quiete 7 honorifice habeant 7 possideant
inperpetuum eandem warennam cum omnibus aliis libertatibus
quas eis concessi 7 carta mea confirmaui . Prohibeo autem ne
aliquis de ministris uel hominibus meis iniuriam uel contumeliam
faciat ecclesie Linc' . de warenna prenominata . nec super ecclesiam
Lincol' uel canonicum Asgerbi se inde intromittat . Preterea concedo

7 dono prebende Asgerbi percursum suum in warennam meam .
scilicet si canonicus illius prebende uel aliquis per eum exmouerit
leporem uel aliam feram ad fugandum infra territorium Asgerbi .
7 introierit in warennam meam *: potest eum persequi 7 capere sine
omni calumpnia 7 querela . Testes huius donationis sunt . G. abbas
Reuesbi . P. abbas Torrenton' . Herbertus prior Espalling' . Willelmus
archidiaconus . Alexander Malabissa . Ricardus Lotheringus . Haco
decanus . Odo Bucheri . Rogerus de Teliolo . Herbertus 7 Osbertus
de Calz . Robertus Carbonellus . Achi.

Marginalia: +   φ.
Text: MS—A.

Folio 18.
Hdl.   .1.8.

*The following document has been entered by a late sixteenth century
hand on folio* 18 *and the dorse.*

103

134. Institution of Gerard de Wenge, chaplain, on the
presentation of the dean and chapter of Lincoln, to the newly-
ordained vicarage of the churches of [Castle] Bytham and
Holywell [co. Lincoln]. The endowment of the vicarage is
described, and the duties incumbent upon the rector and vicar
respectively are defined. At Louth [co. Lincoln], 13 June, 1291.

[1]Tempore domini Oliveri Sutton olim episcopi Lincoln qui
cepit preesse ecclesie Lincoln xiiij[to] kalendas Junii anno Domini
millesimo ducentesimo octogesimo[1]. [19 May, 1280.]

Gerard[2] de Wenge capellanus presentatus per decanum et
capitulum ecclesie Lincoln' ad vicariam in ecclesiis de Bitham et
de Helewell de nouo ordinanda[3] factaque inquisicione per decanum
de Beltisloue[4] super omnibus porcionibus maioribus et minoribus
ad dictas ecclesias pertinentibus ipsarumque porcionum vero valore
ac oneribus tam in ministris iuxta morem preteriti temporis quam
aliis eisdem ecclesiis incumbentibus necnon in quibus portionibus
vnacum manso competente vicariæ ibidem possit[5] convenientius
ordinari per quam quidem inquisicionem est acceptum quod tres
bouate terre et tresdecem acre 7 dimidia spectant ad ecclesiam de
Biyham[6] et valet bouata terre sexdecem solidos, quodque decime
garbarum de Biyham[7] Cunthorp[8] et Creton valent viginti libras et
decime[9] feni xxix solidos Item decime[9] feni de la Lawnde[10] valet
ix solidos decime[9] vero lane 7 agnorum de Bitham[6] Cunthorp[11] 7
Creton valet sexaginta solidos vnacum principale cum omnibus
aliis minutis decimis oblacionibus 7 gallinis valet sex marcis . Item
est ibi pastura ad viginti quatuor boves in parco per annum et
valet viginti solidos Item quod rector potest habere in parco

F

quadraginta porcos 7 vnum per sex septimanas, 7 valet duos solidos, et percipit ecclesia de Biyham[7] pro capella de castro ac decima molendini tres solidos redditus etiam assisus spectant ad ecclesiam de Biham[7] xij solidos vj denarios . Item rectores habent in bosco tresdecim carectatas bosci 7 valent iiij solidos et iiij denarios Item rector habebit de vendicione domini tres feras Item decime garbarum de Hellewell et Ownby[12] valent vndecem marcas et alteragium cum omnibus pertinenciis valet quinque marcas . Est etiam in villa de Byham[13] locus quidam qui consueuit spectare ad ecclesiam de Hellewell qui est mansus competens ad opus vicarii sed[14] sunt ibi quedam domus constructe vt aula et camera tantum Item apud Biyham[7] solet esse vnus capellanus 7 clericus eius et ille[15] sacerdos invenit alium sacerdotem loco suo qui celebrauit apud Cunthorp[11] sex principalibus festis 7 idem sacerdos singulis diebus dominicis venit apud Cunthorp[11] 7 ministrauit parochianis aquam bene-dictam 7 panem benedictum 7 dixit eis memoriam de die 7 preces* Rector etiam inveniet lumen sufficiens circa magnum altare et vnam lampadem Item dictus rector inveniet capellanum idoneum[16] celebrantem in ecclesia de Helewell et ille capelle deseruiet paro-chianis de Helewell et Ounby[12] et inveniet lumen sufficiens circa magnum altare 7 vnam lampadem Inveniet etiam omnia ornamenta ecclesie preter calicem 7 missale et vas ad aquam benedictam in tribus locis videlicet apud Biham[7] Helewell 7 Cunthorp Sustinebit insuper tria cancella scilicet vnum apud Biham[7] aliud apud Hele-well 7 tertium apud Cunthorp Soluet etiam procurationem archidiaconi pro tribus partibus 7 soluet pro[17] sinodalibus vj solidos Episcopus habita deliberacione cum capitulo suo predicto ordinavit quod vicaria predicta consistat in manso competente per capitulum Lincoln' sufficienter edificando 7 in vtroque alteragio de Biham[7] 7 de Helewell cum omnibus pertinentiis suis nullo excepto vnacum decima feni de La Laund[10] et ea que redditur dicte ecclesie de Biham[7] pro capella de castro, ac decima molendini, saluo quod pastura bouum[18] et porcorum in parco ac decima ferarum 7 bosci que ad capitulum predictum spectare debebunt, sub generalitate verborum predicta nullatenus contineantur Ita quod vicarius preter seipsum duos habet[19] capellanos vnum apud Biham[7] 7 alium apud Helewell et ferat omnia onera ordinaria invenietque libros 7 orna-menta, dum tamen defectus in eisdem si quis in presentiarum existat per dictum capitulum plenius suppleatur[20] sed capitulum ipsum cancellos quotiens opus fuerit reficiet 7 reparabit hoc addito quod memoratum capitulum pro decima agnorum et lane iam collecta vicario dicte ecclesie ad ipsius sustentacionem pro anno futuro sexaginta solidos solvere teneatur . Si quid in huiusmodi ordinacione obscurum vel ambiguum aut eidem detrahendum seu adiciendum videatur in futuro interpretandi 7 declarandi seu dictam ordinacionem minuendi et augendi prout episcopo aut successoribus suis videbitur expedire potestate speciale[21] reservata

Deinde idem dominus episcopus prefatum Gerardum ad dictam vicarium admisit idus Junii anno xij° apud Ludam . Et vicarius perpetuus cum onere personaliter ministrandi et continue residendi canonice instituit in eadem iuratusque episcopo canonicam obedientiam in forma consueta prestitoque a dicto Gerardo iuramento de continue residendo in vicaria predicta Scriptum fuit officiali archidiaconi Lincoln' quod ipsum Gerrardum corporalem possessionem de vicaria²² habere faceret in forma predicta.

Marginalia: Bitham. Ordinacio vicarie (contemp.).
Texts: A (a poor text, with many erasures, interlineations, and corrections which, since the document is a late one, have not been noted, except in the matter of proper names). Lincoln Episcopal Registers i, ff. 5d., 6.
Var. R. : ¹⁻¹ om. Reg. ² Gerardo Reg. ³ ordinandam˙ Reg. ⁴ Betteslawe Reg. ⁵ posset Reg. ⁶ corrected from Bitham A ; Bitham Reg. ⁷ corrected from Bitham A ; Byham Reg. ⁸ Cuinthorp' Reg. ⁹ decima Reg. ¹⁰ Launde Reg. ¹¹ Cunthorp' Reg. ¹² Ouneby Reg. ¹³ Byham has been corrected from Bytham A. ¹⁴ set Reg. ¹⁵ corrected from ibi A. ¹⁶ ydoneum Reg. ¹⁷ for pro read in Reg. ¹⁸ boum Reg. ¹⁹ habeat Reg. ²⁰ supleatur Reg. ²¹ specialiter Reg. ²² for de vicaria read dicto vicario Reg.

Note : Bishop Gravesend had, in 1273, appropriated the church of Castle Bytham and, in 1277, the church of Holywell, to the dean and chapter (A nos. 952, 953, which will be printed in a later volume). Counthorpe was a hamlet in the parish of Castle Bytham until 1860, when it was annexed to the parish of Creeton. Holywell with Aunby was, until modern times, a chapelry in the parish of Castle Bytham. They are now in the parish of Careby. The castle was, in 1291, in the possession of the Colville family.

*Folio 18d.

Folio 19.

Hdl.   CARTE REGIS HENRICI SECUNDI.   .1.9.

104

135. Writ of Henry II, confirming to Eynesham abbey whatever has been reasonably given to it, namely, the villages of Eynesham and Rollright and Shifford ; and, in Gloucestershire, Mickleton ; and, in Oxford, the church of Saint Ebbe, two mills near Oxford, and meadows ; and whatever bishop Robert gave in exchange for Newark and Stow, namely, Charlbury, South Stoke, and Woodcote ; in Cambridgeshire, fifteen hides and three virgates in Histon ; the tithe, etc., of Thame, Banbury, Cropredy ; Milton [near Thame] ; the tithe of the wax of the altar of Stow [co. Lincoln] ; and of the gift of Nigel de Oilli one hide which he held of the church of Eynesham, and quitclaimed with the consent of bishop Robert, and three and a half hides in Milcombe ; of the gift of Robert de Graio the tithe of Dornford, Woodlays, and Cornwell ; of the gift of Roger de Kesneto the tithe of his land of Minster [Lovell], and of all his wool in Oxfordshire ; of the gift of Gilbert Basset the tithe of Stratton [Audley] ; of the gift of Ralf Basset his tithe of

one hide in Ashley [probably co. Northampton], and of all his
wool; of the gift of Robert son of Walkelin his tithe of Wickham;
of the gift of Geoffrey of Cropredy two thirds of his tithe; of the
gift of Richard of Newark two thirds of his tithe of Claydon; of
the gift of William son of Nigel one messuage in Oxford; of the
gift of Hardinc of Oxford two messuages, the one within the borough
and the other without; of the gift of Gilbert de Almereio one
messuage outside the borough, except the king's custom; of the
gift of William son of Bernard his tithe. Further, the king has
confirmed to the bishop the power of appointing the abbot with
the king's advice and consent. At Rouen. (1157–1163.)

De beneficiis collatis abbacie de Eigneshami*a*[1] (A marg.).

.H.[2] rex Ang*lorum* 7 dux Norma*nnorum* 7 Aquit*anorum* . 7 comes
And*egauorum* . archiepiscopis . episcopis . abbatibus . comitibus.
baronibus . iustic*iariis* . vice*comitibus* . ministris . 7 omnibus hominibus 7 fidelibus suis totius Angli*ę*[3] Francis 7 Anglis salutem . Sciatis
me concessisse . 7 carta mea presenti confirmasse abbati*ę* de Einegsham quicquid datum est ei[4] rationabiliter . videlicet villam de
Einegsham cum omnibus pertinentiis eius[5] . 7 Rolindricd'[6] . cum
omnibus pertinentiis eius[5] . et Schiford' similiter . et in Gloece*stria*-
sira Micheletuna*m* cum pertinentiis suis . et in Oxenefordi*a* ęcclesiam
sanctę Ebbę . cum omnibus pertinentiis eius[5] . 7 duo molendina
iuxta Oxinefordi*am* . 7 prata . 7 quicquid Robertus Linc' episcopus
dedit pro commutatione Newerce . 7 Stowie . videlicet Cerlebiriam .
ita solidam 7 quietam ut episcopus Robertus tenuit . in bosco[7]
7 plano . 7 in omnibus pertinentiis eius . similiter Stoches cum
omnibus pertinentiis . similiter Wdecotam cum silua quę ad eam
pertinet . et in Cantebrugesir*a* . in Histona .xv. hidas 7 tres uirgatas
terrę . *œ'* decimam de Thama[8] . in annona . in pecudibus 7 lana .
7 caseis . 7 vnum bordarium cum duabus acris . 7 decimam de
Bannebri*a* . 7 de Croperia cum bordariis . similiter Mildeltonę[9]
decimam . 7 decimam cerę altaris de Stowa . et ex dono Nigelli
de Oill*i* unam hidam terrę quam tenebat de ęcclesia de Einegsham[10] .
7 clamauit quietam concessu Roberti predicti Linc' episcopi . 7
ex dono eiusdem tres hidas 7 dimidiam in Midelcumba[11] . ex dono
Ricardi de Graio decimam de Darneford' . 7 de Widel' . 7 de Corne-
well'[12] videlicet omnium illorum quę ad easdem uillas pertinent .
tam de annona quam de lana 7 caseis 7 ceteris pecuniis . ex dono
Rogeri de Kesneto[13] decimam terrę suę[14] de Ministr' . 7 de tota
lana sua de Oxineford' sir*a*[15] . ex dono Gisleberti Basset decimam
de Stratona videlicet duas partes 7 de tota lana sua 7 caseis de tota
terra sua . ex dono Radulfi Basset decimam suam de una hida de
Estlaia . 7 de tota lana sua . ex dono Roberti filii Walquelini totam
decimam suam de Wicheham[16] . ex dono Gaufridi de Croper' duas
partes decimę suę . [17]ex dono . Ricardi de Newerc*a* duas partes decimę

H. Rex Angl' 7 Dux Norm' 7 Aquit' 7 Comes And' Archiep'is Ep'is Abb'ibus Com' Baron' Justic' Vic' 7 oīb;
[a]riis 7 Omnibus hominib; 7 fidelib; suis tocius anglie francis 7 anglis Salt'. Sciatis me concessisse 7 carta mea p'senti
confirmasse Abb'ie de Cinegham quicquid dat'm est ei rōnabilit'. Videlic'. villam de Cinegham cum omnib; p'tinentiis
eius 7 Kolmdred cum omnibus p'tinentiis eius. et Schirlord similit'. Et in aloesf'r Michelenina cum p'tinentiis suis.
Et in B'neford' ecclam sce Elbe. cum omnib; p'tinentiis eius. 7 dno eadem dina iuxta B'neford' 7 p'ta 7 quicquid
Robtus sue ep's dedit p' comunicacione Helwys 7 Helwe. Videlic' certobtiam. ses solidas 7 quietam ut ep' Robtus
tenuit. In bosco 7 plano. 7 in oīb; p'tinentiis eius. simili Stockes cum omnib; p'tinentiis simul Wlteram cum silua
que ad eam p'tinet. Et in Cantebrugesir' Jn hidona ux' hida. 7 tres virgatas terre. et decimam de Hamd'. Jn hinona
in p'culis. 7 Lina 7 casas. 7 q'ndam bordarium cum duab; acris. 7 decima de hannebec. 7 de Croperia cum bordi
ris. Sim Middelcone decima. 7 decimam ecce hilarie de Stokes. et ex dono Nigelli de Velli unam hidam ep' qm' erat
bar de Eccla de Cinegha p'clamauit. quieta concessit Robt' p'dcus sue ep's. 7 ex dono eiusdem ep' hida'. 7 dim'
hiam in ondolenulis. Et dono Ric' de Graio decimam de Barneford' 7 de Vdikel. 7 de Canefeld'. Videlic'. omnium d
totii que ad easdem villas p'tinent. nam de hinona' gren' de lana 7 casas. 7 cens' p'uenit. Et dono Rog'i de keluedo decima
rure sue de Almistr'. 7 de tota lana sua de B'neford sir'. Et dono Gisleb'i basset decima de Harena Videlic' duas partes
7 de tota lana sua 7 casis de tota terra sua. Et dono Radulfi basset decima' suam de una hida de esllam. 7 de tota lana
sua. Et dono Robti filii Walquelini totam decima' suam de Wicheham. Et dono Gaufridi de Croper duas p'tes de
cima sue. Et dono Ric' de Helleye duas p'tes decime sue de Clandona. Et dono Willi filii Nigelli unam domum in
B'neford'. Et dono baydine de B'neford' duas domus. unam infra burgum. 7 aliam extra. Et dono Gisleb'i de Monterio
unam domum. extra burgum. excepta consuetudine regia. Et dono Willi filii hugonis decimam suam. Hec aut' Abb'ia
tota est in manu 7 potestate sue ep'i constituendi Abbem canonico consilio. 7 assensu regis. Q. ea re uolo 7 firmit' p'cipio
q'd Abb'ia p'dicta habeat 7 teneat hec p'dicta b'n 7 Jn pace. 7 honorifice. 7 integre. 7 libe. 7 quiete. 7 ep' hinc habean
eand' libtate' 7 dignitate' Constituendi Abbem in eadem Abb'ia consilio 7 Assensu regio sicut carta H. regis Aui mei testat'
cuius uidi oculis meis. C. R' ex' ob p'dco'. Apd Lerou' philip bone' hilario' Cic' frog' Sagensi ep'is. Theim' Cane' Willo filio
hamon. Willo de kesneto Ran bisex dap'. Ric' de burnex Const' Jostelino de bailol Stepho de belcampo. Roberto de don
francuilla 7 p [...] o h [...] o a l [...] o n i

suę[18] de Claindona[19] . ex dono Willelmi filii Nigelli unam domum
in Oxenefordia . ex dono Hardinc de Oxenefordia duas domos .
unam intra burgum 7 aliam extra . ex dono Gisleberti de Almereio[20]
vnam domum . extra burgum . excepta consuetudine regia . ex
dono Willelmi filii Bernardi decimam suam . Hec autem abbatia .
tota est in manu 7 potestate Linc' episcopi constituendi abbatem
canonice . consilio 7 assensu regis . Quare uolo 7 firmiter precipio
quod abbatia predicta habeat 7 teneat hec predicta bene 7 in pace .
7 honorifice 7 integre . 7 libere 7 quiete . 7 episcopus Linc' habeat
eandem libertatem 7 dignitatem constituendi abbatem in eadem[21]
abbatia . consilio 7 assensu regio . sicut carta .H.[22] regis aui mei
testatur quam uidi oculis meis* . Testibus . Rotrodo Ebroicensi .
Arnulfo Lęxouiensi . Philipo[23] Baiocensi . Hilario[24] Cicestrensi .
Frogerio Sagiensi episcopis . Thoma cancellario . Willelmo filio
Hamonis . Willelmo de Kesneto[25] . Manassero Biset[26] dapifero .
Ricardo de Humet[27] constabulario . Joscelino de Baillol Stephano
de Belcampo[28] . Roberto de Donstanuilla . apvd Rotomagvm ;

Facsimile facing page 84.
Endorsed: (1) Eynesham pro domino (15 cent.). (2) De Eynsam (13 cent.).
The tag or strip to which the seal was attached has been torn away and the foot
of the charter damaged. Size: 10½ x 14 inches.
Marginalia in A: 2| + φ Eigneshαm . va cat.
Texts: MS—Orig. A1/1/15. A. C.ff.14,14d. Pd—E.H.R.xxiv,306 (incomplete).
See Delisle, p. 556.
Var. R.: [1] De abbatia Egnesham C. [2] Henr' C. [3] Anglie repeated C. [4] ei
corrected from est C. [5] suis C. [6] Rolindrid' C. [7] boscho A. [8] Tama C. [9] Milde-
tone C. [10] Einesham C. [11] Midelconba C. [12] Cornewel C. [13] Keneto C. [14] om.
suę C. [15] Oxinefordsir' C. [16] Wicheam C. [17–18] om. ex dono . Ricardi de
Newerca duas partes decimę suę C. [19] Claidona A. [20] Almerio A C. [21] for
eadem read ed' C. [22] Henr' C. [23] Phillip' C. [24] Hylario C. [25] Keneto C. [26] Bisset
C. [27] Humet' C. [28] Belcambo C.
Note: For a similar charter of confirmation granted by Henry I, 25 December,
1109, see Eynesham Cartulary, ed. H. E. Salter, i, 36–7. For the identification of
some of the places, see Salter's notes. All the places are in Oxfordshire unless
otherwise described above.

Folio 19d.

Hdl.   *Carte Regis* HENRICI SECUNDI.

105

136. Writ of Henry II, confirming to Saint Mary of Lincoln
and bishop Robert II the houses which belong to the brethren
of the Temple in London, in the parish of Saint Andrew in Holborn,
with the chapel and gardens, which the bishop bought from the
brethren for one hundred marks and a yearly render of three gold
pieces for all service. At Rouen. (Probably 1162.)

De domibus Lundon'[1] (A marg.).

.H. rex Anglorum[2] . 7 dux Normannorum . 7 Aquitanorum . 7
comes Andegauorum . archiepiscopis . episcopis . comitibus baronibus . iusticiariis . vicecomitibus ministris . 7 omnibus hominibus 7

fidelibus suis Francis 7 Anglis . totius Anglię salutem . Sciatis me
concessisse . 7 carta mea presenti confirmasse ęcclesię beatę Marię
Linc' . 7 Roberto eiusdem ęcclesię episcopo . 7 successoribus suis
episcopis eiusdem ęcclesię domos quę fuerunt fratrum Templi in
London' . in parrochia sancti Andree³ de Holeburn'⁴ . cum capella
7 gardinis . 7 omnibus earum pertinentiis quas idem Robertus de
Kaisneto⁵ Linc' episcopus .C. marcis emit de fratribus Templi
reddendo inde eisdem⁶ fratribus Templi annuatim tres aureos pro
omni seruicio . Quare uolo 7 firmiter precipio quod ęcclesia Linc' . 7
predictus Robertus episcopus . 7 successores eius episcopi . habeant
7 teneant predictas domos . cum capella 7 gardinis . 7 omnibus
earum pertinentiis . sicut fratres Templi eidem Roberto episcopo 7
eius successoribus in perpetuum concesserunt . 7 carta sua confirmauerunt . Testibus . Rogero Eboracensi archiepiscopo . Hylario
Cicestrensi⁷ . Hugone Dunelmensi episcopis .' Thoma cancellario
apvd Rotomagvm ;⁸

Facsimile opposite.
Endorsed : (1) de domibus Lundoniariis (query 12 cent.). (2) pro tribus aureis
annuis (13 cent.).
The foot of the charter, with the tag for the seal, has been torn away. Size :
6⅜ x 7¼ inches.
Marginalia in A: 2] R' φ   De domibus Lund'.
Texts: Orig.A1/1/26.   A.   C,f.14d.   Iiv(9).   Pd—Mon.viii,1275(54).   E.H.R.
xxiv,309-10.   C.C.R.iv,108(9).   Delisle, p. 557 (abs.).
Var. R.: ¹ De templo London' C marg.   ² Anglie A.   ³ Andrréé A.   ⁴ Holeburn A.
⁵ Kaineto C.   ⁶ eiusdem C.   ⁷ Cistr' C.   ⁸ Rothom' C ; Rothomagum Iiv.

106

137. Writ of Henry II, granting to bishop Robert II and his
successors for their buildings and messuages all the land with the
ditch from the wall of the king's bailey at Lincoln on the east side
round the church of Saint Michael to the burial ground of Saint
Andrew, and thence to the city wall towards the east ; and granting
that this gift shall be quit of land gable and *parcagium* ; and that
the bishop may pierce the wall of the king's bailey for the purpose
of making a gate towards the church, and extend his buildings to
either wall.   At Lincoln.   (1155–1158.)

De terra cum fossato de muro ballii ad edificia facienda Linc'
(A marg.).¹

.H. rex Anglorum . 7 dux Normannorum . 7 Aquitanorum . 7 comes
Andegauorum iusticiariis vicecomitibus ministris² 7 omnibus
hominibus . 7³ fidelibus suis totius Anglię⁴ Francis 7 Anglis 7
nominatim⁵ de Lincolia⁶ 7⁷ Lincolię siria⁸ salutem . Sciatis me
dedisse 7 . concessisse . 7⁹ carta mea¹⁰ confirmasse ęcclesię Linc' .
7 Roberto Linc' episcopo¹¹ 7 successoribus eius¹² ad edificia sua
7 domos suas totam terram cum fossato de muro ballii mei Linc'
in orientali parte per circuitum¹³ ęcclesię beati Michaelis usque

H. Rex Angl' [...] dux Norm' et Aquit' et Com' And' Archiepis' Epis' Com'
Baron' Justic' et [...] ministris et omnib; hominib; et fidelib; suis franc' et Anglis
totius Anglie Salt'. Sciatis me concessisse et carta mea presenti confirmasse
Ecclie beate marie line' et Rob'o eiusdem ecclie epo' et successorib; suis epis
eiusdem ecclie domos que fuerunt scm templi in londo'. In parrochia S[...]
Andree de holeburn' cum Capella et Gardinis et Omnib; earum pertin'
[...] quas idem [...] scm templi tenuere tempore [...] [...] de hiis amplius
reddendo inde eisdem [...] templi Damnatam [...] [...] [...] p omni servitio.
Quare volo et firmit' precipio qd' ecclia line' et p[...] Robertus epus et
successores eius epi habeant [...] teneant p[...] domos cum Capella et Gardinis et omnibus earum pertinentiis sicut tra templi qd Rob'o epo et eius successorib; in p[...]etuum concesserunt et carta sua confirmaverunt. T'. Rog' Ebor'
Archiepo'. hs[...] Cicestr'. hugone Dunelm' epis'. thoma Cancellario.
[...]

ad cimiterium sancti Andree 7 a cimiterio sancti Andree usque
ad murum ciuitatis uersus orientem . Et hanc terram concessi 7
dedi ęcclesię Linc' . 7 eidem Roberto episcopo 7 successoribus
eius[12] solutam 7 quietam de langabulo . 7 parcagio 7 omnibus
aliis rebus . Et libere poterit perforare murum[14] ballii mei[15] ad
portam[16] faciendam ad introitum 7 exitum suum habendum uersus
ęcclesiam 7 ita edificare quod edificia sua extendantur in utrunque[17]
murum . Quare uolo 7 firmiter precipio quod ecclesia L[inc' 7[18]]
Robertus episcopus 7 omnes successores eius[18a] teneant predictam
terram bene . 7 in pace . 7 honorifice . 7 quiete . 7[19] cum socca .
7 sacca[20] . 7 thol[21] . 7 them[22] . 7 infanguenethef[23] . Testibus . Rogero
Eboracensi archiepiscopo . [24]Thoma[25] cancellario . [24]Ricardo de[26]
Luci . [24]Warino filio Giroldi[27] camerario . [24]Willelmo[28] filio Hamonis .
[24]Roberto de Donstanuilla[29] . [24]Joscelino[30] de Baillol[31] apvd Lincol'.[32]

Endorsed : (1) XVIII .H.ij. (13 cent.).　(2) de domibus episcopi Lincolie (13 cent.).
(3) Henrici secundi de domibus episcopi (13 cent.).
The vellum is folded over 2½ inches deep at the foot, and there is a tag for the seal.
Size : 6⅞ x 8½ inches.
Marginalia in A :　2| + φ　De domibus Linc'.
Texts : MS—Orig.A1/1/13.　A.　C,f.15.　R38.　Iiv(6).　Pd—*Mon*.vi,1275–6(55).
E.H.R.xxiv,305–6.　*C.C.R*.iv,107(6).　See Delisle, p. 551.
Var. R. : [1] De muro ballii ad faciendam portam episcopi C ; De palacio episcopi
R rubric ; De palacio episcopi et de . . . . eiusdem R marg.　[2] *om.* ministris A C R.
[3] *om.* hominibus . 7 A C R.　[4] *om.* totius Anglię A C R.　[5] *om.* 7 nominatim A C R.
[6] Linc' A C ; Lincol' R.　[7] *insert* de A C R.　[8] Linc' scir' A ; Lincol' sir' C ; Lincolscir'
R.　[9] *insert* presenti A C R.　[10] *om.* mea A C R.　[11] episcopo Linc' A C R.　[12] suis
A C R.　[13] cimiterium A C R.　[14] murum perforare A C R.　[15] *insert* Linc' A C R.
[16] *insert* suam A C R.　[17] utrumque A C R.　[18] *supplied from* A C ; Lincoln' 7 R.
[18a] sui A C R.　[19] *om.* 7 A C R.　[20] soca 7 saca A C R.　[21] toll A ;
tol C R.　[22] team A C R.　[23] infanguenetheof A ; infange neteof C ; infanguenethef R.
[24] *insert* 7 A C R.　[25] T. A C R.　[26] *om.* de A.　[27] Ger' A C R.　[28] W. A R.
[29] Dunest' A C R.　[30] Jocel' C.　[31] Baill' A C R.　[32] Linc' A ; Lincoliam C R.
Note : The ink of the original charter is very much faded, and some of the words
cannot be read without difficulty ; but, with the exception of two words (see Var.
R : 18), and a few of the stops, the text as printed here may be accepted as certain.
In view of the general accuracy of the Registrum Antiquissimum, the differences
of reading here are remarkable. The fact that A is almost always supported by
C and R suggests that they all have their source in another version of the charter.
Iiv agrees with Orig. throughout.

107

138. Writ of Henry II, confirming to the church of Lincoln
and bishop Robert Chesney and his successors the right to have
a market in the town of Banbury every Thursday in the year.
At Rouen. (1155–1162.)

De foro de Bannebir' (A marg.).

.H. rex Anglorum . 7 dux Normannorum . 7 Aquitanorum . 7
comes Andegauorum . archiepiscopis . episcopis[1] . comitibus .
baronibus . iusticiariis vicecomitibus . ministris . 7 omnibus
hominibus . 7 fidelibus suis Francis 7 Anglis* totius Anglie salutem
Sciatis me concess[isse 7 carta me[2]]a presenti confirmasse ęcclesię
beatę Marię Linc' . 7 Roberto de Kaisneto Linc' episcopo . 7 [suc-
cessoribus eius episcopis[2]] Linc' . quod habeant forum . in uilla

de Banneb*iria*³ vnaquaque⁴ die Iouis totius anni . Quare uolo
7 firmiter precipio quod ẹcclesia Linc' 7 Robertus episcopus 7
successores sui episcopi Linc' habeant 7 teneant predictum forum
de Banneb*iria*⁵ bene 7 in pace honorifice . 7 quiete . Testibus .
Hilario⁶ Cicestr*ensi*⁷ . Hugone Dunelmensi episcopis . Thoma
cancellario . a p v d R o t h o m a g v m ;⁸

The last two words are spread out to form the last line.
Endorsed : (1) XXXVIII .H. ij. (13 cent.). (2) H. secundi de foro de Banebiri
(13 cent.). (3) de foro apud Banburye (16 cent.).
There is a tag for the seal. Size : 6⅞ x 5¼ inches.
Marginalia in A : 2| + *preb*' φ De foro Bannebir'.
Texts : MS—Orig. ᴀ1/1/16. A. C,ff.15,15d. Pd—*Mon.*vi,1276(56). *E.H.R.*
xxiv,306. Delisle, p. 556 (abs.).
Var. R.: ¹ *om.* episcopis C. ² *supplied from* A *and* C, *there being a hole in the
charter.* ³ Baneb'r' C. ⁴ umaquaque A. ⁵ Banneb'r' A C. ⁶ Hylario A C.
⁷ Ciscestr' C. ⁸ Rotomagum A C.

Folio 20.

Hdl.   *Carte Regis* HENRICI SECUNDI.   2.0

108

139. Writ of Henry II, giving to the church of Lincoln, at the
request and for love of bishop Robert II, the church of Langford
[co. Oxford], and all the land which Roger bishop of Salisbury
held in the same village, to hold as bishop Roger or Ailric his predecessor best held them in the time of Henry I. At Brill in the
Forest [of Bernwood, co. Buckingham]. (1155–1158.)

De ecclesia de Langeford' 7 terra in eadem villa¹ (A marg.).

H. rex Angl*orum* . 7 dux Norm*annorum* 7 Aqui*tanorum* . 7 comes
And*egauorum* . archiepiscopis . episcopis² . abbatibus . comitibus .
baronibus . iustici*ariis* . vicecomitibus . ministris . 7 omnibus
fidelibus suis Francis 7 Anglis totius Anglie ː salutem . Sciatis me
dedisse 7 in perpetuam elemosinam concessisse ecclesie sancte
Marie Linc' pro amore dei 7 anima regis .H. aui mei . 7 aliorum
antecessorum meorum . 7 peticione 7 amore Roberti episcopi Linc'
ecclesiam de Langéford'³ cum omnibus pertinentiis suis . 7 totam
terram quam Rogerus episcopus Sar*isbir*iensis in eadem villa de
Langéford'³ tenuit . Quare volo⁴ 7 firmiter precipio quod predicta
ecclesia sancte Marie Linc' habeat 7 teneat predictam ecclesiam
de Langéford'³ . et totam terram prenominatam . ita bene 7 in pace
7 libere 7 honorifice 7 quiete . in bosco 7 plano . in pratis 7 pascuis⁵ .
in aquis 7 molendinis . 7 in omnibus locis . cum omnibus libertatibus
7 consuetudinibus 7 quietanciis⁶ 7 aliis pertinentiis suis in omnibus
rebus sicut predictus Rogerus episcopus Sar*isbir*iensis uel Ailricus
predecessor suus umquam⁷ melius liberius honorificentius 7 quietius
tenuerunt tempore .H. regis aui mei . Testibus Toma⁸ cancellario .
H. de Essexa⁹ constabulario . Warino filio Ger*oldi* camerario .

XIII

H[enricus] rex ... Com[itibus] ... Justic[iariis] Vicecomitibus Baronibus ... omnibus fidelibus suis ... Sciatis me concessisse ... dedisse ... de ... Sancte Marie Lincoln ...

... de ... canonicus ... successerit in canonicus ... villa ... e omni ...

... silvis in ... liberam elemosinam. Quare volo ... per ... per eand[em]

villa ... possessione ... in pace ... honorifice teneat libere et quiete de ...

... et hundred ... sacra ... et ... In Langene ... cum omnibus

consuetudinibus ... liberam sicut aliqua prebenda Lincoln ... quietior et liber...

... sic[ut] ... per dictus meus concessi ... Teste ... R[obert]

Episcopo Lincoln ... Philippus ... Episcopus ... Lincoln ...

H[enricus] Rex ... Justic[iariis] ... et ... Comitibus ... Archiepiscopis

Episcopis Abbatibus Justic[iariis] Comitibus Vicecomitibus ... Omnibus hominibus et

fidelibus suis totius anglie Salutem. Sciatis me dedisse et concessisse in puram

... elemosinam ecclesie beate Marie de Lincoln ecclesiam de ... cum

omnibus pertinentiis suis. Quare volo et firmiter precipio quod ecclesia illa

... tenet prefatam ecclesiam de ... libere quiete bene et in

pace honorifice integre cum omnibus pertinentiis suis In bosco In

plano in pratis et pascuis ... et quiete ... consuetudinibus suis ... cum omnibus li-

bertatibus et liberis consuetudinibus suis. Teste Thoma Canc[ellario] ... Episcopo ...

... filio ... Apud ...

Willelmo filio Hamonis . H. filio Geroldi . apud Bruhellam in foresta ;

Facsimile facing page 89.
Endorsed : Henrici secundi de ecclesia de Langeford' (13 cent.).
Part of the tag for the seal remains.　Size : 8⅓ x 5¾ inches.
Marginalia in A : 2 ＋　φ　De ecclesia de Langford'.　va cat.
Texts : MS—Orig. A1/1/35.　A.　C,f.15d.　Iiv(1).　Pd—*Mon*.vi,1276(57).
E.H.R.xxvi, 312.　*C.C.R*.iv,106(1).
Var. R. : ¹ De ecclesia de Langeford' C Iiv.　² *om*. episcopis C.　³ The *e* of *Lange-*
ford' in the original charter is marked with two strokes like acute accents.　H. Salter
(*E.H.R*.xxiv,312n.) suggests that the intention is to indicate a short *e* which is to
be sounded, the preceding *g* being hard.　In no. 179 below, which is written by
another hand, the name appears as *Langueford*'.　⁴ *corrected from* uoluit C.　⁵ paschuis
A.　⁶ quitanc' C.　⁷ unquam A C.　⁸ Thom' A C Iiv.　⁹ Essexia A ; Excessia C.

109

140.　Writ of Henry II, giving to the church of Lincoln the church of Brampton [co. Huntingdon].　At Brill [co. Buckingham]. (1155–1158.)

De ecclesia de Bramton' (A marg.).

.H. rex Anglo*rum*¹ . 7 dux Norm*annorum* . 7 Aquit*anorum* . 7 comes Ande*gauorum* . archiepiscopis . episcopis . abbatibus . iustic*iariis* . comitibus vicecomitibus . ministris . 7 omnibus ho²minibus . 7 fidelibus suis totius Anglię salutem . Sciatis me dedisse 7 concessisse in perpetuam elemosinam ęcclesię beatę Marię de Lincol'³ . ęcclesiam de Brantona cum omnibus pertinentiis suis . Quare uolo 7 firmiter precipio quod ęcclesia illa de Linc' teneat predictam ęcclesiam de Brantona . libere . quiete . bene . 7 in pace . honorifice . integre . cum omnibus pertinentiis suis in bosco⁴ 7 in plano . in pratis 7 pascuis⁵ . in aquis 7 molendinis . cum omnibus libertatibus 7 liberis consuetudinibus suis . Testibus Thoma cancellario . Man*assero* Biset⁶ dapifero . Garino⁷ filio Giroldi⁸ . a p v d　B r e h e l l a m ;⁹

Facsimile opposite.
Endorsed : (1) H. ij. de Brantuna (13 cent.).　.L. (13 cent.).　(2) de ecclesia de
Brantuna (13 cent.).
There is a tag for the seal.　Size : 5⅝ x 5⅝ inches.
Marginalia in A : 2 φ　De Bramton'　va　[cat (*at end of no*. 141)].
Texts : MS—Orig. A1/1/23.　A.　C,ff.15d,16.　Iiii(33).　Pd—*Mon*.vi,1276(58).
C.C.R.iv,104(33).　*E.H.R*.xxiv,308–9.　See Delisle, p. 549.
Var. R. : ¹ Anglie A.　² *From the beginning to* omnibus ho *is repeated in* C.　³ Linc'
A.　⁴ boscho A.　⁵ paschuis A.　⁶ Bisset C.　⁷ Warino Iiii.　⁸ Gerold' A C.
⁹ Brehgllam Iiii.

110

141.　Writ of Henry II, confirming to the church of Lincoln Albert Grellei's gift of the church of Bracebridge with one bovate of land.　At Rouen.　(1156–1169 ; probably 1156–1162.)

De ecclesia de Bracebrig' (marg.).

.H. rex Anglo*rum* . dux Norm*annorum* . 7 Aquit*anorum* . 7 comes Ande*gauorum* . archiepiscopis . episcopis . abbatibus . comitibus .

baronibus . iusticiariis . vicecomitibus . 7 omnibus fidelibus suis tocius Anglie salutem . Sciatis me concessisse 7 presenti carta mea confirmasse ecclesie beate Marie Linc' . ecclesiam omnium sanctorum de Bracebrig' cum una bouata terre . 7 omnibus aliis pertinenciis suis .* in perpetuam elemosinam . Quare uolo 7 firmiter precipio quod ecclesia beate Marie Linc' . 7 episcopi Linc' prefatam ecclesiam de Bracebrig' cum suis pertinenciis bene 7 in pace honorifice 7 quiete teneant . sicut Albertus Grellei eam eis donauit . 7 carta sua confirmauit . Testibus . Rogero Eboracensi . archiepiscopo . 7 .H. Cicestrensi episcopo . apud Rotomagum.

Marginalia : N(Q). De Bracebrig'. [Va (*at beginning of no.* 140)] cat. (*On a label cut out of the side of the leaf except the lower end by which it is attached*) De ecclesia de Bracebrig'.
Text : MS—A.

Folio 20d.

111

142. Writ of Henry II, confirming to the church of Lincoln Henry I's gift of the manor of Kilsby [co. Northampton]. At Rouen. (1155–1162.)

De Kildeb' manerio[1] (marg.).

.H. rex Anglorum . 7 dux Normannorum . 7 Aquitanorum . 7 comes Andegauorum . archiepiscopis . episcopis . comitibus . baronibus . vicecomitibus . iusticiariis . ministris . 7 omnibus hominibus 7 fidelibus suis Francis 7 Anglis tocius Anglie . salutem . Sciatis me concessisse 7 carta mea confirmasse ecclesie beate Marie Linc' . manerium de Kildesbi cum omnibus pertinenciis suis . Quare uolo 7 firmiter precipio quod predicta ecclesia Linc' habeat 7 teneat predictum manerium bene . 7 in pace . honorifice . libere . 7 quiete . 7 integre . in bosco . 7 in plano . in pratis 7 paschuis[2] . 7 in omnibus locis 7 rebus eidem manerio pertinentibus . sicut . H. rex auus meus illud manerium ei dedit . 7 carta sua confirmauit . Testibus . Rogero . Eboracensi[3] archiepiscopo . Hilario Cicestrensi . Hugone Dunelmensi episcopis Thoma cancellario . apud Rotomagum.

Marginalia : N(Q). 2| R' . φ preb' De Kildebi.
Texts : MS—A. C,ff.16,16d. Iiii(34). Pd—*Mon.*vi,1276(60). *C.C.R.*iv,104(34).
Var. R. : [1] De manerio de Kildesbi C. [2] pascuis C I. [3] Eborr' C.

112

143. Writ of Henry II, confirming to the church of Lincoln the franchises and gifts granted by king William, his great-grand-father (see no. 2 above). At Lincoln. (1155–1161.)

Confirmatio libertatum 7 beneficiorum per Willelmum regem ecclesie Linc' collatorum[1] (A marg.).

H' rex Anglorum . dux Normannorum . 7 Æquitanorum[2] . 7 comes Andegauorum . iusticiariis . vicecomitibus . baronibus .

Francis . 7 Anglis . tocius episcopatus Linc'[3] salutem . Sciatis me concessisse [7 confir[4]]masse ecclesie beate Marie Linc'[3] e[and[4]]em libertatem quam rex Willelmus atauus[5] meus concessit edificationi predicte ecclesie 7 mansionibus cimiterii eiusdem ecclesie . Similiter concedo 7 confirmo donationem quam predictus rex Willelmus fecit de terris . 7 ecclesiis . 7 decimis . quas eidem ecclesie donauit . 7 in perpetuam elemosinam carta sua confirmauit . videlicet Welletonam . 7 Slafordam[6] cum appendiciis suis . 7 ecclesias de Chirchetona[7] . 7 de Castra . 7 de Wellingoura . necnon 7 decimas tocius redditus eorundem maneriorum . 7 duas ecclesias in Lincolnia[8] scilicet ecclesiam sancti Laurentii . 7 ecclesiam sancti Martini . 7 Lectonam quam Waldeouus comes per manum predicti regis Willelmi ecclesie Linc'[3] donauit . 7 Waburnam[9] quam rex ecclesie Linc' 7 Remigio episcopo cum pastorali baculo donauit . 7 ecclesiam sancte Marie de Bedeford'[10] . 7 ecclesiam [de Lec[4]]ton' in Bedeford' scire[11] . 7 ecclesiam de Buchingham[12] . 7 ecclesiam de Aeilesbiria[13] cum omnibus pertinentiis earundem ecclesiarum . Testibus . Theod[baldo[14] C[4]]antuariensi archiepiscopo . 7 Romane ecclesie legato . 7 Philippo Baiocensi episcopo . 7 Ernulfo[15] Luxouiensi episcopo . apud Linc'.[16]

Endorsed : (1) de libertate quam rex Willelmus concessit beate Marie 7 cimiterio (13 cent.). 7 quibusdam prebendis eidem collatis . . . 7 Welletone . 7 . . . . (14 cent.). (2) LIII (13 cent.). (3) Asgerby (15 cent.).
There is a fragment of the seal on a tag. Size : 9 x 4¼ inches.
Marginalia in A : 2 ·ȷ· + ·ȷ· φ   N   va [cat (*at the end of no.* 144)].   V   De libert' [ecclesie].
Texts : MS—Orig. A1/1/27. A. C,f.16d. R36. Iv(34). Delisle, pp. 550–1. Pd— *E.H.R.*xxiv,310. *C.C.R.*iv,145(34).
Var. R. : [1] Carta confirmatoria de libertatibus terris ecclesiis 7 decimis concessis per W. regem R rubric ; De libertatibus clausi 7 Welton' Chercheton' 7 Leghton' R marg. [2] Aquit' A C R Iv. [3] Lincol' C. [4] *supplied from* A, *the charter having five holes.* [5] attauus A R. [6] Salfordam A ; Slaffordam Iv. [7] Chirketona C. [8] Lincolia A ; Lincol' C R. [9] Woburnam, *corrected from* Waburnam C. [10] Bedeford C. [11] Bedeford scira A ; Bedefordsir' C. [12] Buchingeham A ; Buchinham C ; Buckingham Iv. [13] Eilesbiria A ; Elesberia C. [14] Theobaldo A C R Iv. [15] Arnulfo A R Iv. [16] Lincoliam A C R.
Note : For the date, see Round, *Ancient Charters*, p. 58.

113

144. Writ of Henry II, confirming the gift made to the church of Lincoln by William son of Clarembald of Searby of the church of Searby with the chapel of Owmby [co. Lincoln]. At Salisbury. (1155–1158.)

De ecclesia de Seuerb*i* (marg.).
.H. rex Angl*orum* . 7 dux Norm*annorum* . 7 Aquit*anorum* . 7 comes And*egauorum* . episcopo Linc' . 7 iustic' . baronibus . vicecom*it'* . 7 omnibus ministris . 7 fidelibus suis de Lincol' scira salutem . Sciatis me concessisse 7 confirmasse ecclesie beate Marie Lincol' . ecclesiam de Sauerbi cum terris 7 capellis 7 decimis 7 omnibus aliis rebus eidem ecclesie* pertinentibus ita bene 7 in

pace libere quiete 7 honorifice tenendam : sicut Willelmus filius
Clarembaldi de Sauerbi eandem ecclesiam de Seuerbi[1] cum decimis
7 terris 7 oblationibus . 7 toftis . 7 cum capella Oudenbi . 7 cum
omnibus rectitudinibus 7 pertinenciis suis in perpetuam elemosinam
predicte ecclesie beate Marie Linc'[2] dedit 7 concessit 7 carta sua
confirmauit . Testibus . Thoma cancellario . Willelmo fratre Regis .
Reginaldo comite Cornubie . Ricardo de Humez . constabulario .
Warino filio Geroldi camerario . Manassero Biset' dapifero .
apud Sarisbiriam.

Marginalia: ♃ φ   [va (*at the beginning of no.* 143)] cat.   De Seuereb'.
Text: MS—A.
Var. R.: [1] eandem ecclesiam de Seuerbi *written in marg. by a similar hand, and
marked for inclusion in the text.*   [2] There is a blank here one and a half inches long
where words have been completely erased, probably due to an error in copying.

*Folio 21.

Hdl.   2 1

114

145. Writ of Henry II, giving licence to bishop Robert II, at his
request, to have his market in his town of Banbury [co. Oxford]
every Thursday. At Lincoln. (Probably January, 1154–1155.)

De mercato de Bannebiria[1] (A marg.).

H. rex Anglorum . 7 dux Normannorum 7 Aquitanorum . 7 comes
Andegauorum . iustic' . 7 baronibus . 7 vicecomit' . 7 omnibus
fidelibus 7 ministris suis de Oxenef'[2] scira : salutem . Sciatis me
dedisse 7 concessisse pro dei amore 7 petitione Roberti Linc'[3]
episcopi : ecclesie sancte Marie Lincolie[4] in perpetuum quod habeat
mercatum suum in villa sua de Banneberia[5] unaquaque septimana
in die Iouis libere 7 quiete 7 honorifice ad tales consuetudines
quales habent alia mercata per Angliam . Testibus . Philippo[6]
Baiocensi . 7 Arnulfo[7] Lexouiensi episcopis . 7 Toma[8] cancellario .
apud Lincoliam.

Facsimile opposite.
Endorsed: (1) XXXVIII .H. ij (13 cent.).   (2) de mercatu in uilla de Bannebiri
(12 cent.).   (3) Henrici secundi de mercatu de Banneb' (12 cent.).
The strip at the foot for the seal, and perhaps a ribband, have been torn off.
Size: 6 x 3⅞ inches (without the strip).
Marginalia in A: ♃ R' . preb' + φ . . . . Bannebir'.
Texts: MS—Orig. a1/1/20.   A. C,f.15.   Iiv(18).   Pd—*Mon.*iv,1276(56).   *E.H.R.*
xxiv,308.   Delisle, pp. 551–2 (abs.).   See *C.C.R.*iv,110(18).
Var. R.: [1] Bannebiria C.   [2] Oxeneford' A; Oxeneford C.   [3] Lincol' A.   [4] Linc'
A; Lincol' C.   [5] Bannebiria A; Banneberia C.   [6] Phill' C.   [7] Arnulf' A C.   [8] Thom'
A C.

115

146. Writ of Henry II, confirming to the church of Lincoln
Henry I's gift of the churches of Derby and Wirksworth *in prebendam*. At York. (Probably 1158.)

De ecclesiis de Derby 7 de Wirkesworth'[1] (marg.).

.H. rex Anglorum . 7 dux Normannorum . 7 Aquitanorum . 7
comes Andegauorum . archiepiscopis . episcopis . abbatibus .
comitibus . baronibus . iusticiariis . vicecomitibus . 7 omnibus
fidelibus[2] tocius Anglie ⁊ salutem . Sciatis me dedisse 7 concessisse
7 presenti carta mea confirmasse deo 7 sancte Marie[3] ecclesie Linc' .
ecclesias de[4] Derebia 7 de[4] Wercesworda[5] in prebendam perpetuo iure
possidendas cum omnibus[6] pertinenciis suis . Quare uolo 7 firmiter
precipio quod ecclesia beate Marie Linc' predictas ecclesias in
perpetuam elemosinam bene 7 in pace honorifice 7 quiete teneat .
cum omnibus libertatibus . 7 liberis consuetudinbus ⁊ que ad easdem
pertinent . Has autem ecclesias cum suis pertinenciis ecclesie Linc'
concedo 7 confirmo . sicut carta Henrici[7] regis aui mei testatur .
Testibus . Ricardo de Luci[8] . Nicholao de Sigillo . Willelmo filio
Johannis . apud Eboracum.[9]

Marginalia : + Hec carta est in cista domini decani cartarum (Q).
Texts: MS—A. C,ff.16d,17. D2. D127. Iiii(32). Pd—Mon.viii,1276(62).
C.C.R.iv,104(32).
Var. R. : [1] De ecclesis de Derebia C marg. [2] insert suis D2 D127. [3] insert 7
C D2 D127. [4] om. de C. [5] Weresworda C ; Werceswrda Iiii ; Wirceworda
D127. [6] insert iuris [sic] 7 D127. [7] Henricus C. [8] Luci C. [9] Eboracum
D127.

116

147. Writ of Henry II, confirming to the church of Lincoln
and bishop Robert II Henry I's grant of toll in their fairs of Stow.
At Westminster. (1155–1158.)

De theloneo in feriis de Stowe (A marg.).

[.H. rex A[1]]nglorum . 7 dux Normannorum 7 Aquitanorum .
7 comes Andegauorum . T. Canthuariensi[2] archiepiscopo . 7 R.
Eboracensi [archiepiscopo . 7[1]] omnibus episcopis 7 abbatibus 7
comitibus 7 baronibus 7 iusticiariis 7 vicecomitibus 7 ministris
7 fidelibus [suis[1]] tocius Anglie . salutem . Sciatis me concessisse .
deo 7 sancte Marie Linc' 7 Roberto Linc' [episcopo[1]] 7 omnibus
[success[1]]oribus suis in perpetuum habendum theloneum in feriis
de [Stowa[1]] scilicet in festo sancte Marie in Augusto . 7 in festo
sancte Marie in Septembri . 7 in illa feria in festo sancti Michaelis .
7 in Pentecosten . sicut rex H. auus meus illud dedit 7 concessit
predicte Linc' ecclesie 7 carta sua confirmauit . Testibus . Toma
cancellario . 7 Ricardo de Humez . conestabulario . 7 Mannassero
Biset dapifero . 7 Warino filio Geroldi camerario . apud Westmonasterium.

Endorsed : (1) de telonio de Stowa (12 cent.). (2) II .H. ij. (13 cent.). (3) episcopo
Linc' (13 cent.).
There is a strip at the foot for the seal. Size : 6 x 3¾ inches.
Marginalia in A : 2↓ +.
Texts: MS—Orig. A1/1/28. A. Iv(28). Pd—E.H.R.xxiv,304. C.C.R.iv, 143–4
(28). Delisle, p. 553 (abs.).
Var. R. : [1] supplied from A, the original charter having been injured. [2] Cantuar' A.

Folio 21d.

Hdl.   .H. Regis *Secundi.*

117

148. Writ of Henry II, confirming to the bishop of Lincoln licence to have a fair at Louth [co. Lincoln] on the octave of Saint Peter and Saint Paul [6 July], which fair shall last for eight days. At Woodstock. (1155–1158.)

De feria in[1] Luda (marg.).

.H. rex Angl*ie* . 7 dux Norma*nnie* . 7 Aquitanie . 7 comes Ande*gauie* . iustic*ie* . vicecom*iti* . 7 omnibus ministris suis de Lincol. scira[2] *:* salutem . Sciatis me concessisse 7 confirmasse episcopo Linc' feriam habere in Luda in octabis apostolorum Petri 7 Pauli que duret octo diebus . Et uolo 7 precipio quod eam habeat . 7 teneat libere . 7 honorifice . 7 plenarie . cum libertatibus . 7 aliis liberis consuetudinibus ferie pertinentibus . Testibus . Thoma cancellario . 7 Ricardo de Luci . 7 Warino filio Geroldi . apud Wdestoch[3].

Marginalia : 2 R' φ de feri*a* Lude.
Texts : MS—A. C,f.17. Iiv(17). Pd—*C.C.R.*iv,110(17).
Var. R. : [1] de C. [2] Linc' sir' C. [3] Wodestoch' Iiv.

118

149. Writ of Henry II. Whereas Rannulf earl of Chester, in the king's presence and with his assent, gave to Saint Mary of Lincoln and bishop Robert II in compensation for the damages which he did to the said church, Marston and Warkworth [co. Northampton], to be held as thirty pounds' worth of land in perpetual alms; with the proviso that if those villages were not worth thirty pounds a year, the earl would make up the amount out of his own inheritance; and whereas Walter of Wahull, in the king's presence, renounced his claim to any right in the said manors, and rendered them to the earl; and also whereas the earl covenanted to cause the heir of Norman de Verdun to quitclaim the manors, and covenanted likewise that if the heirs of William Meschin, or any one else, should claim anything in the said lands, he, the earl, and his heirs would warrant them to the said bishop and church, either by making good the said thirty pounds' worth of land out of their own inheritance, or by giving an exchange to those who claimed the premises. Now the king, willing that the agreement stand firm, has come in as surety on these terms, that if the earl does

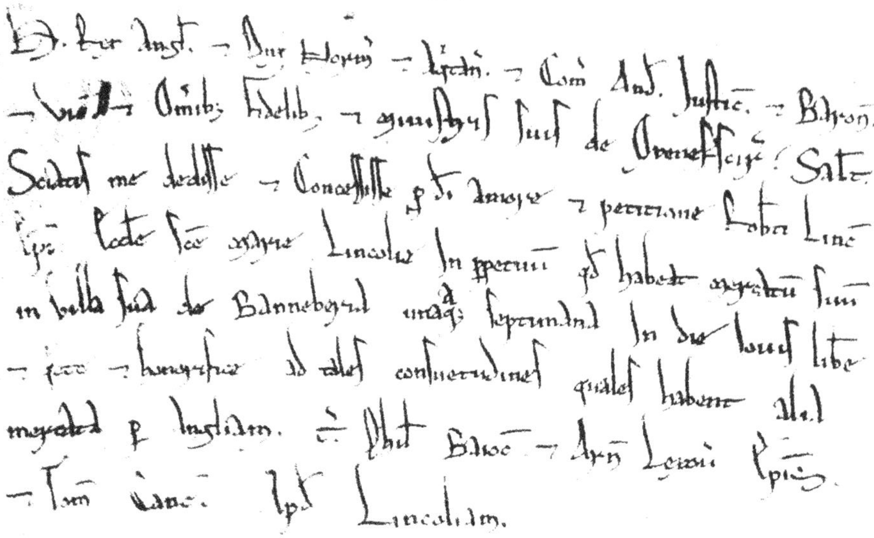

H. Rex Angl. ⁊ Dux Norm. ⁊ Aquit. ⁊ Com. And. Justic. ⁊ Baron.
⁊ Vicit. Omnibᵤ fidelibᵤ ⁊ ... suis de Ormesseie Salt.
Sciat̃ me dedisse ⁊ Concessisse p̃ ... amore ⁊ petitione Robt̃i Linc
in bello suo de Bannebyrd ... sepᵗdn̄l In dᵤ buᵗ libe
⁊ ... ⁊ honorifice ad illas consuetudines quales habent alic̃
... p. Angliam. ⁊ ... Baroñ ⁊ Arñ Loeuui ...
⁊ Ioĩn ... apᵈ Lincolniam.

[second charter, largely illegible]

H. Rex Angl. ... Comit. ... Apᷟtop̃
Comit. ... Rex ... suis Angliæ Salt
Sciat̃ me ... In pᵗena Almolini Concessisse ...
... apᵗe Linc ... Omnibᵤ successorib; suis apᵗpetuã ...
... Linc ... Robt̃ ... Lincᷟ ...
de ... ⁊ ... ... Lincoln. ... omb; ...
... libas ⁊ ... suis In Bosco ... pᵗ ...
... In pᵗis ⁊ libis ⁊ ... ⁊ ... ...
illud ... ... libe ... ⁊ honorifice ... apᵈ ... Regis ...
meg. Tst̃ ... ⁊ ... Comit. ... ...
Com. ... Robt̃o de Auᵗ ... apᵈ ...

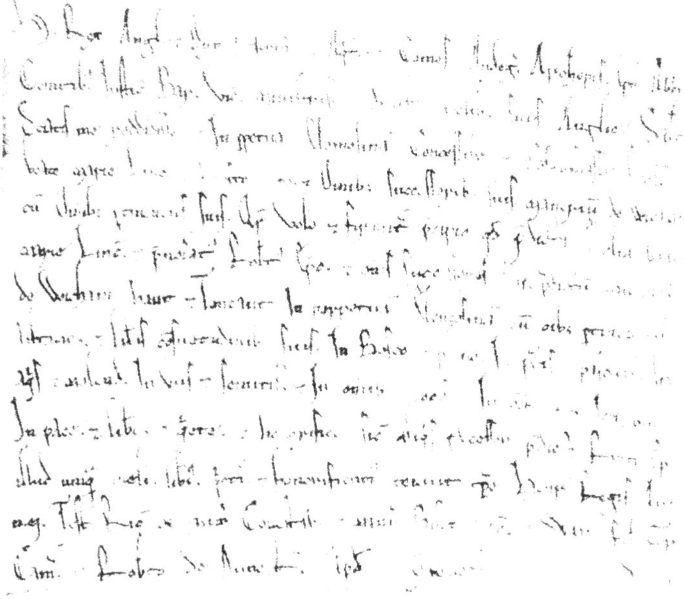

not keep his covenant, he, the king, will, out of his own demesne, make good the thirty pounds' worth of land to the said church and bishop, quit of all secular service and custom. At Evesham [co. Worcester]. (1155–1158.)

De Merston' 7 Wauencurt[1] (marg.).

.H. rex Anglorum . 7 dux Normannorum . 7 Aquitanorum . 7 comes Andegauorum . archiepiscopis . episcopis . abbatibus . comitibus . baronibus . iusticiariis . vicecomitibus . ministris . 7 omnibus fidelibus suis tocius Anglie . 7 Normannie : salutem . Sciatis quod Rannulfus comes Cestrie in presentia mea 7 assensu meo dedit deo 7 sancte Marie Linc' . 7 Roberto episcopo eiusdem loci pro salute animarum patris 7 matris sue . 7 aliorum predecessorum suorum . 7 pro salute anime sue . 7 in recompensatione dampnorum que fecerat ecclesie sancte Marie Linc' . Mestonam . 7 Wauencurt[2] . cum appenditiis suis pro .xxx. libratis terre tenendas libere 7 quiete in perpetuam elemosinam . tali tenore quod si uille ille cum appenditiis suis .xxx. libras annuatim non ualerent : quando episcopus eas reciperet : predictus comes Rannulfus de propria hereditate sua perimpleret sine dilatione . Ibidem remisit calumpniam suam Walterus de Wahella in presentia mea . 7 quicquid iuris habebat in maneriis predictis : ulterius in eis nichil reclamaturus . 7 Rannulfo comiti eadem maneria reddidit . 7 ipse comes ecclesie 7 episcopo illa donauit . Conuencionauit etiam comes Cestrie quod infra terminum proximi festi sancti Michaelis heredi Normanni de Verduno[3] eadem maneria quieta clamare faceret . 7 quicquid ad ea pertinet . nec aliquo tempore aduersus ecclesiam Linc' . uel episcopum calumpniam inde moueret . Similiter conuencionauit legittime comes Rannulfus . quod si heredes Willelmi Meschin uel alius aliquid in predictis terris[4] calumpniarentur : ipse 7 heredes sui adquietarent eas 7 warentizarent[5] episcopo Linc' . 7 ecclesie sancte Marie Linc' . Quod si non faceret : comes Rannulfus uel heres suus si post decessum comitis calumpnia fieret : de propria hereditate sua omni occasione remota illas .xxx. libratas terre ecclesie Linc' . 7 episcopo restitueret . de libera elemosina imperpetuum ab ipsis tenenda 7 possidenda . uel ipsis calumpniatoribus inde escambium daret . Ego autem hanc conuentionem firmam esse uolens interposui me plegium hac conditione . quod si comes Rannulfus eam non teneret : uel de ea exiret[6] : de predictis .xxx. libratis terre in liberam elemosinam date grantum episcopi 7 Lincol' ecclesie non faciens : restituerem eas ecclesie Linc' 7 episcopo de dominio meo in perpetuam 7 liberam elemosinam possidendas . 7 ab omni seculari seruitio 7 consuetudine quietas . Concedo etiam quod ille .xxx. librate quas comes Rannulfus dedit ecclesie Linc' sint quiete ab omni exactione 7 secularibus consuetudinibus . Testibus . H. episcopo Abrinciensi . Thoma* cancellario . Reginaldo comite Cornubie . Ricardo de Humez constabulario . H. de Essexa

constabulario . Warino filio Ger*oldi* . camarario . Man*assero*⁷ Biset
dapifero . Joc*elino* de Baillol' . apud Euesham.

Marginalia: φ Nescitur de Bukyng' (query Q.).
Texts: MS—A. R164. Iiv(10). Pd—*C.C.R.*iv,108–9(10).
Var. R.: ¹ Carta regis pro Merston R marg. ² Wauercurt Iiv. ³ Verdumo Iiv.
⁴ aliquid in predictis terris *repeated in* A *and struck out.* ⁵ *om.* warentizarent R.
⁶ *om.* uel de ea exiret R. ⁷ Manet R.

Folio 22.

Hdl.   *Henrici Regis* SECUNDI   2.2.

ADD. CHART.

150. An earlier form of the preceding charter issued before
Henry became king. At Stamford during the siege. 31 August,
1153.

Merston' (R marg.).

[.H. dux Normann*orum* ꝫ Aquit*anorum* ꝫ comes Andeg*auorum*
omnibus archiepiscopis episcopis comi]tibus baronibus . vicecomitibus . [iustic*iariis* ꝫ omnibus amicis ꝫ fidelibus suis Normann*ie*
ꝫ Angl*ie* salutem ⸗ Sciatis quod Ranulphus comes Cestrie in presencia
mea ꝫ assensu meo dedit deo ꝫ sancte Marie Lincoln'] . ꝫ Roberto
episcopo eiusdem loci pro salute animarum [patris ꝫ matris sue
ꝫ aliorum predecessorum suorum ꝫ pro salute anime sue ꝫ in
recompensacione dampnorum que fecerat ecclesie sancte Marie
Linc' Merstonam ꝫ Wauerc]uurt ⸗ cum appenditijs suis pro . xxx.
libratis [terre tenendas libere ꝫ quiete in perpetuam elemosinam
tali tenore ⸗ quod si ville ille cum appendicijs suis .xxx. libras
annuatim non valuerint ⸗ quando episcopus eas reci]piet ⸗ predictus
comes Rannulphus de propria hereditate sua [perimplebit sine
frustratoria dilatione ⸗ Ibidem remisit calumpniam suam Walterus
de Wahella ⸗ in presencia mea ꝫ quicquid iuris habebat in manerijs
predictis ⸗ vlterius in eis] nichil reclamaturus . ꝫ Rannulpho c[omiti]
eadem maneria re[ddidit ⸗ ꝫ ipse comes ecclesie ꝫ episcopo illa donauit .
Conuencionauit eciam comes Cestrie quatinus infra terminum
proximi festi sancti Michaelis heredi Normanni de] Verdumo¹ eadem
maneria quieta [clama]re faceret ꝫ quicquid [ꝫ quicquid² ad ea
pertinet ⸗ nec aliquo tempore aduersus ecclesiam Linc' vel episcopum
calumpniam inde mouebit . Similiter conuencionauit legitime comes
Ranulphus ⸗ quod si heredes Willelmi Mesc]hini uel alius aliquid
in predictis [terris ca]lumpniarentur ⸗ ipse adq[uietaret eas³ ꝫ
warantizaret episcopo Lincoln' ꝫ ecclesie sancte Marie Linc' ⸗
Quod si non faceret ⸗ comes Ranulphus vel heres suus si post decessum comitis calumpnia ista fieret . d]e propria hereditate sua omni
occasione remota . illas . x[xx. libratas terre Linc' ecclesie ꝫ episcopo
restitueret de libera elemosina inperpetuum ab ipsis tenenda ⸗ ꝫ
possidenda ⸗ vel ipsis calumpniatoribus in esc]ambium daret . Ego
autem hanc conuentionem firmam [esse volens interposui me fide-
iussorem hac condicione ⸗ quod si comes Ranulphus eam non teneret

vel de ea exiret ꞉ de predictis libratis terre sic⁴ in liberam ele]mosinam
date guarantum episcopi 7 Linc' ecclesie non facien[s ꞉ restituerem
eas ecclesie Linc' 7 episcopo de dominio meo in perpetuam 7 liberam
elemosinam possidendas (7 ab omni seculari consuetudine quietas .
Conce]do etiam quod ille .xxx. librate quas Rannulphus com[es
dabit ecclesie Linc' sint quiete ab omni exactione 7 secularibus
consuetudinibus (Facta fuit hec conuencio quadam die Lune in
vigilia sancti Egidii in ob]sidione Stanfordie . Testibus . Ricardo
de Hulmez . W[al]tero [Herefordie (Waltero Wahelle ꞉ con-
stabulariis (Hugone Waac (Geruasio Paganell' (Walchelino
Maminot' (Roberto Dunestanuilla (Warino 7 Henr]ico ꞉ filiis
Geroldi . Willelmo de Coleuilla . Simone filio Wil[lelmi Jocelino
de Bailoll' (Gossumo castellano de Fines⁵ (Roberto filio Walteri (
Pagano de Cheuerci (Ricardo pincerna (Osberto Malebissa (
Hugone⁶ H]ameslap' clerico . apud Stanfordiam ꞉ in obsidione.

Endorsed : . . . rstona.
Slit for seal tag. Size : 4¼ inches from top to bottom.
Texts : MS—Orig. A1/1/40 (a mere fragment, consisting of the left hand end).
R166.
Var. R. : *The words enclosed in brackets are supplied from* R. ¹ *sic.* ² 7 quicquid
repeated R. ³ eas *cancelled* R. ⁴ sic *has been inserted by a rather later hand.*
⁵ *perhaps to be identified with* Fiennes, *near* Calais. ⁶ de *has been omitted here.*

119

151. Writ of Henry duke of the Normans, confirming the gift
which Rannulf earl of Chester made to the church of Lincoln, in
recompense for the damages which he did to it, namely, thirty
pounds' worth of land from his own inheritance. The duke himself
is surety of this covenant insomuch that, should the earl fail to
keep it, he will give to the said church thirty pounds' worth of
land out of his demesne. At Crowmarsh Giffard [co. Oxford],
during the siege. (1153.)

Item de Merston' (marg.).

.H. rex Anglorum . 7¹ dux Normannorum . 7 Aquitanorum . 7
comes Andegauorum . omnibus archiepiscopis . episcopis . comitibus .
baronibus . iusticiariis . vicecomitibus . 7 omnibus amicis 7 fidelibus
suis Normannie . 7 Anglie . salutem . Sciatis me concessisse 7 confirmasse donationem quam Rannulfus comes Cestrie fecit ecclesie
Linc' pro dampnis que illi fecerat .xxx.² videlicet libratas terre
de propria sua hereditate . Quare uolo 7 firmiter precipio quatinus
predicta Lincol' ecclesia illas .xxx.² libratas terre in bono . 7 in pace .
quiete . 7 libere . ab omnibus exactionibus 7 consuetudinibus
secularibus imperpetuum possideat . Ego ipse enim huius
conuentionis tenende fideiussor existo ꞉ in tantum quod nisi
Rannulfus comes illam firmiter 7 inconcusse tenuerit ꞉ ego de
dominio meo proprio illas .xxx.² libratas terre predicte Lincol'
ecclesie dabo . Testibus . Theobaldo³ Cantuariensi archiepiscopo .

G

Rogero Cant*uarie* arch*idiacono*[4] . Willelmo comite Gleo*cestrie*[5] .
Rogero comite Herefo*rdie* . apud Craum*er*sam[6] in obsidione.[7]

Marginalia: + R'. preb' De Merstona.
Texts: MS—A. R165. Iv(30). Pd—*C.C.R.*iv,144(30).
Var. R.: [1] *om.* rex Angl' 7 R Iv. [2] triginta Iv. [3] Teobaldo R. [4] arch*idiacono* R.
[5] Sl'o R Iv, *due to a misreading of the initial letter.* [6] Crasam R. [7] obsudione R.

120

152. Writ of Henry II, commanding that the canons of Lincoln
shall hold their tenements, possessions, and lands within the city,
and within and without the borough, as they best held them when
the king last crossed the sea ; and that they shall not be put in plea
until he returns to England, unless he otherwise direct.   At
Tinchebrai. (1155–1166.)

De libertatibus canonicorum (marg.).

.H. rex Ang*lorum* . 7 dux Norm*annorum* . 7 Aquit*anorum* . 7
comes Ande*gauorum* . vicecom*iti* . Linc' scire salutem . Precipio
quod canonici Lincol' teneant omnia tenementa sua 7 omnes res
suas 7 terras 7 possessiones suas infra ciuitatem 7 infra burgum 7
extra . 7 in omnibus locis ita bene 7 in pace libere quiete integre
honorifice 7 iuste sicut melius 7 liberius tenuerunt quando nouissime
transfretaui . Et non ponantur inde in placitum donec in Ang*lia*
redeam nisi precepero . Et nisi feceris ; iustic*ia* mea faciat . Teste .
M'. Bisset dapifero . apud Tenerchebra.

Marginalia: N(Q) V Nota (Q). Carta Ashbye. preb' (13 cent.). (*It is improbable that this marginal note refers to this charter.*)
Text: MS—A.

121

153. Writ of Henry II, commanding H. de Pontn' and the
sheriff of Huntingdonshire to cause bishop Robert II to have in peace
all his corn from the assarts which were in the time of Henry I ;
and that all the corn from the assarts which were made after that
king's death shall be gathered and remain upon the land until the
king otherwise directs. At Nottingham. (1154–1168.)

De essartis (marg.).

.H. rex Ang*lorum* . 7 dux Norm*annorum* . 7 Aquit*annorum* . 7
comes Ande*gauorum* . H. de Pontn' . 7 vicecomite suo de Huntedon-
scira . salutem . Precipio quod faciatis habere in pace Roberto
episcopo Linc' omnia bladia sua de essartis que fuerunt tempore
.H. regis aui mei . Et de assartis que fuerunt facta post mortem
regis . H. predicti bladia omnia colligantur 7 remaneant super
eandem terram donec inde aliud precipiam . Teste . Ricardo de
Hum*ez* constabulario . apud Notingeham.

Marginalia: T. [Va]cat.
Text: MS—A.
Note: H. de Pontn' is unknown. Perhaps the name should be extended
' Pontiniaco '.

122

154. Writ of Henry II, declaring that he has restored and confirmed to the church of Lincoln and bishop Robert II and his successors the manor of Wickham [co. Oxford], to hold as any of the bishop's predecessors best held it in the time of king Henry I. At Oxford. (1154–1158.)

De manerio de Wicham (A marg.).

.H. rex Anglo*rum* . 7 dux Norm*annorum* 7 Aquit*anorum* . 7 comes Andeg*auorum* . archiepiscopis . episcopis[1] . abbatibus . comitibus . iustic*iariis* . baronibus . vicecomitibus . ministris . 7 omnibus fidelibus suis Anglie ⁊ salutem . Sciatis me reddidisse 7 in perpetuam elemosinam concessisse 7 confirmasse ecclesie beate Marie Linc' . 7 Roberto episcopo . 7 omnibus successoribus suis . manerium de Wicham cum omnibus pertinentiis suis . Quare volo 7 firmiter precipio quod predicta ecclesia* beate Marie Linc' . 7 prenominatus Robertus[2] episcopus . 7 omnes successores sui . predictum manerium de Wicham habeant 7 teneant in perpetuam elemosinam cum omnibus pertinentiis 7 libertatibus . 7 liberis consuetudinibus suis . in bosco 7 plano . in pratis 7 pascuis[3] . in aquis 7 molendinis . in viis 7 semitis . 7 in omnibus locis 7 in omnibus rebus ita bene . 7 in pace . 7[4] libere . 7 quiete . 7 honorifice ⁊ sicut aliquis predecessorum predicti Roberti episcopi illud umquam[5] melius . liberius . quietius . 7 honorificentius tenuit tempore Henrici regis aui mei . Testibus . Ricardo de Humez conestabulario[6] . 7 Mann*assero* Biset dapifero . 7 Warino filio Ger*oldi* camerario . 7[4] Roberto de Dunest*anuilla* . apud Oxenef or dam.[7]

Facsimile facing page 92.

Endorsed : (1) H'ij. de Wicham (12 cent.).　(2) de manerio Wicham (12 cent.). (3) XVII .H. ij. (13 cent.).

Tag for the seal.　Size : 6¼ x 6¼ inches.

Marginalia in A : ♃ φ De Wicham'.

Texts : MS—Orig. A1/1/12.　A. P15.　Iv(29).　Pd—*E.H.R.*xxiv,305.　*C.C.R.* iv,144(29).　See Delisle, p. 552.

Var. R.: [1] The part of P which contained the preceding words is missing.　[2] Rob' *interlineated* A ; *om.* Robertus P.　[3] paschuis A.　[4] *om.* 7 P.　[5] unquam A.　[6] constab' A P.　[7] Oxenfordam P.

Note : ' Wicham ' may safely be identified as Wickham, in Bodicote.　In 1166 Richard de Stokes, one of the knights of the bishop of Lincoln, held three fees (*Red Book of the Exchequer* i, 375); and in 1208-9 Robert de Stokes, a knight of the bishop's, held three fees in Wickham, Swalcliffe, Fawler (in Charlbury), and Epwell (in Swalcliffe) (*Book of Fees* i, 39).

Folio 22d.

Hdl.　　　　　　　　　HENRICI *Regis Secundi.*

123

155. Writ of Henry II, confirming to the church of Lincoln and bishop Robert II Henry I's grant of the wapentake of Well ; and confirming the same king's precept to the barons, vavasours,

and lords within the wapentake (see no. 60 above).   At York.
(1155–1166.)

De Welle wapentacho (A marg.).

.H'. rex Anglorum 7 dux Normannorum 7 Aquitanorum 7 comes
Andegauorum . omnibus baronibus 7 vauasoribus 7 omnibus dominis
qui terras tenent infra Wellewapentacum ؛ salutem . Sciatis me concessisse 7 presenti carta mea confirmasse ęcclesic Linc'[1] 7 Roberto
episcopo Linc' Wellewapentac de me tenendum . Quare uolo 7
firmiter precipio quod omnes ueniatis ad placita 7 wapentacum episcopi
Linc' per summonitionem ministrorum suorum . 7 faciatis ei omnes
rectitudines 7 rectas consuetudines in omnibus rebus quas ei debetis
de terris uestris ad illud wapentacum . ita plenarie . sicut umquam[2]
melius 7 plenius alicui antecessorum suorum ؛ fecistis . Et nisi
feceritis ؛ ipse uos iusticiet per pecuniam uestram donec faciatis
ei quicquid iuste 7 ex consuetudine wapentaci ؛ facere debetis .
Istud[3] wapentacum ęcclesie Linc'[1] 7 Roberto episcopo de me tenendum
concedo 7 confirmo ؛ sicut carta Henrici regis aui mei ؛ testatur .
Testibus . Rogero Eboracensi archiepiscopo . Hugone Dunolmensi[4]
episcopo . Ricardo de Luci . 7 Manassero Bisset[5] dapifero apud
Eboracum.[6]

Facsimile opposite.
Endorsed: (1) XXVII .H. ij. (13 cent.).   (2) de Welle wapentac (13 cent.).
(3) Henrici ij. de Welle wapentac' (12 cent.).
The strip at the foot for the seal, and perhaps a ribband, have been torn off.
Size: 6⅜ x 3¼ inches (without the strip).
Marginalia in A: 2⅃ + R' N φ Welle wapentac.
Texts: MS—Orig. A1/1/17. A. S28 (only the last eight words remain). P16.
Iv(24).   Pd—E.H.R.xxiv,307.   C.C.R.iv,142–3(24).   Delisle, p. 560 (abs.).
Var. R.: [1] Lincol' P.   [2] unquam A Iv.   [3] Illud P.   [4] Dunelm' A P Iv.   [5] Biset
A S P.   [6] Eboracvm P.

124

156. Writ of Henry II, commanding the sheriff of Lincolnshire
to cause a recognition to be made by the oath of lawful citizens of
Lincoln to show whether the canons of Lincoln were seised, on
the day on which king Henry I was alive and dead [1 December,
1135], of the land near the water of the city, which Martell gave
them.   At Tinchebrai.   (1155–1166.)

De terra Martelli[1] (A marg.).

.H. rex Anglorum 7 dux Normannorum 7 Aquitanorum 7 comes
Andegauorum . vicecomiti Linc'[2] sire[3] ؛ salutem ; Precipio tibi
quod sine dilatione facias recognosci per sacramentum legalium
ciuium Linc'[4] ؛ si canonici Linc'[2] fuerunt saisiti de terra quam
Martellus eis dedit iuxta aquam ciuitatis ؛ anno 7 die quo rex .H.
auus meus fuit uiuus 7 mortuus . 7 postea iniuste 7 sine iudicio
dissaisiti ؛ tunc precipio quod sine dilatione 7 iuste inde resaisiantur .
et teneant bene 7 in pace 7 iuste . libere 7 quiete 7 honorifice . Et

H. Rex Angl' 7 Dux Norm' 7 Aquit' 7 Com' And'. Ciuib3 Baronib3 7 Vauasoribg 7 oibg suis q'
eneas tenent infra Wellouuapent. Salt. Sciatis me accessisse 7 p'senti carta mea affirmasse Eccle
Line 7 Rob'to ep'o Line Wellouuapent de me tenend. Quare uolo 7 firmit' p'cipio q3 uenianr
ad placit' 7 Wapent ep'i Line p' summonicem ministror suor 7 faciatis ei g'cuetudines 7 recta
g'cuetudines in eisd' rebg q'f ei debent de cerp' s'uicijs ad ill' Wapent. ita plenarie sic uniq' m'lis'
7 plen' itc'ue Incessit' sug' forefacts. Et si feceris. Ipse uos iusticiet p' pecunia uinam de
uos faciatis ei q'qd iustu 7 ex g'cuetudinib3 Wapent' ei facn deberis. Istud Wapent eccle Line
7 Rob'to ep'o de me tenent' q'eds 7 affirmo sicut carta henr' Reg' aui mei t'. T.
Rog' ebor' Archiep's. Hug' Durelm' ep'o. Ricart' de Luci. 7 Manass' Biss' dap' ap' etonac'.

H. Rex Angl' 7 Dux Norm' 7 Ag' 7 Com' And' oibg Line'sg' Salt.
Sciatis q' qd q'n bitas sacei recognosc' p' iu'dm' leg'liu Line q'
canonici Line fuere saisiti de t'ra q'm Masoell' cul sedem uer' q'm
tenuerit. Anno 7 die q' bor' h. Rex me bue aui 7 morcu' 7 sca Line'g'
ti bit' Reg' usto ei corpus q3 su bitae 7 iube sca p'bla'stam' ec teneant
b'n 7 in pace 7 iuste libe q'etam' 7 honorifice. 7 n pernanc' in p'iudic'
do in Angl' p'd'ca n p'nc'. Et n l'dil' belse mih faciam'. T.
Bisg dap' ap's Tonnebr'gen.

H. Rex Angl' 7 Dux Norm' 7 Ag'ann' 7 Com' And' Iustic' Vic' Baron' 7 oibg Minist'
7 fidelib3 suis Francis 7 Anglis de Line'sg' Salt. Volo 7 p'cipio q' ecclia sca Marie de Line
7 Canonici eid' eccle teneant 7 habeant in p'nda'. Manerin de Welleton Bn' 7 in pace.
itc' 7 q'ete 7 honorifice 7 plenarie cu oibg p'nencijs Manerin sic' Rex Will'. 7 Rex Ho.
auus m's ei deder' 7 Carta sua affirmauer'. T. Ric' de Luci 7 Will'mo fil' harn'.
7 Man' Bisg dap' 7 Reinf de Esser' ap' Line'.

non ponantur inde in placitum donec in Angl*iam* redeam nisi precepero . Et nisi feceris ·′ iustic*ia* mea faciat . Teste . M. Bis*et*[5] dapifero apud Tenechebrai.[6]

Facsimile opposite page 100.
Endorsed : (1) XLIII .H. ij. (13 cent.).　　(2) de terra canonicorum iuxta aquam (13 cent.).
Strip at the foot for seal, and ribband.　Size : 6 x 3½ inches.
Marginalia : R' De terra Martelli.
Texts : MS—Orig. A1/1/22.　A.　S29.　R46.　Pd—*E.H.R.*xxiv,308.　Delisle, p. 565.
Var. R. : [1] De terra quam Martellus dedit S marg. ;　De terra pertinente ad prebendam de Thorngate R rubric. [2] Lincol' A S. [3] scire S A. [4] Lincol' S. [5] Mann' Biset A S. [6] Tenechebrai R.

125

157. Writ of Henry II, granting to the church of Lincoln and its canons the tithes of all moneys from all his forests in the counties of Northampton, Huntingdon, Buckingham, and Oxford, as they best had them in the time of Henry I.　At Lincoln.　(1155–1158.)

De decimis foresta*riorum*[1] (marg.).

.H. rex Angl*orum* ⁊ dux Norm*annorum* ⁊ Aquit*anorum* ⁊ comes Ande*gauorum* . iustic*iariis* . ⁊ vicecomitibus . ⁊[2] baronibus ⁊ forestariis . ⁊[2] ministris . ⁊ omnibus fidelibus suis de Norhamte scira . ⁊ Hunted' scira[3] . ⁊ Buchingeham scira . ⁊ Oxenef' scira . salutem . Sciatis me concessisse ecclesie sancte Marie Linc'[4] . ⁊ canonicis eiusdem ecclesie decimas omnium denariorum de omnibus forestis meis de quatuor predictis comitatibus ita bene ⁊ in pace ⁊[2] libere ⁊ quiete ⁊[2] *plenarie ⁊ integre habendas sicut eas melius ⁊ plenius[5] ⁊ integrius habuerunt tempore regis .H. aui mei . Testibus . Th*oma* cancellario . ⁊ Warino filio G*eroldi* camerario . ⁊ Mann*assero* Biset dapifero . apud Lincoliam.

Marginalia : ⅔ ·j· De decimis foresta*riorum* . [Va]cat V. φ
Texts : MS—A.　S30.　P17.　R47.
Var. R. : [1] Carta de decimis omnium denariorum de forestis quatuor comitatuum subscriptorum R rubric. [2] *om.* ⁊ P. [3] schir' R. [4] Lincol' S P. [5] *om.* ⁊ plenius R.

Folio 23.

Hdl.　　　　*Henrici* REGIS SECUNDI.　　　　　.2.3.

126

158. Writ of Henry II, confirming to the church of Lincoln his grandfather's gift of the churches in Lincoln which their priests held of the king (see no. 45 above).　At Lincoln.　(Probably January, 1154–1155.)

De omnibus ecclesiis Linc' (marg.).

.H. rex Angl*orum* . dux Norm*annorum* . ⁊ Aquit*anorum* . ⁊ comes Ande*gauorum* . iustic' . vice*comit'* . baronibus . Francis ⁊ Anglis de Lincol' scira[1] salutem . Sciatis me concessisse ⁊ confirmasse ecclesie beate Marie Linc'[2] in perpetuam elemosinam

donationem illam quam Henricus[3] rex auus meus fecit eidem ecclesie
de omnibus ecclesiis Lincol' que sunt intra murum 7 extra murum
quas presbiteri earumdem ecclesiarum· de ipso rege tenebant cum
omnibus ad easdem ecclesias pertinentibus . Testibus . Theobaldo[4] .
Cantuariensi archiepiscopo . 7 Romane ecclesie legato . 7 Philippo
Baiocensi episcopo . 7 Ernulfo[5] Luxouiensi episcopo . apud
Lincoliam.

Marginalia: + preb' De ecclesiis Linc' va cat V N † vide plus in folio
7 et folio 27 (the reference being to no. 45 above and no. 196 below).
Texts: MS—A. S31. P18. R42.
Var. R.: [1] Linc' scir' R.   [2] Lincol' S.   [3] .H. P.   [4] Teobald' S.   [5] Arnulpho R.

127

159. Writ of Henry II, confirming to the church of Lincoln
and bishop Robert II and his successors Henry I's grant of the manor
of Kilsby [co. Northampton] (see no. 43 above). At Nottingham.
(1155–1158.)

De Kildesby[1] (A marg.).
.H. rex Anglorum . 7 d[ux Normannorum . 7 Aquitanorum[2]] .
7 comes Andegauorum . i[usticiariis . baronibus . vicecomitibus .
7[2]] omnibus fidelibus suis Francis 7 Anglis ꞉ salutem . Sciatis me
c[oncessisse deo 7 sancte Marie[2]] 7 ecclesie Lincoliensi[3] . 7 Roberto
episcopo . 7 omnibus success[oribus suis episcopis Linc'[2]] manerium
de Kylesbya[4] cum soca 7 saca 7 omnibus [aliis consuetudinibus
suis sicut[2]] unquam[5] melius fuit tempore regis Eduardi[6] . 7 reg[is
Willelmi . 7 regis Henrici aui[2]] mei . 7 sicut carta predicti regis .
H. aui [mei testatur quod illud manerium[2]] predicte ecclesie Lincol'[7]
reddidit cum omnib[us predictis libertatibus 7 consuetudinibus[2]]
suis . Testibus . Rogero archiepiscopo Eboracensi . 7 [Thoma[8]
cancellario . 7 comite Reginaldo[2] .] apud Notingeham.

Endorsed: (1) . . . .   (2) de manerio Kylesbi (13 cent.).
(3) XXXIII .H. ij. (13 cent.).
Strip for seal, and narrow ribband below it. The right hand end of the charter
has perished. Size: 5⅝ x 3½ inches.
Marginalia in A: ⚹
Texts: MS—Orig. A1/1/19. A. S32 (ends with the words Kylesbia cum). P19
(ends with the words regis Willelmi). Iv(26). Pd—E.H.R.xxiv,307. C.C.R.iv,143
(26). Delisle, p. 560 (abs.).
Var. R.: [1] De manerio de Kildesbi S.   [2] supplied from A.   [3] Lincol' P.   [4] Kylesbia
A S P Iv.   [5] umquam P.   [6] Edwardi A; Eadwardi P.   [7] Lincolie A.   [8] Toma Iv.

128

160. Writ of Henry II, confirming to the church of Lincoln
Henry I's grant of twelve bovates in Burgh [on Bain] and six bovates
in [South] Willingham [co. Lincoln] (see no. 42 above). At
Argentan. (1155–1162.)

De .xii. bouatis terre .vj. in Burgo .vi. in Wollingham (marg.).
.H. rex Anglorum 7 dux Normannorum . 7 Aquitanorum . 7

comes And*egauorum* . archiepiscopis . episcopis . abbatibus .
comitibus . baronibus . iustic*iariis* . vicecomitibus . ministris . 7
omnibus fidelibus suis Anglie salutem . Sciatis me concessisse 7
confirmasse deo 7 ecclesie Lincol' .xii. bouatas terre . quas Radulfus
Basset disrationauit esse in dominio meo . videlicet .vi. bouatas
in Burgo . 7 .vi. bouatas in Wellingeham[1] . Quare uolo 7 firmiter
precipio quod eas teneat bene 7 in pace 7 libere 7 quiete 7 honorifice
cum soca 7 saca 7 tol 7 team 7 infangenthef cum omnibus libertatibus
7 liberis consuetudinibus cum quibus tenet alias terras suas sicut
carta .H. regis[2] aui mei testatur . Testibus . Philippo episcopo
Baio*censi* . Ernulfo episcopo Lexou*iensi* . Thoma cancellario .
Roberto de Nouo Burgo . Willelmo filio Hamonis . apud Argen-
tomum[3].

Marginalia : 2 φ + De xii bouatis . . . . .
Texts : MS—A. Iiv(4).   Pd—*C.C.R.*iv,107(4).
Var. R. : [1] Welingeham Iiv.   [2] regis H. Iiv.   [3] Argentonium Iiv.

129

161. Writ of Henry II, granting to bishop Robert II and his
successors licence to have a yearly fair in their town of Louth,
beginning on the third Sunday after Easter, and lasting for eight
days. At Woodstock. (1155–1158.)

De feria in Luda (marg.).

.H. rex Angl*orum* . 7 dux Norm*annorum* . 7 Aquit*anorum* . 7
comes And*egauorum* . archiepiscopis . episcopis . abbatibus .
comitibus . iustic*iariis* .[1] vicecomitibus . ministris . 7 omnibus
fidelibus suis Francis 7 Anglis[2] tocius Anglie salutem . Sciatis me
concessisse Roberto episcopo Linc' 7 omnibus successoribus suis
ut habeant singulis annis unam feriam in Luda uilla sua[3] . 7 incipiat
feria illa dominica die tercia post diem Pasche . 7 duret .viii. dies .
Et uolo* 7 firmiter precipio quod ecclesia Lincol' 7 Robertus episcopus
7 successores sui habeant 7 teneant in perpetuam elemosinam
feriam illam cum omnibus illis libertatibus 7 consuetudinibus quas
ferie mee[4] habent in regno meo Anglie . Testibus . Thoma[5] cancellario .
7 Warino filio Ger*oldi* camerario . 7 Mann*assero*[6] Biset dapifero . 7
Ricardo de Campiuilla . apud Wodestocam[7].

Marginalia : 2 R' De feria Lude.
Texts : MS—A. Iiv(20).   Pd—*C.C.R.*iv,110–11(20).
Var. R. in Iiv : [1] *insert* baronibus.   [2] Anglicis.   [3] villa sua de Luda.   [4] mee ferie.
[5] T.   [6] M.   [7] Wudestocam.

Folio 23d.
Hdl.   CARTE . REGIS .*H. Secundi.*

130

162. Writ of Henry II, commanding the barons of the Exchequer to allow to the sheriff of Lincolnshire and the reeves of
Lincoln in the king's *firma* of Lincoln thirteen pence every year

in respect of landgable for the land which the king gave to the
church of Lincoln and bishop Robert II and his successors for their
buildings; and, further, in the year in which *parcagium* shall go
by way of Lincoln, to allow them seven shillings and seven pence
because the king gave the land quit of all secular service and custom.
At Lincoln. (1155–1158, probably 1157.)

De .xiii. denariis computandis ad scaccarium pro terra domini
episcopi in Linc'[1] (marg.).

.H. rex Angl*orum* . 7 dux Norm*annorum* . 7 Aquit*anorum* . 7
comes Andeg*auorum* . baronibus . de scacario[2] *:* salutem . Computate
vice*comiti* de Lincol' scira . 7 prepositi*is*[3] . Linc' . singulis annis in
firma mea Lincol'[4] .xiii. denarios . de langabulo pro terra quam
dedi ecclesie Lincol'[4] 7 Roberto episcopo Lincol'[4] 7 successoribus
in perpetuam elemosinam ad edificia sua . Et preter hoc anno
quo *parcagium* ibit per uiam[5] Lincol'[4] *:* computate eis . vii. solidos .
7 .vii. denarios . quia ego dedi terram illam deo 7 sancte Marie
7 episcopis Lincol'[4] in perpetuam elemosinam ad edificia sua
solutam[6] . quietam ab omni seculari seruitio 7 consuetudine .
Testibus . Thoma cancellario . 7 R'. comite Legrecest*rie* . 7 Ricardo .
de Hum*ez* constabulario . 7 Warino filio Ger*oldi* camerario . apud
Lincol'.[7]

Marginalia: 2 ·j· preb' uillam De terra Linc'.
Texts: MS—A. S33 (*the part preceding* ego dedi terram *is missing*). R21.
Var. R.: [1] Carta de allocacione xiij denariorum de langabulo pro palacio episcopi
R rubric. [2] scaccario R. [3] prepositis R. [4] Linc' R. [5] villam R ; *in* A uillam *is
written opposite in marg.* [6] *insert* 7 S R. [7] Lincoliam S R.

131

163. Writ of Henry II, confirming to the church of Lincoln
Henry I's gift of the manor of Nettleham (see no. 61 above). At
Winchester. (1155–1158.)

De manerio de Netelham (marg.).

.H. rex Anglorum . 7 dux Norm*annorum* . 7 Aquit*anorum* . 7
comes Andeg*auorum* . archiepiscopis . episcopis . comitibus .
baronibus . iustici*ariis* . vicecomitibus . ministris . 7 omnibus
fidelibus suis tocius Anglie Francis 7 Anglis salutem . Sciatis me
concessisse 7 confirmasse ecclesie sancte Marie de Linc'[1] in perpetuam elemosinam manerium de Netelham cum omnibus pertinenciis suis . quod rex .H. auus meus concessu Matildis regine
aue méé cuius[2] tunc erat eidem ecclesie dedit 7 per cartam suam
confirmauit . Quare uolo 7 firmiter precipio quod predicta ecclesia
teneat manerium illud bene 7 in pace 7 libere 7 quiete 7 integre
7 honorifice cum omnibus pertinenciis suis . in boscho[3] . 7 plano .
in pratis . 7 paschuis[4] . in viis . 7 semitis . in aquis . 7 molendinis .
7 in omnibus rebus cum omnibus libertatibus 7 liberis consuetudinibus cum quibus rex .H. auus meus 7 Matild*is* regina aua mea illud

tenebant die qua illud predicte ecclesie concesserunt . sicut carta eiusdem regis Henrici . aui mei testatur . Testibus . Thoma cancellario . 7 Ricardo de⁵ Hum*ez* constabulario . 7 Mann*assero* Biset dapifero . 7 Warino filio Ger*oldi* camerario . Willelmo filio Hamonis . Joscelino de Baillol'⁶ . apud Wintoniam.

Marginalia : 2.　φ　De Net . . . .
Texts : MS—A.　S34 (*some words are illegible through decay*).　P6 (*the text is missing before* eiusdem regis aui mei testatur).　Iii(3).　Iv(31).　Pd—*C.C.R.*ii,271(3). See *C.C.R.*iv,144(31).
Var. R. : ¹ Lincol' S.　² cuius *is written on an erasure* A.　³ bosco S Iii Iv. ⁴ pascuis S Iii Iv.　⁵ *om*. de P.　⁶ Baioll' P.

132

164. Writ of Henry II, confirming to the church of Lincoln the grant of the church of Corringham with two and a half carucates which were Brand the priest's (see no. 35 above). At Oxford. (1155–1158.)

De ecclesia de Coringham' 7 .ii. carucatis terre 7 dimidia (marg.).

.H. rex Angl*orum* . 7 dux Norm*annorum* . 7 Aquit*anorum* . 7 comes Ande*gauorum* . archiepiscopis . episcopis . comitibus . vicecomitibus . baronibus . 7 omnibus ministris 7 fidelibus suis Francis 7 Anglis salutem . Sciatis me concessisse 7 in perpetuam elemosinam confirmasse pro anima patris mei 7 antecessorum meorum deo 7 ecclesie sancte Marie de Linc'¹ ecclesiam de Coringeham . 7 omnia pertinentia ecclesie cum duabus carrucatis terre 7 dimidia que fuerunt Brand presbiteri . Quare uolo 7 firmiter precipio quod predicta ecclesia Linc'¹ teneat 7 habeat predictam ecclesiam de Coringeham² 7 duas carrucatas terre 7 dimidiam in prebendam libere 7 quiete 7 honorifice 7 plenarie in bosco 7 plano in pratis *7 pasturis³ in uiis 7 semitis 7 in omnibus aliis rebus cum socha . 7 sacha . 7 tol . 7 theam . 7 infangenthef⁴ 7 omnibus libertatibus 7 liberis consuetudinibus . Testibus . Thoma cancellario . 7 Ricardo de Luci . 7 Willelmo filio Hamonis . 7 Man*assero* Biset dapifero . apud Oxneford*iam*.⁵

Marginalia : 2.　φ　va　cat　De Cor . . . . .
Texts : MS—A.　S35.　P7.　Iiv(3).　Pd—*C.C.R.*iv,106(3).
Var. R. : ¹ Lincol' S P ; Lincoln' Iiv.　² Coringeh' S P.　³ pascuis P.　⁴ team 7 infangeneyef Iiv.　⁵ Oxene. . . . . S ; Oxeneford' P.

*Folio 24.

Hdl.　　　　　*Carte . Regis .* Henrici . Secundi.　　　　.2.4.

133

165. Writ of Henry II, confirming to bishop Robert II, for his life, Henry I's grant of the third penny of the wapentake of Stow to the bishop's predecessor. At Winchester. (1155–1158.) No. 178 below is another copy of this writ.

De firma de wapentac Stow'[1] (marg.).

.H. rex Anglorum . 7 dux Normannorum . 7 Aquitanorum[2] . 7 comes Andegauorum . vicecomiti suo de Lincol' scira[3] . 7 omnibus baronibus suis Francis 7 Anglis[4] de Lincol' scira salutem . Sciatis me concessisse Roberto Lincol'[5] episcopo tercium denarium de wapentac del[6] Stowa[7] ad firmam pro .x. libris[8] . numero uno quoque anno quam diu uixerit . sicut rex .H. auus meus illum dederat 7 concesserat predecessori suo Roberto Lincol' episcopo . Testibus . Thoma[9] cancellario . 7 Warino filio Geroldi camerario . apud Wintoniam.

Marginalia: 2| ɸ preb' . . . De tercio denario De iii denario . . Well' wap'. +
Texts: MS—A133. A146. S36. P10. Iv(27). Pd—C.C.R.iv,143(27).
Var R.: [1] De decem libris pro wapentac de Estou S marg.; De decem libris pro wapentac de Stow P marg. [2] C.C.R. (but not Iv) omits 7 Aquit'. [3] Linc' scira A146; Linc' sir' P. [4] Angl' Iv. [5] Linc' A146 P. [6] de P. [7] Estowa A146 Iv; Stouwa S P. [8] per .x. libras S P. [9] Tom' Iv.

134

166. Writ of Henry II, confirming to the church of Lincoln and the canons thereof William II's gift of the manor of Welton [by Lincoln] (see no. 3 above). At Lincoln. (1154–1158.)

De manerio de Welleton'[1] (A marg.).

H. rex Anglorum 7 dux Normannorum 7 Aquitanorum 7 comes Andegauorum . iustic' . vicecomit' . baronibus . 7 omnibus ministris 7 fidelibus suis Francis 7 Anglis de Linc'[2] scira . salutem . Volo 7 precipio quod ecclesia sancte Marie de Linc'[2] 7 canonici eiusdem ecclesie . teneant 7 habeant in prebendam ⁚ manerium de Welletona . bene . 7 in pace 7 libere . 7 quiete . 7 honorifice . 7 plenarie . cum omnibus pertinentibus manerii . sicut . rex Willelmus . 7 rex .H.[3] auus meus eis dederunt . 7 carta sua confirmauerunt . Testibus . Ricardo de Luci . 7 Willelmo filio Hamonis . 7 Manassero Biset[4] dapifero . 7 Henrico de Essexa[5] . apud Linc'.[6]

Facsimile facing page 100.
Endorsed: (1) Confirmatio H. ij. de Welletuna (13 cent.). (2) de maneria de Welletun' (13 cent.). (3) xij visa (query Q).
Strip for seal, and a ribband below it. Size: 6¾ x 2⅝ inches.
Marginalia in A: 2 . . . ɸ preb' va cat + De . . . .
Texts: MS—Orig. A1/1/38. A. S37. P11 (the text ends with the words manerium de Welletona). R35. Pd—E.H.R.xxiv,311. See Delisle, pp. 549–50.
Var. R.: [1] Welletona S; Welletun P. [2] Lincol' A S. [3] Henr' S. [4] Biset A S. [5] Essex A S. [6] Lincol' A; Lincoliam S.

135

167. Writ of Henry II, commanding that the canons of Lincoln shall hold their prebends as they best had them in the time of Henry I. At Oxford. (1155–1162.)

De libertatibus canonicorum[1] (marg.).

.H. rex Anglorum . 7 dux Normannorum 7 Aquitanorum . 7 comes Andegauorum . iusticiariis . vicecomitibus . 7 omnibus ministris suis in quorum ballia canonici Lincol' terras uel prebendas habent . salutem . Precipio quod canonici Linc'[2] teneant 7 habeant prebendas suas in ecclesiis 7 decimis . in domibus . 7 terris . in hominibus . 7 denariis . 7 in omnibus aliis rebus ita libere . 7 quiete . 7 honorifice . 7 plenarie sicut unquam habuerunt tempore regis .H. aui mei . cum[3] soch 7 sach[4] 7 tol aut thiam[5] 7 infangenþef[6] . [7]Testibus . Thoma cancellario . 7 Ricardo de Humez constabulario . 7 Willelmo de Lanualaþon[8] . 7 Hugone de Pirariis . apud Oxenefordiam.[9]

Marginalia : 2. preb' + va cat V iij⁰ + ·j· De lib' . . . . Nota (Q). Texts : MS—A. S38. R37.
Var. R. : [1] De libertatibus concessis canonicis Lincoln' 7 de socca 7 sacca thol 7 team 7 infangenethef' R rubric ; Libertates terre in ballio R marg. ; De libertatibus prebendarum S marg. [2] Linc' interlineated A ; Lincol' S. [3] cum soch . . . infangenþef written in marg. and marked for insertion in text S. [4] socca 7 sacca R. [5] thol 7 them R. [6] infangenethef R. [7] S inserts an extra clause which, however, is marked va cat—Et va prohibeo nequis eis super hoc iniuriam uel contumeliam faciat cat. [8] Lanualayo R. [9] Oxeneford R.

136

168. Writ of Henry II, confirming to the church of Lincoln Robert de Stotvill's gift as testified by the charter of Henry I (see no. 44 above). At Westminster. (1154–1171.)

De domibus Roberti de Stoteuill'[1] (A marg.).

H. rex Anglorum 7 dux Normannorum 7 Aquitanorum . 7 comes Andegauorum . ar[chiepiscopis . episcopis . comitibus . vicecomitibus .[2]] baronibus . 7 omnibus fidelibus suis Francis 7 Anglis . salutem . Sciatis me concessisse 7 confirmass[e in perpetuam elemosinam[2]] 7 prebendam ꞏ/ deo 7 ecclesie sancte Marie de Linc'[3] . pro anima patris mei 7 antecessorum meorum . omnes domos quas R[obertus de[2]] Stoteuilla[4] dedit 7 concessit deo 7 predicte ecclesie . Quare uolo . 7 firmiter precipio quod ecclesia sancte Marie Linc'[3] teneat 7 habeat domos illas bene . 7 in pace . 7 libere . 7 quiete . 7 honorifice . 7 plenarie . cum omnibus libertatibus . 7 liberis consuetudinibus . et sicut carta regis .H.[5] aui mei testatur . Testibus . Roberto comite Legrecestrie[6] . 7 Ricardo de Humez constabulario . 7 Manassero* Biset[7] dapifero . 7 Willelmo filio Hamonis . 7 Nigello de Broch' . apud Westmonasterium.

Endorsed : (1) XXXVIII (13 cent.). (2) xvij visa (13 cent.). (3) de prebenda Philippi (12 cent.).
Strip for seal, and ribband below it. Size : 7¼ x 3¼ inches.
Marginalia in A : 2. φ va cat V.
Texts : MS—Orig. A1/1/21. A. S39 (the text ends with the words libere 7 quiete). R41. Pd—E.H.R.xxiv,308. Delisle, pp.563–4 (abs.).
Var. R. : [1] Scotr' R marg. [2] supplied from A, the text of the original charter having been injured. [3] Lincol' A S. [4] Scot' R. [5] Henr' A. [6] Legrecest' A. [7] Biset A.
Note : This land seemingly formed part of the endowment of the prebend of Thorngate (see page 277, below).

*Folio 24d.
Hdl.   HENRICI REGIS Secundi

137

169. Writ of Henry II, in almost the same words as no. 160 above. At Nottingham. (1154–1162.)

De .xii. bouatis terre in Burgo 7 Wollingham' (marg.).

.H. rex An*gl*orum . 7 dux Norm*annorum* . 7 Aquit*anorum* . 7 comes Ande*gauorum* . comitibus . baronibus . vice*comit*' . ministris 7 omnibus fidelibus suis de Lincol' scira salutem . Sciatis me concessisse 7 confirmasse[1] deo 7 sancte Marie de Lincol' .xii. bouatas terre quas Radulfus Basset disrationauit esse in dominio meo . scilicet .vi. bouatas in Burgo . 7 .vi. bouatas in Wellingeh*am'* . Quare uolo 7 firmiter precipio quod predicta ecclesia eas teneat bene 7 in pace 7 libere 7 quiete 7 honorifice 7 plenarie cum socha . 7 sacha 7 tol 7 theam 7 infangenþef 7 cum omnibus libertatibus 7 liberis consuetudinibus sicut carta regis Henrici aui mei testatur . Testibus . Thoma cancellario . 7 Ricardo de Luci . 7 Man*assero* Biset dapifero . 7 Roberto de Wateuill' . apud Notingeham.

Marginalia : ♃ + + φ De . xii . bouatis . . . . . .
Text : MS—A.
Var. R. : [1] 7 confirmasse *inserted in marg., and marked for insertion in text.*

138

170. Writ of Henry II, confirming to the church of Lincoln and bishop Robert II Henry I's grant of a fair at the bishop's castle of Newark (see no. 48 above). At York. (1154–1156.)

De feria de Newerc (A marg.).

.H'. rex An*gl*orum 7 dux Norm*annorum* 7 Aquit*anorum* 7 comes Ande*gauorum* . archiepiscopis . episcopis . abbatibus . comitibus . baronibus 7 omnibus fidelibus suis tocius An*gl*ie ⁛ salutem . Sciatis me concessisse 7 presenti carta mea confirmasse ecclesie Linc' 7 Roberto episcopo Linc' . 7 successoribus suis unam feriam de .v. diebus ad castellum suum de Niwerc*a* . scilicet die festi beate Marie Magdalene 7 .iiij.[1] primis precedentibus diebus . Quare uolo 7 firmiter precipio quod omnes illi undecumque sint qui illuc uenerint causa emendi uel uendendi meam firmam pacem habeant in eundo 7 redeundo . Et prohibeo ne quis eos iniuste disturbet . uel mercat*um*[2] eorum unde in feria suas rectas dederint consuetudines . super .x. libras forisfacture . Et hanc predictam feriam cum libertatibus suis concedo 7 confirmo episcopo Linc'[3] ⁛ sicut carta Henrici regis aui mei testatur . Testibus . Rogero archiepiscopo Eborac*ensi* . H. Dunolm*ensi*[4] episcopo . 7 Ricardo de Luci[5] ⁛ apud Eboracum.

Endorsed : (1) VII .H. ij. (13 cent.). (2) De feria de Newerc*a* (13 cent.). (3) De feria quinque diebus ad castellum de Newerc (13 cent.).
Strip for seal, and a ribband below it. Size : 6¼ x 6¼ inches.
Marginalia in A : ♃. φ
Texts : MS—Orig. A1/1/29. A. Iiv(19). Pd—*E.H.R.*xxiv,304–5. *C.C.R.*iv, 110(19). Delisle, p. 561 (abs.).
Var. R. : [1] iiij*or* A. [2] mercatum A. [3] Lincol' A. [4] Hug' Dunelm' A. [5] Luzi A.

139

171. Writ of Henry II, confirming to the church of Lincoln and the canons thereof Henry I's grant of a vineyard in Lincoln (see no. 23 above). At Woodstock [co. Oxford]. (1155–1162.)

De vinea Linc' (marg.).

.H. rex Anglorum . 7 dux Normannorum 7 Aquitanorum . 7 comes Andegauorum . iustic' . vicecomit' . baronibus . [1]7 omnibus[1] ministris suis 7 fidelibus de Lincol'[2] scira salutem . Sciatis me concessisse 7 confirmasse deo 7 sancte Marie Lincol'[2] 7 canonicis eiusdem ecclesie ; uineam meam Linc' cum omnibus uinéé pertinentibus . Quare uolo 7 firmiter precipio quod predicta ecclesia 7 canonici uineam illam cum omnibus pertinenciis teneant 7 habeant bene 7 in pace 7[3] libere 7 quiete 7 honorifice 7 plenarie sicut carta regis .H. aui mei[4] testatur . Testibus . Thoma cancellario . 7 Ricardo de Luci[5] . 7 Manassero Biset dapifero . apud Wdestocham.[6]

Marginalia: ♃ 7 postea folio 164 (the reference being to A856) (Q).
Texts: MS—A139. A856. S40 (the text preceding the words precipio quod is wanting). R801.
Var. R.: [1–1] om. 7 omnibus A856 where a blank space is left for these words. [2] Linc' A856 R. [3] om. 7 R. [4] nostri R. [5] Luzi A856. [6] Wudestok' R.

140

172. Writ of Henry II, commanding that bishop Robert II shall hold his ferry of Newton [on Trent, co. Lincoln] as his predecessors best held it in the time of Henry I, and as it was acknowledged in the shire [court]. At Angers. (1155–1162.)

De passagio de Newentona[1] (marg.).

.H. rex Anglorum . 7 dux Normannorum . 7 Aquitanorum . 7 comes Andegauorum . iustic' . 7 vicecomit' . 7 ministris suis de Lincol' scira[2] salutem . Precipio quod Robertus episcopus Linc'[3] teneat bene 7 in pace 7 quiete 7 iuste passagium suum de Newentona sicut antecessores sui* melius tenuerunt tempore regis Henrici aui mei . 7 sicut recognitum est in comitatu . Teste . Thoma cancellario . apud Angeriacum.

Marginalia: φ.
Texts: MS—A. S41. Iiv(15). Pd—C.C.R.iv,110(15).
Var. R.: [1] Newentona S marg. [2] Linc'scyra Iiv. [3] Lincol' S Iiv.

*Folio 25.

Hdl.   *Henrici Regis* SECUNDI.   .2.5.

141

173. Writ of Henry II, commanding that those who serve the church of Lincoln shall have their liberties and customs as they best had them in the time of Henry I. At 'Wigoan.' (1155–1162.)

De libertatibus seruientum [*sic*] ecclesie Linc'[1] (marg.).

.H. rex Ang*lorum* . 7 dux Norm*annorum* 7 Aquit*anorum* . 7 comes Andeg*auorum* . vicecom*it*' . 7 prepositis suis Lincol' salutem . Precipio quod proprii seruientes sancte Marie Linc' habeant omnes libertates suas 7 consuetudines in omnibus rebus sicut unquam melius habuerunt tempore regis .H. aui mei . Et prohibeo ne quis eis super hoc iniuriam faciat . nec in nouas consuetudines ponat . Teste . Thoma cancellario . apud Wigoan'.

Marginalia: va cat V d' Nota(Q).
Texts: MS—A. S42.
Var. R.: [1] *for* ecclesie Linc' *read* sancte Marie S marg.

142

174. Writ of Henry II, commanding that those who serve the church of Lincoln shall be free of all things, as they were in the time of Henry I. At Woodstock. (1154–1171.)

De eodem[1] (A marg.).

.H'. rex Ang*lorum* 7 dux Norm*annorum* 7 Aquit*anorum* 7 comes Andeg*auorum* . iustic' . 7 vicecom*it*' 7 preposit*is* 7 burgensibus Linc' . salutem . Precipio quod seruientes ecclesie sancte Marie de Linc' sint ita liberi de omnibus rebus sicut fuerunt tempore regis .H. aui mei . Teste . Man*assero* Bis*et* dapifero 7 Nigello de Broc apud Wudestoc*am*.[2]

Facsimile opposite.
Endorsed: (1) LII (13 cent.). (2) de libertate seruiencium ecclesie (12 cent.).
The strip for the seal has been torn off: the ribband below it remains. Size: 5½ x 2⅝ inches.
Marginalia in A: 2 preb' + φ + ·j· va cat V.
Texts: MS—Orig. ʌ1/1/24. A. S43. R40. Pd—*E.H.R.*xxiv,309.
Var R.: [1] De libertatibus seruientium sancte Marie S marg.; De libertatibus concessis seruientibus ecclesie Linc' R marg. [2] Wdestoch' A S; Wodestok' R.

143

175. Writ of Henry II, commanding the reeves of Lincoln to cause an acknowledgment to be made by the oaths of the most ancient and lawful men of that city, before the sheriff of Lincolnshire, of the franchises which the bishops of Lincoln had in their land at Lincoln and in burgage in the time of Henry I, and of what franchises the clerks of the city had at the same time; and, in accordance with the acknowledgement, to cause bishop Robert II and his men of Lincoln and the clerks of the city to have those franchises, and to demand no new customs from them. The king also commands the reeves to cause the bishop to hold his tenements in the city as any one of his predecessors best held them in the time of Henry I. At Woodstock. (1155–1165.)

H. Rex Angl' 7 Dux Norm' 7 Aq' 7 Com And' 7 Iusti... 7
...uic' 7 burgen' ib; linc. Sal'. Scipio qd seruicac' eccl'e ...
... in linc. sunt ita libe'i de omib; reb; sicut 7 ...
... degn' h. dns m'. ...

H. Rex Angl' 7 Dux Norm' 7 Aq' 7 Com And' pposit'i 7 ...ib; Lnc
sal'. Scipio qd ius falconarii m' 7 heor' fuit 7 filii sui 7 filii sui
fuit i pace 7 gen de placit'i 7 ...t 7 Geldis 7 Assisis 7 oib; consue
tudinib; q ad me ptinent. ppt' seruic' suu qd i' debet de accipitrib; 7
falconib; ...grend' Qf uolo qd manuteneatis 7 honoretis eu 7 iuue
... ad seruiciu meu facieñdu 7 firma pace iuste illi teneatis. T. T.
m' Cancell' 7 ... Bifer' ap' Westmon'

... h'eo electione 7 fieade'it de thom' abbe elect ... ...melb; ...
...nat 7 ...or qd fiead'is ei ipm mlnu benedicat'is ... ...api ...
... de ...melb. 7 mlnu ... ... no ...
... ...nustin' de ...melb ...
eide. T. Well' ...t' a't'b ...p' ...billa.

... ...
... ...melb.

De inquisitione facienda super libertatibus episcopi in burgagio Linc' (marg.).

.H. rex . Angl*orum* . 7 dux Norm*annorum* . 7 Aquit*anorum* . 7 comes Ande*gauorum* . prepositis Linc' ? salutem . Precipio nobis quod sine dilatione faciatis recognosci per sacramenta antiquorum 7 legalium hominum ciuitatis Linc' coram vicecom*ite* de Lincol' scir*a* . in summonitionem vicecom*itis* . libertates quas episcopi Linc'[1] habuerunt in terra sua Linc' . 7 in burgagio suo tempore regis .H. aui mei . 7 quas libertates clerici ciuitatis Linc' habuerunt eodem tempore . Et sicut recognitum fuerit ita sine dilatione faciatis habere Roberto Linc' episcopo 7 hominibus suis Linc' 7 clericis ciuitatis Linc' omnes illas libertates . 7 nullas nouas consuetudines ab eis exigatis . Et faciatis eundem episcopum tenere omnia tenementa sua de ciuitate Linc' bene 7 in pace 7 libere 7 honorifice cum omnibus libertatibus 7 liberis consuetudinibus suis sicut unquam aliquis antecessorum suorum melius 7 liberius tenuit tempore regis .H. aui mei . Teste . Johanne de Oxene*fordia* . apud Wdestoc'.[2]

Marginalia: φ R' ·ꝓ· d' N Nota (Q).
Texts: MS—A. Iv(23). Pd—*C.C.R.*iv,142(23).
Var. R.: [1] Lincol' Iv. [2] Wodestoc' Iv.

144

176. Writ of Henry II, commanding his reeves of Lincoln to render to the canons of Lincoln eighteen pounds yearly from the king's *firma* of Lincoln instead of those eighteen pounds which the canons were wont to have from the king's manor of Kirton [in Lindsey]. At Westminster. (1155–1175.)

De .xviii. libris de firma Linc' (marg.).

.H. rex Angl*orum* . 7 dux Norm*annorum* . 7 Aquit*anorum* . 7 comes Ande*gauorum* . prepositis suis Linc' . salutem . Precipio uobis quod reddatis canonicis Linc'[1] . xviii. libras . de firma mea Linc'[1] annuatim pro illis .xviii. libris . quas solebant habere de manerio meo de Kerketon*a* . 7 reddatis eis ad terminos quibus michi redditis firmam meam . Teste . comite Reginaldo . apud Westmon*asterium*.

Marginalia: 2 φ va cat.
Texts: MS—A. S44. R33.
Var. R.: [1] Lincol' S.

145

177. Writ of Henry II, giving to the church of Lincoln eighteen pounds of the *firma* of his city of Lincoln, in exchange for those eighteen pounds which the said church had from the king's manor of Kirton [in Lindsey]. At Westminster. (1154–1160.)

De eadem firma .xviii. libr'¹ (marg.).

.H. rex Anglorum . 7 dux Normannorum 7 Aquitanorum . 7
comes Andegauorum . archiepiscopis . episcopis . abbatibus . baronibus . iusticiariis . vicecomitibus . 7 omnibus fidelibus suis Francis
7 Anglis tocius Anglie salutem . Sciatis me dedisse ecclesie sancte
Marie Linc'² .xviii. libras de redditu ciui*tatis méé Lincol' in
escambio pro illis .xviii. libris . quas habebat in manerio meo
de Kerchetona³ . Quare uolo 7 firmiter precipio quod predicta
ecclesia illas .xviii. libras in perpetuam elemosinam libere 7 quiete
7 honorifice habeat ad terminos statutos quibus ministri mei Lincol'
michi reddunt redditus meos . Testibus . Theobaldo archiepiscopo
Cantuariensi⁴ . N. episcopo de Ely⁵ . Ricardo episcopo Lundoniensi⁶ .
H. episcopo Abrincensi . R. comite Cornubie . R. comite Legrecestrie .
R. de Humez constabulario apud Westmonasterium.

Marginalia : 2 φ va cat.
Texts : MS—A. S45 (*the text ends with the words* quas habebat in manerio). R.34.
Var. R.: ¹ Carta de octodecim libris firme in Linc' datis ecclesie in excambio
pro xviii libris in Kirketon' R rubric. ² Lincol' S. ³ Kirketona R. ⁴ Canth' R.
⁵ Eli R. ⁶ Lond' R.
Note : *The pipe roll of 31 Henry I* (p. 109) records a payment to the canons of
Lincoln in alms of £18 by tale. King Stephen gave to the canons £18 pounds in
land in the wapentake of Corringham in exchange for £18 which they were wont
to have in Kirton and Caistor for tithes *in prebenda* (nos. 83 and 89 above). This
arrangement seemingly did not persist ; for Henry II in the present text charges
the payment upon the *firma* of the city of Lincoln, and the pipe roll of his second
year has an entry, the equivalent of which appears upon the succeeding rolls : *In
decimis constitutis canonicis Lincol' .xviii. li. pro .xviii. li. quas habebant in Chirche-
tun'* (*The Great Rolls of the Pipe for 2, 3 and 4 Henry II*, p. 28). It would seem,
therefore, that the present charter and no. 176 should be placed very early in
Henry's reign. For the original grant of these tithes see no. 2 above.

Folio 25d.
Hdl. HENRICI . REGIS . *Secundi.*

146

178. Writ of Henry II. *This writ is marked* vacat *in the margin
of* A *because it is identical with no. 133 above.*

Marginalia : 2 + va cat.

147

179. Writ of Henry II, confirming to Saint Mary of Lincoln
his gifts of the church of Langford [co. Oxford] and of land there,
and also of the church of Brampton [co. Huntingdon] (see no. 139
and no. 140 above). At Brill in the Forest [of Bernwood, co.
Buckingham]. (1155–1158.)

De ecclesiis de Langeford' 7 Bramton' . 7 terris in Langeford'
(A marg.).

.H. rex Anglorum . 7 dux Normannorum . 7 Aquitanorum . 7
comes Andegauorum . archiepiscopis . episcopis . abbatibus .
comitibus . baronibus . iusticiariis . vicecomitibus . ministris . 7
omnibus hominibus 7 fidelibus suis totius Anglię Francis 7 Anglis

salutem . Sciatis me dedisse 7 carta mea presenti confirmasse .
ęcclesię beatę Marię Linc' . in perpetuam elemosinam pro amore
dei 7 anima regis .H. aui mei . 7 aliorum antecessorum meorum .
7 petitione 7 amore Roberti Linc' episcopi . ęcclesiam de Langeford'
in Oxineford' sira . cum omnibus pertinentiis eius . 7 totam terram
quam Rogerus episcopus *Sarisbiriensis* tenuit in eadem uilla de
Langueford'[1] . Et ecclesiam de Brantona in Huntend' sira[2] cum
omnibus pertinentiis eius . Quare uolo 7 firmiter precipio quod
predicta Linc' ecclesia habeat 7 teneat predictas ęcclesias 7 totam
terram prenominatam . ita bene . 7 in pace . libere . honorifice .
quiete . in bosco 7 plano in pratis 7 pascuis in aquis 7 molendinis .
7 in omnibus locis . cum omnibus libertatibus . 7 consuetudinibus
7 quietantiis . sicut aliqui prefatas ęcclesias . 7 terram prenominatam
unquam melius . liberius . honorificentius 7 quietius tenuerunt
tempore .H. regis aui mei . Testibus . Thoma cancellario . Henrico
de Exesia constabulario . Warino filio Giroldi camerario . Willelmo
filio Hamonis . Henrico filio Giroldi . a p v d   B r v h e l l a m[3]
i n   f o r e s t a.

Endorsed: (1) H'.ij. de Langhefordia 7 Brantuna (13 cent.). (2) de ecclesia
Langheford 7 Brantona (13 cent.).
Tag for seal. Size: 8¼ x 8⅜ inches.
On a narrow slip of parchment attached to the charter—De ecclesia 7 manerio
de Langeford' (14 cent.).
Marginalia in A: 2 + + preb' φ va cat.
Texts: MS—Orig. A1/1/36. A. Iiii(36). Pd—*E.H.R.*xxiv,312–13. *C.C.R.*iv,
105(36). Delisle, p. 549 (abs).
Var. R.: [1] Langeford' A Iiii. [2] Huntendsir' A. [3] Bruhgllam in forgsta A.;
Bruhgllam in foresta Iiii. (This reading of *g* for *e* is due to the fact that in the
original charter the name is spread out in order to fill up the last line, the top of
the *e* in *Brvhellam* and *foresta* being extended, with the result that it somewhat
resembles *g*.)

148

180. Writ of Henry II, granting licence to bishop Robert II to
till and have twenty acres of land newly brought into cultivation
at Lyddington [co. Rutland]. At London. (1154–1159.)

De essartis apud Lidingt' (marg.).

.H. rex Angl*orum* . 7 dux Norm*annorum* 7 Aquit*anorum* . 7
comes Andeg*auorum* . balliuis suis de Rotelanda salutem . Concedo
quod Robertus episcopus Linc' excolat 7 habeat bene 7 in pace
7 quiete viginti acras de essartis apud Lidentonam . Teste . Ricardo
de Hume*z* constabulario apud Lond*oniam* . per magistrum
Aluredum.

Marginalia: preb' φ.
Texts: MS—A. Iiv(7). Pd—*C.C.R.*iv,107(7).

Folio 26.
Hdl.   *Henrici . Regis .* SECUNDI.   .2.6.

149

181. Writ of Henry II, commanding that the canons of Lincoln shall have the manor of Friesthorpe [co. Lincoln] as they best had it on the day on which Henry I was alive and dead [1 December, 1135]. At Northampton. (Query circa 1155.)

De manerio de Fristorp (marg.).

.H.[1] rex Anglo*rum* . 7 dux Norman*norum* . 7 Aquit*anorum* . 7 comes Andeg*auorum* . iustic' . 7 vicec*omit'* suis de Lincol' scyra[2] *.'* salutem . Precipio quod canonici Linc' teneant ita bene 7 in pace 7 iuste 7 libere 7 quiete manerium de Fristorp[3] sicut illud tenuerunt die qua rex .H. auus meus fuit uiuus 7 mortuus . Et prohibeo ne quis eos inde iniuste ponat in placitum . ne inde audiam clamorem pro penuria recti . Teste . comite Reg'[4] . apud Norh*antonam*.

Marginalia : 2
Texts: MS—A. R77. Iiv(5). Pd—*C.C.R.*iv,107(5).
Var. R. : [1] R *leaves a blank space for* H. [2] Lincolscir' R. [3] Festorp' R. [4] Rogero R ; Rog' Iiv.
Note : The evidence is probably slightly in favour of the witness being earl Roger (of Hereford) rather than earl Reginald (of Cornwall), and the date has been suggested in accordance with that opinion.

150

182. Writ of Henry II, granting licence to the church of Lincoln and bishop Robert II to have in their manor of Banbury [co. Oxford] one yearly fair lasting throughout the week of Pentecost. At Rouen. (1155–1163.)

De feria in Bannebir*ia* (A marg.).

.H. rex Anglo*rum* . 7 dux Norman*norum* . 7 Aquit*anorum* . 7 comes Andeg*auorum* . iustic*iariis* . vicecomitibus . ministris . 7 omnibus fidelibus suis Francis 7 Anglicis totius Anglie *.'* salutem . Sciatis me concessisse 7 confirmasse[1] deo 7 ecclesie sancte . Marie Linc' . 7 Roberto Linc' . episcopo 7 successoribus suis vnam feriam per annum in manerio suo de Bannebiria . Et concedo quod feria predicta duret per totam septimanam . Pentecoste*n* . Quare volo 7 firmiter precipio quod illa feria predicta habeat omnes illas liber-tates 7 liberas consuetudines 7 quietantias quas habent alie ferie mee per Angliam . Et prohibeo quod nullus disturbet euntes ad feriam illam uel redeuntes de feria *.'* super .x. libras forisfacture . Testibus . Arn*ulfo* . Lexoui*ensi* . Ph*ilippo* . Baioc*ensi* . Rotroldo Ebroic*ensi*[2] episcopis . Man*assero* Bis*et* dapifero . Willelmo filio Hamonis apud Rothomagu*m*.

Facsimile opposite.
Endorsed : (1) XXXII .H. ij. (13 cent.). (2) de feria Bannebiri (12 cent.). (3) de feria de Bannebiri (13 cent.). (4) H ij. (13 cent.).
Strip for seal, half of it being torn off ; and ribband below it. Size : 11¼ x 4⅝ inches.
Marginalia in A : 2| R' preb'.
Texts: MS—Orig. A1/1/18. A. Iv(25). Pd—*E.H.R.*xxiv,307. *C.C.R.*iv,143(25). Delisle, p. 558 (abs.).
Var. R. : [1] *om.* 7 confirmasse Iv. [2] Eboric' A.

H. Rex Angl' z Dux Norm. z Aquit' z Com. And. Iust.. vicec. ... ... Angl.. (Omib;
fidelibs suis francis z Anglis suis totci Angl' Salt'. Sciat me concessisse z confirmasse Deo z ecc'tie Sce.
Marie lincol. z Rotbo linc. epo z successoribs suis vnam feriam per annum in Bidierie Vilra de Banneburia.
Et concedo qd feria p'dicta duret per totam feptimanam . pentecost'. Quare volo z firmit' p'cipio qd
illa feria p'dicta habeat omnes illas libertates z liberas consuetudines z quietancias qual' alie ferie
mee p'p Angl'. Et p'hibeo qs nullus disturbet eumd. ad feriam illa ut redeuntes se feria fugia; e libtas
forisftac.. Teft. Hug. lincoln. ep. Bawoc. Parobtos. Caponi epis. Galfr. Br. Joh. Willmo fil. Ham Alex.. Jochanea.. z.

151

183. Writ of Henry II, granting licence to the church and bishop of Lincoln to have their market in their town of Sleaford on one day in the week, provided that it do not injure the neighbouring markets. At Woodstock. (1154–1189.)

De mercato in Slaford' (marg.).

.H. rex Angl*orum* . 7 dux Norm*annorum* . 7 Aquitan*orum* 7 . comes Ande*gauorum* . iustic' . vice*comit'* . 7 omnibus ministris 7 fidelibus suis de Lincolnesira[1] salutem . Concedo quod ecclesia Linc' . 7 episcopus Linc' ecclesie habeat mercatum suum in villa sua de Slafordia[2] per unum diem in ebdomada . si non nocuerit uicinis mercatis . Quare uolo 7 firmiter precipio quod predicta ecclesia 7 episcopi eiusdem ecclesie illum mercatum habeant 7 teneant bene 7 in pace 7 libere 7 honorifice . 7 omnes qui ad mercatum illum uenerint habeant meam firmam pacem in eundo . 7 morando 7 redeundo . Et prohibeo ne aliquis super hoc eis inde aliquam iniuriam uel contumeliam faciat . Testibus . Roberto Legre*cestrie* comite . 7 Ricardo de Luci[3] . 7 Johanne de Oxen*efordia* . apud Wdestoc*am*[4].

Marginalia: 2| preb' R'.
Texts: MS—A. Iiv(16). Pd—*C.C.R.*iv,110(16).
Var. R. in Iiv: [1] Lincolnisir'. [2] Slaffordia. [3] Lucy. [4] Wodestoc'.

152

184. Writ of Henry II, giving to bishop Robert II and the church of Lincoln, in perpetual alms, fifty-three acres of their assarts of Bugden and Spaldwick [co. Huntingdon]. At Canterbury. (1155–1158.)

De essartis apud Buggenden' 7 Spaldewich' (marg.).

.H. rex Angl*orum* . 7 dux Norm*annorum* . 7 Aquitan*orum* . 7 comes Ande*gauorum* . iustic' . vice*comit'* . 7 omnibus ministris suis de Huntedon' scir*a* salutem . Sciatis me dedisse . 7 in perpetuam elemosinam concessisse Roberto episcopo 7 ecclesie beate Marie Lincol'[1] .liii. acras de essartis suis de Bugdena[2] . 7 de Spaldewica . Et uolo 7 firmiter precipio quod episcopus 7 ecclesia beate Marie Linc' illas teneant ita bene 7 in pace 7 honorifice sicut tenent aliam suam[3] terram . Et sint ita libere 7 quiete in omnibus rebus . sicut sua alia terra est . Testibus . T. cancellario . 7 . R. comite Legre*cestrie* . 7 Ricardo de Luci . 7 Warino filio Ger*oldi* camerario . apud Canthuar*iam*.

Marginalia: 2| φ preb'.
Texts: MS—A. Iiv(8). Pd—*C.C.R.*iv,107–8(8).
Var. R. in Iiv: [1] Linc'. [2] Bugendena. [3] suam aliam.

Folio 26d.

The next two charters seem to be written by another early hand.

153

185. Writ of Henry II, commanding that the church of Chesterfield [co. Derby] shall have all its liberties, customs, and tenements, as it best had them in the time of Henry I, and as it has been acknowledged by the lawful men of the halimote and of the wapentake; and that it shall hold all the lands and renders which the parishioners gave it after the death of Henry I, as the charter of Roger bishop of Chester witnesses. At Nottingham. (1157–1158.)

De ecclesia de Cesterfelda (marg.).

.H. rex Anglie[1] . dux Normannie[2] . 7 Aquitannie[3] . [4]comes Andegauie[5] . iusticiariis . 7 vicecomiti suis de Nothingham syra[6] 7 de Derbi syra[7] salutem . Precipio quod ecclesia de Cestresfelda[8] teneat 7 habeat omnes libertates 7 omnes consuetudines 7 omnia tenementa sua in pratis 7 pascuis 7 nemoribus 7 in omnibus rebus . ita bene 7 in pace . [9]libere 7 quiete . 7 iuste 7 honorifice . 7 integre sicut melius 7 liberius tenuit tempore regis .H. aui mei . et sicut recognitum est per legales homines de halimato 7 de wapintac . Et preter hec[10] teneat omnes terras 7 redditus quos parrochiani post mortem[11] regis .H. aui mei eidem ecclesie dederunt . sicut carta Rogeri episcopi Cestrensis . testatur . Et prohibeo ne quis eidem ecclesie vel rebus ad eandem pertinentibus in aliquo forisfaciat . Teste . Nigello de Broch[12] apud Nothingham.[13]

Texts: MS—A. D60 (*an inspeximus, which may be identified with* Iv(21), *beginning with the words* Inspeximus eciam quamdam aliam cartam eiusdem progenitoris nostri in hec verba .H. rex). Iv(21). Pd—*C.C.R.*iv,141(21).
Var. R.: [1] Angl' D. [2] Normannie D. [3] Aquitan' D. [4] *insert* 7 D Iv. [5] Andegauie D. [6] Notyngehamsira D; Notinghamsira Iv. [7] Derbisira D Iv. [8] Cestrefelda D Iv. [9] *insert* 7 D Iv. [10] post hoc D Iv. [11] pre morte D Iv. [12] Broc D Iv. [13] Notingham D; Nottingeham Iv.

154

186. Writ of Henry II, confirming the gift of William II of the churches of Orston, Chesterfield, Ashbourne, and Mansfield to the church and bishop of Lincoln (see no. 14 above). At Windsor. (1162–1165.)

De ecclesiis de Oskington' Cesterfeld' . Esseburn' . Mammesfeld' . 7 capellis (A marg.).

.H. rex Anglorum[1] . œ' dux Normannorum . œ' Aquitanorum . 7 comes Andegauorum . archiepiscopis . episcopis . comitibus baronibus . iusticiariis . vicecomitibus . ministris . œ' omnibus hominibus . 7 fidelibus suis totius Anglię Francis 7 Anglis[2] salutem . Sciatis me concessisse . œ' carta mea confirmasse . ęcclesię beatę Marię Linc' . 7 episcopo donationem quam Willelmus rex Anglię antecessor meus dedit eis in perpetuam elemosinam . videlicet ęcclesiam de Oschintona[3] . œ' quicquid ad eam pertinebat tempore regis Edwardi . œ' ęcclesiam de Cestrefelt[4] . œ' eclesiam[5] de Esseburna . œ' ęcclesiam de Mamesfelt[6] . œ' capellas quę sunt in berwitis[7] quę adiacent predictis maneriis Quare uolo œ' firmiter precipio quod predicta ęcclesia Linc' . predictas ęcclesias . œ' capellas habeat œ' teneat

bene . 7 in pace . libere . quiete . honorifice . integre & plenarie
cum omnibus pertinentiis suis . in terris & decimis . 7 in omnibus
rebus . sicut carta Willelmi regis Anglię antecessoris mei quam uidi
testatur . Testibus . Thoma Cantuariensi archiepiscopo . Henrico
Wintoniensi[8] Hilario Cicestrensi episcopis . Roberto comite Legrecestrie . Ricardo de Luci[9] . Raginaldo[10] de sancto Walerico . Ricardo
de Humeto constabulario . apvd Windesores[11] ;

Written at the foot: Confirmatur (13 cent.).
Endorsed: (1) H. secundi De Oskenton (12 cent.). (2) Carta Henrici regis super
ecclesiis de Oskigton . Cesterfeld' . Esseburne . 7 Manesfeld' (13 cent.).
The tag for the seal, with part of the charter below the text, has been torn away.
Size: 8 x 9¾ inches.
Texts: MS—Orig. A1/1/25. A. D3. Iiii(35). Pd—*E.H.R.*xxiv,309. *C.C.R.*iv,
104–5(35). Delisle, p. 559 (abs.).
Var. R.: [1] Anglie A. [2] Anglicis Iiii. [3] Oschinthona A. [4] Cestrefeld A ; Cestre-
felt' D. [5] ecclesiam A Iiii. [6] Mamesfeld A ; Mamesfelt' D. [7] berewicis Iiii.
Wynton' D. [9] Lucia A. [10] Reginald' A. [11] Wyndesores D ; Windesore Iiii.

ADD. CHART.

187. Writ of Henry II, commanding W[alter] bishop of Chester
and Froger the archdeacon to cause the king's church of Darley
[co. Derby] to have the tithes and customary dues of Winster
[co. Derby] as it best had them in the time of Henry I and king
Edward. At Bridgnorth. (1155–1158 ; probably May–July, 1155.)

H. rex Anglorum 7 dux Normannorum 7 Aquitanorum 7 comes
Andegauorum .W. episcopo Cestrensi 7 Frogero archidiacono
salutem Precipio uobis quod faciatis habere ecclesie mee de Derlega
decimas 7 consuetudines de Winesterna ita sicut eas melius habuit
tempore regis .H. aui mei 7 tempore regis Edwardi Et si omnes
in predicta villa manentes decimas reddere noluerint (facite inde
quod ad vestrum pertinet ministerium et vicecomites Notingham .
forisfacturam meam inde accipiant Testibus . Willelmo fratre regis
Ricardo de Humez constabulario apud Brugiam.

Marginalia: 2 Froiero.
Texts: MS—D130. Iv(20). Pd—*C.C.R.*iv,141(20).

ADD. CHART.

188. Writ of Henry II, addressed to the reeves and citizens of
Lincoln, commanding that Ivo the king's falconer, and his wife,
and his sons and daughter shall be quit of royal pleas and suits
and gelds and assizes and customary dues, on account of the service
of procuring sparrow-hawks and falcons which he owes ; and
desiring them to maintain and help Ivo to do the king's service.
At Westminster. (1154–1158.)

H'. rex Anglorum 7 dux Normannorum 7 Aquitanorum . 7 comes
Andegauorum . prepositis 7 ciuibus Linc' salutem . Precipio quod

Iuo falconarius meus 7 vxor sua . 7 filii sui 7 filia sua sint in pace
7 quieti de placitis 7 querelis 7 geldis . 7 assisis . 7 omnibus consuetudinibus que ad me pertinent . propter seruicium . suum quod
michi debent de accipitribus 7 falconibus perquirendis . Quare uolo
quod manuteneatis 7 honoretis eum 7 iuuetis ad seruicium meum
faciendum . 7 firmam pacem iuste[1] illi teneatis . Testibus . Toma
cancellario . 7 Manassero Biset . apud Westmonasterium.

Facsimile facing page 110.
No endorsement.
Strip at foot for seal, with ribband below it.   Size :   6 x 3½ inches.
Texts :   MS—Orig. A1/1/37.   R637.
Var. R. :   [1] om. iuste R.

189. Writ of Henry II, commanding Matthew de Curcy to
warrant to Philip son of William son of Osbert, canon of Lincoln,
twelve shillings of rent which Matthew gave to the church of Lincoln
in augmentation of Philip's prebend, or to give him an exchange
of equal value. At Woodstock. (1156–1166.)

Carta de .xij. solidis annui redditus ad augmentum (rubric).

.H. rex Anglorum 7 dux Normannorum 7 Aquitanorum 7 comes
Andegauorum Matheo de Curcy ꞉ salutem . Precipio tibi quod
iuste warantizes Philippo filio Willelmi filii Osberti canonico Linc'
.xij. solidos redditus quas [sic] dedisti in elemosinam ecclesie Linc'
in augmentum prebende ipsius Philippi sicut carta tua testatur (
vel iuste dones ei escambium ad vaillanciam . Et nisi feceris vicecomes Linc' faciat fieri ne amplius inde clamorem audiam ꞉ pro
penuria recti . Teste . comite Gaufrido apud Wudestocam.

Text :   MS—R20.
Note :   The prebend referred to in the text may be Thorngate (see no. 168
above, endorsement).

190. Writ of Henry II, commanding the reeve and citizens of
Lincoln that Siward the canon shall hold his lands in the city of
Lincoln, and especially that which was Gurret the moneyer's and
Ailred his son's, as his predecessors best held them in the time of
Henry I; and forbidding that he be put in plea unless the king
enjoins it with his own mouth. At London. (1155–1175.)

De terris Siwardi in Linc' 7 precipue de illis que fuerunt Gurreti
monetarii (rubric).

.H. rex Anglorum 7 dux Normannorum 7 Aquitanorum 7 comes
Andegauorum preposito 7 ciuibus Linc' ꞉ salutem . Precipio quod
Siwardus canonicus teneat bene 7 in pace 7 iuste omnes terras suas
in vrbe Linc' 7 nominatim illam que fuit Gurreti monetarii 7 Ailredi
filii sui 7 ita libere 7 quiete 7 honorifice 7 iuste teneat ꞉ sicut antecessores sui melius vel liberius tenuerunt tempore Regis .H. aui

mei . Et prohibeo quod inde non ponatur in placitum ; nisi hoc prius ore meo precipiam . Teste . comite Reginaldo . apud Londo*niam*.

Marginalia : Gurret'.
Text : MS—R43.

ADD. CHART.

191. Writ of Henry II, addressed to the reeve and citizens of Lincoln, commanding that Siward the canon shall hold his lands in the city of Lincoln, and especially the land which was Guthred his kinsman's near Bailgate, as his predecessor best held it in the time of Henry I ; and forbidding that he be put in plea without the king's express command.　(1155–1175.)

De eisdem terris (rubric).

.H. Anglo*rum* 7 dux Norm*annorum* 7 Aquit*anorum* 7 comes Ande*gauorum* vicecomiti 7 preposito 7 ciuibus Linc' salutem (Precipio quod Siwardus canonicus teneat bene 7 in pace (libere 7 iuste omnes terras suas in vrbe Linc' 7 nominatim terram que fuit Guthtredi cognati sui iuxta portam Ballii (sicut antecessores sui melius 7 liberius tenuerunt tempore Regis .H. aui mei . Et prohibeo ne inde ponatur in placitum) nisi nominatim precepero . Et nisi feceritis iusticia mea faciat . Teste .W. filio Johannis apud [*blank*].

Text : MS—R44.

ADD. CHART.

192. Writ of Henry II, commanding that Geoffrey, his chaplain, shall hold his prebend of Lincoln as any one of his predecessors best held it in the time of Henry I. At Caen.　(1156–1175 ; probably circa 1160.)

De quietacione prebende Gaufridi capellani in Lincoln' (rubric).

.H. rex Anglo*rum* 7 dux Norm*annorum* 7 Aquit*anorum* 7 comes Ande*gauorum* vicecomiti Linc'scire 7 prepositis 7 ciuibus Linc' salutem . Precipio quod dominus Gaufridus capellanus meus teneat prebendam suam de Linc' bene 7 in pace 7 honorifice 7 integre sicut aliquis antecessorum suorum eam melius vel liberius tenuit tempore regis aui mei (quia non paterer quod aliquis ei vel rebus eius iniuriam faceret vel contumeliam . Teste . episcopo Ebro*icensi* . apud Cadom*um*.

Text : MS—R45.

ADD. (EXTRAN.) CHART.

193. Writ of Henry II, confirming to the church and canons of Lincoln one carucate in Keal of the gift of William de Romara II. At Rouen.　(Probably September, 1177.)

De terra de Kales (marg.).

H'. rex Anglorum 7 dux Normannorum 7 Aquitanorum . 7 comes .
Andegauorum archiepiscopis . episcopis abbatibus . comitibus .
baronibus . iusticiariis . vicecomitibus 7 omnibus ministris 7 fidelibus
hominibus suis tocius Anglie salutem . Sciatis me concessisse 7
presenti carta confirmasse ecclesie beate Marie Linc' 7 canonicis
eiusdem ecclesie unam carrucatam terre . in Kales cum omnibus
pertinentiis suis . ex dono Willelmi de Romara . Quare uolo 7 firmiter
precipio quod ecclesia Linc' 7 canonici eiusdem ecclesie teneant
predictam carrucatam terre bene . 7 in pace honorifice 7 quiete .
sicut carta Willelmi testatur . Testibus . Rogero archiepiscopo .
Eboracensi . 7 .J. episcopo Cistrerensi [sic] . apud Rotomagvm.

Text: MS—C,f.16.

ADD. (EXTRAN.) CHART.

194. Writ of Henry II, confirming to the church of the canons
of the order of Sempringham [i.e. Saint Katherine's priory] which
bishop Robert II, with the assent of his chapter, founded near the
city of Lincoln, the prebend of Canwick [co. Lincoln], and five
bovates in Wigsley [co. Nottingham], and the churches of Newark
[co. Nottingham], Norton Disney, Marton, and Newton [on Trent],
[co. Lincoln], and two messuages, houses, and land in the borough
and fields of Newark, and the chapel of Saint Philip and Saint
James founded in Newark castle and in olden time given to the
mother church with the tenth penny of the whole toll of the borough
except in the time of fairs, and three bovates in Balderton [co.
Nottingham] with messuages and four shillings' worth of land
which master Malger held in Newark. Also confirming the grant
by bishop Robert and the chapter to the said canons of the church
of Bracebridge [co. Lincoln], and of the cure and custody of the
hospital of Saint Sepulchre, Lincoln, and the possessions of its
poor men and brethren. At Westminster. (1154–1166.)

H. rex Anglorum 7 dux Normannorum 7 Aquitanorum 7 comes
Andegauorum archiepiscopis episcopis abbatibus comitibus baronibus
iusticiariis vicecomitibus ministris 7 omnibus fidelibus suis tocius
Anglie salutem . Sciatis me ad peticionem Roberti secundi Lincoln'
episcopi 7 capituli Lincoln' concessisse 7 presenti carta mea confirmasse ecclesie canonicorum ordinis de Sempingham quam prefatus
Robertus episcopus Lincol' assensu capituli sui fundauit iuxta
ciuitatem Lincoln' 7 canonicis ibidem deo seruientibus prebendam
de Canewich cum omnibus pertinenciis suis 7 quinque bouatas
terre in Wiggesle cum omnibus pertinenciis suis 7 ecclesias de
Newerc 7 de Norton' 7 de Martun' 7 de Newetun' cum omnibus

pertinenciis suis 7 duas mansuras in burgo de Newerc 7 domos cum terra ab aquilonali parte 7 orientali matris ecclesie de Newerc 7 quatuor bouatas terre in campis de Newerc cum mansuris 7 .xx. acras in bruera 7 mansuram quam prius habuerat ipsa ecclesia de Newerc cum duabus bouatis terris in campis eiusdem ville 7 capellam apostolorum Philippi 7 Jacobi in castello eiusdem ville . fundatam 7 antiquitus matri ecclesie datam cum decimo denario tocius telonei de burgo de Newerc exceptis nundinis 7 tres bouatas terre in Baldertun cum mansuris 7 quatuor solidatas terre quas magister Malgerus tenuit in Newerc . Concessi etiam eis ecclesiam de Bracebrigge cum una bouata terre 7 mansura 7 cum omnibus pertinenciis suis in Bracebrigge (Predictorum uero canonicorum cure 7 custodie hospitale sancti Sepulchri Linc' 7 possessiones omnes pauperum 7 fratrum illius concessi 7 presenti carta confirmaui . Quare uolo 7 firmiter precipio quod predicta ecclesia canonicorum 7 prenominati canonici omnia supradicta in puram 7 perpetuam elemosinam habeant 7 teneant 7 possideant libere 7 quiete 7 honorifice sicut carte prenominati Roberti episcopi 7 capituli Lincol' testantur . Hec omnia concessi predicte ecclesie pro anima regis .H. aui mei 7 pro anima .M. imperatricis matris mee 7 pro salute mea 7 A. regine 7 heredum meorum 7 pro statu regni mei . Testibus Rogero Eboracensi archiepiscopo Hugone Dunolmensi Hylario Cistrensi episcopis Reginaldo comite Cornubie Rogero de Mubrai Reginaldo de Curtenai apud Westmonasterium.

Texts : MS—*Charter Roll*, 1 Edward III, mem. 13 (an inspeximus, dated at York, 2 July, 1327). Pd—*C.C.R.*iv,52(28). Associated Architectural Societies' *Reports and Papers* xxvii, 323–4.

ADD. CHART.

195. Writ of Henry II, ratifying the election of Thomas abbot elect of Grimsby, and commanding the chapter of Lincoln to cause him to receive benediction and consecration as abbot, and to maintain him and his abbey. At Brill [co. Buckingham]. (1175–1189; probably 1179.)

.H. dei gracia rex Anglorum . 7 dux Normannorum . 7 Aquitanorum . 7 comes Andegauorum . capitulo ecclesie sancte Marie Lincoln' : salutem . Sciatis quod ratam habeo electionem que facta est de Thoma abbate electo de Grimesbi . Et ideo mando uobis 7 precor quod faciatis ei imponi manum benedictionis 7 faciatis eum consecrari in abbatem ecclesie sancti Augustini de Grimesbi . 7 manuteneatis eum 7 abbatiam suam 7 non permittatis quod aliquis ei forisfaciat . Teste . Willelmo filio Aldelmi dapifero apud Brohillam.

Facsimile facing page 110.
No endorsement.
Strip for seal, on which is written by the scribe of the charter, ' Capitulo Lincoln' pro abbate de Grimesbi.' Size : 6⅜ x 2 inches.
Text : MS—Orig. ▲1/1/39.

Folio 27.
Hdl.   CARTE REGIS RICARDI . 7 JOHANNIS.   .2.7.

155

196. Writ of Richard I, commanding the reeves of Lincoln to cause the churches of the precentor and canons of Lincoln, within the walls and without, to be in the same condition as when Henry II was alive and dead [6 July, 1189], and as they were on the day of his own coronation [3 September, 1189]. At Westminster. 20 February (1190).

De ecclesiis cantoris 7 canonicorum Lincoln' (marg.).

.R. dei gracia rex Anglorum . dux Normannorum . Aquitanorum . comes Andegauorum . prepositis de Lincol'[1] salutem . Precipimus uobis quod ecclesias cantoris 7 canonicorum Lincol'[1] intra muros 7 extra faciatis esse in eodem statu 7 eadem pace qua erant quando pater noster rex . H. fuit uiuus 7 mortuus . 7 in qua erant die coronationis nostre . Nec patiamini quod inde molestentur nisi per nos uel capitalem iusticiam nostram . Teste . episcopo Dunelmensi[2] apud Westmonasterium .xx. die Februarii.

Marginalia : + .1. ·j· Vide folio huius libri 7 et 23 ad hoc signum + (*the reference being to no.* 45 *and no.* 158 *above*).
Texts : MS—A. R48A.
Var. R. : [1] Linc' R.   [2] Dunelmens' R.

156

197. Writ of Richard I, rendering to the church of Lincoln and bishop Hugh I the manor of Marston [Saint Lawrence, co. Northampton], which the bishop had claimed in the king's court as the right of his church ; and commanding that the bishop shall hold the manor as the church of Lincoln ever best held it. At Winchester. 20 April, (1194).

De manerio de Merstona (A marg.).

Ricardus dei gratia rex Anglorum . dux Normannorum . Aquitanorum . comes Andegauorum ; archiepiscopis . episcopis . abbatibus . comitibus . baronibus . iusticiariis . vicecomitibus . 7 omnibus ministris 7 fidelibus suis ; salutem . Sciatis nos reddidisse ecclesie Lincoliensi . 7 Hugoni eiusdem ecclesie episcopo . manerium de Merstona cum pertinentiis suis . quod idem episcopus tanquam ius ecclesie sue in [curia nostra[1]] petierat . Quare uolumus 7 firmiter precipimus quod ecclesia Lincol'[2] 7 predictus .H. Lincol' episcopus 7 successores sui predictum manerium de Merstona cum pertinentiis suis . habeant 7 teneant bene 7 in pace . libere 7 quiete . plenarie in[te[1]]gre 7 honorifice . in bosco 7 plano . in pratis 7 pascuis . in viis 7 semitis . in aquis 7 molendinis . 7 in omnibus aliis pertinentiis . 7 cum omnibus libertatibus 7 liberis consuetudinibus suis . sicut unquam ecclesia Lincol' idem manerium melius 7 liberius tenuit . et sicut carta regis .H. patris nostri testatur ; quod tenere debeat .

XVIII

Testibus . H. Cant*uariensi* archiepiscopo .R. Lond*oniensi* .G.
Roffen*si* .W. Hereforden*si* .H. Exon*iensi* .S. Cicestr*ensi* . episcopis .
comite Rogero le Bigot . Willelmo de Breosa . Rogero de Mortuo
mari[3] . Willelmus[4] Mares*callo*[5] . Hugone Bard*ulf* . Willelmo de
Warenn*a* . Simone de Pateshull' .xx. die Aprilis *:* apvd Wintoniam.

Facsimile facing page 122.
Endorsed : (1) R'. reg*is* de Merstona (contemp.). (2) Carte de Marstona (contemp.).
There is a tag for the seal. Size : 8¼ x 5 inches.
Marginalia in A : .ij. Norhantscir' (query Q).
Texts : MS—Orig. a1/1/41. A. R169. Iiv(21). Pd—*C.C.R.*iv,111(21).
Var. R : [1] *supplied from A, there being a hole in the original charter.* [2] Linc' A ;
Lincoln' R. [3] mari R. [4] Will'o A Iiv ; Will' R. [5] Marescall' R.

157

198. Writ of Richard I, releasing the demand for a mantle
which he had made upon the bishop, and which Henry II and his
predecessors had made upon the church of Lincoln. At Le Mans.
(22 June, 1195.)

De exigentia mantelli (marg.).

Ricardus dei gratia rex Ang*lorum* dux Norma*nnorum* . Aquit-
anorum . comes Ande*gauorum* . archiepiscopis . episcopis . abbatibus .
comitibus . baronibus . iusti*ciariis* . vicecomitibus . balliuis . 7 omnibus
fidelibus[1] tocius terre sue salutem . Sciatis nos pro amore dei 7
beate Marie semper uirginis matris eius . 7 pro salute nostra 7
antecessorum 7 successorum nostrorum remisisse in puram 7 perpetuam elemosinam deo 7 beate Marie 7 ecclesie Lincol'[2] imperpetuum exigentiam mantelli quam feceramus de episcopo Linc' .
7 quam dominus rex Henricus pater noster 7 predecessores sui de
predicta ecclesia Linc' fecerant . eandemque ecclesiam imperpetuum
de predicta exigentia mantelli de nobis 7 heredibus nostris presenti
carta nostra quietam clamamus . Quare uolumus 7 firmiter precipimus quod predicta ecclesia Linc' imperpetuum sit quieta de
predicto mantello de nobis 7 heredibus nostris . Si quis autem
successorum nostrorum hanc nostram elemosinam 7 quietantiam
infringere presumpserit *:* indignationem 7 maledictionem omnipotentis dei 7 gloriose uirginis Marie matris eius incurrat . donec
resipiscat . 7 a sua temeritate desistat . Testibus hiis . Johanne
comite Morit*onie* . fratre nostro . Willelmo Marescallo . comite
Willelmo * Saresbir*ie* . Ricardo comite de Clara . magistro Philippo
archidiacono Cant*uariensi* . Radulfo Foliot archidiacono Hereforden*si* . Bochardo thesaurario Eboracen*si* . 7 aliis multis . Datum per
manum magistri Eustachii decani Saresbir*ie* uicem agentis cancellarii
nostri apud Cenomann*um* .xxiii. die Junii . anno .v[3]. regni nostri.

Marginalia : 2| .iii. φ.
Texts : MS—A. Iv(40). Pd—*C.C.R.*iv,146–7(40).
Var. R. : [1] *insert* suis Iv. [2] Linc' Iv. [3] sexto Iv. (*The reading* sexto *is probably*
correct, for the payment appears in the Pipe Roll of 7 *Richard for the first time.*)

Folio 27d.
Hdl.   . REGIS . RICARDI .

158

199. Writ of Richard I. The king has granted to the church of Lincoln and bishop Hugh I and his successors that all their lands and their men shall be quit of fines for murder and of payments pertaining to murder. Further, the king has granted to the church and bishop one hundred acres of ancient assart, quit of regard of the forest, namely, fifty acres at Buckden in the hundred of Toseland, and twenty-five acres at Spaldwick in the hundred of Leightonstone [co. Huntingdon], and twenty-five acres at Lyddington, co. Rutland; likewise fifty acres of new assart at Buckden. Moreover the king has confirmed to them the adgistment of their woods, and licence to take wood, whether green or dry, for their needs without view of the foresters, saving to the king his hunting and the regard inspection every third year. At Westminster. 25 January, 1189–1190.

De murdro . De . c. acris de ueteri essarto . scilicet apud Buggenden' ∴ L. apud Spaldewich' .xxv. apud Lidington' .xxv.[1] (marg.).

Ricardus dei gratia rex Angl*orum* . dux Norman*norum* . Aquit*anorum* . comes Andeg*auorum* . archiepiscopis . episcopis . decanis . archidiaconis . abbatibus . comitibus . baronibus . iustic*iariis* . vicecomitibus . bailliuis . prepositis . forestariis . ministris . ⁊ omnibus fidelibus suis salutem . Sciatis nos pro salute nostra ⁊ pro anima patris nostri regis .H. ⁊ pro animabus omnium antecessorum nostrorum concessisse ⁊ presenti carta nostra confirmasse deo ⁊ ecclesie beate Marie Linc' . ⁊ .H. episcopo Linc' . ⁊ omnibus successoribus suis in liberam ⁊ puram ⁊ perpetuam elemosinam quod omnes terre sue ⁊ homines sui sint quieti de murdro . ⁊ de denariis ad murdrum pertinentibus . Concessimus etiam eis centum acras de ueteri essarto cum p*ur*presturis infra easdem factis quietas de[2] reguardo[3] in perpetuum . quinquaginta scilicet apud Buggeden' in Tolleslundhundr*ed* . ⁊ .xxv. apud Spaldewic[4] in Lectonestanhundr*ed* . et .xxv. apud Lidinton'[5] in Roteland' . Similiter de nouo essarto quinquaginta acras cum presturis[6] infra eadem[7] factis apud Buggeden[8] quietas imperpetuum de reguardo ⁊ de omni exactione . Preterea concessimus ⁊ confirmauimus eis adgistamentum boscorum suorum quandocumque ⁊ ubicumque uoluerint in propriis boscis[9] . ⁊ ut capiant in boscis suis omnia sua necessaria in uiridi ⁊ sicco sine uisu ⁊ liberatione forestariorum salua ueneratione[10] nostra quam nobis retinuimus . ⁊ saluo nobis reguardo in tercio anno . Quare uolumus ⁊ firmiter precipimus quod predicta ecclesia beate Marie Linc' . ⁊ .H. episcopus eiusdem loci ⁊ omnes successores sui ⁊ homines eorum omnes has predictas quietantias habeant ⁊ teneant imperpetuum bene ⁊ in pace . libere . pacifice . ⁊ honorifice . cum omnibus aliis libertatibus ⁊ liberis consuetudinibus quas

habuerunt tempore patris nostri regis .H. 7 omnium aliorum
antecessorum[11] nostrorum . Et prohibemus ne quis[12] aliquod
grauamen aut molestiam . aut iniuriam de predictis quietanciis[13]
7 libertatibus faciat . Testibus . H. Dunelm*ensi* .R. London*iensi*
.G. Winton*iensi* . episcopis . comite Willelmo Saresbirien*si* . Willelmo
Marescallo . Galfrido filio Petri . Hugone Bardulf . Dat' apud
Westm*onasterium* . per manum Willelmi de Longo Campo Elyensis[14]
episcopi cancellarii nostri .xxv. die Januarii regni nostri anno
primo.

Marginalia : .iiii.
Texts: MS—A. R48. Iv(39). Pd—*C.C.R.*iv,146(39).
Var. R. : [1] Carta de quietacione murdri 7 de denariis pertinentibus ad murdrum
ac de boscis maneriorum episcopi R rubric. [2] de *repeated* R. [3] *corrected from*
regauardo A. [4] Spladewic R. [5] Lidington R. [6] purpresturis R Iv. [7] easdem
R Iv. [8] Buggeden' R. [9] *for* boscis *read* suis R. [10] *sic;* uenatione R Iv. [11] *insert*
suorum R. [12] *insert* eis R Iv. [13] quietanciis *written in marg. of* A, *and marked
for insertion in the text.* [14] Eliens' R.

Folio 28.
Hdl.   .2.8.

159

200. Decree of John [Gynwell], bishop of Lincoln, uniting the
priory of Wothorpe [co. Northampton], to which the parish church
of Wothorpe is of old annexed, to the priory of Saint Michael,
Stamford, which has become impoverished after the last general
pestilence. At Kibworth [co. Leicester]. 11 June, 1354.

Vniuersis sancte matris ecclesie filiis ad quos presentes littere
peruenerint Johannes permissione diuina Lincoln' episcopus salutem
in omnium saluatore Sua nobis dilecte in Christo filie priorissa
7 conuentus prioratus sancti Michaelis iuxta Staunford' ordinis
sancti Benedicti nostre diocesis peticione monstrauerunt quod ipse
tanto debitorum onere sunt depresse ac redditus 7 prouentus dicti
prioratus ad tam irrecuperabilem sterilitatem post vltimam
generalem hominum pestilenciam moderno tempore sunt redacti .
quod ad earumdem priorisse 7 conuentus sustentacionem hospital-
itatemque . tenendam 7 alia eis incumbencia onera supportanda ⸴
non sufficiunt hiis diebus nec sperantur verisimiliter sufficere in
futuro nisi de eis de aliquo alio subuencionis remedio succuratur .
Vnde nobis humiliter supplicabant vt prioratum de Wirthorp'
nostre diocesis eis 7 domui earundem vicinum ad tantam inopiam
iam redactum quod ad vnam monialem necessaria ministranda non
sufficiunt prouentus eiusdem vna cum ecclesia parochiali eiusdem
loci ad dictum prioratum de Wirthorp' ab antiquo notorie pertinente
in quo prioratu post dictam pestilenciam vnica dumtaxat monialis
remansit superstes ex causis premissis eis 7 earum successoribus
ac prioratui sancti Michaelis predicti modo quo odor sacre religionis
solebat 7 nunc inuenitur in omnibus pululare viuere 7 annectere

dignaremur in earum vsus proprios cum suis iuribus et pertinenciis
vniuersis perpetuo possidendum . Nos igitur super hiis premissa
inquisicione diligenti per quam inuenimus predicta omnia veritatem
continere) habitoque cum capitulo nostro super hiis tractatu
debito 7 solempni ostensaque nobis domini uestri Rogeri super
hoc eis concessa licencia speciali ac consensu nobilis viri domini
Thome de Holand militis qui heredem 7 filiam comitis Cancie quondam
dicti prioratus de Wirthorp' patroni duxit in vxorem ad hoc per
suas litteras expresse accedente eundum prioratum de Wirthorp'
cum ecclesia parochiali eiusdem loci dicto prioratui de Wirthorp'
ab antiquo annexa vna cum aliis suis iuribus 7 pertinenciis vniuersis
prefatis priorisse 7 conuentui sancti Michaelis 7 earum successoribus
ac ipsarum prioratui supradicto ex causis premissis de quarum
veritate est nobis in forma iuris sufficiens facta fides obseruatis
quoque aliis iuris solempniis quibuscunque in hac parte requisitis
saluo iure cuiuscunque . vnimus annectimus 7 incorporamus 7 in
vsus proprios concedimus perpetuo possidendum volentes 7 expresse
concedentes quod quando dictum prioratum de Wirthorp' per
mortem cessionem seu amocionem priorisse eiusdem vel alio
quouismodo vacare . contigerit extunc liceat dicte priorisse 7
conuentui sancti Michaelis per se vel per procuratorem suum
corporalem possessionem dicte prioratus de Wirthorp' iurium 7
pertinenciarum ipsius omnium 7 singulorum libere ingredi 7
apprehendere . nostra aut alterius licencia super hoc minime requisita
Saluis tamen nobis 7 successoribus nostris in omnibus iuribus . 7
consuetudinibus episcopalibus 7 nostre ecclesie Linc' dignitate
Volumus insuper 7 ordinamus quod omnes fructus redditus 7
prouentus dictorum prioratus de Wirthorp' 7 ecclesie parochialis
eiusdem . in vsus commune infirmarie ac necessariorum coquine
monalium prioratus sancti Michaelis predicti 7 non in vsus alios
conuertantur . Et inueniant dicti priorissa 7 conuentus sancti
Michaelis   vnum capellanum in ecclesia parochiali de Wirthorp'
diuina officia cotidie celebrantem 7 parochianis eiusdem die 7
nocte cum indiguerint sacramenta ecclesiastica debite ministrantem
7 omnia alia onera eiusdem ecclesie consueta 7 debita supportabunt
In   quorum   omnium   testimonium   atque   fidem   presentem
processum fieri mandamus ac sigilli nostri appensione fecimus
communiri . Actum 7 datum apud Kybbeworth' . iij idus Junii
anno Domini Mᵒ cccᵐᵒ quinquagesimo quarto et consecracionis
nostre septimo.

Text : MS—A (written by a fourteenth century hand).

Folio 28d.

160

201. Letters of the subdean and chapter of Lincoln, confirming
the foregoing union. At Lincoln. 19 June, 1354.

Vniuersis sancte matris ecclesie filiis ad quos presentes littere peruenerint subdecanus 7 capitulum ecclesie beate Marie Linc' decano eiusdem absente salutem in omnium saluatore. Nouerit vniuersitas vestra quod cum venerabilis in Christo pater 7 dominus dominus Johannes dei gracia Linc' episcopus prioratum de Worthorp' Linc' diocesis cum suis iuribus 7 pertinenciis vniuersis vna cum ecclesia parochiali eiusdem loci dicto prioratui de Worthorp' ab antiquo annexa habito primitus nobiscum tractatu diligenti concurrentibus . quoque aliis iuris solempniis in hac parte necessariis priorisse 7 conuentui domus monialium sancti Michaelis extra Staunford' . eiusdem Linc' diocesis et earum successoribus . ac ipsum prioratui supradicto sub certa forma vnierit annexerit 7 incorporauerit ac in vsus proprios perpetuo possidendum concesserit Nos subdecanus et capitulum prefati vnionem annexionem et apropriacionem predictas sic de consensu nostro factas quantum in nobis est approbamus ratificamus et confirmamus per presentes In cuius rei testimonium sigillum commune capituli nostri presentibus est appensum Hiis testibus magistro Antonio de Goldesburgh' precentore ecclesie Linc' domino Johanne de Welburn' thesaurario ecclesie predicte magistris Hamone Belers tunc subdecano Radulfo de Erghom' domino Ada de Lymberg' canonicis Linc' 7 aliis Dat' in capitulo nostro Linc' xiij° kalendas Julij anno Domini millesimo ccc^{mo} liiij^{to}.

Text : MS—A.

Folio 29.   2.9

Hdl.   CARTE REGIS JOHANNIS.

161

202. Writ of John, notifying the knights, free tenants, and men of the abbey of Eynsham [co. Oxford] that he has rendered to bishop Hugh II the bishop's abbey of Eynsham, and commanding them to be obedient to the bishop. At Porchester [co. Southampton]. 17 July, 1213.

De Egnesham' (marg.).

.J. dei gracia rex Angl*ie* . dominus Hibernie . dux Norm*annie* . 7 Aquit*anie* . comes Andeg*auie* . militibus . libere tenentibus 7 omnibus hominibus abbatie de Einesham salutem . Sciatis quod reddidimus venerabili patri nostro domino .H. Linc' . episcopo . abbatiam suam de Einesham[1] cum omnibus pertinenciis . libertatibus . 7 liberis consuetudinibus suis . Et ideo uobis mandamus quatinus ei decetero inde sitis intendentes 7 respondentes . Teste . me ipso apud Porecestr*iam* .xvii. die Julii anno regni nostri .xv°.

Texts : MS—A. Iv(42). Pd—*C.C.R.*iv,147(42).
Var. R. : [1] Eynesham Iv.

162

203. Writ of John, notifying to the prior and convent of Eynsham that he has rendered to bishop Hugh II the bishop's abbey of Eynsham, and commanding them henceforth to be obedient to the bishop. At Portsmouth. 14 July, 1213.

De Egnesham' (marg.).

.J. dei gracia rex Angl*ie* . dominus Hibernie . dux Norm*annie* . 7 Aquitan*ie* . comes Andeg*auie* . priori 7 conuentui de Einesham[1] *?* salutem . Sciatis quod reddidimus venerabili patri nostro domino .H. Linc' episcopo abbatiam suam de Einesham[1] cum pertinenciis suis . Et ideo uobis mandamus quod ei decetero sitis intendentes . Et in huius rei testimonium has litteras nostras patentes uobis inde mittimus . Teste . me ipso apud Portesm*utam* .xiiii. die Julii anno regni nostri .xvº.

Marginalia : ♃.
Texts : MS—A.   Iv(41).   Pd—*C.C.R.*iv,147(41).
Var. R. : [1] Eynesham Iv.

163

204. Charter of John, granting licence to William [of Ely], his treasurer, canon of Lincoln, to have every year at his prebend of Leighton[-Buzzard, co. Bedford] one fair lasting three days, namely, on the vigil of the Invention of the Cross [3 May] and the two following days, and to have a weekly market every Wednesday. Dated by the hand of Hugh of Wells, archdeacon of Wells. At Christchurch [co. Southampton]. 12 November, 1208.

De feria apud Lecton' (marg.).

Johannes[1] dei gracia rex Angl*ie* . dominus Hibernie . dux Norman*nie* . 7 Aquitan*ie* . comes Andeg*auie* . archiepiscopis . episcopis . abbatibus . comitibus . baronibus . iustic*iariis* . vicecomitibus . prepositis . 7 omnibus balliuis 7 fidelibus suis[2] salutem . Sciatis nos concessisse 7 hac carta nostra confirmasse Willelmo thesaurario nostro[3] ecclesie Linc' canonico quod habeat unam feriam apud prebendam[4] de Lectona[5] singulis annis per tres dies duraturam . Scilicet[6] vigilia inuentionis sancte Crucis 7 duobus diebus subsequentibus[7] . 7 quod habeat ibidem unum mercatum singulis septimanis per diem Mercurii . Ita tamen quod feria illa 7 mercatum illud non sint ad nocumentum uicinarum feriarum 7 uicinorum mercatorum . Quare uolumus 7 firmiter precipimus quod predictus Willelmus[8] 7 successores sui predicte prebende canonici habeant predictam feriam 7 predictum mercatum apud Lectonam[5] imperpetuum . bene 7 in pace libere 7[9] quiete[10] 7 honorifice cum omnibus libertatibus 7 liberis consuetudinibus ad huiusmodi feriam 7 mercatum pertinentibus sicut supradictum est . Testibus . domino .P.[11] Winton*iensi* episcopo . Willelmo comite Deuon*ie* .

Willelmo Briwerr'[12] . Petro filio Hereberti[13] . Willelmo de Cantilupo .
Willelmo Malet . Roberto de Vallibus . Galfrido Luterel[14] . Johanne
filio Hugonis . Data per manum Hugonis[15] de Wellis archidiaconi
Wellensis[16] apud Christi Ecclesiam .xii. die Nouembris anno regni
nostri decimo.

Marginalia : 2 H'.
Texts : MS—A. Charter roll, 10 John, mem. 2. Pd—*Rotuli Charterum* i, 183.
See *C.C.R.*v, 294(3).
Var. R. : [1] *For* Johannes *read* J. Ch. roll. [2] *The salutation is shortened in* Ch.
roll. [3] nostro *interlineated*. [4] *insert* suam Ch. roll. [5] Lecton' Ch. roll. [6] *insert*
in Ch. roll. [7] sequentibus Ch. roll. [8] W. Ch. roll. [9] *om.* 7 Ch. roll. [10] *add* 7 integre
Ch. roll. [11] *om.* P. Ch. roll. [12] W. Briw' Ch. roll. [13] Herb' Ch. roll. [14] Gaufr'
Luterello Ch. roll. [15] *for* Hugonis *read* H. Ch. roll. [16] Well' Ch. roll.

Folio 29d. No. 205 is written by a later hand, about 1260.

164

205. Charter of John, granting to the church of Lincoln and
bishop Hugh II, in compensation for damages in the time of the
general interdict, the manor of Winthorpe near Newark [co. Notting-
ham], which is of the bishop's fee, and was pledged to Aaron the
Jew, and came, after Aaron's death, into the hand of Henry, the
king's father, as his escheat ; also granting and quitclaiming ten
pounds sterling which the bishop and his predecessors were wont
to render yearly to the king and his predecessors in respect of the
wapentake of Stow ; granting also to the bishop and his successors
licence to enclose, impark, or assart their woods of Lyddington
[co. Rutland], and Buckden and Spaldwick, and the grove of
Stow [in Long Stow] [co. Huntingdon], and the spinney of
Crouch, near Banbury [co. Oxford], quit of view of foresters and
pleas of the forest, saving however to the king his hunting ; granting
also that they may divert the way which leads from Kimbolton
[co. Huntingdon] towards Huntingdon, through part of Buckden
wood, so that that way may be the boundary between their said
wood and the adjoining wood of Brampton [co. Huntingdon] ;
granting also that they may have their fairs for three or four days
every year, and their markets one day a week, in all their manors.
Dated at the New Temple, London. 21 January, 1214–1215.

De manerio de Wimpthorp (A marg., query by Q).

Johannes dei gratia rex Anglie dominus Hybernie dux Normannie
7 Aquitanie comes Andegauie . archiepiscopis . episcopis . abbatibus .
comitibus . baronibus . iusticiariis . forestariis . vicecomitibus .
prepositis . 7 omnibus balliuis 7 fidelibus suis .' salutem[1] . Sciatis
nos pro amore dei 7 pro salute anime nostre 7 omnium antecessorum
7 heredum nostrorum in recompensationem quoque ablatorum .
iniuriarum 7 dampnorum ecclesie beate Marie Linc'[2] . 7 venerabili

I

patri Hugoni Linc'[2] episcopo secundo illatorum tempore generalis
interdicti ./ dedisse . concessisse . 7 presenti carta nostra confirmasse
deo 7 ipsi ecclesie Linc' 7 predicto episcopo 7 successoribus suis
in perpetuum . in puram . liberam . 7 perpetuam elemosinam
manerium de Wimeltorpe[3] iuxta Neowercha[4] cum omnibus pertinenciis suis quod est de feodo ipsius episcopi Linc' . 7 forisuadiatum
fuit uersus Aaron[4a] iudeum . 7 deuenit in manum domini regis .H.
patris nostri post mortem eiusdem Aaron[4a] tanquam exscaeta[5] sua ./
habendum eidem episcopo 7 successoribus suis 7 ecclesie Linc'[2]
in perpetuum . quietum ab omni seculari seruitio 7 exactione cum
omnibus libertatibus 7 liberis consuetudinibus quas habet aliquod
liberiorum maneriorum ipsius episcopi . Dedimus etiam 7 concessimus 7 omnino quietas clamauimus in perpetuum eidem ecclesie
Linc'[2] 7 predicto episcopo 7 successoribus suis decem libras
sterlingorum quas ipse episcopus 7 predecessores sui nobis 7 antecessoribus nostris annuatim reddere consueuerunt de wapentacco
de Stowa[6] . Concessimus etiam quod idem episcopus 7 successores
sui possint claudere 7 parcos facere si uoluerint . uel essartare :
quantum . quando . 7 ubi uoluerint boscos suos de Lidintona[7] .
7 Buggedena . 7 Spaldewich' . 7 grauam de Stowa[8] . 7 spinetum de
Cruch' iuxta Bannebiria . 7 pro uoluntate sua de boscis illis facere .
dare . uendere . 7 capere . 7 capi facere sine uisu 7 omni contradiccione forestariorum . 7 regardatorum . 7 omnium ministrorum
suorum . 7 inde quicquid ceperint . uel capi fecerint . dederint uel
uendiderint . attrahere possint 7 attrahi facere libere 7 pacifice
cum libertate chemini absque reclamatione . contradiccione . 7
impedimento forestariorum quacumque . occasione . Et quod bosci
illi 7 essarta inde facta 7 facienda ./ sint quieta de uasto . 7 regardo .
7 uisu forestariorum . viridariorum . 7 regardatorum . Et quod
ipsi 7 omnia dominica sua 7 omnes homines dominicorum suorum
sint quieti de sectis swanimotorum 7 omnium aliorum placitorum
foreste . 7 de espaltamentis canum . 7 de omnibus summonitionibus .
placitis . querelis . 7 occasionibus ad forestam 7 forestarios pertinentibus ./ salua nobis tantum uenatione nostra . saluis nichilominus
predicto episcopo 7 successoribus suis in perpetuum omnibus
predictis libertatibus 7 quietantiis[9] . Et quandocumque de predictis
boscis parcos fecerint ./ extunc omnino sint deafforestati tam de
uenatione quam de omnibus aliis ad forestam 7 forestarios pertinentibus . Concessimus itaque quod tresturnare possint uiam[10]
que se extendit a Kenebautona[11] uersus Huntendoniam per quandam
partem bosci de Buggedena ./ ut decetero sit uia illa inter boscum
suum predictum . 7 boscum contiguum de Brantona[12] in[13] diuisa
eorundem boscorum . Preterea concessimus quod predictus episcopus
7 successores sui habeant ferias singulis annis per tres uel[14] quattuor
dies duraturas . 7 mercata singulis septimanis per unum diem per
omnia maneria sua ubi . 7 quando . ea[15] habere uoluerint 7 habere
possint absque nocumento uicinarum feriarum 7 uicinorum merca-

torum ; cum omnibus libertatibus 7 liberis consuetudinibus ad huiusmodi ferias 7 mercata pertinentibus . Nos uero 7 heredes nostri predictum manerium de Wimelthorpe[16] cum omnibus pertinentiis suis . omnes quoque donationes . concessiones . libertates . quietas clamantias predictas . predicto episcopo 7 successoribus suis tanquam puram . liberam 7 perpetuam elemosinam nostram ; contra omnes homines[17] warantizabimus in perpetuum . Quare uolumus 7 firmiter precipimus quod predicta ecclesia Linc'[2] 7 predictus Hugo Linc'[2] episcopus 7 successores sui in perpetuum habeant 7 teneant omnia predicta bene . 7 in pace . libere . quiete . 7 integre . in omnibus locis 7 rebus cum omnibus libertatibus . 7 liberis consuetudinibus 7 quietantiis supradictis sicut predictum est ; tamquam puram . liberam . 7 perpe*tuam elemosinam nostram . quietam penitus ab omni seculari seruitio 7 exactione in perpetuum . Testibus domino . S. Cantuariensi archiepiscopo . W. Londoniensi . P. Wintoniensi . E. Elyensi[18] . E. Herefordiensi . J. Bathoniensi 7 Glastoniensi episcopis . W. Marescallo comite Penbrochie . [19]W. comite Warenne . S. comite Wintonie . Willelmo[20] Briwerr' . Roberto filio Walteri . J. Marescallo[19] . 7 Thoma[21] de Erdintona[22] . Data per manum magistri Ricardi de Marisco cancellarii nostri apud Nouum Templum London' vicesimo primo die Januarii[23] ; anno regni nostri sextodecimo.

Endorsed : (1) III (13 cent.). (2) .j. (13 cent.). (3) Carta Johannis regis de Vimelthorp et aliis (15 cent.).
Tag for seal torn away. Size : 7¾ x 12.
Marginalia in A : 2|.
Texts : MS—Orig. A1/1/44. A. Orig. A1/1/50 (inspeximus, no. 228 below). Orig. A1/1/60 (inspeximus, no. 228 below). Iiv(23). Charter roll, 16 John, mem. 5. Pd—*Rotuli Chartarum* i, 203–4. See *C.C.R.*i,5 ; iv,111(23).
Var. R. : [1] Rot. ch. *shortens the salutation.* [2] Lincoln' Orig.50 Iiv. [3] Wymeltorp' A ; Wimelthorp' Orig.50. [4] Newerc' A ; Neuwerch' Orig.50. [4a] *the first two letters of* Aaron *have each an acute accent.* [5] excaeta Orig.50. [6] Stouwa A Orig.50 ; Stow' Orig.60. [7] Lidington' Orig.50 ; Lidintun' Orig.60 ; Lydinton' Iiv. [8] Stouwa Orig.50. [9] quitanciis Orig.50 Iiv. [10] uiam possint A. [11] Kenebautun' Orig.60. [12] Brantun' Orig.60. [13] cum A. [14] *insert* per Orig.50 Orig.60. [15] eam A. [16] Wymeltorp' A Iiv ; Wimeltorp Orig.60. [17] *om.* homines A. [18] Helyens' A. [19–19] *om.* W. comite Warenne . . . J. Marescallo A. [20] W. Orig.60. [21] Tom' Orig.60. [22] Erdington Orig.50 ; Erdintun' Orig.60. [23] Nouembris Iiv (which is the date of the variant charter, no. 206 below).
Note : Crouch spinney was in the parish of Banbury, and Crouch Hill still appears on the map, two miles to the south-west of that place.

*Folio 30.

Hdl. .3.0.

ADD. CHART.

206. Charter of John, similar in part to the preceding charter, 21 November, 1214.

Johannes dei gratia rex Anglie . dominus Hibernie . dux Normannie et Aquitanie . comes Andegauie . archiepiscopis . episcopis . abbatibus . comitibus . baronibus . iusticiariis . forestariis . vicecomitibus . prepositis . et omnibus balliuis et fidelibus suis ; salutem .

Sciatis nos pro amore dei [7¹] pro salute anime nostre 7 omnium antecessorum 7 heredum nostrorum dedisse . concessisse 7 hac carta nostra confirmasse deo 7 ecclesie beate Marie Lincoln' 7 venerabili patri Hugoni Lincoln' episcopo 7 successoribus suis inperpetuum in liberam puram 7 perpetuam elemosinam manerium de Wimelthorpe iuxta Neowercha cum omnibus pertinentiis suis quod est de feodo episcopi Linc' . 7 forisuadiatum fuit uersus Aaron² iudeum . 7 deuenit in manum domini regis .H. patris nostri post mortem eiusdem Aaron² tanquam excaeta sua . Habendum eidem episcopo 7 successoribus suis 7 ecclesie Lincoln' in perpetuum quietum ab omni seculari seruicio 7 exactione cum omnibus libertatibus 7 liberis consuetudinibus quas ipsum manerium habet uel quas aliquod maneriorum ipsius episcopi habet . Dedimus etiam et concessimus 7 omnino quietas clamauimus in perpetuum eidem ecclesie Linc' 7 predicto episcopo 7 successoribus suis decem libras argenti quas ipse episcopus 7 predecessores sui nobis 7 antecessoribus nostris annuatim reddere consueuerunt de wapentacco de Stowa . Concessimus etiam quod idem episcopus uel successores sui possint claudere 7 parcos facere si uoluerint uel essartare boscos suos de Lidintona 7 Bugendena 7 Spaldewic cum graua de Stowa . 7 pro uoluntate sua de boscis illis facere 7 capere sine contradictione 7 uisu forestariorum . Et quod bosci illi 7 essarta inde facta 7 facienda sint quieta de uasto 7 regardo 7 uisu forestariorum 7 regardatorum . Et quod ipsi 7 dominica sua 7 homines dominicorum suorum sint quieti de sectis swanimotorum 7 omnium aliorum placitorum foreste . 7 de espeltamentis canum . 7 de omnibus querelis 7 occasionibus ad forestarios pertinentibus . Salua nobis tantum uenatione nostra . 7 saluis predicto episcopo 7 successoribus suis in perpetuum omnibus predictis libertatibus 7 quitanciis . Et quandocunque de predictis boscis [par¹]cos fecerint ꞉ extunc omnino sint deafforestati tam de uenatione quam de omnibus aliis ad forestam 7 forestarios pertinentibus . Preterea concessimus quod predictus episcopus 7 successores sui habeant ferias singulis annis per tres uel quattuor dies duraturas 7 mercata singulis s[eptimana¹]s per unum diem per omnia maneria sua ubi 7 quando ea habere uoluerint 7 habere possint absque nocumento uicinarum fer[iarum 7¹] uicinorum mercatorum cum omnibus [li¹]bertatibus 7 liberis consuetudinibus ad huiusmodi ferias 7 mercata pertinentibus . Nos uero 7 heredes nostri predictum manerium [de¹] Wimelthorpe cum omnibus pertinentiis suis predicto episcopo 7 successoribus suis tanquam puram 7 perpetuam elemosinam nostram contra [omnes h¹]omines warantizabimus . Quare uolumus 7 firmiter precipimus . quod predicta ecclesia Linc' 7 predictus .H. episcopus [7 succe¹]ssores sui in perpetuum habeant 7 teneant predictum manerium de Wimelthorpe cum omnibus pertinentiis 7 libertatibus suis predictis . . . . . d habeant in perpetuum quitanciam predictarum decem librarum argenti . 7 predictas libertates de predictis boscis suis . 7 quod . . . . dominica sua 7 omnes homines dominicorum suorum quieti sint de omnibus que ad forestam 7 forestarios pertinent sicut pre*dictum est* . . . . . . *predictus* episcopus 7 successores sui habeant predictas ferias 7 mercata sicut supradictum est . Et quod omnia pre*dicta* . . . . pace . libere 7 quiete . integre 7 honorifice in omnibus locis 7 rebus cum omnibus libertatibus et . . . . ciis supradictis . Testibus . domino .S. Cant*uariensi* archiepiscopo . W. Lond*oniensi* . P. Winton*iensi* . E. Elien*si* . . . . episcopis . W. Marescallo comite Penbro*chie* .W. comite Warenne .S. comite Wintoni*e* . Willelmo . . . .[3] 7 Thoma de Erdinton*a* . Data per manum magistri Ricardi de Marisco can*cellario* . . . . *vice*simo primo die Nouembris . anno regni nostri sexto decimo.

Endorsed : (1) III. (2) Carta Johannis regis de Wymelthorp remissione x li. pro Stow et de aliis (14 cent.). (3) . . . . .
Text : MS—Orig. A1/1/44a (the charter has several holes, and the bottom left hand corner has been torn off).
Var. R. : [1] *supplied from* Orig. A1/1/45 (no. 205 above). [2] *The first two letters of* Aaron *have each an acute accent.* [3] *The witnesses are probably the same as in* Orig. A1/1/45.

ADD. CHART.

207. Letters patent of John, addressed to bishop Hugh II, promising peace and safety, and asking him to come to England. At Temple Ewell [co. Kent]. 24 May, 1213.

De pace promissa . . episcopo Lincoln' (R rubric).

.J. dei gratia rex Angl*ie* (dominus Hibern*ie* .⁊ dux Aquit*anie* . Norm*annie* comes Andeg*auie* .⁊ venerabili patri in Christo .H. eadem gratia Linc' episcopo salutem . Sciatis quod secundum formam mandati domini 7 venerabilis patris nostri .I. dei gratia summi pontificis veram pacem ac plenam securitatem vobis prestamus necnon ceteris tam clericis quam laicis hoc negocium quod inter nos 7 ecclesiam Anglicanam versatum est contingentibus (Nec vos nec vestros ledemus vel ledi faciemus aut permittemus in personis vel rebus . vobisque dimittimus omnem indignacionem 7 in gratiam nostram vos recipimus 7 tenebimus bona fide (Et quod vos non impediemus nec faciemus aut permittemus aliquatenus impediri quo minus libere vestrum exequamini officium 7 plena iurisdiccionis vestre auctoritate prout debetis vtamini . Et super hiis vobis iuramenta 7 litteras patentes fidelium nostrorum venerabilium patrum domini .H. Dublinens*is* archiepiscopi .P. Winton*iensis* 7 .J. Norwicens*is* episcoporum (7 preterea .xii. baronum nostrorum scilicet .G. filii Petri comitis Essex*ie* iustic*iarii* nostri .R. comitis Bolon*ie* .R. comitis Cestr*ie* .W. Marescall*i* comitis Pembroc .W. comitis Warenne .W. comitis Arundell' .W. comitis de Ferrar*iis* (Willelmi Briwerr' (Roberti de Ros (Gilberti filii Reinfridi (Rogeri de Mortuo Mari 7 Petri filii Herberti fecimus exhiberi .⁊ quod ipsi

bona fide studebunt vt hec pax 7 securitas firmiter obseruetur .
Et si forte quod deus auertat per nos ipsos vel alios contrauenerimus ;
ipsi pro ecclesia contra violatores securitatis 7 pacis mandatis
apostolicis inherebunt (Nos que perpetuo ecclesiarum vacancium
custodiam amittamus . Et ideo vos rogamus quatinus ad nos secure
7 sine dilacione in Angliam venire festinetis . Si quid autem in hoc
scripto omissum vel minus plene factum fuerit ; cum in Angliam
veneritis secundum formam mandati apostolici perficietur . Et in
huius rei testimonium has litteras nostras patentes vobis mittimus
Testibus dominis .H. Dublinensi archiepiscopo .P. Wintoniensi
episcopo .G. filio Petri comite Essexie .W. Marescallo comite Pembroc
apud Templum de Ewell' .xxiiijto. die Maij . anno regni nostri
quintodecimo.

Marginalia : Nota.
Text : MS—R49.
Note : A similar letter, addressed to the archbishop of Canterbury, and of the
same date, is enrolled on the patent roll, with a note that letters were sent to each
bishop who was with the archbishop beyond the sea, namely, the bishops of London,
Hereford, Ely, Bath, and Lincoln, and to the prior and monks of Canterbury (*Rotuli
Litt. Pat.* i, 98b, 99).

ADD. CHART.

208. Letters patent of John, informing bishop Hugh II that
he has granted peace and security to the Church of England,
according to the form of peace sent by the pope through Pandulf
the legate, whereby the king, in return for his submission to the
pope, and absolution from excommunication, has made oath to
give security to the bishops and others, and to make restitution
for damages. At Beer [Regis, co. Dorset]. 28 June, 1213.

De pace reformata inter regem 7 .. episcopum Lincoln' (R
rubric).

Johannes dei gracia rex Anglie . dominus Hibernie . dux Normannie
7 Aquitanie . comes Andegauie . venerabili patri in Christo .H.
eadem gracia Lincoln' episcopo . salutem . Sciatis quod ueram
pacem 7 plenam securitatem uobis 7 uestris prestamus necnon
ceteris tam clericis quam laicis negocium quod inter nos 7 ecclesiam
Anglicanam diutius uersatum est contingentibus . secundum formam
pacis nobis a domino papa per Pandulfum clericum suum trans-
missam . que talis est . In primis itaque solempniter 7 absolute
iurabimus . stare mandatis domini pape coram eius legato uel
delegato[1] super omnibus pro quibus excommunicati sumus ab ipso .
7 ueram pacem ac plenam securitatem prestabimus venerabilibus
viris .S. Cantuariensi . archiepiscopo .W. Londoniensi .E. Eliensi
.E. Herefordiensi .J. Bathoniensi . 7 .H. Lincolniensi[2] episcopis .
priori quoque ac monachis Cantuarie . 7 .R. filio Walteri ac Eustacio
de Vescy . necnon ceteris clericis ac laicis hoc negocium contingentibus . Prestando simul coram eodem legato uel delegato publice

iuramentum . quod ipsos cum suis nec ledemus nec ledi faciemus
uel permittemus in personis uel rebus . Eisque dimittemus omnem
indignacionem . 7 in graciam nostram recipiemus eosdem . ac
tenebimus bona fide . Quodque prefatos archiepiscopum 7 episcopos
non impediemus . nec faciemus aut permittemus aliquatenus
impediri . quominus ipsi libere suum exequantur officium . 7 plena
sue iuridictionis auctoritate prout debent utantur . Et super hiis
tam domino pape quam archiepiscopo 7 singulis episcopis nostras
patentes litteras exhibebimus . facientes ab episcopis 7 comitibus
ac baronibus nostris quot 7 quos prefati archiepiscopi 7 episcopi
postulauerint iuramenta 7 eorum patentes lit[teras ex³]hiberi .
quod ipsi bona fide studebunt . ut hec pax 7 securitas firmiter
obseruetur . Et si forte quod [deus³] auertat per nos ipsos uel alios
contrauenerimus⁴ (ipsi pro ecclesia contra uiolatores securitatis
7 pacis mandatis apostolicis inherebunt . nosque perpetuo uacantium
ecclesiarum custodiam amittamus . Quod si forte nequiuerimus
eos ad hanc ultimam iuramenti partem inducere . videlicet quod
si per nos ipsos uel alios contrauenerimus . ipsi pro ecclesia contra
uiolatores securitatis 7 pacis mandatis apostolicis inherebunt ; nos
propter hoc domino pape ac ecclesie Romane per nostras patentes
litteras obligabimus omne ius patronatus quod habemus in ecclesiis
Anglicanis . Et omnes litteras que pro securitate predictorum sunt
exhibende ; prefatis archiepiscopo 7 episcopis ante suum ingressum
in Angliam transmittemus . Si uero nobis placuerit . sepefati archiepiscopus 7 episcopi prestabunt saluo honore dei 7 ecclesie iuratoriam⁵
7 litteratoriam cautionem . quod ipsi nec per se nec per alios contra
personam uel coronam nostram aliquid attemptabunt . nobis predictam eis securitatem 7 pacem seruantibus illibatam . De ablatis
autem plenam restitutionem . 7 de dampnis recompensationem
sufficientem omnibus impendemus . tam clericis omnibus quam
etiam laicis uniuersis ad hoc negocium pertinentibus . non solum
rerum . set etiam libertatum . 7 restitutas conseruabimus libertates .
archiepiscopo quidem 7 episcopo Linc' a tempore sue confirmationis .
aliis a tempore discordie inchoate . Nec obstabit aliqua pactio uel
promissio uel concessio . quominus 7 dampna recompensentur ;
7 restituantur ablata . tam uiuorum quam etiam defunctorum .
Nec de hiis aliquid retinebimus pretextu seruicii quod debuerat
nobis impendi . set postea debita nobis pro seruicio recompensatio
tribuetur . statimque omnes quos detinemus clericos faciemus
absolute dimitti . ac restitui proprie libertati . 7 etiam laicos qui
occasione huius negocii detinentur . incontinenti quoque post
aduentum illius qui nos debebit absoluere faciemus [de p³]arte
restitutionis ablatorum octo milia librarum legalium sterlingorum
pro persoluendis debitis 7 faciendis expensis in nun[cii³]s predictorum archiepiscopi 7 episcoporum ac monachorum Cantuarie
assignari . sine impedimento quolibet per potestatem nostram ad
eos libere deferenda . ut expediti reuertantur in Angliam . honorifice

reuocati . videlicet .S. Cant*uariensi* archiepiscopo duo millia 7 quingentas libras .W. Lond*oniensi*[6] ⁒ septingentas 7 quinquaginta libras .E. Eliensi ⁒ mille 7 quingentas libras .E. Heref*ordiensi*[7] ⁒ septingentas 7 quinquaginta libras .J. Bathon*iensi* septingentas 7 quinquaginta libras .H. Linc' septingentas 7 quinquaginta libras . priori 7 monachis Cant*uarie* ⁒ mille libras . Set protinus absque mora postquam pacem istam duxerimus acceptandam ⁒ resignari faciemus archiepiscopo 7 episcopis 7 clericis ac ecclesiis uniuersis in manibus nunciorum uel procuratorum ipsorum ⁒ omnia inmobilia cum administratione libera eorundem . 7 in pace dimitti . Interdictum etiam uulgariter utlagatio nuncupatum quod proponi fecimus contra personas ecclesiasticas . publice reuocabimus . protestando per nostras litteras[8] patentes archiepiscopo tribuendas ⁒ id ad nos de personis ecclesiasticis nullatenus pertinere . quodque illud decetero contra personas ecclesiasticas nullatenus faciemus proponi . Reuocantes preterea utlagationem laicorum ad hoc negocium pertinentium . 7 remittentes hominia quod post interdictum recepimus ab ecclesiarum hominibus preter regni consuetudinem 7 ecclesiasticam libertatem . Si uero super dampnis uel ablatis aut eorum quantitate uel estimatione questio fuerit de facto suborta ⁒ per legatum aut delegatum domini pape receptis probacionibus publice terminetur . Et hiis omnibus rite peractis ⁒ relaxabitur sentencia interdicti . Su[per ceteris[3]] autem capitulis sique fuerint dubitationes suborte de quibus merito ualeat dubitari nis[i[3]] per legatum uel delegatum domini pape de partium fuerint uoluntate sopite ⁒ ad ipsius referantur arbitrium . ut super hiis quod ipse decreuerit ⁒ obseruetur . Et super hiis uobis[9] iuramenta 7 litteras patentes fidelium nostrorum . uenerabilium patrum .H. Dublin*ensis* archiepiscopi . 7 .J. Norwic*ensis* 7 .P. Winton*iensis* episcoporum . 7 duodecim baronum nostrorum scilicet .G. filii Petri[10] comitis Essex*ie* .R. comitis Bolon*ie* .W. comitis de Ferrar*iis*[11] .R. comitis Cestr*ie* .W. Marescall*i* comitis Penbroch*ie*[12] .W. comitis Warenne .W. comitis Arundell' ⟨ Willelmo[*sic*] Briwerr' . Roberti de Ros . Gileberti[13] filii Reinfr*idi* . Rogeri[14] de Mortuo Mari[15] . Petri filii Herb*erti*[16] fecimus exhiberi . quod ipsi bona fide studebunt . ut hec pax 7 securitas firmiter obseruetur . Et in huius rei testimonium has litteras patentes sigillo nostro signatas uobis transmittimus . Teste . me ipso apud Bera*m* .xxviij. die Junii . anno regni nostri quintodecimo ;

Endorsed : (1) Pacis prouisio inter .J. regem 7 prelatos post gwerram (13 cent.). (2) Domino Lincoln' (contemp.). (3) I ⸳į⸳
    Tag for seal, with the remains of a black leather cover which covered it. Size : 5¾ x 11¼ inches.
    Texts : MS—Orig. A1/1/42. R51.
    Var. R. : [1] *om.* uel delegato R. [2] Linc' R. [3] *supplied from* R, *the charter having been injured.* [4] contrauenimus R. [5] iuramentum R. [6] London' R. [7] Hereford' R. [8] litteras nostras R. [9] uobis *interlineated* Orig. [10] *for* G. filii Petri *read* fil' Gilberti R. [11] Ferrar' R. [12] Penbroc R. [13] Gilberti R. [14] Rogero R. [15] *insert* 7 R. [16] Henrici R.

209. Notification by John that he has made oath that, by Easter, 1214, he will make full restitution and compensation for losses and damages inflicted upon clerks and laymen. At Portchester. 13 July, 1213.

De restitucione dampnorum illatorum per regem (rubric).

.J. dei gracia rex Anglie ⟩ dominus Hibernie ⟩ dux Normannie ⟩ Aquitanie 7 comes Andegauie omnibus ad quos presens scriptum peruenerit ⫶ salutem . Nouerit vniuersitas vestra nos tactis sacrosanctis ewangeliis iurasse ⫶ quod infra pascha proximum anni regni nostri quintidecimi[1] de ablatis plenam restitucionem 7 de dampnis recompensacionem sufficientem impendemus tam clericis omnibus quam eciam laicis vniuersis ad negocium quod inter nos 7 Anglicanam ecclesiam diucius versatum est pertinentibus ⟩ Et quod non obstabit aliqua pactio vel promissio seu concessio ⫶ quo minus 7 dampna recompensentur 7 restituantur ablata tam viuorum quam eciam defunctorum . Et quod de oblatis nichil retinebimus pretextu seruicii quod nobis debuerit impendi ⟩ Set postea debita nobis pro seruicio ⟩ recompensacio tribuetur ⟩ 7 quod infra Natale proximum de parte restitucionis ablatorum archiepiscopo Cantuariensi 7 Londoniensi ⟩ Eliensi ⟩ 7 .M. bone memorie Wigorniensi ⟩ Herefordensi ⟩ Bathoniensi 7 Lincolniensi episcopis . . priori Cantuarie ⟩ Roberto filio Walteri ⟩ Eustachio de Vescy 7 magistro Simoni de Langeton' quindecim milia marcarum legalium sterlingorum persoluemus 7 totum residuum de restitucione 7 recompensacione facienda omnibus ⫶ soluemus infra predictum Pascha ⟩ nisi de gracia predictorum archiepiscopi 7 episcoporum terminus vltime solucionis scilicet Pasche predicti vlterius prorogetur . Teste me ipso apud Portcestram .xiij. die Julii anno regni nostri quinto decimo.

Marginalia : Nota.
Text : MS—R50.
Var. R. : [1] sic.

210. The Charter of Liberties, commonly called MAGNA CARTA, dated at Runnymede [co. Surrey], between Windsor and Staines. 15 June, 1215.

The charter is not printed here because it appears in type and engraved facsimile in The Statutes of the Realm i, 9–13, *and in* Appendix to Reports of the Public Records Commissioners (1819), no. 3. *The Lincoln copy of the Great Charter was also selected for reproduction in type and engraved facsimile in* Facsimilies of National Manuscripts (Ordnance Survey Office), part i, no. XVI, *and* Table of the Charters *because it was the handsomest extant of the four original copies. The charter has also been printed by* Stubbs, Select Charters, pp. 296–306, *and by others. The charter at Lincoln, like the original at Salisbury, shews no trace of any seal, and Dr R. L. Poole conjectures that the great seal was attached to the original kept in the Exchequer* (E. H. R. xxviii, 449).

Texts at Lincoln : MS—Orig. A1/1/45. R52. Pd—as above.
Size : 18¼ x 17¾ inches.

211. Charter of John, granting to the church of Lincoln and bishop Hugh II, in compensation for waste made by the king and his men in respect of Stow Park, in the time of the general interdict in England, the royal wood of Harthay [co. Huntingdon], with licence to enclose, impark, or assart it, quit of pleas of the forest, saving the king's hunting, until the wood is disafforested. At Oxford. 18 July, 1215.

Johannes dei gratia rex Anglie dominus Hybernie dux Normannie 7[1] Aquitanie[2] comes Andegauie . archiepiscopis . episcopis . abbatibus . comitibus . baronibus . iusticiariis . forestariis . vicecomitibus . prepositis . 7 omnibus balliuis 7 fidelibus suis ⁊ salutem[3]. Sciatis nos pro amore dei 7 pro salute anime nostre 7 omnium antecessorum 7 heredum nostrorum . in recompensationem quoque uasti 7 exilii facti per nos 7 nostros de parco de Stowa[4] tempore generalis interdicti in Anglia . dedisse 7 concessisse . 7 presenti carta nostra confirmasse deo 7 ecclesie beate Marie Linc'[5] 7 venerabili patri Hugoni Linc'[6] episcopo secundo 7 successoribus suis in perpetuum . in puram . liberam . 7 perpetuam elemosinam boscum nostrum de Herteia[7] in Huntedunesyra[8] cum omnibus pertinentiis . libertatibus . 7 liberis consuetudinibus suis . in plano . pratis . pascuis . 7 pasturis . habendum 7 tenendum eidem episcopo 7 successoribus suis 7 Linc'[5] ecclesie in perpetuum . adeo libere . quiete . integre . 7 pacifice . sicut nos 7 antecessores nostri ipsum boscum unquam melius . liberius . 7 integrius tenuimus . quietum etiam ab omni seculari seruitio 7 exactione . Concessimus etiam quod idem episcopus 7 successores sui possint claudere 7 parcum facere si uoluerint uel essartare[9] quantum . quando . 7 ubi uoluerint boscum illum cum pertinentiis suis . 7 pro uoluntate sua de bosco illo facere . dare . uendere . 7 capere . 7 capi facere sine uisu 7 omni contradictione . forestariorum . viridariorum[10] . 7 regardatorum . 7 omnium ministrorum . suorum . 7 inde quicquid[11] ceperint . uel capi fecerint . dederint uel uendiderint . attrahere possint 7 attrahi facere . libere . 7 pacifice cum libertate chemini absque reclamatione 7 contradictione 7 impedimento forestariorum ⁊ quacumque occasione . Et quod boscus ille cum pertinentiis 7 essarta inde facta 7 facienda sint quieta de uasto 7 regardo 7 uisu forestariorum . viridariorum . 7 regardatorum . Et quod omnes homines in bosco illo 7 essartis inde factis 7 faciendis 7 pertinentiis eorum manentes ⁊ sint quieti de sectis swanimottorum 7 omnium placitorum foreste . 7 de espeltamentis canum . 7 de omnibus summonitionibus . placitis . querelis . 7 occasionibus ad forestam 7 forestarios pertinentibus ⁊ salua tantum nobis uenatione nostra . Saluis nichilominus predicto episcopo 7 successoribus suis in perpetuum omnibus predictis libertatibus 7 quitantiis[11a]. Et quandocumque de predicto bosco

parcum fecerint (extunc omnino sit deafforestatus tam de uenatione
quam de omnibus aliis ad forestam 7 forestarios pertinentibus .
Quare uolumus 7 firmiter precipimus quod predicta ecclesia Lincoln'
7 predictus Hugo Linc' episcopus[11b] 7 successores sui in perpetuum
habeant 7 teneant predictum boscum de Herteia[7] cum omnibus
pertinentiis suis in plano . pratis . pascuis . 7 pasturis . bene . 7 in
pace . libere . quiete . 7 integre . in omnibus locis 7 rebus cum omnibus
libertatibus 7 liberis consuetudinibus 7 quietantiis supradictis (
sicut predictum est . tanquam puram . liberam . 7 perpetuam
elemosinam nostram . quietam penitus ab omni seculari seruitio
7 exactione in perpetuum . Quam nos 7 heredes nostri eis[12] contra
omnes homines warantizabimus in perpetuum . Hiis testibus .
Henrico Dublin*ensi*[13] archiepiscopo . Petro Winton*iensi* . Joscelino
Bathon*iensi*[14] 7 Glaston*iensi* . Waltero Wigorn*ensi* : episcopis .
Willelmo Marescall*o* comite Penbrocie[15] . Willelmo comite
Saresbyrie[16] . Rand*ulfo* comite Cestr*ie* . Willelmo comite de
Ferrar*iis*[17] . Willelmo Briwerr'[18] . Petro filio Hereberti[19] . Philippo
de Albiniaco[20] . Willelmo de Harecurt' . 7 Briano de Insula .
Data per manum magistri Ricardi de Marisco cancellarii nostri
apud Oxon*iam*[21] octauodecimo die Julij : anno regni nostri septimo
decimo.

Endorsed : (1) II .j. (13 cent.). (2) Carta regis Johannis de Herteia (15 cent.).
(3) Johannis regis (14 cent.).
Tag for seal torn away. Size : 8¼ x 9⅜ inches.
Texts : MS—Orig. A1/1/43. Orig. A1/1/53 (inspeximus, no. 237 below). Charter
rolls, 17 John, mem. 7 ; also *ibid.* 11 Henry III, mem. 28 ; and *ibid.* 13 Henry III,
schedule, mem. 2. Iiv(24). Pd—*Rotuli Chartarum* i, 214. See *C.C.R.*i,8,105 ;
iv,111(24).
Var. R. : [1] *om.* 7 Orig.53. [2] *insert* 7 Orig.53. [3] *The salutation is shortened in*
Ch. Roll. [4] Stouwa Orig.53. [5] Lincoln' Orig.53. [6] Lincoln' Orig.53 Ch. roll.
[7] Herteya Ch. roll. [8] Huntingdon' sira Orig.53 ; Huntedonesir' Ch. roll. [9] assartare
Ch. roll. [10] *om.* viridariorum Ch. roll. [11] quicquit Ch. roll. [11a] quietanciis Orig.53.
[11b] *insert* secundus Orig.53. [12] *om.* eis Ch. roll. [13] Dupplin' Ch. roll. [14] Baton'
Ch. roll. [15] Penbroc Ch. roll. [16] Sarr' Orig.53 ; Sar' Ch. roll. [17] Ferrariis Ch.
roll. [18] Briwer' Ch. roll. [19] Herberti Orig.53. [20] de Albinniac' Orig.53 ; Dealban'
Ch. roll. [21] Oxoniam Ch. roll.
Note : Harthay wood was in the parish of Brampton, co. Huntingdon and
originally, it may be presumed, it formed part of the forest of Weybridge (*The
Place-Names of Bedfordshire and Huntingdonshire*, English Place-Name Society iii,
232–4). High Harthay still appears on the ordnance map.

ADD. (EXTRAN.) CHART.

212. Charter of John, confirming the settlement made between
Robert [Fitz Parnell], earl of Leicester, and bishop William and
the chapter of Lincoln touching the manor of Knighton [co.
Leicester] and the bishop's land at Leicester. The bishop and
chapter have quitclaimed the manor of Knighton and the land
at Leicester to the earl for the service of one knight's fee, saving
to the bishop and church of Lincoln the church of Saint Margaret
with the chapel of Knighton, which church is a prebend of Lincoln.
For this settlement, the earl, with assent of P[aul] the abbot and

the convent of Leicester, has given to the bishop and church of
Lincoln the village of Asfordby with the advowson of its church
and six carucates and three bovates in Seagrave [co. Leicester],
and whatever the abbot and convent held there; and the king,
with the assent of the bishop and church of Lincoln, has rendered
to the earl Farthinghoe and Syresham [co. Northampton], which
were given by the earl's grandfather to bishop Robert Chesney
and the church of Lincoln. At Westminster. 24 March, 1203–1204.

Conuentio facta inter episcopum Linc' 7 comitem Leice*strie*.

Johannes dei gracia 7c. Sciatis quod de assensu venerabilis
patris nostri domini H. Cant*uariensis* archiepiscopi 7 nostro est
hec finalis concordia facta in vigilia Annunciationis beate Marie
anno regni nostri v^to. apud West*monasterium* coram predicto
domino Cant*uariensi* 7 coram nobis) 7 coram dominis London*iensi*
Roff*ensi* Sarr*isbiriensi* Elyen*si* Norwic*ensi* Wigor*niensi* Bathon*iensi*
episcopis de eorum consilio 7 assensu 7 coram G. filio Petri comite
Essex*ie* 7c. iustic*ia* coram W. comite Mare*scallo*) W. comite
Arundell*i*) W. comite Sarr*isbirie* .W. comite Warenn*e* . comite
R. Bigot .A. comite Ebroic*ensi* .W. de Braosa .W. Briwerr*a* . 7
aliis baronibus 7 fidelibus nostris ibidem 7c. presentibus Inter
Robertum filium Roberti comitem Leirc*estrie* petentem 7 Willelmum
episcopum Linc' 7 capitulum Lincol' tenentes de Knicteton' cum
pertinenciis 7 de tota terra quam idem episcopus 7 antecessores
sui habuerunt infra murum Leirc*estrie* 7 in suburbio . unde placitum
fuit inter eos videlicet) quod predictus episcopus 7 capitulum
Linc' reddiderunt 7 quietum clamauerunt 7 concesserunt predicto
comiti 7 heredibus suis in perpetuum sicut ius 7 hereditatem suam
Knicteton' cum pertinenciis suis 7 totam predictam terram quam
ipsi habuerunt infra murum Leirc*estrie* 7 in suburbio . habenda 7
tenenda sibi 7 heredibus suis iure hereditario de predicto episcopo
7 successoribus . suis) 7 ecclesia Linc') in perpetuum) per seruicium
.j. militis pro omni seruicio salua predicto episcopo Linc' 7 ecclesie
Linc' ecclesia sancte Margarete cum capella de Knicteton' 7 aliis
pertinenciis suis) que scilicet ecclesia cum pertinenciis suis est
prebenda ecclesie Linc' . Predictus uero episcopus in presencia
nostra 7 omnium predictorum recepit inde homagium predicti
comitis . Pro hac concordia reddicione quieto clamio 7 concessione
dedit predictus comes coram domino Cant*uariensi* 7 nobis 7 aliis
tam episcopis quam baronibus supradictis predicto episcopo 7
successoribus suis 7 ecclesie Linc' de assensu 7 voluntate P. tunc
abbatis Leice*strie* 7 conventus eiusdem loci totam villam de Esse-
fordebi cum advocatione ecclesie eiusdem ville) 7 molendinis) 7
omnibus pertinenciis suis 7 sex carrucatas 7 tres bovatas terre in
Segrave cum pertinenciis suis 7 quicquid idem abbas 7 conuentus
ibidem tunc tenuerunt sicut predictus abbas 7 conuentus ea
tenuerunt . habenda 7 tenenda in liberam 7 perpetuam 7 puram

elemosinam libera 7 quieta ab omni seculari seruicio 7 exactione .
Per hanc autem concordiam reddidimus de assensu prefati episcopi
Linc' 7 capituli predicto comiti 7 heredibus suis Ferlingho 7 Sigeresh'
) que date fuerunt per concordiam episcopo Linc' 7 ecclesie Linc'
tempore Roberti de Chedney tunc episcopi Linc' inter quem 7
antecessores predicti comitis erat controversia de predictis terris
) scilicet) de Knicteton' cum pertinenciis 7 predictis terris infra
murum Leir*cestrie* 7 in suburbio) habenda 7 tenenda predicto
comiti 7 heredibus suis sicut ius 7 hereditatem suam quieta de
predicto episcopo 7 successoribus suis 7 ecclesia Linc' inperpetuum .
Concessum est autem a predictis episcopo 7 capitulo Linc' 7 comite
7 abbate 7 conventu Leir*cestrie* quod si aliqua instrumenta penes
aliquam partium remanserint) que de predictis terris) uel ecclesiis
uel aliqua earum uel de pertinenciis alicuius earum fecerint men-
tionem) eis nullo tempore utantur contra formam predicte concordie .
Predictam uero uillam de Essefordeby cum advocatione ecclesie
eiusdem ville 7 aliis pertinenciis suis predictis . 7 predictas sex
carrucatas terre 7 tres bovatas in Sagrave cum pertinenciis suis) 7
quicquid idem abbas 7 conventus tunc ibidem habuerunt warantizabunt sicut tenentur 7 debent predictus comes 7 heredes sui predicto
episcopo 7 successoribus suis 7 ecclesie Linc' in perpetuum . 7 idem
episcopus 7 successores sui 7 ecclesia Lincol' warantizabunt sic
tenentur 7 debent predicto comiti 7 heredibus suis inperpetuum
Knicteton' cum pertinenciis suis 7 totam predictam terram quam
predictus episcopus 7 antecessores sui 7 capitulum Linc' habuerunt
infra murum Leir*cestrie* 7 in suburbio . Nos igitur predictam concordiam ratam habentes eam presenti scripto 7 sigilli nostri munimine confirmauimus 7 ad peticionem nostram dominus Cant*uariensis*
7 alii coepiscopi sui suprascripti sigilla sua huic scripto apposuerunt
7 subscripserunt . 7 ad maiorem securitatem presens scriptum in
modum cyrographi confectum est 7 utrique partium sua pars
tradita est.

Text : MS—Charter roll, 5 John, mem. 8. Pd—*Rotuli Chartarum* i, 125.

Add. Chart.

213. Charter of John, confirming a grant made by the abbot
and convent of Leicester to William bishop of Lincoln of the village
of Asfordby [co. Leicester], with the advowson of its church, and
of six carucates and three bovates in Seagrave [co. Leicester]. At
Wallingford [co. Berks]. 20 April, 1204.

Johannes dei gracia rex Angl*ie* dominus Hybernie dux Normann*ie*
7 Aquitann*ie* comes Andeg*auie* archiepiscopis episcopis abbatibus
comitibus baronibus iustic*iariis* vicecomitibus prepositis 7 omnibus
balliuis 7 fidelibus suis) salutem[1]. Sciatis Robertum comitem
Leyrcestrie[2] de consensu 7 voluntate Pauli[3] abbatis 7 conuentus
Leircestrie[2] coram nobis 7 coram domino .H. Cant*uariensi*

archiepiscopo 7 aliis multis tam episcopis quam baronibus nostris dedisse 7 concessisse 7 carta sua confirmasse Willelmo episcopo Lincoln'⁴ 7 successoribus suis 7 ecclesie Lincoln'⁴ imperpetuum totam villam de Esefordeby⁵ cum aduocacione ecclesie eiusdem ville 7 cum molendinis 7 omnibus aliis pertinenciis suis et sex carucatas 7 tres bouatas terre in Segraua⁶ cum pertinenciis suis 7 quicquid idem abbas 7 conuentus Leyrcestrie² tunc ibidem tenuerunt) habenda 7 tenenda eidem episcopo 7 successoribus suis 7 ecclesie Lincoln'⁴ in liberam puram 7 perpetuam elemosinam quieta ab omni seculari seruicio . Quare volumus 7 firmiter precipimus⁷ quod predictus episcopus Linc' 7 successores sui 7 ecclesia Linc' habeant 7 teneant omnia predicta tenementa cum omnibus pertinentiis suis imperpetuum bene 7 in pace libere 7 quiete 7 integre in liberam puram 7 perpetuam elemosinam sicut predictum est . Testibus . G. filio Petri comite Essex*ie*) R. comite Cestr*ie*) Warino filio Geroldi) Roberto de Veteri ponte) Petro de Stok' . Dat' per manum domini .S. Cicestr*ensis* electi) apud Wallingeford*am* .xx. die Aprilis anno regni nostri quinto.

Texts : MS—Iiv(22). Charter roll, 5 John, mem. 7. Pd—*Rotuli Chartarum* i, 126. *C.C.R.*iv,111(22).
　Var. R. in Charter roll : ¹ *The salutation is shortened.* ² Leirc'. ³ *read P. for* Pauli. ⁴ Linc'. ⁵ Essefordby. ⁶ Segrave. ⁷ *for* volumus 7 firmiter precipimus *read* 7c.

ADD. (EXTRAN.) CHART.

214. Charter of John, confirming to the church of Lincoln the prebend of Carlton [Kyme] [North Carlton, co. Lincoln], which Philip of Kyme constituted a prebend of the church of Lincoln, saving to Philip's son, Simon, the advowson of that prebend. At Woodstock [co. Oxford]. 17 January, 1208.

Carta de prebenda de Karleton'.

J. dei gracia 7c. Sciatis nos concessisse 7 presenti carta nostra confirmasse deo 7 ecclesie beate Marie Lincoln' . prebendam de Karleton' cum omnibus pertinenciis suis) quam Philippus de Kima concessit 7 constituit prebendam Linc' ecclesie hoc retento Simoni de Kyma 7 heredibus suis qui heres ipsius Philippi est ut liceat sibi 7 heredibus suis quociens eadem prebenda uacauerit clericum idoneum presentare qui auctoritate 7 consilio domini episcopi Linc' eiusdem prebende canonicus instituatur sicut carte Walteri 7 Hugonis Lincoln' episcoporum quas inde habet rationabiliter testantur . Hiis testibus) Roberto filio Walteri . Hugone le Bigod . Ricardo de Perci . Willelmo de Kantil*upo* . Radulfo Gernu*n* . Luca de Trubevill' . Galfrido Luterel . Dat' per manum H. de Well*is* . archidiaconi de Well*is* . apud Wdestok') xvij. die Januarii) anno regni nostri nono.

Texts : MS—Charter roll, 9 John, mem. 4. Pd—*Rotuli Chartarum* i, 174.

ADD. (EXTRAN.) CHART.

215. Letters patent of John, pardoning to bishop Hugh II all the debts which he owed to the king before Saint Cecilia's day [22 November], 1214, to the approximate sum of six hundred marks. At the New Temple, London. 22 November, 1214.

J. dei gracia rex Angl*ie* dominus Hibern*ie* dux Norm*annie* 7 Aquit*anie* 7 comes Andeg*auie* omnibus fidelibus suis has litteras inspecturis salutem . Sciatis quod perdonauimus venerabili patri Hugoni Lincoln' episcopo omnia debita que nobis debuit ante diem sancte Cecilie anno regni nostri sextodecimo vsque ad summam circiter sexcentarum marcarum . Et in huius rei testimonium has litteras nostras patentes ei inde fieri fecimus . Teste me ipso apud Nouum Templum London' xxij die Nouembris anno regni nostri sextodecimo.

Text: MS—Iv(43).　Pd.—See *C.C.R.*iv,147(43).

Nos. 216-217 are an insertion by a sixteenth century hand.

165

216. Composition by which Roger the dean and the chapter of Lincoln demise the church of Scothorne [co. Lincoln] to the abbot and canons of Barlings for a yearly render of ten shillings, saving the portion which belongs to the prebend of Richard of Linwood, canon of Lincoln. The dean and chapter also grant all their right in two bovates in Scothorne to the abbot and canons for a yearly render of four shillings. (1203–1206.)

Composicio facta inter capitulum Lincoln' et abbatem et conuentum de Barlyng*es* de ecclesia de Scosthorne.

Hec est amicabilis composicio facta inter Rogerum decanum et capitulum Lincoln' ecclesie ex parte vna . et abbatem et canonicos de Barling*es* ex alia super ecclesia de Scosthorne de qua controuersia agebatur inter eos . videlicet quod predicti decanus et capitulum dimiserunt eijsdem abbati et canonicis ecclesiam de Scosthorne perpetuo et pacifice possidendam Reddendo annuatim commune Lincoln' ecclesie decem solidos ad duos terminos . Scilicet in pascha . quinque solidos . et in festo sancti Michaelis . quinque solidos . Salua porcione pertinente ad prebendam que est Ricardi de Lindwd' canonici Lincoln' ecclesie scilicet duabus partibus decimarum de dominio . Preterea concesserunt prenominati decanus et capitulum prefatis abbati et canonicis totum ius quod habebant in duabus bouatis terre in Scosthorne Habend*um* inperpetuum . Soluendo ex inde singulis annis eidem commune quatuor solidos pro omni seruicio ad eosdem terminos . Et ut hec dicta composicio rata et inconcussa permaneat . vtraque pars presenti scripto sigilla sua apposuit . Testibus Radulp*ho* . abbate de Bartheneia . Thoma

abbate de Kirkested' . Hugone abbate de Reuesby Galfrido abbate
de Tupholm . Jordano abbate de Thorneh'[1] . Waltero priore de
Thornholm . Roberto Bard*ulf* . Hugone de Sancto Edwardo et
canonicis ecclesie Lincoln' . Eudone preposito.

Text : MS—A.
Note : [1] Evidently a mistake for ' Thornton.'   Jordan de Villa was elected
abbot of Thornton in 1203.

166

217. Agreement made between R[oger] dean of Lincoln and
Robert abbot of Barlings with respect to certain tithes in Scothorne,
which from of old have belonged to the prebend of All Saints in
Hungate. (1203–1206.)

Finalis concordia facta inter decanum et capitulum Lincoln' et
abbatem et conuentum de ecclesia de Scosthorne.

Hec est finalis concordia facta inter .R. decanum Lincoln' ecclesie
ex vna parte . et Robertum abbatem et conuentum* de Barling' ex
altera procurante et consenciente .R. Bard*ulf* fratre 7 herede .
Hugonis Bard*ulf* super duabus partibus decimarum de dominico
quondam Hugonis Bard*ulf* . et dominico Radulfi Trehampton in
Scosthorn tam in garbis quam minutis decimis . ab antiquo ad
prebendam Linc' . scilicet Omnium Sanctorum in Hundegate spectantibus videlicet quod .R. de Linwud tunc temporis eiusdem
prebende canonicus et singuli eius successores duas partes decimarum garbarum de dictis dominicis bene 7 in pace cum omni
integritate . participent . Ita quod collectores decimarum tam ex
parte dictorum abbatis et conuentus quam pro tempore canonici ;
iuramento astringantur de collectione fideliter pro debita porcione
facienda pro duabus vero partibus decimarum minutarum
vtriusque dominici Predicti abbas 7 conuentus soluent annuatim
inperpetuum predicto R. canonico et successoribus suis viginti
solidos in ecclesia Lincoln' . scilicet . decem solidos ad natale sancti
Johannis Baptiste . et decem solidos ad festum Omnium Sanctorum .
In hac etiam conuencione adiectum est quod abbas et conuentus
de Barling*es* quo minus hec concordia fideliter obseruetur nullo
vmquam vteretur priuiligeo [*sic*] set vtrimque in perpetuum stabilis
et illibata permanebit In huius autem rei robur et testimonium
sigilla capituli Lincoln' et abbatis et conuentus de Barling*es* presenti
cirographo dictam concordiam continenti appensa sunt.

Text : MS—A.
*Folio 30d.

167

218. Confirmation of the foregoing agreement by William
bishop of Lincoln. (1203–1206.)

Confirmacio episcopi Linc' de ecclesia de Scosthorne data
abbati et conuentui.

XIX

14¾ in. × 11¾ in.

Omnibus Christi fidelibus ad quos presens scriptum peruenerit Willelmus Dei gracia Linc' episcopus salutem eternam in Domino . Noueritis quod nos ratam et gratam habemus composicionem factam inter dilectos filios R. decanum et capitulum Lincoln' ex vna parte . et abbatem et canonicos de Barlinges ex altera super ecclesiam de Scosthorne de qua inter eos agebatur controuersia prout in autentico inter eos super hoc confecto continetur Eam que auctoritate nostra prout rite facta est confirmamus et presenti scripto cum sigilli nostri patrocinio communimus (Saluis in omnibus episcopalibus consuetudinibus et Lincoln' ecclesie dignitate . Testibus magistris .G. de Rowelle . A. de Sancto Edmundo T. de Fiskerton . canonicis Linc' magistro .W. filio Fulconis R. de Calc-welle . R. de Stowe . R. de Rowell' clericis et multis aliis.

Text : MS—A.

ADD. CHART.

219. Henry III : Charter of the Forest, dated at Saint Paul's, London. 6 November, 1217.

Enricus[1] dei gracia rex Anglie . dominus Hybernie . dux Normannie . Aquitanie . [2]comes Andegauie . archiepiscopis . episcopis . abbatibus . prioribus . comitibus . baronibus . iusticiariis . forestariis . vicecomitibus . prepositis . ministris .
5   [3]balliuis . 7 omnibus fidelibus suis[3] ⁒ salutem . Sciatis quod intuitu dei . 7 pro salute anime nostre . 7 animarum ante-cessorum . 7 successorum nostrorum . ad exaltationem sancte ecclesie . 7 emendationem regni nostri . concessimus 7 hac presenti carta confirmauimus . pro nobis 7 heredibus nostris
10   in perpetuum . de consilio venerabilis patris nostri domini Gualonis . tituli sancti Martini presbiteri cardinalis . 7 apos-tolice sedis legati . domini Walteri Eboracensis . archiepiscopi . Willelmi Londoniensis episcopi . 7 aliorum . episcoporum . Anglie . et Willelmi Marescalli comitis Penbrocie . rectoris
15   nostri . 7 regni nostri . 7 aliorum fidelium . comitum . 7 baronum nostrorum . Anglie . has libertates subscriptas tenendas in regno nostro Anglie . in perpetuum . In primis . Omnes foreste quas Henricus rex auus noster afforestauit ⁒ uideantur per probos[4] 7 legales homines . Et si boscum aliquem
20   alium quam suum dominicum afforestauerit ⁒ ad dampnum illius cuius boscus fuerit ⁒ deafforestetur[5] . Et si boscum suum proprium afforestauerit ⁒ remaneat foresta . salua communa de herbagio . 7 aliis in eadem foresta . illis qui eam prius habere consueuerunt . Homines qui manent extra forestam ⁒
25   non ueniant de cetero coram iusticiariis nostris de foresta per communes summonitiones ⁒ nisi sint in placito . uel plegii alicuius uel aliquorum . qui attachiati sunt propter forestam . Omnes autem bosci qui fuerunt afforestati per regem Ricardum auunculum nostrum . uel per regem Johannem patrem nostrum .

K

30 usque ad primam coronationem nostram ; statim deafforesten-
    tur . nisi fuerit dominicus boscus noster . archiepiscopi .
    episcopi . abbates . priores . comites . 7 barones . 7 milites .
    7 libere tenentes . qui boscos suos habent in forestis ; habeant
    boscos suos sicut eos habuerunt tempore prime coronationis
35 predicti regis Henrici . aui nostri . ita quod quieti sint in
    perpetuum de omnibus purpresturis . vastis . 7 essartis⁶
    factis in illis boscis post illud tempus . usque ad principium
    secundi anni coronationis nostre . Et qui de cetero vastum .
    purpresturam . uel essartum⁷ . sine licentia nostra in illis
40 fecerint ; de vastis . purpresturis⁸ . 7 essartis⁶ respondeant .
    Reguardores nostri eant per forestas ad faciendum reguardum
    sicut fieri consueuit tempore prime coronationis predicti
    regis Henrici . aui nostri . 7 non aliter . Inquisitio uel visus
    de expeditatione canum existentium in foresta de cetero
45 fiat quando debet fieri reguardum . scilicet de tercio anno
    in tercium annum . 7 tunc fiat per visum 7 testimonium
    legalium hominum . 7 non aliter . Et ille cuius canis inuentus
    fuerit tunc non expeditatus ; det pro misericordia tres solidos .
    Et de cetero nullus bos capiatur pro expeditatione . Talis
50 autem sit expeditatio per assisam communiter . quod tres
    ortilli abscidantur sine pelota de pede anteriori . Nec expedi-
    tentur canes de cetero ; nisi in locis ubi consueuerunt expe-
    ditari tempore prime coronationis regis Henrici . aui nostri .
    Nullus forestarius uel bedellus de cetero faciat scotale . uel
55 colligat garbas . uel auenam . uel bladum [aliud] uel agnos .
    uel porcellos . uel aliquam collectam faciat⁹ . Et per visum
    7 sacramentum duodecim reguardorum . quando facient
    reguardum ; tot forestarii ponantur ad forestas custodiendas ;
    quot¹⁰ [ad illas cus]todiendas rationabiliter uiderint sufficere .
60 Nullum suanimotum de cetero teneatur in regno nostro nisi
    ter in anno . videlicet in principio quindecim dierum ante
    festum sancti Michaelis . quando [agistatores conueni]unt
    ad agistandum dominicos boscos nostros . Et circa festum
    sancti Martini . quando agistatores nostri debent recipere
65 pannagium nostrum . Et ad ista duo suanimota conueniant
    forestarii . [viridarii 7 agistatores] . 7 nullus alius per distric-
    tionem . Et tercium suanimotum teneatur in initio quindecim
    dierum ante festum sancti Johannis Baptiste . pro feonatione
    bestiarum nostrarum . Et ad istud [suanimotum tenendum]
70 conueniant forestarii . 7 viridarii . 7 non¹¹ alii per distric-
    tionem . Et preterea singulis quadraginta diebus per totum
    annum ; conueniant ¹²forestarii . 7 viridarii¹² . ad uidendum
    attachiamenta de fores[ta] tam de viridi . quam de venatione .
    per presentationem ipsorum . forestariorum . 7 coram ipsis
75 attachiatis . Predicta autem suanimota non teneantur nisi
    in comitatibus in quibus teneri consueuerunt . Vnusquisque

liber homo agistet boscum suum in foresta ⫶ pro uoluntate
sua 7 habeat pannagium suum . Concedimus etiam quod
unusquisque liber homo possit ducere porcos suos per
80   dominicum boscum nostrum libere . 7 sine impedimento .
ad agistandum eos in boscis suis propriis . uel alibi ubi
uoluerit . Et si porci alicuius liberi hominis una nocte pernoctauerint in foresta nostra ⫶ non inde occasionetur . ita
quod aliquid de suo perdat . Nullus de cetero amittat uitam
85   uel menbra ⫶ pro venatione nostra . Set si aliquis captus
fuerit 7 conuictus de captione venationis ⫶ grauiter redimatur .
si habeat unde redimi [*possit*] . Et si non habeat unde redimi
possit ⫶ iaceat in prisona nostra per unum annum . 7 unum
diem . Et si post unum annum 7 unum diem plegios inuenire
90   possit ⫶ exeat a prisona . Sinautem ⫶ abiuret regnum nostrum¹³
[Angl*ie* . Quicunque . archie]piscopus . episcopus . comes .
uel baro . transierit per forestam nostram ⫶ liceat ei capere
unam uel duas bestias . per visum forestarii si presens fuerit .
sinautem ⫶ faciat cornari ne uideatur furtiue [hoc facere .
95   Vnusquisque li]ber homo de cetero sine occasione faciat in
bosco suo . uel in terra sua quam *habeat* in foresta ⫶ molendinum . viuarium . stagnum . marleram . fossatum . uel
terram arabilem extra [cooperatum in terra arabili] . ita
quod non sit ad nocumentum alicuius vicini . Vnusquisque
100   liber homo habeat in boscis suis aerias ancipitrum¹⁴ . 7 spar-
uariorum¹⁵ . falconum . aquilarum . 7 de heyruns¹⁶ . Et habeat¹⁷
similiter [mel quod inuentum fuerit in] boscis suis . Nullus
forestarius de cetero qui non sit forestarius de feodo¹⁸ . eddens
nobis firmam pro ballia sua ⫶ capiat chiminagium aliquod
105   in ballia sua . forestarius autem [de feudo firmam nobis
redd]ens pro ballia sua ⫶ capiat chiminagium . videlicet
pro careta per dimidium annum . duos denarios . 7 per alium
dimidium annum ⫶ duos denarios . et pro equo qui portat
summagium ⫶ per dimi[dium annum vnum obolum] 7 per
110   alium dimidium annum ⫶ unum obolum . Et non nisi de illis ⫶
qui de extra balliam suam tanquam mercatores ueniunt
per licentiam suam in balliam suam . ad buscam . meyre-
mum¹⁹ . [corticem . uel carbonem em]endum . 7 alias
ducendum ad uendendum ubi uoluerint . et de nulla alia
115   careta uel summagio ⫶ aliquod chiminagium capiatur . Et
non capiatur chiminagium ⫶ nisi in locis illis ⫶ ubi [*antiquitus
capi solebat*] 7 debuit . Illi autem qui portant super dorsum
suum buscam . corticem . uel carbonem ad uendendum .
quamuis inde uiuant ⫶ nullum de cetero dent chiminagium .
120   De boscis autem aliorum ⫶ [*nullum detur chim*]inagium
forestariis nostris . preterquam de dominicis boscis nostris .
Omnes vtlagati pro foresta tantum ⫶ a tempore regis Henrici .
aui nostri usque ad primam coronationem nostram ⫶ ueniant

ad [*pacem nostram si*]ne impedimento . 7 saluos plegios
125 inueniant quod de cetero non forisfacient[20] nobis de foresta
nostra . Nullus castellanus uel alius teneat placitum de foresta .
siue de viridi . siue de venatione . set[21] quilibet forestarius
de feodo[22] . attachiet placita de foresta . tam de viridi quam
de venatione . 7 ea presentet viridariis prouinciarum . 7
130 cum inrotulata fuerint . 7 sub sigillis viridariorum inclusa :
presententur capitali forestario . cum in partes illas uenerit
ad tenendum placita foreste . 7 coram eo terminentur . Has
autem libertates de forestis : concessimus omnibus . Saluis
archiepiscopis . episcopis . abbatibus . prioribus . comitibus .
135 baronibus . militibus . 7 aliis . tam personis ecclesiasticis .
quam secularibus . Templariis . 7 Hospitalariis . libertatibus .
7 liberis consuetudinibus . in forestis . 7 extra . in warenniis .
7 aliis : quas prius habuerunt . Omnes autem istas consuetudines predictas 7 libertates quas concessimus in regno nostro
140 tenendas quantum ad nos pertinet erga nostros : omnes de
regno nostro tam clerici quam laici obseruent . quantum
ad se pertinet : erga . suos . Quia uero [23]nondum sigillum[23]
habuimus : presentem cartam sigillis venerabilis patris nostri .
domini Gualonis[24] . tituli . sancti Martini presbiteri cardinalis .
145 7[25] apostolice sedis legati . et Willelmi Marescalli comitis
Penbrocie[26] . rectoris nostri . 7 regni nostri . fecimus sigillari .
Testibus prenominatis . 7 aliis multis.[27]

Facsimile opposite page 145.
Endorsed : Carta de foresta sub sigillo episcopi (13 cent.).
Seal on tag : Pointed oval, 1⅞ x 1¼ inches, green wax ; ecclesiastical figure vested
in alb and chasuble with maniple, hands uplifted ; the head missing : [SIGILL'
G]VAL[E. T' SC'I MARTINI PRE . . . .]. The seal of William Marshall is missing. Size :
14⅜ x 11¾ inches.
Texts : MS—Orig. A1/1/46. The charter has been injured on the lower part
of the left hand margin, and the missing words have been supplied in square brackets
from the only other original copy that is known to exist, namely, the copy in Durham
cathedral, which is printed both in type and engraved facsimile in *Statutes of the
Realm* i, 20–1, and *Appendix to Reports* of the Public Records Commission (1819),
no. IV. The legate's seal is in a more perfect condition than that of the Lincoln
charter. The Lincoln charter, however, has suffered less injury than the Durham
copy, and is the best existing text. For secondary copies of the charter see *Statutes
of the Realm* i, Table of the Charters. Where both the Lincoln and the Durham
copies are defective the missing words have been supplied conjecturally in italic
type, enclosed within square brackets, from these secondary copies. Pd—(In
addition to the works already mentioned) Stubbs, *Select Charters*, pp. 348–51.
G. J. Turner, *Select Pleas of the Forest*, Selden Soc. xiii, pp. cxxxv-vii. See
R. L. Poole's note in *E.H.R.* xxviii, 448–51.
Var. R. in the Durham Cathedral charter : [1] *for* Enricus *read* Henricus. (*In the
Lincoln copy space is left for the initial* H.)   [2] *insert* 7.   [3–3] omnibus balliuis 7 fidelibus
suis.   [4] bonos.   [5] deafforestentur.   [6] assartis.   [7] assartum.   [8] *om.* purpresturis.
[9] faciant.   [10] quod.   [11] *for* non *read* nulli.   [12–12] viridarii 7 forestarii.   [13] *om.*
nostrum.   [14] [an]ciptum.   [15] *insert* 7.   [16] heyrinis.   [17] habeant.   [18] feudo.   [19] mere-
mum.   [20] forisfaciant.   [21] sed.   [22] feudo.   [23–23] sigillum non dum.   [24] G.   [25] *om.* 7.
[26] Penbrok'.   [27] *add* Dat' p[er *manus predictorum domini legati* 7 *Willelmi Mares*]calli
apud sanctum Paulum London*ie* Q . . . . . . [*die No*]uembris anno regni nostri
. secundo.
Note : The Forest charter was published at a grand council held at Saint Paul's,
on 6 November, 1217, when also a re-issue of Magna Carta was published. This

date is given in the transcript of the Durham copy of the Forest charter printed from type in *Statutes of the Realm* (p. 21) ; but in the engraved facsimile in the same work the day of the month begins with Q, while the rest of the word has perished. Since the date cannot be earlier than November the 6th, Q indicates *Quartodecimo* or *Quintodecimo*. The word *Sexto* in the printed text was probably taken by the Record Commission editors from the lost Exchequer original.

ADD. CHART.

220: Henry III : Charter of the Forest, dated at Westminster. 11 February, 1225.

De libertatibus regni Angl*ie* de foresta (R. rubric).

Henricus dei gracia rex Angl*ie* . dominus Hibern*ie*[1] . dux Norm*annie* . Aquit*anie* . 7 comes Andeg*auie* . archiepiscopis . episcopis . abbatibus . prioribus . comitibus . baronibus . iusticiar*iis* forestariis . vicecomitibus prepositis ministris
5 Et omnibus balliuis 7 fidelibus suis[2] . salutem . Sciatis quod[3] intuitu dei[4] 7 pro salute anime nostre 7 animarum[5] antecessorum[6] 7[7] successorum nostrorum ad exaltacionem sancte ecclesie 7 emendacionem regni nostri spontanea 7 bona uoluntate nostra dedimus 7 concessimus archiepiscopis . episcopis .
10 comitibus . baronibus 7 omnibus de regno nostro . has libertates subscriptas tenendas in regno nostro Angl*ie* in perpetuum . In primis omnes foreste quas Henricus rex[8] auus noster afforestauit uideantur per bonos 7 legales homines ⟩ 7 si boscum aliquem alium[9] quam suum dominicum afforest-
15 auerit ad dampnum illius cuius boscus[10] fuerit ⸴ deafforestetur ⟩ Et si boscum suum proprium afforestauerit ⸴ remaneat foresta ⟩ salua communa de herbagio 7 aliis in eadem foresta illis qui prius ea[11] habere consueuerunt ⟩ Homines[12] qui manent extra forestam non ueniant decetero coram iusticiar*iis*[13]
20 nostris de foresta per communes summoniciones nisi sint in placito uel plegii alicuius uel aliquorum qui attachiati sint[14] propter forestam . Omnes autem bosci qui fuerunt[15] afforestati per regem Ricardum auunculum nostrum ⟩ uel per regem Johannem patrem nostrum usque ad primam coronacionem
25 nostram . statim deafforestentur ⟩ nisi fuerit[16] dominicus boscus noster . Archiepiscopi . episcopi . abbates . priores . comites . barones . milites . 7 libere tenentes [17]qui boscos suos habent[17] in forestis ⸴ habeant boscos suos sicut eos habuerunt tempore prime coronacionis predicti[18] regis Henrici aui nostri .
30 ita quod quieti sint in perpetuum de omnibus purpresturis . vastis ⟩ 7 assartis[19] ⟩ factis in illis boscis post illud tempus usque ad principium secundi anni coronacionis nostre ⟩ Et qui decetero vastum ⟩ [20]purpresturam ⟩ uel assartum sine licencia[20] nostra in illis fecerint[21] . de vastis ⟩ purpresturis[22] .
35 7 assartis[23] respondeant ⟩ Regardores[24] nostri eant per forestas ad faciendum regardum[25] sicut fieri consueuit tempore prime coronacionis predicti[26] regis Henrici aui nostri . 7 non aliter .

Inquisicio uel uisus de expeditacione canum existencium in
foresta[27] decetero fiat ⁏ quando debet fieri[28] reguardum[29])
40 scilicet de tercio anno in tercium annum) 7 tunc fiat per
uisum 7 testimonium legalium hominum 7 non aliter . Et
ille cuius canis inuentus fuerit tunc non expeditatus ⁏ det
pro misericordia tres solidos) Et de cetero nullus bos capiatur
pro expeditacione) Talis autem sit expeditacio per assisam
45 communiter . quod tres ortilli abscindantur[30] sine pelota de
pede anteriori . Nec expeditentur canes decetero nisi in locis
ubi consueuerunt expeditari) tempore prime coronacionis
predicti[31] regis Henrici aui nostri . Nullus forestarius uel
bedellus decetero faciat scotall'[32] uel colligat garbas uel
50 auenam uel bladum aliud[32a] uel agnos uel purcellos) nec aliquam
collectam faciat) Et per uisum 7 sacramentum duodecim
reguardorum[33] quando facient reguardum[34]) tot forestarii
ponantur ad forestas custodiendas . quot ad illas custodiendas[35]
rationabiliter uiderint sufficere) Nullum swanimotum decetero
55 teneatur in regno nostro) nisi ter in anno . videlicet in principio
quindecim dierum ante festum sancti Michaelis) quando
agistatores[36] conueniunt ad agistandum dominicos boscos
nostros ⁏ Et circa festum sancti Martini quando agistatores
nostri debent recipere pannagium nostrum . Et ad ista duo
60 swanimota conueniant forestarii . viridarii 7 agistatores)
7 nullus alius[37] per districtionem) Et tercium swanimotum
teneatur in inicio quindecim dierum ante festum sancti Johannis
Baptiste . pro feonacione bestiarum nostrarum . Et ad istud[38]
swanimotum tenendum ⁏ conueniant forestarii 7 viridarii)
65 7 non alii per districtionem . Et[39] preterea singulis quadraginta
diebus per totum annum conueniant viridarii . 7 forestarii[40]
ad uidendum[41] attachiamenta de foresta tam de uiridi quam
de venacione per presentacionem [42]ipsorum forestariorum[42] 7
coram ipsis attachiatis) Predicta autem swanimota non
70 teneantur nisi in comitatibus in quibus teneri consueuerunt)
Vnusquisque liber homo agistet boscum suum[43] in foresta
pro uoluntate sua ⁏ 7 habeat pannagium suum) Concedimus
eciam quod unusquisque liber homo ducere possit porcos
suos per dominicum boscum nostrum libere 7 sine impedi-
75 mento ad agistandum eos in boscis suis propriis uel alibi
ubi uoluerit . Et si porci alicuius liberi hominis una nocte
pernoctauerint in foresta nostra ⁏ non inde occasionetur[44] ⁏
ita quod[45] aliquid de suo perdat) Nullus decetero amittat
uitam uel menbra[46] pro uenacione nostra . Set si aliquis
80 captus fuerit 7 conuictus de capcione uenacionis ⁏ grauiter
redimatur si habeat unde redimi possit) Et si[47] non habeat
unde redimi possit ⁏ iaceat in prisona nostra per unum annum
7 unum diem . 7 si post unum annum 7 unum diem plegios
inuenire[48] possit ⁏ exeat a prisona[49]) sin autem ⁏ abiuret

85   regnum Anglie . Quicunque . archiepiscopus . episcopus .
comes . uel baro ueniens ad nos ad mandatum nostrum
transierit per forestam nostram . liceat ei capere unam uel
duas bestias per uisum forestarii si presens fuerit) sinautem :'
faciat cornare[50] . ne uideatur furtiue hoc facere . Idem liceat
90   ei[51] in redeundo facere sicut predictum est . vnusquisque
liber homo decetero sine occasione faciat in bosco suo[52] uel
in terra sua quam habet in foresta . molendinum . viuarium .
stagnum . marleriam[53] . fossatum) uel terram arrabilem .
extra coopertum in terra arabili . ita quod non sit ad nocu-
95   mentum alicuius vicini . Vnusquisque liber homo habeat in
boscis suis aerias . ancipitrum speruariorum[54] falconum .
aquilarum . 7 de heyruns[55]) 7 habeat similiter mel quod
inuentum fuerit in boscis suis . Nullus forestarius decetero
qui non sit forestarius de feudo[56] nobis reddens firmam[57]
100   pro ballia[58] sua :' capiat chiminagium[59] aliquod in ballia[58] sua
forestarius autem de feudo[56] firmam nobis reddens pro ballia[58]
sua :' capiat chiminagium[59] . videlicet pro careta[60] per dimidium
annum[61] duos denarios . 7 [62]per alium dimidium annum .
duos denarios . Et[62] pro[63] equo qui portat summagium per
105   dimidium annum :' unum[64] obulum[65] . 7 per alium dimidium
annum unum[64] obulum[65]) 7 non nisi de illis qui de[66] extra
balliam[67] suam tanquam mercatores ueniunt per licenciam
suam in balliuam[68] suam ad buscam . meremium . corticem .
uel carbonem emendum 7 alias ducendum ad uendendum
110   ubi uoluerint Et de nulla alia careta[69] uel summagio aliquo
cheminagium[70] capiatur) Et non capiatur cheminagium[70] :'
nisi in locis illis :' ubi[71] antiquitus capi solebat 7 debuit . Illi
autem qui portant super dorsum suum buscam . corticem .
uel carbonem ad uendendum quamuis inde uiuant nullum
115   decetero dent cheminegium[72]) Omnes vtlagati pro foresta
tantum a tempore regis Henrici aui nostri usque ad primam
coronacionem nostram :' ueniant ad pacem nostram sine
impedimento :' et saluos plegios inueniant :' quod decetero
non forisfacient nobis de foresta nostra) Nullus castellanus
120   uel alius[73] teneat placita de foresta siue de viridi siue de
uenacione . Set quilibet forestarius de feudo[74] attachiet[75]
placita de foresta tam de viridi quam de uenacione) 7 ea
presentet viridariis prouinciarum) 7 cum inrotulata fuerint
7 sub sigillis viridariorum inclusa :' presententur capitali
125   forestario[76] cum in partes illas uenerint[77] ad tenendum placita
foreste 7 coram eo terminentur) Has autem[78] libertates de
forestis concessimus omnibus . saluis . archiepiscopis . episcopis .
abbatibus . prioribus . comitibus . baronibus . militibus . 7
aliis tam personis ecclesiasticis . quam secularibus . Templariis .
130   Hospitalariis :' libertatibus 7 liberis consuetudinibus in forestis
7 extra in warennis 7 aliis . quas prius habuerunt . Omnes

autem istas consuetudines predictas 7 libertates quas concessimus in regno nostro tenendas quantum ad nos pertinet
erga nostros ⫶ omnes de regno nostro [79]tam clerici quam
135   laici[79] obseruent quantum ad se pertinet erga suos . Pro hac
autem[80] concessione 7 donacione libertatum istarum 7 aliarum[81]
contentarum in maiori carta nostra de aliis[82] libertatibus ⫶
archiepiscopi . episcopi . abbates . priores . comites . barones .
milites . 7[83] libere tenentes 7 omnes de regno nostro dederunt
140   nobis quintamdecimam partem omnium mobilium suorum .
Concessimus eciam eisdem pro nobis 7 heredibus nostris quod
nec nos nec heredes nostri aliquid perquiremus per quod
libertates in hac carta contente infringantur . uel infirmentur .
Et si ab aliquo [84]aliquid contra hoc[84] perquisitum fuerit ⫶
145   nichil . ualeat 7 pro nullo habeatur ⫶ Hiis testibus[85] . domino .
Stephano Cantuariensi archiepiscopo[86] . Jocelino Bathoniensi[87] .
Petro Wintoniensi . Hugone Lincolniensi . Ricardo Sarresbiriensi . Benedicto Roffensensi . Willelmo Wygorniensi .
Johanne Eliensi . Eustachio Londoniensi . Hugone Here-
150   fordensi . Radulfo Cicestrensi . Willelmo Exoniensi episcopis .
abbate Sancti Edmundi . abbate Sancti Albani . abbate de
Bello . abbate Sancti Augustini Cantuariensi[88] . abbate[89]
Eueshamie . abbate[89] Westmonasterii . abbate de Burgo
Sancti Petri . abbate Radingie[90] . abbate[89] Abbendonie . abbate
155   Malmesbirie[91] . abbate[89] Winchecumbie . abbate de Hida .
abbate Certeseye[92] . abbate de Sireburna . abbate de Cerna[93] .
abbate de Abbodesbiria[94] . abbate Middeltone[95] . abbate de
Seleby . abbate de Wyteby . abbate Cirencestrie[96] . Huberto
de Burgo iusticiario . Randulfo comite Cestrie 7 Lincolnie .
160   Willelmo comite Sarresbirie[97] . Willelmo comite Warenne .
Gileberto de Clare comite Gloucestrie[98] 7 Hertfordie . Willelmo
de Ferrariis comite de Derebeia . Willelmo de Mandauilla[99]
comite Essexie . Hugone le Bigod[100] comite Norfolcie .
Willelmo comite Albemarlie[101] . Humfrido comite Herefordie .
165   Johanne constabulario Cestrie . Roberto de Ros . Roberto
filio Walteri . Roberto de Veteri Ponte . Willelmo Briwera[102] .
Ricardo de Munfichet[103] . Petro filio Hereberti . Matheo [filio
Herberti ⟩ Willelmo de[104]] Albiniaco[105] . Roberto Gresleia[106] .
Reginaldo[107] de Brausa[108] . Johanne de Munemue[109] . Johanne
170   filio Alani . Hugone de Mortuo Mari . Waltero de Bello Campo .
Willelmo de Sancto Johanne . Petro de Malo[110] La[cu ⟩ Briano
de Insula . Thoma de Multona[111] ⟩ Ricardo de Argentin[104] ⟩]
Galfrido de Neuilla . Willelmo Maudut[112] . Johanne de Balun[113] .
Dat' apud Westmonasterium vn[decimo die Februarij .
175   anno regni nostri . nono[104]].

Texts : MS—Orig.A1/1/47.　R59　Durham cathedral MSS(original). *Ibid.*
Cartularium III, f. 211.　B.M., Add. Charter 24,712.　The Lincoln original has
been injured at the foot on the right hand side, and twenty-one words are lost.
The Durham original is less perfect.　The original in the B.M. is perfect, and still
has the royal seal attached, though it has been damaged at one edge and repaired.
The three original texts and that of R are collated here.　　　Pd—Blackstone,
Charters, pp. 60–67.　*Statutes of the Realm* i, 26–7.

Var. R.: [1] Hybern' Dur.　[2] *insert* presentem cartam inspecturis Dur.　[3] *insert*
nos Dur.　[4] *for* Dei *read* dedi Add.ch.　[5] *om.* 7 animarum Add.ch.　[6] *insert* nostrorum
Add.ch.　[7] *insert* animarum Add.ch.　[8] rex Henricus Add.ch.　[9] *om.* alium R.
[10] *insert* ille Dur.　[11] eam Dur. Add.ch.　[12] *insert* vero Dur.　[13] iusticiariis Dur.
Add.ch.　[14] sunt Dur. Add.ch.　[15] fuerint Dur. Add.ch.　[16] sit Dur. ; *om.* fuerit R.
[17–17] qui habent boscos suos Dur.　[18] *om.* predicti Dur.　[19] essartis Dur.　[20–20] vel
purpresturam sine licencia Dur.　[21] *insert* vel essartum Dur.　[22] *om.* purpresturis
Add.ch.　[23] essartis Dur. ;　*add* 7 purpresturis Add.ch.　[24] reguardores Add.ch. ;
regardatores R.　[25] reguardum Add.ch. ; *om.* regardum R.　[26] *om.* predicti Dur.
[27] in foresta existencium Add.ch.　[28] fieri debet Dur.　[29] regardum Dur.　[30] abscidantur
Dur. Add.ch. R.　[31] *om.* predicti Add.ch. R.　[32] scottallas Dur. ; scotalam Add.ch. ;
scottall' R.　[32a] aliquod Dur.　[33] regardorum Dur. ; regwardorum Add.ch. ; reguarda-
torum R.　[34] regardum Dur.　[35] *om.* custodiendas Add.ch.　[36] *insert* nostri Dur.
[37] nulli alii Dur.　[38] illud Dur. ; istum Add.ch.　[39] *om.* Et Dur.　[40] forestarii 7 viridarii Dur.　[41] faciendum Dur.　[42–42] forestariorum ipsorum Dur.　[43] *insert* quem habet
Dur.　[44] occasionentur R.　[45] *for* ita quod *read* unde Dur.　[46] membra Add.ch. R.
[47] *for* Et si *read* Si autem Dur.　[48] *insert* non R.　[49] de prisona Dur.　[50] cornari Dur.
Add.ch.　[51] eis Dur. Add.ch.　[52] *om.* suo R.　[53] marlerum Dur.　[54] espervariorum
Dur.　[55] heyrinis Dur. ; *for* de heyruns *read* ardearum Add.ch.　[56] feodo Dur. Add.ch.
R.　[57] firmam nobis reddens Dur.　[58] balliua Dur. R ; baillia Add.ch.　[59] cheminagium
Dur. Add.ch.　[60] caretta Dur. R ; *om.* pro careta Add.ch.　[61] *insert* pro carretta
Add.ch.　[62–62] *om.* per alium dimidium annum . duos denarios . Et R.　[63] *insert*
vno R.　[64] *om.* unum Dur.　[65] obolum Dur. R.　[66] *om.* de R.　[67] balliuam Dur. R ;
bailliam Add.ch.　[68] bailliam Add.ch.　[69] caretta Dur. Add.ch. R.　[70] chiminagium R.
[71] *for* illis *.' ubi *read* in quibus Dur.　[72] cheminagium Dur. Add.ch. ; chiminagium R.
[73] *om.* uel alius Dur.　[74] feodo Dur. Add.ch. R.　[75] atachiet Add.ch.　[76] *insert* nostro
Dur.　[77] venerit Dur. R.　[78] *om.* autem R.　[79–79] *om.* Dur.　[80] *for* autem *read* igitur
Dur.　[81] *insert* libertatum Dur.　[82] *om.* aliis Add.ch.　[83] *om.* 7 Dur. Add.ch.
[84–84] contra hoc aliquid Add.ch.　[85] *Only the more important various readings in the
names of the witnesses in the several texts are given in the following notes.* Dur. *and*
Add.ch. *generally give an initial for the christian names of the bishops, abbots, and
earls* ; R *generally agrees with the Lincoln original.*　[86] Dur. *and* Add.ch. *insert* E Lond'
here instead of later.　[87] Batthon' Add.ch.　[88] Cantuariensi Add.ch.　[89] *insert* de Dur.
[90] de Rading' Dur. ; Reding' Add.ch.　[91] de Maumebir' Dur.　[92] de Certes' Dur. ;
Certenens' Add.ch. ; Certeseie R.　[93] Cerna Add.ch.　[94] Abotebir' Dur. ; Abbendesbir'
Add.ch.　[95] de Middelton' Dur. Add.ch.　[96] de Cirencestr' Dur. ; de Cyrencestr'
abbatibus Add.ch.　[97] Sarresbyr' Add.ch.　[98] Glouern' Add.ch.　[99] Mandeuill' Dur.
Add.ch.　[100] Bigot Add.ch.　[101] Aubemarl' Add.ch. ; Alberm' Add.ch.　[102] Brigwerr'
Dur.　[103] Muntfichet Add.ch.　[104] *supplied from* Add.ch.　[105] Auben' Add.ch.
[106] Grell' R.　[107] Rog' R.　[108] Brahus Dur. ; Breaus' R.　[109] Multon R.　[110] Mala
Dur.　[111] Muleton Dur. Add.ch.　[112] Mauduit Dur. ; Mauditt Add.ch.　[113] Baalun
Dur. Add.ch.

ADD. CHART.

221. Henry III : The Great Charter, dated at Westminster.
11 February, 1225.

Carta de libertatibus concessis ecclesie 7 regno Anglie (R
rubric) . Magna Carta (R marg.).

Henricus dei gracia rex Anglie dominus Hibernie dux
Normannie Aquitanie 7 comes Andegauie archiepiscopis
5　episcopis abbatibus prioribus comitibus baronibus vicecomitibus (prepositis ministris 7 omnibus balliuis 7 fidelibus
suis presentem cartam inspecturis salutem . Sciatis quod nos

intuitu dei 7 pro salute anime nostre 7 animarum antecessorum
7 successorum nostrorum ad exaltacionem sancte ecclesie 7
10 emendacionem regni nostri spontanea 7 bona voluntate nostra
dedimus 7 concessimus (archiepiscopis episcopis[1] comitibus (
baronibus 7 omnibus de regno nostro[2] Anglie inperpetuum .
In primis concessimus deo 7 hac presenti carta nostra confirmauimus pro nobis 7 heredibus nostris inperpetuum (quod
15 Anglicana ecclesia libera sit 7 habeat[3] iura sua integra 7
libertates suas illesas . Concessimus eciam 7 dedimus[4] omnibus
liberis hominibus regni nostri pro nobis 7 heredibus nostris
imperpetuum omnes libertates subscriptas habendas 7 tenendas
eis 7 heredibus suis de nobis 7 heredibus nostris . Si quis
20 comitum vel baronum nostrorum de nobis tenencium[5] in
capite per seruicium militare mortuus fuerit ∴ 7 cum decesserit ∴
heres eius plene etatis fuerit 7 releuium debeat ∴ habeat
hereditatem suam per antiquum releuium (scilicet heres vel
heredes comitis de baronia comitis integra ∴ per centum
25 libras (heres vel heredes baronis de baronia integra per
centum libras (heres vel heredes militis de feodo militis
integro ∴ per centum solidos ad plus (7 qui minus debuerit ∴
minus det secundum antiquam consuetudinem feodorum .
Si autem heres alicuius talium fuerit infra etatem ∴ dominus
30 eius non habeat custodiam eius nec terre sue antequam
homagium eius ceperit . et postquam talis heres fuerit in
custodia ∴ cum ad etatem peruenerit ∴ scilicet viginti 7 vnius
anni ∴ habeat hereditatem suam sine releuio 7 sine fine .
Ita tamen quod si ipse dum infra etatem fuerit fiat miles ∴
35 nichilominus terra remaneat in custodia dominorum suorum
vsque ad terminum predictum . Custos terre huiusmodi
heredis qui infra etatem fuerit ∴ non capiat de terra heredis
nisi racionabiles exitus 7 racionabiles consuetudines 7
racionabilia seruicia 7 hoc sine destruccione 7 vasto hominum
40 vel rerum . Et si nos commiserimus custodiam alicuius talis
terre vicecomiti vel alicui alii qui de exitibus[6] terre illius
nobis debeant[7] respondere ∴ 7 ille destructionem de custodia
fecerit vel vastum ∴ nos ab illo capiemus emendam 7 terra
committatur[8] duobus legalibus 7 discretis hominibus de feodo
45 illo (qui de exitibus nobis respondeant ∴ vel ei cui eos
assignauerimus . Et si dederimus vel vendiderimus alicui
custodiam alicuius talis terre ∴ 7 ille destructionem inde
fecerit vel vastum ∴ amittat ipsam custodiam 7 tradatur
duobus legalibus 7 discretis hominibus de feodo illo qui
50 similiter nobis respondeant ∴ sicut predictum est . Custos
autem quam diu custodiam terre habuerit ∴ sustentet domos (
parcos (viuaria[9] (stagna (molendina (7 cetera ad terram
illam pertinencia de exitibus terre eiusdem 7 reddat heredi
cum ad plenam etatem peruenerit ∴ terram suam totam

55   instauratam de carucis 7 omnibus aliis rebus ⸴ ad minus
secundum quod illam recepit . Hec omnia obseruentur de
custodiis archiepiscopatuum episcopatuum abbatiarum prior-
atuum ecclesiarum 7 dignitatuum[10] vacancium que ad nos
pertinent (excepto quod custodie huiusmodi[11] ⸴ vendi non
60   debeant[12] . Heredes maritentur absque disparagacione .
Vidua post mortem mariti sui statim 7 sine difficultate[13]
habeat maritagium suum 7 hereditatem suam nec aliquit[14]
det pro dote sua 7[15] pro maritagio suo vel[16] hereditate sua ⸴
quam hereditatem maritus suus 7 ipsa tenuerunt die obitus
65   ipsius mariti (Et maneat in capitali mesuagio[17] mariti sui per
quadraginta dies post obitum ipsius mariti[18] (Infra quos
assignetur ei dos sua ⸴ nisi prius fuerit ei[19] assignata ⸴ vel
nisi domus illa sit castrum (Et si de castro recesserit ⸴ statim
prouideatur ei domus competens in qua possit honeste morari
70   quousque dos sua ei assignetur ⸴ secundum quod[20] predictum
est (Et habeat racionabile estouerium suum interim de
communi . Assignetur autem ei pro dote sua tercia pars
tocius terre mariti sui que sua fuit in vita sua (nisi de minori
dotata fuerit ad hostium ecclesie . Nulla vidua distringatur
75   ad se maritandam ⸴ dum voluerit viuere[21] sine marito ⸴ ita
tamen quod securitatem faciat[22] (quod se non maritabit sine
assensu nostro si de nobis tenuerit ⸴ vel sine assensu domini
sui ⸴ si de alio tenuerit . Nos vero vel balliui nostri non
saisiemus[23] terram aliquam ne[24] redditum pro debito aliquo (
80   quamdiu catalla debitoris presencia sufficiant ad debitum
reddendum ⸴ 7 ipse debitor paratus sit inde satisfacere (Nec
plegii ipsius debitoris distringantur ⸴ quamdiu ipse capitalis
debitor sufficiat ad solucionem debiti . Et si capitalis debitor
defecerit in solucione debiti non habens vnde reddat aut
85   reddere nolit cum possit ⸴ plegii respondeant pro debito
7 si voluerint habeant terras 7 redditus debitoris ⸴ quousque
sit eis satisfactum de debito (quod ante pro eo soluerint[25]
(nisi capitalis debitor monstrauerit ⸴ se inde esse quietum
versus eosdem plegios . Ciuitas London' habeat omnes anti-
90   quas libertates 7 liberas consuetudines suas . Preterea volumus
7 concedimus quod omnes alie ciuitates 7 burgi 7 ville 7
barones de quinque portibus[26] (7 omnes portus habeant
omnes libertates 7 liberas consuetudines suas . Nullus distringatur ad faciendum maius seruicium de feodo militis
95   nec de alio libero tenemento quam inde debetur . Communia
placita non sequantur curiam nostram set teneantur in aliquo
loco certo . Recogniciones de noua disseisina 7 de morte
antecessoris ⸴ non capiantur nisi in suis comitatibus 7 hoc
modo . [27]Nos vel si extra regnum fuerimus capitalis iusti*ciarius*
100   noster[27] . per vnumquemque comitatum semel in anno qui
cum militibus comitatuum capiant in comitatibus assisas⸴

predictas (7 ea que in illo aduentu suo in comitatu per
justiciarios predictos ad dictas assisas capiendas missos
terminari non possunt :' per eosdem terminentur alibi in itinere
105 suo . 7 ea que per eosdem propter difficultatem aliquorum
articulorum terminari non possunt :' referantur ad justic*iarios*
nostros de Bancco[28] 7 ibi terminentur . Assise de vltima
presentacione semper capiantur coram iustic*iariis*[29] de Bancco[28]
7 ibi terminentur . Liber homo non amercietur pro paruo
110 delicto nisi[30] secundum modum ipsius delicti (Et pro magno
delicto secundum magnitudinem delicti :' saluo contenento[31]
suo . Et mercator eodem modo :' salua mercandisia[32] sua .
Et villanus alterius quam noster :' eodem modo amercietur :'
saluo wainagio suo . si incidit[33] in misericordiam nostram
115 (et nulla predictarum misericordiarum ponatur :' nisi per
sacramentum proborum 7 legalium hominum de visneto .
Comites 7 barones non amercientur :' nisi per pares suos
7 non nisi secundum modum delicti . Nulla ecciastica[34] persona
amercietur secundum quantitatem beneficii sui ecclesiastici :'
120 set secundum laicum tenementum suum 7 secundum quantitatem delicti . Nec villa nec homo distringatur facere pontes
ad riparias :' nisi qui ab[35] antiquo 7 de iure[36] debent[37] . Nulla
riparia decetero defendatur :' nisi ille que fuerunt in defenso
tempore .H.[38] aui nostri per eadem loca 7 eosdem terminos
125 sicut esse consueuerunt tempore suo . Nullus vicecomes
constabularius coronatores vel alii balliui nostri teneant
placita corone nostre . Si aliquis tenens de nobis laicum
feodum moriatur 7 vicecomes vel balliuus noster ostendat
litteras nostras patentes de sumonicione nostra de debito
130 quod defunctus nobis debuit :' liceat vicecomiti vel balliuo
nostro attachiare 7 imbreuiare catalla defuncti inuenta in
laico feodo ad valenciam illius debiti per visum legalium
hominum (Ita tamen quod nichil inde[39] amoueatur donec
persoluatur nobis debitum quod clarum fuerit 7 residuum
135 relinquatur executoribus ad faciendum testamentum defuncti .
Et si nichil nobis debeatur ab ipso :' omnia catalla cedant
defuncto (saluis vxori ipsius 7 pueris suis racionabilibus
partibus suis . Nullus constabularius vel eius balliuus capiat
blada vel alia catalla alicuius qui non sit de villa :' vbi castrum
140 situm est nisi statim inde[39] reddat denarios (aut respectum
inde habere possit de voluntate venditoris . Si autem de
villa ipsa fuerit :' infra quadraginta dies precium reddat .
Nullus constabularius distringat aliquem militem ad dandum
denarios pro custodia castri :' si ipse eam facere voluerit
145 in propria persona sua vel per alium probum hominem (si
ipse eam facere non possit propter racionabilem causam .
Et si nos duxerimus eum vel miserimus in excercitum[40] :'
erit quietus de custodia secundum quantitatem temporis quo

per nos fuerit in excercitu[41] (de feodo pro quo fecit seruicium
150 in excercitu[41] . Nullus vicecomes vel balliuus noster vel alius
capiat equos vel carettas alicuius pro cariagio faciendo ⸴
nisi reddat liberacionem antiquitus statutam (scilicet pro
caretta ad duos equos decem denarios per diem (7 pro caretta
ad tres equos quatuordecim denarios per diem . Nulla caretta[42]
155 alicuius ecclesiastice persone vel militis vel alicuius domine
capiatur per balliuos nostros[43] predictos (Nec nos nec balliui
nostri nec alii capiemus alienum boscum ad castra vel alia
agenda nostra ⸴ nisi per voluntatem ipsius[44] cuius boscus
ille fuerit . Nos non tenebimus terras eorum qui conuicti
160 fuerint de felonia . nisi per vnum annum 7 vnum diem . 7
tunc reddantur terre dominis feodorum . Omnes kidelli
decetero deponantur penitus per Thamisiam[45] vel[46] Medeweiam
7 per totam Angliam nisi per costam[47] maris . Breue quod
vocatur . Precipe ⸴ decetero non fiat alicui de aliquo tene-
165 mento ⸴ vnde liber homo perdat curiam suam . Vna mensura
vini sit per totum regnum nostrum . 7 vna mensura ceruisie (
7 vna mensura bladi (scilicet quarterium Londonie . 7 vna
latitudo pannorum tinctorum 7 russettorum 7 haubergettorum .
scilicet due vlne infra listas . De ponderibus[48] sit vt de
170 mensuris . Nichil decetero detur[49] pro breui inquisicionis
ab eo qui inquisicionem petit de vita vel de[50] membris (set
gratis concedatur 7 non negetur . Si quis[51] teneat de nobis
per feodi firmam (vel soccagium (vel[52] burgagium . 7 de alio
teneat terram[53] per seruicium militare ⸴ nos non habebimus
175 custodiam heredis nec terre sue que est de feodo alterius
occasione illius feodi firme vel soccagii vel burgagii . Nec
habebimus custodiam illius feodi firme vel soccagii (vel
burgagii ⸴ nisi ipsa feodi firma debeat seruicium militare .
Nos non habebimus custodiam heredis vel[54] terre alicuius
180 quam tenet de alio per seruicium[55] occasione alicuius
parue serianterie quam tenet de nobis per seruicium reddendi
nobis cultellos vel sagittas vel huiusmodi . Nullus balliuus
ponat decetero aliquem ad legem manifestam nec[56] ad
iuramentum simplici loquela sua sine testibus fidelibus ad
185 hoc inductis . Nullus liber homo[57] capiatur vel[58] imprisonetur
vel[58] dissaisietur[59] de[60] libero tenemento suo vel libertatibus
vel liberis consuetudinibus suis aut vtlagetur aut exulet aut
aliquo[61] modo destruatur nec super eum ibimus nec super
eum mittemus (nisi per legale iudicium parium suorum vel
190 per legem terre . Nulli vendemus nulli negabimus aut
differemus rectum vel iusticiam . Omnes mercatores nisi
publice antea prohibiti fuerint ⸴ habeant saluum 7 securum
exire de Anglia 7 venire in Angliam 7 morari 7 ire per Angliam
tam per terram quam per aquam ad emendum vel vendendum
195 sine omnibus toltis maltis[62] per antiquas 7 rectas consuetudines

preterquam in tempore guerre[63] . Et si sint de terra contra
nos guerrina[64] 7 si tales inueniantur in terra nostra in principio
guerre[63] ⸓ attachientur sine dampno corporum vel rerum
donec sciatur a nobis vel a capitali iusticiar*io* nostro (quomodo
200 mercatores terre nostre tractentur qui tunc inueiantur [*sic*][65] in
terra contra nos guerrina[64] . Et si nostri salui sint ibi alii
salui sint in terra nostra . Si quis tenuerit de aliqua eschaeta[66]
sicut de honore Walingfordi*e*[67] Bolon*ie* (Notingham[68] Langcastr*ie* vel de aliis eschaetis[69] que sunt in manu nostra 7 sint
205 baronie 7 obierit ⸓ heres eius nec[70] det aliud releuium nec
faciat nobis aliud seruicium quam faceret baroni si illa[71]
esset in manu baronis (7 nos eam[72] eodem modo tenebimus
quo baro eam tenuit . Nec nos occasione talis baronie vel
eschaete[73] habebimus aliquam eschaetam[74] vel custodiam
210 aliquorum hominum nostrorum nisi alibi tenuerit de nobis
in capite ille qui tenuit baroniam vel eschaetam[74] . Nullus
liber homo decetero det amplius alicui vel vendat de terra
sua quam vt de residuo terre sue possit sufficienter fieri
domino feodi[75] debitum quod pertinet ad feodum illud .
215 Omnes patroni abbatiarum qui habent cartas regum Angl*ie*
de aduocacione vel antiquam tenuram vel possessionem ⸓
habeant earum custodiam cum vacauerint sicut habere debent
7 sicut supra declaratum est . Nullus capiatur vel inprisonetur
propter appellacionem[76] femine de morte alterius quam viri
220 sui . Nullus comitatus decetero teneatur ⸓ nisi de mense in
mensem 7 vbi maior terminus esse solebat ⸓ maior sit . Nec
aliquis vicecomes vel balliuus suus[77] faciat turnum suum
per hundredum nisi bis in anno 7 non nisi in loco debito 7
consueto (videlicet[78] post Pascha 7 iterum post festum sancti
225 Michaelis (et visus de francco[79] plegio tunc fiat ad illum
terminum sancti Michaelis sine occasione . Ita scilicet quod
quilibet habeat libertates suas quas habuit 7 habere consueuit tempore .H. regis[80] aui nostri vel quas postea per-
quisiuit . Fiat autem visus de francco[79] plegio sic . videlicet
230 quod pax nostra teneatur 7 quod thedhinga[81] integra sit
sicut esse consueuit 7 quod vicecomes non querat occasiones
(7 quod contentus sit de[82] eo quod vicecomes habere consueuit de visu suo faciendo tempore .H. regis[80] aui nostri .
Non licet[83] alicui decetero dare terram suam alicui domui
235 religiose . ita quod illam[84] resumat tenendam de eadem
domo . Nec liceat alicui[85] terram alicuius sic accipere (quod
tradat eam illi[86] a quo eam[87] recepit tenendam . Si quis autem
decetero terram suam alicui domui religiose sic dederit . 7
super hoc conuinctatur[88] donum suum penitus cassetur (7
240 terra illa domino suo illius feodi incurratur . Scutagium
decetero capiatur sicut capi consueuit[89] tempore .H. regis[80]
aui nostri 7 salue sint archiepiscopis (episcopis (abbatibus (

prioribus [90]templariis (hospitelariis (comitibus baronibus[90]
7 omnibus aliis tam ecclesiasticis [91]personis quam secularibus[91]
245 libertates 7 libere consuetudines quas prius habuerunt .
Omnes autem istas consuetudines predictas 7 libertates quas
concessimus in regno nostro tenendas quantum ad nos pertinet
erga nostros ∴ omnes de regno nostro tam clerici quam laici
obseruent quantum ad[92] pertinet erga suos . Pro hac autem
250 concessione 7 donacione libertatum istarum 7 aliarum[93]
contentarum in carta nostra de libertatibus foreste ∴ archiepiscopi episcopi (abbates (priores (comites (barones (milites
7[94] libere tenentes 7 omnes de regno nostro dederunt nobis
quintam decimam partem omnium mobilium suorum . Con-
255 cessimus eciam eisdem pro nobis 7 heredibus nostris (quod
nec nos nec heredes nostri aliquid perquiremus per quod
libertates in hac carta contente ∴ infringantur vel infirmentur
(7 si ab aliquo aliquid contra hoc perquisitum fuerit ∴ nichil
valeat 7 pro nullo habeatur . Hiis testibus domino Stephano
260 Cantuariensi archiepiscopo[95]) Eustachio Londoniensi) Jocelino
Bathoniensi (Petro Wintoniensi (Hugone Lincolniensi (
Ricardo Sarresbiriensi (Benedicto Roffensi (Willelmo
Wigorniensi (Johanne Eliensi (Hugone Herefordensi (
Radulfo Cicestrensi (Willelmo Exoniensi episcopis (abbate
265 sancti Edmundi (abbate sancti Albani (abbate de Bello (
abbate sancti Augustini Cantuar' (abbate Eueshamie[96]
abbate Westmonasterii (abbate de Burgo sancti Petri (abbate
Radingie (abbate Abbendonie (abbate Malmesbirie[97] (abbate
Winchecumbie[98] (abbate de Hyda (abbate Certeseye (
270 abbate de Sireburna (abbate de Cerna (abbate de Abbodesbiria[99] (abbate de Middelton' (abbate de Seleby (abbate
de Wyteby (abbate de Cirencestria (Huberto de Burgo
iusticia (Randulfo comite Cestrie 7 Linc' (Willelmo comite
Sarresbirie (Willelmo comite Warenne (Gilberto de Clare
275 comite Gloucestrie 7 Hertfordie (Willelmo de Ferrariis comite
de Derbeia (Willelmo de Mandeuilla comite Essexie (Hugone
le Bigod comite Nortfolchie (Willelmo comite Albemarlie[100] (
Humfrido comite Herefordie (Johanne constabulario Cestrie (
Roberto de Ros (Roberto filio Walteri (Roberto de Veteri
280 Ponte (Willelmo Briwera[101] (Ricardo de Munfichet (Petro
filio Herberti (Matheo filio Herberti (Willelmo de Albiniaco (
Roberto Grell'[102] (Reginaldo de Breusa[103] (Johanne de
Munnemue (Johanne filio Alani (Hugone de Mortuo Mari (
Waltero de Bello Campo (Willelmo de Sancto Johanne (
285 Petro de Malo[104] Lacu (Briano de Insula (Thoma de Mul-
ton[105] (Ricardo de Argentein' (Galfrido de Neuilla (Willelmo
Maudut[106] (Johanne de Balun[107] (Dat' apud Westmonasterium vndecimo die Februarii . anno regni nostri nono.

Texts : MS—R58. The only known original copies of this charter are preserved
in Durham Cathedral and at Lacock abbey in Wiltshire. The present text has been

collated with the former of these originals. There is a copy in the Red Book of the Exchequer, ff. 183-4.   Pd—Blackstone, *Charters*, pp. 47-59. *Statutes of the Realm* i, 22-5 (both in type and engraved facsimile).   See Stubbs, *Select Charters*, pp. 353-4.

Var. R. in the Durham Cathedral charter : [1] *add* abbatibus prioribus. [2] *insert* has libertates subscriptas tenendas in regno nostro. [3] *insert* omnia. [4] *om.* 7 dedimus. [5] *for* de nobis tenencium *read* siue aliorum tenencium de nobis. [6] exibus. [7] debeat. [8] committetur. [9] *om.* viuaria. [10] dignitatum. [11] huiusmodi custodie. [12] debent. [13] *insert* aliqua. [14] aliquid. [15] *for* 7 *read* uel. [16] *insert* pro. [17] *for* mesuagio *read* mesagio ipsius. [18] *insert* sui. [19] ei fuerit. [20] quod secundum. [21] uiuere uoluerit. [22] faciet. [23] seisiemus. [24] nec. [25] soluerunt. [26] portubus. [27]-[27] *The text is corrupt : the Durham copy reads* Nos vel si extra regnum fuerimus capitalis Justiciari*us* noster mittemus iusticiarios ; *the copy in the Red Book reads* Nos si extra regnum fuerimus capitalis Justiciari*us* noster mittet iusticiarios. [28] Banco. [29] *insert* nostris. [30] *for* nisi *read* set. [31] contenemento. [32] mercandisa. [33] inciderit. [34] ecclesiastica. [35] *for* ab *read* ex. [36] *insert* facere. [37] debet. [38] *for* H. *read* regis Henrici. [39] *om.* inde. [40] exercitum. [41] exercitu. [42] *insert* dominica. [43] *om.* nostros. [44] *for* ipsius *read* illius. [45] Tamisiam. [46] *for* vel *read* &'. [47] *for* costam *read* costeram. [48] *insert* uero. [49] detur nichil decetero. [50] *om.* de. [51] *for* quis *read* aliquis. [52] *insert* per. [53] terram teneat. [54] *for* vel *read* nec. [55] *insert* militare. [56] *for* nec *read* uel. [57] *insert* decetero. [58] *for* vel *read* aut. [59] disseisiatur. [60] *insert* aliquo. [61] *insert* alio. [62] malis. [63] gwerre. [64] gwerrina. [65] inuenientur. [66] escaeta. [67] Walingeford'. [68] Notingeham'. [69] *om.* eschaetis. [70] *for* nec *read* non. [71] *for* illa *read* ipsa. [72] *om.* eam. [73] escaete. [74] escaetam. [75] *insert* seruicium ei. [76] appellum. [77] *om.* suus. [78] *insert* semel. [79] franco. [80] *regis* Henrici. [81] tethinga. [82] *om.* de. [83] liceat. [84] *for* illam *read* eam. [85] *insert* domui religiose. [86] *for* eam illi *read* illam ei. [87] *for* eam *read* illam. [88] conuincatur. [89] *for* consueuit *read* solebat. [90]-[90] comitibus baronibus . templariis hospitalariis. [91]-[91] quam secularibus personis. [92] *insert* se. [93] *insert* libertatum. [94] *om.* 7. [95] *An initial only is given for the christian names of the bishops and earls. Only the more important variations of reading in the list of witnesses are given.* [96] de Euesham'. [97] de Maumebur'. [98] de Winchecumb'. [99] Abotebir'. [100] Aubermarl'. [101] Brigwerr'. [102] Gresl'. [103] Brahus'. [104] mala. [105] Muleton'. [106] Mauduit. [107] Baalun.

Note : The Great Charter was re-issued at the same time as the Charter of the Forest (see no. 220, page 148 above) in return for a tax of a fifteenth on *mobilia* or personal property (Stubbs, *Constitutional History* ii, 37 ; Ramsey, *Dawn of the Constitution*, p. 39).

ADD. CHART.

222. Letters patent of Henry III, declaring that, whereas at the siege of Bedford castle which he has undertaken on account of the manifest excesses of Fawkes de Bréauté, Stephen archbishop of Canterbury and the other prelates of the province of Canterbury have furnished an aid of half a mark from every plough-team in demesne, and two shillings from every plough-team of their knights, free tenants, and villeins, and have furnished men from their demesnes and fees to transport engines of war for assaulting the castle, the king, not wishing that the liberty of the Church should be prejudiced, has granted that this gift shall not be drawn into a precedent. At Bedford. 18 August, 1224.

Carta ne auxilium concessum domino regi propter obsidionem castri Bede*fordie* trahatur in consuetudinem vel preiudicium concedencium (R. rubric).

H. dei gracia rex Angl*ie* . dominus Hyberni*e* . dux Norm*annie* . Aquitan*ie* . 7 comes Ande*gauie* . omnibus ad quos presens scriptum

peruenerit ⫶ salutem . Cum propter graues 7 manifestos excessus
Falkasii[1] de Breaute quibus nos 7 regnum nostrum multipliciter
perturbauit . de consilio fidelium nostrorum castrum Bedefordie
obsideremus ⫶ venerabilis pater .S. Cantuariensis archiepiscopus
tocius Anglie primas 7 sancte Romane ecclesie cardinalis . 7
suffraganei sui qui nobiscum gratis venerunt ad excercitum[2] . aliique
prelati prouincie Cantuariensis sola ducti deuocione qua sui gracia
nos fuerant amplexati de mera gracia 7 liberalitate[3] sua auxilium
prouiderunt nobis[4] faciendum ⫶ ad tantos excessus forcius 7 facilius
corrigendos . ordinantes per se ipsos ut singuli dictorum archiepiscopi . episcoporum 7 aliorum prelatorum qui separatas habent
porciones a conuentibus suis[5] de singulis carucis terrarum quas
tenent in dominico [6]darent nobis dimidiam marcam[6] Item de carucis
militum 7 libere tenencium 7 rusticorum predictorum archiepiscopi
7 suffraganeorum 7 aliorum prelatorum memoratorum . 7 de
carucis similiter illorum qui tenent de militibus 7 libere tenentibus
ipsorum duo nobis solidi conferrentur . De carucis eciam abbatum .
priorum . 7 aliorum prelatorum qui non habent separatas porciones a conuentibus suis 7 militum[7] libere tenencium 7 rusticorum
suorum . 7 similiter de carucis eorum qui tenent de dictis militibus
7 libere tenentibus ⫶ darentur nobis duo solidi . Preterea de sola
gracia 7 mera liberalitate[3] sua concesserunt quod homines de
dominicis 7 feodis suis venirent in excercitum[2] ad trahendum
ingenia . 7 ad alia negocia quantum in eis esset expedienda . que
ad expugnandum[8] castrum neccessaria viderentur . Qui quidem
per balliuos[9] nostros alicubi infra libertates ecclesie 7 ipsorum
prelatorum aliter quam hactenus fieri consueuerit[10] summoniti
fuerunt 7 conpulsi[11] ut accepimus ad hoc faciendum . Nos igitur
nolentes occasione gracie 7 liberalitatis[12] nobis ut diximus inpense[13] .
ecclesie dei uel archiepiscopo uel aliis prelatis predictis uel successoribus suis terris . feodis . uel hominibus eorum preiudicium
libertatis sue uel grauamen aliquod unquam generari . nec graciam
sic nobis exhibitam . ad debitum uel consuetudinem posse retorqueri ⫶
omnia premissa per has litteras nostras patentes protestamur ex
sola gracia 7 liberalitate[3] processisse . 7 hoc numquam[14] occasione
predicta in consuetudinem trahi posse uel debere . Et in huius
rei testimonium has litteras nostras patentes inde fieri fecimus
7 sigillo nostro signari . Teste me ipso apud Bedefordiam . decimo
octauo die Augusti anno regni nostri octauo . presentibus . H. de
Burgo iusticie nostro[15] . W. comite Sarrisbirie . W. comite
Warenne . G. comite Gloucestrie . 7 Hertfordie . W. de Mandeuilla[16]
comite Essexie . comite H.[17] Bigod . H.[18] comite Herefordie .
H.[18] comite Warewici . J.[19] constabulario Cestrie . W. Briwer' .
P. filio Hereberti . W. de Albiniaco . Thoma de Multon'[20] . J. de
Munemue[21] . Roberto de Curtenay . Johanne filio Roberti . Ricardo
de Munfichet . W. de Lancastria[22] . P. de Brus[23] . Ricardo de Percy .
W. de Ros . 7 aliis.

Endorsed : (1) Subsidium concessum regi non trahendum ad consequenciam (13 cent.). (2) de obsidione castri Bedefordie (13 cent.). (3) XIII . H. iij. (13 cent.). Tag for seal. Size : 6⅜ x 6¼ inches.
Texts : MS—Orig. A1/1/48. R53. Pd—*Patent Rolls*, 1216–1225, 464–5.
Var. R. : ¹ Falkesii Pat. ² exercitum Pat. ³ libertate R. ⁴ nobis prouiderunt R. ⁵ *insert* 7 Pat. ⁶⁻⁶ daretur nobis dimidia marca Pat. ⁷ *insert* 7 Pat. ⁸ expungnandum Pat. ⁹ bailliuos Pat. ¹⁰ consueuit Pat. ¹¹ compulsi R. Pat. ¹² libertatis R. ¹³ impense R. ¹⁴ nuncquam R. ¹⁵ *om.* nostro Pat. ¹⁶ Maundeuill' Pat. ¹⁷ *insert* le Pat. ¹⁸ *om.* H. Pat. ¹⁹ *om.* J. Pat. ²⁰ Multun R. ; Muleton Pat. ²¹ Monemue Pat. ²² Langcastr' R. ²³ Bruis Pat.
Note : The king laid siege to Bedford castle on 20 June, 1224, and with its surrender on 15 August the campaign against Fawkes de Bréauté came to an end. The expenses of the campaign were met by a scutage (known as the Scutage of Bedford) of two marks on each knight's fee held by the lay tenants in chief, and by the carucage mentioned in the present text. Sir James Ramsey (*The Dawn of the Constitution*, p. 37) says that the lay tenants paid the carucage as well as the scutage ; but S. K. Mitchell (*Studies in Taxation under John and Henry III*, pp. 153–6) adduces evidence which goes far to prove that the carucage was paid by the churchmen only. Mitchell argues that *caruca* is used in the sense of *carucata*, and that even if the teams were counted, the purpose of the enumeration was not to levy a tax on them, but to find out the amount of land under cultivation (pp. 133–4). For the authorities see Ramsey and Mitchell *loc. cit.*

ADD. CHART.

223. Letters of Henry III, addressed to the abbots, priors, and the other religious in the diocese of Lincoln. The king appeals to them to furnish in accordance with the command of pope Honorius III, a fifteenth from their benefices and goods ; with an effective aid from their benefices and goods from which he has not received the fifteenth ; and grants that, in future, tithes of hay and of mills shall be given from the royal demesnes ; and further, that he will endeavour to secure that the magnates of the realm shall make a similar offering of tithes. At Westminster. 27 May, 1226.

Carta de eodem (R rubric).

H. dei gracia rex Anglie . dominus Hibernie . dux Normannie Aquitanie 7 comes Andegauie dilectis sibi in Christo abbatibus prioribus 7 ceteris viris religionis 7 omnibus ecclesiasticis personis in diocesi Lincoln' constitutis salutem . Condolens affectu paterno dominus Papa insufficientie nostre . scripsit dudum venerabilibus patribus archiepiscopis episcopis 7 vniuerso clero regni nostri monens attentius 7 mandans ut optentu pietatis subsidium efficax 7 compentens de beneficiis suis nobis . facerent uniuersi quatinus ipsorum prestationibus adniti paci ecclesie 7 regni nostri commodius possemus 7 fortius prouidere . Moti igitur misericorditer ad succurrendum nobis immo potius ipsis in nobis prelati terre nostre *.·* pridem consenserunt de quintadecima mobilium suorum nobis subuenire consensum pium operum effectu prosequentes . Cum igitur a liberalitate uestra *.·* dependeat¹ consummatio negotii predicti . benignitatem uestram rogamus attentius quatinus necessitatibus nostris compati uelitis affeccione sincera quod quidem exspectamus² alias de uoluntatibus uestris nullo precedente mandato . Tale

igitur 7 tam efficax auxilium nobis in hac parte facere curetis de
benefitiis 7 bonis uestris de quibus quintamdecimam non recepimus
vt ecclesie Romane de collato nobis per nos beneficio ad graciarum
actiones teneri 7 uobis singulis 7 vniuersis in negotiis uestris promouendis adesse debeamus promptiores . Cupientes autem non
solum facere set 7 faciendo aliis exemplum prebere ea³ que communi ecclesie 7 cleri conueniant utilitati 7 honori ad consilium
venerabilium patrum Cantuar*iensis* archiepiscopi 7 coepiscoporum
su[orum conces⁴]simus ut decime feni 7 molendinorum omni
cauillatione cessante de singulis dominicis nostris in regno nostro
decetero prestentur . hoc idem singulis balliuis nostris per litteras
nostras mandantes . laborabimus etiam bona fide ut magnates
regni nostri simili prestationi decimarum decetero⁵ consenciant
litis dispendio cessante . Teste me ipso apud Westm*onasterium*
.xxvij. die Maij . anno regni ⁶decimo.

Endorsed : (1) C . . . . regis Henrici . iij. de concessione decime molendinorum
7 feni . post .xv . concessa (13 cent.).   (2) XII .H. iij. (13 cent.).
   Strip for seal ; the ribbon below it is torn away.   Size : 5¾ x 4½ inches.
   Texts : MS—Orig. A1/1/51.   R53B.   Pd—Similar letters, addressed to the dean
and chapter of Chichester, are printed in *Rotuli Litterarum Clausarum* ii, 152.
   Var. R. : ¹ dependat R.   ² expectamus R.   ³ ea *is interlineated* Orig.   ⁴ *supplied
from* R, *the orig. having been injured.*   ⁵ *om.* decetero R.   ⁶ *insert* nostro R.
   Note : The government did not attempt to collect from the beneficed clergy
the aid of the fifteenth granted by the grand council in February, 1224–5 (above,
no. 221, note).   On 3 February of that year a letter from pope Honorius III exhorted
the clergy to make a grant to the king (*Patent Rolls*, 1216–1225, p. 585), and
fifteen months later this letter, with one from the king, dated 27 May, 1226 (see
the present text), was sent out to the clergy by archbishop Stephen with letters
of his own.   The archbishop proposed a grant of a twelfth or a fourteenth ; and
in October, 1226, a council of deans, archdeacons, and regulars, which was summoned by him, met in London, and granted a sixteenth of their revenues according
to the valuation of the twentieth in 1216 (see no. 224 below).   The aid was to be
paid, half in February, 1226–7, and half in June, 1227.   On 20 October a writ was
directed to the sheriffs of Nottingham, Derby, Oxford, Bedford and Buckingham,
and Lincoln, commanding them to help the dean and chapter of Lincoln to obtain
from their knights and free tenants a reasonable aid towards the sixteenth which
they themselves had granted to the king from their churches, prebends, and lands
(*Rotuli Litterarum Clausarum* ii, 143).   In November, 1229, the dean and chapter
of Lincoln, amongst others, had paid nothing in respect of the sixteenth, and the
archdeacons of Northampton, Buckingham, Huntingdon, and Stow, who were
collectors for parochial benefices, had still to render account at the Exchequer
(*Cal. Close Rolls*, 1227–1231, p. 380).   Mitchell (pp. 169–71) gives a full account
of the sixteenth, from which most of the present note is derived.

ADD. CHART.

224. Letters patent of Henry III : whereas the clergy, under
orders from pope Innocent III, have granted to the king, as a
voluntary gift, a sixteenth of their benefices according to the
valuation made at the time when a twentieth was collected in aid
of the Holy Land, for the preservation of the peace of the church
and realm, the king declares that this shall not be drawn into a
custom.   At Westminster.   20 October, 1226.

Carta de eodem (R rubric).

.H. dei gracia rex Anglie dominus Hibernie dux Normannie 7 Aquitanie comes Andegauie venerabili patri in Christo .H. eadem gracia Lincoln' episcopo salutem . Cum propter vrgencia negocia nostra dominus papa Honorius tercius archiepiscopis episcopis regni nostri per litteras apostolicas dedisset in mandatis vt clerum Anglie sibi subditum monerent diligenter 7 inducerent quod de beneficiis suis competens auxilium caritatiue nobis facere deberent ad conseruacionem pacis ecclesiastice 7 regni nostri ⸫ clerus prefatus ad faciendum premissa prona deuocione inductus liberaliter concessit 7 benigne sextam decimam partem beneficiorum suorum secundum estimacionem competentem vnius anni factam scilicet tempore quo collecta fuit vicesima in succursum Terre Sancte nobis per manus suas proprias collectam largiri (ita quod ex hac gracia gratis 7 liberaliter tunc nobis impensa processu temporis ecclesiis vel ecclesiasticis personis seu beneficiis nullum posset aliquatenus preiudicium generari . Nos igitur nolentes occasione gracie 7 libertatis nobis vt premissum est affectu fauorabili impense ecclesie dei archiepiscopis episcopis aliis ve prelatis clericis aut ecclesiasticis seu viris religiosis vel ecclesiasticis possessionibus quibuscumque vel feodis vel hominibus eorum preiudicium au[1] grauamen aliquod aliquo tempore generari ⸫ nec similem prestacionem trahi posse in consuetudinem vel debitum ⸫ presentibus litteris nostris cum multiplici graciarum accione protestamur beneficium taliter nobis collatum ex sola liberali gracia cleri processisse . nec illud a nobis vel heredibus nostris occasione vel exemplo tali in debitum vel consuetudinem trahi posse . In cuius rei testimonium has litteras nostras patentes fieri fecimus . Teste meipso apud Westmonasterium .xx. die Octobris . anno regni nostri decimo . Dat' per manum venerabilis patris .R. Cicestrensis episcopi cancellarii nostri coram .H. de Burgo iusticiario nostro .J. Bathoniensis 7 .R. Sarrisbiriensis episcopis.

Text : MS—R53A. Pd—Similar letters, addressed to the bishop of Hereford, are printed in *Patent Rolls*, 1225–1232, p. 64.
Var. R. : [1] *for* aut.
Note : See Note to the preceding charter.

ADD. CHART.

225. Letters patent of Henry III : whereas the prelates and other ecclesiastical persons of the realm, who hold in chief, have granted to the king an aid of two marks for every shield from all their fees, both from those for which they are answerable when scutage is paid and from those which they retain for their own use ; and the king has granted to the prelates that for furnishing the aid they shall have forty shillings for each knight's fee which is held of them ; the king, in order that this aid shall not be drawn into a precedent, grants that no injury shall hereafter accrue to the prelates. At Westminster. 13 April, 1231.

Carta de eodem (rubric).

.H. dei gracia rex Anglie (dominus Hibernie (dux Normannie Aquitanie 7 comes Andegauie (omnibus ad quos presens scriptum peruenerit salutem . Cum peteremus a prelatis Anglie quod nobis auxilium facerent pro magna necessitate nostra de qua eis constabat (videlicet episcopis (abbatibus (abbatissis (prioribus 7 priorissis qui de nobis tenent in capite (ipsi nobis liberaliter concesserunt auxilium tale (scilicet de singulis feodis militum suorum quadraginta solidos de tot feodis de quot ipsi tenentur nobis respondere quando faciunt nobis seruicium militare . Et nos concessimus eisdem prelatis quod ad predictum auxilium nobis faciendum ; habeant de singulis feodis militum que de eis tenentur quadraginta solidos . Nos igitur nolentes quod ex hac eorum concessione nobis facta de mera liberalitate sua 7 non alia racione ecclesiis suis vel eorum successoribus possit preiudicium aliquod generari vel ecclesiastice libertati in aliquo derogari ; per has litteras nostras patentes hoc duximus protestandum . Nolumus eciam quod propter hanc concessionem nostram quam fecimus ; aliquid nobis vel heredibus nostris acrescat vel decrescat . Teste meipso apud Westmonasterium .xiij°.[1] die Aprilis . anno regni nostri .xv°.

Text : MS—R54. Pd—*Patent Rolls*, 1225–1232, p. 429.

Var. R. : [1] xiiij *Pat. Rolls*, ut supra.

Note : In order to provide money for the war with France the lay barons granted to the king a scutage at the rate of three marks (£2) per knight's fee. The clergy, in a synod held at Saint Paul's, on 6th October, 1230, opposed the levy of the scutage (probably on the principle of the non-liability of the clergy to foreign service enunciated by Saint Hugh of Lincoln in 1197), but agreed to give the three marks, not as scutage, but by way of an extraordinary aid (Ramsey, *The Dawn of the Constitution*, p. 54 ; Mitchell, *op. cit.* 180–95).

ADD. CHART.

226. Letters patent of Henry III : the king declares that the aid given by the prelates of two marks for every shield shall not prejudice them at any time as a precedent. At Westminster. 3 May, 1236.

Carta de eodem (rubric).

Henricus dei gracia rex Anglie dominus Hibernie dux Normannie 7 Aquitanie comes Andegauie omnibus ad quos presentes littere peruenerint salutem . Sciatis quod cum nuper rogassemus archiepiscopos episcopos abbates priores 7 alias personas ecclesiasticas de regno nostro quod pro vrgenti necessitate nostra nobis inpenderent ; ipsi gratis 7 spontanea voluntate sua ; communiter nobis concesserunt quoddam auxilium de omnibus feodis suis tam de illis de quibus nobis respondent quando scutagium datur quam de aliis que retinent ad opus suum videlicet duas marcas de scuto . Ne igitur huiusmodi concessio 7 auxilii prestacio possit aliquo tempore trahi in consequenciam ; concedimus pro nobis 7 heredibus nostris 7 presencium tenore protestamur quod pro gracia hac vice nobis facta *: predictis archiepiscopis episcopis (abbatibus prioribus 7 aliis personis ecclesiasticis vel eorum successoribus (aut ecclesiis suis inposterum *: in nullo derogetur . In cuius rei testimonium has litteras patentes fieri fecimus . Teste meipso apud Westmonas-terium tercio[1] die Maij anno regni nostri vicesimo.

Text : MS—R55. Pd—*Cal. Patent Rolls*, 1232-1247, 145(abs.).
Var. R. : [1] quarto *Cal. Pat. Rolls*.

ADD. CHART.

227. Letters patent of Henry III, notifying that whereas he has granted to Ralf son of Nicholas, his seneschal, the custody of the lands which were Eustace of Mortain's, which lands were of the honour of Peverel now in the king's hand, he has requested bishop Hugh II to give to Ralf the custody of the lands of the bishop's fee which were Eustace's, to wit, Dunsby [near Bourne, co. Lincoln] and Branston [co. Leicester], until the lawful age of Eustace's heir.   At Abingdon.   15 August, 1234.

H. dei gracia rex Angl*ie* . dominus Hibern*ie* . d[ux] Norm*annie* [A]quit*anie* . 7 comes And*egauie* omnibus ad quos presentes littere peruenerint salutem . Sciatis quod cu[m dedi]mus . . . . 7 concessissemus dilecto 7 fideli nostro Radulfo filio Nichol*ai* senescallo nostro custodiam terrarum que fuerunt Eus[tachii] de Moretoina[1] . que sunt de honore Peu*erell*' qui est in manu nostra Habendam 7 tenendam vsque ad legitimam etatem heredis ipsius Eustach*ii* *:* rogauimus venerabilem patrem Hugonem Lincoln' episcopum secundum *:* quod pro amore nostro dar[et 7 conc]ederet eidem Radulfo custodiam terrarum que fuerunt predicti Eustachii que sunt de feodo ipsius episcopi . videlicet de Dunnesby[2] . 7 Brauntestona . Habendam 7 tenendam usque ad legitimam etatem heredis ipsius Eustachii . Ipse uero episcopus sui gracia peticionem nostram benigne exaudiuit . Et sic predictus senescallus noster dictam custodiam predictarum terrarum que de feodo ipsius episcopi sunt *:* de consciencia 7 voluntate nostra de dono ipsius episcopi recepit .. Et in huius rei robur 7 testimonium *:* hoc presentibus litteris protestamur . Hiis . testibus . venerabilibus . patribus . H. Roff*ensi* . 7 W. Karl*eolensi* episcopis . Ricardo comite Cornub*ie* fratre nostro . G. Mares*callo* comite Pembroch*ie* . Godefrido de Craucumb' 7 aliis . Dat' per manum venerabilis patris . R. Cices-tr*ensis* episcopi . cancellarii nostri . apud Abbendon*iam* . quinto decimo die Augusti . anno regni nostri decimo [octauo[3]].

Endorsed : (1) X (13 cent.).   (2) .H. iij. (13 cent.).
Tag and seal torn away.   Size : 6½ x 5 inches.
Text : MS—Orig. A1/1/54 (the charter has been injured, and the missing words have been supplied conjecturally within square brackets). Patent roll, 18 Henry III, mem. 7. Pd—*Cal. Patent Rolls*, 1232-1247, pp. 64-5.
Var. R. in Patent roll ; [1] Moreton.   [2] Dunesby.   [3] *this word is illegible in* Orig.

ADD. CHART.

228. Charter of Henry III, inspecting and confirming the charter of his father, John, dated at the New Temple, 21 January, 1214–15 (no. 205 above), granting the manor of Winthorpe near Newark and other gifts to the church of Lincoln and bishop Hugh II. At Westminster. 12 February, 1227.

Henricus dei gracia rex Anglie dominus Hybernie[1] . dux Normannie 7 Aquitannie comes Andegauie . archiepiscopis . episcopis . abbatibus . prioribus . comitibus . baronibus iusticiariis forestariis . vicecomitibus . prepositis 7 omnibus bailliuis[2] 7 fidelibus suis . salutem . Inspeximus cartam domini patris nostri Johannis[3] illustris Anglorum regis in hec verba. [*Here is recited king John's charter in full.*] Nos itaque predictam donationem concessionem 7 confirmationem predicti domini patris nostri ratam 7 gratam habentes ∴ eam presenti carta nostra confirmamus . Quare volumus 7 firmiter precipimus . quod predicta ecclesia Lincoln'[4] 7 predictus Hugo Lincoln'[4] episcopus 7 successores sui in perpetuum habeant 7 teneant omnia predicta bene . 7 in pace . libere . quiete . 7 integre . in omnibus locis 7 rebus . cum omnibus libertatibus 7 liberis consuetudinibus 7 quietantiis supradictis sicut[5] predictum est ∴ tanquam[6] puram . liberam . 7 perpetuam elemosinam predicti domini patris nostri 7 nostram quietam penitus ab omni seculari seruicio 7 exactione in perpetuum . Hiis testibus . dominis Eustachio Londoniensi . Ricardo Sarrisbiriensi . episcopis . Huberto de Burgo iusticiario nostro . Willelmo de Sancto Johanne . Willelmo de Cantelupo[7] . Ricardo de Argenteom[8] . 7 Godefrido de Craucumb' senescallis nostris . Stephano de Segraue[9] . 7 aliis . Dat' per manum venerabilis patris Radulfi Cicestrensis episcopi 7 cancellarii nostri apud Westmonasterium duodecimo die Februarii anno regni nostri vndecimo.

<small>Endorsed : V .H. iij (13 cent.). (Orig. no. 60 is endorsed : De Wimeltorp' 7 parcis faciendis (13 cent.). De confirmatione manerii de Wimeltorp (13 cent.)).
Tag for seal torn away. Size : 9¼ x 18 inches. (No. 60 : tag for seal torn away. Size : 8⅝ x 15 inches.)
Texts : MS—Orig. A1/1/50. Orig. A1/1/60. *Charter Roll*, 11 Henry III, part 1, mem. 32. Pd—See *C.C.R.*i,5.
Var. R. : [1] Hibernie no. 60.　[2] balliuis no. 60.　[3] J. no. 60.　[4] Linc' no. 60.
[5] sicud no. 60.　[6] tamquam no. 60.　[7] Cantilupo no. 60.　[8] Argentuem' no. 60.
[9] Seygrau' no. 60.</small>

ADD. CHART.

229. Charter of Henry III, granting to bishop Hugh II and his successors that no market which has been or shall be established after the king's first coronation, outside the royal demesne, shall continue to the detriment of the markets which the bishop had before that coronation. At Westminster. 5 February, 1227.

Henricus dei gracia rex Anglie . dominus Hybernie . dux Normannie 7 Aquitanie . comes Andegauie . archiepiscopis . episcopis .

abbatibus . prioribus . comitibus . baronibus . iusticiariis . vicecomitibus . prepositis . 7 omnibus bailliuis 7 fidelibus suis ꞏꞏ salutem .
Sciatis nos concessisse 7 presenti carta nostra confirmasse venerabili
patri Hugoni Lincoln' episcopo 7 successoribus suis inperpetuum .
quod nullum mercatum quod post primam coronacionem nostram
leuatum sit uel de cetero leuabitur extra dominica nostra ad nocumentum alicuius mercatorum suorum que idem episcopus habuit
ante coronacionem illam stet uel teneatur aliquo tempore . Hiis
testibus . dominis Eustachio Londoniensi . Joscelino Bathoniensi .
7 Ricardo Sarrisbiriensi . episcopis . Huberto de Burgo iusticiario
nostro . Willelmo de Eyneford' . senescallo nostro . Willelmo Briwerr' .
7 aliis . Dat' per manum venerabilis patris Radulfi Cicestrensis .
episcopi 7 cancellarii nostri apud Westmonasterium . quinto die
Februarii . anno regni nostri vndecimo.

Endorsed : De mercatis generaliter non leuandis (13 cent.).
Tag and seal torn away. Size : 8 x 6 inches.
Text : MS—Orig. A1/1/59.

ADD. CHART.

230. A renewal of the preceding charter. At Fulham. 15 May,
1229.

Henricus dei gracia rex Anglie . dominus Hybernie . dux Normannie 7 Aquitannie . comes Andegauie . archiepiscopis . episcopis .
abbatibus . prioribus . comitibus . baronibus . iusticiariis . vicecomitibus . [prepositis . 7 omnibus bailliuis 7 fidelibus] suis ꞏꞏ salutem .
Sciatis nos concessisse 7 presenti carta nostra confirmasse venerabili
patri Hugoni Lincoln' episcopo 7 successoribus suis imperpetuum .
quod nullum mercatum quod post primam coronacionem nostram
leuatum sit uel de cetero leuabitur extra dominica nostra ad
nocumentum alicuius mercatorum suorum que idem episcopus
habuit ante cor[onacionem illam stet uel teneatur aliquo] tempore .
Hiis testibus) dominis Ricardo Dunholmensi episcopo) Waltero
Karleolensi episcopo thesaurario nostro) Huberto de Burgo)
comite Cantie iusticiario nostro) Johanne de Munemue) Stephano
de Segraue) Radulfo de Trubleuill') Hugone Dispensatore Henrico
filio Aucheri) Ricardo de Gray) Henrico de Capella 7 aliis . Dat'
per manum venerabilis patris R[adulfi Cicestrensis episcopi 7
can]cellarii nostri apud Fuleham' quintodecimo die Maii) anno regni
nostri terciodecimo.

Text : MS—Iiv(25). Charter roll, 13 Henry III, schedule, mem. 2. Pd—See
C.C.R.i,104 ; ibid.iv,111(25).
Var. R : The words enclosed in brackets are supplied from the Charter roll.

ADD. CHART.

231. Charter of Henry III, granting to bishop Hugh II that
in future the market of [Chipping] Warden, co. Northampton,
shall not be held, which Henry de Braybroc set up during the
king's minority and caused to be held, notwithstanding the king's

charter to the bishop (no. 229 above); confirming also to the bishop king John's grant of the markets of Thame [co. Oxford] and Biggleswade [co. Bedford]. At Westminster. 30 April, 1227.

Henricus dei gracia rex Angl*ie* . dominus H[ibernie dux Norm*annie* 7 Aquitan*ie* comes And*egauie* archiepiscopis episcopis abbatibus prioribus[1]] comitibus . baronibus . iustic*iariis* . vicecomitibus [prepositis 7 omnibus balliuis 7 fidelibus suis salutem . Sciatis nos pro salute anime nostre 7 anima[1]]rum omnium antecessorum 7 heredum nostrorum con[cessisse 7 presenti carta nostra confirmasse venerabili patri Lincoln' episcopo Hugoni secundo et suc[1]]cessoribus suis imperpetuum . quod decetero non stet uel [vnquam leuetur aut teneatur mercatum de Wardon' in comitatu Norhamt*onie* quod[1]] Henricus de Braybroch[2] dum minoris essemus etatis [leuauit ibidem . Et quod post generalem prohibicionem nostram per litteras nostras factam de huiusmo[1]]di mercatis ⸴ nichilominus teneri fecit . antequam litteras [nostras 7 mandatum[3] super hoc optineret licet cartam nostram dicto episcopo fecissemus per quam ei con[1]]cessimus . quod nullum mercatum quod post primam coronacionem [nostram leuatum esset vel extunc leuaretur extra dominia nostra ad nocumentum alicuius merca[1]]torum suorum que habuit ante coronacionem illam staret vel te[neretur aliquo tempore . Concedimus eciam 7 presenti carta nostra confirmamus pro nobis 7 here[1]]dibus nostris dicto episcopo 7 successoribus suis imperpetuum . mercata de Tame 7 de [Bicleswade que clare memorie illustris rex Angl*ie* pater noster dicto[1]] episcopo 7 successoribus suis concessit 7 dedit . et que idem episcopus hactenus in pace semper [tenuit . Habenda 7 tenenda eidem episcopo 7 successoribus[1]] suis decetero in pace ⸴ absque omni impedimento 7 contradiccione cum omnibus libertatibus 7 liberis consuetudinibus ad huiusmodi mercata pertinentibus . Volentes 7 concedentes quod predictus episcopus 7 successores sui habeant 7 teneant imperpetuum omnes predictas libertates 7 concessiones nostras . in liberam . puram 7 per[petu[1]]am elemosinam . Prohibentes insuper super forisfacturam nostram . ne quis contra premissam concessionem 7 confirmacionem nostram ueniat aliquo tempore . Hiis testibus . dominis Joscelino Bathon*iensi* . Ricardo S*arresbiriensi* . Waltero Karleol*ensi* . Galfrido [Elyensi episcopis .L. capellano[1]] decano sancti Martini . H[ubert[4]]o[5] de Burg*o* comite Cantie iustic*iario* nostro . Radulfo filio Nicholai ⸴ senescallo nostro [Henrico de A[1]]thelega . Dat' per manum ve[nerabilis pat[4]]ris Radulfi Cycestr*ensi* episcopi cancellarii nostri apud Westm*onasterium* [xxx die Aprilis anno 7c. xj°[1]].

Endorsed : Contra mercatum de Wardon' . pro mercatis nostris (13 cent.). . . . . .
Tag and seal torn away. Size : 9 x 7¼ inches.
Texts : MS—Orig. A1/1/49 (about half the charter has perished). Charter roll, 11 Henry III, part i, mem. 9. Pd—*C.C.R.*i,33(abs.)
Var. R. : [1] *supplied from* Ch. roll. [2] Braybroc Ch. roll. [3] 7 mandatum *repeated* Ch. roll. [4] *supplied conjecturally.* [5] *the Christian names of the first six witnesses are represented by their initial letters in* Ch. roll.

ADD. (EXTRAN.) CHART.

232. A renewal of the preceding charter. At Fulham. 15 May, 1229.

Henricus dei gracia rex Anglie dominus Hibernie dux Normannie 7 Aquitanie comes Andegauie archiepiscopis episcopis abbatibus prioribus comitibus baronibus iusticiariis vicecomitibus prepositis 7 omnibus balliuis 7 fidelibus suis salutem . Sciatis nos pro salute anime nostre 7 animarum omnium antecessorum 7 heredum nostrorum concessisse 7 presenti carta nostra confirmasse venerabili patri Lincoln' episcopo Hugoni secundo et successoribus suis imperpetuum quod decetero non stet uel vnquam leuetur aut teneatur mercatum de Wardon' in comitatu Norhamtonie quod Henricus de Braibroc[1] dum minoris essemus etatis leuauit ibidem . Et quod post generalem prohibicionem nostram per litteras nostras factam de huiusmodi mercatis nichilominus teneri fecit antequam litteras nostras 7 mandatum super hoc optineret licet cartam nostram dicto episcopo fecissemus per quam ei concessimus quod nullum marcatum[2] post primam coronacionem nostram leuatum esset vel extunc leuaretur extra dominia nostra ad nocumentum alicuius mercatorum suorum que habuit ante coronacionem illam staret vel teneretur aliquo tempore . Concedimus eciam 7 presenti carta nostra confirmamus pro nobis 7 heredibus nostris dicto episcopo 7 successoribus suis imperpetuum . mercata de Tame 7 de Bicleswade[3] que clare memorie illustris rex Anglie pater noster dicto episcopo 7 successoribus suis concessit 7 dedit . et que idem episcopus hactenus in pace semper tenuit . Habenda 7 tenenda eidem episcopo 7 successoribus suis decetero in pace absque omni impedimento 7 contradiccione cum omnibus libertatibus 7 liberis consuetudinibus ad huiusmodi mercata pertinentibus . Volentes 7 concedentes quod predictus episcopus 7 successores sui habeant 7 teneant imperpetuum omnes predictas libertates 7 concessiones nostras in liberam puram 7 perpetuam elemosinam . Prohibentes insuper super forisfacturam nostram ne quis contra premissam concessionem 7 confirmacionem nostram ueniat aliquo tempore . Hiis testibus dominis Ricardo Dunolmensi episcopo Waltero Karleolensi episcopo thesaurario nostro Huberto de Burgo comite Kancie iusticiario nostro Johanne de Monemue Stephano de Segraue Radulfo de Trubleuile Hugone Dispensatore Henrico filio Aucheri Ricardo de Gray Henrico de Capella 7 aliis . Dat' per manum venerabilis patris Radulfi Cicestrensis episcopi cancellarii nostri apud Fuleham quinto decimo die Maij anno regni nostri terciodecimo.

Texts : MS—Iv(44). Charter roll, 13 Henry III, part i, schedule, mem. 2. Pd— See *C.C.R.*i,105 ; *ibid.*iv,147(44).
Var. R. : [1] Braybrok' Ch. roll. [2] *sic.* [3] Biclaswade Ch. roll.

ADD. (EXTRAN.) CHART.

233. *Inspeximus* and confirmation by Henry III of an indenture, dated 1227, whereby Roesia of Kyme, with the advice of Philip of Kyme, her son and heir, granted her manors of South Elkington and Cawthorpe [in the parish of Covenham], in Lindsey [co. Lincoln], on the Monday before the Exaltation of the Cross to bishop Hugh II, at a farm of twenty marks a year. At Westminster, 11 October, 1227.

H. rex 7c' salutem . Inspeximus cirografum factum inter venerabilem . patrem . Linc' episcopum Hugonem secundum ex una parte 7 Roes*iam* de Kyma 7 Philippum de Kyma filium 7 heredum suum 7 heredum ex altera de Suthelkinton' [cum pertinenciis[1]] 7 Kalthorp' cum pertinenciis maneriis ipsius Roesie in Lindes*eia* in hec verba . Anno ab incarnacione domini Mᵒ Cᵒ Cᵒ xxvijᵒ[2] . conuenit inter dominum Linc' episcopum Hugonem secundum ex una parte 7 Roesia de Kym[a 7[1]] Philippum de Kyma filium 7 heredum suum ex altera de Suthelkinton cum pertinenciis 7 Calthorp' cum pertinenciis maneriis ipsius Roesie in Lindes*eia* videlicet quod eadem Roesia de consilio dicti Philippi filii 7 heredis sui concessit 7 tradidit die Lune proxima ante exaltacionem sancte Crucis eodem anno ipsi episcopo maneria predicta ad firmam pro viginta marcis annuis habenda 7 tenenda sibi et ei vel hiis cui vel quibus ea assignare voluerit cum omnibus pertinenciis suis usque ad .x. annos proximos sequentes completos integre 7 quiete in hominibus terris tenementis pratis pascuis 7 pasturis bosco 7 plano viis 7 semitis redditibus 7 seruiciis releuiis 7 excaetis 7 omnibus aliis pertinenciis [suis[1]] ipsam Roesiam 7 Philippum filium suum 7 heredes suos interim contingentibus) absque ullo penitus retenemento Quas quidem viginti marcas annuas de firma idem episcopus ipsi Roesie 7 Philippo filio 7 heredi suo premanibus pacauit) de toto ipso decennio integre scilicet ducentas marcas sterlingorum 7 sic de tota firma predicti decennii idem episcopus 7 attornati sui quieti sunt omnino erga ipsam Roesiam 7 Philippum filium suum 7 heredes suos 7 omnes suos ad quos quocunque titulo predicta maneria possent deuenire) usque ad diem Lune proximam ante exaltacionem sancte Crucis in fine predictorum .x. annorum completorum quo predicta Roesia 7 Philippus filius suus vel heres eorum qui tunc superstes fuerit si ipsi forte quod deus auertat interim decesserint recipiet maneria predicta sine bladis et cum tanto warecto quantum dictus episcopus recepit in primo anno predicte firme sue 7 tot domos per visum 7 testimonium legalium hominum quot similiter tunc recepit) secundum quod in alio cirografo inter eos super hoc confecto continetur . Remanentibus eidem episcopo vel ei vel hiis cui vel quibus ea assignauerit integre 7 absque ulla diminucione) bladis omnibus que seminata fuerint in dominicis

illorum maneriorum[3] in ultimo anno cum operationibus 7 consuetudinibus ad ea metenda et colligenda sicut domini ea habere
deberunt non obstante eo quod restitucio maneriorum eis prius
facta fuerit ut predictum est quam predicta Roesia 7 Philippus
filius suus blada illius anni in predictis maneriis seminata quo
hanc firmam recepit sepedictus episcopus sibi integre retinuerunt .
Conuenit eciam inter eos quod ipsa Roesia 7 Philippus 7 heredes
eorum predicta maneria cum omnibus pertinenciis ut predictum
est warantizabunt predicto episcopo 7 ei vel hiis cui vel quibus
ea assignare voluerit contra omnes homines tamque liberam 7
puram elemosinam ipsius episcopi 7 assignatorum suorum liberam
prorsus 7 quietam per totum illud decennium ab omni seculari
seruicio 7 exactione consuetudine 7 demanda) saluo domino rege
auxilio vicecomitis debito 7 consueto 7 saluo domino feodi scutagio
suo quando illud per annum currere contigerit que homines dictorum
maneriorum acquietabunt per manum . balliuorum dicti episcopi
vel attornatorum suorum ꝛ nec licebit ipsis Roesie vel Philippo
filio suo aut heredibus suis per se vel per aliquem ex parte sua
interim manum mittere ad predicta maneria vel homines vel alia[4]
pertinencia ipsorum maneriorum vel de hiis ullo modo se intro-
mittere ꝛ set omnia ea tenebuntur tam ipsa Roesia 7 Philippus
quam heredes sui bene 7 in pace dimittere 7 warantizare ipsi episcopo
7 ei vel hiis cui vel quibus ea assignaverit absque ulla alia [diminu-
cione[1]] sui vel suorum usque ad terminum supradictum[5] . Si vero
sepedictus episcopus vel is vel hii cui vel quibus predicta maneria
assignauerit domos vel quecunque edificia in terris illis interim
fecerint) licebit eis omnia predicta amouere quandocunque voluerint
nisi per grantum ipsorum 7 consensum ea remanserint dictis
Roesie vel Philippo filio suo aut heredibus suis per[6] legale precium
legalium hominum 7 hec omnino erit in opcione ipsius episcopi
uel attornatorum suorum . Adiectum est eciam in hac conuencione
quod si idem episcopus vel attornati sui processu temporis aliquid
addendum vel mutandum viderint de forma huius cirografi ad
majorem sui vel suorum [huius conuencionis[1]] securitatem) eadem
Roesia 7 Philippus filius suus 7 heredes sui id facere tenebuntur
ad [mandatum[1]] suum absque omni contradiccione 7 dilacione
bona fide . Hec autem omnia predicta tam ipsa Roesia quam
Philippus filius suus absque dolo 7 male ingenio firmiter 7 fideliter
tenenda pro se 7 heredibus suis [iurauerunt[1]] tactis sacrosanctis
ewangeliis . 7 super hoc tam se quam omnia sua mobilia . 7 immobilia
7 christianitatem suam supposuerunt iurisdiccioni ipsius episcopi
vel capituli sui [Linc'[1]] utrum ipse episcopus vel eius attor[nati
maluerint[1]] ut liceat eis omni appellacione remota 7 condicione [si
quam hoc in[1]] aliquo umquam [mouerint[1]] in ipsos [animaduertere[1]]
secundum quod decreuerint donec inde [plene[1]] fuerit satisfactum .
Insuper eadem Roesia 7 Philippus filius suus plegios inuenerunt
pro se 7 heredibus suis subscriptis videlicet Simonem de Chauncy

Willelmum de Well' Willelmum de Benigworth' Willelmum de
Magneby Radulfum de Barkeworth' Philippum de Timberland'[7]
Adam de Merla Jordanum de Esseby Simonem de Hauton[8] Robertum
filium Isabelle de Steping' Galfridum de Thorp' 7 Simonem
de Bekering' qui singuli tactis sacrosanctis ewangeliis [iurauerunt[1]]
quod quicquid de ipsa Roesia vel Philippo filio suo aut heredibus
suis vel de maneriis sepedictis[9] cum pertinenciis suis aut de aliquibus
in predicta conuencione contentis aliquo casu contigerit infra
terminum memoratum quominus predicta conuencio plene 7 integre
obseruetur) ipsi omnes et singuli tenebuntur in solidum ad [con-
seruand'[1]] indempnes in omnibus 7 per omnia ipsum episcopum
7 eum vel eos cui vel quibus predicta assignauerit secundum formam
predicte conuencionis usque ad terminum memoratum 7 inde se
7 omnia sua mobilia 7 immobilia 7 christianitatem suam obligauerunt
et contradicione 7 apellacione remota eodem modo quo 7 Roesia 7
Philippus filius suus se obligauerunt pre[10] premissis sicut predictum
est . Et preterea eadem Roesia 7 Philippus filius suus [7 plegii sui[1]]
concesserunt pro se 7 heredibus suis sub debito predicti iuramenti
quod ipsi vel heredes sui nichil impetrabunt a curia domini regis
[vel alia curia quominus[1]] per censuram ecclesiasticam compelli
possent ad predictam conuencionem tenendam 7 si aliquid forte
impetratum fuerit pro nichilo habebitur 7 vim non habebit . Ad
hoc conuenit inter predictum episcopum 7 dictam Roesiam 7
Philippum filium suum 7 plegios eorum similiter sub debito predicti
iuramenti quod si ipse episcopus infirmitate vel morte obierit quod
deus avertat uel alio quocunque casu contingente non attornasset
infra terminum predictum cui vel quibus vellet predicta maneria
assignari cum pertinenciis ut predictum est) quod Robertus archidiaconus 7 Johannes precentor Linc' 7 Galfridus filius Bald' 7
Radulfus de Warauill'[11] assignent predicta maneria cum pertinenciis
habenda 7 tenenda cui vel quibus decreuerint in pios usus pro
anima ipsius episcopi conuertenda usque ad finem decennii memorati
sicut ipse episcopus assignare posset per predictam conuencionem)
vel eciam quod duo vel unus eorum si alii decessissent quod absit
vel alius vel alii quem vel quos idem episcopus loco suo per litteras
suas patentes ad hoc attornauerit idem inde facere possint omni
occasione 7 contradicione postpositis sine aliquo impedimento
ipsius Roesie vel Philippi filii sui aut heredum suum[12] . Ad maiorem
autem securitatem huius conuencionis factum est hoc scriptum[13]
in modum cirographi 7 parti que remanet dictis Roesie 7 Philippo
filio suo appositum est sigillum dicti episcopi parti eciam que eidem
episcopo remanet apposita sunt sigilla dictorum Roesie 7 Philippi
filii sui . Hiis testibus . Radulfo filio Reginaldi tunc vicecomite
Linc' . Henrico de Braybroc . Simone de Roppele . Galfrido de
Sausucomar[14] . Radulfo filio Simonis . Johanne Coleman . Hugone
de Harington' . Alexandro de Pointon' . Hugone Bretun[15] .
Willelmo Burdet . Haroldo filio Umfridi . Hugone de Ringesdon' .

Johanne de Braytoft . 7 Osberto Arsich' militibus . Johanne
filio Reginaldi 7 Johanne de Burgo clericis . Nos itaque predictam
conuencionem inter predictum Linc' episcopum Hugonem
secundum 7 predictos Roesiam de Kima 7 Philippum filium 7
heredem suum de predictis maneriis cum pertinenciis factam ratam
7 gratam habemus 7 eam pre[senti carta nostra confirmamus¹]
volentes 7 firmiter precipientes quod predictus episcopus 7 attornati
sui quos per se vel per alium secundum formam predicti cirografi
constituerit habeant 7 teneant usque ad terminum memoratum
predicta maneria cum omnibus pertinenciis suis 7 libertatibus 7
quietanciis premissis bene 7 in pace libere 7 quiete integre 7 honorarie
sicut predictum est . Hiis testibus . E. Londoniensi . R. Sarresbiriensi . H. Herefordensi . W. Carleolensi . G. Elyensi . Thoma
Norwicensi . 7 . H. Roffensi episcopis . H. de Burgo . 7c' . Philippo
de Albiniaco . [Radulfo¹] de Trublevill' . Radulfo filio Nicholai .
Henrico de Trublevill' . Johanne filio Philippi . Henrico de Capella .
7 aliis . Dat' 7c' . apud Westmonasterium .xj. die Octobris .
anno 7c'.xj.

Texts : MS—Charter roll, 11 Henry III, part ii, mem. 2 (the text is sometimes
illegible at the right hand edge). Pd—C.C.R.i,62–3(abs.).
   Var. R. : ¹ supplied from No. 234 below. ² xxiij° No. 234. ³ maneriorum illorum
No. 234. ⁴ aliquam No. 234. ⁵ predictum No. 234. ⁶ for per read vel No. 234.
⁷ Cumberland No. 234 (but the reading of the text is right). ⁸ Halton' No. 234. ⁹ prenominatis No. 234. ¹⁰ super No. 234. ¹¹ Wareuill' No. 234. ¹² suorum No. 234.
¹³ insert inter eos No. 234. ¹⁴ Saususemar' No. 234. ¹⁵ Britone No. 234.

ADD. (EXTRAN.) CHART.

234. Another *inspeximus* and confirmation of the same indenture.
At Fulham. 15 May, 1229.

Texts : MS—Charter roll, 13 Henry III, part i, schedule, membranes 2 and 1.
Pd—See C.C.R.i,105(abs.).
Var. R. : See no. 233 above.

ADD. CHART.

235. Charter of Henry III, granting licence to bishop Hugh II
and his successors to have deer-leaps at their parks of Buckden
and Spaldwick [co. Huntingdon] and Lyddington [co. Rutland].
At Fulham, 15 May, 1229.

Henricus dei gracia rex Anglie . dominus Hybernie . dux Normannie 7 Aquitannie . comes Andegauie ꞉ archiepiscopis . episcopis .
abbatibus . prioribus . comitibus . baronibus . iusticiariis . vicecomitibus . forestariis . prepositis . 7 omnibus balliuis 7 fidelibus
suis ꞉ salutem . Sciatis nos concessisse 7 presenti carta nostra confirmasse venerabili patri Lincoln' episcopo Hugoni secundo 7
successoribus suis inperpetuum quod habeant saltatoria ad parcos
suos de Buggeden' . 7 de Spaldewich' 7 de Lidington' cum omnibus
libertatibus ad huiusmodi saltatoria pertinentibus . Quare uolumus
7 firmiter precipimus quod idem episcopus 7 successores sui habeant

7 teneant inperpetuum predicta saltatoria bene 7 in pace sicut
predictum est . Hiis testibus . dominis . Ricardo Dunolm*ensi*
episcopo . Waltero Karleolen*si* episcopo . thesaurario nostro .
Huberto de Burgo comite Cantie iusticiar*io* nostro . Johanne de
Monemue . Stephano de Segraue . Radulfo de Trubleuill*a* . Hugone
Dispensatore . Henrico filio Auch*eri* . Ricardo de Gray . Henrico de
Capella . 7 aliis . Dat' per manum venerabilis patris Radulfi
Cicestr*ensis* episcopi cancellarii nostri apud Fuleham' quinto
decimo die Maij . anno regni nostri terciodecimo.

Endorsed : (1) .H. III (13 cent.).   (2) De saltatoriis (13 cent.).
Tag and seal torn away. Size : 6¼ x 7 inches.
Texts : MS—Orig. A1/1/52. Iv(45). Pd—See *C.C.R.*i,105 ; *ibid.*iv,147(45).

ADD. (EXTRAN.) CHART.

236. An earlier issue of the preceding charter. At Westminster.
27 May, 1227.

H. rex 7c. salutem . Sciatis nos concessisse 7 presenti carta nostra
confirmasse venerabili patri Linc' episcopo Hugoni secundo 7
successoribus suis inperpetuum quod habeant saltatoria ad parcos
suos de Buggeden' . 7 de Spaldewich' 7 de Lidington' cum omnibus
libertatibus ad huiusmodi saltatoria pertinentibus . Quare uolumus
7c. quod idem episcopus 7 successores sui habeant 7 teneant inperpetuum predicta saltatoria bene 7 in pace sicut predictum est . Hiis
testibus J . Bath*oniensi* episcopo W . Carleolen*si* [episcopo] . H. de
Burgo 7c. comite W. Mar*escallo* Radulpho filio Nicholai senescallo
nostro Willelmo filio Warini Henrico de Aldithele 7 aliis . Dat'
7c. apud Westm*onasterium* xxvij. die Maij anno 7c. xjº.

Text : MS—Charter roll, 11 Henry III, mem. 3.

ADD. CHART.

237. Charter of Henry III, inspecting and confirming the charter
of his father, John, dated at Oxford, 18 July, 1215 (no. 211 above),
granting Harthay wood, co. Huntingdon, to bishop Hugh II. At
Fulham. 15 May, 1229.

Henricus dei gratia rex Angl*ie* . dominus Hybern*ie* . dux Normann*ie* . Aquitann*ie* 7 comes Andeg*auie* . archiepiscopis . episcopis .
abbatibus . prior*ibus* . comitibus . baronibus . iustici*ariis* . forestariis .
vicecomitibus . prepositis . 7 omnibus bailliuis 7 fidelibus suis .
salutem . Inspeximus cartam domini patris nostri Johannis illustris
Anglorum regis in hec uerba. [*Here is recited king John's charter
in full.*] Nos itaque donationem . concessionem . 7 confirmationem
predicti domini patris nostri gratam 7 ratam habemus pro nobis
7 heredibus nostris 7 eam presenti carta nostra confirmamus . Hiis
testibus . dominis Ricardo Dunholm*ensi* episcopo . Waltero
Karleol*ensi* episcopo . thesaurario nostro . Huberto de Burgo

comite Cant*ie* iustic*iario* nostro . Johanne de Munemue . Stephano
de Segraue . Radulfo de Trubleuill' . Hugone Dispensatore . Henrico
filio Auch*eri* . Ricardo de Gray . Henrico de Capella . 7 aliis . Dat'
per manum venerabilis patris Radulfi Cicestr*ensis* episcopi cancellarii
nostri . apud Fuleham' . quintodecimo die Maij . anno regni nostri
terciodecimo.

Endorsed : I .H. iij (13 cent.). De Herteia (13 cent.).
Tag for seal torn away. Size : 10 x 9 inches.
Texts : MS—Orig. A1/1/53. Charter Roll, 13 Henry III, part i, schedule, mem. 2.
Pd—See *C.C.R.*i, 105.
Note : Another inspeximus of king John's charter was granted at Westminster,
12 February, 1226–7 (*C.C.R.*i,8).

ADD. (EXTRAN.) CHART.

238. Charter of Henry III, granting to bishop Hugh II and his
successors that, at whatever time of the year they may die, they
shall have their movables and the fruits of corn sown before their
death and of copses and vineyards until the feast of Michaelmas
next following their death. At Oxford. 15 July, 1231.

Henricus dei gracia rex Angl*ie* dominus Hibern*ie* dux Norm*annie*
7 Aquit*anie* comes And*egauie* archiepiscopis episcopis abbatibus
prioribus comitibus baronibus iustic*iariis* forestariis vicecomitibus
prepositis ministris 7 omnibus balliuis 7 fidelibus suis ⟩ salutem
Sciatis nos intuitu dei 7 pro salute anime nostre 7 omnium antecessorum 7 heredum nostrorum concessisse pro nobis 7 heredibus
nostris in liberam puram 7 perpetuam elemosinam venerabili patri
Lincoln' episcopo Hugoni secundo 7 successoribus suis imperpetuum
quod non obstante consuetudine aliqua qua nos vel antecessores
nostri aliquo tempore vsi fuerimus quacumque parte anni idem
episcopus vel aliquis successorum suorum decesserit habeat omnia
bona sua mobilia 7 omnes fructus tam de bladis in terra sua
seminatis ante mortem suam quam fructus virgultorum 7 vinearum
eodem anno scilicet vsque ad festum sancti Michaelis proximum
post mortem eorundem prouenientes Ita quod nec nos nec aliquis
heredum nostrorum nec aliquis balliuorum nostrorum inde in
aliquo se vnquam intromittat vel ad ea manum extendat set
liberum sit eidem episcopo 7 successoribus suis 7 executoribus
eorum inde facere 7 disponere omnino pro voluntate sua absque
impedimento nostri vel heredum nostrorum vel balliuorum
nostrorum . Concessimus eciam quod executores eorum absque
impedimento nostri vel heredum nostrorum vel balliuorum nostrorum
habeant aisiamenta curiarum grangiarum torcularium granariorum
7 aliarum domorum que eorundem episcoporum fuerunt ad reponenda 7 conseruanda bona sua predicta in eis donec rationabiliter
debeant prouisoribus fructuum anni sequentis per eosdem executores
liberari . Quare volumus 7 firmiter precipimus quod quacumque
parte anni idem episcopus vel aliquis successorum suorum decesserit

non obstante predicta consuetudine qua nos vel antecessores nostri
aliquo tempore vsi fuerimus habeat omnia bona sua mobilia 7
omnes fructus tam de bladis in terra sua seminatis ante mortem
suam quam fructus virgultorum 7 vinearum eodem anno scilicet
vsque ad festum sancti Michaelis proximum post mortem in eorundem
prouenientes . Ita quod nec nos nec aliquis heredum nostrorum
nec aliquis balliuorum nostrorum in aliquo se vnquam intromittat
vel ad ea manum extendat set liberum sit eidem episcopo 7 successoribus suis 7 executoribus eorum inde facere 7 disponere omnino
pro voluntate sua absque impedimento nostri vel heredum nostrorum
vel balliuorum nostrorum . et quod executores eorum absque
impedimento nostri vel heredum nostrorum vel balliuorum nostrorum
habeant aisiamenta curiarum grangearum torcularium granariorum
7 aliarum domorum que eorundem episcoporum fuerunt ad reponenda
7 conseruanda bona sua predicta in eis donec rationabiliter debeant
prouisoribus fructuum anni sequentis per eosdem executores liberari
sicut predictum est . Hiis testibus dominis Rogero London*iensi*
Waltero Karleolen*si* thesaurario nostro Thoma Norwicenci[1] Hugone
Eliens*i*[2] episcopis Huberto de Burgo comes Kanci*e*[3] iustic*iario*
nostro . W. comes Warenne Godefrido de Craucumb' senescallo
nostro Hugone Despensatore Henrico de Capella 7 aliis . Dat'
per manum venerabilis patris Radulfi Cicestr*ensis* episcopi cancellarii
nostri apud Oxon*iam* quintodecimo die Julij anno regni nostri
quintodecimo.

Texts : MS—Iv(46).   Pd—*C.C.R.*iv,147–8 (46) (abs.).
Var. R. :   [1] Norwicens' Ch. roll.   [2] Elyens' Ch. roll.   [3] Canc' Ch. roll.

ADD. (EXTRAN.) CHART.

239. Charter of Henry III, granting to bishop Hugh II and
his successors that, at whatever time of the year they may wish
to make their will, they shall have full power to dispose by their
will of all their goods moveable and immoveable ; and that neither
the king nor any other secular person shall lay hand on the said
goods, or interfere with the execution or provisions of the will.
At Westminster.   27 March, 1234.

Henricus dei gracia rex Angl*ie* dominus Hibern*ie* dux Norma*nnie*
Aquit*annie* 7 comes Ande*gauie* archiepiscopis episcopis abbatibus
prioribus comitibus baronibus iustic*iariis* vicecomitibus prepositis
ministris 7 omnibus balliuis 7 fidelibus suis salutem . Sciatis nos
intuitu dei 7 pro salute anime nostre 7 animarum antecessorum
7 heredum nostrorum concessisse venerabili patri Hugoni Linc'
episcopo quod quocunque tempore vel termino anni idem episcopus
vel successores sui episcopi Lincoln' ante obitum suum testamentum
suum condere voluerint . idem episcopus 7 successores sui episcopi

M

Lincoln' liberam habeant disposicionem testamentum suum condere
de omnibus rebus suis mobilibus 7 immobilibus tam de bladis in
terris seminatis quam aliis quod quidem testamentum pro nobis
7 heredibus nostris[1] firmum esse volumus 7 stabile . Ita quod nec
nos nec heredes nostri manum apponere possumus[2] nec eciam vicecomes constabularius vel alius balliuus noster vel heredum nostrorum
vel alia quecunque secularis persona manum apponere possint ad
bona ipsius episcopi vel successorum suorum episcoporum Linc'
mobilia vel immobilia vel blada sua in terris seminata vel alia que
idem episcopus 7 successores sui episcopi Linc' in testamento suo
assignauerint nec aliquod impedimentum nos vel heredes nostri
innectemus nec eciam vicecomes constabularius vel alius balliuus
noster vel heredum nostrorum vel alia quecunque secularis persona
innectere possint quominus libere plene 7 pacifice disponere
possint executores testamenti predicti episcopi 7 successorum
suorum episcoporum Lincoln' de bonis eorundem secundum
quod in testamento suo ordinauerint vel dictorum executorum
disposicioni ordinanda reliquerint . Quare volumus 7 firmiter
precipimus pro nobis 7 heredibus nostris quod quocumque tempore
vel termino anni predictus episcopus et successores sui episcopi
Lincoln' ante obitum suum testamentum suum condere voluerint :
idem episcopus 7 successores sui episcopi Lincoln' liberam habeant
disposicionem testamentum suum condere de omnibus rebus suis
mobilibus 7 immobilibus tam de bladis in terris seminatis quam
aliis quod quidem testamentum pro nobis 7 heredibus nostris
imperpetuum firmum esse volumus 7 stabile . Ita quod nec nos
nec heredes nostri manum apponere possimus nec eciam vicecomes
constabularius vel aliquis balliuus noster vel heredum nostrorum
vel alia quecumque secularis persona manum apponere possint
ad bona ipsius episcopi vel successorum suorum episcoporum
Linc' mobilia vel immobilia vel blada sua in terris seminata vel
alia que idem episcopus 7 successores sui episcopi Linc' in testamento suo assignauerint nec aliquod impedimentum nos vel heredes
nostri innectemus nec eciam vicecomes constabularius vel alius
balliuus noster vel heredum nostrorum vel alia quacunque[3] secularis
persona manum innectere . possint quominus libere plene 7 pacifice
disponere possint executores testamenti predicti episcopi 7 successorum suorum episcoporum Linc' de bonis eorundem secundum
quod in testamento suo ordinauerint vel dictorum executorum
disposicioni ordinanda reliquerint sicut predictum est . Hiis testibus
venerabili patre P. Wintoniensi episcopo . S. de Segraue . iusticiario
Anglie . J. comite Linc' 7 constabulario Cestrie Hugone Dispensario
Radulfo filio Nicollai Radulfo Gernun . Godefrido de Crawcumb
Galfrido Dispensario Galfrido de Kauz Johanne de Plesseto 7
aliis . Dat' per manum venerabilis patris Radulfi Cicestrensis
episcopi cancellarii nostri apud Westmonasterium vicesimo septimo
die Marcij anno regni nostri decimo octauo.

Texts : MS—Iv(48).   Pd—*C.C.R.*iv, 148(48)(abs.).
Var. R. : [1] *insert* inperpetuum Ch. Roll.   [2] possimus Ch. roll.   [3] quecumque
Ch. roll.

ADD. CHART.

240. Charter of Henry III, granting licence to bishop Hugh II and his successors to have the fairs at Marton [co. Lincoln] which the bishop had at Stow, namely, one fair on the Assumption of Saint Mary [15 August], and another on the Nativity of Saint Mary [8 September], and a third on the feast of Saint Michael [29 September] ; and to hold them for as many days at Marton as the bishop and his predecessors did at Stow. At Westminster. 19 October, 1234.

Henricus dei gracia rex Angl*ie* . dominus Hybern*ie* . dux Norm*annie* . Aquit*annie* . 7 comes Ande*gauie* . archiepiscopis . episcopis . abbatibus . prioribus comitibus . baronibus . iustic*iariis* . vicecomitibus . prepositis . ministris . 7 omnibus balliuis 7 fidelibus suis salutem . Sciatis nos intuitu dei . 7 pro salute anime nostre . 7 animarum antecessorum . 7 heredum nostrorum . concessisse . 7 presenti carta nostra confirmasse . pro nobis 7 heredibus nostris . venerabili patri Lincoln' . episcopo . Hugoni secundo . quod ipse 7 successores sui inperpetuum habeant 7 teneant ferias apud Marton*am* .⁊ quas idem episcopus habuit apud Stouwe[1] . videlicet vnam in Assumptione beate Marie . 7 aliam in Natiuitate beate Marie . 7 terciam .⁊ in festo sancti Michaelis . Ita quod quelibet earundem feriarum per tot dies duret apud Marton*am* .⁊ per quot durare consueuit apud Stouwe[1] . Et predictus episcopus . 7 successores sui inperpetuum habeant omnes libertates . 7 liberas consuetudines in predictis feriis apud Marton*am* .⁊ quas predictus episcopus . 7 predecessores eius prius habuerunt in feriis apud Stouwe . Quare volumus 7 firmiter precipimus pro nobis 7 heredibus nostris quod predictus episcopus 7 successores sui in perpetuum habeant 7 teneant predictas ferias apud Marton*am* .⁊ quas idem episcopus habuit apud Stouwe . videlicet vnam in Assumptione beate Marie . 7 aliam in Natiuitate beate Marie . 7 terciam in festo sancti Michaelis . Ita quod quelibet earumdem feriarum per tot dies duret apud Marton*am* .⁊ per quot durare consueuit apud Stouwe . bene 7 in pace . libere . quiete . 7 integre . cum omnibus libertatibus . 7 liberis consuetudinibus quas prefatus episcopus . 7 predecessores sui prius habuerunt in feriis apud Stouwe[1] .⁊ sicut predictum est . Hiis testibus . venerabilibus patribus . R. Dunelm*ensi* . J. Baitthon*iensi* . H. Roff*ensi* . 7 W. Karleol*ensi* . episcopis . J. comite Cestr*ie* . 7 Huntind*onie* . H. de Boun . comite Herefordie . Hugone Dispens*atore* . Henrico de Aldithel*ega* . Radulfo filio Nicholai . Godefrido de Craucumb' . Galfrido Dispens*atore* . Henrico de Capella . 7 aliis . Dat' per manum venerabilis patris Radulfi . Cycestr*ensis*

episcopi . cancellarii nostri apud West*monasterium* . decimo nono
die Octobris . anno regni nostri decimo octauo.

Endorsed : (1) De feriis habendis apud Marton*am* (14 cent.).   (2) III. (13 cent.).
(3) .H. iij. (13 cent.).
Tag and seal torn away. Size : 9¼ x 9 inches.
Texts : MS—Orig. A1/1/55.   Iv(47).   Pd—*C.C.R.iv*, 148(47)(abs.).
Var. R. : ¹ Stowe Iv.

ADD. CHART.

241. Charter of Henry III, granting to John of Lexington and
his heirs free warren in his demesne lands in Tuxford and Warsop
[co. Nottingham], and Aston [le Walls, co. Northampton]; and
granting to the said John and his heirs and to Matthew [Stratton]
archdeacon of Buckingham and his successors, tenants of the
prebend of Horley, free warren in their demesne lands of Horley
and Hornton [co. Oxford]; granting also to John and his heirs
licence to hunt and take the fox, the wolf, the hare, and the cat
in the royal forest in Nottinghamshire outside the king's demesne
warrens. At Westminster. 6 March, 1238–9.

Henricus dei gracia rex Angl*ie* dominus Hybern*ie* dux Norm*annie*
Aquitann*ie* ⁊ comes Andeg*auie* . archiepiscopis . episcopis .
abbatibus . prioribus . comitibus baronibus iustic*iariis* . vicecomitibus
. prepositis . ministris . ⁊ omnibus balliuis ⁊ fidelibus suis salutem .
Sciatis nos concessisse ⁊ hac carta nostra confirmasse pro nobis
⁊ heredibus nostris . dilecto ⁊ fideli nostro Johanni de Lessington'
quod ipse ⁊ heredes sui inperpetuum habeant liberam warennam
in dominicis terris suis in Touxford' . Warsop' ⁊ Aston' . Concessimus eciam eidem Johanni ⁊ Matheo archidiacono Bokyng-
ham*ie* pro nobis ⁊ heredibus nostris . quod idem Johannes ⁊ heredes
sui ⁊ predictus Matheus ⁊ successores sui tenentes prebendam de
Hornilegh' habeant inperpetuum liberam warennam in dominicis
terris suis in Hornilegh' ⁊ Horninton' Ita quod nullus warennas
illas intrare possit ad fugandum in eis sine licencia ⁊ voluntate
predicti Johannis ⁊ heredum suorum ⁊ predicti Mathei ⁊ successorum suorum . Concessimus eciam eidem Johanni pro nobis
⁊ heredibus nostris quod ipse ⁊ heredes sui inperpetuum libere
⁊ sine inpedimento fugare ⁊ capere possint per totam forestam
nostram in comitatu Notingham*ie* . vulpem . lupum . leporem . ⁊
cattum . exceptis dominicis warennis nostris . Quare volumus ⁊
firmiter precipimus pro nobis ⁊ heredibus nostris quod predictus
Johannes ⁊ heredes sui ⁊ predictus Matheus ⁊ successores sui habeant
in perpetuum predictas warennas cum omnibus libertatibus ⁊
liberis consuetudinibus ad huiusmodi warennas pertinentibus . Ita
quod nullus warennas illas intrare possit ad fugandum in eis sine
licencia ⁊ voluntate predicti Johannis ⁊ heredum suorum ⁊ predicti
Mathei ⁊ successorum suorum . Et prohibemus ne quis intret

warennas illas ad fugandum in eis sine licencia 7 voluntate predicti Johannis 7 heredum suorum 7 predicti Mathei 7 successorum suorum . super forisfacturam nostram decem librarum volumus eciam 7 precipimus pro nobis 7 heredibus nostris quod idem Johannes 7 heredes sui inperpetuum libere 7 sine inpedimento fugare 7 capere possit per totam forestam nostram in comitatu Notingham' . vulpem . lupum . leporem . 7 cattum exceptis dominicis warennis nostris sicut predictum est . Hiis testibus . S. de Monte Forti comite Leycestrie . W. de Ralega thesaurario Exonie . Henrico de Turbleuilla Ricardo de Gray . Johanne filio Galfridi Herberto filio Mathei . Roberto de Mucegros . Johanne de Plesseto . Galfrido de Langeleia . Thoma de Albo Monasterio 7 aliis Dat' per manum nostram apud Westmonasterium sexto die Martij anno regni nostri vicesimo tertio.

Written at the foot : Ista carta tripplicata sub cera residet penes dominum Ricardum de Sutton' inter cartas eiusdem.

Size : 9¼ x 5½ inches.

Text : MS—D. & C. A1/1/56 (a fourteenth century copy of the original charter).

Note : John of Lexington, the grantee, died in or before January, 1246–7, seised *inter alia* of the manor of Tuxford with the hamlet of Warsop which he held of the king in chief by the service of one knight's fee ; of £20 of land in Appletree [in the parish of Aston le Walls] and Aston le Walls ; and of ten hides of land in Horley of the fee of Brandon, held of John de Verddun. His heir was his brother, Henry Lexington, bishop of Lincoln (*Cal. Inq.* i, no. 378). The bishop died in August, 1258, seised of the villages of Tuxford and Warsop, which were held in dower by the lady Margaret, his brother's widow ; and his heirs were his nephews, Richard Markham (*de Marcham*) and William Sutton (*ibid.*, no. 402 ; *Visitation of Nottinghamshire*, Harl. Soc. iv, pp. 141–2).

The sir Richard Sutton, who is mentioned in the footnote to the charter as holding the original charter, was, no doubt, the son of Robert Sutton, and the grandson of the William Sutton mentioned above (Thoroton, *History of Nottinghamshire*, ed. Throsby, iii, 108–10, 220, 367). In 1303 this Richard Sutton held of the king in chief half a knight's fee in Warsop and Eakring, co. Nottingham (*Feudal Aids* iv, 98) ; in 1316 he held Aston and Appletree (*ibid.*, p. 20) ; and in the same year he and Neupolyn (i.e. Napoleone cardinal-deacon of Saint Adrian), prebendary of Sutton cum Buckingham, held the village of Horley cum Hornton between them (*ibid.*, p. 166).

The usual name of the prebend of ' Hornilegh,' as it is called in the text, is Sutton cum Buckingham.

ADD. CHART.

242. Letters patent of Henry III, addressed to the dean and chapter of Lincoln, reciting letters from the king, directed to Robert [Grosseteste] bishop of Lincoln, with respect to the bishop's allegation that John Maunsell, king's clerk, had applied a force to keep the prebend of Thame. At Chester, 2 September, 1241.

Quedam littera directa decano et capitulo Linc' (R rubric).

.H. dei gracia rex Anglie *:* dominus Hibernie *(* dux Normannie Aquitannie 7 comes Andegauie dilectis sibi in Christo decano 7 capitulo Linc' salutem in Domino . Noueritis uos litteras nostras venerabili in Christo patri .R. eadem gracia episcopo Linc' salutem in domino . Venientes ad nos ex parte uestra de Leycestria 7 Huntendonia archidiaconi magistri .R. de Rauelingeham 7 .L.

clerici litteras vestras deferentes vt hiis que ex parte vestra nobis
proponerent aurem preberemus benignam (Ipsos benigne recepimus
7 peticiones infrascriptas quas in nostra plenius exposuerunt presencia intelleximus diligenter Peticiones autem nobis fuerunt
porrecte 7 exposite in hunc modum . Petit episcopus Linc' quod
cum Johannes Maunsel clericus se manu armata in ecclesiam de
Thame intruserit 7 manu armata eam detineat occupantem[1] ꝉ vobis
auxilium eidem 7 fauorem vt dicitur prestantibus vt sicut illam
precipiatis amoueri cum in preiudicium ecciastice [sic] libertatis 7
contra coronam 7 dignitatem predicta manifeste perpetrentur .
Item petit idem episcopus quod cum vicecomes Oxonie in pleno
comitatu Oxonie preceperit omnibus in comitatu ex parte vestra
vt omnes venirent cum equis 7 arcuis ad summonicionem suam
apud Thame in subsidium Johannis Maunsel 7 suorum ad tenendum
contra ipsum ecclesiam de Thame quod illud mandatum faciatis
reuocari cum in preiudicium ecclesiastice libertatis 7c. Item predictus vicecomes attendens apud Thame in propria persona
iniunxerit balliuo episcopi ex parte vestra manutenere predictum
Johannem intrusum in sua seisina in dicta ecclesia non obstante
sentencia lata in omnes fautores coadiutores ipsius Johannis vt
predictum mandatum reuocetis cum in preiudicium ecclesiastice
libertatis 7c . Item cum dictus Johannes propter manifestam eius
offensam sentencia excommunicacionis meruerit innodari ne per
eius communionem grex domini maculetur ꝉ ipsum vobis 7 consilio
vestro 7 familie vestre excommunicatum denunciat 7 a vobis 7
consilio vestro 7 aliis Christi fidelibus vitandum . Item cum predicta
manifeste contra libertates 7 coronam 7 dignitatem vestram que
sicut alii fideles nostri episcopus seruare tenetur ꝉ attemptentur ꝉ
nisi saniori consilio predicta emendentur ꝉ cum maius sit Deum
offendere quam hominem 7 melius sit incidere in manus hominum
quam peccare in conspectu Domini ꝉ necesse habet episcopus manum
suam agrauare 7 episcopatum suum interdicto supponere 7 aliter
si fuerit necesse procedere . E contra vero dilectus clericus noster
dictus .J. Maunsel qui tunc temporis presens erat coram nobis
proposuit quod peticiones predicte exaudiende non erant pro eo
quod nec manu armata in ecclesia[2] de Thame se intrusit nec ipsam
violenter detinet occupatam Set verum est quod auctoritate apostolica sibi rite 7 canonice collata extitit 7 eadem auctoritate possessionem ipsius ecclesie adeptus fuit 7 ante aliquam sentenciam in
eum latam ꝉ ad sedem apostolicam probabiliter 7 racionabiliter
appellauit (propter quod nec excommunicari potuit . Et si hoc
factum sit occasione . sentencie que nulla est ꝉ nec a nobis neque
a consilio nostro nec aliis Christi fidelibus debet aliquatenus euitari (
Vnde si predictas peticiones exaudiremus ꝉ ecclesiastica libertas
que post appelacionem iustam maxime a non suo iudice nulla
excommunicacionis vel suspencionis aut interdicti sentencia aliquem
ligari permittit 7 eadem 7 corona atque regalis dignitas que debiliores

per potentiores pati non debent opprimi nec permittere aliquem
iniuste vexari (Set quemlibet de iure 7 consuetudine regni in iure
suo 7 seisina sua seu possessione tueri eneruari 7 confundi pocius
viderentur quam eisdem si non exaudiantur preiudicium generari .
Licet autem de predictis ex parte ipsius Johannis fuerimus ad
instruccionem nostram certificati summarie ? tamen ad cautelam
nobis offerimus . quod si in curia nostra vultis ostendere quod
nos vel nostri aliquam violenciam tueamur (vel quod aliquid
faciamus per quod libertati ecclesiastice vel corone 7 dignitati
nostre preiudicium aliquod generetur (cum alias non sufficiat
dicere nisi 7 probetur nec nos vel nostros ex hiis que supra sunt
proposita culpabiles senciamus parati sumus corrigere 7 iuxta
consideracionem predicte curie reuocare . Et si hoc vobis non
sufficit quatenus predicta spiritualitatem respiciunt ? offerimus nos
paratos vna vobiscum arbitros eligere quorum sentenciam seruabimus
7 faciemus inuiolabiliter obseruari . Rogamus igitur paternitatem
vestram quatinus a predictis comminationibus nostris 7 effectum
ipsarum cessetis si placuerit . Ita quod in preiudicium nostrum
vel regni vel nostrorum nullam sentenciam proferatis cum in predictis offeramus nos 7 parati sumus per omnia stare iuri 7 sequi
consilium peritorum communiter electorum . Quod si forte ea que
vobis offerimus renueritis ? nos **propter** predicta ex parte nostra
uobis oblata 7 non admissa ? pro statu nostro 7 regni 7 consilii
nostri 7 nostrorum 7 specialiter terre in diocesi vestra site ne ad
aliquas procedatis sentencias nec pendente appellacione vel oblacione aliquod innouetis ? ad sedem apostolicam appellamus Rogamus
eciam vt circa predicta tale consilium habeatis 7 taliter procedatis ?
ne deuiantes a iusticia in manibus dei pocius quam hominum ?
incidatis . In cuius rei testimonium has litteras nostras vobis
transmittimus patentes . Teste meipso apud Cestr*iam* .ij. die
Septembris anno regni nostri .xxvᵒ. Cum igitur pro iuris nostri
conseruacione ad dominum papam interposuerimus appellacionem
legitimam 7 uos iura nostra teneamini conseruare ? dilecionem
nostre necnon discrecionem de qua fiduciam reportamus pleniorem
mandandam duximus 7 rogandam quatinus si forsitan prefatum
episcopum presumptuose contigerit episcopatum suum ecclesiastico
supponere interdicto in preiudicium regie dignitatis 7 appellacionis
nostre predicte ? vos nichilominus diuina celebretis (precipue
cum dominum papam communem iudicem habemus qui nobis in
iure nostro nullatenus deerit domino concedente Vos igitur in hoc
facto taliter vos geratis ? quod discrecionem vestram debeamus
specialiter commendare 7 iura nostra conseruare tempore oportuno .
In cuius rei testimonium has litteras vobis transmittimus patentes .
Teste meipso apud Cestr*iam* eisdem die 7 anno.

Text : MS—R56.
Note : See *Cal. Pat. Rolls*, 1232–1247, p. 257, where the king's letter to the bishop
of Lincoln is dated 8 August, 1241, instead of 2 September as in the text,
Var. R. : ¹ *recte* occupatam. ² *recte* ecclesiam.

ADD. CHART.

243. Letters patent of Henry III, granting to master Nicholas de Heigham and his heirs those houses in the city of Lincoln which were John Maunsell's, and which are the king's escheat by John's death. At Kenilworth. 12 July, 1266.

H dei gracia rex Angl*ie* dominus Hibern*ie* 7 dux Aquit*annie* omnibus ad quos presentes littere peruenerint salutem Sciatis quod ad instanciam dilecti 7 fidelis nostri Rogeri de Leyburn' dedimus 7 concessimus quantum in nobis est dilecto nobis magistro Nicholao de Hegham domos illas cum redditibus 7 omnibus aliis pertinenciis suis in ciuitate Lincoln' que fuerunt Johannis Maunsell' defuncti 7 que sunt escaeta nostra per mortem eiusdem Johannis vt dicitur Habend*as* 7 tenend*as* de nobis 7 heredibus nostris eidem Nicholao 7 heredibus suis imperpetuum saluo iure cuiuslibet . faciendo . seruicium inde debitum 7 consuetum . In cuius rei testimonium has litteras nostras fieri fecimus patentes . Teste me ipso apud Kenilwrth' .xij. die[1] Julij anno regni nostri L°.

Endorsed : Carta regis facta Nicholao de Hegham de domibus cum redditibus 7 pertinentiis in Lincoln' que fuerunt Johannis Maunsell et tunc escaeta (14 cent.).
Tag for seal.   Size :   7 x 3 inches.
Texts :   MS—Orig. A1/1/57.   Pd—*Cal. Patent Rolls*, 1258–1268, 615.
Var. R. :   [1]xj die *Cal. Pat. Rolls.*
Note :   John Maunsell was parson of Wigan, chancellor of Saint Paul's, London, and provost of Beverley.   His inquisition post mortem is dated 16 April, 1266 (*Cal. Inq.* i, no. 621).   Nicholas Heigham became archdeacon of Oxford in 1275, and dean of Lincoln in 1280, and died in 1288.

ADD. (EXTRAN.) CHART.

244. Commission to Henry de Bathonia to enquire touching the petition of the dean and canons for licence to lengthen their church towards the east. At Westminster. 5 November, 1255.

Rex Henrico de Bathon*ia* salutem cum dilecti nobis in Christo decanus et canonici Linc' ecclesie nobis supplicauerint quod licenciam eis concederemus elongandi ecclesiam suam uersus orientem per remotionem muri orientalis ciuitatis nostre Linc' qui est ex opposito eiusdem ecclesie ignorantes utrum hoc fieri posset sine dampno nostro et detrimento aut nocumento eiusdem ciuitatis : constituimus uos ad inquirendum per sacramentum proborum 7c. utrum esset ad dampnum nostrum aut detrimentum uel nocumentum ciuitatis predicte si concederemus predictis decano et canonicis quod elongare possint predictam ecclesiam suam et remouere predictum murum uersus orientem necne et si esset ad dampnum nostrum uel detrimentum seu nocumentum predicte ciuitatis . ad quod dampnum quod detrimentum et quod nocumentum . Et si non esset ad dampnum . 7c. per que loca et per quas diuisas posset predicta ecclesia elongari . et predictus murus remoueri . sine dampno nostro et detrimento ac nocumento eiusdem ciuitatis . Et ideo uobis mandamus quod in propria persona uestra accedatis ad predictam ciuitatem et in presencia maioris et balliuorum et aliorum ciuium eiusdem ciuitatis dictam inquisitionem sicut predictum est facias . et quid inde inueneritis nobis in reuersione uestra ad nos distincte et aperte scire facias . Mandauimus enim uicecomiti nostro Linc' quod ad diem 7c. uenire faciat coram uobis tot et tales 7c. de balliua sua per quos 7c. in cuius testimonium 7c. teste Rege apud Westmonasterium qvinto die Nouembris.

Texts : MS—Patent Roll, 40 Henry III, mem. 22d.　Pd—*Mon.*viii,278(66).

ADD. CHART.

245. Letters patent of Henry III, recording his approval of the enclosure and extension of walls round the church of Lincoln, which have been made with the king's licence and with the consent of his citizens of Lincoln. At Westminster, 19 July, 1256.

De clausura ecclesie (rubric).　De clausura (marg.).

.Henricus dei gracia rex Angl*ie* dominus Hibern*ie* dux Norm*annie* Aquit*annie* 7 comes Andeg*auie* omnibus balliuis 7 fidelibus suis ad quos presentes littere peruenerint salutem . Sciatis nos pro nobis 7 heredibus nostris gratam habere 7 acceptam clausuram 7 elongacionem murorum que de licencia nostra 7 de consensu ciuium nostrorum Linc' circa ecclesiam Lincoln' facta est ad ampliacionem ecclesie predicte secundum quod inter decanum 7 capitulum eiusdem ecclesie 7 ciuos[1] predictos de vtriusque partis prouisione conuenit . Ita quod placea infra dictam clausuram contenta dicte ecclesie Linc' prout dicti decanus 7 capitulum expedire viderint inter ipsos 7 dictos ciues conuenit applicetur . In cuius rei testimonium has litteras nostras eisdem 7 capitulo fieri fecimus patentes . Teste meipso apud Westm*onasterium* decimo nodo[2] Julij (anno regni nostri quadragesimo.

Text : MS—R57.
Var. R. : [1] *recte* ciues.　[2] *recte* nono.

ADD. CHART.

246. Writ of Henry III, forbidding the canons of the church of All Saints, Derby, which is the king's free chapel, and exempt from ordinary jurisdiction, to render obedience to the bishop of Coventry and Lichfield and the archdeacon of Derby. At Westminster. 28 January, 1271.

H. dei gracia rex Angl*ie* dominus Hibern*ie* 7 dux Aquit*annie* omnibus 7 singulis canonicis ecclesie omnium Sanctorum de[1] Derby salutem (Quia libertate ecclesie Omnium Sanctorum Derbeye que est libera capella nostra 7 per priuilegia sedis apostolice nobis indulta 7 ab omni ordinaria iurisdiccione funditus exempta illesa volumus conseruari ⫶ vobis mandamus districtius inhibentes ne Couentr*ensi*

7 Liche*feldensi* episcopo archidiacono Derbeye vel eorum officialibus decanis seu clericis quibuscunque pretextu iurisdiccionis ordinarie in aliquibus pareatis vel intendatis contra libertates 7 priuilegia nostra predicta (Teste . meipso apud Westmo*nasterium* xxviij. die Januarii . anno regni . nostri . lv^{to}.

Marginalia in D : 🖙 🖙 Breue regium quod episcopus Liche*feldensis* non exerceat iurisdictionem in decanatu Omnium Sanctorum Derb'.
Texts : MS—D4. Iv(49). Pd—*C.C.R.*iv,148(49)(abs.).
Var, R. : ¹ de *is interlineated*.

Folio 169.
Hdl. .1.6.9.

Note by Q : Prima pars. Primus titulus. De priuilegiis. apud .A.

On the surviving part of a tag sewn to the edge of folio 169 :
Confirm' . . . . . 7 decan'.

876

247. Confirmation by pope Nicholas II, addressed to Wulfwig bishop of Dorchester, confirming to Wulfwig's church all that belongs to it, and especially the diocese of Lindsey and the church of Stow [co. Lincoln] with Newark [co. Nottingham] which Ailric archbishop of York wrongfully seized. 3 May, 1061.

[*The title at the head of the document has been carefully erased, perhaps by Q in order that his note* (see marginalia) *might be substituted.*]

Nicholaus episcopus seruus seruorum dei Wlwino uenerabili episcopo Dorcacastrensi suisque successoribus ibique¹ canonice promouendis imperpetuum . Cum magna nobis sollicitudine insistit cura pro uniuersis dei ecclesiis ac piis locis uigilandum
5 ne aliquam necessitatis iacturam sustineant . Sed proprie utilitatis stipendia consequantur . Ideo conuenit nos tota mentis integritate eisdem uenerabilibus locis ut ea que sua sunt stabilita permaneant prouide² . Igitur quia petisti a nobis karissime fili cum Edwardi³ regis legatis atque litteris
10 nostri uidelicet amici ut per nostri priuilegii paginam tue ecclesie tibique necnon successoribus tuis omnia perpetualiter confirmaremus . que prefate ecclesie iuste 7 legaliter competunt . suggestioni tue gratanter annuentes per huius nostre constitucionis decretum 7 apostolice sedis liberale edictum
15 concedimus 7 confirmamus tibi sicut supra legitur tuisque successoribus ibidem canonice promouendis inperpetuum . queque prefate ecclesie pertinent . tam que in presentiarum possidet uel possedit 7 maxime parrochiam Lindisi ecclesiamque Stou cum Newerca⁴ 7 appendiciis quas iniuste
20 Aluricus archiepiscopus Eboracensis inuasit . uti per legatorum nostrorum dicta 7 per antecessorum testimonia 7 scripta

agnouimus . quamque in futuro quocumque modo diuinis
7 humanis legibus adquire[5] poterit scilicet prenominata
ecclesia cum omnibus rebus 7 possessionibus suis ac pertinenciis
25 mobilibus 7 inmobilibus seseque mouentibus castris scilicet .
cassis . uillis . territoriis . ecclesiis cum primitiis 7 decima-
tionibus cum omnibus quoque que pia deuotio fidelium sacris
contulit sibi uel contulerit oblationibus[6] pro salute uiuorum
quamque etiam mortuorum . statuentes per huius nostre
30 apostolice sedis cui deo auctore presidemus auctoritatem 7
nostri edicti inuiolabilem constitucionem . ut neque rex .
neque archiepiscopus . siue dux . siue marchio . seu comes .
aut uicecomes . nec alia siue magna siue[7] persona cuiuscumque
dignitatis uel ordinis contra hoc nostrum priuilegium pre-
35 sumat prefatam ecclesiam aut te karissime confrater tuosque
inperpetuum successores de bonis suis deinuestire aut
inquietare . aut aliquid ibi contra sanctos canones constituere
uel ordinare sed ita sicut predicta ecclesia que omnia pre-
libauimus melius firmius ue a sue constitucionis initio tenuit
40 teneas possideasque tam tu quam successores tui sub con-
stitucione huius pagine 7 apostolica sanctione . Si quis igitur
quod non optamus contra hoc nostrum priuilegium uenire
temptauerit ⫶ 7 sicuti ab apostolica auctoritate preceptum
ac corroboratum est ⫶ permanere non dimiserit . sciat se
45 anathematis uinculo innodatum . 7 cum Iuda traditore 7
Dathan 7 Abyron partem habere nisi forte resipuerit . 7
digne satis fecerit . Qui uero pio intuitu in omnibus obseruator
extiterit custodiens huius priuilegii nostri[8] constituta ad
cultum dei respicientis benedictionis gratiam a misericordis-
50 simo domino deo nostro consequatur ⫶ 7 uite eterne particeps
fieri mereatur . Datum .v. nonas . Maii[9] per manus Bernardi
episcopi sancte ecclesie Prenestrine[10] . anno ab incarnatione
domini millesimo . sexagesimo .jⁿ. anno .iijⁿ. pontificatus
Nicholai pape .ij. indictio .xiiij^{ma}.

Marginalia : *opp. l. 1*, I. Confirmacio de ecclesia) castris) decimis 7 rebus aliis
(Q). *opp. l. 19*, Nota archiepiscopus Eboracensis iniuste inuasit (Q). *opp. l. 45*,
Judas proditor Dathan 7 Abyro (Q).
Texts : MS—A. C,*ff.*18-19. Pd : Wilkins i, 315. Mansi xix, 875. Migne,
lat. cxliii, 1356. Jaffé-Löwenfeld, no. 4461.
Var. R. : [1]*for* ibidem, *cp. l. 16*. [2]prouidere C. [3]Eadwardi C. [4]Neuuerca C.
[5]adquirere C. [6]*insert* tam C. [7]*insert* parua C. [8]nostri priuilegii C. [9]Mai C.
[10]Prenestine C.

Note by Dr W. Holtzmann : This bull of Nicholas II, though the original text
has not survived, is one of the earliest genuine documents issued by a pope during
the reformation of the church in the eleventh century ; and it supplies valuable
evidence in regard to the ecclesiastical politics of Edward the Confessor. There
can be no doubt whatever about its genuineness. The bull is dated 3 May, 1061,
and a few days earlier, on 25 April, a similar bull was granted to bishop Giso of
Wells, which is the earliest original extant bull known to me in England (facsimile
in Hickes, *Thesaurus Linguarum Veterum Septentrionalium* i, after p. 177). A
comparison of the Lincoln and Wells documents shews that the two texts are
nearly identical, and suggests that the papal notary used the same model for both
documents. We are not yet sufficiently acquainted with the styles of the several

papal writers of the period to enable us to say which of them composed the text of the Lincoln bull. The slight differences between the Lincoln and Wells documents may be easily explained: the Wells bull is dated by the cardinal-bishop Humbert of Silva Candida, a famous churchman and diplomatist from the time of the pontificate of Leo IX (A.D. 1049–1054); the Lincoln bull, on the other hand, is dated by Bernard, cardinal-bishop of Palestrina. Now, Humbert died 5 May, 1061; and the last bull in which his name as *bibliothecarius apostolicae sedis* appears is a document in favour of Saint Mary of Saintes, 30 April, 1061. All the later bulls of Nicholas II, who died in Florence, 27 July, 1061, are dated by Bernard of Palestrina or his lieutenants. Since, in those days, the chancellors (or *bibliothecarii*, as they were called) played a great part in forming the texts of the bulls, we may venture to ascribe the difference between the Lincoln and Wells bulls to the personal influence of the two chancellors.

If doubts have been at times entertained about the genuineness of the Lincoln bull, they can have been founded only upon the clause, ‘*et maxime parrochiam Lindisi*,’ for Lindsey was claimed by the archbishop of York. The bishop of Lincoln, however, also claimed it, and was able finally to establish his right about the year 1091, when archbishop Thomas renounced his claim (see no. 4 above). The settlement then arrived at was confirmed by pope Paschal II, 19 April, 1103 (Raine, *Historians of the Church of York and its Archbishops* iii, 28, no. 12). This bull of Nicholas II, if, as is here claimed, its genuineness is established, is important documentary evidence for King Edward’s mission to the pope (*cum Edwardi regis legatis*), of which the story is told only by the later English chroniclers.

Folio 169d.

877

248. Confirmation by pope Honorius II, addressed to bishop Alexander, of various possessions of the church of Lincoln. At the Lateran. 30 January, 1126.

Honorius episcopus seruus seruorum dei venerabili fratri Alexandro Lincolniensi[1] episcopo eiusque successoribus canonice promouendis imperpetuum[2]. Pia 7 diligens materne cura sollicitudinis teneros filios consueuit dulciter educare .
5   7 adultis unde sustentari ualeant sagaciter prouidere . Proporcionaliter itaque sancta Romana ecclesia . in fide Petri fundata omnium ecclesiarum optinet[3] principatum . paruulos 7 inbecilles lacte sapientie sue nutrit . Prouectis autem 7 deuotis profundioris scientie pabula subministrat[4]. Et ut
10   liberius diuinis uacare possint obsequiis apostolice sedis munimine ab hostium incursione defendit . Hac igitur inducti ratione Lincolniensem[5] ecclesiam cui deo auctore dilecte in domino frater Alexander episcope presides sub apostolice sedis tutelam excipimus . 7 contra prauorum hominum
15   molestiam auctoritatis eius defensione 7 priuilegio communimus . Bona ergo 7 possessiones quas iuste[5a] 7 legittime possidet . uel infuturum largiente domino canonice poterit adipisci ꞏ firma tibi tuisque successoribus 7 per uos ecclesie Lincolniensi[1] 7 illibata permaneant . In quibus hec propriis
20   duximus nominibus annotanda . videlicet in ciuitate Lincolnie[6] burgum quod uocatur [15]Willigtorp . [16]Hundegatam . ecclesiam Omnium Sanctorum . [17]Netelham . Ludam . Stou . Nortonam[7] . [18]Newercam . [19]Slaford’[8] . [20]Lidentonam

[21]Espaldewic . Buchendenam . manerium situm iuxta
25 [22]Legrecestram ciuitatem . [23]Chilesbei . [24]Croposeiam[9] .
Banebiriam[9a] . Taman[10] . [25]Nundentonam . [26]Dorchecestriam .
[27]Woburnam[11] . abbatiam de [28]Egenesham cum omnium
supradictorum pertinenciis . parrochialem[12] episcopalem
[29]Lindesiam . [30]Nicholasira[13] . Léécestrasira[13a] . [31]Hamtona-
30 sira . Buchinghamsira . Oxinafordsira[14] . Huntendonasira .
[32] Herefortsira pars . Decernimus ergo ut nulli omnino
hominum clerico uel laico liceat prefatam ecclesiam temere
perturbare . aut eius possessiones auferre . uel ablatas retinere .
minuere . uel temerariis uexationibus fatigare . Sed omnia
35 integra conseruentur usibus ecclesiasticis pro futura . Si qua
igitur ecclesiastica secularis ue persona hanc nostre constitucionis paginam sciens ꝰ contra eam temere[14a] temptauerit .
secundo tercio ue commonita si non satisfactione congrua
emendauerit potestatis honorisque sui dignitate careat .
40 reamque se diuino iuditio existere de perpetrata iniquitate
cognoscat . ꝯ a sacratissimo corpore ac sanguine dei ꝯ domini[14c]
ꝯ redemptoris nostri Ihesu Christi aliena fiat atque in
extremo examine districte ultioni subiaceat . Cunctis autem
eidem loco iusta[14b] seruantibus sit pax domini nostri Ihesu
45 Christi quatinus ꝯ hic fructum bone actionis percipiant ꝯ
apud districtum iudicem premia eterne pacis inueniant .
Amen . Amen . Datum Laterani per manum Aimerici sancte
Romane ecclesie diaconi cardinalis . ꝯ cancellarii .iii. kalendas
Februarii . indictione .iiii. incarnationis dominice . anno .
50 Mᵒ. Cᵒ. xxᵒ. vᵒ. pontificatus autem domini[14c] Honori [14d]pape
secundi anno secundo.

Marginalia : *opp. l. 1*, II. Confirmacio sicut ante . nominibus expressis (Q).
Texts : MS—A. C,ff.19–20. Pd—Wilkins i, 406. Migne, lat. clxvi, 1246.
Jaffé-Löwenfeld, no. 7241 (calendared). *Mon.*vi,1276–7(64).
Var. R. : [1] Lincoliensi C. [2] inperpetuum C. [3] obtinet C. [4] summministrat C.
[5] Lincoliensem C. [5a] *altered from* iniuste C. [6] Lincolie C. [7] Northonam C.
[8] Slafortd' C. [9] Cropereiam *altered from* Cropeseiam C. [9a] Baneberiam C.
[10] Tamam C. [11] Voburnam C. [12] parrochiam C. [13] Nicholasira C. [13a] Leeces-
trasira C. [14] Oxinafortdsira C. [14a] uenire *is missing here in* A. [14b] *altered from*
iuxta A ; iuxta C. [14c] d'ni C. *The correct spelling is* domni. [14d] Honorii C.
Identifications : [15] Willingthorpe (see Note below). [16] Hungate, a street and
district in Lincoln, in which the church of All Saints (now destroyed) was situate.
[17] Nettleham, Louth, Stow Saint Mary, Bishop Norton, co. Lincoln. [18] Newark,
co. Nottingham. [19] Sleaford, co. Lincoln. [20] Lyddington, co. Rutland. [21] Spaldwick, Buckden, co. Huntingdon. [22] Leicester. [23] Kilsby, co. Northampton. [24] Cropredy, Banbury, Thame, co. Oxford. [25] probably an attempt to indicate ' Milton '
(near Thame) : cp. page 7, l. 1, above, and page 191, l. 1, below. [26] Dorchester,
co. Oxford. [27] Wooburn, co. Buckingham. [28] Eynsham, co. Oxford. [29] Lindsey.
[30] Lincolnshire. [31] Northamptonshire. [32] Hertfordshire.
Note : Willingthorpe (lines 20–1)—The present text speaks of Willigtorp as a
borough in the city of Lincoln. In no. 249 below, lines 23–5, the equivalent words
are ' Westegata cum suis appendiciis tam extra muros ipsius ciuitatis quam infra '.
In no. 250, line 18, and no. 251, line 19, the place appears as ' manerium de Lincolia scilicet Willingtorp,' and in no. 254, lines 15–16, as ' manerium de Willintorp '.
These passages shew that Willingthorpe is to be identified with the little manor
(*maneriolum*) with one carucate which bishop Remigius had, in 1086, adjoining the city
of Lincoln, with sake and soke, and with toll and team (*The Lincolnshire Domesday*

pp. 4, 5). The name of Willingthorpe has been found only in one other context, namely, a confirmation by Robert II bishop of Lincoln to William son of Fardain of four dwellings (*mansiones*) in Willingtorp at (*ab*) the north side of Willingtorp, with all that belongs to them, free and quit of all service except *burgagium*, a service which points to the tenement being in a suburb of Lincoln (Stenton, *Danelaw Charters*, p. 343 and note). The suburb of Westgate was an extensive area out-side the walls, near the west gate of the Roman city, lying to the west and north-west of the castle. The city generally suffered extensive waste in the time of the Conqueror (*The Lincolnshire Domesday*, pp. 6, 7) and Westgate in particular was much damaged during the siege of the castle by Stephen in 1141, and remained for the most part depopulated till recent times.

*below, Folio 170.

Hdl.   .1.7.0.

†below, Folio 170d.

878

249. Similar confirmation by pope Innocent II, addressed to bishop Alexander.   At the Lateran.   28 April, 1139.

Innocentius episcopus seruus seruorum dei venerabili fratri Alexandro Lincolniensi[1] episcopo eiusque successoribus canonice promouendis inperpetuum . Cum omnibus ecclesiis 7 ecclesi*asticis personis debitores ex iniuncto nobis a deo
5 apostolatus officio atque beniuolentia[1a] existamus . illis tamen propensiori caritatis studio nos conuenit prouidere . quos erga beati Petri 7 nostra obsequia promptiores ac deuotiores esse cognoscimus . hoc nimirum intuitu uenerabilis frater Alexander episcope tuis desideriis fraterna benignitate imper-
10 timur assensum 7 Lincolniensem[2] ecclesiam cuius[3] auctore domino amministras . presentis scripti patrocinio com-munimus . Statuentes ut quascumque possessiones quecumque bona idem locus in presentiarum iuste 7 canonice possidet . aut in futurum largitione regum uel principum oblatione
15 fidelium seu aliis iustis modis deo propitio poterit adipisci . firma tibi tuis successoribus necnon canonicis eiusdem ecclesie imperpetuum 7 illibata permaneant . In quibus hec propriis duximus exprimenda uocabulis . Abbatiam uidelicet de [23]Egenesham . cum suis tenementis[3a] . [24]Neewerc cum suis
20 appendiciis . 7 cum iusticia regali de tribus . wapentac[4] quam reges Anglorum ecclesie contulerunt . [25]Stou cum suis appendiciis . Nortonam . Ludam . Nethelham[5] . 7 terram quam habet prefata ecclesia in Lincolnia[6] . scilicet [26]Westegata cum suis appendiciis tam extra muros ipsius ciuitatis quam
25 infra . 7 terram quam dedit Stephanus rex tam tibi quam successoribus tuis ad faciendas episcopales domos cum .xx[ti]. solidatis terre ad restituendas easdem domos a parte australi[7] . cum[8] sancti Michaelis in eadem terra sita . ecclesia Omnium Sanctorum 7 cum aliis ecclesiis supradicte ciuitatis . [27]Esla-
30 ford'[9] . [28]Holmum cum suis appendiciis . manerium de [29]Legecestria extra muros 7 infra . ubi sunt due ecclesie

cum .xxx[ta]. duabus mansionibus burgensium . [30]Baneberia .
7 Croperia cum suo hundreto 7 libertatibus[10a] suis . Dorcacestria
cum suo hundreto 7 libertatibus[10a] suis . [10]Dorcacestria cum suo

35   hundreto 7 libertatibus[10a] suis[10] . 7 Tama . 7 Mideltona . cum
suo hundreto 7 libertatibus[10a] suis . [31]Kildebi cum suis appendiciis . [32]Waburna[11] cum suis appendiciis . [33]Bicheleswada .
[34]Espaldeswic . quod manerium datum fuit Lincolniensi[1]
ecclesie in recompensatione cuiusdam partis sue parrochie

40   que uocatur [35]Cantebrugesiram 7 modo est [36]Helyensis[12]
episcopatus . 7 [37]Bugendena . Nichilominus eciam confirmamus
libertatem eiusdem Lincolniensis[13] ecclesie cum sua parrochia
scilicet Lincolniesiram[14] cum [38]Lindesia tota . Norhamte-
sciram cum Rotelanda . Legecestresciram . Oxenefordsciram[15] .

45   Buchinghamsciram . Bedefordsciram . Huntendonesciram .
cum maxima parte de [39]Herefordscira . terras eciam confirmamus quas rex Stephanus recompensauit predicte ecclesie .
7 canonicis ibidem deo seruientibus pro .x[cem] . 7 .viii. libris
denariorum quas solebant habere canonici largitione regum

50   in [40]Kyrketona 7 Castra maneriis videlicet in [41]Torp .iii.
carrucat*as* terre . 7 .iii. bouat*as* . in Blitona 7 in Wartona
.v. carruat*as* terre . 7 .vij. bouat*as* . in Pileham .ij. carruatas .
7 .v. bouat*as* . terre . 7 duo[1a] partes .i. bouate . in Gillebi 7 in
Wartona . vij. bouat*as* . 7 ad [42]Trentam .ix. bouat*as* . 7

55   dimid*iam* . Preterea [43]Waltonam . ecclesiam de Aleberes
cum suis appendiciis . ecclesiam de [44]Lectonam[16] . ecclesiam
de Buchingeham cum suis appendiciis . ecclesiam de [45]Sutona
cum suis appendiciis . manerium de [46]Welletona cum suis
appendiciis . ceterasque eiusdem ecclesie canonicorum posses-

60   siones ecclesiasticas .† firmam predicte ecclesie 7 ipsis canonicis
confirmamus . Lectonam[44] eciam 7 terram de Bedeford tam infra
burgum quam extra cum suis libertatibus . relaxationem
quoque seruicii militum ipsius episcopatus Lincolniensis[13]
quod predecessores tui in castro Lincolnie[17] facere consueuer-

65   ant ? vnde Henricus rex gloriose memorie tercium militem
ecclesie Lincolniensi[1] 7 tibi ac successoribus tuis relaxauit .
quod nimirum seruitium castro tuo de [24]Newerca fieri concessit
. 7 scripto suo firmauit . nichilhominus[17a] tibi 7 successoribus
tuis imperpetuum auctoritate apostolica confirmamus .

70   Obeunte uero te venerabilis frater Alexander episcope uel
tuorum quolibet successorum . nullus in Lincolniensi[1] ecclesia
qualibet surreptionis astucia seu uiolentia preponatur . nisi
quem clerus 7 populus comuni[17b] assensu aut pars consilii sanioris
secundum dei timorem 7 sanctorum canonum scita duxerunt[18]

75   eligendum . Porro libertatem ab illustri uiro Stephano
Anglorum rege ecclesie ipsi concessam nos quoque autoritatis[19]
nostre munimine roboramus . Inter cetera uero eiusdem
libertatis insignia illud specialiter huic decreto duximus

inserendum . ut in obitu tuo uel successorum tuorum dum
80 episcopalis sedes uacauerit[20] *.* nullus prorsus episcopalia uel
ecclesiastica bona usurpare presumat *.* sed potius ecclesie
omnes 7 earum possessiones in libera clericorum custodia 7
potestate consistant ad usus futuri pontificis 7 utilitatem
eiusdem ecclesie integre conseruande . Nulli ergo omnino
85 fas sit uos uel ecclesiam uestram super hac nostra constitu-
cione uel confirmatione temere perturbare . aut eius possessiones auferre . uel ablatas retinere . minuere . seu quibuslibet
fatigare molestiis . sed omnia integra conseruentur eorum
pro quorum gubernatione 7 sustentatione concessa sunt
90 usibus omnimodis profutura . Si qua sane in posterum
ecclesiastica secularis ue persona hanc nostre constitucionis
paginam sciens contra eam temere uenire temptauerit secundo
tercio ue commonita nisi reatum suum congrue emendauerit .
potestatis honorisque sui dignitate careat . reamque se diuino
95 iudicio existere de perpetrata iniquitate cognoscat . 7 a
sacratissimo corpore ac sanguine dei 7 domini redemptoris
nostri Ihesu Christi aliena fiat . atque in extremo examine
districte subiaceat ultioni . Cunctis autem eidem loco sua
iura seruantibus sit pax domini nostri Ihesu Christi quatinus
100 7 hic fructum bone actionis percipiant . 7 apud districtum
iudicem premia eterne pacis inueniant . Amen . Amen . Amen .
Datum Laterani[21] per manum Aimerici Sancte Romane ecclesie
diaconi . cardinalis . 7 cancellarii .iiii. kalendas . Maii . indictione .ij[a]. incarnationis dominice anno . M⁰. c⁰. xxx⁰. viii⁰.[21a]
105 pontificatus uero domini[22] Innocentii pape secundi . anno . x⁰.

Marginalia : *opp. l. 1—III. opp. l. 4,* Confirmacio consimilis (Q). *opp. ll. 37–40,*
Nota escambium pro episcopatu Eliensi (Q). *opp. ll. 77–90,* Nota (in the left hand
margin to direct attention to the clause, and a head with a cowl is drawn in the opposite
margin).
Texts : MS—A. C,ff.20–23. Pd—Migne, lat. clxxix, 466. Jaffé-Löwenfeld,
no. 8024 (calendared). *Mon.*viii,1277(65).
Var. R. : [1] Lincoliensi C. [1a] sic. [2] Lincoliensem C. [3] *insert* regimen C. [3a] teni-
mentis C. [4] wappentac C. [5] Netelham C. [6] Lincolia C. [7] *insert* ecclesie C.
[8] *insert* ecclesia C. [9] Eslafortd' C. [10-10] *These words are a repetition in A of the
clause which immediately precedes them.* C omits them. [10a] libertalibus
altered from liberalibus C. [11] *corrected from* Caburna C. [12] Heliensis C. [13] Lincoliensis C. [14] Lincoliesciram C. [15] Oxenefortdsciram C. [16] Lectona C. [17] Lincolie C. [17a] nichilhominus, *the h being cancelled,* C. [17b] communi C. [18] duxerint,
which has been corrected from dixerint C. [19] auctoritatis C. [20] uocauerit C. [21] Laturni
C. [21a] viiii⁰ C (*April in the tenth year fell in* 1139) ; *the reading of A is apparently
wrong.* [22] domni C.
Identifications : [23] Eynsham, co. Oxford. [24] Newark, co. Nottingham. [25] Stow
Saint Mary, Bishop Norton, Louth, Nettleham, co. Lincoln. [26] Westgate in the city of
Lincoln, = Willingthorpe (see no. 248, Note, above). [27] Sleaford, co. Linc. [28] Holmum, see Note, below. [29] Leicester. [30] Banbury, Cropredy, Dorchester, Thame,
Milton (by Thame), co. Oxford. [31] Kilsby, co. Northampton. [32] Wooburn,
co. Buckingham. [33] Biggleswade, co. Bedford. [34] Spaldwick, co. Huntingdon.
[35] Cambridgeshire. [36] Ely, co. Cambridge. [37] Buckden, co. Huntingdon. [38] Lindsey.
[39] Hertfordshire. [40] Kirton in Lindsey, Caistor, co. Lincoln. [41] Northorpe (and
Southorpe), Blyton, Wharton, Pilham, Gilby, co. Lincoln. [42] the river Trent.
[43] Walton and Aylesbury, co. Buckingham. [44] Leighton Buzzard, co. Bedford.
[45] King's Sutton, co. Northampton. [46] Welton by Lincoln.

Note by Dr W. Holtzmann : This bull is dated at (Rome) Lateran, 28 April, 1139. On the third of April the (second) Lateran Council took place (cp. the acts printed by Mansi xxi, 526). From this bull it may be gathered that bishop Alexander of Lincoln, or one who occupied a place almost as his representative, was present at the council. Other Englishmen whose presence at the council may likewise be inferred from the fact that documents in their favour were issued by the papal chancery, are the bishops of Salisbury, Ely, and Coventry and Lichfield, and the abbots of Westminster, Saint Augustine's at Canterbury, Evesham, and Ramsey (Jaffé-Löwenfeld, *op. cit.*, nos, 7999, 8004, 8005, 8016a, 8025–8, etc.).

Note : Holmum (line 30). The only place of the name of Holme among the permanent possessions of the church of Lincoln was Holme in Biggleswade ; but *Holmus* in the present text cannot be identified with it. In Domesday Book (vol. i, p. 217, col. 1) Ralf de Insula held ten hides in Biggleswade and two hides in Holme, which are both described as manors. In 1132 (see no. 53 above) Henry I granted to bishop Alexander the manor of Biggleswade, and it is plain that Holme was included in the gift ; and from that time onwards, Holme is included in that manor (see *Book of Fees* ii, 869 ; *Feudal Aids* i, 4). Further, though the argument must not be allowed too much weight, the possessions of the church of Lincoln are, in the papal bulls, named in a rough geographical order, and *Holmus*, it will be observed, is associated rather with places in the counties Lincoln and Northampton than with places in Buckingham. The only place with which it is possible to identify *Holmus* is Holme Spinney (in Beckingham, co. Lincoln) which, with land in Rutland and Northampton, had been pledged to bishop Alexander 1123–1133, seemingly by Walter de Gant, for three hundred marks (see no. 69, and note, above). This sum indicates an estate which was certainly of sufficient importance to deserve a place in papal confirmations. The geographical situation of the lands which were pledged to the bishop suits the order of the possessions in the bulls. The fact that Holme Spinney was no more than a temporary possession of the bishops of Lincoln need cause no difficulty ; and it is perhaps significant in this connection that while *Holmus* appears in the bulls of 1139, 1146, 1149 and 6 June, 1163 (249, *l.* 30 ; 250, *l.* 32 ; 251, *l.* 34 ; 254, *l.* 30), each one of which follows much the same form, it is not to be found in the bulls of 1146 and 5 June, 1163 (nos. 252 and 255), which contain another and a fuller list of possessions. The de Gants evidently redeemed their land, for Holme Spinney continued to be their property.

* *below*, Folio 171.

Hdl.   .1.7.1.

† *below*, Folio 171d.

879

250. Similar confirmation by pope Eugenius III, addressed to bishop Robert II. At Tusculum. 13 April, 1149.

Eugenius episcopus seruus seruorum dei venerabili fratri Roberto Lincolniensi[1] episcopo eiusque successoribus canonice substituendis imperpetuum . In eminenti specula sedis apostolice disponente domino constituti ex iniuncto nobis officio
5 fratres nostros episcopos tam uicinos quam longe positos debemus diligere . 7 ecclesiis sibi a deo commissis suam iusticiam conseruare . huius rei gracia uenerabilis frater in Christo Roberte episcope tuis iustis postulationibus clementer annuimus . 7 Lincolniensem[2] ecclesiam cui deo[3] *preesse
10 dinosceris sub beati Petri 7 nostra protectione suscipimus . 7 presentis scripti priuilegio communimus . Statuentes ut quascumque possessiones quecumque bona inpresentiarum iuste 7 canonice possides aut infuturum liberalitate regum . largitione principum . oblatione fidelium . seu aliis iustis

N

15 modis deo propitio poteris adipisci ⸱⸴ firma tibi tuisque successoribus 7 per uos Lincoliensi ecclesie illibata permaneat⁴ .
in quibus hec propriis duximus exprimenda uocabulis .
manerium de Lincolia scilicet ⁹Willingtorp cum reliquis
appendiciis ipsius manerii . et in ipsa ciuitate terram que
20 est inter ecclesiam sancti Michaelis 7 fossatum ciuitatis .
sicut fossatum se extendit in murum ciuitatis . 7 in eodem
loco ipsum fossatum 7 murum ad faciendos introitus domorum
episcopalium . et in proximo loco circa prefatam ecclesiam
beati Michaelis .xxᵗⁱ. solidatas terre de dominio regis .
25 manerium de Stou cum nundinis 7 libertatibus 7 consuetudinibus 7 omnibus appendiciis suis . manerium de ¹⁰ Nortuna
cum libertatibus 7 omnibus appendiciis suis . Netelham cum
appendiciis suis . manerium de ¹¹Luda . ¹² Eslaford cum
castro 7 foro 7 omnibus libertatibus 7 appendiciis suis .
30 Castrum de ¹³Newerch⁵ cum omnibus libertatibus consuetudinibus 7 ceteris appendiciis suis . manerium de ¹⁴ Legecestria cum omnibus appendiciis suis . ¹⁵Chilihtingtonam ¹⁶Hol-
mum cum appendiciis suis . ¹⁷Childebiam cum pertinenciis
suis . abbatiam de ¹⁸Egenesham cum foro 7 omnibus liber-
35 tatibus 7 pertinenciis suis . ¹⁹Hardingtonam cum pertinenciis
suis . ²⁰Baneberiam cum castro 7 foro 7 libertatibus 7 pertinenciis suis . ²¹Cropereiam cum pertinenciis suis . ²²Thamam⁶
cum libertatibus 7 pertinenciis suis . ²³Dorcestram cum
omnibus libertatibus 7 pertinenciis suis . ²⁴Woburnam cum
40 pertinenciis suis . ²⁵Buchendenam cum libertatibus 7 pertinenciis suis . ²⁶Spaldewic cum pertinenciis suis . ²⁷Bicheles-
wadam cum libertatibus 7 pertinenciis suis . In Bedefordia
domus episcopi cum terra sua . ecclesiam quoque de ²⁸Bran-
tona manerio regis quod est iuxta Huntendonam . Preterea
45 presentis decreti auctoritate sancimus . ut uniuersi Lincoliensis
episcopatus fines quieti deinceps omnino 7 integri tam tibi
quam successoribus tuis conseruentur . sicut tu ipse 7 predecessores tui eos hactenus quiete 7 legittime possedistis .
Apostolica quoque auctoritate interdicimus ut nullus omnino
50 siue rex seu quelibet prepotens persona . aut eorum ministri
decedentibus episcopis castra Lincoliensis ecclesie causa
custodie uel alia qualibet occasione occupare presumat . sed
in casatorum qui ligii homines sunt custodia ipsius ecclesie
7 in eiusdem ecclesie potestate permaneant . donec in potes-
55 tatem episcopi qui canonice fuerit substitutus libere redeant .
Decernimus ergo ut nulli omnino hominum liceat prefatam
beate Marie Lincoliensem ecclesiam temere perturbat⁷ . aut
eius possessiones auferre . uel ablatas retinere . minuere . aut
quibuslibet indebitis uexationibus uel molestiis fatigare . sed
60 omnia integre⁷ᵃ conseruentur uestris ac pauperum Christi
usibus omnimodis profutura . salua sedis apostolice auctoritate .

† Si qua igitur in futurum ecclesiastica secularis ue persona hanc nostre constitucionis paginam sciens contra eam temere uenire temptauerit secundo tercio ue commonita si non
65 satisfactione congrua emendauerit potestatis honorisque sui dignitate careat . reamque se diuino iuditio existere de perpetrata iniquitate cognoscat . 7 a sacratissimo corpore ac sanguine dei 7 domini redemptoris nostri Ihesu Christi aliena fiat . atque in extremo examine districte ultioni sub-
70 iaceat . Cunctis autem eidem ecclesie iusta seruantibus sit pax domini nostri Ihesu Christi quatinus 7 hic fructum bone actionis percipiant . 7 apud districtum iudicem premia eterne pacis inueniant . Amen . Amen . Amen . Datum Tusculani per manum Greci sancte Romane ecclesie diaconi cardinalis
75 agentis uicem Widonis sancte Romane ecclesie diaconi . cardinalis . 7 cancellarii . idus Aprilis . indictione .xi. Incarnationis dominice anno . M°. C°. XL°. viii.⁸ pontificatus uero domini⁸ᵃ Eugenii .III. pape . anno quinto.

Marginalia : De eodem (Q), *opp. l. 1*, IIII. *opp. l. 34*, Nota.
Texts : MS—A. C,ff.23–5.
Var. R. : ¹ Lincoliensi C. ² Lincoliensem C. ³ *insert* auctore C. ⁴ permaneant C. ⁵ Newerca C. ⁶ Tamam C. ⁷ *recte* perturbare A C. ⁷ᵃ integra C. ⁸ viiii C (*April in the fifth year fell in* A.D. 1149). *The date in C is to be preferred ; the indiction should be* xii. ⁸ᵃ domni C.
Identifications : ⁹ Willingthorpe (see no. 248, Note, above). ¹⁰ Bishop Norton, co. Lincoln. ¹¹ Louth, co. Lincoln. ¹² Sleaford, co. Lincoln. ¹³ Newark, co. Nottingham. ¹⁴ Leicester. ¹⁵ Knighton, co. Leicester. ¹⁶ see no. 249, Note, above. ¹⁷ Kilsby, co. Northampton. ¹⁸ Eynsham, co. Oxford. ¹⁹ Yarnton, co. Oxford. ²⁰ Banbury, co. Oxford. ²¹ Cropredy, co. Oxford. ²² Thame, co. Oxford. ²³ Dorchester, co. Oxford. ²⁴ Wooburn, co. Buckingham. ²⁵ Buckden, co. Huntingdon. ²⁶ Spaldwick, co. Huntingdon. ²⁷ Biggleswade, co. Bedford. ²⁸ Brampton, co. Huntingdon.
Note by Dr W. Holtzmann : This bull affords valuable information about the papal chancery. It is given by *Grecus sanctae Romanae ecclesiae diaconus cardinalis agens vicem Widonis sanctae Romanae diaconi cardinalis et cancellarii*. Wido occurs as chancellor in the date-clauses of bulls from 17 December, 1146, till 6 May, 1149. In this period if Wido is hindered, his place is generally taken by Hugo, cardinal-priest of S. Lorenzo in Lucina, as *vicem gerens*. Grecus only appears in the present bull. Indeed, our knowledge of him in any capacity is very slight. In a few bulls, between 11 and 20 March, 1149, he subscribes with his full title, cardinal-deacon of SS. Sergio e Baccho (cp. M. Brixius, *Die Mitglieder des Kardinalkollegiums von* 1130–1181, a useful thesis of the university of Strassburg (Berlin, 1912), p. 54). His subscription in the present text is therefore a valuable supplement to the list of papal vice-chancellors drawn up by Bresslau in his *Handbuch der Urkundenlehre*, 2nd ed. (Leipzig, 1912), i, 245.

below, Folio 172.
Hdl.   .1.7.2.

880

251. Similar confirmation by pope Eugenius III, addressed to bishop Alexander. At Trastevere. 9 February, 1146.

Eugenius episcopus seruus seruorum dei venerabili fratri Alexandro Lincoliensi episcopo eiusque successoribus canonice substituendis imperpetuum . Ex iniuncto nobis a deo apostolatus officio fratres nostros episcopos tam uicinos quam

5 longe positos debemus diligere ⁊ 7 ecclesiis in quibus domino
   militare noscuntur suam iusticiam conseruare . vt quemad-
   modum patres uocamur in nomine ita nichilominus com-
   probemur in opere . Huius rei gracia venerabilis frater in
   Christo Alexander episcope tuis iustis postulationibus clementer
10 annuimus . 7 Lincoliensem ecclesiam cui deo auctore preesse
   dinosceris . sub beati Petri 7 nostra protectione suscipimus .
   7 presentis scripti priuilegio communimus . Statuentes ut
   quascumque possessiones quecumque bona inpresentiarum
   iuste 7 canonice possides aut infuturum liberalitate regum .
15 largitione principum . oblatione fidelium seu aliis iustis modis
   prestante domino poteris adipisci firma tibi tuisque successoribus 7 per uos Lincoliensi ecclesie¹ illibata permaneant .
   in quibus hec propriis duximus exprimenda uocabulis .
   manerium de Lincolia scilicet ⁵Willingtorp cum reliquis
20 appendiciis ipsius manerii . Et in ipsa ciuitate terram que
   est inter ecclesiam sancti Michaelis 7 fossatum ciuitatis sicut
   fossatum se extendit in murum ciuitatis . et in eodem loco
   ipsum fossatum 7 murum ad faciendos introitus domorum
   episcopalium . et in proximo loco circa prefatam ecclesiam
25 beati Michaelis uiginti solidatas terre de dominio regis .
   manerium de Stou cum nundinis 7 libertatibus 7 consuetudinibus 7 omnibus appendiciis suis . manerium de
   ⁶L   ² cum libertatibus 7 omnibus appendiciis . ⁷Nethel-
   ham³ cum appendiciis suis . manerium de ⁸Luda . Eslaford'
30 cum castro 7 foro 7 omnibus libertatibus 7 appendiciis suis .
   castrum de ⁹Newerca cum omnibus libertatibus consuetudinibus 7 ceteris appendiciis suis . manerium de ¹⁰Legre-
   cestria cum omnibus appendiciis suis in ciuitate Cnichting-
   tunam . ¹¹Holmum cum omnibus appendiciis suis . ¹²Childe-
35 biam cum pertinenciis suis . abbatiam de ¹³Egnesham cum
   foro 7 omnibus liber*tatibus 7 pertinenciis suis . ¹⁴Harding-
   tonam cum pertinenciis suis . ¹⁵Baneberiam cum castro 7
   foro 7 omnibus libertatibus 7 pertinenciis suis . Croperiam
   cum pertinenciis suis . Tamam cum omnibus libertatibus 7
40 pertinenciis suis . Dorcacestram cum omnibus libertatibus 7
   pertinenciis⁴ suis . ¹⁶Woburnam cum pertinenciis suis .
   ¹⁷Buchendenam cum omnibus libertatibus 7 pertinenciis suis .
   Spaldewic cum omnibus pertinenciis suis . ¹⁸Bicleswadam
   cum omnibus libertatibus 7 pertinenciis suis . in Bedefordia
45 domos episcopi cum terra sua . Preterea presentis decreti
   auctoritate sanctimus . ut uniuersi Lincoliensis episcopatus
   fines quieti deinceps omnino 7 integri tam tibi quam successoribus tuis conseruentur . sicut tu ipse 7 predecessores
   tui eos hactenus quiete 7 legittime possedistis . apostolica
50 quoque auctoritate interdicimus ut nullus omnino siue rex
   seu quelibet prepotens persona aut eorum ministri decedentibus

episcopis castra Lincoliensis ecclesie causa custodie uel alia
qualibet occasione occupare presumat . sed in casatorum qui
ligii homines sunt ipsius ecclesie custodia 7 in eiusdem ecclesie
55 potestate permaneant . donec in potestatem episcopi qui
canonice fuerit substitutus libere redeant . Decernimus ergo
ut nulli omnino hominum liceat prefatam beate Marie
Lincoliensem ecclesiam temere perturbare aut castra ipsius
siue bona uel possessiones auferre aut ablata retinere . minuere
60 seu quibuslibet indebitis uexationibus uel molestiis fatigare .
Sed omnia integra conseruentur . uestris ac pauperum Christi
usibus omnimodis profutura . salua sedis apostolice auctoritate . Si qua igitur in futurum ecclesiastica secularis ue persona
huius nostre constitucionis paginam sciens contra eam temere
65 uenire temptauerit secundo tercio ue commonita nisi reatum
suum congrua satisfactione correxerit ; potestatis honorisque
sui dignitate careat . reamque se diuino iuditio existere de
perpetrata iniquitate cognoscat . 7 a sacratissimo corpore
ac sanguine dei 7 domini redemptoris nostri Ihesu Christi
70 aliena fiat . atque in extremo examine districte ultioni subiaceat . Cunctis autem eidem ecclesie iusta seruantibus sit
pax domini nostri Ihesu Christi . quatinus 7 hic fructum
bone actionis percipiant . 7 apud districtum iudicem premia
eterne pacis inueniant . Amen . Amen . Amen . Datum Trans-
75 tiberim per manum Romane sancte ecclesie[4a] presbiteri .
cardinalis . 7 cancellarii .v. idus . Februarii . indictione .viii.
incarnationis dominice . anno millesimo . c°. xl°. v°. [sic] pontificatus uero domini pape Eugenii .iii. anno .i°.

Marginalia : De eodem (Q).

Texts : MS—A. C,ff.25,25d (the text is incomplete, ending with the name
' Buchendenam ' in l. 42).

Var. R. : [1] insert 7 C. [2] Nortuna C (A leaves the name blank after the initial letter
L). [3] Netelham C. [4] om. 7 pertinenciis C. [4a] recte per manum Roberti sancte
Romane ecclesie (see no. 252, l. 141, below). The indiction should be viiii.

Identifications : [5] Willingthorpe (see no. 248, Note, above). [6] Bishop Norton,
co. Lincoln. [7] Nettleham, co. Lincoln. [8] Louth, Sleaford, co. Lincoln. [9] Newark,
co. Nottingham. [10] Leicester, Knighton, co. Leicester. [11] see no. 249, Note, above.
[12] Kilsby, co. Northampton. [13] Eynsham, co. Oxford. [14] Yarnton, co. Oxford.
[15] Banbury, Cropredy, Thame, Dorchester, co. Oxford. [16] Wooburn, co. Buckingham. [17] Buckden, Spaldwick, co. Huntingdon. [18] Biggleswade, co. Bedford.

Note by Dr W. Holtzmann : The dating clause, l. 75, is corrupt : it should run,
per manum Roberti sancte Romane ecclesie, as in no. 252, l. 141, below. The chancellor Robert gave all the bulls between 4 January, 1145, and 22 September, 1146.
He was Robert Pullen, an Englishman by origin, cardinal-priest of S. Martino,
and formerly a professor at Oxford, a famous philosopher and theologian (see D.B.N.).

*below, Folio 172d.
†below, Folio 173.
Hdl.   1.7.3.
‡below, Folio 173d.

881

252. Similar confirmation by pope Eugenius III, addressed to
the canons of Lincoln, in which the possessions of the prebends

are distinguished from those of the common.   At Trastevere.
6 February, 1146.

   Eugenius episcopus seruus seruorum dei dilectis filiis
canonicis ecclesie beate Marie Lincoliensis[1] tam presentibus
quam futuris canonice substituendis imperpetuum . Com-
misse nobis apostolice sedis nos[2] hortatur auctoritas . ut
5 locis 7 personis eius auxilium deuotione debita implorantibus
tuicionis presidium impendere debeamus . Quia sicut iniusta
petentibus nullus est tribuendus effectus ⁊ ita legittima 7
iusta postulantium non est differenda peticio eorum presertim qui cum honestate uite 7 laudabili morum composicione
10 gaudent omnipotenti domino deseruire . Eapropter * dilecti
in domino filii venerabilis fratris nostri Alexandri episcopi
uestri precibus inclinati uestris iustis postulationibus clementer
annuimus 7 prefatam beate dei genitricis semperque virginis
Marie ecclesiam in qua diuino mancipati estis obsequio sub
15 beati Petri 7 nostra protectione suscipimus[3] . 7 presentis
scripti priuilegio communimus . Statuentes ut quascumque
possessiones quecumque bona in presentiarum iuste 7 canonice
possidetis aut in futurum concessione pontificum . liberalitate
regum . largitione principum . oblatione fidelium . seu aliis
20 iustis modis prestante domino poteritis adipisci ⁊ firma uobis .
uestrisque successoribus illibata permaneant . in quibus hec
propriis duximus exprimenda uocabulis . Welletonam cum
appendiciis suis . ecclesiam de [40]Kirchetona[4] cum appendiciis
suis . ecclesiam de Castra cum appendiciis suis . ecclesiam
25 de Wellingoura cum appendiciis suis . et terram quam rex
Stephanus dedit in excambium pro decimis trium predictorum
maneriorum[5] Chirketone[6] . Castre[7] . 7 Wellingoure . in
ciuitate Linc' ecclesiam sancti Martini . 7[8] ecclesiam sancti
Laurencii . 7 reliquas eiusdem ciuitatis ecclesias in proprio
30 feudo regis sitas . 7 in prebendas canonicorum collatas . .
[41]Lectonam cum appendiciis suis . ecclesiam beate Marie
Bedefordensem cum appendiciis suis . ecclesiam [42]Lectonien-
sem cum appendiciis suis . ecclesiam [43]Buchingehamensem
in prebenda dedit cum appendiciis suis . ecclesiam Eles-
35 beriensem[9] cum appendiciis suis . domos quoque omnes
[44]iuxta pontem Lincoliensem[1] quas Robertus de Stuteuilla
dedit in prebendam ecclesie Linc'[10] . ecclesiam de [45]Empinge-
ham cum omnibus decimis eiusdem uille . 7 terris ad eam
pertinentibus . ecclesiam Omnium Sanctorum in Lincolia[1]
40 cum terris 7 decimis ad eam pertinentibus . ecclesiam sancti
Johanni[11] de [46]Newport[12] cum appendiciis suis 7 dimidiam
carrucatam terre que fuit Aie sacerdotis . mansionem unam
in uico magno inter fabros . ecclesiam de [47]Duneham cum
pertinenciis suis . totam decimam de dominio Roberti de[13]
45 Bussei in [48]Acham . vnam carrucatam terre in eadem villa .

et ecclesiam de [49]Karletona cum appendiciis suis . ecclesiam
de Turlebia[14] cum appendiciis suis . duas partes decime in
[50]Canewic[15] de terra Marcelli[15a] de Taneio[16] 7 Hugonis generi
eius quam tenebant de rege uel de honore [51]Pontisfracti .
50 7 pasturam in eadem uilla . ecclesiam de [52]Oschintuna cum
omnibus pertinenciis suis . ecclesiam de [53]Cestrefelda cum
pertinenciis suis . ecclesiam de Esseburna cum pertinenciis
suis . ecclesiam de [54]Mamesfelda . 7 capellas omnes in berewicis
ad predicta .iiii[or]. maneria pertinentibus cum terris 7 decimis
55 que ad predictas ecclesias pertinent . 7 cum libertate quam
habuerunt a tempore Ingelranni[17] canonici Lincoliensis[1]
usque nunc . ecclesias de [55]Derbia[18] de Werchewarda[19] . de
[56]Legretuna . 7 de [57]Edenestou . cum appendiciis earum .
vndecim bouatas terre in [58]Binnebroch quas Osbertus uice-
60 comes tenebat . ecclesiam de Coringeham cum duabus carrucatis terre 7 dimidia 7 reliquis pertinenciis suis . ecclesiam de
[59]Chetena cum pertinenciis suis . ecclesiam de [60]Gretuna[20]
cum pertinen† ciis suis . ecclesiam de [61]Donintuna . ecclesiam
de [62]Nessentuna cum terris . decimis . 7 consuetudinibus ad
65 eas pertinentibus . In ciuitate Lincol'[1] .xiiii. libras . de decima
reddituum eiusdem ciuitatis . ecclesiam de [63]Norcheleiseia[21]
cum pertinenciis suis . ecclesiam de [64]Langeford in Oxene-
fordesira cum omnibus pertinenciis suis . ecclesiam de
[65]Lectona in Huntedunesira cum pertinenciis suis . ecclesiam
70 de [66]Bodesford . de Scamelbi[22] . 7 de Meltona in Lindisi cum
omnibus ad easdem ecclesias pertinentibus 7 uillam de
[67]Asgerbia . 7 quicquid infra terminos agrorum eiusdem uille
continetur . Et hoc quod habetis in ecclesia de [68]Roucebi[23] .
[69]Horneleiam . 7 ecclesiam de [70]Suttuna in Hamtunesira[24]
75 cum pertinenciis suis . [71]Waltunam in Buchingehamsira .
7 dimidium [72]Mideltune . 7 ecclesiam eiusdem uille cum
pertinenciis suis . ecclesiam de Tama cum pertinenciis suis .
ecclesiam de Banebiria . 7 ecclesiam de Croperia cum capellis
suis . duas partes decime de dominio de [73]Childesbi[25] .
80 totam decimam de dominio episcopi in [74]Stou[26] . 7 duas
partes decime parrochianorum eiusdem uille . ecclesiam
sancte Margarete de [75]Legrecestria cum pertinenciis suis .
ecclesiam de [76]Luda cum appendiciis suis . ecclesiam de
Eslaford[27] cum pertinenciis suis . ecclesiam de [77]Buchendena
85 cum pertinenciis suis . duas partes decime de dominio de
[78]Stottuna . decimam de dominio de Spaldewic[28] . duas
partes decime de dominio de [79]Gretewella . Sciendum uero est
quod supradicta in prebendas fratrum diuisa sunt . Subscripta autem in commune cedunt . dimidia pars oblationis
90 altaris sancte Marie Linc' . virgultum ubi fuit uinea regis .
ecclesia sancti Nicholai de Newport[29] . cum pertinenciis suis .
terra ubi fuit uinea Colsueni . in magno uico Linc' mansio

in qua ⁸⁰Tebertus mansit . in ⁸¹Wikeford³⁰ terra que fuit
Osulfi . quatuordecim mansiones in burgo Linc' in diuersis
95 locis . terram quam Azo dedit canonicis iuxta magnum pontem .
due bouate terre in campis Linc' . decima terre que fuit Petri
filii Durandi . triginta solid' ab archidia*conatu* Linc' . decime
forestarum regis de episcopatu Linc' . triginta solid' de
⁸²Waltuna³¹ . ecclesia de ⁸³Eintuna . ⁸⁴feudum Picoti de
100 ⁸⁴Fristorp³² . terra que fuit Gocelini³³ filii Lamberti in
⁸⁵Cheleseia . decima de terra Haconis in Cukewald³⁴ . due
partes decimarum de dominio in ⁸⁶Spirlintuna³⁵ . ⁊ Ingeham .
⁊ Fallinguerda . ⁊ Kyrchebeia³⁶ . Quedam mansio iuxta
magnum pontem . ecclesia de ⁸⁷Scottorna ⁊ sita in feudo
105 Gaufridi de Noua Uilla . due partes decime de carrucata terre
que fuit Alueredi in ⁸⁸Scallebya³⁷ . ecclesia de ⁸⁹Schillingetona
cum pertinenciis suis . decima de terra Colegrimi in ⁹⁰Beltuna .
⁊ in Gunewardebeia . ⁊ in Fulebech . ⁊ in Stoches . ⁊ in ea
.iiiiᵒʳ. bouate terre . ⁊ unum molendinum super aquam de
110 ⁹¹Graham in Waltuna decima de ⁹²Burch . ⁊ de Wilgebia³⁸ .
Decem solidate terre in ⁹³Normannebia iuxta Stou ex donatione Adelidis de Condeio . ⁊ Rogeri filii eius . Prefati quoque
episcopi uestri precibus annuentes iuxta uotum ⁊ rationabilem
ipsius prouinciam³⁹ sanctimus ut de prebendis canonicorum
115 decedentium post decessum eorum per annum debita ipsorum
uel seruientium eorum mercedes persoluantur . Quod autem
superfuerit . uel si debitum ‡ non habuerint ⁊ totum in usus
fratrum cedat . Obeunte uero eiusdem Lincoliensis¹ ecclesie
episcopo nullus ibi qualibet surreptionis astucia seu uiolentia
120 episcopus statuatur . nisi quem canonici ipsius ecclesie
secundum deum ⁊ sanctorum patrum decreta canonice
prouiderint eligendum . Decernimus ergo ut nulli omnino
liceat eandem ecclesiam temere perturbare . aut eius bona
uel possessiones auferre . uel ablatas retinere . minuere . seu
125 quibuslibet uexationibus fatigare . sed omnia integra conseruentur . eorum pro quorum gubernatione ⁊ sustentacione
concessa sunt . usibus omnimodis profutura . Salua sedis
apostolice auctoritate . ⁊ episcopi uestri canonica iusticia ⁊
reuerentia . Si qua igitur in futurum ecclesiastica secularis
130 ue persona huius nostre constitucionis paginam sciens contra
eam temere uenire presumpserit ⁊ secundo tercio ue commonita nisi reatum suum congrua satisfactione correxerit ⁊
potestatis honorisque sui dignitate careat . eamque³⁹ᵃ se diuino
iuditio existere de perpetrata iniquitate cognoscat . ⁊ a
135 sacratissimo corpore ac sanguine dei ⁊ domini redemptoris
nostri Ihesu Christi aliena fiat . atque in extremo examine
districte ultioni subiaceat . Cunctis autem eidem ecclesie
iusta seruantibus sit pax domini nostri Ihesu Christi . quatinus
⁊ hic fructum bone actionis percipiant . ⁊ apud districtum

140　iudicem premia eterne pacis inueniant . Amen . Datum
Transtiberim per manum Roberti sancte Romane ecclesie
presbiteri cardinalis 7 cancellarii .viii. idus . Februarii .
indictione .viiii. Incarnationis dominice anno . M°. C°. XL°. V°.
pontificatus uero domini[39b] Eugenii .iii. pape . anno .i°.

Marginalia : De eodem (Q). *opp. l. 36*, Nota pro prebenda de Thorngate . Stut-
vill (see p. *277*, below). *opp. l. 48*, Nota pro Hedeham (the reference is not
apparent). *opp. l. 67*, Ox (Q). *opp. l. 72*, Asgerby 🖙 (Q). *opp. l. 80*,
Stowe. *opp. l. 82*, prebenda Laic*estr'*. *opp. l. 86*, 🖙. *opp. l. 89*, De
communa (Q). *opp. l. 90*, pro terris in Linc' (Q). *opp. l. 92–5*, Mansiones
(Q). *opp. l. 96*, .ij. bouata terre . Linc' (Q). *opp. l. 98*, Nota de decimis forestarum.
opp. ll. 105–6, Scalby. *opp. ll. 105–7*, Decime parciales Ingham Scalby Belton
7c. (Q). *opp. l. 110*, Walton (Q). *opp. ll. 113–17*, Nota annum post mortem ad
quid (Q).
　Texts : MS—A. P20 (much injured ; only about half the text remains). Dij
55/2/5 (an inspeximus, see no. 253 below).
　Var. R. : [1] Linc' Dij.　[2] *om.* nos Dij.　[3] suscepimus Dij.　[4] Kirketona Dij.
[5] maneriorum predictorum Dij.　[6] Chirchetone P ; Kirketon' Dij.　[7] Castra Dij.
[8] *om.* 7 Dij.　[9] Elesbiriam Dij.　[10] Lincol' P.　[11] Johannis P Dij.　[12] Newpport P ;
Neuport Dij.　[13] *om.* de Dij.　[14] Thurlebia Dij.　[15] Canewyc Dij.　[15a] *recte* Martelli.
[16] Taneyo Dij.　[17] Ingeleranni Dij.　[18] Derebia Dij.　[19] Werchewrda Dij.　[20] Gret-
tuna P.　[21] Norcheleseia P.　[22] Scamelby Dij.　[23] Rouceby Dij.　[24] Hametunsira
Dij.　[25] Childesby Dij.　[26] Stow Dij.　[27] Eslafford Dij.　[28] Spaldewyc Dij.　[29] Neu-
port P Dij.　[30] . . cheford P.　[31] Waltunia Dij.　[32] Fristrop P ; Fristhorp' Dij.
[33] Gozelini P.　[34] Cuchewald P.　[35] Spirlingtona Dij.　[36] Kyrkebeia Dij.　[37] Scallebia
P.　[38] Wilgebia Dij.　[39] prouidenciam Dij.　[39a] *recte* reamque.　[39b] *recte* domni.
　Identifications : [40] Kirton in Lindsey, Caistor, Wellingore, co. Lincoln.　[41] Leighton
Bromswold, co. Huntingdon.　[42] Leighton Buzzard, co. Bedford.　[43] Buckingham,
Aylesbury, co. Buckingham.　[44] in Thorngate, Lincoln (see p. 277, below).　[45] Empingham, co. Rutland.　[46] Newport in Lincoln.　[47] Dunholme, co. Lincoln.　[48] Hougham,
co. Lincoln.　Robert de Bussei is evidently identical with Robert the priest who
before 1086 had one carucate in Hougham of the king in alms ; and had at that
time with the same land been made a monk of Stow Saint Mary ; but, it is added,
it was not lawful for anyone to have the land except by grant of the king (*The
Lincolnshire Domesday*, 7/55). Cp. no. 3 above. In no. 255, *l.* 52, below, Robert's
name is given as ' de Baffet.' The Bussei family was for long an important one in
Hougham.　[49] South Carlton, Thurlby (near Lincoln), co. Lincoln.　[50] Canwick,
co. Lincoln.　[51] Pontefract, co. York.　[52] Orston, co. Nottingham.　[53] Chesterfield,
Ashbourne, co. Derby.　[54] Mansfield, co. Nottingham.　[55] Derby, Wirksworth, co.
Derby.　[56] South Leverton, co. Nottingham.　[57] Edwinstowe, co. Nottingham.
[58] Binbrook, Corringham, co. Lincoln.　[59] Ketton, co. Rutland.　[60] Gretton, co.
Northampton.　[61] Duddington, co. Northampton (cp. no. 255, *l.* 97, below).
[62] Nassington, co. Northampton.　[63] North Kelsey, co. Lincoln.　[64] Langford, co.
Oxford.　[65] Leighton Bromswold, co. Huntingdon.　[66] Bottesford, Scamblesby,
Melton Ross (in Lindsey), co. Lincoln.　[67] Asgarby (near Spilsby), co. Lincoln.
[68] Rauceby, co. Lincoln.　[69] Horley, co. Oxford.　[70] King's Sutton, co. Northampton.
[71] Walton, co. Buckingham.　[72] Milton (near Thame), Thame, Banbury, Cropredy,
co. Oxford.　[73] Kilsby, co. Northampton.　[74] Stow Saint Mary, co. Lincoln.
[75] Leicester.　[76] Louth, Sleaford, co. Lincoln.　[77] Buckden, co. Huntingdon.
[78] Staughton, Spaldwick, co. Huntingdon.　[79] Greetwell, co. Lincoln.　[80] ' The land
of Saint Mary on which Tedbert dwells in the high street has not paid geld' (*The
Lincolnshire Domesday*, p. 7, no. 19). See no. 255, *l.* 123, below.　[81] Wigford in
Lincoln.　[82] Waltuna (query in Grantham).　[83] Hainton, co. Lincoln.　[84] Friesthorpe, co. Lincoln.　In 1086 Colsuain, Picot's father, had three carucates in
Friesthorpe, which were sokeland of his manor of Ingham.　The subtenants were
Roger and Anschetel (*The Lincolnshire Domesday*, 26/10, 11).　In 1115–1118 Robert
de Haia, who was then Colsuain's successor, held seven bovates in Friesthorpe,
while Saint Mary of Lincoln held the remainder of Colsuain's three carucates, i.e.
two carucates and one bovate, of which Nigel was sub-tenant (*ibid.* p. 241, nos.
4, 6).　The latter tenement is to be identified with Picot's fee in the text.　The
manor of Friesthorpe was confirmed to the canons by Henry II (no. 181, above),
and formed part of their lay fee (*Valor Eccles.* iv, 11).　[85] Kelsey, Cuxwold, co.

Lincoln. [86] Spridlington, Ingham, Faldingworth, and Kirkby (by Osgodby), co. Lincoln. [87] Scothorn, co. Lincoln. [88] Scawby, co. Lincoln (see *The Lincolnshire Domesday*, 26/16). [89] Skillington, co. Lincoln. [90] Belton (near Grantham), Gonerby, Fulbeck, and Stoke, co. Lincoln. [91] Grantham, Walton (in Grantham), co. Lincoln. [92] The corresponding clause in no. 255 below is ' decimam de Burg 7 de Wilchebi.' The latter place is to be identified with Silk Willoughby (see *Valor Eccles.* iv, 9, 121b). Burch or Burg is probably the extinct village of Burg in or near Kirkby Laythorpe, mention of which has previously been found only in Domesday Book (*The Lincolnshire Domesday*, pp. li, lii, and 67/3, 4, 6, and 68/26). It is perhaps significant that under the head of *decimœ partiales* in the *Valor Eccles.*, iv, 9, Willoughby iuxta Sleford and Kirkby Lathorp appear. [93] Normanby by Stow, co. Lincoln.

ADD. CHART.

253. An *inspeximus* of the preceding confirmation by W[alter de Gray], archbishop of York. (1216–1255.)

Omnibus Christi fidelibus ad quos presens scriptum peruenerit .W. dei gracia Ebor*acensis* archiepiscopus Angl*ie* primas eternam in domino salutem . Nouerit vniuersitas uestra nos subscripta priuilegia Linc' ecclesie inspexisse in
5   hec uerba . Eugenius episcopus [*etc., as in* no. 252 *above*].

Slit for seal tag : the tag and seal are missing. Size : 15¼ x 12¼ inches.
Text : MS—Dij/55/2/5.
Var. R. : see no. 252 above.

below, Folio 174.
Hdl.   1.7.4.

882

254. Similar confirmation by pope Alexander III, addressed to bishop Robert II. At Tours. 6 June, 1163.

Alexander episcopus seruus seruorum dei uenerabili fratri Roberto Lincol' episcopo eiusque successoribus canonice substituendis inperpetuum . Sicut iniusta petentibus nullus est attribuendus assensus . ita 7 iusta postulantium non est
5   differenda peticio . Quocirca uenerabilis in Christo frater Roberte episcope tuis iustis postulationibus clementer annuimus . 7 Lincoliens' ecclesiam cui deo auctore preesse dinosceris . sub beati Petri 7 nostra protectione suscipimus . 7 presentis scripti priuilegio communimus . Statuentes ut
10 quascumque possessiones quecumque bona inpresentiarum iuste 7 canonice possides . aut infuturum liberalitate regum . largitione principum . oblatione fidelium . seu aliis iustis modis deo propicio poteris adipisci . firma tibi tuisque successoribus 7 illibata permaneant . in quibus hec propriis
15 duximus exprimenda uocabulis . manerium de Lincolia scilicet [6]Willintorp . cum reliquis appendiciis ipsius manerii . 7 in ipsa ciuitate terram que est inter ecclesiam sancti Michaelis 7 fossatum ciuitatis sicut fossatum se extendit in murum ciuitatis . 7 in eodem loco ipsum fossatum 7 murum ad
20 faciendos introitus domorum episcopalium . in proximo loco

circa prefatam ecclesiam beati Michaelis .xx. solidatas terre
de dominio regis . manerium de ⁷Stou ; cum nundinis .
libertatibus . consuetudinibus . 7 appendiciis suis . ¹manerium
de ⁸Nortuna cum libertatibus 7 omnibus appendiciis suis¹ ·
25 ⁹Netelham cum appendiciis suis . manerium de ⁴⁴Luda . ¹⁰Esla-
ford cum castro . foro . 7 omnibus libertatibus . 7 appendiciis
suis . castrum de ¹¹Newerca cum omnibus libertatibus .
consuetudinibus . 7 appendiciis suis . manerium de ¹²Legre-
cestria cum omnibus appendiciis suis . ¹³Childebiam cum
30 pertinenciis suis . ¹⁴Chinchungtona . ¹⁵Holmum cum appendiciis suis . abbatiam de ¹⁶Egnesham cum foro 7 libertatibus
7 omnibus pertinen*ciis suis . ¹⁷Hardingtonam cum pertinenciis suis . ¹⁸Bannebiriam cum castro . foro . libertatibus .
7 pertinenciis suis . ¹⁹Cropereiam cum pertinenciis suis .
35 ²⁰Tamam cum libertatibus 7 pertinenciis suis . ²¹Dorcacestram
cum omnibus libertatibus 7 pertinenciis suis . ²²Woburnam
cum pertinenciis suis . ²³Bugedenam cum libertatibus 7
pertinenciis suis . ²⁴Spaldewic cum pertinenciis suis . ²⁵Bicles-
wadam cum libertatibus 7 pertinenciis suis . in ²⁶Bedefordia
40 domum episcopalem cum terra sua . ecclesiam de ²⁷Brantona
in manerio regis . manerium de ²⁸Tingerhest cum ecclesia
7 omnibus pertinenciis suis . domum episcopi Lundoniis .
auctoritate militum Templi Lincoliensi episcopo . 7 eius
successoribus imperpetuum concessam . 7 domum episcopi in
45 ciuitate Lincol' iuxta baliam ab austro . ius etiam episcopale
quod tam tu quam predecessores tui a quadraginta retro
annis in abbatiis inferius positis habuisse noscimini . videlicet
in abbatia de ²⁹Rameseia . de ³⁰Burgo . de ³¹Crulanda . de
³²Bardtheneia . de ³³Messendena . de ³⁴Dorkecestria² . de
50 ³⁵Legrecestria³ . de ³⁶Hoseneia . de ³⁷Brunna . de ³⁸Torintona .
de ³⁹Grimesbia . de ⁴⁰Weburna . de ⁴¹Guardona . de
⁴²Kirchebia⁴ . de ⁴³Reuesbia . de ⁴⁴Luda . 7 in aliis abbatiis
premonstratensis ordinis tibi auctoritate apostolica nichilominus confirmamus . Preterea presentis decreti auctoritate
55 sanctimus ut uniuersi Lincol' episcopatus fines ; quieti deinceps
omnino 7 integri tibi tuisque successoribus conseruentur .
sicut tu ipse 7 predecessores tui eos hactenus quiete 7 legittime
possedistis . Apostolica quoque auctoritate interdicimus ut
nullus omnino siue rex siue quelibet prepotens persona aut
60 eorum ministri decedentibus episcopis castra Linc' ecclesie
causa custodie uel alia qualibet occasione occupare presumat .
sed in casatorum qui ligii homines sunt custodia ipsius ecclesie
7 in eiusdem ecclesie potestate permaneant . donec in potestatem episcopi qui canonice fuerit substitutus libere redeant .
65 Decernimus ergo ut nulli omnino hominum liceat prefatam
beate Marie Lincol' ecclesiam temere perturbare . aut eius
possessiones auferre . uel ablatas retinere . minuere , seu

quibuslibet uexationibus perturbare . Sed illibata omnia
7 integre conseruentur . uestris ac pauperum Christi usibus
70 omnimodis pro futura . salua sedis apostolice auctoritate .
Si qua igitur in futurum ecclesiastica secularis ue persona
hanc nostre constitucionis paginam sciens contra eam temere
uenire temptauerit .⁊ secundo tercio ue commonita nisi
presumptionem congrua satisfactione correxerit .⁊ potestatis
75 honorisque sui careat dignitate . reamque se diuino iuditio
existere de perpetrata iniquitate cognoscat . ⁊ a sacratissimco⁵
corpore ⁊ sanguine dei ac domini redemptoris nostri Ihesu
Christi aliena fiat . atque in extremo examine districte subiaceat
ultioni . Cunctis autem eidem ecclesie sua iura seruantibus
80 sit pax domini nostri Ihesu Christi . quatinus ⁊ hic fructum
bone actionis percipiant . ⁊ apud districtum iudicem premia
eterne pacis inueniant . Amen . Amen . Amen . Datum Turon'
per manum Hermanni sancte Romane ecclesie subdiaconi ⁊
notarii .viii. idus Junii indictione .xiᵃ. incarnationis dominice
85 anno . Mᵒ. Cᵒ. LXIII. pontificatus uero domini Alexandri
pape .iii. anno .iiiiᵗᵒ.

Marginalia: *l. 1*, De eodem (Q). *opp. l. 38*, †
Texts : MS—A. P21 (only a few fragments remain).
Var. R. : ¹⁻¹ *omitted by* A, *supplied from* P.   ² Dorkecest' P.   ³ Legecestria P.
⁴ Kyrchebia P.   ⁵ *sic.*
Identifications : ⁶ Willingthorpe (see no. 248, Note, above).   ⁷ Stow St Mary, co.
Lincoln.   ⁸ Bishop Norton, co. Lincoln.   ⁹ Nettleham, co. Lincoln.   ¹⁰ Sleaford, co.
Lincoln.   ¹¹ Newark, co. Nottingham.   ¹² Leicester.   ¹³ Kilsby, co. Northampton.
¹⁴ Knighton, co. Leicester.   ¹⁵ Holme (see no. 249, Note, above).   ¹⁶ Eynsham, co.
Oxford.   ¹⁷ Yarnton, co. Oxford.   ¹⁸ Banbury, co. Oxford.   ¹⁹ Cropredy, co. Oxford.
²⁰ Thame, co. Oxford.   ²¹ Dorchester, co. Oxford.   ²² Wooburn, co. Buckingham.
²³ Buckden, co. Huntingdon.   ²⁴ Spaldwick, co. Huntingdon.   ²⁵ Biggleswade, co.
Bedford.   ²⁶ Bedford.   ²⁷ Brampton, co. Huntingdon.   ²⁸ Fingest, co. Buckingham.
²⁹ Ramsey, co. Huntingdon.   ³⁰ Peterborough, co. Northampton.   ³¹ Croyland, co.
Lincoln.   ³² Bardney, co. Lincoln.   ³³ Missenden, co. Buckingham.   ³⁴ Dorchester,
co. Oxford.   ³⁵ Leicester.   ³⁶ Oseney, co. Oxford.   ³⁷ Bourne, co. Lincoln.   ³⁸ Thornton, co. Lincoln.   ³⁹ Grimsby, co. Lincoln.   ⁴⁰ Woburn, co. Bedford.   ⁴¹ Warden,
co. Bedford.   ⁴² Kirby Bellars, co. Leicester.   ⁴³ Revesby, co. Lincoln.   ⁴⁴ Louth
Park, co. Lincoln.

*below, Folio 174d.
†below, Folio 175.
Hdl.   1.7.5.
‡below, Folio 175d.
§below, Folio 176.
Hdl.   1.7.6.

883

255. Similar confirmation by pope Alexander III, addressed
to Adelmus the dean and the canons of Lincoln. At Tours.
5 June, 1163.

Alexander episcopus seruus seruorum dei dilectis filiis
Alelmo¹ decano ⁊ canonicis ecclesie beate Marie Lincol' tam

presentibus quam futuris canonice substituendis imperpetuum . * Effectum iusta postulantibus indulgere . 7 uigor
5   equitatis 7 ordo exigit rationis . presertim quando petentium
uoluntatem 7 pietas adiuuat . 7 ueritas non relinquit . Eapropter dilecti in domino filii uestris iustis postulationibus
clementer annuimus . 7 prefatam ecclesiam in qua diuino
mancipati estis obsequio . ad exemplar patris 7 predecessoris
10 nostri sancte recordationis Eugenii pape sub beati Petri 7
nostra protectione suscipimus . 7 presentis scripti priuilegio
communimus . Statuentes ut quascumque possessiones .
quecumque bona . eadem ecclesia in presentiarum iuste 7
canonice possidet ? aut in futurum concessione pontificum .
15 largitione regum . uel principum . oblacione fidelium . seu
aliis iustis modis prestante domino poterit adipisci ? firma
uobis uestrisque successoribus ? 7 illibata permaneant . in
quibus hec propriis duximus exprimenda uocabulis . In
Lincol'scira . ⁴Welletonam cum omnibus appendiciis suis .
20 7 villam de ⁵Asgereby . 7 quicquid infra territorium eiusdem
uille continetur . duodecim bouatas terre in ⁶Binnebroc quas
Osbertus uicecomet¹ . tenuit . totam terram quam Radulfus
Ruffus in ⁷Willingham 7 in Surrea habuit in prebenda sua .
ecclesiam de ⁸Kerketona . ecclesiam de Castra . ecclesiam
25 de Wellinghouer' . ecclesiam de Duneham . ecclesiam de
⁹Karletona . ecclesiam de Turleby . ecclesiam de Coringham .
ecclesiam de Norkeleseie . ecclesiam de Scamelesby . ecclesiam
de Lafford' . quicquid iuris habetis in ecclesia de ¹⁰Roucebi .
7 quicquid iuris habetis in ecclesia de Hibaldestou . ecclesiam
30 de Luda cum omnibus decimis . terris . 7 pertinenciis earundem
ecclesiarum . in ciuitate Linc' . ecclesiam sancti Martini .
ecclesiam sancti Laurencii . 7 reliquas eiusdem ciuitatis ecclesias
in proprio feudo regis sitas . ecclesiam ¹¹sancte Marie . ecclesiam sancti Stephani . ecclesiam sancte Fidis in soca episcopi .
35 ecclesiam sancti Johannis in Newport . ecclesiam sancti
Leonardi . quarum quedam cedunt in prebendas canonicorum .
quedam uero ad ¹²cantariam pertinent . 7 ecclesiam Omnium
Sanctorum in ballio ciuitatis sitam cum mansionibus circum-
quaque adiacentibus . 7 quibusdam aliis mansionibus in
40 ¹³Estgata . 7 cum quadam mensura in parrochia sancti
Augustini . 7 cum quadam ¹⁴carrucata terre in campis Linc' .
cum decimis eiusdem carrucate . 7 aliis decimis quatuor
culturarum pertinentium ad prebendam Humfridi subdecani .
simul cum centum solidis annuis in archidiaconatu Lincol' ?
45 de redditu episcopi . que ad cancellariam eiusdem ecclesie
pertinet . ¹⁵mansuras quoque omnes quas Robertus de
Stuteuilla dedit in prebendam ecclesie Lincol' iuxta pontem
Linc' . dimidiam carrucatam terre que fuit Haiax sacerdotis .
7 aliam dimidiam carrucatam in eis campis de prebenda

50 Dauidis . mansionem unam in uico magno inter fabros .
aliam mansionem in eodem uico de prebenda Radulfi Rufi .
totam decimam de dominio Roberti de Baffet[2] in [16]Hacham .
7 unam carrucatam terre in eadem uilla . duas partes decime
in [17]Canewic de terra Martelli de Taneio . 7 Hugonis generi
55 eius . quam tenebant de rege . uel de honore Pontisfracti .
7 pasturam in eadem uilla . duas partes decime de dominio
[18]Gretewelle . duas partes omnium decimationum dominii
Walteri de Mundauilla ⁏ † in [19]Kynerebi . duas partes decimationum de dominio eiusdem in [20]Hellesham . 7 totam
60 decimam de dominio suo in [21]Houresbi . item in prefata
ciuitate decem 7 octo libras annuas de redditu regis in eadem
ciuitate . item de feudo Helfridi prepositi 7 Fulconis generi
eius ⁏ quatuor libras terre in eadem ciuitate quas dederunt
in prebendam ecclesie Linc' . 7 quatuor libras quas in aug-
65 mentum eiusdem prebende episcopus Robertus concessit .
7 dedit annuas de redditu suo in archidiaconatu Lincol' .
preterea beneficium illud quod in Linc'sira parrichiani[1]
eiusdem sire ab antiquo concesserunt . 7 dederunt ecclesie
Linc' annuatim reddendo de singulis aratris suis . scilicet
70 una traua bladi . quod uulo[3] appellatur sancte Mariecorn .
duas partes decime de dominio de [18]Gretewella . totam
decimam de dominio episcopi in [22]Nortona . duas partes
omnium decimationum de dominio de [23]Scotorn' . totam
decimam de dominio episcopi de [24]Lestou . 7 duas partes
75 decime omnium parrochianorum . 7 duas mansuras cum logis
pertinentibus ad easdem mansuras . vnam bouatam terre
in [25]Brancebi . 7 unum pratum in [26]Coringham quod pertinet
ad Stou[24] . totam decimam de dominio episcopi in [27]Netelham .
in blado 7 molendinis . In Notinghamsira ⁏ ecclesiam de
80 [28]Farendona . ecclesiam de Baldertona . centum solidos
annuos in archidiaconatu Legrecestrie de redditu episcopi .
ecclesiam de [29]Scarla . ecclesiam de Gretona . ecclesiam de
Cliftona de feudo episcopi . 7 quadraginta solidos annuos
in archidiaconatu Lincol' de redditu episcopi . ecclesiam de
85 [30]Oschintona . ecclesiam de [31]Cestrefelda . ecclesiam de
Esseburna . ecclesiam de [32]Mamesfelda . capellas omnes in
berewicis ad predicta .iiijor. maneria pertinentibus . ecclesias
de [33]Derebia . ecclesiam de Werkeworda . ecclesiam de
[34]Leertona . ecclesiam de Edenestoua . cum terris . decimis .
90 7 ceteris pertinenciis omnium predictarum ecclesiarum .
ecclesiam de [35]Stokes . ecclesiam de Chodingtona . cum
omnibus pertinenciis suis . totam decimam de dominio episcopi .
in [36]Newerch . 7 Farendona . 7 Baldertona . In Lecestresira ⁏
ecclesiam [37]sancte Margarete cum omnibus pertinenciis suis .
95 duas partes decime de dominio de [38]Keldesbi . in Norhant'sira ⁏
ecclesiam de [39]Chetenea cum capella de Tikesoura . ecclesiam

de ⁴⁰Gretona . ecclesiam de Dodingtona . ecclesiam de Nessintona . ecclesiam de ⁴¹Ledingtona . assignatam loco prebende de ⁴²Canewic . quam episcopus consensu capituli pauperibus
100 assignauit . ecclesiam de ⁴³Sutton' cum capellis . decimis . terris . ⁊ omnibus pertinenciis predictarum ecclesiarum . In Huntedun'sira ⸴ manerium de ⁴⁴Lechtona cum omni integritate sua . ecclesiam de Bugdendena . ecclesiam de Brantona . cum omnibus pertinenciis earundem . totam decimam de dominio
105 episcopi in ⁴⁵Stou . ⁊ duas partes decime parrochianorum eiusdem uille . duas partes decime de dominio de ⁴⁶Stoton' . decimam de dominio de Spaldewich . ecclesiam de Lectona subdecanatui Linc' ab episcopo Alexandro primo assignatam . cum capella de ⁴⁷Sala . ⁊ omnibus pertinenciis suis . ecclesiam
110 beate Marie ⁴⁸Bedeford' . ecclesiam Lectona cum omnibus pertinenciis suis . In Buchinghamsira manerium ⁴⁹Waltonam . ecclesiam Elesbirie . ecclesiam de Buchingham . cum capellis . decimis . ⁊ ceteris pertinencii¹ earundem . In Oxenford'sira ⸴ manerium ⁵⁰Orneleie . ⁊ dimidiam Mideltonam . ⁊ ecclesiam
115 eiusdem uille . ecclesiam de ⁵¹Tama . ecclesiam de Bannebiria . ecclesiam de Cropereia . ecclesiam de Langeford' ⸴ cum capellis . decimis . terris . ⁊ omnibus pertinenciis earundem . ‡ Specialiter ad communam pertinentia ⸴ dimidiam partem oblationum altaris sancte Marie Lincol' . virgultum ubi fuit ⁵²uinea
120 regis . ecclesiam sancti Nicholai de ⁵³Neuport . ecclesiam ⁵³sancti Egidii . ecclesiam de ⁵⁴Heinton' . ecclesiam de Scellitona . cum omnibus pertinenciis suis . terram ubi fuit uinea Colsuein' . in ⁵³magno uico ⸴ mansuram ⁵⁵Teberti . in ⁵⁶Wicheford ⸴ terram Osulfi . quatuordecim mansiones
125 passim in burgo Linc' . terram Azonis iuxta ⁵³pontem magnum . duas bouatas terre in campis Linc' . decimam terre Petri filii Dorandi . triginta solidos annuos ab archidiaconatu . Linc' . decimam forestarum regis de episcopatu Linc' . viginti solidos de ⁵⁷Waltona . feudum Picoti de ⁵⁸Fristorp . terram
130 Gocelini in ⁵⁹Cheleseia . decimam de terra Haconis in ⁶⁰Cucuwald . duas partes decimarum de dominio Willelmi filii Symonis in ⁶¹Sperlintona . Ingaham . ⁊ Faldingword' . ⁊ Kyrcheby . quandam mansuram iuxta ⁶²pontem . ecclesiam de ⁶³Scotorna . sitam in feudo Galfridi de Noua Uilla . duas
135 partes decime carrucate terre Alueredi in ⁶⁴Scallebi . decimam terre Colgrimi in ⁶⁵Beltona . ⁊ in Gunwordebi . ⁊ in Fulebech . ⁊ in Stoches . ⁊ in ea quatuor bouatas terre . ⁊ unum molendinum super aquam de ⁶⁶Graham . ⁊ Waltona . decimam de ⁶⁷Burg . ⁊ de ⁶⁸Wilchebi . decem solidatas terre in ⁶⁹Nor
140 mannebi . iuxta Stou . ex donatione Adelidis ⁊ Rogeri filii eius . Prefati quoque episcopi uestri precibus annuentes iuxta uotum ⁊ rationabilem ipsius prouidentiam sanctimus . ut de prebendis canonicorum decedentium post decessum eorum

145 per annum debita eorum uel seruientium eorum mercedes
persoluantur . quod autem superfuerit uel si debitum non
habuerint ; totum in usus fratrum cedat . Centum solidos
annuos de dono episcopi . vnam carrucatam terre in [70]Cala .
de dono Willelmi Romara . dimidiam carrucatam in [71]Burtun
super Trentam . per adquisitionem Reginaldi quatuor solidos
150 in molendino de [72]Kirchebi . vnam bouatam in [73]Linwd' .
vnam bouatam in Crochesbi . tres solidos in Barwa . in terra
Petri de Gousele . in ballio ; unam mansuram de feudo Roberti
de Aresci . duas bouatas terre in [74]Hicham . dimidiam marcam
in Rieb' . 7 in Swalwe . de terra Humfridi de Terleia ; tres
155 solidos de dono episcopi . tres solidos de terra Roberti filii
Fulconis de Sireham ; ex dono episcopi . Decernimus ergo
ut nulli omnino hominum liceat supradictam ecclesiam temere
perturbare . aut eius possessiones auferre . uel ablatas retinere
minuere . seu quibuslibet uexationibus fatigare . Sed illibata
160 omnia 7 integra conseruentur . eorum pro quorum gubernatione 7 sustentatione concessa sunt ; usibus omnimodis
profutura . salua sedis apostolice auctoritate . 7 diocesanorum
episcoporum canonica iusticia . Si qua igitur in futurum
ecclesiastica secularis ue persona hanc nostre constitucionis
165 paginam sciens contra eam temere uenire temptauerit ;
secundo tercio ue commonita nisi presumptionem suam congrua satisfactione correxerit ; potestatis honorisque sui
dignitate careat . reamque se diuino iudicio existere de
perpetrata iniquitate cognoscat . 7 a sacratissimo corpore
170 ac sanguine dei 7 domini redemptoris nostri Ihesu Christi
aliena fiat . atque in extremo examine districte ultioni
subiaceat . Cunctis autem eidem loco sua iura seruantibus ;
sit pax domini nostri Ihesu Christi . quatinus § 7 hic fructum
bone actionis percipiant ; 7 apud districtum iudicem premia
175 eterne . pacis inueniant . Amen . Amen . Amen . Datum
Turon' per manum Hermanni sancte Romane ecclesie
subdiaconi . 7 notarii . nonas . Junii . indictione .xi[a]. incarnacionis dominice anno . M[o]. C[o]. lx[o]. iii[o]. pontificatus uero domini
Alexandri pape tercii anno quarto.

Marginalia : *l. 1*, De eodem (Q). *opp. l. 46*, Nota pro Thorngate. *opp. l. 67*,
Lincol' (Q). *opp. l. 70*, seyntemaricorn. *opp. l. 71*, minute decime prediales.
opp. l. 79, Notingham. *opp. l. 83*, Clifton'. *opp. ll. 91–3*, Stookes cum Codington.
Nota ecclesiis de Stokes 7 Chodingtona pertinent decime de terris dominicis
episcopi in campis de Newerk Farendona 7 Baldertona . de quibus fit hic
mencio in hoc privilegio (Q). *opp. l. 93*, Leicest' (Q). *opp. l. 99*, pro Canewick.
opp. ll. 98–9, Nota quomodo episcopus Linc' . assignauit Lydingtona ecclesie
Lincoln' loco prebende de Canwyke quam dedit pauperibus hospitalis sancte
Katerine. *opp. l. 100*, 🖙. *opp. l. 102*, Hun' (Q). *opp. l. 108*, Nota pro subdecano. *opp. l. 111*, Buc' (Q). *opp. l. 113*, Ox' (Q). *opp. l. 118*, nota que
pertinent ad communam 🖙. *opp. l. 128*, de decima forestarum regis in diocesi.
opp. l. 130, ... *opp. l. 129*, xx solid' Walton' (Q). *opp. l. 132*, Ingeham' . . . .
(Q). *opp. l. 135*, 🖙. *opp. l. 135*, Scalby Belton. *opp. l. 145*, ... prebend'
canonic' 🖙 (Q). *opp. l. 153*, Ryby 7 Swallowe. *opp. l. 179*, huc.

Text: MS—A.
Var. R.: ¹ sic. ² see no. 252, p. 201, note 48. ³ for uulgo.
Identifications: In Lincolnshire—⁴ Welton (by Lincoln). ⁵ Asgarby (by Spilsby).
⁶ Binbrook. ⁷ Cherry Willingham and Southrey. ⁸ Kirton in Lindsey, Caistor,
Wellingore, Dunholme. ⁹ South Carlton, Thurlby (by Lincoln), Corringham, North
Kelsey, Scamblesby, Sleaford. ¹⁰ Rauceby, Hibaldstow, Louth. ¹¹ St Mary
le Wigford. ¹² the precentory. ¹³ Eastgate in Lincoln. ¹⁴ see *The Lincolnshire
Domesday*, p. 5, no. 10. ¹⁵ in Thorngate (see pages 277–290 below). ¹⁶ Hougham
(see no. 252, note 48, above). ¹⁷ Canwick. ¹⁸ Greetwell. ¹⁹ Kingerby. ²⁰ Elsham.
²¹ Owersby. ²² Bishop Norton. ²³ Scothorne. ²⁴ Stow St Mary. ²⁵ Bransby.
²⁶ Corringham. ²⁷ Nettleton.
    ²⁸ Farndon, Balderton, co. Nottingham. ²⁹ South Scarle, Girton, Clifton (near
Newark), co. Nottingham. ³⁰ Orston, co. Nottingham. ³¹ Chesterfield, Ashbourne, co. Derby. ³² Mansfield, co. Nottingham. ³³ Derby, Wirksworth, co.
Derby. ³⁴ South Leverton, Edwinstowe, co. Nottingham. ³⁵ East Stoke, Coddington, co. Nottingham. ³⁶ Newark, Farndon, Balderton, co. Nottingham. ³⁷ St
Margaret's, Leicester. ³⁸ Kilsby, co. Northampton. ³⁹ Ketton, Tixover, co. Rutland.. ⁴⁰ Gretton, Duddington, Nassington, co. Northampton. ⁴¹ Lyddington, co.
Rutland. ⁴² Canwick, co. Lincoln. ⁴³ King's Sutton, co. Northampton. ⁴⁴ Leighton
Bromswold, Buckden, Brampton, co. Huntingdon. ⁴⁵ Long Stow, co. Huntingdon.
⁴⁶ Staughton, Spaldwick, Leighton Bromswold, co. Huntingdon. ⁴⁷ Sale (now
extinct), in the parish of Leighton Bromswold. Its approximate site is indicated
by the present Salome Wood, one-and-half miles north-east of Leighton (Mawer
and Stenton, *The Place-names of Bedfordshire and Huntingdonshire*, p. 246). The
place appears as 'Salna' in 1248 (Lincoln Record Soc. xi, 295–6). ⁴⁸ Bedford,
Leighton Buzzard, co. Bedford. ⁴⁹ Walton, Aylesbury, Buckingham, co. Buckingham. ⁵⁰ Horley, Milton (by Thame), co. Oxford. ⁵¹ Thame, Banbury, Cropredy,
Langford, co. Oxford.
    In Lincolnshire—⁵² in Lincoln (cp. no. 23, above). ⁵³ in Lincoln. ⁵⁴ Hainton,
Skillington. ⁵⁵ see no. 252, note 80, above. ⁵⁶ Wigford in Lincoln. ⁵⁷ See no. 252,
l. 82, where the amount is given as thirty shillings. ⁵⁸ Friesthorpe (see no. 252,
note 84, above). ⁵⁹ Kelsey. ⁶⁰ Cuxwold. ⁶¹ Spridlington, Ingham, Faldingworth, Kirkby Laythorpe. ⁶² in Lincoln. ⁶³ Scothorne. ⁶⁴ Scawby. ⁶⁵ Belton
(near Grantham), Gonerby, Fulbeck, Stoke. ⁶⁶ Grantham, Walton (in Grantham).
⁶⁷ See no. 252, note 92, above. ⁶⁸ Silk Willoughby. ⁶⁹ Normanby by Stow.
⁷⁰ Cheal (in Gosberton). ⁷¹ Gate Burton (cp. Registrum Antiquissimum, no. 257).
⁷² Kirkby (by Osgodby). ⁷³ Linwood, Croxby, Barrow. ⁷⁴ Hykeham, Riby,
Swallow.

884

256. Confirmation by pope Alexander [III], addressed to the
dean and chapter of Lincoln, of the liberty which bishop Robert II,
about the time of his promotion, granted to them in their prebends,
and in the churches belonging to their common, and to the
subdeanery, and to the church of Leighton [Bromswold, co.
Huntingdon] which pertains to the subdeanery. At Tusculum.
13 September (1171–1180).

    Alexander episcopus seruus seruorum dei dilectis filiis
decano 7 capitulo Lincolnien*sibus*¹ salutem . 7 apostolicam
benedictionem . Quotiens a uiris ecclesiasticis deuote requiritur
ut eis super hiis que rationabiliter possident apostolice con-
5 firmationis suffragium conferamus ad concedendum que
postulant ⸴ faciles inueniri debemus . 7 eorum rationabilibus
uotis gratuitum impertiri consensum . Eapropter dilecti in
domino filii uestris iustis postulationibus benignius annuentes ⸴
libertatem quam bone memorie Robertus quondam episcopus

10 uester uobis in prebendis uestris 7 in ecclesiis ad communionem
uestram pertinentibus 7 subdecanatui ecclesie uestre 7 ecclesie
de Lecten' ad eundem subdecanatum pertinenti circa tempora
sue promotionis concessit . 7 scripto proprio suo sigillo roborato
firmauit ꝫ sicut eam hactenus pacifice habuistis ꝫ deuotioni
15 uestre auctoritate apostolica confirmamus . 7 presentis scripti
patrocinio communimus . Statuentes ut nulli omnino hominum
liceat hanc paginam nostre confirmationis infringere uel ei
aliquatenus contraire . Siquis autem hoc attemptare presumpserit ꝫ indignationem omnipotentis dei 7 beatorum
20 Petri 7 Pauli apostolorum eius ꝫ se nouerit incursurum .
Datum Tuscul' . idus Septembris.

Marginalia in A 884: *opp. l. 1*, .V. (resuming the numbering from no. 250 above).   *opp. l. 2*, ▨▨▨   non
(*erased*) reperitur originale (14 cent.).   patet (15 cent.).
opp. l. 7, Confirmacio pro prebendis et ecclesiis de communa (16 cent.).   (*Another head is drawn very faintly
in marg.*)
    Marginalia in A 66 : Carta venerabilis Alexandri summi
pontificis (rubric).   *opp. l. 1*, Confirmacio iurisdictionis
scribitur alibi (Q).
    Texts : MS—A884.   A66.   Ix(4).   Pd : Wilkins i, 539.
Jaffé-Löwenfeld, no. 13574 (calendared).
    Var. R. : ¹ Lincoln' Ix.
    Note : Bishop Robert's charter will be found at no.
287, below.
    Note by Dr W. Holtzmann : The date 1171–1180 here and in no. 257 is derived
from the itinerary of pope Alexander III.

Nota pro subdecano

opp. l. 14 (13 cent.)

885

257. Mandate of pope Alexander [III]: the pope, having
received a report that certain canons, although they receive their
prebends in full, yet disdain to attend the divine offices in their
church, and that certain canons who, having been disgraced by
crime and having sworn to forsake it, do not blush to return to it,
commands the dean and chapter of Lincoln to fine in their benefices
those who will not attend the services constantly or for the greater
part of the year, and to inflict such penalty as they shall see fit
on those who cannot establish their innocence by purgation, and
on those who revert to the crimes which they have abjured.   At
Tusculum.   9 September (1171–1180).

    Alexander episcopus seruus seruorum dei dilectis filiis
decano 7 capitulo Lincolien*sibus*¹ salutem . 7 apostolicam
benediccionem . De negligentia 7 remissione pastoralis solici-
tudinis merito possemus redargui . 7 circa officium nostrum
5 desides iudicari ꝫ si errata corrigere 7 ab ecclesia dei enormi-
tates postponeremus 7 prauas consuetudines radicitus extir-
pare . Relatum est siquidem auribus nostris quosdam esse

in ecclesia uestra canonicos qui licet prebendas suas absque
diminutione percipiant ; in ipsa tamen ecclesia diuinis obsequiis
10   uacare contempnunt . Quidam uero sunt ibi qui sicut dicitur
postquam de crimine infammati[2] fuerint 7 ab eo decetero
abstinere iuramento firmarunt ; neglecta fama 7 iuramento
contempto ad idem quasi canes ad uomitum non erubuerunt
reuerti . Quia igitur hec si uera sunt non possumus absque
15   diminutione fame uestre ac detrimento animarum uestrarum
incorrecta relinquere ; discretioni uestre per apostolica scripta
percipiendo mandamus . quatinus canonicos illos qui se ab
obsequiis ecclesie uestre absentant sollicite moneatis 7 inducere
modis omnibus laboretis . ut sicut gaudent de accepta cum
20   integritate prebenda ; ita per se ipsos assidue aut per maiorem
partem anni ecclesie uestre deseruiant . Quod si monitis
uestris parere contempserint 7 in eadem ecclesia [3]non fuerint
assidui[3] . aut per maiorem partem anni eidem ecclesie non
deseruierint ; eos in propriis * beneficiis prout uideritis ex-
25   pedire mulctetis . Illi autem qui de aliquo crimine infamati
se purgare uoluerint ; secundum ordinem suum 7 qualitatem
7 quantitatem delicti ; suam innocentiam purgent . 7 tam
hiis qui se purgare non possunt . quam ceteris que[4] ad eadem
crimina que abiurarunt non erubuerunt reuerti ; penam sicut
30   expedire uideritis iuxta modum culpe infligere non post-
ponatis . Et in hiis omnibus eam discretionem 7 moderantiam
habeatis ut zelo rectitudinis 7 ecclesiastice iusticie non liuore
inuidie uideamini prouocari . 7 conuersis locum satisfaciendi
7 in melius emendandi commissa . conuertendis autem spei
35   solatium 7 indulgentie tribuatis . 7 ceteri hec audientes nedum
ipsi timeant similia perpetrare . Dat' Tusculan' .v. id*us*
Septembris.

Marginalia : *opp. l. 1*, .VI.   *opp. l. 4*, non (*cancelled*) reperitur originale (14 cent.).
reperitur nunc anno domini m° cccc^mo vj° (15 cent.).   *opp. l. 23*, Nota pro
maiori anni (14 cent.).   *opp. l. 30*, Recidere debent (14 cent.).
    Text : MS—A. Ix(5) (imperfect).   Pd : Wilkins i, 539.   Jaffé-Löwenfeld, no.
13572 (calendared).
    Var. R. : [1] Linc' Ix.   [2] infamati Ix.   [3-3] assidui non fuerint Ix.   [4] *recte* qui.

* *Folio 176d.*

886

258.   Confirmation by pope Eugenius [III], addressed to bishop
Alexander, of king Stephen's grant of the chapelry of Blyth [co.
Nottingham] to the church of Lincoln as a prebend. At Viterbo.
23 December (1146).

    Evgenivs episcopus seruus seruorum dei venerabili fratri
Alexandro Lincoliensi episcopo salutem . 7 apostolicam
benediccionem . Quotiens illud a nobis petitur quod racioni
7 honestati conuenire dinoscitur animo nos decet libenti

5   concedere . 7 petencium desideriis congruum impertiri suffra-
    gium . Ea propter venerabilis frater in Christo Alexander
    episcope tue 7 ecclesie Lincoliensis quieti in posterum proui-
    dentes capellariam de Blia quam Stephanus illustris rex
    Anglorum ecclesie beate Marie Lincoliensi prebendam pia
10 deuotione concessit . 7 dimisit . nos eidem ecclesie presentis
    scripti pagina confirmamus . Nulli ergo omnino hominum
    liceat te uel Lincoliensem¹ super hac nostra confirmatione 7
    eiusdem regis concessione perturbare seu quibuslibet molestiis
    fatigare . Si quis autem huius nostre confirmationis paginam
15 sciens contra eam temere uenire temptauerit secundo tercio
    ue commonitus nisi reatum suum congrva satisfactione
    correxerit indignationem omnipotentis dei 7 beatorum Petri
    7 Pauli apostolorum eius incurrat . atque in extremo examine
    districte ultioni subiaceat . Dat' . Viterbi .x. kalendas .
20 Ianuarii.

Marginalia : *opp. l. 1*, .VII.
Text : MS—A.
Var. R. : ¹ecclesiam *has been omitted by the scribe.*
Note : Stephen's charter will be found at no. 100, above. The earliest date
for that charter is 1146, and the present text proves that it is also the latest
date to which it can be assigned.
Note by Dr Holtzmann : The itinerary of pope Eugenius III shews that 1146
was the only year in which he was at Viterbo on 23 December.

With no. 886 the original hand ceases, and the charters from no.
887 onwards are entered by a late thirteenth century hand—probably
that of Q2.

887

259. Mandate of pope Honorius [II], commanding the barons
and others, great and little, throughout the diocese of Lincoln, to
honour and help their church and the canons dedicated to its service,
and not to retain or take away the goods bestowed upon it. At
the Lateran. 30 January (1126).

    Honorius episcopus seruus seruorum dei . vniuersis baronibus .
    7 aliis maioribus 7 minoribus per Lincolniensem parochiam .
    salutem 7 apostolicam benediccionem . In lege domini
    scriptum est . Honora patrem tuum 7 matrem tuam ut sis
5   longeuus super terram . Attencius igitur spirituali matri
    idest sancte ecclesie vt uita eterna in celestibus habeatur .
    honor 7 beneficia sint humiliter conferenda Vniuersitatem
    ergo uestram exhortamur in domino vt sanctam matrem
    uestram Lincolniensem ecclesiam 7 canonicos suo famulatui
10 dicatos . honoretis diligatis 7 de hiis poscessionibus vobis
    a deo collatis attencius adiuuetis . Neque aliquis vestrum
    possessiones 7 bona eidem ecclesie a parentibus suis uel ab
    aliis attributa retinere . uel aliqua temeritate auferre pre-
    sumat . quod si quis attemptare presumserit iram dei 7

15 spiritualis matris sue se non dubitet incursurum . Dat' .
　　Laterani .iij. kalendas Februarii.

Marginalia: *opp. l. 1*, .VIII.
Texts: MS—A. S59 (only a fragment remains).
Note by Dr W. Holtzmann : This bull evidently belongs to the same year as
no. 248 above, which is given in the second year of the pontificate of Honorius II.
The years of pontificate are reckoned from the consecration, which took place
21 December, 1124 ; the second year therefore begins with 21 December, 1125 ;
the fourth indiction runs from 1 September, 1125, till 30 August, 1126 ; it follows,
therefore, that the *annus incarnationis* is reckoned according to the style of the
annunciation or, more exactly, according to the *calculus Florentinus*, which is
identical with the later *mos Anglicus*.

At foot of folio 176*d*.　　　　.VIII.　　　　.vndecima pecia.

Folio 177.
Hdl.　　　　　　　Prima pars (Q).　　　　.1.7.7.

888

260. Indult by pope Innocent [IV] granting to the dean and
chapter that, when the bishop visits the churches which are subject
to them, they shall not be bound to furnish procurations beyond
the definitive limit of persons and horsemen determined by the
Lateran council. At Lyons. 11 December, 1247.

　　Innocentius episcopus seruus seruorum dei dilectis filiis
decano 7 capitulo Linc' . salutem . 7 apostolicam benediccionem . Cum in Lateranensi consilio[1] prouida fuerit deliberacione statutum vt ne prelati que sua sunt non que Ihesu
5 Christi querentes subditos suos cum ad eos visitaturi accedunt
grauarent in procurationibus personarum 7 euectionum
mediocritatem obseruent . licet super eo quod ius commune
concedit superflue peti videatur concessio specialis quia .
tamen plus timeri solet quod speciali conceditur indulgencia (
10 quam quod edicto concluditur generali . auctoritate vobis
presencium indulgemus . vt episcopum uestrum cum ad
ecclesias uobis subiectas impensur*us* in eis officium visitationis accesserit (recipere ac procurare minime teneamini (
nisi circa illas (diffinitam mediocritatem huiusmodi personarum
15 7 euectionum in eodem concilio (duxerit obseruandam[1] .
Nulli ergo omnino hominum liceat hanc paginam nostre concessionis infringere (uel ei ausu temerario contraire . Si
quis autem hoc attempta[1] presumpserit (indignationem
omnipotentis dei 7 beatorum Petri 7 Pauli apostolorum eius
20 (se nouerit incursurum . Datum Lugdun' .iij. idus Decembris
pontificatus nostri anno quarto.

Marginalia: *opp. l. 1*, .IX.　　*opp. l. 3*, .i.　　*opp. l. 12*, de visitacione episcopi.
Text: MS—A.
Var. R.: [1] *sic*.
Note : The duty of providing for the entertainment of the bishop or archdeacon,
when he visits parish churches, is laid by the common law of the Church upon the
persons visited. This duty, which included the entertainment of the visitor's

retinue, is known by the name of procurations. At first these procurations were
fulfilled by furnishing victuals and other provisions in kind ; but by a constitution
of archbishop Stratford it was put in the choice of the incumbent whether he would
entertain the visitor with provisions or compound for the duty by a certain sum
of money. This was the origin of the custom, which still obtains, of paying a fixed
sum for procurations. The Third Lateran Council, 1179, limited the retinue of a
bishop, for which procurations might be demanded, to twenty or thirty horsemen
(Gibson, *Codex Juris Ecclesiastici Anglicani*, pp. 973–5).

889

261. Indult of pope Innocent [IV] granting, at the request of
the bishop of Lincoln, to the chapter of Lincoln and the rectors of
the parishes of the city and diocese of Lincoln, that they shall not
be bound to pay procuration by reason of the visitation of the
diocesan bishop for the time being, in respect of the churches situate
in the prebends of the canons, or of the common fund of the chapter,
or of the other parish churches of the city and diocese of Lincoln.
At Lyons.   2 August, 1250.

Innocentius episcopus seruus seruorum dei . Dilectis filiis
capitulo Lincolniens*ibus* (7 rectoribus parochialium ecclesiarum
ciuitatis et dio*cesis* Lincolniens*is* (salutem 7 benediccionem
apostolicam . Precibus venerabilis fratris nostri . episcopi
5 Lincolniens*is* benignum impercientes assensum vt racione
visitacionis ecclesiis sitis in prebendis canonicorum uel
commune capituli Lincolniens*is* 7 aliis ecclesiis parochialibus
ciuitatis 7 dio*cesis* Lincolniens*is* a diocesano episcopo qui
pro tempore fuerit impendende procuracionem eidem episcopo
10 soluere minime teneamini auctoritate vobis presencium
indulgemus . Nulli ergo omnino hominum liceat hanc paginam
nostre concessionis infringere (uel ei ausu temerario contraire .
Si quis autem attemptare presumpserit indignacionem omnipotentis dei 7 beatorum Petri 7 Pauli apostolorum eius
15 se nouerit incursurum . Dat' Lugdun' .iiij. nonas Augusti
pontificatus nostri anno octauo.

Marginalia : *opp. l. 1*, .X. .ii. *opp. l. 7*, de eodem.
Text : MS—A.
Note : In view of the general and undisputed duty of procurations which rested
upon rectors of churches, this document, in spite of the generality of its wording,
must be interpreted as referring to the rectors of churches belonging to the prebends and the common of the church of Lincoln. The fact that the privilege
was granted at the request of bishop Grosseteste seems to indicate that it was part
of the settlement of the dispute between himself and the chapter about jurisdiction
(see no. 273, below).

890

262. Mandate of pope Innocent [IV] commanding the archdeacon
of Saint Albans not to allow the chapter and the rectors to be
molested contrary to the tenor of the next preceding indult.   At
Lyons.   2 August, 1250.

Innocencius episcopus seruus seruorum dei . dilecto filio
archidiacono sancti Albani Lincolnien*sis* dio*cesis* (salutem . 7
apostolicam benediccionem . Precibus venerabilis fratris nostri . .
Lincolnien*sis* benignum impercientes assensum vt racione
5 visitacionis ecclesiis suis in prebendis canonicorum uel commune
capituli Lincolnien*sis* 7 aliis ecclesiis parochialibus ciuitatis
7 dio*cesis* Lincolnien*sis* a diocesano episcopo (qui pro tempore
fuerit inpendende procuracionem dilecti filii capitulum
Lincolnien*se* 7 rectores parochialium ecclesiarum ciuitatis
10 7 dio*cesis* Lincolnien*sis* eidem episcopo minime soluere
teneantur (auctoritate litterarum nostrarum eis duximus
indulgendum . Quocirca discrecioni tue per apostolica scripta
mandamus quatinus prefatos capitulum 7 rectores non permittas contra concessionis nostre tenorem super hiis ab
15 aliquibus indebite molestari . Molestatores huiusmodi (per
censuram ecclesiasticam (appellacione postposita compescendo . non obstante si aliquibus de partibus illis quod
excommunicari (suspendi uel interdici non valeant a sede
apostolica sit indultum 7 quauis alia ipsius sedis indulgencia (
20 per quam id impediri uel differri possit 7 de qua specialiter
oporteat in presentibus fieri mencionem . Dat' Lugdun'
.iiij. nonas Augusti pontificatus nostri anno octauo.

Marginalia : *title*, Execucio de eodem (Q).
Texts : MS—A.

Folio 177d.
Hdl.　　　Copie litterarum apostolicarum pro septimis (14 cent.)

891

263. Confirmation by pope Innocent [IV] of an ordinance
made by the dean and chapter, on the authority of a precept of
pope Alexander [III] (see no. 257, above), that a canon who does
not make residence in the church of Lincoln continually, or for
the greater part of the year, shall pay one-seventh of the revenues
of his prebend to the common of the dean and chapter. At
Perugia. 22 January, 1252.

Innocencius episcopus seruus seruorum dei dilectis filiis
. . decano 7 capitulo Lincolnien*sibus* . salutem 7 apostolicam
benediccionem . Iustis petencium desideriis dignum est nos
facilem prebere concensum 7 vota que a racionis tramite non
5 discordant effectu prosequente complere . Sane porrecta
nobis . ex parte vestra peticio continebat (quod cum felicis
recordacionis Alexander papa . predecessor noster . . decano
7 capitulo Linc' ecclesie suis dedisset litteris in preceptis (
vt canonicos ipsius ecclesie nisi moniti ab eisdem decano
10 7 capitulo in dicta ecclesia essent assidue aut per maiorem

partem anni deseruirent in ea (multarent in propriis beneficiis
prout expedire viderent . iidem decanus 7 capitulum auctoritate
huiusmodi precepti deliberacione prouida statuerunt (ut canonicus qui in eadem ecclesia residenciam predictam facere non
15   curauerit (monitus a . . decano 7 capitulo ecclesie nominate .
septimam partem prouentuum prebende sue Lincolnien*sis*
quam diu absens fuerit soluat commune decani 7 capituli
predictorum . Quare nobis humiliter supplicastis ut cum in
poscessione[1] percipiendi existatis partem predictam statutum
20   huiusmodi confirmare de benignitate sedis apostolice dignaremur . Nos igitur vestris supplicacionibus inclinati (quod a
predictis decano 7 capitulo prouide factum est (in hac parte (
ratum 7 gratum habentes illud (auctoritate apostolica (confirmamus (7 presentis scripti patrocinio communimus . Nulli
25   ergo omnino hominum liceat hanc paginam nostre confirmacionis infringere uel ei ausu temerario contraire . Si quis autem
hoc attemptare presumserit (indignacionem omnipotentis dei
7 beatorum Petri 7 Pauli apostolorum eius se nouerit incursurum . Dat' Perusii .xj. kalendas . Februarii pontificatus
30   nostri . anno . nono .

Marginalia : *opp. l. 1*, .XI.
Text : MS—A.
Var. R. : [1] *sic.*
Note : The name given to the seventh part mentioned in the text was *Septimae*
or *Septisms*, and the payment was made on the *taxatio* or rateable value or estimated net annual income of each prebend.   A canon was said, in technical language,
to pay the ' septism ' of his ' taxation ' (*Linc. Cath. Statutes* i, 129 ; ii, pp. cc, cci ;
iii, 577, 656*n*).   John de Schalby gives, in tabular form, a ' taxatio prebendarum
secundum quam soluitur septima non residencium ' (*ibid.*, iii, 171–2).

892

264.   Mandate of pope Innocent [IV] to [Richard] the abbot
and the prior of Roche and the prior of Worksop.   Whereas the
pope has confirmed an ordinance which has prevailed for forty years
and more in the church of Lincoln, that those canons who do not
make personal residence for the third part of the year shall deliver
a seventh part of the yield of their prebends to the canons who
reside, the pope commands the abbot and priors not to allow the
dean and chapter to be molested contrary to the tenor of this indult.
At Perugia.   18 December, 1251.

Innocencius episcopus seruus seruorum dei . dilectis filiis
. . abbati . 7 . . priori de Rupe Cisterciensis ordinis . ac . .
priori de Wirichsob Ebor*acensis* dioc*esis* . salutem . 7 apostolicam benediccionem . Peticio dilectorum filiorum . . decani
5   7 capituli Lincolnien*sium* nobis exibita continebat . quod
in eorum ecclesia per quatraginta annos 7 amplius est pacifice
obseruatum vt canonici eidem[1] ecclesie qui per terciam par**t**em

anni residenciam in ea non faciant personalem septimam
partem prouentuum prebendarum suarum exibeant canonicis
10 residentibus in eadem 7 ipsi sint in pocessione¹ pacifica percipiendi huiusmodi porcionem . Nos igitur eorundem decani
7 capituli supplicacionibus inclinati huiusmodi consuetudinem
ratam 7 gratam habentes eam auctoritate apostolica duximus
confirmandam . Quocirca discrecioni vestre per apostolica
15 scripta mandamus . quatinus dictos decanum 7 capitulum non
permittatis super hiis contra confirmacionis nostre tenorem
ab aliquibus indebite molestari . molestatores huiusmodi per
censuram ecclesiasticam appellacione postposita compescendo .
non obstante si est aliquibus ab apostolica sede indultum quod
20 interdici suspendi uel excommunicari non possint per litteras
apostolicas que de indulto huiusmodi non fecerint mencionem
sine aliqua alia indulgencia sedis eiusdem per quam effectus
presencium inpediri valeat uel differri . Quod si non omnes
hiis exequendis potueritis interesse . duo vestrum ea nichil-
25 hominus exequantur . Dat' Perusii .xv. kalendas Ianuarii
pontificatus nostri . anno nono.

Marginalia: *title*, de eodem.
Texts: MS—A. Pd.—*Cal. Papal Letters* i, 275 (abs.).   Élie Berger, tom. iii
(Paris, 1897), p. 14, no. 5515 (abs.).
Var. R.: ¹ *sic.*
Note: The prior of Roche as an addressee is omitted in Bliss's abstract (*Cal.
Papal Letters*), but that writer is not always very accurate. Berger gives the
conseruatores as ' prior et abbas de Rupe, Cistertien. ordinis, ac prior de Wirichsob,
Eboracen. dioc.', with the same date as the mandate. It is strange that the prior
is named before his abbot. In no. 265, below, he is not mentioned.

893

265. Mandate of pope Innocent [IV] to [Richard] abbot of
Roche, the prior of Worksop, and the archdeacon of Nottingham
in the church of York, to restrain those who would hinder the
dean and chapter from receiving from the canons who do not make
residence the seventh part of the yield of the prebends. At Perugia.
27 January, 1252.

Innocencius episcopus seruus seruorum dei . dilectis filiis
. . abbati de Rupe Cisterciensis ordinis 7 . . priori de Wirichsob Eboracen*sis* diocesis 7 . . archidiacono Notinghamie in
ecclesia Eboracen*si** salutem et apostolicam benediccionem .
5 Porrecta nobis ex parte dilectorum filiorum . . decani 7
capituli Lincolniens*ium* peticio continebat (quod cum felicis
recordacionis Alexander papa predecessor noster . . decano 7
capitulo Lincolniens*is* ecclesie suis dedisset litteris in preceptis vt canonicos ipsius ecclesie nisi moniti ab eisdem decano
10 7 capitulo in dicta ecclesia essent assidue (aut per maiorem
partem anni deseruirent in ea multarent in propriis beneficiis
prout expedire viderent . iidem decanus 7 capitulum auctoritate

huiusmodi precepti deliberacione prouida statuerunt (ut
canonicus qui in eadem ecclesia residenciam predictam facere
15 non curauerit monitus a . . decano 7 capitulo ecclesie memorate . septimam partem prouentuum prebende sue Lincolnien*sis* quam diu absens fuerit (soluat commune decani
7 capituli predictorum . Quare nobis iidem decanus 7 capitulum
nobis humiliter supplicarunt (ut cum in poscessione[1] per-
20 cipiendi existant partem predictam statutum huiusmodi
confirmare de benignitate sedis apostolice dignaremur . Nos
igitur eorum supplicacionibus inclinati (quod a predictis
decano 7 capitulo prouide factum est in hac parte ratum 7
gratum habentes illud auctoritate apostolica duximus con-
25 firmandum . Quocirca discrecioni vestre per apostolica scripta
mandamus (quatinus non permittatis prefatos decanum
7 capitulum super hiis contra confirmacionis nostre tenorem
ab aliquibus indebite molestari . molestatores huiusmodi per
censuram ecclesiasticam appellacione postposita compescendo .
30 quod si non omnes hiis exequendis potueritis interesse (duo
vestrum ea nichilhominus exequantur . Dat' Perusii .vj.
kalendas . Februarii pontificatus nostri anno nono.

Marginalia: *title*, De eodem (Q).
Text: MS—A.
Var. R.: [1] *sic.*

Folio 179 [178 *has been missed out in numbering the leaves*].

Hdl.   De priuilegiis (Q).

894

266. Confirmation by pope Innocent [IV] of the custom which
has prevailed in the church of Lincoln for forty years and more,
that the canons who do not make personal residence in the church
during the third part of the year shall deliver the seventh part of
the revenues of their prebends to the canons who reside. At
Perugia. 18 December, 1251.

Innocencius episcopus seruus seruorum dei . dilectis filiis
. . decano 7 capitulo Lincolnien*sibus* salutem 7 apostolicam
benediccionem . Peticio uestra nobis exhibita contineat[1] quod
in ecclesia vestra per quatraginta annos 7 amplius est pacifice
5 obseruatum ut canonici eiusdem ecclesie qui per terciam
partem anni residenciam in ea non faciunt personalem septimam partem prouentuum[2] prebendarum suarum exhibeant
canonicis residentibus in eadem 7 vos estis in possessione
pacifica percipiendi huiusmodi porcionem . nos igitur vestris
10 supplicacionibus inclinati huiusmodi consuetudinem ratam 7
gratam habentes eam auctoritate apostolica confirmamus 7
presentis scripti patrocinio communimus . Nulli ergo omnino

hominum liceat hanc paginam nostre confirmacionis infringere
uel ei ausu temerario contraire . Si quis autem hoc attemptare
15 presumpserit indignacionem omnipotentis dei 7 beatorum
Petri 7 Pauli apostolorum eius se nouerit incursurum . Dat'
Perusii .xv. kalendas Ianuarii pontificatus nostri anno .
nono.

Marginalia: *title*, de eodem (Q). *opp. l. 5*, Nota quod dicitur recidere [*sic*] per
terciam partem anni (14 cent.).
Texts: MS—A. Pd.—*Cal. Papal Letters* i, 275 (abs.). Élie Berger, tom. iii
(Paris, 1897), p. 14, no. 5515 (abs.).
Var. R.: ¹ *sic*. ² *corrected from* prouenituum.

895

267. Letter of pope Alexander [IV], beseeching [Godfrey de
Ludham] archbishop of York not to demand the revenues of the
first year after vacancy of the churches of Mansfield and [South]
Leverton [co. Nottingham], which are in his diocese (since these
churches were assigned to the deanery of Lincoln), by virtue of a
papal indult giving him the revenues of the first year after vacancy
of churches in the city and diocese of York, since the said indult
was not intended to include the income of churches assigned to
parsonages and dignities of other dioceses. At Anagni. 24 April,
1259.

　　Alexander episcopus seruus seruorum dei . venerabili
fratri . . archiepiscopo Eboracensi (salutem 7 apostolicam
benediccionem . Ex parte dilecti filii . . decani Lincolniensis
fuit propositum coram nobis quod cum tibi a . sede apostolica
5 sit indultum (ut prouentus primi anni beneficiorum que in
ciuitate ac diocesi Eboracensibus usque ad certum tempus
vacare contigerit (possis percipere in solucionem debitorum
quibus premitur Eboracensis ecclesia conuertendos (in
decanatu Lincolniensi vacante prouentus primi anni eccle-
10 siarum de Mammefeld' 7 de Leyretona eiusdem diocesis que
predicto decanatui pro eius supportandis oneribus sunt
concesse pretextu indulti huiusmodi contendis percipere in
ipsius decani preiudicium 7 grauamen . vnde nobis humiliter
supplicauit (ut cum ecclesie ipse ab antiquo dicto decanatui
15 assignate fuerint* pro ipsius oneribus supportandis (7 decani
Lincolnienses qui fuere pro tempore illas pacifice tenuerint
7 quiete prouidere in hac parte sibi paterna diligencia curaremus . Cum itaque nostre intencionis non fuerit per tale
indultum concedere tibi prouentus ecclesiarum assignatarum
20 personatibus 7 dignitatibus aliarum diocesum pro ipsarum
oneribus supportandis (etiam si ecclesie ipse in tua diocesi
predicta consistant fraternitati tue per apostolica scripta
mandamus (quatinus indultum ipsum ad huiusmodi ecclesias

non extendens (earum fructus ab eodem decanatu eius
25 pretextu non exigas (sed ipsos dictum decanum libere percipere
7 absque qualibet molestacione permittas . alioquin dilecto
filio . . priori sancte Fredeswide Oxonie Linc' diocesis litteris
nostris iniungimus (ut te 7 quemlibet alium pro te ac predicta
Eboracensi ecclesia (ab ipsius decani super eisdem fructibus
30 molestacione desistere monicione premissa auctoritate nostra
sublato cuiuslibet appellacionis impedimento compellat (non
obstantibus indulto (huiusmodi 7 indulgencia qua tibi a predicta sede dicitur esse concessum (quod interdicti¹ (suspendi (
uel excommunicari non possis per litteras apostolicas plenam
35 7 expressam non facientes de indulto huiusmodi mencionem
7 qualibet alia prefate sedis indulgencia per quam effectus
presencium impediri valeat uel differri . Dat' Anagnie .viij.
kalendas . Maij pontificatus nostri anno quinto.

Marginalia : opp. l. 1, .XII. opp. l. 5, Nota pro decano (14 cent.).
Text : MS—A.
Var. R. : ¹ recte interdici.

*Folio 179d.

896

268. Mandate of pope Alexander [IV], commanding the prior
of Saint Frideswide, Oxford, to enforce the execution of the next
preceding mandate. At Anagni. 24 April, 1259.

Alexander episcopus seruus seruorum dei . dilecto filio . .
priori sancte Fredeswide Oxonie Lincolniensis¹ diocesis salutem
et apostolicam benediccionem . Ex parte dilecti filii . . decani
Lincolniensis fuit propositum coram nobis quod cum venerabili
5 fratri nostro . . archiepiscopo Eboracensi a sede apostolica
sit indultum ut prouentus primi anni beneficiorum que in
ciuitate ac diocesi Eboracensibus² usque ad certum tempus
uacare contigerit possit idem archiepiscopus percipere in
solucionem debitorum quibus premitur Eboracensis² ecclesia
10 conuertendos ? ipse decanatu Lincolniensi¹ uacante prouentus
primi anni ecclesiarum de Mammefeld³ et de Leyrtona eiusdem
diocesis que predicto decanatui pro eius supportandis oneribus
sunt concesse pretextu indulti huiusmodi contendit percipere
in ipsius decani preiudicium et grauamen . Vnde nobis pre-
15 fatus decanus humiliter supplicauit ut cum ecclesie ipse ab
antiquo dicto decanatui concesse fuerint pro ipsius oneribus
supportandis et decani Lincolnienses¹ qui fuere pro tempore
illas pacifice tenuerint et quiete prouidere in hac parte sibi
paterna diligencia curaremus . Cum itaque nostre intencionis
20 non fuerit per tale indultum concedere ipsi arch[iepiscopo⁴]
prouentus ecclesiarum assignatarum personatibus et dignitatibus aliarum diocesum pro ipsorum oneribus supportandis
eciam si ecclesie ipse [in] sua diocesi [predicta consis⁴]tant

eidem archiepiscopo nostris damus litteris in mandatis ut
25 ipsum indultum ad huiusmodi ecclesias non extendens earum
fr[uctus ab eod⁴]em decano [eius⁴] pretextu non exigat set
ipsos dictum decanum libere percipere 7 absque qualibet
molestacione permittat . Quocirca discrecioni [tue per⁴]
apostolica scripta mandamus quatinus si mandatum nostrum
30 super hoc dictus archiepiscopus neglexerit adimplere tu ipsum
et quemlibet alium pro ipso et predicta ecclesia Eboracen*si*²
ab ipsius decani super eisdem fructibus molestacione desistere
monicione premissa auctoritate nostra sublato cuiuslibet
appellacionis impedimento compellas⁵ non obstantibus indulto
35 huiusmodi 7 indulgencia qua eidem archiepiscopo a predicta
sede dicitur esse concessum quod interdici suspendi uel excommunicari non possit per litteras apostolicas plenam 7
expressam non facientes de indulto huiusmodi mencionem .
et qualibet alia prefate sedis* indulgencia per quam effectus
40 presencium impediri ualeat uel differri . Dat' Anagnie viij
kalendas Maii pontificatus⁶ anno quinto.

Marginalia in A : *title*, Executor*ia* de eodem (14 cent.).
Texts : MS—Orig. ᴅij/57/1/2. A.
Endorsed : (1) . . . . nacione fruct*uum* primi anni de beneficiis decanatus Linc'
in Ebor' diocesi soluat' (13 cent.). (2) . . . . Henr' noster procurator iste signaretur
ad dupplicandum (14 cent.). (3) Testamentes de prebendes proued before the
deane and chapter with their inuentoryes and some proued in ye olde mynster
fee (16 cent. This endorsement has nothing to do with the present text).
The name ' Hayneton ' has been written three times by a 15th century hand
at the head of the original charter.
Seal torn away. Size : 15¾ x 11½ inches.
Var. R. in A : ¹ Linc'. ² Ebor'. ³ Mammesfelde. ⁴ *supplied from A, the original
having been injured.* ⁵ copellas. ⁶ *insert* nostri.

Folio 180.

Hdl.   De priuilegiis (Q).

897

269. Mandate of pope Clement [IV], enjoining [William of
Langton] dean of York to prevent those who shall molest the dean
and chapter of Lincoln contrary to the indults of privileges granted
by the apostolic see. At Viterbo. 20 June, 1268.

Clemens episcopus seruus seruorum dei . dilecto filio . .
decano Ebor*acensi* (salutem 7 apostolicam benediccionem . Sub
religionis habitu studio vacantibus pie uite ita debemus esse
propicii (quod in diuinis benep*l*acitis exequendis malignorum
5 non possint obstaculis impediri . Cum igitur dilecti filii . .
decanus 7 capitulum ecclesie Lincolnien*sis* a nonnullis sicut
accepimus (qui nomen domini in uacuum recipere non for-
midant (diuersas paciantur iniurias et iacturas (nos uolentes
7 eorundem decani 7 capituli prouidere quieti 7 peruersorum
10 conatibus obuiare discrecioni tue per apostolica scripta mandamus (quatinus ipsos decanum 7 capitulum fauoris oportuni

presidiis prosequens non permittas eos contra indulta priui-
legiorum sedis apostolice ab aliquibus indebite molestari .
molestatores huiusmodi per censuram ecclesiasticam appella-
15 cione postposita compescendo . actenus prouisurus ne de hiis
que cause cognicionem exigunt (uel que indulta huiusmodi
non contingunt (te aliquatenus intromittas . Nos enim si
secus presumpseris (tam presentes litteras (quam eciam
processum (quem per te illarum auctoritate haberi contigerit (
20 omnino carere viribus (ac nullius fore decernimus firmitatis .
Huiusmodi ergo mandatum nostrum sic sapienter 7 fideliter
exequaris (vt eius fines quomodo . libet non excedas . Presentibus post triennium minime valiturus¹ . Dat᾽ Viterbii
.xij. kalendas Iulii . pontificatus nostri anno quarto.

Marginalia: *opp. l. 1*, .XIII.   *opp. l. 22*,
Text: MS—A.
Var. R.: ¹ *recte* valituris.

898

270. Mandate of pope Honorius [IV], enjoining [Robert of
Wainfleet] abbot of Bardney publicly in the churches to admonish
those sons of iniquity, who withhold tithes and other possessions
from the dean and chapter of Lincoln, to restore them and make
due satisfaction; and should they fail to do this within the time
appointed by him, the abbot shall inflict on them the sentence of
excommunication. At Rome. 9 February, 1286.

Honorius episcopus seruus seruorum dei . dilecto filio . .
abbati monasterii de Bardeneye . Linc' diocesis (salutem 7
apostolicam benediccionem . Significauit¹ nobis dilecti filii . .
decanus 7 capitulum ecclesie Linc') quod nonnulli iniquitatis
5 filii quos prorsus ignorant) decimas) redditus) census)
legata) instrumenta publica) terras) domos) prata) pascua)
nemora) molendina) possessiones) 7 alia bona ad ecclesiam
ipsam spectancia temere . ac maliciose . occultare et occulte .
detinere presumunt) non curantes ea ipsis decano 7 capitulo
10 exhibere . in animarum suarum periculum . et predicte ecclesie
non modicum detrimentum . super quo iidem decanus 7
capitulum apostolice sedis remedium implorarunt . Quocirca
discrecioni tue per apostolica scripta mandamus) quatinus
omnes huiusmodi detentores occultos decimarum) reddituum
15 7 aliorum bonorum predictorum ex parte nostra publice in
ecclesiis coram populo per te uel per alium moneas) ut infra
competentem terminum quem ei² prefixeris ea predictis
decano 7 capitulo a se debita restituant 7 reuelent) ac de
ipsis plenum² et debitam eis satisfactionem impendant . Et
20 si non impleuerint infra alium terminum competentem quem
eis ad hoc peremptorie duxeris prefigendum ex tunc in eos

generalem excommunicacionis sentenciam proferas 7 eam ubi
7 quando expedire videris facias usque ad satisfactionem
condignam solempniter publicari . Dat' . Rom' apud
25 sanctam Sabinam .vj. idus . Februarii . pontificatus nostri .
anno . primo.

Marginalia: *opp. l. 1*, .XIIII. *opp. ll. 2–10*, Sentencia per apostolicam [sedem],
super detentores decimarum reddituum legatorum terrarum domorum pratorum
pascuarum molendinorum possessionum 7 aliarum [*sic*] bonorum ad capitulum
pertinencium (14 cent.).
Text: MS.—A.
Var. R.: ¹ *recte* Significauerunt.　² *sic*.

899

271. Mandate of [Robert of Wainfleet] abbot of Bardney,
enjoining the archdeacons of the diocese of Lincoln or their officials
to cause the next preceding mandate of pope Honorius to be published in every parish church; and, failing restitution by the
offenders before the feast of the Exaltation of the Holy Cross [14
September], to cause a general sentence of the greater excommunication to be promulged. At Bardney. 4 July, 1286.

. . permissione diuina abbas monasterii de Bardeneya Linc'
diocesis (executor in hac parte mandati apostolici deputatus :
venerabilibus viris 7 discretis dominis . . archidiaconis uel
eorundem . . officialibus vniuersis per dictam diocesim
5 constitutis (salutem in eo quem peperit uterus virginalis .
Litteras sanctissimi patris nostri (domini Honorii pape .iiij^ti.
recepimus formam 7 tenorem continentes de uerbo
ad uerbum inferius* annotatos . Honorius episcopus seruus
seruorum [*the next preceding mandate is recited word for word*].
10 Harum igitur auctoritate litterarum vobis in uirtute obediencie
qua sedi apostolice tenemini) firmiter iniungendo mandamus)
quatinus quilibet vestrum in singulis ecclesiis parochialibus
sui archidiaconatus diebus dominicis 7 festiuis infra missarum
solempnia post lecta ewangelia) indicto districtius interim
15 parochianis 7 ceteris tunc presentibus silencio) omnes 7 singulos
huiusmodi decimarum reddituum censuum legatorum) instru-
mentorum publicorum) terrarum) domorum) pratorum)
pascuarum) nemorum) molendinorum) possessionum necnon bonorum aliorum ad ecclesiam Linc' spectantium ante-
20 dictam) temere 7 maliciose detentores occultos) per locorum
capellanos publice moneri faciat) ut citra festum Assumpcionis
beate virginis : premissa que decano 7 capitulo memoratis
debentur ab ipsis) reuelent 7 restituere non omittant) ac
eciam de premissis plenariam prout iustum fuerit) eis satis-
25 factionem) impendant . Qui si sic moniti) id efficere non
curauerint : prefigat ex tunc) nichilominus ex habundanti
palam 7 expresse eisdem detentoribus occultis in genere

festum exultacionis[1] sancte Crucis tunc proximo futurum pro
termino peremptorio ⟩ vt infra dictum festum prefatis decano
30 7 capitulo ⟩ plenarie satisfaciant in hac parte . alioquin ⸲ in
ipsos maioris excommunicacionis sentenciam publice 7 sollempniter ⟩ pulsatis campanis ⟩ candelis accensis in singulis
ecclesiis archidiaconatus sui singulis diebus dominicis 7
festiuis intra missarum sollempnia silencio tunc presentibus
35 sicut premittitur imposito ⸲ promulgari faciat generalem .
quousque iidem detentores occulti premissorum ad cor reuersi ⟩
beneficium absolutionis a nobis forma iuris exinde meruerint
optinere . aliudque super hoc ex parte nostra receperitis in
mandatis . Et quid in premissis feceritis ⸲ nobis seu pocius
40 dictis decano 7 capitulo distincte 7 aperte litteris vestris
patentibus harum seriem continentibus ⟩ vna cum nominibus
eorundem ⟩ de quibus per famam ⟩ seu rei euidenciam . vel alio
modo legittimo nobis constiterit in hac parte ⸲ citra festum
Omnium Sanctorum significare curetis . Valete semper in
45 Christo Ihesu 7 virgine gloriosa . Dat' apud Bardeneyam .iiij.
nonas . Iulii . anno domini . M⁰ . CC⁰ octogesimo sexto.

Marginalia: *title*, Execucio de eodem (*query* Q). *opp. l. 1*, nota. *opp. l. 46*, anno
1286 (modern).
Text: MS—A.
Var. R.: [1] *sic.*

Folio 180d.
At foot of folio 180d. Item de eodem (query Q).

Folio 181.
Hdl.   De priuilegiis (Q).

900

272. Mandate of W[illiam de la Gare] archdeacon of Lincoln,
enjoining the deans throughout his archdeaconry to execute or
cause to be executed the next preceding mandate of the abbot of
Bardney. At Corringham [co. Lincoln]. 21 July, 1286.

.W. archidiaconus Linc' dilectis sibi in Christo vniuersis
. . decanis per archidiaconatum Linc' constitutis salutem
in omnium saluatore . Litteras religiosi viri domini . . dei
gracia abbatis de Bardeneye executoris in hac parte mandati
5 apostolici deputati nuper recepimus 7 inspecsimus sub hac
forma uerborum . . Permissione diuina abbas monasterii de
Bardeneye 7 cetera ut proximo supra . Nos itaque uolentes
reuerenter ut tenemur executorii antedicti mandatis . immo
veracius apostolicis in hac parte parerere[1] . ac premissa eo
10 libencius prosequi cum effectu ⟩ quo reuerendam matricem
ecclesiam nostram prefatam cui ex affectu pecculiariter
tenemur astricti ⸲ contingere dinoscuntur ⸲ vobis in uirtute
obediencie . nec non sub pena canonice districcionis firmiter

iniungimus 7 mandamus) quatinus diligenter inspecto huius
15　mandati tenore) 7 eciam plenius intellecto ⸴ vnusquisque
vestrum quatenus ad ipsum pertinet in hac parte) omnia
7 singula in eodem mandato contenta iuxta formam 7 tenorem
ipsius ⸴ vice nostra 7 auctoritate predicta) adhibitis super
hoc omnimoda diligencia 7 fauore) demandet siue faciat
20　execucionem debite demandari . Et quid exinde feceritis ⸴
nobis citra festum Omnium Sanctorum superius annotatum)
distinctius 7 apercius intimetis per vestras patentes litteras
harum seriem continentes) Valete) Dat' apud Coringham
.xv. kalendas Augusti anno domini . Mᵒ. CCᵒ. octogesimo
25　sexto.

Marginalia: *opp. l. 24*, aᵒ *1286* (modern).
Text: MS—A.
Var. R.: ¹ *sic.*

901

273. Notification by pope Innocent [IV] to [Robert Grosse-
teste] bishop of Lincoln of the definitive papal sentence that the
bishop is to be admitted to visit the dean and chapter, canons,
clerks of the choir, and servants, and also the vicars, chaplains, and
parishioners of the prebendal churches and of the churches of
dignities and of the common; and to correct abuses; and
that the dean and chapter shall not pay procuration for visitation
in their cathedral church; but that the canons shall not be bound
to take an oath of obedience to the bishop. At Lyons. 25 August,
1245.

Innocentius episcopus seruus seruorum dei . venerabili fratri
. . episcopo Linc') salutem 7 apostolicam benedictionem . Inter
cetera que nostrum animum qui uniuersali regimini quamuis
immeriti disponente domino presidemus insultibus impetunt
5　successiuis ⸍ illud nos frequenti meditacione purget¹ ut ecclesie
causarum calumpniis agitare non deficiant sub dispendiis
questionum et litibus que propter intricaciones 7 diffugia
parcium videntur fieri quodammodo immortales ⸍ finis debitus
imponatur . Cum igitur inter te ex parte vna et . . decanum
10　7 capitulum Linc' ex altera ⸴ super eorum 7 ecclesiarum
prebendalium ac ecclesiarum de dignitatibus 7 communia
visitatione 7 reformacione morum ac correctione tam decani
quam canonicorum 7 clericorum chori 7 eciam ministrorum .
ac vicariorum 7 capellanorum 7 parochianorum dictarum
15　omnium ecclesiarum nec non reuerencia 7 obediencia canonica
tibi ab eis prestanda 7 quibusdam aliis dignitatem 7 officium
episcopale contingentibus suborta fuisset materia questionis)
nos post diuersas commissiones hinc inde ab apostolica sede
ad iudices diuersos obtentas 7 processus habitos per easdem

P

20 causam ipsam finem sibi cupientes imponi ad examen nostrum
duximus reuocandam . Cumque tu et . . procurator ²partis
alterius² in nostra essetis presencia constituti fuit ex tua
parte propositum) quod cum ex diligencia pastoralis officii
tenearis de iure communi capitulum Linc' 7 omnes ecclesias
25 prebendales 7 ecclesias de dignitatibus 7 communia³ visitare)
ac ea secundum formam iuris que ad visitacionis spectant
officium adimplere) cum tam capitulum quam ecclesie tibi
sint de iure communi subiecte necnon excessus tam decani
quam canonicorum vniuersorum 7* singulorum 7 clericorum
30 de choro 7 ministrorum eorundem . vicariorum que⁴ eciam
capellanorum 7 parochianorum predictarum ecclesiarum corrigere) ac eorum mores ne ipsorum sanguis de tuis requiratur
manibus reformare) causas eciam omnium predictorum quas
ad inuicem eos promouere⁵ contingeret . uel ipsi contra alios
35 tue diocesis uel alii contra ipsos siue sint ciuiles siue criminales
examinare ac decidere ad te tanquam ad ordinarium pertineat)
dum tamen ad ecclesiasticum forum spectent . . Decanus
7 capitulum Linc' se tibi super hiis contra iusticiam opponebant propter quod premissa libere non poteras prout officii
40 tui cura exigit adimplere . Adiciebas preterea quod cum sis
caput Linc' ecclesie 7 a te tanquam a capite ante electionem
decani Linc' celebrandam tuus de iure sit ⁶requirendus assensus⁶
ipsi tua requisita licencia se debere ad electionem decani
procedere asseuerant . super quo tibi petebas iusticiam
45 exiberi . Dicebas preterea quod cum decanus in sui⁷ confirmacione 7 canonici cum prebende ipsis conferentur iurare
tibi de iure canonicam obedienciam teneantur . iidem id
hactenus indebite facere non curarunt . Proponebas insuper
quod cum lege dioceana decanatus dignitatum 7 prebendarum
50 vacancium sequestracio ad te de iure pertineat) Prefati
decanus 7 capitulum se tibi super hoc contra iusticiam
opponebant . Quare petebas super premissis ius tuum declarari (
ac adiudicari tibi per diffinitiuam⁸ sentenciam teque ad
visitacionis officium in capitulo Linc' 7 ecclesiis prebendalibus
55 de dignitatibus 7 communia³ 7 ad correctionem excessuum
7 morum reformacionem omnium predictorum (non obstante
decani 7 canonicorum reclamacione admitti debere diffinitiue
pronunciari ac imponi eis ⁹perpetuum silencium⁹ nisi sedis
apostolice priuilegio uel alio iure speciali iuste tueri se possent
60 super impedimentis 7 obstaculis supradictis . Petebas eciam
procuracionem racione visitationis capituli debitam 7 expensas
faciendas in lite ac ut ipsi quocienscumque te ad ecclesiam
Linc' venire contigerit contra te pulsare faciant 7 exibeant
tibi reuerenciam tanquam patri . quodque decanus aliquem
65 canonicum ad iurandum ei canonicam obedienciam nisi
dignitas episcopalis 7 auctoritas excipiatur¹⁰) decetero non

compellat . nec cogat canonicos iurare aliquas consuetudines
que sint contra canonicas sancciones (neque statuta que
sint contra canones 7 auctoritatem aut dignitatem episcopalem
70 ulterius in capitulo isto edat . Petebas insuper ut cum prebendarum 7 ecclesiarum de dignitatibus 7 communia[3] [11]visitatio
ad te de iure communi pertineat (quod decanus decetero ab
earum[11] visitacione desistere per sentenciam cogeretur . Procurator uero partis alterius litem contestando respondit (
75 narrata non esse vera ut narrabantur 7 petita fieri non debere .
Lite igitur super hiis legittime contestata racionibus quoque
ac allegacionibus utriusque partis diligenter auditis nos
postquam fuit cause conclusum deliberacione habita diligenti . de fratrum nostrorum consilio pronunciauimus te ad
80 visitacionem tam decani 7 capituli quam canonicorum clericorum chori ac ministrorum vicariorum eciam capellanorum
ecclesiarum 7 parochianorum ad omnes predictas ecclesias
pertinencium . 7 ad correccionem excessuum ac morum
reformacionem libere admittendum . Pro visitacione[11a] in
85 cathedrali ecclesia facienda procuracio a capitulo non prestetur .
Excessus tamen canonicorum cathedralis ecclesie qui consueuerunt corrigi per capitulum per ipsum iuxta eiusdem
ecclesie consuetudinem hactenus pacifice obseruatam ad
comonicionem[12] 7 iussionem tuam successorumque tuorum
90 infra conpetentem[13] terminum eis prefigendum a te uel eisdem
successoribus corrigantur . Alioquin ex tunc tu uel successores
ipsi deum habentes pre oculis ipsos ut animarum cura requirit
per censuram ecclesiasticam corrigatis . Mandamus eciam
ut predicti canonici tibi canonicam obedienciam 7 reuerenciam
95 exibeant 7 obseruent . obligare se tamen[14] ad hoc iuramento
manuali prestacione seu promissione minime teneantur .
cum ad hoc consuetudine non iuueris In ceteris petitis ab
impetitione tua prefatos decanum 7 capitulum absoluentes .
Nulli ergo omnino hominum liceat hanc paginam nostre
100 diffinicionis infringere uel ei ausu temerario contraire . Si
quis autem hoc attemptare presumpserit indignacionem
omnipotentis dei 7 beatorum Petri 7 Pauli apostolorum eius
se nouerit incursurum . Dat' . Lugdun'[15] .viij. kalendas .
Septembris pontificatus nostri anno tercio.

Marginalia : *a title has been erased.* opp. *l. 1,* .XV. opp. *l. 50,* Nota pro
vacatione dignitatuum 7 prebendarum (14 cent.). opp. *l. 88,* Nota.
    Texts : MS—A.   Black Book, ff. 16–17d. The text of the bull is recited in
the Black Book in an *inspeximus* of bishop Grosseteste, which begins :
    Omnibus Christi fidelibus ad quos presens scriptum peruenerit) Robertus
    Dei gracia Lincolniensis episcopus) salutem in Domino . Litteras domini
    pape[16] non cancellatas) nec abolitas) aut aliqua parte sui viciatas inspeximus
    in hec verba,
and ends :
    In huius igitur rei testimonium ; presenti scripto . sigillum nostrum duximus
    apponendum. (No date.)

and has the marginal note:
> Sentencia lata in curia Romana in causa mota inter quondam Robertum Grosetesth episcopum Lincolniensem ac . . . decanum et capitulum ecclesie Linc'.

The text of the Black Book has many corrections. Pd—*Linc., Cath. Statutes* i, 315–19. *Cal. Papal Registers, Papal Letters* i, 219 (abs.). Elie Berger, tom. i (Paris, 1884), p. 221, no. 1457. A. Potthast, *Regesta pontificum Romanorum*, no. 11833 (abs.).

Var. R. in Black Book: [1] perurget. [2-2] alterius partis. [3] communa. [4] *om.* que. [5] mouere. [6-6] assensus requirendus. [7] sua. [8] diffinitam. [9-9] silencium perpetuum. [10] excipiantur. [11-11] *om. Linc. Cath. Statutes.* [11a] *insert* autem. [12] commonicionem. [13] competentem. [14] tamen se. [15] Lugdon'; *printed* Bugdun' *in Linc. Cath. Statutes.* [16] pape *erased.*

*above, *Folio 181d.*

Hdl.   Prima pars .   Primus titulus (Q).

Folio 182.

Hdl.   Primus titulus prime partis (Q).

902

274. Mandate of pope Innocent [III], enjoining [Geoffrey Henlaw] bishop of Saint David's to preserve the dean and chapter of Lincoln from disturbance in their ancient customs which the pope has thought good to confirm to them. At the Lateran. 18 December, 1208.

Innocencius episcopus seruus seruorum dei[1] (venerabili fratri[2] . . episcopo Meneuensi salutem 7 apostolicam benediccionem . Cum antiquas 7 racionabiles consuetudines hactenus pacifice in Linc' ecclesia obseruatas (que canonicis non
5   obuiant institutis sicut racionabiliter dilecti filii . . decani 7 capitulum Linc' optinent (eis 7 per eos eidem ecclesie auctoritate apostolica duxerimus confirmandas (districtius inhibentes (ne quis consuetudines huiusmodi temere infringere uel immutare presumat fraternitati tue per apostolica scripta
10   mandamus (quatinus dictos decanum 7 capitulum non permittas super hiis contra confirmacionis 7 inhibicionis nostre tenorem ab aliquibus indebite molestari . molestatores huiusmodi per censuram ecclesiasticam appellacione postposita conpescendo . Non obstante si aliquibus de partibus illis a
15   sede apostolica sit indultum (quod suspendi uel interdici aut excommunicari non possint nisi de indulto huiusmodi sibi concesso (plena 7 expressa seu de uerbo ad uerbum in nostris litteris mencio habeatur . Dat' Lateran' .xv. kalendas Januarii pontificat' nostri anno vndecimo.

Marginalia: *opp. l. 1*, .XVI.   *opp. l. 4*, 🖙 .b. (indicating in conjunction with ' .a.' in the margin of no. 275 that the two charters are to be transposed, though there does not seem to be any valid reason for transposition). *opp. l. 10*, reperitur originale.
Text: MS—A.
Var. R.: [1] *The first five words were written by Q, who left Q2 to complete the document.* [2] *corrected from* patri.

903

275. Confirmation by pope Alexander [IV], to the dean and chapter, of the ancient and laudable customs observed in the church of Lincoln. At the Lateran. 4 April, 1256.

Alexander episcopus seruus seruorum dei . dilectis filiis
. . decano 7 capitulo Lincolnien*sibus*¹ . salutem . 7 apostolicam
benediccionem . Cum a nobis petitur quod iustum est 7
honestam tam uigor equitatis tam² ordo exigit racionis . vt
5   id per solicitudinem officii nostri ad debitum perducatur
effectum . Ea propter dilecti in domino filii uestris iustis
postulacionibus grato concurrentes assensu ad instar felicis
recordacionis Innocencii pape predecessoris nostri antiquas .
7 racionabiles consuetudines [hatenus³] pacifice in uestra
10   ecclesia obseruatas) que canonicis non obuiant institutis)
sicut [eas racion⁴]abiliter obtinetis⁵) uobis 7 per uos eidem
ecclesie) auctoritate apostolica confirmamus) 7 presentis
scripti patrocinio communimus districtius inhibentes ne quis
consuetudines huiusmodi temere infringere uel immutare
15   presumat . Nulli ergo omnino hominum liceat hanc paginam
nostre confirmacionis 7 inhibitionis infringere uel ei ausu
temerario contraire . Si quis autem hoc attemptare presumpserit indignacionem omnipotentis dei 7 beatorum Petri
7 Pauli apostolorum eius se nouerit incursurum . Dat' Lateran'
20   .ij. [nonas⁴] Aprilis pontificatus [nostri⁴] . anno secundo.

Endorsed : (1) Immo confirmacio generalis consuetudinum ecclesie Linc'. (*query*
Q).   (2) 7 de non immutand' (14 cent.).   (3) Confirmacio d*omini* Alexandri
pape iiij⁴ⁱ ; (13 cent.).   (4) Priuilegium domini Alexandri pape (13 cent.).   (5) XVI
(corresponding with the marginal number in A).
Seal torn off. Size : 10½ x 9½ inches.
Marginalia in A : *title*, De eodem (Q).   .a. (cp no. 274 marg.).   reperitur originale
(14 cent.).
Texts : MS—Orig. Dij/57/1/3. A.
Var. R. : ¹ Linc' A.   ² quam A.   ³ *sic* ;   *supplied from* A, *the original having
been injured.*   ⁴ *supplied from* A.   ⁵ optinetis A.

904

276. Indult of pope Alexander [IV], granting to the dean and chapter of Lincoln that they shall not, against their will, be summoned to judgement more than two days' journey from their church. At Viterbo. 3 July, 1257.

Alexander episcopus seruus seruuorum¹ dei (dilectis filiis
. . decano 7 capitulo Linc' (salutem 7 apostolicam benediccionem . Vestris supplicacionibus inpartientes benignum
assensum (vt per litteras apostolice sedis (uel legatorum
5   ipsius ultra duas dietas ab ecclesia uestra super que infra
illas habetis non possitis inuiti ad iudicium euocari auctoritate
vobis presencium indulgemus (nisi eedem ipsius sedis littere

plenam 7 expressam fecerint de hac indulgencia mencionem .
Nulli ergo omnino hominum liceat hanc paginam nostre con-
10 cessionis infringere (uel ei ausu temerario contraire . Si quis
autem hoc attemptare presumserit (indignacionem omnipotentis Dei 7 beatorum Petri 7 Pauli apostolorum eius se
nouerit incursurum (presentibus post triennium minime
valituris . Dat' Viterbii .v. nonas Julii pontificatus nostri
15 anno tercio.

Marginalia : *title*, Ne vltra duas dietas ab ecclesia (Q).   *opp. l. 1*, .XVII. .xvij.
Text : MS—A.
Var. R. : ¹ *sic*.

At this point the transcripts of papal bulls come to an end, and the
remaining third of folio 182 has been filled by Q with the titles, etc.,
of other bulls which, as he intended, were to be copied into the new
edition of the Registrum Antiquissimum.   The series of large roman
numerals in the margin is continued ; but the later series of arabic
figures ceases until the episcopal charters begin with A905.   It
has been possible to supply, from various sources, most of the bulls
indicated by Q, and for the sake of convenience these documents are
here numbered A904a to A904d.

[904a]

277. .XVIII. De capellis de Aylesbir' appropriatis capitulo
(Q).

Adrianus etc.) littere papales sunt in [*query* primo *interlineated*]
cofino longo . sub predicto numero (Q).

The note littere papales etc. *probably refers to the papal documents*
in general, and not merely to the bulls about Aylesbury.   The predictus
numerus *is* I *or* A, *that is, the* primus titulus prime partis *of the*
proposed new Registrum. (See p. 186 above.)

The bull about the chapels of Aylesbury is no longer to be found
at Lincoln, but its provisions may be deduced from the next document,
no. 278, which also indicates that the pope in no. 277 is Adrian V,
and the date 1276.

[904b]

278. XIX De diuisione prebende prebende [*sic*] de Aylesbiria
(Q).

Nicolaus episcopus seruus seruorum (Q).

The original text has disappeared, but fortunately the bull is recited
in the charter of bishop Oliver Sutton which is printed below.

Notification by bishop Oliver that he has received a mandate
of pope Nicholas [IV], to this effect :

The pope informs the bishop that, the late Percival de
Lavagna, brother of the late pope Adrian [V], who obtained

the archdeaconry of Buckingham, and also a canonry and prebend, having died at Rome, he has reserved those benefices to his own gift; and he commands the bishop to confer the archdeaconry, and also the prebend which the bishop has by apostolic authority divided into two parts, on men of English birth and lawful parentage, who are either masters of theology or doctors in decrees or professors in civil law; and the pope enjoins that he on whom the archdeaconry shall be conferred shall reside personally, but that after his death it shall remain in its former liberty; and that those who shall be appointed to the prebends shall in future make perpetual residence. At Saint Mary Major's, Rome, 22 April, 1290.

The bishop, therefore, on the authority of this mandate, has conferred the archdeaconry of Buckingham on master Richard of Saint Frideswide, doctor in canon law; and regarding the prebend of Aylesbury [co. Buckingham], which formerly consisted of the church of Aylesbury with the chapel of Milton [near Thame, co. Oxford], he has, by papal authority, thought good to divide it into two parts, namely, the church of Milton, which was formerly a chapel, but shall henceforth be a separate prebend, and the church of Aylesbury; saving to the chapter of Lincoln the chapels of Quarrendon, Bierton, Stoke [Mandevill], and Buckland [co. Buckingham], which formerly belonged to the prebend of Aylesbury, but were granted by papal authority to the bishop himself. Further, the bishop has conferred the newly ordained prebend of Aylesbury on Richard de Hetherington, and the newly established prebend of Milton on John of Monmouth. August, 1290.

Vniuersis ad quorum noticiam presens scriptum peruenerit ⁚ Oliuerus permissione diuina Linc'[1] episcopus salutem in salutis auctore . Mandatum sanctissimi patris domni Nicolai pape quarti recepimus sub hac forma . Nicolaus episcopus
5 seruus seruorum dei venerabili fratri . . episcopo Lincolnen'[1] salutem 7 apostolicam benedictionem . Ad tuam volumus peruenire noticiam quod quondam Perceuallus de Lauannia felicis recordacionis Adriani pape predecessoris nostri germanus ⟩ qui sicut tua discrecio non ignorat in ecclesia Linc'[1]
10 archidiaconatum Buckinghamie nec non 7 canonicatum ac prebendam optinuit dum viuebat ⟩ nuper in urbe sicut domino placuit debitum nature persoluit . Nos autem archidiaconatum 7 canonicatum ac prebendam predictos donacioni nostre duximus reseruandos ⟩ decernentes irritum 7 inane si secus
15 scienter uel ignoranter de ipsis per quoscumque quauis

auctoritate contigerit attemptari . Verum personam tuam
honorare uolentes 7 aliquibus probis viris de regno Anglie de
archidiaconatu 7 canonicatu ac prebenda prouideri predictis
ut ex eo erga deum 7 Romanam ecclesiam ipsorum virorum
20 deuocio augeatur ⁊ 7 alii eorum exemplo ad uertutum studia
propencius[1a] excitentur ⁊ archidiaconatum 7 canonicatum ac
prebendam eosdem per te auctoritate nostra benigne dis-
ponendo prouidimus conferendos . Volumus igitur 7 per
apostolica tibi scripta districte precipiendo mandamus quati-
25 nus predicta prebenda per te auctoritate nostra diuisa in
duas prefatum archidiaconatum 7 prebendas ipsas sic diuisas
aliquibus probis viris de Anglicanis partibus oriundis) qui
de legittimo matrimonio procreati) 7 uel in theologica facultate
magistri aut in decretis doctores) uel in iure ciuili professores
30 existant) super quibus tuam intendimus conscienciam onerare
auctoritate nostra conferas 7 assignes ita quod singule singulis
conferantur) faciens illum cui prefatum archidiaconatum
contuleris in archidiaconum Bokinghamie[2] in prefata ecclesia
prout est moris admitti) ac illos quibus prebendas easdem
35 duxeris conferendas in ecclesia ipsa in canonicos recipi 7 in
fratres) stallis sibi in choro 7 locis in capitulo cum plenitudine
iuris canonici assignatis) ac eis de archidiaconatus 7 prebendarum ipsarum fructibus) redditibus) prouentibus 7
obuencionibus uniuersis integre responderi . Contradictores
40 per censuram ecclesiasticam appellacione postposita compescendo . Non obstantibus quibuslibet ipsius ecclesie statutis
7 consuetudinibus contrariis iuramento confirmacione sedis
apostolice uel quacunque alia firmitate vallatis seu si aliqui
apostolica uel alia quauis auctoritate in eadem ecclesia in
45 canonicos sint recepti uel ut recipiantur insistant aut si super
aliquorum prouisione in eadem ecclesia specialiter uel in
partibus illis generaliter scripta apostolica sunt directa quibus
omnibus illos quibus dictum archidiaconatum 7 prebendas
ipsas sic diuisas contuleris in eorum uolumus assecucione
50 preferri) set quo ad alios personatus dignitates canonicatus
7 prebendas) ac beneficia nullum per hoc preiudicium generari)
seu si aliquibus communiter uel diuisim a sede sit indultum
eadem quod ad receptionem uel prouisionem alicuius minime
teneantur) quodque ad id compelli) seu quod interdici sus-
55 pendi uel excommunicari non possint) 7 quod de personatibus
dignitatibus canonicatibus 7 prebendis uel beneficiis ad eorum
collacionem) ordinacionem) uel disposicionem spectantibus
nulli ualeat prouideri per litteras apostolicas non facientes
plenam 7 expressam de indulto huiusmodi mencionem 7
60 qualibet alia prefate sedis indulgencia generali uel speciali
per quam effectus presencium impediri valeat uel differri)
7 de qua cuiusque toto tenore de uerbo ad uerbum fieri debeat

in nostris litteris mencio specialis . Volumus autem quod is
cui archidiaconatum contuleris supradictum personaliter quoad
65   uixerit resideat in eodem) set post eius obitum in pristina
remaneat libertate . ac illis[1a] quibus de prebendis ipsis siue
per te siue successores tuos aut alios auctoritate quacunque
contigerit in posterum[3] prouideri ⁑ continuam in illis residenciam facere teneantur . Quod vero in hac parte duxeris
70   faciendum ⁑ nobis plene seriatim 7 distincte per tuas litteras
harum seriem continentes studeas quantocius intimare sic te
in hac parte fideliter habiturus) ut exinde possis a nobis non
inmerito conmendari . Dat' Rome apud sanctam Mariam
Maiorem decimo kalendas Maii) pontificatus nostri anno
75   tercio . Huius igitur auctoritate mandati viro prouido 7
discreto magistro Ricardo de Sancta Fretheswida[4] doctori in
iure canonico 7 alias habenti condiciones in ipso mandato
expressas secundum formam eiusdem mandati archidiaconatum
Bokinghamie[2] contulimus memoratum cum onere residendi
80   personaliter in eodem . Consequenter autem ad prebendam
de Aylesbiry que in dicta Lincolniensi ecclesia eiusdem[5]
Perceualli fuerat dum viuebat) oculos dirigentes ⁑ saluis
capitulo Lincoln'[1]) de Querndon') Birton') Stokes) 7 Bokland'
capellis cum suis pertinenciis) que ad ipsam prebendam
85   prius notorie pertinebant secundum concessionem 7 assigna-
cionem de illis sibi factam 7 a sede apostolica confirmatam
ipsam in ecclesia de Aylesbiry[6] cum capella de Milton') primitus
consistentem auctoritate prefata in duas prebendas duximus
diuidendam . Ita quod ecclesia de Milton') que prius fuit capella
90   cum suis pertinenciis per se decetero sit vna prebenda ab
ecclesia de Aylesbiry separata . 7 ecclesia ipsa de Aylesbiry
cum suis pertinenciis) saluis semper capitulo Lincolniensi
de Querendon') Birton') Stokes 7 Bokland' capellis cum suis
pertinenciis superius nominatis alia sit prebenda . Stallum
95   uero prebende de Aylesbiry eundem fore ordinauimus qui ad
ipsam pertinuit ab antiquo) 7 quod stallus de Milton' sit ex
alia parte chori ultimus stallorum pertinencium ad prebendas .
Psalmi autem qui solebant ad prebendam dum fuit integra
pertinere ⁑ ita diuidantur) quod ad prebendam de Aylesbiry
100   pertineant psalmi) Cum inuocarem 7 Verba mea . Et ad
prebendam de Milton' Domine ne in furore 7 Domine
Deus meus . Dictam quidem prebendam de Aylesbiry sic de
nouo ordinatam magistro Ricardo de Hetherington' 7 prebendam de Milton' de nouo taliter constitutam magistro
105   Johanni de Monemuta doctoribus in sacra theologia) 7 alias
habentibus condiciones) in mandato supradicto contentas
secundum formam eiusdem mandati cum plenitudine iuris
canonici contulimus) 7 ipsos de eisdem installari fecimus)
ac eis locum in capitulo assignari cum onere in prebendis

110 ipsis personaliter residendi . Nichilominus suplere[1a] parati .
si quid defuerit quod auctoritate predicta per nos agendum
fuerat in hac parte . In quorum omnium testimonium sigillum
nostrum presentibus duximus apponendum . Act' mense
Augusti . anno domini . millesimo ducentesimo nonagesimo)
115 7 pontificatus nostri vndecimo.

Endorsed on no. 50: Diuisio prebende de Aylesbyr' 7 commisio facta domino
episcopo vt conferret eam diuersis qui in ecclesia residerent (14 cent.).
Endorsed on no. 51: Diuisio prebende de Aylesbyr' (14 cent.).
No. 50: Tag for seal torn away. Size: 12½ x 18 inches. No. 51: Tag for seal.
Size: 13 x 16¾ inches.
Texts: MS—Orig. Dij/66/2/50. Orig. Dij/66/2/51. Both these texts are original
documents, the charter being issued in duplicate.
Var. R. in no. 51: [1]Lincolnien'. [1a]sic. [2]Buckinghamie. [3]imposterum. [4]Fre-
thesyda. [5]insert domini. [6]Aylesbir'.
Note: The psalms assigned to the prebend of Aylesbury (psalms 4 and 5) and
to the prebend of Milton Ecclesia (psalms 6 and 7) are those given in the Black
Book. In the case of Milton, however, the entry is an addition at the foot of the
list, since the list is older than the separation of Milton Ecclesia from Buckingham
(Linc. Cath. Statutes i, 301, 306, 306n). Psalms 2 and 3 are now assigned to Bucking-
ham: those assigned to Milton Ecclesia are unchanged.
Note by Dr W. Holtzmann: For Percival Fiesco, youngest brother of pope
Adrian V, and the role that he played in Italian politics, see R. Davidsohn,
Geschichte von Florenz, vol. ii, part 2 (Berlin, 1908), pp. 303-49; Natalie Schöpp,
Papst Hadrian V (Heidelberg, 1916), passim, specially p. 204.

[904c]
279. XX. Declaratio residencie pro Aylesbir' et Miltona (Q).

This document is no longer to be found at Lincoln.

[904ð]
280. XXI. De canonizacione sancti Hugonis episcopi (Q).

*The papal bulls relating to the canonization of Saint Hugh are no
longer to be found at Lincoln. The texts printed below are taken
from J. F. Dimock's edition of the bulls as they are given at the end
of the Brownlow MS. of the Life of Saint Hugh* (Giraldi Cambrensis
Opera vii, 243-6, Rolls Series).

280a. *Bulla specialis domini papæ Honorii tertii, de canonizatione beatissimi et gloriosissimi Hugonis Lincolniensis episcopi.*

Honorius episcopus, [servus[1]] servorum Dei, venerabili
fratri episcopo, et dilectis filiis, capitulo, clero, et populo
Lincolniensi, salutem et apostolicam benedictionem . " Non
repulit Dominus plebem suam "[2] : nec eam expertem gratiæ
5 suæ reliquit aut gloriæ, Qui terminos gentium secundum
numerum Angelorum suorum legitur statuisse[3]. Quinimmo,
licet electi dicantur pauci respectu multitudinis vocatorum,
certum est tamen quod ex tanto fidelium numero eligitur
maxima multitudo . Unde prophetæ, conquerenti se solum

10   esse relictum, aliis interemptis, responsum est a Domino,
"Reliqui mihi septem milia virorum, qui ante Baal genua
non curvaverunt"[4]. Et beatus evangelista Johannes,[5] cum
revelatum sibi numerum signatorum ex duodecim tribubus
conspexisset, vidit turbam magnam, quæ dinumerari non
15   poterat, amictam stolis candidis, et tenentem palmas in
manibus coram Deo . Porro justus et misericors Dominus
fideles suos, quos prædestinavit ad vitam, omnes quidem
coronans in patria, quosdam eorum, secundum multitudinem
divitiarum sapientiæ ac misericordiæ suæ, glorificavit in via,
20   ut frigescentem jam in pluribus caritatis igniculum accendat
mirabilium novitate suorum, et pravitatem confundat here-
ticam, dum, ad catholicorum tumulos faciens miracula radiare,
ostendit per gloriam post exitum vitæ hujus illis exhibitam,
eos tenuisse dum viverent fidem rectam . Ipso igitur piæ
25   recordationis Hugonem Lincolniensem episcopum, quem in
vita sua non solum virtutibus sed etiam signorum osten-
sionibus illustraverat, faciente post obitum crebrioribus
miraculis coruscare, vos, frater episcope, et filii capitulum
ejusdem, per apostolicam sedem ascribi sanctorum catalogo
30   instanti devotione ac devota instantia postulastis . Cum
autem vestra petitio diu fuisset necessaria maturitate suspensa,
eo quod, cum hujusmodi judicium divinum sit potius quam
humanum, reformidat mortalis infirmitas judicare de illis,
qui, veste mortalitatis exuta, cum Christo creduntur vivere
35   ac regnare, demum vobis propter miraculorum frequentiam
petitionem prædictam humiliter replicantibus, nos, ne ministerium nostrum divinæ dignationi mirificanti sanctum suum
subtrahere videremur, venerabili fratri nostro Stephano
Cantuariensi archiepiscopo, sanctæ Romanæ ecclesiæ car-
40   dinali, et dilecto filio abbati de Fontibus, dederimus in mandatis, ut, cum opera pietatis in vita et miraculorum signa
post mortem ad hoc quod quis reputetur sanctus in militanti
ecclesia requirantur, licet ad sanctitatem fidelis animæ opera
sola sufficiant in ecclesia triumphanti, quærerent super
45   utriusque solicite veritatem, et quod invenirent curarent
nobis fideliter intimare, quatinus per eorum relationem
instructi procederemus in negotio prout nobis Dominus
inspiraret . Qui, juxta mandati nostri tenorem, primo de
illius conversatione ac vita, et deinde de miraculis, inquisi-
50   tionem facientes per testes omni exceptione majores et
astrictos juramenti vinculo diligentem, invenerunt ipsum
sanctæ conversationis odore aliis præfuisse dum viveret, et
insignium miraculorum multitudine in vita et post obitum
claruisse . Quæ, quia pro sua multitudine non possent sub
55   brevitate narrari, præsenti paginæ non duximus inserenda :
melius æstimantes scripturæ gloriosam ejus historiam

universam relinquere, quam paucis auctoritatem bullæ nostræ
appositione præstando, eam reliquis quodammodo derogare .
Ipsis autem miraculis, quæ inquisitores prædicti nobis sub
60 sigillis suis prout in mandatis acceperant transmiserunt,
examinatis per venerabilem fratrem nostrum P. Sabien'
episcopum diligenter, ea demum in auditorio nostro fecimus
solempniter recitari . Et cum sanctitatem morum, et signorum
virtutem, ad favorem petitionis jam dictæ concurrere vide-
65 remus, divinum et humanum secuti judicium, de divina
misericordia et ejusdem sancti meritis confidentes, ipsum,
de fratrum nostrorum et episcoporum qui apud apostolicam
sedem erant consilio, sanctorum catalogo duximus ascriben-
dum; statuentes ut in die depositionis ejusdem festivitas
70 annis singulis devote celebretur . Quocirca universitati vestræ
per apostolica scripta mandamus, quatinus ejusdem sancti
memoriam cum celebritate debita venerantes, ejus apud
Deum suffragia humiliter imploretis . Dat' Viterbii xiii. kal.
Marcii pontificatus nostri anno quarto.[6]

Text: Brownlow MS (as above).
Var. R. and notes: [1] *servus is omitted by mistake in the Brownlow MS.* [2] Rom.
xi, 2. [3] Deut. xxxii, 8. [4] Rom. xi, 4. [5] Apoc. vii, 3–9. [6] 17 February, 1220.

280b. *Bulla generalis domini papæ Honorii de canonizatione et
translatione beati Hugonis Lincolniensis episcopi.*

Honorius episcopus, etc. universis Christi fidelibus, præ-
sentem paginam inspecturis, salutem et apostolicam benedictionem . Divinæ dignatio pietatis sanctos et electos suos,
in cœlestis regni felicitate locatos, ad hoc[1] in terra miraculorum
5 coruscatione clarificat, ut fidelium per hæc excitata devotio
eorum suffragia digna veneratione deposcat . Cum igitur
sanctæ recordationis Hugonem Lincolniensem episcopum,
quem, sicut nobis plenarie constitit,[2] divini muneris largitas
tam in vita, quam etiam post vestem mortalitatis exutam,
10 insignium miraculorum multitudine illustravit, sanctorum
catalogo conscripserimus,[3] universitatem vestram monemus
et exhortamur in domino, quatinus ejus apud deum patro-
cinia devotis[4] mentibus imploretis . Cum autem venerabile
corpus ejus a loco in quo est transferri oporteat et honorifi-
15 centius collocari, nos omnibus qui ad solempnitatem translationis ejusdem, die quo transfertur, aut etiam infra ejus
octavas, et his quoque qui revolutis annis ipso translationis
die ad ejus tumbam cum devotione accesserint, de dei misericordia ac beatorum Petri et Pauli apostolorum ejus auctoritate
20 confisi, quadraginta dies de injunctis sibi pœnitentiis relaxamus.
Dat' Viterbii xiii. kal. Marcii, pontificatus nostri anno quarto.[5]

Texts: Brownlow MS. (as above). A similar bull, but with no mention of the
translation, is given in Rymer, *Fœdera* i, 165, from the original in the Tower ; and
in Wendover, iv, 64,

Var. R. and notes: [1] ad huc Rymer Wend. [2] constituit Brownlow MS ; constat Rymer Wend. [3] adscripsimus Rymer Wend. [4] devote Rymer Wend. [5] 17 February, 1220.

Note by Dr W. Holtzmann : No. 280b has been very often printed in Italian publications, chiefly in the first edition of Rainaldus, *Annales ecclesiastici ad annum* 1220. Also in *Bullarium Romanum*, ed. Charles Cocquelines, vol. iii (Romae 1740) 213, no. 42, and ed. Taurinensis iii, 367 ; Justus Fontanini *Codex constitutionum quas summi pontifices ediderunt in solemni canonizatione sanctorum* (Romae 1729) 52, no. 35 ; Bulaeus *Hist. uniuersitatis Parisiensis* iii, 104 ; Tromby *Storia del patriarco S. Brunone e del suo ordine Cartusiano* v, append. 83, no. 71 ; and probably also in other histories of the Carthusian order, e.g. Charles Lecouteulx, *Annales ordinis Cartusiensis* (Carreriae, 1887), which I have not been able to see. Also in publications of the Vatican registers, where the bull is inserted : Horoy, *Med. aevi bibl. patrist., Honorii pape iii opera* iii, 388, no. 82, and 420, no. 49 ; Pietro Pressutti *I regesti del pontefice Onorio* iii, vol. i (Roma 1888), 387, no. 2334 ; A. Potthast, *Regesta pontificum Romanorum*, no. 6195 ; also in Matthaei Parisien. *Chronica maiora*, ed. Luard, iii, 58 (from Wendover).

280c. *Item alia bulla de translatione ejusdem.*

Honorius, &c. venerabili fratri episcopo Lincolniensi salutem et apostolicam benedictionem . Cum venerabile corpus beati Hugonis a loco in quo est transferendum sit et dignius collocandum, fraternitati tuæ per apostolica scripta
5 [mandamus[1]], quatinus, convocatis prælatis et aliis quos videris convocandos, corpus ipsum in locum opportunum cures cum debita[2] solempnitate transferre, faciens illud cum digna honorificentia collocari . Dat' Viterbii, pontificatus nostri anno quarto.[3]

Text: Brownlow MS (as above).
Var. R. and note: [1] mandamus *is omitted by mistake in the Brownlow MS.* [2] *after* debita *is* et *in the Brownlow MS. Perhaps the bull had* debita reverentia (*or some such word*) et solempnitate. [3] A D. 1220.

Folio 182d [*blank*].

[904e]

280d. Processus canonizacionis beati Roberti in certa rotula est in cofino sub hoc titulo . non scribatur (Q).

The efforts to obtain canonization for bishop Grosseteste began about 1288, *shortly before Q made this entry in the Registrum Antiquissimum ; but both the earlier and the later attempts were unsuccessful. For an account of the proceedings see an article by Canon R. E. G. Cole in* Associated Societies' Reports *xxxiii,* 1–34. *There is no papal document at Lincoln relating to the proceedings.*

ADD. CHART.

281. Indult of pope Innocent [IV], granting to the bishops of the province of Canterbury that procurations shall not be paid to the archbishop when, as metropolitan, he visits parish churches. At Perugia. 27 May, 1252.

Innocencius episcopus seruus seruorum dei ⟩ venerabilibus
fratribus vniuersis episcopis Cantuariensis prouincie ⟩ salutem
et apostolicam benediccionem.

Attendentes quod prouincia Cantuar' claris semper con-
5 sueuit pollere prelatis ⟩ qui officii sui debitum laudabiliter
exequentes ⟩ studuerunt circa greges sibi creditos curam
impendere vigilem et salubrem visitando eos oportune ⟩ ac
in alijs prouide gubernando . Considerantes eciam quod
ecclesie seculares non collegiate vestrarum ciuitatum et
10 diocesium in quibus singulares rectores et vicarii et nulli
alij sunt clerici instituti . tum quia erga ipsas a suis prelatis
sollicitudo debita in visitacione ac alijs adhibetur . tum quia
in eis clericorum collegia non existunt a metropolitano vestro
quasi nunquam indigeant visitari ⟩ et propter hoc ipsas racione
15 visitacionis metropolitice in procuracionibus aggrauari nolentes ⟩
Vobis et eisdem ecclesijs de fratrum nostrorum consilio
auctoritate apostolica perpetuo indulgemus ⟩ Vt idem metropolitanus ab ipsis ecclesijs procuraciones que racione visitacionis debentur nullatenus decetero exigere ⟩ vel eas exac-
20 cionibus pecuniarijs aggrauare valeat ⟩ nec eedem ecclesie
ad illarum exhibicionem aliquatenus teneantur . Decernentes
quascumque sentencias talium occasione procuracionum vel
exaccionum contra easdem ecclesias vel rectores et vicarios
ipsos seu alios dictus metropolitanus aut alter ipsius auctori-
25 tate tulerit ⟩ vacuas penitus et inanes ⟩ nisi forte ad singulorum
requisicionem ⟩ vel de omnium aut maioris partis vestrum
consilio et assensu ⟩ illas duxerit visitandas ⟩ et tunc secundum
ipsarum facultates moderate iuxta constitucionem nostram
super hoc editam pro suis procuracionibus expendatur . Nulli
30 ergo omnino hominum liceat hanc paginam nostre concessionis
et constitucionis infringere ⟩ vel ei ausu temerario contraire .
Si quis autem hoc attemptare presumpserit ⟩ indignacionem
omnipotentis dei ⟩ et beatorum Petri et Pauli apostolorum
eius se nouerit incursurum.
35   Dat' Perusij .vj. kalendas . Junij (pontificatus nostri (
anno nono.

Marginalia: Indulgencia super procurationibus a parochialibus ecclesiis non
prestandis archiepiscopo . . visitanti.
    Texts : MS—Black Book, ff. 21d—22. Martilogium, f. 5. Pd—*Linc. Cath.
Statutes* i, 323.

ADD. CHART.

282. Mandate of pope Alexander [IV]. Whereas some of the
canons of Lincoln refuse to contribute to the expenses which the
dean and chapter must needs incur in preserving the rights of
their church, the pope commands the dean and precentor of York
to compel such canons to contribute. At the Lateran. 15 May, 1256.

Alexander episcopus seruus seruorum dei . dilectis filiis
.. decano et .. precentori Eboracen*sibus* salutem et apostolicam benediccionem . Ex parte dilectorum filiorum ..
decani et capituli ecclesie Lincolnien*is* nostris est auribus
5 intimatum . quod magister Willelmus de Sewelle Nicolaus
dictus Grecus et quidam alii eiusdem ecclesie canonici in
expensis quas eosdem decanum 7 capitulum pro conseruandis
iuribus et libertatibus ipsius ecclesie et subditorum eius
hactenus subire oportuit cum eis contribuere indebite con-
10 tradicunt quamquam prebendarum suarum ipsius ecclesie
percipiant cum integritate prouentus in eorundem decani et
capituli non modicam lesionem . Quare ipsi decanus 7
capitulum supplicarunt humiliter sibi super hoc misericorditer
prouideri . Cum igitur dignum sit ut ipsi canonici qui bonorum
15 eiusdem ecclesie sunt participes onerum minime sint ex-
pertes (discretioni uestre per apostolica scripta mandamus
quatinus si est ita canonicos ipsos ad contribuendum cum
ipsis decano et capitulo in expensis huiusmodi ut tenentur
monitione premissa appellacione remota per censuram eccle-
20 siasticam compellatis . Non obstante aliqua indulgencia per
quam huiusmodi mandati effectus (impediri ualeat uel differri .
Quod si non ambo hiis exequendis potueritis interesse (alter
uestrum ea nichilominus exequatur . Dat' Lateran' id*ibus*
Maij pontificatus nostri anno secundo ;

Endorsed : Contra prebendarios nolentes contribuere in expensis ecclesie (query
Q).
The seal has been torn off with a small piece at the foot of the charter. Size :
10¼ x 8¼ inches.
Text : MS—Orig. Dij/57/1/7.
Note : Nicholas Grecus frequently appears as a witness to the acts of bishop
Grosseteste (L.R.S. xi, index). He was still a canon of Lincoln in 1278 (*Linc. Cath.
Statutes* ii, pp. ccviii, 802). William de Sewelle cannot be traced.

ADD. CHART.

283. Mandate of pope Innocent [II], commanding the legate
Henry bishop of Winchester and T[heobald] archbishop of Canterbury
and his suffragans to confirm the sentence of excommunication
pronounced by A[lexander] bishop of Lincoln against [Robert] earl
of Leicester, who is withholding bishop Alexander's castle of
Newark [co. Nottingham], and to provide that the bishop shall
come to them. At the Lateran. 5 ides of . . . . . . (Probably
1140.)

[I]Nnocentius episcopus seruus seruorum dei . venerabilibus fratribus . He . Wintoniensi episcopo apostolice sedis
legato . T'. Cantuariensi archiepiscopo eiusque suffraganeis
salutem 7 apostolicam [be]nedictionem . Principes terrarum
5 qui deberent ecclesias ec[clesia]sticas personas 7 earum bona

manutenere . [7 a pra]uorum incursibus defensare . peccatis
exigen[tibus mutati] sunt in tirannos personas ecclesiasticas
[indebitis exa]ctionibus 7 oppressionibus inquietant . [. . . . . .
eorumque] bona ecclesiastica uiolenter occupant [et detinent
10   occupata] . Perlatum siquidem est . ad [aures nostras)
quod uenera]bilis frater noster .A. Lincoliensis [episco-
pus contra Robertum comitem] Leecestrie qui castrum
Niwerc . [quod sui iuris est) occupauit 7] uiolenter detinet .
excommu[nicationis sententiam promu]lgauit . Et nos quidem
15   . . . .
ta]lem raptorem ab ipsius [. . . . .
. . . .]antes .· per [*probably about six lines missing for the latter part of which there
may be suggested :* fraternitati uestre per apostolica scripta
20   mandamus) quatinus sententiam) quam idem .A. contra
predictum .R. canonice promul]gauerit simili modo firmetis .
7 obseruari faciatis . Ipsum quoque fratrem nostrum in suis
7 ecclesie sue oportunitatibus iuuare ac manutenere fraterna
caritate curetis 7 ut ad uos[1] absque inpedimento uenire
25   ualeat cum omni diligentia prouideatis . Dat' . Lat'. v
idus . . . .

Text : MS—S58. A considerable part of the leaf which contains the text has
perished. The words enclosed within square brackets have been suggested by
Dr W. Holtzmann for the purpose of filling up the lacunæ.

Var. R. : [1] An apparently early hand has cancelled the *u* of *uos* by placing a dot
below it, and has written *e* above the *u*, thus changing the word into *eos*. The
sense, however, requires *uos*. If the damage to the document was done at an early
date, the correction may have been made by one who, on account of the incom-
pleteness of the text, failed to appreciate its meaning.

Note by Dr W. Holtzmann : This document supplies very valuable evidence
in regard to the struggle between king Stephen on the one hand and bishop Roger
of Salisbury and his *nepotes*, bishop Alexander of Lincoln and Bishop Nigel of Ely,
on the other. The story of the conflict has been often told by ancient and modern
writers, but documentary evidence for it is very scarce. For the bishop of Ely
we have some letters in the third (and still unpublished) book of the Liber Eliensis :
for Lincoln the present text is the only document that is known. It shews that
bishop Alexander had taken care to launch an appeal to the pope against his
oppressors, among whom the existing part of this badly injured text of the pope's
letter mentions only Robert earl of Leicester. It would be very interesting to
know whether anything, however slight, was said which would illustrate the
attitude of the pope on the arrival of the bad news about his creature, king Stephen.
While we may with considerable confidence supply the missing words in the smaller
gaps, we cannot have a similar assurance about the words which have perished
in the main *lacuna*. Relying, however, on the letters to the bishop of Ely mentioned below, I would suggest the following re-construction of the text, the suggested words being printed in italic type :

Et nos quidem *predictam sententiam contra* talem raptorem ab ipsius *castri
domino latam confirm*antes per apostolica *scripta fraternitati vestre mandamus
et mandando precipimus, quatenus ipsi episcopo ad sua bona recuperanda
opem et consilium prebeatis et ipsam sententiam, quam idem venerabilis frater
noster A. contra predictum comitem R. canonice promulg*auerit, simili modo . . . . .

The struggle began with the arrest of the bishops at Oxford, 24 June, 1139 (cp.
Stubbs, *Constitutional History* i, § 114). At this time the pope was in Southern Italy,
and he did not return to the Lateran till 3 October. His letter, therefore, cannot
have been written before 12 October at the earliest. This would be after the
legate's council of Westminster, 29 August to 1 September. But probably the

date of the letter must be placed in 1140, and it is significant that the pope, on 5 October in that year, wrote a similar letter in favour of bishop Nigel of Ely (Jaffe-Löwenfeld, *op. cit.*, no. 8101 ; Liber Eliensis, lib. iii, cap. 64 ; British Museum, Cotton MS, Titus A i, f. 37, and Tiberius A vi, f. 114 ; Dean and Chapter of Ely, MS of the Liber Eliensis (13 cent.), f. 147).

ADD. CHART.

284. Notarial copy, dated 13 June, 1345, of a bull of pope Alexander [III] in favour of the prior and convent of Merton [co. Surrey], dated at the Lateran. 2 July, 1179.

Alexander seruus seruorum dei dilectis filiis Roberto priori ecclesie sancte Marie de ²Mertona eiusque fratribus tam presentibus quam futuris regularem vitam profess[is in perpetuum . Ad hoc uniuersalis ecclesie] cura nobis a prouisore
5　omnium bonorum deo commissa est vt religiosas diligamus personas 7 beneplacentem deo religionem studeamus modis omnibus propagare [. Nec enim deo gratus aliquando famulatus impenditur] nisi ex caritatis radice procedens in puritate religionis fuerit conseruatus Eapropter dilecti in domino
10　filii vestris iustis postulacionibus [clementer annuimus 7 prefatam ecclesiam ⟩ in qua diuino mancipati] estis obsequio sub beati Petri 7 nostra proteccione suscipimus 7 presentis scripti priuilegio communimus ⟨ In primis siquidem statuente[s ⟩ ut ordo canonicus ⟩ qui secundum deum 7 beati Augustini]
15　regulam in ipsa ecclesia institutus esse dinoscitur perpetuis ibidem temporibus inuiolabiliter obseruetur ⟨ Preterea quascumque possessiones quecumque bona [in presentiarum iuste 7 canonice possidetis aut] in futurum concessione pontificum ⟨ largicione regum vel principum ⟨ oblacione fidelium ⟨ seu
20　aliis iustis modis ⟨ prestante domino poteritis adipisc[i ⟨ firma uobis uestrisque successoribus 7] illibata permaneant ⟨ in quibus hec propriis duximus exprimenda vocabulis ⟨ Locum ipsum in quo predicta ecclesia de ²Merton' sita est . ecclesiam de ³Kyngeston' [cum omnibus pertinenciis] suis ⟨ ecclesiam
25　de Codyngton' ⟨ ecclesiam de ⁴Vpton' ⟨ 7 manerium quod habetis in eadem villa ⟨ ecclesiam de Huccham ⟨ ecclesias de ⁵Gildeford' ⟨ ecclesiam de Iuh[erst cum omnibus pertinenciis suis ⟨ ecclesiam de] ⁶Schirefeld ⟨ ecclesiam de Sutton' ⟨ terram de ⁷Aldynton' ⟨ ecclesiam de ⁸Norton' ⟨ cum omnibus per-
30　tinenciis suis ⟨ ecclesiam de ⁹Kymeto[n' cum] omnibus pertinenciis suis [ecclesiam de ¹⁰Stan]sted' ⟨ ecclesiam de ¹¹Standon' ⟨ ecclesiam de ¹²Honesdon' ⟨ ecclesiam de ¹³Middelton' ⟨ ecclesiam de ¹⁴Gillynges ⟨ ecclesiam de ¹⁵Clyua ⟨ ec[clesiam] de ¹⁶Gudemecestria [⟨ ecclesiam de] Mundebiria ⟨ redditum
35　viginti solidorum in molendinis de Huntindon' ⟨ ecclesias de ¹⁷Matolask' 7 de Plumsted' ⟨ redditum sexaginta solidorum apud [¹⁸. . . . .]ide ad opus o[. . . . .] ¹⁹Burnes

Q

7 de Brugges cum pertinenciis suis (ecclesiam de Hardres (
ecclesiam de Ryhers' (ecclesiam de [20]Cumba (ecclesiam
40 de [21]Kaynes (7 ecclesiam de [22]Flore 7 ecclesiam de [23]Ber[ton' (
7 ecclesiam] de [24]Taronta (7 ecclesiam de [25]Somerford' (
ecclesiam de [26]Meldon' (ecclesiam de [27]Ramesdon' (ecclesiam
de [28]Ditton' (ecclesiam de Clopham (7 ecclesiam de Awlton'
(cum omnibus pertinenciis suis et heremitorium quod fuit
45 Rogeri heremite iuxta Blecchyngleye (7 terram de Toles-
worth' (7 vineam quam habetis apud [18]Sutton' (libertates
quoque 7 (immunitates (quas dilectus filius noster Henricus
illustris Anglorum rex (diuino vobis intuitu cartis suis auten-
ticis confirmauit ratas decernimus perpetuo permanere (
50 Obeunte vero te nunc eiusdem loci priore (vel tuorum quolibet
(successorum (nullus ibi (qualibet subrepcionis astucia (
seu principis aut alterius potestatis violencia preponatur nisi
quem fratres communi consensu vel fratrum pars sanioris
concilii secundum dei timorem (7 beati Augustini regulam
55 7 sanctorum patrum statuta (prouiderint eligendum ⁊ In
parochialibus autem ecclesiis vestris liceat vobis de fratribus
vestris vel de aliis honestis personis presbiteros eligere (et
diocesano episcopo presentare (quibus si ydonei fuerint
episcopus curam animarum committat (vt ei de spiritualibus
60 vobis vero de temporalibus 7 si fratres . superfuerint (de
ordinis insuper obseruancia debeant respondere . Sane de
noualibus vestris (que propriis manibus aut sumptibus
colitis siue de nutrimentis animalium vestrorum vbicunque
sint (decimas a vobis nullus presumat exigere ⁊ Sepulturam
65 quoque ipsius loci (liberam esse concedimus (vt eorum
deuocioni 7 extreme voluntati (qui se illic sepeliri deliberauer-
int (nisi forte excommunicati sint vel interdicti ullus obsistat
(salua tamen iusticia illarum ecclesiarum a quibus mortuorum
corpora assumuntur (Cum autem generale interdictum terre
70 fuerit (liceat vobis clausis ianuis (exclusis excommunicatis
7 interdictis (non pulsatis campanis (suppressa voce (diuina
officia celebrare (Inhibemus eciam ne terras aut ecclesias (
seu aliquod beneficium ecclesie vestre collatum (liceat alicui
personaliter dari seu alio mod[o] alienari sine communi
75 cons[en]su tocius capituli (aut maioris 7 sanioris partis .
Si que vero donaciones seu alienaciones aliter quam dictum
est facte fuerint (eas irritas esse censemus (Pretere[a] nouas
7 indebitas exactiones (ab archiepiscopis (vel episcopis (
archidiaconis (seu decanis (aliis ve quibuslibet ecclesiasticis
80 personis (7 maxime pro dedicacione ecclesiarum siue pro aliis
ecclesiasticis sacramen[tis] in ecclesiis vestris fieri omnino
prohibemus nisi tantum synodalia 7 episcopalia que de
canonum iure debentur (Inhibemus quoque ne quis infra
parochias ecclesiarum vestrarum (ecclesiam aut oratorium

85 (sine ass[ensu] diocesani episcopi 7 vestro edificare pre-
   sumant¹ (saluis tamen priuilegiis Romane ecclesie (nec
   cuiquam liceat religionem domus vestre (secundum regulam
   beati Augustini constitutam vel iura vestra seu racionabiles
   instituciones a patribus vestris scripto commendatas (sine
90 maioris 7 sanioris partis capituli concilio¹ 7 assensu corrumpere
   vel mutare (minuere vel aliquid superaddere (quod religioni
   siue saluti vestre vel salubribus patrum videatur institu-
   cionibus obuiare (Prohibemus ad hec (ne aliqui canonici
   seu conuersi sub professione vestre domus astricti (sine
95 conssensu¹ 7 licencia prioris 7 maioris ac sanioris partis capituli
   vestri pro aliquo fideiubeant (vel ab alio peccuniam¹ mutuo
   accipiant (vltra precium prouidencia capituli constitutum (
   quod si facere forte presumpserint (non teneatur conuentus
   sine cuius licencia 7 consensu hoc egerint pro hiis aliquatenus
100 respondere (Adicimus eciam ne aliquam ecclesiarum vestrarum
   alicui conc[edere liceat nisi q]uis velit 7 debeat in propria
   ministrare persona . sed pocius in singulis ecclesiis vestris
   presbiteri collocentur ydonei (qui deo in illis digne valeant
   deseruire (Liceat autem (vobis clericos vel laicos e seculo
105 fugientes (ad conuersionem vestram liberos 7 absolutos sine
   contradiccione aliqua retinere (laici vero conuersi priori 7
   canonicis religionis 7 professionis vestre vbique subditi 7
   obedientes existant (nec sine prioris 7 conuentus consciencia
   7 assensu quicquam de possessionibus vestris disponere
110 audeant vel mutare ꞉ Paci quoque 7 tranquillitati vestre
   paterna sollicitudine prouidere volentes auctoritate apostolica
   prohibemus (vt infra clausuras locorum seu grangiarum
   vestrarum nullas violenciam vel rapinam seu furtum (com-
   mittere aut ignem apponere (seu hominem capere (vel inter-
115 ficere audeat (Prohibemus insuper vt nullus in vos vel in
   ecclesias vestras excommunicacionis seu interdicti sentenciam
   absque manifesta 7 racionabili causa audeat promulgare (
   Decernimus ergo vt nulli omnino hominum liceat prefatam
   ecclesiam temere perturbare (aut eius possessiones auferre (
120 vel oblatas¹ retinere (aut minuere (seu aliquibus vexacionibus
   fatigari¹ (sed omnia integra conseruentur (eorum p[ro quorum]
   gubernacione ac sustentacione concessa sunt vsibus omnimodis profutura (salua apostolice sedis auctoritate (
   7 diocesani episcopi canonica iusticia (Si qua igitur in futurum
125 ecclesiastica secularis ve persona hanc [nostre constitucionis]
   paginam (sciens contra eam temere venire temptauerit (
   secundo tercio ve commonita (si non satisfacione congrua
   id emendauerit (potestatis honorisque sui dignitate careat
   (reamque [se diuino iudicio exi]stere de perpetrata iniqui-
130 tate cognoscat (7 a sacratissimo corpore dei 7 domini
   redemptoris nostri Ihesu Christi aliena fiat (atque in extremo

examine (diuine vltioni subiaceat (Cunctis autem eidem
loco sua iura seruantibus sit pax domini nostri Ihesu Christi .
quatinus ⁊ hic fructum bone accionis percipiant ⁊ apud
135 districtum iudicem premia eterne pacis inueniant . amen .
Dat' Lateranen'[1a] per manum Alberti sancte Romane ecclesie
presbiteri cardinalis ⁊ cancellarii .vj. nonas Julij . indiccione .
xj.[1b] incarnacionis dominice anno millesimo . C^{mo}. lxxviiij^{no}.
pontificatus domni Alexandri pape tercij anno .xix^{no}.

140   Facta est collacio ⁊ concordat cum originali pro
Roche.

[Notary's   Et ego Johannes de Marlesforde clericus
mark]   Exon*iensis* diocesis apostolica auctoritate
JOHANNES   notarius publicus vltima die mensis
145 MARLESFORDE. Junij anno domini millesimo CCC^{mo}
                 xlv^{to} indiccione decima tercia pontifi-
catus sanctissimi patris ac domni d[omni] Clementis
diuina prouidencia pape vj^{ti} anno quarto in ecclesia
sancti Pauli London' supradictas litteras apostolicas vera
150 bulla plumbea . more Romane curie bullatas sanas ⁊
integras ac omni suspicionis vicio vt prima facie apparuit
carentes (coram me notario publico . tanquam coram
publica ⁊ autentica persona ac magistro Edmundo de
Pontefracto Willelmo Papiloun Ricardo Maunstede
155 Johanne de Gadeston' et aliis testibus ad hoc vocatis
⁊ rogatis (per magistrum Johannem de Tetforde clericum
procuratorem religiosorum virorum prioris ⁊ conuentus
de Merton' predictarum exhibitas vidi palpa[ui] con-
sideraui et diligenter inspexi hancque veram copiam et
160 cum dictis apostolicis litteris originalibus in omnibus
concordantem iuxta veram ⁊ diligentem collacionem
habitam cum esdem[1] (manuque propria me subscripsi
signumque meum publicum apposui per dictum procuratorem rogatus ⁊ requisitus in testimonium pre-
165 missorum.

No endorsement. Size : 13½ x 14¾ inches.
Text : Orig.ᴅɪj/57/1/5 . . . The right hand top corner has perished, and there are
several holes elsewhere. The words which are consequently lost (apart from those
in lines 24–41) have been supplied by Dr W. Holtzmann, and are enclosed within
square brackets. Since they consist of standard papal formulæ, with the exception
of the phrase in line 101, they may be accepted as certain. The missing words
in lines 24–41 have been supplied by the editor. The copies of papal bulls have
disappeared from the Merton priory cartulary (British Museum, Cotton MSS,
Cleopatra C. VII), and the present text preserves seemingly the only surviving copy
of this bull. There is no record of the circumstances which led to its finding a
place in the cathedral church of Lincoln.
Var. R.: [1] sic. [1a] the adjective seems to have been used erroneously instead of
the substantive Laterani (sing.) or Lateranis (plur.). [1b] the indiction should be xij.
Identifications : [2] Merton, co. Surrey. [3] Kingston on Thames, Cuddington, co.
Surrey. [4] Upton, Hitcham, co. Buckingham. [5] Guildford, Ewhurst, co. Surrey.
[6] Sherfield on Loddon, Bishop's Sutton, co. Southampton. [7] Alderton, co. Wiltshire (see Note below). [8] Midsomer Norton, co. Somerset. [9] Kimpton, co. Bucking-

ham. [10] Stanstead Abbots, co. Hertford. [11] Stondon, co. Bedford. [12] Hunsdon, co. Hertford. [13] Milton Bryant, co. Bedford. [14] Yelling, co. Huntingdon. [15] Kings Cliffe, co. Northampton. [16] Godmanchester, Alconbury, Huntingdon, co. Huntingdon. [17] Matlask, Plumstead (by Holt), co. Norfolk. [18] Unidentified. [19] Patrixbourne, Bridge, Lower Hardres, and Ryarsh, co. Kent. [20] Coombe Keynes, co. Dorset. [21] Caen, in Normandy (*see Note below*). [22] Flore, co. Northampton. [23] Barton, co. Cambridge. [24] Tarrant Keynton, co. Dorset. [25] Somerford Keynes, co. Gloucester. [26] Malden, co. Surrey. [27] Ramsden (formerly a chapelry in the parish of Shipton under Wychwood), co. Oxford. [28] Long Ditton, Clapham, Carshalton, Blechingley, Talworth (in the parish of Long Ditton), co. Surrey.

Note : (1) Aldynton' (line 29)—This place must be identified with Alderton, in Wiltshire, because Merton priory had one hide there (*in Aldintona*) of the gift of Aliz de Condi and Roger [de Condi] and his heir, in 1177 (A. Heales, *The Records of Merton Priory*, page 27). Roger was one of the bishop of Lincoln's knights, and this fact may possibly account for a copy of the present text being found at Lincoln (see page 291, below).

(2) The identification of Kaynes (line 40) with Caen, in Normandy, is confirmed by the fact that the prior and canons of Merton, in the year 1200, obtained confirmation from king John of the exchange of their church of ' Kaannes in Normannia ' for tithes and churches in England which belonged to the prior and monks of Saint Fromond in the diocese of Bayeux (*Rotuli Chartarum*, page 36).

ADD. CHART.

285. Notice of an indulgence granted by the pope [query Gregory IX] to the hospital of S. Maria della Stella near Rome in the city of Spoleto, which the pope wishes to be frequented by pilgrims. (Query circa 1234.)

Domnus papa iniungit nobis [ca]p[el]lanis ut iniungamus parochianis nostris in remissionem[1] peccatorum suorum ut sint coadiutores 7 benefactores noui hos[pi]talis beate Marie de Stella prope Romam in ciuitate de Spoleta[2] ubi de prouisione
5   do*mn*i pape omnibus transiuntibus[2] 7 peregrinis ad terram sanctam tam militibus quam armigeris tam clericis omnia necessaria inueniuntur ibi fiunt omnia[3] opera misericordie pro quibus dominus promittit uitam eternam Vnde do*mn*us papa omnibus benefactoribus predicte domus vii. partem
10   penitencie iniuncte peccata oblita uota fracta offensas patrum 7 matrum siue manuum iniectione[4] misericordie[5] relaxat .I. annum . c[6] 7 XL dies quotiens Christi fideles suas dederint elemosynas cum stacionibus et peregrinationibus sancte Romane ecclesie eis conced[it. . .] [Summa] stacionum
15   XLIIIJ anni cum VII quatragenis[2] 7 si quis cum aliqua sentencia excommunicacionis per ignoranciam innodatus si[7] de bonis suis congrue ad pre[dictam domum cum con]silio sacerdotis sui parochialis transmiserit est penitus absolutus de vsuris rapinis et [bon]is male adquisitis nisi sciatur cui ex [debito sint]
20   reddenda) a domno papa est absolutus et de omnibus uotis excepto uoto Ierosolimitano Sacerdote[8] uero et [cleri]ci istut[2] negocium deligente[9] et fideli[ter] exponentes quicquid in diuinis officiis omiserint a do*mn*o papa est remissum[10] . Summa aliarum remissi[onum] a uenerabilibus cardinalibus[11]
25   archiepiscopis episcopis . . . IJ.[12] anni , Summa missarum ab

abbatibus prioribus 7 aliis uiris religiosis .xxxIII. Iniunctum est a domno papa omnibus presbiteris parochialibus [in uirtu]te obediencie ut omnia supradicta parochianis suis exponant 7 elemosinas personaliter [colli]gant . Reddantur
30　collecta pro [tempore] 7 loco statuto sub pena canonica cum breue.

Text : MS—Orig.Dij/57/1/6. This rather difficult document has been transcribed by Dr W. Holtzmann. The words enclosed in square brackets have been supplied conjecturally.
Size : 8¼ x 3 inches.
Var. R. : ¹ remissionem *seems to be intended* ; *the text has* remisc'm, *and an additional final minim has been cancelled.* ² sic. ³ fiunt *is repeated after* omnia. ⁴ *for* iniectiones. ⁵ intuitu *seems to have been omitted.* ⁶ *or perhaps* c.i. (*the document is nearly illegible here*). ⁷ *query for* sit. ⁸ *for* Sacerdotes. ⁹ *for* diligenter. ¹⁰ *perhaps for* remissarum. ¹¹ *the text has* cadt, *which must represent* cardinalibus. ¹² *The number ends with* ij, *but the preceding numerals are indecipherable.*
Note by Dr W. Holtzmann : This notice was apparently written by an English visitor at the papal curia, and was destined to be published by an English bishop in his diocese. It seems to be only a draft, as is suggested by many carelessnesses in the text. A hospital of Sta Maria della Stella in Spoleto is mentioned in a map of Spoleto drawn by Giovanni Parenzi in 1613 (see the reproduction in Achille Sansi, *Storia del commune di Spoleto dal secolo XII al XVII*, parte i (Foligno, 1879), at the end of the volume), but I have not been able to find any notice about the foundation of that hospital in the local literature on Spoleto. So for dating the document we have to fall back upon palaeographical evidence. The kind of writing shows characteristics of the thirteenth century. The measure of the indulgences also places the document in the same century. The processions to the churches of stations, very common in Rome in the earlier centuries, ceased to be in use in the thirteenth and fourteenth centuries, and the devotion of the fourteen crossway stations of our Lord is later. The papal curia stayed in Spoleto some time in 1234 under Gregory IX ; and perhaps we may place the document with all reserve in that or one of the following years.

ADD. (EXTRAN.) CHART.

286. Confirmation by pope Eugenius III to Alvered the abbot and his brethren of Dorchester [co. Oxford] of the church of Saint Peter of Dorchester, and of the liberties which it had by the grant of Remigius bishop of Lincoln, when the episcopal see was translated from Dorchester to Lincoln, and of other possessions of their church. At Trastevere. 5 February, 1146.

¹Eugenius episcopus servus servorum dei . Dilectis filiis Alveredo abbati ecclesiæ beati Petri de Dorcacestria eiusque fratribus tam præsentibus quam futuris regularem vitam professis in perpetuum¹ . Ad hoc nobis ecclesiæ catholicæ
5　cura a summo pastore deo commissa est, ut dei servos paternis affectibus diligamus et eo amplius studeamus devotionem ipsorum modis omnibus confovere, quo ferventius ipsi disciplinis ecclesiasticis et sanctorum patrum regulis inhærere noscuntur . Tunc enim deo apostolicus impenditur
10　famulatus, si sanctorum locorum salubris institutio, rigor et ordo nostris patrociniis in religionis puritate serventur . Ea propter dilecti in domino filii venerabilis fratris nostri Alexandri Lincoliensis episcopi precibus inclinati vestris

iustis postulationibus clementer annuimus et prædecessoris
15 nostri bonæ memoriæ papæ Coelestini[2] vestigiis inhærentes
præfatam beati Petri ecclesiam, in qua divino mancipati
estis obsequio, sub eiusdem apostolorum principis et nostra
protectione suscipimus et præsentis scripti privilegio communimus . In primis siquidem statuentes ut ordo canonicus
20 secundum beati Augustini regulam perpetuis ibi temporibus
inviolabiliter conservetur . Quascumque præterea possessiones,
quæcumque bona inpræsentiarum iuste et canonice possidetis,
aut in futurum concessione pontificum, liberalitate regum,
largitione principum, oblatione fidelium seu aliis iustis modis
25 præstante domino poteritis adipisci, firma vobis vestrisque
successoribus et illibata permaneant . In quibus hæc propriis
duximus exprimenda vocabulis, ipsam videlicet ecclesiam
beati Petri de Dorcacestria cum libertatibus suis, quas habuit
rationabili concessione Remigii Lincoliensis episcopi, ex quo
30 sedes episcopalis ad beatæ Mariæ Lincoliensem ecclesiam
auctoritate apostolica ab ea translata fuit, cum decimis et
capellis suis scilicet capella de [12]Bensintuna, capella de
[13]Cliftona, capella de [14]Baldenduna, capella de [15]Chiselentona,
capella de [16]Stodeham, capella de [17]Drætona, terram quam
35 tenuit Hunfredus presbyter, terram de Brademera cum prato,
pastura et aliis pertinentiis suis, molendinum de [18]Tamisia,
molendinum de [19]Tamensi, quod est ultra pontem ex parte
orientali, ita tamen ut inde Lincoliensi episcopo xx solidos
annuatim persolvatis, totam curtem et croftam, que fuit
40 Hunfredi presbyteri, decem bordarios, domos episcopales et
quicquid infra murum habetis . extra murum a parte
occidentali terram quæ est inter prædictam partem muri et
viam, qua itur ad domum Dunningi, totum ambitum
grangiarum episcopalium et croftam retro ipsum ambitum
45 grangiarum, gardinum et totam culturam retro ipsum
gardinum extensam usque molendinum de Queneford, in qua
centum acræ continentur, pasturam sive pratum quod est
inter prædictam culturam et aquam, pratum de Suiftelac,
quod eidem pasturæ sive prato rivulo intercurrente continuatur,
50 viginti acras de dominio episcopi[3] de [20]Midentona cum prato
eis pertinente . Obeunte vero te, nunc eiusdem loci abbate,
vel tuorum quolibet successorum nullus ibi qualibet[4] sub-
reptionis astutia seu violentia præponatur, nisi quem fratres
communi consensu vel fratrum pars consilii sanioris secundum
55 dei timorem et beati Augustini regulam providerint eligendum .
Decernimus ergo ut nulli omnino hominum liceat præfatum
locum temere perturbare, aut eius possessiones auferre vel
ablatas retinere, minuere, seu quibuslibet vexationibus fatigare,
sed omnia integra conserventur, eorum, pro quorum guber-
60 natione et sustentatione concessa sunt, usibus omnimodis

profutura, salva sedis apostolicæ auctoritate et Lincoliensis
episcopi canonica iustitia et reverentia . Si qua igitur in
futurum ecclesiastica secularisve persona huius nostræ con-
stitutionis paginam sciens contra eam temere venire tempta-
65 verit secundo tertiove commonita, si non reatum suum congrua
satisfactione correxerit potestatis honorisque sui dignitate
careat reamque se divino iudicio existere de perpetrata
iniquitate cognoscat, et a sacratissimo corpore et sanguine
dei et domini redemptoris nostri Ihesu Christi aliena fiat,
70 atque in extremo examine districte ultioni subiaceat . Cunctis
autem eidem loco sua iura servantibus sit pax domini nostri
Ihesu Christi, quatinus et hic fructum bonæ actionis percipiant,
et apud districtum iudicem præmia æternæ pacis inveniant .
AMEN . Amen.
75   R[5] . Ego Eugenius catholicæ ecclesiæ episcopus[6] . B V[7] .
          + Ego Conradus Sabinensis episcopus.
          + Ego Albericus Hostiensis episcopus.
          + Ego Ymarus Tusculanus episcopus.
          Ego Gregorius presbyter cardinalis tituli Calixti.
80   Ego Guido presbyter cardinalis tituli sancti Grisogoni.
          + Ego Hubaldus presbyter cardinalis tituli sanctæ
              Praxedis.
          + Ego Guido presbyter cardinalis tituli sanctorum
              Laurentii et Damasi.[8]
85   + Ego Bernardus presbyter cardinalis tituli sancti
              Clementis.
              + Ego Oddo diaconus cardinalis sancti Bertii[9]
                  ad velum aureum.
              + Ego Guido diaconus cardinalis sanctorum Cosmæ
90   et Damiani.
              + Ego Gregorius diaconus cardinalis tituli sancti
                  Andreæ.[9a]
              + Ego Berardus diaconus cardinalis sanctæ Romanæ
                  ecclesiæ.[10]
95   Dat. trans Tiberim per manum ROBERTI sanctæ Romanæ
ecclesiæ presbyteri cardinalis et cancellarii nonas Februarii
indictione VIIII incarnationis dominicæ anno MCXLVI,
pontificatus vero domini[11] Eugenii III papæ anno I.

Text : Bodleian Library, Rawlinson MSS D404, f. 140, an eighteenth century
copy made from an unknown source. The present text is printed from a copy made
by Dr W. Holtzmann, who considers the Rawlinson text a very good copy with
no more than a few mistakes in the subscriptions, which in bulls of the time of
Eugenius III are often difficult to read since they were the autographs of cardinals
who were not always calligraphists.
Var. R. etc. : [1-1] *underlined : in the upper margin is the copyist's note*—Literæ
nigris lineis subtensæ constant ex uncialibus, Italicis, oblongis. *On the opposite
folio* 139d *the copyist has written an erroneous note on* In PPM (*which stands for* in
perpetuum): forsan : in perpetuam memoriam. [2] Coelestini *is underlined.*
[3] episcopi *is interlineated.* [4] *the copyist has the note*—litera (q) exesa. [5] *The Rota
is drawn here, with the legend,* Fac mecum domine signum in bonum. [6] *The*

copyist has omitted the s.s. (*i.e.* subscripsi) *in the subscriptions of pope and cardinals.*
[7] B V. (*i.e.* Benevalete) *appears in an ornamental design.* [8] *sic, instead of* sancti
Laurentii in Damaso (*S. Lorenzo in Damaso*). [9] *recte* sancti Georgii (*S. Giorgio
in Velabro*). [9a] *There is no title of a cardinal deacon of* S. Andrea. *The text is
apparently a mis-reading by the copyist for* S. Angeli, *where cardinal deacon Gregory
appears during the whole of the pontificate of Eugenius III.* [10] *The order of the
subscriptions of the cardinals is somewhat confused in the copy, and they are printed
in what Dr Holtzmann considers to be the correct sequence.* [11] *recte* domni.

Identifications : In the county of Oxford—[12] Bensington. [13] Clifton Hampden.
[14] Baldon Toot. [15] Chiselhampton. [16] Stadhampton. [17] Drayton Saint Leonard.
[18] Thames river. [19] Tame river ; Dorchester bridge crosses the Tame, and a mill
to the east of the bridge would be on the Tame. [20] Milton (by Thame).

Note : The Reverend H. E. Salter has printed another bull of pope Alexander III,
A.D. 1163, in favour of Dorchester Abbey (*The Report of the Oxfordshire Archæological Society* for 1909).

Folio 183.

*A tag is sewn to this folio to mark the beginning of this division
of the volume, and on it is written—(query* Libertates) prebend'
(*14 cent.*).

Notes by Q : .III. titulus . de iurisdiccione Capituli 7 Canonicorum
apud .C. Originalia sunt in vno cofino sub predicto signo.

905

287. Charter of bishop Robert [II], exempting the prebends
of the church of Lincoln from all episcopal rights and demands ;
so that the archdeacons shall have no power to demand anything
from the prebends or from the churches which belong to the common
of the church of Lincoln, or to implead their men ; but the canons
shall have the same liberty in their prebends that the canons of
Salisbury have in theirs. The bishop also grants the same liberty
to the church of Leighton [Bromswold, co. Huntingdon] which is
known to belong to the subdeanery, and to the church of All Saints
in the Bail which belongs to the chancellorship. (Circa 1160.)

    Carta Roberti dei gracia Linc' episcopi (A 65, rubric).
    Robertus dei gracia Linc'[1] episcopus . omnibus fidelibus
dei . salutem . Nouerit vniuersitas vestra nos remisisse
omnibus prebendis Linc'[1] ecclesie imperpetuum omnia iura
5 episcopalia 7 omnes exactiones . Et volumus quod[2] canonici
Linc' perpetuam in prebendis suis 7 omnibus possessionibus
que ad prebendas pertinent ꞓ libertatem habeant . Ita quod
de cetero nulli liceat archidiacono uel archidiaconorum officiali
de prebendis uel de eclesiis que ad communionem Linc'[1]
10 ecclesie pertinent ꞓ aliquid exigere uel homines eorum im-
placitum[3] ponere . sed eandem omnino habeant canonici

libertatem in prebendis suis . quam habent canonici Sales-
biriens*is* ecclesie in suis . Prefatam uero libertatem subdecanatui[4] 7 ecclesie Lectunie[5] que ad subdecanatum pertinere
15 dinoscitur *:* necnon 7 ecclesie[6] Omnium Sanctorum in ballio
que de cancellaria est nostre ecclesie perpetuo concedimus .
7 presentis sigilli nostri attestatione communimus 7 cor-
roboramus[7] . Testibus . Martino thesaurario[8] . Radulfo sub-
diacono[9] . Galfrido capellano domini regis . Willelmo de
20 Bugd*en*'[10] capellano . Fulco[11] de Schaisn'[12] canonico . magistro
Radulfo medico . Laurencio . Gilberto[13] de Sempingham[14] .
Mill'o[15] Clement' priore de Helesham[16] . Thoma canonico de
Grimesby . 7 magistro Malgero[17].

Marginalia in A 905: *opp. l. 15*, Ecclesia Omnium Sanctorum. In A 65: De
iurisdiccione capituli 7 scribitur alibi in proprio titulo (Q). In Black Book: De
libertate prebendarum ecclesie Lincolniensis.
Texts: MS—A905. A65. Ix(1). Black Book, f.14. Pd—*L.C.S.* i, 309–10.
Var. R.: [1] Lincoln' Ix BlBk. [2] *insert* omnes A65 Ix BlBk. [3] in placitum
A65 Ix. [4] subdecanatui A65; subdiaconatui Ix BlBk; *altered from* subdiaconatui
A905. [5] Lectunie A65 Ix. [6] ecclesia A65. [7] corroborauimus A65. [8] A65 *omits
all but the first witness, and has* 7c. [9] subd' Ix; subdecano BlBk. [10] Buged'
Ix; Bugeden' BlBk. [11] Fulcon' Ix. [12] Chaisn' Ix BlBk. [13] Gilliberto BlBk.
[14] Semplingham Ix; Semplingam BlBk. [15] *This must be intended for Willelmo
although all the texts have* Mill'o ; *for William Clement occurs as prior of Elsham in
1208* (Final Concords (*Lincolnshire Records*) i, 83). *Though the interval is a long
one, the occurrence of the same name at the two dates cannot be treated as a mere
coincidence. As prior he witnessed charters late in the twelfth century* (Stenton,
Danelaw Charters, *pp. 227, 345*). *Before he became prior, he was one of bishop
Robert's chaplains early in the reign of Henry II* (ibid., p. 39). [16] Helessam BlBk.
[17] *altered from* Aalgero A905; Malgero Ix; Aalgero (*with the* l *interlined*)
BlBk. *Master Malger was one of bishop Robert's clerks, and witnessed his charters*
(Stenton, Danelaw Charters, *pp. 3, 39, 151, 191, etc.*).
Note: Of the charters registered in this section of the Registrum Antiquissimum,
nos. 287, 289, 290, 294, 296, 298, 300 were transcribed into the Black Book, *circa*
1320 (for the references see below under the several charters) ; no. 287 is entered
earlier in the Registrum Antiquissimum at no. 65 ; and the texts of nos. 287, 288
and 289, with two papal bulls, nos. 256 and 257 above, are given in an *inspeximus*
of the privileges of the church of Lincoln by W. archbishop of York, whom the
handwriting shews to have been Walter Gray (1216–1255). This *inspeximus* is
here referred to as Ix. On these charters, see *Linc. Cath. Statutes* i, 108–9 ;
ii, 112, 115–16, 307–11.
On the subject of the rights of the chapter of Lincoln, see the monumental work
of Henry Bradshaw and Christopher Wordsworth, *Lincoln Cathedral Statutes*. With
reference to the transference of episcopal rights to cathedral chapters, Mr Bradshaw
writes :—
'For the purpose of an effective home government, St Osmund had transferred to his Chapter almost all the episcopal rights which he possessed, not
only in the Cathedral Church itself, but throughout the diocese, wherever the
churches or lands were in possession of the Chapter.
'The Charter of King Henry I (between 1107–23) reveals to us the existence
of (if it was possible) still greater independence at York ; the very appoint-
ment of the Canons by the Archbishop being subject to the consent of the
Dean and Chapter.
'Shortly before 1150 the new Bishop of Lincoln (Robert de Chesney) had
been persuaded on his accession to the see to bestow upon his Chapter the
fullest privileges which had been accorded to the Chapter at Salisbury by
their founder ; and this example was followed by other Bishops both in England
and Scotland. No Bishop, no Archdeacon, no diocesan officer of any kind,
could thenceforth lift a finger against anyone, even a parishioner, living on
this privileged ground ; the Chapter-house was the one place in which the
offender could be brought to account. Immunities of this kind were granted

by Bishop after Bishop, and confirmed by successive Popes, until by the middle of the thirteenth century, even the Bishop's ordinary duty of visitation had come to be looked upon as an intolerable infringement of the rights of the Chapter. The Bishop certainly appointed the Canons and all the dignitaries except only the Dean, who was in most places elected freely by the Chapter; but with this the power of the Bishop seemed to reach its fullest limit. Certain kinds of statutes required, or at any rate received, the Bishop's assent; but as statutes were for the most part looked upon as a declaration of the " ancient custom of the Church " which there was no gainsaying, it is clear that during the whole of this period the Dean and the rest of the Chapter, if only they could work harmoniously together, would find little difficulty in carrying everything before them ' (*Linc. Cath. Statutes* i, 36–7).

In 1245, however, on an appeal to Rome, bishop Grosseteste obtained a bull (printed above, no. 273)

' in which, while the duty of punishing delinquents is maintained for the Dean, and only passes out of his hands to the Bishop in case of the Dean's negligence, the Bishop's jurisdiction is asserted as that of visitor not of the cathedral church and chapter alone, but over " all prebendal churches, and churches of the dignities and of the ' communa ' " and " of the vicars, chaplains and parishioners belonging to the said churches " ' (*ibid.* ii, p. clxxxi).

' The result has been, that each successive Bishop of Lincoln has had secured to him a position, not only as visitor, but as, in all respects, the *principale caput* of the chapter ; and his pre-eminence at Lincoln has been long since established more firmly than that of the Bishop in some of the sister churches, where the Bishop is in certain respects dependent on the chapter even after his election ' (*ibid.*, p. cl).

906

288. Confirmation by bishop William [of Blois] of bishop Robert's grant of privileges (no. 287, above), with an addition concerning the churches of Searby [co. Lincoln], Leighton Bromswold [co. Huntingdon], and All Saints [in the Bail], Lincoln. (1203–1205.)

Omnibus Christi fidelibus ad quos presens scriptum peruenerit ⫶ Willelmus dei gracia Linc'[1] episcopus (salutem in domino   Ex inspeccione autentici instrumenti bone memorie Roberti quondam Linc'[1] episcopi predecessoris nostri cog-
5   nouimus ipsum remisisse omnibus prebendis Linc' ecclesie inperpetuum[2] omnia iura episcopalia 7 omnes exacciones . 7 quod omnes canonici Linc'[1] ecclesie ⫶ in prebendis suis 7 omnibus possessionibus que ad prebendas pertinent ⫶ perpetuam habeant libertatem . Ita quod nulli liceat archidiacono
10   uel archidiaconorum officialibus de prebendis uel possessionibus ad communam pertinentibus aliquid exigere . uel parochianos[3] prebendarum Linc'[1] ecclesie in placitum ponere . Nos igitur prefatam indulgenciam ab ipso factam ratam habentes eam presenti scripto 7 sigillo nostro duximus confirmare . Hoc
15   adicientes ut ecclesia de Seuerby que ad luminaria Linc'[1] ecclesie est assignata . 7 ecclesia de Lehton' que fuit de subdecanatu Linc'[1] . et ecclesia Omnium Sanctorum in Linc'[1] que pertinet ad cancellariam Linc'[1] ecclesie ⫶ eadem plene gaudeant libertate . Precipimus etiam ut in omnibus causis
20   tractandis 7 decidendis quecunque in parochiis[4] prebendarum

emerserint ∴ ipsi canonici omnimoda 7 perpetua gaudeant
libertate 7 libera vtantur potestate . Quod ut ratum habeatur
7 firmum ∴ presentis scripti testimonio 7 sigillo nostro
roborauimus . Hiis testibus . Rogero de Rolueston' decano
25 Linc'¹ ecclesie . magistro Willelmo de Montibus cancellario .
magistro Willelmo de Bramfeld' subdecano . magistro Girardo⁵
de Rowell' . magistro Waltero Blundo . Hugone de Sancto
Eadwardo⁶ 7 multis aliis.

Marginalia : *title*, De eodem confirmacio cum adieccione (Q). *opp. l. 15*, Seuerby
(Q).
Texts : MS—A. Ix(3).
Var. R. in Ix : ¹ Lincoln'. ² imperpetuum. ³ parrochianos. ⁴ parrochiis. ⁵ Gi-
rardo. ⁶ Edwardo.

907

289. Confirmation by bishop Hugh [I] of bishop Robert's grant
of privileges (no. 287 above), with the same addition as in no. 288.
(1191–1195.)

Omnibus Christi fidelibus ad quos¹ scriptum peruenerit
hoc² ∴ Hugo dei gratia Lincoln' . episcopus . salutem in
domino . Ex inspectione autentici instrumenti bone memorie .
Roberti quondam Lincoln' episcopi predecessoris nostri
5 cognouimus ipsum remisisse³ omnibus prebendis Linc'⁴ ecclesie
in perpetuum⁵ omnia iura episcopalia 7 omnes exactiones . 7
quod omnes canonici Lincoln' ecclesie ∴ in prebendis suis 7
omnibus possessionibus⁶ que ad prebendas pertinent ∴ perpetuam habeant libertatem . ita quod nulli liceat archidiacono
10 uel archidiaconorum officialibus de prebendis uel possessionibus
ad communam [pertine⁷]ntibus aliquid exigere . uel parrochianos prebendarum Linc'⁴ ecclesie in placitum ponere .
Nos igitur prefatam indulgentiam ab ipso fact[am rat⁷]am
[habe⁷]ntes ∴ eam presenti * scripto 7 sigillo nostro duximus
15 confirmare . Hoc adicientes ut ecclesia de Seuerebi . que ad
luminaria L[inc' ec⁷]clesie est assignata 7 ecclesia de Lehton*a*
que est de subdecanatu⁸ Linc'⁴ . 7 ecclesia Omnium Sanctorum
in Linc' . que pertinet ad cancellariam Lin[c'⁷]⁴ ecclesie .
eadem plene gaudeant libertate . Precipimus etiam ut in
20 omnibus causis tractandis 7 decidendis quecumque in parrochiis prebendarum emerserint ∴ ipsi canonici o[mnimo⁷]da
7 perpetua gaudeant libertate . 7 libera utantur potestate .
Quod ut ratum habeatur 7 firmum ∴ presentis scripti testimonio 7 sigillo nostro roborauimus . Hiis testibus . Hamone
25 decano Linc' ecclesie . Roberto . archidiacono . Huntedon*ie* .
magistro Rogero de Rolueston' . Johanne sacrista . Galfrid[o
de⁷] Lichelad' . magistro Ricardo de Swalwecl*iua* . Roberto
de Capella . magistro Girardo de Rowell' . Hugone . de Sancto
Edwardo⁹ . E[ustachio⁷] de Wilton' . 7 aliis , , ,

Omnib(us) s(an)c(t)e matris eccl(es)ie filiab(us) ad quos p(rese)ns scriptum p(er)venerit. Hugo d(e)i gra(tia) Lincoln(iensis) ep(iscopu)s salt(em) i(n) d(omi)no. Et i(n) p(er)petuo duraturu(m) ut futuru(m)

bone memorie. Rob(er)ti quondam Linc(ol)n(iensis) ep(iscop)i p(re)decessor(is) n(ost)ri cognovim(us) ip(su)m remisisse om(n)ib(us) p(re)bend(is) Linc(olniensis) eccl(es)ie i(n) p(er)petuu(m)

om(n)ia iura ep(iscopa)lia [domi]nis exactiones. q(uo)d om(n)i a(m)odo Linc(ol)n(iensis) eccl(es)ie. i(n) p(re)bend(is) su(is) om(n)i(n)o poss(ess)ionib(us) que ad p(rese)n(tem)

[p(re)]ti(n)ent: ep(iscop)alem h(abe)at libertate(m) i(n)a gr(ati)a t(ant)u(m) beate dignd(icacone) ut archidiacon(is) officialib(us) de p(re)bend(is) ut pos-

[se]ss(i)onib(us) ad co(mmun)a(m) ... unde aliquid exigat ut p(ar)rochianos p(rese)ntar(i) Linc(olniensis) eccl(es)ie i(n) pl(ac)itu(m) pone. H(is) q(ue) p(re)bendam in[d]ui

que ad luminaria ... [li]t(er)e est assignata i(n) eccl(es)ia d(e) leir(on). u(e)s est de sub(scri)ptam l(itte)re i(n) eccl(es)ia f(r)a. in li(n)ie que gra

nec ad cancellaria(m) li(n) ... eccl(es)ie. eadem pl(e)ne q(uan)dem liberta(te) libert(atem) p(re)cipim(us) s(er)va n(ost)ris causis s(er)vand(i) i gaudeb(is)

q(ui)cu(m)q(ue) i(n) p(ar)rochiis p(re)bend(ar)i(s) e(m)er(s)e(r)it(ur). ip(s)i ca(n)onicis v(e)l ... p(er)petua gaudeant liberta(te). i l(iber)a ma(n)u p(er)cipia(n)t.

Q(uo)d ut rat(um) h(abe)at i f(ir)mu(m). p(re)sens s(cri)ptu(m) si(gilli) n(ost)ro roboram(us). H(is) t(estib)us Mag(ist)ro W(illelmo) ... eccl(es)ie. Rob-

[er]tus. burned(on). Magistro Roberto de solvest(on). Joh(anne) capell(an). W(illelmo) ... W(illelmo) Mag(ist)ro ... de Scar[m]eet. Roberto de

Capella. magistro Gualf(rido) de Roxell. Hug(one) de fo(n)t. edwardo. ...

Facsimile facing page 252.

Endorsed : (1) H. de prebendis . 7 aliis possessionibus (13 cent.). (2) Confirmatio Hugonis episcopi Linc' super iurisdiccione in prebendalibus 7 ecclesiis de communa (13 cent.). (3) Tercia exhit' (15 cent.). (4) Memorandum pro Bachyler contra Rauenser' . v. idus Octobris anno domini 1346 . G.T. (contemp.). (5) St Hugh—confirmation of a grant of bp Robert remitting episcopal rights in the prebendal churches (19 cent.).

Tag for seal. Size: 9½ x 6¼ inches.

Marginalia in A907 : *title*, De eodem confirmacione (Q). *opp. l. 1*, ☞. In A909 : *title*, De eodem confirmacio (Q). *opp. l. 21*, Nota.

Texts: MS—Orig. Dij/55/2/8. A907. A909 (*a second copy of the charter : the differences are given in Var. R. below*). Ix(2).

Var. R.: [1] *insert* presens A909. [2] A907 *transfers* hoc *to follow* quos ; *om.* hoc A909 Ix. [3] remississe Ix. [4] Lincoln Ix. [5] imperpetuum Ix. [6] *insert* suis A909. [7] *supplied from* A907, *since there are holes in the original text.* [8] sub-deaconatu A907 A909. [9] Eadwardo A909.

* *Folio 183d.*

Hdl.   . [Titulus] C (Q).   iurisdiccio (Q).

908

290. Notification by bishop Robert [II] to the archdeacons throughout the diocese that he has exempted the canons of Lincoln from the subjection which the archdeacons were wont to demand in respect of the prebends of the canons. (Circa 1160.)

Robertus dei gracia Linc'[1] episcopus . omnibus archidiaconis per episcopatum Linc' constitutis . salutem . Nouerit vniuersitas vestra nos inperpetuum[2] absoluisse omnes canonicos Linc'[1] ecclesie a subieccione quam de prebendis eorum 7

5   earum pertinenciis . tam in prebendis quam in[3] hominibus . 7 omnibus ad eas pertinentibus ∴ exigere quondam consueuistis . Testibus . Martino thesaurario . [4]Gaufrido capellano . Rog'[4] . magistro Radulfo 7 magistro Henrico . Fulcone[5] 7 Willelmo capellano.

Marginalia : *title*, De eodem (Q). *opp. l. 1*, ☞. In P : De absolucione canonicorum Linc' 7 prebendarum earundem.

Texts: MS—A (written at the foot of f. 183). P2. Black Book, f. 14. Pd—*Linc. Cath. Statutes* i, 310.

Var. R.: [1] Lincol' P ; Lincoln' BlBk. [2] imperpetuum BlBk. [3] *om.* in BlBk. [4]-[4] Galfrido capellano regis P ; Gaufrido capellano regis BlBk, *which is no doubt correct.* [5] Fulc' P ; Fulco BlBk.

909

291. Another copy of no. 289 above.

Marginalia : Nota.

909a

292. *Inspeximus* and confirmation by H[ubert] archbishop of Canterbury of bishop Hugh's charter (no. 289 above). (1200–1205.)

H. dei gracia Cantuar*iensis* archiepiscopus tocius Anglie primas . omnibus Christi fidelibus ad quos presens scriptum peruenerit ∴ eternam in domino salutem . Nouerit vniuersitas vestra nos cartam bone memorie .H. quondam Linc' episcopi

5 in hac forma inspexisse . Omnibus Christi fidelibus ad quos
scriptum peruenerit hoc . Hugo dei gracia Linc' episcopus (
salutem in domino . Ex inspeccione autentici instrumenti
bone memorie Roberti quondam Linc' episcopi predecessoris
nostri cognouimus ipsum remisisse omnibus prebendis Linc'
10 ecclesie inperpetuum omnia iura episcopalia . et omnes
exactiones . 7 quod omnes canonici Linc' ecclesie ; in prebendis
suis 7 omnibus possessionibus que ad prebendas pertinent ;
perpetuam habeant libertatem . ita quod nulli liceat archidiacono uel archideaconorum¹ officialibus de prebendis uel
15 possessionibus ad comunam pertinentibus aliquid exigere uel
parochianos prebendarum Linc' ecclesie in placitum ponere .
Nos igitur prefatam indulgenciam ab ipso factam ratam
habentes ; eam presenti scripto 7 sigillo nostro duximus
confirmare . Hoc adicientes ut ecclesia de Seuerby que
20 luminaria Linc' ecclesie est assignata . 7 ecclesia * de Lehton'
que est de subdeaconatu¹ Linc' . et eciam ecclesia Omnium
Sanctorum in Linc' que pertinet ad cancellariam Linc' ecclesie
eadem plene gaudeant libertate . Precipimus eciam ut in
omnibus causis tractandis 7 decidendis quecunque in parochiis
25 prebendarum emerserint ipsi canonici omnimoda 7 perpetua
gaudeant libertate (7 libera utantur potestate . Quod ut
ratum habeatur 7 firmum ; presentis scripti testimonio 7
sigillo nostro roborauimus . Hiis testibus . Hamone decano
Linc' ecclesie . Roberto archidiacono Huntedonie . magistro
30 Rogero de Rolueston' . Johanne sacrista . Gaufrido de Lichelad' . magistro Ricardo de Sualewecliua . Roberto de Capella .
magistro Girardo de Rowell' . Hugone de Sancto Edwardo .
Eustacio de Wilton' . 7 aliis . Vt igitur quod a predictis
episcopis .R. 7 .H. in hac parte racionabiliter factum est
35 maiorem optineat firmitatem ; eorum indulgenciam 7 concessionem sicut racionabiliter facte sunt presentis scripti
serie 7 sigilli nostri apposicione duximus confirmandas . Hiis
testibus . magistro .H. archidiacono Richemundie . magistro
Simone de Siwell' . thesaurario Lichefeld' . magistro Johanne
40 de Tinemutha . magistro Roberto Ralbo . magistro Adam de
Walsingham . Roberto de Bristoll' . 7 aliis.

Marginalia: *title,* De eodem confirmacio archiepiscopi (Q). *opp. l. 1,* ☞ .
Text: MS—A.
Var. R.: ¹ *sic.*

Folio 184.
Hdl.   .C. (Q).

910

293. Ordinance of bishop William [of Blois], made with the
goodwill of the dean and chapter, providing that every one who is

a canon of Lincoln when he closes his latest day shall have the
power of disposing of the fruits of his prebend for one year from
the day of his death ; and that every one of the vicars of the
prebendaries shall receive every year half a mark beyond his
accustomed stipend. (1203–1205.)

    Willelmus dei gracia episcopus Linc' dilectis in Christo
filiis . decano 7 capitulo Linc' ecclesie salutem . 7 benediccionem . Licet ex officii nostri debito singulorum per diocesim
nostram constitutorum utilitatibus paterna sollicitudine
5 prouidere teneamur ꞉ vestris tamen comodis . 7 profectibus
7 animarum vestrarum saluti . qui deo 7 beate uirgini nostrum
inpenditis obsequium . uberiori prouidencia adesse uolumus
sicut 7 debemus . Hinc est quod habita deliberacione cum
Rogero de Rolueston' decano 7 capitulo Linc' ecclesie de
10 communi eorum consilio 7 uoluntate ꞉ statuimus ut vnusquisque
uestrum siue debitis sit oneratus siue non ꞉ de fructibus 7
obuencionibus prebende sue a die obitus sui usque in annum
conpletum¹ liberam habeat pro uoluntate sua disponendi
facultatem . ita ut illi soli hoc gaudeant beneficio ꞉ qui
15 existentes canonici Linc' ecclesie diem clauserint extremum .
Prouidimus eciam ut singuli vicarii prebendarum dimidiam
marcam ultra consueta stipendia singulis annis percipiant .
Vt autem hec nostra ordinacio perpetuam optineat firmitatem
eam presenti scripto . 7 sigilli nostri patrocinio roboramus .
20 Testibus magistris .W. de Bramfeld subdecano .G. archidiacono Bedfordie . Alexandro de Bedefordia . Philippo de
Malbertorp' . Gerardo de Rowell' .T. de Fiskerton'² Linc'
ecclesie canonicis . magistro .W. filio Fulconis . Eudone preposito 7 aliis.

Marginalia: *title*, De anno post obitum canonici (Q).
Texts: MS—A (written at the foot of folios 183d. and 184). Pd—*Linc. Cath.
Statutes* i, 115–16.
Var. R.: ¹ completum BlBk. ² *printed* Silkerton *in Linc. Cath. Statutes.*

911

294. Mandate of bishop Hugh [I], informing the archdeacons
and deans that the dean and chapter have the power of exercising
canonical justice against those who detain anything from the common ; and commanding them to execute the sentence of the dean
and chapter. (Circa 1191–1195.)

    Hugo dei gracia Linc'¹ episcopus ꞉ dilectis filiis archi-
diaconis decanis 7 aliis officialibus per episcopatum Lincoln'
constitutis salutem 7 benediccionem . Vniuersitati vestre
notum fieri uolumus . nos dilectis in Christo filiis nostris
5 decano 7 capitulo Linc'¹ ecclesie² uel si decanus absens fuerit
subdecano . 7 eidem capitulo . hanc indulgenciam fecisse ꞉

ut omnes iniustos detentores commune sue ⁊ omnes qui uel
hominibus³ seu possessionibus ad eandem communam⁴ pertinentibus . iniuriam molestiam uel grauamen intulerint
10 liberum sit eis ecclesiastica censura cohercere . ⁊ in eos usque
ad condignam satisfactionem ⸴ canonicam iusticiam exercere .
Saluo in omnibus iure episcopi ⁊ eius potestate . Nec liceat
uobis excommunicatos uel interdictos ab eis absoluere citra
mandatum episcopi uel capituli . Precipimus autem ut
15 sentencia que ab ipsis lata fuerit ⸴ per uos execucioni
mandetur.

Marginalia: *title*, De iurisdiccione . capituli (Q). *opp. l. 1*, . Nota . pro capitulo.
Texts: MS—A. Black Book, ff. 13d., 14. Martilogium, ff. 3, 3d. Pd—*Linc.*
Cath. Statutes i, 309.
Var. R.: ¹ Lincoln' BlBk. ² *om.* ecclesie Martilogium. ³ *insert* suis Martilogium.
⁴ communem Martilogium.

912

295. Mandate of bishop Walter [of Coutances], charging the
archdeacons to execute ecclesiastical justice, when required by the
dean and chapter so to do, against those who detain anything from
the common. (1183–1185.)

Wal*terus* dei gratia Lincol'¹ episcopus dilectis in Christo
filiis omnibus archidiaconis ⁊ officialibus eorum in [episco-
patu²] Lincol'¹ constitutis ⸴ salutem gratiam ⁊ benedictionem . Quanto propinquius ⁊ familiarius decanus ⁊ Lincoln'
5 capitulum uidentur nobis pre ceteris filiis nostris adherere ⸴
tanto firmius ⁊ plenius uolumus iura eorum in omnibus
illibata ⁊ integra conseruari . ne pro defectu nostro debeant
aliquid incommodum sustinere . Inde est quod uestram
prudentiam attentius duximus exhortari districtius man-
10 dantes . quatinus si quis subditorum uestrorum aliquid de
communia Lincol'¹ ecclesie detinere presumpserit . ⁊ commoni-
tus eisdem filiis ⁊ [cano²]nicis nostris satisfacere noluerit ⸴ in
ipsum iusticiam ecclesiasticam infra quindecim dies postquam requisiti fueritis ⸴ exercere non differatis . Si quis autem
15 uestrum in executione huius mandati nostri negligens uel
remissus inuentus fuerit ⸴ noueritis nos in predictum decanum
Lincol'¹ auctoritatem exequendi mandati nostri plenius
transtulisse ⅋ sentenciam quam propter hoc rationabiliter
tulerit ⸴ ratam ⁊ inuiolabilem habituros . ⁊ ut eandem ratam
20 habeatis precipimus . Si uero prefatus decanus interesse
non poterit ⸴ eandem auctoritatem . in subdecanum uel
alium canonicum qui uices eorum in hac parte suppleat ⸴
duximus transferendam . Vobis igitur * districtius mandamus
ut sentenciam quam super hoc rationabiliter dederint . ratam
25 habeatis . ⁊ faciatis usque ad congruam satisfactionem firmius
obseruari . saluo iure ⁊ dignitate nostra . His testibus .
magistro Johanne Cornub*ia* . magistro Radulfo Constan*ciensi* .

Ricardo R[ogero² .] Nicholao capellanis . Willelmo . Osberto clericis . 7 multis aliis.

Facsimile opposite page 256.
Endorsed: (1) De execucione sentenciarum capituli (Q). (2) .W. de libertatibus commune (13 cent.). (3) Quod archidiaconi teneantur exequi sentencias latas per capitulum (13 cent.). (4) .v. (5) Due litere episcoporum connexe (14 cent.). (6) iij vis'.
The tag for the seal has been torn away with a portion of the foot of the charter (there is a hole for a string in the top left hand corner). Size: 6¾ x 6 inches.
Marginalia in A: *title*, De eodem . 7 infra ad. [a word or words erased] (Q). *opp. l. 23*, Nota (Q).
Texts: MS—Dij/60/2/1. A.
Var. R.: ¹ Linc' A. ² *supplied from A, the original charter having been injured.*

* *Folio 184d.*

912a

296. Mandate of bishop Richard [Gravesend], commanding the archdeacons and deans to execute the sentences of the dean and chapter. At Buckden [co. Huntingdon]. 17 August, 1259.

Ricardus miseracione diuina Linc'¹ episcopus (dilectis in Christo filiis . . archidiaconis . eorum . . officialibus . 7 . . decanis per ciuitatem 7 diocesim Linc'¹ constitutis salutem graciam 7 benediccionem . Cum iudicia merito censeantur
5   frustratoria nisi exequcioni² legitime valeant demandari ꞉ vobis mandamus firmiter iniungentes quatinus sentencias quas dilecti filii . . decanus 7 capitulum Linc'¹ promulgauerint in malefactores suos nostre iurisdiccioni subiectos qui libertates aut liberas consuetudines eorum uiolauerint
10   uel offenderint in rebus uel personis ꞉ ad ipsorum requisicionem sine difficultate qualibet execqucioni demandetis . Incitacionibus faciendis quociens per eosdem interpellati fueritis ꞉ eisdem promtius³ 7 celerius obtemperantes . Dat' apud Bugeden' . xvj. kalendas . Septembris . pontificatus nostri
15   anno primo . Valete semper in domino.

Marginalia in A: *title*, De execucionibus faciendis sentenciarum capituli (Q).
In BlBk: De execucionibus mandatorum decani et capituli Lincolniensis per archidiaconos . . . officiales . . . et decanos Lincolniensis diocesis faciendis.
Texts: MS—A. Black Book i, ff. 14, 14d. Pd—*Linc. Cath. Statutes* i, 310–11.
Var R. in BlBk: ¹ Lincoln'. ² execucioni. ³ prompcius.

913

297. Mandate of bishop William [of Blois] similar to that of his predecessor, bishop Hugh [I] (no. 298 below). (1203–1206.)

Willelmus dei gracia Linc' episcopus omnibus archidiaconis . 7 officialibus per diocesim Linc' ecclesie constitutis) salutem 7 dei benediccionem . Cum cura 7 solicitudo Linc' ecclesie quam deo auctore regendam suscepimus . nos admodum
5   inuitent . ea que hactenus ninus bene fuerint ordinata in meliorem statum redigere . Canonicorum ibidem deo iugiter

R

famulantium comodo inposterum pro futuro inuigilare
tenemur . Mouemur siquidem nec illud clausis oculis decetero
preterire possumus . quod eciam uos mouere deberet . 7 non
10 mouemini ad quos specialius pertinet cura 7 solicitudo Linc'
ecclesie . quod cum tantam habeat filiorum multitudinem
ipsi eam contempnunt ut saltem eam semel in anno secundum
secundum [*sic*] consuetudinem ecclesie nostre . que in aliis
ecclesiis episcopalibus celebris habetur ꝛ eam in propria
15 persona uel de suis facultatibus condignas oblaciones mittendo
negligant uisitare . Quod quidem ex negligencia clericorum
pocius quam laicorum simplicitate . nouimus accidisse .
Quocirca vniuersitati vestre auctoritate qua fungimur precipimus . quatinus decanis ⟩ personis ⟩ presbiteris ⟩ per
20 nostram diocesim constitutis in ue*r*tute obediencie iniungatis .
ut in singulis parochiis singuli capellani fideles sibi commissos
ad hoc sufficientes auctoritate nostra inducant . quod de
singulis domibus aliqui in festo Pentecostes ad locum consuetum 7 processionibus destinatum singulis annis satagant
25 conuenire ꝛ oblaciones condignas in remissionem peccatorum
suorum . 7 in signum obediencie 7 recordacionis matris sue
Linc' ecclesie offerentes . Iubeatis eciam ut singuli decani
personis ⟩ presbiteris sibi commissis auctoritate nostra precipiant ꝛ quatinus uniuersi attenta solicitudine prouideant
30 ut nominibus parochianorum suorum seorsum notatis . decanis
suis cum clericis nostris in Pentecos*te* ad hoc destinandis .
sciant per nominum annotaciones fideliter respondere . qui
secundum mandatum nostrum ut filii obedientes ⟩ uel uenerint
ꝛ uel miserint . 7 qui mandatum nostrum transgredientes
35 venire uel mittere neglexerint.

Marginalia : *title*, De oblacionibus Pentecoste*s* (Q). *opp. l. 14*, Nota.
Text : MS—A.   In the Black Book, f. 13, in allusion to the present charter,
after the copy of bishop Hugh's charter (no. 298 below), there is the note : ' Consimi-
lem litteram concessit episcopus Willelmus successor Hugonis predicti.'

914

298. Mandate of bishop Hugh [I], commanding the archdeacons
to cause the faithful of every household in the diocese to be moved
to a more regular observance of the yearly processions at Pentecost.
(1186–1200.)

Hugo dei gracia Linc' episcopus omnibus archidiaconis
7 officialibus per diocesim Linc'[1] ecclesie[2] constitutis salutem
7 dei benediccionem . Cum cura 7 solicitudo Linc'[1] ecclesie
quam deo auctore regendam suscepimus . nos admodum
5 inuitent . ea que hactenus minus bene fuerint ordinata in
meliorem statum * redigere . canonicorum ibidem deo iugiter
famulantium comodo inposterum pro futuro inuigilare tenemur ꝛ mouemur siquidem nec illud clausis oculis decetero

preterire possumus . quod eciam uos mouere deberet . 7 non
10　mouemini . ad quos specialius pertinet cura 7 solicitudo ³Linc'¹
ecclesie³ . quod cum tantam habeat filiorum multitudinem ipsi
eam contempnunt . vt saltem eam semel in anno secundum
consuetudinem ecclesie nostre que in aliis ecclesiis episcopalibus
celebris habetur ꞏ꞉ eam in propria persona uel de suis facultati-
15　bus condignas oblaciones mittendo negligant visitare . Quod
quidem ex negligencia clericorum potius quam laicorum
simplicitate ꞏ꞉ nouimus accidisse . quocirca vniuersitati uestre
auctoritate qua fungimur precipimus quatinus decanis personis presbiteris per nostram diocesim constitutis in uirtute
20　obediencie iniungatis ut in singulis parochiis singuli capellani
fideles sibi commissos ad hoc sufficientes auctoritate nostra
inducant quod de singulis domibus aliqui in festo⁴ Pentecostes ad locum consuetum 7 processionibus destinatum
singulis annis satagant conuenire ꞏ꞉ oblaciones condignas in
25　remissionem peccatorum suorum . 7 in signum obediencie ꞏ꞉
7 recordacionis matris sue Linc'¹ ecclesie offerentes . Jubeatis
etiam ut singuli decani personis presbiteris sibi commisis
auctoritate nostra precipiant . quatinus vniuersi attenta
solicitudine prouideant vt nominibus parochianorum suorum
30　seorsum notatis decanis suis⁵ cum clericis nostris in Pente-
coste⁶ ad hoc destinandis sciant per nominum annotaciones
fideliter respondere qui secundum mandatum nostrum ut
filii obedientes uel uenerint ꞏ꞉ uel miserint 7 qui mandatum
nostrum transgredientes uenire uel mittere neglexerint⁷.

Marginalia : *title*, De eisdem (Q). *opp. l. 5*, de eadem (Q).
Texts : MS—A. Black Book, f. 13. Martilogium, ff. 2d, 3. Pd—*Giraldus Cam-
brensis* vii, 200–1. *Linc. Cath. Statutes* i, 307–8.
Var. R. : ¹ Lincoln' BlBk. Martilogium. ² *om.* ecclesie Martilogium. ³⁻³ ecclesie
Lincoln' Martilogium. ⁴ festis Martilogium. ⁵ *om.* suis Martilogium. ⁶ Pentecostes
Martilogium. ⁷ necglexerint Martilogium.
Note : By ancient custom some of the inhabitants of every parish were bound
to repair to the mother church of their diocese at Whitsuntide, in order that they
might join in the usual processions, and make the accustomed oblations. These
offerings, to which every house was required to contribute, were called Pentecostals
or Whitsun-farthings (Gibson, *Codex Juris Ecclesiastici Anglicani* ii, 976–7). It
appears from the present text that these duties had been neglected, and Dr R. M.
Woolley suggests that Saint Hugh's effort to secure a greater regularity in their per-
formance was due to the urgent need of money for the re-building of the cathedral
(*St Hugh of Lincoln*, p. 59).

* *Folio* 185.
Hdl.　　　　　　　　　　　　　　　.C. (Q).

915

299. Grant by bishop William [of Blois] similar to that of his
predecessor, bishop Hugh [I] (no. 300 below).　(1203–1206.)

.W. dei gracia Linc' episcopus . dilectis in Christo filiis
decano 7 capitulo Linc' ecclesie salutem . 7 dei benediccionem .
Quia feruens habemus desiderium ut ad honorem dei 7 beate

virginis genitricis eius Marie In ecclesia Linc' debita cele-
5 britate singulis quibus temporibus prout decet diuina celebrentur ; ad id competenter 7 comode prosequendum canonicorum 7 vicariorum ibi residencium utilitati prospicere
cupientes . tibi decane 7 canonicis residentibus . 7 si decanus
fuerit absens tibi subdecane 7 canonicis residentiam facienti-
10 bus . hanc potestatem indulgemus ; vt nostra auctoritate
licitum sit vobis cohercere omnes canonicos qui non faciunt
residenciam per detencionem prebende sue ; idoneos vicarios
loco suo constituant . 7 de communi consilio canonicorum
residencium ; eis honestam 7 sufficientem sustentacionem
15 prouideant . Preterea vobis hanc etiam facimus indulgenciam .
ut omnes iniustos detentores commune vestre 7 omnes qui
uel hominibus uel possessionibus ad eandem communam
pertinentibus iniuriam . molestiam . uel grauamen intulerint ;
liberum sit vobis ecclesiastica censura cohercere . 7 in eos
20 usque ad condignam satisfactionem ; canonicam iusticiam
exercere . Saluo in omnibus iure episcopi 7 eius potestate .
Nec liceat archidiaconis . decanis uel aliis officialibus Linc'
episcopatus excommunicatos aut interdictos a uobis ; absoluere citra mandatum episcopi uel uestrum . Precipimus
25 autem ut sentencia que a vobis lata fuerit ; per archidiaconos
uel decanos seu alios episcopatus officiales execucioni mandetur.

Marginalia : *title*, De vicariis constituendis in choro . 7 iurisdiccione capituli (Q).
opp. l. 11, Nota ad compellendum canonicos non residentes inuenire vicarios
(14 cent.).
Text : MS—A. In the Black Book, f. 13d., in allusion to the present charter,
after the copy of bishop Hugh's charter (no. 300 below), there is the note : ' Con-
similem litteram concessit episcopus Willelmus successor Hugonis predicti.'

Folio 185d.
Hdl.   .C. (Q).

916

300. Grant by bishop Hugh [I] to the dean and chapter of
licence to compel all canons who do not make residence to appoint
suitable vicars to fill their place; and also of liberty to exercise
canonical justice against those persons who do injury to the
common. (1186–1200.)

Hugo dei gracia Linc'[1] episcopus . dilectis in Christo filiis
decano 7 capitulo Linc'[2] ecclesie salutem 7 dei benediccionem .
Quia feruens habemus desiderium ut ad honorem dei 7 beate
virginis genitricis eius Marie in ecclesia Linc'[2] debita cele-
5 britate singulis quibus[3] temporibus prout decet diuina
celebrentur ; Ad id competenter 7 comode [4]prosequendum
canonicorum[4] 7 vicariorum ibi residencium utilitati prospicere

cupientes . tibi decane 7 canonicis residentibus . 7 si decanus
fuerit absens tibi subdecane 7 canonicis residenciam facientibus
10 hanc potestatem indulgemus ; ut nostra auctoritate licitum
sit vobis [5]cohercere omnes canonicos[5] qui non faciunt residenciam per detencionem prebende sue ; ut idoneos vicarios
loco suo constituant 7 de communi consilio canonicorum
residencium ; eis honestam 7 sufficientem sustentacionem
15 prouideant . Preterea vobis hanc [6]etiam facimus[6] indulgenciam ut omnes iniustos detentores commune vestre 7
omnes qui uel hominibus uel possessionibus ad eandem communam pertinentibus iniuriam[7] . molestiam . uel grauamen
intulerint . liberum sit uobis ecclesiastica censura cohercere
20 7 in eos usque ad condignam satisfaccionem ; canonicam
iusticiam excercere[8] Saluo in omnibus iure episcopi 7 eius
potestate . Nec liceat archidiaconis . decanis . uel aliis
officialibus Linc'[1] episcopatus . excommunicatos aut interdictos a uobis ; absoluere citra mandatum episcopi uel uestrum .
25 Precipimus autem ut sentencia que a vobis lata fuerit ; per
archidiaconos uel decanos seu alios episcopatus officiales
execucioni mandetur.[9]

Marginalia in A: *title*, De eodem (Q). In Black Book : De vicariis a singulis
canonicis non residentibus constituendis. De cohercione detentorum commune
ecclesie Lincolniensis et iniuriatorum eiusdem.
Texts : MS—A. Black Book, ff. 13, 13d. Martilogium, f. 3. Pd—*Giraldus Cambrensis* vii, 201–2. *Linc. Cath. Statutes* i, 308–9.
Var. R. : [1] Lincoln' BlBk Martilogium   [2] Lincoln' BlBk.   [3] quibusque BlBk.
Martilogium.   [4-4] canonicorum prosequendum Martilogium.   [5-5] omnes canonicos
cohercere Martilogium.   [6-6] facimus eciam Martilogium.   [7] inuriam BlBk.
Martilogium.   [8] exercere BlBk.   [9] demandatur Martilogium.

917

301. Grant by bishop Hugh [I] similar to no. 300 above. (1186–
1200.)

Hugo dei gracia Linc' episcopus ; dilectis in Christo filiis
decano 7 capitulo Linc' ecclesie ⟩ salutem 7 dei benediccionem . Quia feruens habemus desiderium ut ad honorem
dei 7 beate virginis genitricis eius Marie in ecclesia Linc'
5 debita celeberitate[1] singulis quibusque temporibus prout decet
diuina celebrentur ; Ad id competenter 7 comode prosequendum canonicorum 7 vicariorum ibidem residencium
utilitati prospicere cupientes tibi decane ; 7 canonicis residentibus . 7 si decanus[2] fuerit absens . tibi subdecane 7
10 canonicis residenciam facientibus hanc potestatem indulgemus . ut nostra auctoritate licitum sit vobis cohercere omnes
canonicos qui non faciunt residenciam per detencionem
prebende sue . vt idoneos vicarios loco suo constituant 7 de
communi consilio canonicorum residencium ; eis honestam 7
15 sufficientem sustentacionem prouideant . Preterea vobis hanc
eciam facimus indulgenciam . vt in omnes iniustos detentores

commune vestre) liberum sit vobis ecclesiasticam iusticiam
exercere . Saluo in omnibus iure episcopi 7 eius potestate.

Marginalia: *title*, De eodem (Q). *opp. l. 1*, Nota (Q). *opp. l. 10*, Nota.
Text: A.
Var. R.: ¹ *sic.* ²7 canonicis *struck out.*

918

302. Notification by bishop Alexander to Adelmus the dean
and the chapter that he has given the dignity of the office of precentor to their canon, Roger de Almaria ; and that he has
ordained as the possession of this dignity all the churches in the
borough of Lincoln of the demesne and gift of king Henry [I]
which have not as yet been confirmed by episcopal privilege *in
prebendam* or to the common. The bishop has also confirmed
to Roger the school of song. (March, 1147–February, 1148.)

Alexander dei gracia Linc' episcopus . Adelmo decano 7
personis 7 uniuerso capitulo Linc' salutem . Memini ut uos
ipsi nostis ecclesiam uestram diu a precentoris uacasse officio
quod ei necesse . est habere continuum . Ipsius igitur inper-
5 fectioni cosulere¹ desiderans huius officii dignitatem concessi
7 dedi honesto uiro Rogero de Almaria canonico nostro nobis
simul 7 uobis cognitione ac conuersatione probato qui bonorum
examine uirorum . domini uidelicet Radulfi abbatis S[ancti²]
Albani . Roberti archidiaconi Linc' Roberti archidiaconi
10 Legrecestrie . Dauidis archidiaconi de Buccehinamia³ . magistri
Hamonis [7 al²]iorum [qui²] nobiscum erant canonicorum consilio hoc dignus est inuentus officio . huius dignitatis possessionem esse constitui omnes ecclesias nostras de burgo Linc' de
dominio⁴ 7 dono regis Henrici que adhuc in prebendam siue
15 in comunionem⁵ nec meo nec antecessorum meorum sunt
priuilegio confirmate . ecclesiam uidelicet sancti Micahelis
iuxta portam . ecclesiam sancti Petri in uico parcamenariorum
. ecclesiam sancti Georgii . ecclesiam sancte Trinitatis .
ecclesiam sancti Edmundi ecclesiam sancti Swuituni⁶ . Et
20 extra muros ecclesiam sancte Trinitatis . ecclesiam sancti
Rumoldi . ecclesiam sancti Bauonis . ecclesiam sancti Augustini . In Estgata⁷ . ecclesiam sancti Petri . In Wicheford'⁸
iuxta pontem ecclesiam sancti Johannis . ecclesiam sancte
Trinitatis . ecclesiam sancti Petri . ecclesiam sancti Micahelis .
25 ecclesiam sancte Margarete . ecclesiam sancti Marchi⁹ . scolam
quoque de Cantu 7 alias simul dignitates que ad hunc honorem
pertinere dinoscuntur eidem Rogero concedimus 7 confirmamus.

Facsimile opposite.
Endorsed : Ecclesiæ Lincoln' præcentoratui annexe (18 cent.).
Tag for seal. Size : 6¾ x 3¾ inches.

Rotbertus Dei gratia Lincolniensis episcopus. Adel decano et personis et universis canonicis hunc salutem. ... cum in nos ... nostri ... ecclesia nostra ... a personis vacasse officio ... in nec ... Ipsius ... inspectione consulte, desiderans ... huius officii dignitate congessi et dedi ... mense ... pro Roma ... et almaria canonico meo ... nobis simul et nobis cognatione ... apud ... plene ... quod ... eramus et ... ibi ... Rodulfi Alberti ... eam. Robertus Archidiaconus Lincolniensis ... legere, ... Archidiaconus de Bucchim ... canonicorum consilio ... et universitatis officio, huius dignitate ... et ecclesias nostras de Burgo Lincolniensi de domini ... Rogerii ... que adhuc in prebenda ... nec meos nec successorum meorum se privilegio ... ecclesia ... Sancti Michaelis iuxta portam ... meo ... Ecclesia Sancti Georgii. Ecclesia Sancti ... Ecclesia Sancti Edmundi Ecclesia Sancti ... Ecclesia Sancte ... Ecclesia Sancti Rumoldi ... Ecclesia Sancti Bavonis. Ecclesia Sancti Augustini, ... ecclesia Sancti Petri. In ... iuxta portam Ecclesia Sancti Iohannis. Ecclesia Sancte ... Ecclesia Sancti Petri. Ecclesia Sancti ... Ecclesia Sancte Margarete Ecclesia Sancti ... quoque de eorum et alias simul dignitates que ad hunc honore prime dinoscuntur eidem Rogerio concedimus et confirmamus.

R... gratia Lincolniensis episcopus Omnibus fidelibus Dei salutem. Noverit universitas vestra nos dedisse et concessisse omnibus ecclesiis que ad canonicatum Lincolniensis ecclesie pertinent ... libertate et eundo immunitare in perpetuum quod concessimus dedimus ecclesiis et prebendarum canonicorum et de ecclesie ... in ... nostra quod dedimus de eisdem libertatibus ... Testibus ... cancellario et ... subdecano et Gaufrido capellano et ... filio Godefridi ...

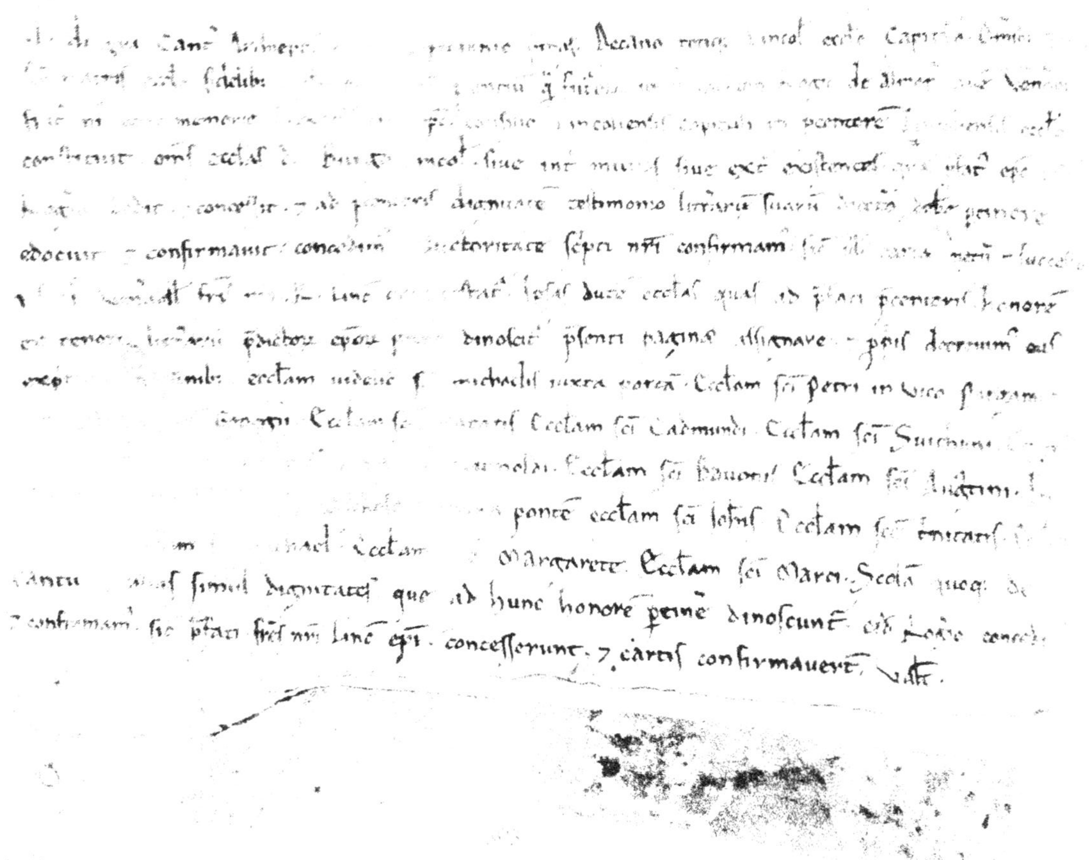

Marginalia in A : *title*, Confirmacio archiepiscopi de iurisdiccione superius (*recte* inferius) est (Q). *opp. l. 10*, scribatur cum dignitatibus * sequens (Q). [Q *does not seem to have indicated any place in the Registrum Antiquissimum for the charters relating to dignities.*]

Texts : MS—Orig. Dij/63/1/8. **A.**

Var. R. in A : ¹ consulere. ² *supplied from A, because of a hole in the original charter.* ³ Bucchingham. ⁴ *dominio.* ⁵ communionem. ⁶ Swithuni. ⁷ Estegata. ⁸ Wikeford. ⁹ Marci.

Note ; Of the parishes enumerated in the present text only those of Saint Michael on the Mount, Saint Swithin, Saint Peter in Eastgate, Saint Peter at Gowts, and Saint Mark have survived to the present day. Of the churches named only that of Saint Peter at Gowts still stands. The other surviving parishes have churches built at later dates and, in some instances, on different sites. An account of the parishes of Lincoln will be supplied in a later volume of this series.

919

303. Confirmation by T[heobald] archbishop of Canterbury of bishop Alexander's charter (no. 302 above).   (1148–1161 ; probably circa 1150.)

.T. dei gratia Cant*uariensis* archiepiscopus . 7 totius Britannie primas . Decano totique Lincol'¹ ecclesie capitulo . omnibus quoque sancte matris ecclesie fidelibus ⁊ salutem . Nouerit tam presentium quam futurorum uniuersitas . quum .
5　Rogerio² de Almar*ia* quem venerabilis frater noster bone memorie Alexander Linc' episcopus . consillio Lincoliensis¹ capituli in precentorem Lincoliensis¹ ecclesie constituit ⁊ omnes ecclesias de burgo Lincol'¹ . siue intra muros siue extra existentes . quas prefatus episcopus eidem Rogerio²
10　dedit . 7 concessit . 7 ad precentoris dignitatem testimonio litterarum suarum decetero debere pertinere edocuit . 7 confirmauit ⁊ concedimus 7 auctoritate scripti nostri confirmamus . sicut illius carta necnon 7 successoris eius venerabilis fratris nostri .R. Linc' episcopi testatur . Ipsas autem
15　ecclesias quas ad prefati precentoris honorem ex tenore litterarum predictorum episcoporum pertinere dinoscitur ⁊ presenti paginæ assignare . 7 propriis decreuimus eas exprimere nominibus . ecclesiam uidelicet sancti Michaelis iuxta portam . ecclesiam sancti Petri in vico pargamenariorum³ .
20　ecclesiam sancti Georgii . ecclesiam sancte Trinitatis . ecclesiam sancti Eadmundi⁴ . ecclesiam sancti Suithuni . Et extra muros ecclesiam sancte Trinitatis . ecclesiam sancti Rumoldi . ecclesiam sancti Bauonis . ecclesiam sancti Augustini . In Estgata⁵ ecclesiam sancti Petri . In Wicheford'⁶ iuxta⁷ pontem
25　ecclesiam sancti Johannis . ecclesiam sancte Trinitatis . ecclesiam sancti Petri . ecclesiam sancti Michaelis . ecclesiam sancte Margarete . ecclesiam sancti Marci . scolam quoque de Cantu . 7 alias simul dignitates que ad hunc honorem pertinere dinoscuntur . eidem Rogerio² concedimus 7 confirmamus .
30　sicut prefati fratres nostri Linc' episcopi ⁊ concesserunt . 7 cartis confirmauerunt , Valete,

Facsimile opposite page 263.
Endorsed : Lincon 𝕭 (13 cent.).
Strip for seal at foot, below which a riband has been torn off. Size : 6⅞ x 5¾ inches.
Texts : MS—Orig. Dij/63/1/9. A.
Var. R. in A : ¹ Linc'. ² Rogero. ³ percamenorum. ⁴ Edmundi. ⁵ Estegata.
⁶ Wikeford'. ⁷ om. iuxta.

ADD. CHART.

304. Grant by bishop Robert [II] to the churches which belong to the precentorship of the same liberty and exemption as he has granted to the prebendal churches of the canons. (Circa 1160–1167.)

.R. dei gracia Linc' episcopus omnibus fidelibus dei salutem . Nouerit uniuersitas uestra nos dedisse 7 concessisse omnibus ecclesiis que ad cantariam Linc' ecclesie pertinent eandem libertatem 7 eandem immunitatem inperpetuum
5 quas concessimus 7 dedimus ecclesiis prebendarum canonicorum eiusdem ecclesie sicut in carta nostra quam dedimus de eisdem libertatibus continetur . Testibus Hamone cancellario . 7 Radulfo subdecano 7 Galfrido capellano . 7 Willelmo filio Godefridi. Valete.

Facsimile opposite page 262.
Endorsed : Lyncon 𝕭 (13 cent.).
Strip for seal at foot, below which is a narrow riband. Size : 5¼ x 3¼ inches.
Text : MS—Orig. Dij/63/1/10.

ADD. CHART.

305. Confirmation by bishop Hugh [I] of bishop Robert's grant (no. 304 above). (1189–1192.)

Omnibus [Christi] fidelibus ad quos presens scriptum peruenerit . Hugo dei gracia Linc' episcopus salutem in domino . Nouerit uniuersitas uestra nos ratam [habentes 7] gratam libertatem 7 immunitatem quam bone memorie Robertus
5 predecessor noster quondam Linc' episcopus concessit ecclesiis de cantaria Linc' ecclesie . volumus itaque 7 precipimus . ut eedem ecclesie ea plene gaudeant libertate qua gaudent ecclesie prebendarum Linc' ecclesie . sicut in scripto nostro quod ecclesiis prebendarum indulsimus ⁊ plene continetur .
10 saluo denario beati Petri . de quo nichil immutamus . Quod ut ratum 7 inconcussum permaneat . presenti scripto 7 sigilli nostri patrocinio confirmamus . Testibus . Haimone Linc' ecclesie decano . magistro Stephano cancellario . magistro Rogero de Rolueston' magistro Ricardo de Swalewecliua .
15 Roberto de Capella . Hugone de Sancto Edwardo . Eustachio de Wilton' . 7 aliis multis.

Endorsed : Lyncon 𝕭 (13 cent.).
Tag for seal. Size : 7¼ x 3¼ inches.
Text : MS—Orig. Dij/63/1/11 : (the words enclosed in square brackets are illegible).

306. Grant by bishop Robert [II], from his rent of the arch-deaconry of Lincoln, to the common of the canons residing in the church of Lincoln of one hundred shillings a year for making bread and beer. (1148–1168.)

De redditu .c. solidorum (marg.).

Robertus . dei gratia Linc' episcopus . Omnibus sancte matris ecclesie filiis salutem . Nouerit uniuersitas uestra nos dedisse ⁊ concessisse . ⁊ presenti carta nostra confirmasse de redditu nostro archidiaconatus Linc' .c. solidos annuos inperpetuum in communam canonicorum residentium in ecclesia Lincol' . ad panem ⁊ ceruisam faciend' . scilicet .l. *sunt* ad pascha . ⁊ l. ad festum beati Michaelis . . Testibus . Waltero abbate de Kyrchest' . Radulfo abbate de Parco Lude . Roberto cellarario de Parco Lude . Gilleberto de Sempingeha*m* . Dauid abbate de Berling' . Waltero priore de Kyrchest' . Willelmo de Amu*n*dauill' dapifero . Valete.

Text : MS—P3.

307. Mandate of bishop Robert [II] addressed to his arch-deacons and their officers. The bishop, assenting to the request and advice of the chapter, has granted to the parishioners of the archdeaconries that, on account of their poverty and remoteness, they may for the present year pay their Pentecostal dues to their mother church [of Lincoln] when and where the archdeacons shall provide, and shall have the same remission of sins as those who come to the mother church ; and he therefore commands the archdeacons to summon the parishioners to meet at suitable places and times. (1147–1168.)

De processionibus totius episcopatus (marg.).

Robertus . dei gratia Lincol' episcopus . archidiaconis suis .H. de .N. ⁊ eorum ministris salutem . Precibus ⁊ consilio capituli ecclesie nostre assentientes . parrochianis uestrorum archidiacona-tuum propter eorum inopiam ⁊ remotionem permittimus quatinus quod sue matrici ecclesie ad sollempnitatem Pentecost' debent exibere in archidiaconatibus uestris ubi ⁊ quando prouidebitis hoc anno exibeant . ⁊ eandem ibi peccatorum veniam quam ⁊ eis qui ad matricem eclesiam uenient eis concedimus . Vobis itaque mandamus ⁊ precipimus quatinus eos benigne ⁊ diligenter sum-moneatis . ut congruis locis ⁊ temporibus prout uobis utile uidebitur contra nuncios capituli ad debitum ecclesie sue persoluendum sollempniter conueniant . Valete.

Text : MS—P5.

Note : The initials ' H. de N.' apparently are fictitious, for there is no known archdeacon to whom they point.

ADDENDUM

ADD. CHART.

308. Writ of Henry II, granting to bishop Robert [II] warren between Stow and Newark; and forbidding that any one shall chase or take hares without his licence, under forfeiture of ten pounds. At Rouen. (1158–1163.)

H. rex Anglo*rum* dux Norm*annorum* 7 Aquit*anorum* 7 comes Ande*gauorum* iustic*iariis* vicecomitibus 7 omnibus ministris suis tocius Angl*ie* salutem. Concedo quod Robertus episcopus Linc' habeat warennam inter Stowe 7 Newerc'. Et prohibeo ne quis in ea fuget vel capiat leporem sine licencia eius super .x. libras forisfacture. Testibus . episcopo Cicestr*ensi* 7 Jocelino de Bail*ol* apud Roto-mag*um*.

Texts: MS—Iiv(14). Pd—*C.C.R.*iv, 109(14).
Note: Cp. no. 110, above.

APPENDIX I

EPISCOPAL RESIDENCES AT LINCOLN

I

Westgate

Henry I granted to bishop Robert Bloet licence to make a way of egress in the wall of the king's castle of Lincoln for the convenience of the bishop's house (*ut faciat exitus* (or *exitum*) *in muro castelli mei ad sua necessaria facienda ad domum suam*), provided that the wall were not thereby weakened.[1] The *murum castelli* has sometimes been explained as meaning the south wall of the first Roman city, which ran on the south side of the cathedral church. The only ground for this suggestion seems to be the assumption that the site of the Old Palace, which is bounded on the north by that wall, was already in the possession of the bishop. It will, however, appear below[2] that the site was not granted to the bishop until the time of king Stephen. Further, it is impossible to explain *castellum* as referring to the Roman city, for in the early part of the twelfth century the *castellum* of Lincoln meant the fortified enclosure of the castle as distinguished from the mound and keep.[3] The word *murus* is interesting, for it indicates, what some have doubted, that as early as 1115 the *castellum* had a containing wall of stone ; for *murus* can hardly be applied to an earthwork or a palisade. The presence, too, of herring-bone coursing seems to point to a date not long after the Conquest for certain parts at least of the existing walls.

The bishop of Lincoln's charter of 1166 shews that he had fortyfive military tenants, holding one hundred and four knights' fees, and of these tenants all but two, with one fee apiece, held by a feoffment granted before the death of Henry I.[4] The grant of so large a body of knights indicates that it was part of William the Conqueror's policy that the bishop should have a large share in defending a part of the kingdom which was remote from the seat of government.

[1] Above, pages 20, 21.
[2] Page 269.
[3] For a discussion of the meaning of *castellum*, see Round, *Geoffrey de Mandeville*, pages 328–46.
[4] *Red Book* i, 374–6.

Henry I, by a writ dated 1123–33, gave to bishop Alexander licence to assign the third part of the knights of the bishopric to the bishop's castle at Newark, that thenceforth they might perform castle-guard there[1] ; and a papal confirmation of 1139 shews that it was at Lincoln castle that the knights of the bishopric had been accustomed to do service.[2] In the same way, Stephen, 1136–1138, allowed bishop Alexander to transfer the castle-guard which he owed at Dover castle to the bishop's castle at Newark or elsewhere.[3]

Where then was bishop Bloet's house to which the new gate was designed to open a way ? It cannot have been near the church, for the main gate was on the eastern side of the castle, opposite the west end of the church, and a new gate at that point would have been unnecessary. But just outside the walls, in the suburb on the western side of the castle, the bishop had the little manor (*maneriolum*) of Willingthorpe or Westgate,[4] and if he made his residence there, a gate in the western wall of the castle is indicated. Such a gate is still to be seen near the north-west corner of the castle, and it may be suggested as probable that this is the gate which the bishop obtained leave to make. It was known as the Sallyport. Its architecture suits the date, and its massive proportions made it a source of strength rather than of weakness to the wall. Just to the north of this gate, and at a slightly lower level, buried in the side of the castle ditch, is the Roman West gate of the city, which the Normans did not make use of in building the castle, a fact which, perhaps, suggests that a gate in the west wall was not part of the original plan of the castle. The Roman gate was discovered on 11 April, 1836, while an individual named Ball was filling up part of the castle ditch. Excavation revealed a considerable part of the gate, but, unfortunately, the work was stopped by the fall of a large mass of masonry on the north side of the Sallyport, which demolished the central part of the gate.[5] The accompanying illustrations, taken from engravings, shew the formidable strength of the Sallyport and the position of the Roman gate. Under the title, ' *De Decimis* ', in the Registrum Antiquissimum,[6] is the entry, *circa* 1290, ' De arrea sub colle vltra nouam

[1] Above, page 35.
[2] Above, page 191.
[3] Above, page 59.
[4] Above, pages 189–90.
[5] *Gentleman's Magazine*, June, 1836.
[6] Reg. Ant., no. 968.

LINCOLN CASTLE: The Sallyport

The Roman West Gate, 1836, with the west wall of the Castle in the background

terram retro castellum que dicitur gardinum episcopi decime '. This garden was presumably connected with the bishop's house, which might be accurately described as at the back of the castle.

II

Eastgate

In 1130–1133 Henry I gave to bishop Alexander the gate of Eastgate with the tower (*turri*) which was over it, in order that he might use it as a lodging for himself (*ad se hospitandum*).[1] Instead of *cum turri* two texts read *cum terris*. The former is the better reading, for it is far more likely that *terris* was read for the less common word *turri* than *vice versa* ; and if, as is likely, the second and third letters were represented by a compendium, the mistake would be the more easily made. The Roman East gate stood on the north side of the present street of Eastgate, a few yards to the east of the East Bight. It is described by Gough as being entire in 1740, and as being of the same proportions as New-port. Towards the end of the eighteenth century, it was destroyed by Sir Cecil Wray, baronet, to make room for a new house which he was building.[2] Nothing is known about bishop Alexander's occupation of the gate, but it is at least remarkable that one of the gates of the city should be assigned to him.

III

The Old Palace

By a charter, dated at Rouen, 1135–8, king Stephen grants to bishop Alexander (a) the land which is between Saint Michael's church and the ditch as the ditch reaches to the city wall, and (b) adjoining this ditch, and round the said church, land of the king's demesne worth twenty shillings a year, with sake and soke and all the other franchises that it had while it was in the king's demesne. Further, the king grants that if the bishop shall build on the land a house for a dwelling-place for himself, the church of Lincoln and the bishop and his successors shall have the land in perpetual possession quit of all customary dues. Further, (c) the king grants to the bishop, in the same place, the actual ditch and city wall to make a way of ingress for himself and to do what is convenient for his building.[3]

[1] Above, page 34.
[2] *A Survey of the Antiquities of the City of Lincoln*, page 39.
[3] Above, pages 54–5.

By a charter, dated at Lincoln, 1155–8, Henry II grants to bishop Robert Chesney, for his buildings and houses, all the land with the ditch from the wall of the king's bailey (*ballii mei*) at Lincoln, on the east side round the church of Saint Michael to the cemetery of Saint Andrew's church, and thence to the city wall towards the east. The king grants this land free and quit of land-gable and *parcagium*[1] and all other matters. He also gives the bishop leave to pierce the wall of the king's bailey for the purpose of making a gate for coming and going towards the church, and to extend his buildings to both walls.[2]

The form of Henry's charter suggests that it was a new grant rather than a confirmation of Stephen's gift. Further, it does not include the land and ditch between Saint Michael's churchyard and the city wall. Nor does it repeat the gift of the wall itself. It may be that Stephen's grant had lapsed, or had become insecure, since Alexander had not fulfilled the condition that he should build a house of residence for himself (*si . . . domum sibi edificauerit ad propriam sui mansionem*). After 1138 the bishop fell upon troublous times, and had little opportunity for building. As the accompanying plan shews, the boundaries described in these charters are unusually precise. They correspond exactly with the lines of the modern map. To take the items of Stephen's charter:

(a) is approximately the area J K P M in the plan. The ground sloped steeply from the city wall J to M, K to P, and the usual flat bottom of the Roman ditch would form a convenient road of approach eastward to the bishop's house. The bishops presumably at all times had access by the ditch or through Saint Michael's churchyard to their house, as the bishop has to-day[3]; and traces of more than one doorway may be seen in the wall K P. But it is improbable that any bishop after Alexander was possessed of the soil of the ditch. In the seventeenth century, all the land up to the city wall was part of the churchyard, which for a reason that is at present unknown, like other churchyards in Lincoln, belonged to the city. Part of the sloping bank had then been cut down perpendicularly to within a few yards of the wall in order to provide

[1] This is interpreted as a payment for the maintenance of the king's park-paling (Du Cange). *Cp.* above, page 104.

[2] Above, pages 86–7.

[3] There was a carriage way to the palace through the churchyard, but this way was closed shortly before 1840 (*A Survey of the Antiquities of the City of Lincoln*, page 32).

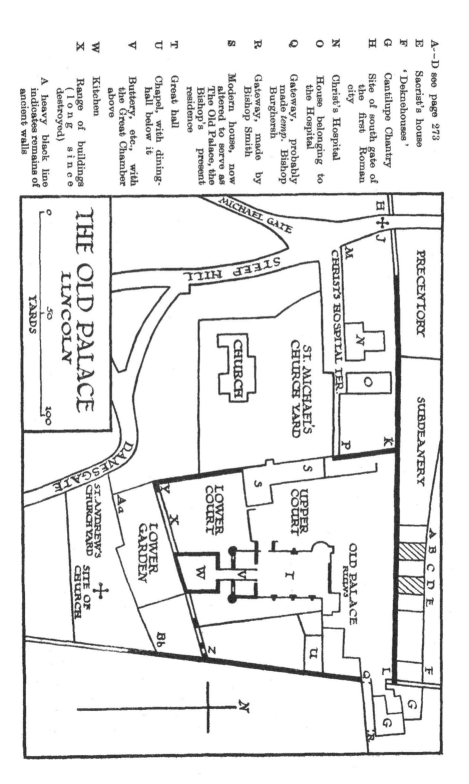

A.–D see page 273

E Sacrist's house

F 'Deknehouses'

G Cantilupe Chantry

H Site of south gate of the first Roman city

N Christ's Hospital

O House belonging to the Hospital

Q Gateway, probably made *temp.* Bishop Burghersh

R Gateway, made by Bishop Smith

S Modern house, now altered to serve as The Old Palace, the Bishop's present residence

T Great hall

U Chapel, with dining-hall below it

V Buttery, etc., with the Great Chamber above

W Kitchen

X Range of buildings (long since destroyed)

A heavy black line indicates remains of ancient walls

THE OLD PALACE
LINCOLN

0   50   100
YARDS

a level site for Christ's Hospital which was founded in 1602 (N in plan). On 12 September, 1699, the city renewed to the governors of the school a lease of the land on which stood the hospital ' where the Hospitall boyes are now kept,' with a little tenement or dwelling-house adjoining (O), for the old rent of three shillings and fourpence and a fat pig to Mr Major or two shillings and sixpence. East of the dwelling-house there was a little orchard which, on 2 October, 1675, the governors leased to Dr James Gardiner, the subdean,[1] whose house was built high above it on the city wall.

(b) is the area K L Z Y in the plan, which was given by Stephen and also by Henry II.

(c) Both kings gave to the bishops the ditch K L Q P, the steep bank of which still remains in the grounds of the Old Palace. Further, Stephen gave to bishop Alexander the wall K L, while Henry II merely gave bishop Robert leave to make a doorway through it to provide access to his church.[2] This wall was part of the south wall of the first Roman city, and it had ceased to be necessary to the defence of the city, because the Romans had afterwards extended the east and west walls southwards, and had connected them with a new south wall at the foot of the hill. The second wall mentioned in Henry's writ (*quod edificia sua extendantur in utrunque murum*) was part of the east wall of the later Roman city (L Z), the most part of which exists to-day.

To complete the enclosure of the site, a massive wall was built on the west side in the twelfth or thirteenth century (K Y). This wall, though in parts rebuilt, stands to-day. At Y there are indications that it was continued from Y to Z to form the southern boundary of the site. The area Y Z Bb Aa, which is now the bishop's lower garden, was, presumably, part of Saint Andrew's churchyard in the twelfth century. The late Dr E. Mansel Sympson[3] states that bishop Burghersh, in 1330, obtained a royal licence, for the enlargement of the area of the palace, by grant from the mayor of Lincoln, but the present writer has not found the evidence for this. The only possible addition to the site was the area Y Z Bb Aa.

---

[1] Minutes of Christ's Hospital, from notes supplied by Mr J. W. F. Hill.
[2] Papal confirmations dated 1146 and 1163 (above, pages 196, 202) err in mis-placing the words *in eodem loco* of Stephen's charter, and thus make the gift refer to the part of the wall J to K.
[3] *Lincoln* (Ancient Cities Series), page 294.

It is to be observed that what Stephen describes as *murum ciuitatis* is styled *murum ballii mei* in Henry II's charter.[1] The bailey or bail originally included the whole of the upper city within the Roman walls, with the place adjoining the castle on the west, called ' La Batailplace,'[2] the whole of which area was within the jurisdiction of the constable of the castle. Afterwards the Close was taken out of the Bail. In letters close, dated 4 August, 1331, the boundaries of the bailey are described as follows :

" that the castle of Lincoln with a place adjoining called ' La Batailplace ' with adjoining ditches is within the bailey of the castle, and that the bailey extends from the West Postern (*West-posterna*) of the bailey going round to Neuportyate and thence going round to Le Estgatyate, and thence to the eastern end of the shrine (*feretri*) of St Hugh in the monastery of Lincoln,[3] and thence southwards to the south part of the messuage called ' Becumhous '[4] with all that messuage, and thence westwards to Le Suthbailyate, and thence crossing about the castle to the said West Postern of the bailey, and that all gates, walls, and ditches about the bailey with the houses built in the ditches are appurtenant to the said bailey and are of the bailey."[5]

The gate which bishop Chesney obtained leave to make formed the main entrance to the palace, and it necessarily had a gatehouse capable of defence. Its position is determined, by the charters of Stephen and Henry II as well as by the appearance of the wall and by tradition, as having been opposite to the south transept of the church. A B C, and perhaps D, in the plan mark its site. On the south side of the south wall of A there is the head of a small Norman doorway the lower part of which is buried in the ground. In the north face of the wall there are the remains of a fireplace, probably of the Norman period, which belonged to an upper room. B also has been occupied by a building. A and B now form part of the garden of the subdeanery. C has a fireplace similar to the one in A in the north face of the wall, and signs of a doorway in the same face. It has been used by the dean and chapter, at one time as a workshop, etc., and now as a store-house for coke. D is

[1] Above, pages 55, 87.

[2] This area, in which the Lawn Hospital now stands, was, like the castle and its ditches, formerly extra-parochial.

[3] The dean and canons obtained a licence in 1255 to remove the east wall of the city in order that they might lengthen their church by extending it beyond the wall (above, pages 184–5).

[4] In a commission of oyer and terminer, 8 March, 1389–90, this messuage is called ' Deknehouses ' (*Cal. Pat. Rolls*, 1388–1392, p. 220). The name suggests that it was the residence of some of the clergy who served the cathedral.

[5] *Cal. Close Rolls*, 1330–1333, page 255.

S

marked in old plans as a building, and it is uncertain whether it formed part of the gate. E is the site of the sacrist's house. D and E are now included in the garden of the Cantilupe Chantry. F is the site of the 'Deknehouses' mentioned above. It is probable that C was the middle of the gate; for at that point the whole of the Roman wall has been rebuilt, a proceeding which would be rendered necessary if it was there that the wall had been originally pierced for the main archway of the gate.

The authorities for the building of the bishop's house are the *Vita Sancti Remigii* of Giraldus and the *Martilogium* of John of Schalby, canon of Lincoln and bishop's registrar, who died in 1333. Giraldus says of bishop Chesney (1147–1168), ' domos episcopales, cum terra quoque ubi sitæ fuerant comparata sumptibus magnis, Lincolniæ fecit.'[1] Schalby makes no mention of any building being done by Chesney, and the earliest remains of the ancient palace are certainly later than Chesney's time. Of Saint Hugh (1186–1200) Giraldus says, ' He began to construct splendid (*egregias*) episcopal buildings.'[2] Schalby says, ' He began to build a splendid (*egregiam*) episcopal hall.'[3] Part of the southernmost portion of the building, including the kitchen, and perhaps some portion of the great hall, and part of the buildings further east, may belong to the end of the thirteenth century. At this point Giraldus' work ends. Schalby relates that Saint Hugh's work was finished by bishop Hugh of Wells, ' He finished, with costly work, the episcopal hall which was begun by Saint Hugh in splendid style, and the kitchen.'[4] The work was still unfinished in 1224, for on 30 December, 1223, Henry III directed the mayor and bailiffs of Lincoln to allow bishop Hugh to dig and take stone in the ditch (*fossato*) of the city, near his house, for building his house at Lincoln, if stone can there be taken without damage to the city.[5] And, on 29 April, 1324, the king commanded Hugh de Nevill to cause the bishop to have forty trees (*fusta*) in the king's forest of Sherwood (*Sirewud'*), where they can best and most conveniently and at least distance be got, for the use of the bishop, to make beams and joists (*gista*) for his hall at Lincoln.[6] This great hall measured 85 feet from north to

---

[1] *Giraldus Cambrensis* vii, 35. See NOTE on p. 276, below.
[2] *Ibid.*, page 41.
[3] *Ibid.*, page 200.
[4] *Ibid.*, page 204.
[5] *Rotuli Litterarum Clausarum* i, 580.
[6] *Ibid.*, page 595.

south and 58 feet from east to west, and its roof was supported by two arcades with pillars of Purbeck marble.

On 28 September, 1329, bishop Henry Burghersh, who was the king's chancellor, obtained licence from the king

" in consideration of his profitable services and the great place he holds in the direction of the king's affairs, and for his successors, bishops of Lincoln, to repair, raise, crenellate and turrellate the walls of his palace which adjoins the precinct of St Mary's, Lincoln, now partly enclosed with a stone wall, crenellated and turrellated, and if necessary to make new walls in the circuit of the palace, and to crenellate and turrellate them as often as and as they think fit. Further grant to them, in frank almoin, of the old wall, and the soil on which it is situated, adjoining the palace towards the east, which wall contains 18½ perches *per virgam viginti pedum de ulna regia*, and the like licence to crenellate, etc., the same. Further, grant that both the soil on which the wall is situated and the palace shall have the immunity and ecclesiastical liberty of the church, its cemetery and other places within the precincts, all offenders in the former to be held violators of the liberties of Holy Church just as if they had offended in the latter."[1]

And again on 9 August, 1330, a grant,

" for the affection which the king bears to Henry, bishop of Lincoln, the chancellor, that the bishop's palace with a wall and the land whereon the wall stands, adjoining the palace on the east, and lately granted to the bishop by the king, and the dwelling houses of the dean and chapter, canons, vicars, choristers and other ministers of the cathedral church, and all houses, plots and places within the precinct, shall have the same immunity and ecclesiastical liberty as the cathedral or the cemetery thereof, so that any trespassers therein shall be held to be violators of Holy Church."[2]

The grant of the eastern wall of the later Roman city L to Bb, enabled bishop Burghersh to make at Q a new gateway to his house, towards the east, which, being on comparatively level ground, was far more convenient than the original gateway at A to D, which involved a very steep approach. This gateway was rebuilt in the nineteenth century. The outer gateway at R, which bears the arms of bishop William Smith (1496–1514), was probably his work. Bishop William Alnwick (1436–1449) erected a new chapel (U), and the entrance tower at the north-east corner of the great

[1] *Cal. Patent Rolls*, 1327–1330, page 453.
[2] *Ibid.*, page 548.

hall, and other buildings. The great hall (T) was still standing in the time of 'Gervase Holles, about 1640.'[1] The whole of the site slopes steeply downhill towards the south, and massive buttresses supposed to be the work of bishop Williams (1621–1641), were found necessary to support the southern end of the buildings. Leland, about 1540, describes the palace as ' hangginge *in declivio.*'[2]

It is beyond the purpose of this appendix to give a full description of the buildings, and the reader may be referred to an article, entitled ' The Ancient Episcopal Palace, Lincoln,' by the late Mr. E. J. Willson in *Memoirs . . . of the County and City of Lincoln*, published by the Archæological Institute (London: 1850), pages 1–19, and *A Survey of the Antiquities of the City of Lincoln*, pages 32–5.

NOTE: In spite of the fact that, as stated on p. 274, above, no part of the remains of the Old Palace are earlier than the time of Saint Hugh, the words of the papal bull of 1163 (above, page 203, ll. 44, 45), 'domum episcopi in ciuitate Lincol' iuxta baliam ab austro ', probably indicate that bishop Robert Chesney began to build a house on the site.

[1] *Associated Architectural Societies' Reports and Papers,* xxxi, 379–83.
[2] *Leland's Itinerary* (ed. E. Toulmin Smith), v. 123.

APPENDIX II

THORNGATE AND THE CONDET FAMILY

I

Thorngate

A marginal note in No. 252, lines 35–7 (above, page 198), ' Nota pro prebenda de Thorngate,' and a similar note in No. 255, lines 46–7 (above, page 205), indicate that the houses near the bridge of Lincoln, which Robert de Stutevill gave *in prebendam* to the church of Lincoln, formed part, perhaps the original portion, of the prebend of Thorngate. Henry I's charter confirming the gift, circa 1107, states that Hugh son of Baldric held the houses in the time of the Conqueror.[1] Though Hugh had land in Lincoln in 1086, these particular tenements cannot be identified.[2] When the papal confirmations, Nos. 252 and 255, describe the houses as being near ' the bridge of Lincoln,' it is probable that we are to understand the *pons magna* in High street which spanned the Witham. Martel also gave land near the river to this prebend.[2a]

The only existing account of the district of Thorngate is to be found in the important manuscript history of Lincoln, *Annales Lincolnienses*, compiled by J. Ross, 1850–1860, which is preserved among Lord Monson's archives at Burton hall. According to Ross, Thorngate extended from Wigford causeway on the west to the confluence of the river Witham and Sincil dyke on the east, and was bounded on the east and south by Sincil dyke, and on the north by the parishes of Saint Swithin and Saint Augustine.[3] Ross suggests that the area was perhaps not yet inhabited in 1086, and that it was a swamp overgrown with thorns until it was reclaimed chiefly as a result of the reopening of the Foss dike.[4] He thinks that Thorngate, which appears to have comprised both banks of the Witham, was, some fifty years later, becoming the most populous part of the city, and that ' the increased value of land for mercatorial buildings contracted the stream of the river.'[5] This district, he says, formed the parish of Saint Denis, which was united to the

[1] Above, page 32.
[2] *The Lincolnshire Domesday*, page 6, nos. 19, 24.
[2a] Above, pages 100–1.
[3] Liber i, 162 ; Liber iii, 109.
[4] Liber i, 459–60.
[5] *Ibid.*

parishes of Saint Swithin and Saint Augustine as early as the fourteenth century, when, no doubt, the church of Saint Denis, which was situate east of Thorn bridge, disappeared, so that all memory of its site was forgotten.[1] Its endowments were appropriated to the prebend of Thorngate.[2] Precentor Venables states that the site of the church was on the north bank of the Witham, 'a little to the east of the present bridge,'[3] but that seems an impossible position since the parish of Saint Augustine and perhaps the parish of Saint Rumbold bounded upon that part of the river. It seems that Venables' mistake is due to his misinterpretation of one of Ross's rather elaborate sentences.

Wigford causeway, which Ross mentions as the western boundary of Thorngate, followed the course of the present Sincil street, forming a parish boundary (see plan). Sincil dyke at that time continued its course northwards as far as the present Norman street, where it turned eastwards approximately along the line of that street, again forming a parish boundary. A Lincoln corporation lease, circa 1830, contains a plan shewing the old bed of the stream which was then being filled up.[4] The fact that Sincil street on the west and Norman street on the south formed, in the fourteenth century, and still form, the boundaries of Saint Swithin's parish confirms the limits of Thorngate as given by Ross. North of the river, Thorngate was bounded on the west by the parish of Saint Benedict. The accompanying plan will enable the reader to follow the description of Thorngate with greater ease.

It is unfortunate that the beautifully written volumes which Ross compiled with amazing industry are almost entirely lacking in references to his sources, but the impression left on the mind of a reader, who is well acquainted with the manuscript evidence, is that Ross was a careful and accurate historian, who gave some indication when his conclusions were doubtful. Most of his statements about Thorngate may be verified, and his suggestion may be correct, namely, that the area of Thorngate was reclaimed as a result of the improvement of the Foss dyke for the purpose of navigation between the Trent and Lincoln, which took place in 1121,[5] an event which no doubt had the effect of increasing the

---

[1] Liber i, p. 162.
[2] Ibid. iii, 109.
[3] Associated Architectural Societies' Reports and Papers xix, 335.
[4] Marrat's map (1817) shews the old course of Sincil dyke.
[5] Symeon of Durham (Rolls Series) ii, 260.

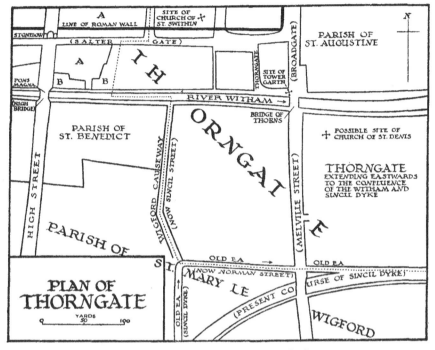

PLAN OF THORNGATE

YARDS
0   50   100

A   Parish of Saint Peter at Arches

B   Parish of Saint Benedict

A black line indicates the Roman south wall of the City

A dotted line indicates the southern and western boundaries of the Parish of Saint Swithin

Later names of streets, etc., are enclosed in brackets

value of the river-frontages at Lincoln. The union at an early
date of the parish of Saint Denis with that of Saint Swithin is
confirmed by the fact that, as early as circa 1250, in charters of
land in Thorngate, the property is stated to be in the parish of
Saint Swithin.[1] In the fourteenth century, tenements are described
as being in Thorngate in the parish of Saint Swithin, and abutting
upon the water of Witham towards the north, and towards the
south upon *le Oldea* or *le Aldea* which is to be identified with Sincil
dyke.[2] Union with the parish of Saint Augustine is unlikely, for
while no charters have been found to indicate that that parish
extended southwards beyond the river, a charter of land in Saint
Swithin's parish describes a tenement as extending from the little
bridge (*de paruo ponte*) towards the west to the king's way towards
the east[3]; and another Saint Swithin's charter states that certain
land lies on the east side of Thorn bridge (*pons de Thorn'*) on the
south side of the water.[4] These descriptions suggest that the whole
of Thorngate was added to the parish of Saint Swithin. Ross's
statement that the church of Saint Denis was situate to the east
of Thorn bridge points in the same direction.

The little bridge just mentioned was Thorn bridge which spanned
the river at or very near the present Magpie bridge, and opposite
to the tower and gate at the corner of the city wall, where the
Green Dragon hotel now stands on a plot which formerly was called
the Towergarth. The bridge was also nearly opposite the present
little street called Thorngate which leads from Saint Swithin's
square to the Witham. It is described, in a charter of *circa* 1332,
as 'Pons spinarum,'[5] and it is marked as 'Thorne bridge—Pont de
l'Espine' in a 'Plan de Lincolne,' perhaps of the early part of the
seventeenth century, in which the names are given in French.[6]
In the Gough MSS[7] there is a note, made in 1737, perhaps by
Thomas Sympson: 'Lower down the River [than the High Bridge]
stands another Bridge of one Arch, called Thorn Bridge; the date
of 1602 upon the East Side of it shows the age of the present building, though no doubt there was one before.' Marrat's map of

[1] Bardney Abbey Cartulary (B.M., Cotton MS, Vespasian, E xx), f. 258d.
[2] *Ibid.*, f. 257d. Dean and Chapter muniments, Dii/76/1, 36, and 39.
[3] *Ibid.*, 76/1/40.
[4] Registrum, no. 836.
[5] Dean and Chapter muniments, Dij/76/1/33.
[6] Brit. Mus., Add. MS 11,564, f. 39 ; reproduced in *The Archæological Journal*
xxxviii, 170.
[7] Bodleian Library, Gough MS, Lincoln i, p. 262.

Lincoln (1817) and Padley's map (1867) give it as Thorn Bridge ; but Padley in a later edition (1868) calls it Witham Bridge.

The charters mentioned above are not later than the earlier part of the fourteenth century, and they confirm Ross's suggestion that the union of parishes took place at an early date. Further, the church of Saint Denis is not mentioned in the episcopal registers of institutions which begin *circa* 1220, nor, so far as is known, in charters or other documents. It would be interesting to know the evidence on which Ross relied, for it is unlikely that he invented a church of Saint Denis. But here a further difficulty occurs ; for the prebend is now designated All Saints, Thorngate. This would postulate a church of that dedication in Thorngate, but for such a church no evidence has been found. If the church of Saint Denis was situate to the east of Thorn bridge, there would scarcely have been room for another parish, however small, in Thorngate to the west of Thorn bridge. In the various public records, in the episcopal registers of institutions from 1290 to 1812, and in the *Calendars of Papal Letters*, the prebend is invariably called Thorngate. The first occurrence of the addition ' All Saints ' is in a *Speculum Diœceseos circa* 1735, an office list of benefices for use in the Diocesan Registry. This addition did not creep into the registers of institutions until 1847, since which date it has persisted to the present day. It is at least probable that the interpolation is an error, and it would seem desirable to revert to the well-established and distinctive title of Thorngate.

Ross says that the wealthier citizens had halls or dwellings in Thorngate, and that the Kymes had a mansion there. The *Hundred Rolls*[1], 3 Edward III, state that Philip of Kyme had a manor house in the parish of Saint Swithin, but evidence that it was in Thorngate is not yet forthcoming, unless it be supplied by an inquisition *ad quod damnum*, 6 Edward II, for Philip to have a grant of a messuage in Thornbridge gate, late inhabited by the brethren of the Penance of Jesus Christ.[2] In the thirteenth century Bardney abbey held land in Thorngate in the parish of Saint Swithin.[3]

The writer is indebted to the kindness of Lord Monson for access

[1] Vol. i, p. 312.
[2] P.R.O., *Lists and Indexes* xvii, 135.
[3] Bardney Abbey Cartulary, ff. 258d, 259, 259d.

to Ross's manuscripts and books. If some of Ross's sources have appeared in print since his day, his collections preserve a large amount of material which is not elsewhere to be found.

II

Thorngate Castle and the Condet Family

The evidence about Thorngate given above now makes it possible to identify the *castellum de Torngat*[1] as a castle situate in Thorngate, just outside the walls of the later Roman city of Lincoln. Adelidis, Adelis, or Alice de Condet had pledged her castle of Thorngate and her lands in Kent, Nottinghamshire, and Lincolnshire to king Stephen, who granted the pledge to bishop Alexander.

Alice de Condet

The extant accounts of Alice's ancestry[2] are derived from the *Stemma Willelmi Longspée, Comitis Linc. et Sarum, ab Osberto de Casneto Domino de Cavenby et Glentham deductum* in the Leger Book of Barlings abbey.[3] It is stated there that Osbert Chesney (*de Casneto*), long before the coming of William the Conqueror, lord of Caenby (*Cavenby*) and Glentham, founded the church of Saint Nicholas within his principal manor of Caenby, and endowed it with the tithes of the village. Further, that in the time of the Conqueror, sir William de Casneto, lord of Caenby and Glentham, begat, by Constance his wife, an only daughter, Adelidis, whom he gave in marriage to Sir Osbert de Cundi, of which Robert[4] [*sic*] and Adelidis Roger was son and heir, who gave to the brethren of Lyskes,[5] of the Premonstratensian order,[6] his toft of five acres with two bovates and pasture for seven hundred sheep in Glentham and Caenby, with chace and rechace from the one to the other, in free, pure, and perpetual alms. The facts which are certain in this story are that Alice married Robert de Condet, and that she and Roger their son had a lordship in Caenby and Glentham. A pedigree

[1] Above, page 61.

[2] Dugdale, *Baronage* i, 336 ; Gervase Holles, Lansdowne MS 207a, f. 457 ; W.O. Massingberd, *Associated Architectural Societies' Reports and Papers* xxvi, 22–3.

[3] P.R.O., Exchequer, Treasury of Receipt, Miscellaneous Books, 71, page 12 (printed by Dugdale, *Mon.* vii, 917).

[4] In another edition of the *Stemma* (Leger Book, p. 18) ' Osbert ' is substituted for ' Robert.'

[5] This is the abbey of Licques, near Boulogne, Pas-de-Calais, the mother-house of Newhouse abbey.

[6] The edition on page 18 adds here, ' after the death of his father, with the assent and consent of Adelidis his mother.' It appears from *C.C.R.* i, 89, that the abbot and convent of Newhouse, who held this land of the canons of Liskes, gave it to Barlings abbey.

shewing the descent so far as it is known will help the reader to
follow the story :

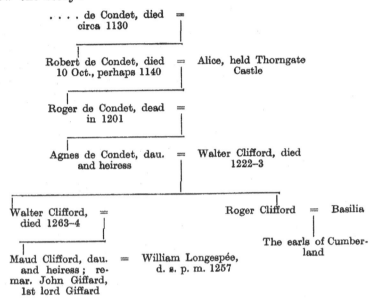

While it would be easy to allow too much weight to the *Stemma*,
it is probable that it contains a substratum of fact. Perhaps we
may conclude that Caenby and Glentham belonged to the Chesney
family,[1] whose heiress married a de Condet ; but that there is
considerable confusion in the generations. It would suit the
chronology better if the Chesney heiress married the father (perhaps
Osbert) of Robert de Condet rather than Robert himself, and if
Alice also belonged to the next generation. This might explain the
confusion between Osbert and Robert in the *Stemma*, and might
account for the fact that Alice, as will be seen, appears to have
been a person of greater consequence than merely the heiress of a
small estate. The story of the *Stemma*, namely, that the pre-
Conquest lord of Caenby and Glentham was a Chesney, recalls
the description by Giraldus Cambrensis of bishop Robert Chesney
as ' vir generosus, natione quidem Anglicus, sed cognatione
Normannus,' that is, English on his father's side.[2] In 1086, the
bishop of Lincoln held four carucates in Caenby (*Couenebi*) which
were inland of his manor of Stow, and three carucates and six

---

[1] Mr. Salter's account of this family in the *Eynsham Cartulary* i, 411–23, does
not contain anything about the ancestry of the Chesneys of Caenby and Glentham.
[2] Vol. vii, p. 34.

bovates in Glentham which were sokeland of the same manor.[1]
In 1115–18, the bishop had in the two places seven carucates and
six bovates, of which Martel de Taneio held two carucates and
four bovates.[2] With this exception, the names of the bishop's
tenants in these villages are not given in any of the feudal surveys.
The statement in the *Stemma*, however, that Alice de Condet and
Roger her son held Caenby and Glentham is confirmed by Roger's
grant, already mentioned, to the canons of Licques, by the descent
of the manor of Caenby to Roger's daughter, Agnes de Condet,
who married Walter Clifford senior[3]; by the fact that Walter
Clifford junior, the son of Walter and Agnes, presented to the
rectory of Caenby in 1235 and 1244[4]; and by the gift to Barlings
abbey, by Maud de Clifford and William de Longspée her husband,
of their manor in, and advowson of, Caenby.[5]

Here it will be convenient to collect the available evidence about
Alice de Condet. At a date before 6 February, 1146, king Stephen
granted to bishop Alexander the pledge which Alice gave the king
of her castle of Thorngate and of her lands, namely, Wickham
[breux] in Kent, Grimston in Nottinghamshire, and [South] Carlton,
Thurlby [near Lincoln], Eagle, and Skellingthorpe, in Lincolnshire,
with the wardship of Alice's son, until the son should be of such
an age that he could hold the land and be made a knight.[6] By
1146, then, Alice's husband, Robert de Condet, was dead. In the
Obituary of Lincoln cathedral the date of his death is given as
10 October, but the year is not specified.[7] Alice, with Roger her
son, who was then only a few years old, issued a notification
that on the day of Robert's burial, they had given and placed
upon the altar of the church of Lincoln, for the health of his soul,
three bovates of their land and three messuages in Normanby
[by Stow]. This grant of three bovates was, *circa* 1160–1165,
renewed and confirmed by Roger to the use of the common of the
canons with the condition that he should hold the land of them in
return for a yearly payment of ten shillings, and the proviso that,
if war should trouble the country, the land should return into the

---

[1] *The Lincolnshire Domesday*, 7/3, 7/5.
[2] *Ibid.*, page 239.
[3] Below, page 292.
[4] L.R.S. xi, 134, 146.
[5] *Mon.* vii, 918.
[6] Above, page 61.
[7] *Giraldus Cambrensis* vii, 161.

hands of the canons, and the payment of ten shillings should cease, until peace was restored. The latter grant is witnessed by Robert de Cundi, who was perhaps brother to Roger.[1] This gift by Alice and Roger of ten shillings' worth of land in Normanby by Stow was confirmed by a papal bull, 6 February, 1146.[2] But it seems that Robert's death must be placed in or before 1140. He was dead at the time of Stephen's charter to bishop Alexander. That charter was given at Lincoln, and its probable date is the early part of the year 1141, when Stephen was besieging Rannulf earl of Chester and his half-brother, William of Roumare, in Lincoln castle. Alice's husband, Robert de Condet, died therefore not later than 10 October, 1145, and probably in or before 1140.

'Aliz de Condi' gave twelve bovates in Empingham (*Hemping-ham*) to the Knights of the Temple.[3] And she and Roger her son gave two messuages in Eakring, co. Nottingham, to Rufford abbey, temp. Henry II :

Aeliz de Cundeio et Rogerus filius suus omnibus hominibus suis Francis et Anglis et omnibus filiis sancte ecclesie salutem Sciatis nos concessisse et dedisse in elemosinam perpetuam deo et ecclesie sancte Marie de Ruffordia et monachis ibidem deo seruientibus duas mansuras in Eicring duas acras continentes scilicet mansuram que fuit Arneuin et mansuram que fuit Turchill pratos [*sic*] liberas et quietas ab omni terreno seruicio et omnibus consuetudinibus Hiis testibus Osberto de Wynchleia cum ceteris.[4]

Alice and Roger also gave one hide in Alderton, in Wiltshire, in fee and inheritance, to Merton priory.[5]

Alice, with her son Roger's consent, gave to the church of Saint Mary Magdalene, Hartsholme, for the soul of Robert 'de Cundeio,' her lord, the render of the heath and marsh of Skellingthorpe :

A. de Cund' . omnibus hominibus Francis . 7 Anglis . atque universis ecclesie filiis salutem . Notum sit uobis presentibus 7 futuris . dedisse me in elemosina redditum bruerie . 7 maresii de Eskelinguehop' ecclesie sancte Marie Magdalene de Hertesholm . concessu Rogeri filii mei . ut prenotata ecclesia in perpetuum debeat ob salutem anime mee . 7 domini mei Roberti de Gundeio [*sic*] .

[1] Registrum Antiquissimum, nos. 242, 243. These charters will be printed in a later volume.
[2] Above, page 200 ; cp. above, page 207.
[3] *Mon.* vii, 829.
[4] Brit. Mus., Harleian MS 1063, f. 17.
[5] Brit. Mus., Cotton MSS, Cleopatra cvii, f. lxxxvii, no. 72. See above, page 245.

nec non antecessorum 7 heredum meorum . Testibus . Rogero filio Columbani . 7c.[1]

She also confirmed Baldwin fitz Gilbert's gift of Hartsholme, in the parish of Skellingthorpe, to Bardney abbey and the church of Saint Mary Magdalene of Hartsholme :

Notum sit tam futuris quam presentibus quod ego Baldewinus filius Gileberti 7 uxor mea Adelina 7 heres noster Rogerus concedimus Hertesholm liberam perpetualiter in elemosinam ecclesie dei 7 sancti Oswaldi ac beate Marie Magdalene . cum terra 7 marisco per uiam iacentem inter uiuarium 7 terminos Bulthamie usque in fossam . item a uiuario per cornarium fossate monachorum usque in fossam . 7 de pastura 7 de mora quantum volunt liberam 7 quietam . hominibus suis eandem consuetudinem reddentibus quam homines de Sceldinghop reddunt . Hanc donacionem facimus pro salute nostra 7 pro animabus parentum 7 amicorum nostrorum Huius rei sunt testes . Robertus capellanus . Suartebrandus sacerdos . Willelmus diaconus . 7c.[2]

Universis hominibus suis . Francis 7 Anglis . atque omnibus ecclesie filiis . presentibus 7 futuris . A. de Cundeio ? salutem . Noscat presentia uestra . atque successorum uestrorum me concessisse donum quod Baldewinus filius Gileberti dedit ecclesie sancte Marie Magdalene de Hertesholm . 7 monachis ibidem deo servientibus prout carta eiusdem testatur . ut ita inperpetuo maneat . Preterea concedo ecclesie predicte . Morton' . cum tota terra arabili . 7 nemore . 7 molendino . 7 stagno . 7 prato quod est circa Hertesholm . 7 dimidio prato de Brodeholme . 7 Godewinecroft . supra fossam . nec non cum pastura . 7 Brudella . 7 in Torpeio tres bovatas 7 dimidiam cum prato . 7 pertinentibus suis . Testibus . Gaufrido Columbano . 7c.[3]

Hartsholme was, seemingly, a cell of Bardney abbey. Baldwin fitz Gilbert (of Clare), the grantor, was a son of Gilbert fitz Richard (of Clare), by Adelis, daughter of Hugh count of Clermont, and in 1138 he founded Bourne abbey. He married Adelidis, daughter and heiress of Richard de Rullos, lord of Deeping and Bourne, and his grandson, Baldwin Wake, died seised of an estate in Skellingthorpe.[4]

Alice de Condet is mentioned in a remarkable way at the end

[1] Brit. Mus., Cotton MS., Vespasian, E xx, f. 207.
[2] Ibid., f. 206d.
[3] Ibid., f. 207. The writer is indebted to Professor F. M. Stenton for calling his attention to these three charters.
[4] See Stenton, Facsimiles of Early Charters (Northampton Record Society iv), pages 53–4, 82–3. Associated Architectural Societies' Reports and Papers vi, 18 (pedigree). Cal. of Inquisitions ii, p. 261.

of the important charter by which king Stephen, probably in 1151,[1] purchased the adherence to his cause of earl Rannulf of Chester, who more than once transferred his allegiance from the king to the empress Maud and her son, duke Henry. The original charter was preserved in Pontefract castle until 1325, when, after the attainder and death of Thomas earl of Lancaster, Edward II ordered his charters and other muniments at Pontefract and elsewhere to be delivered to the treasurer and chamberlains of the Exchequer. The documents found at Pontefract were summarized in a roll which is preserved in the Public Record Office.[2] Some of the originals are now in the same place, but many of them, including Stephen's charter, have been lost, a loss which is all the more to be deplored since the summary in the roll supplies a very poor text. Dugdale prints an abstract in English from an ancient cartulary of Lyre abbey, 'formerly in Pontefract castle, as plainly appears from the collections of Robert Glover, Somerset [Herald].'[3] This abstract omits the grant of the honour of Lancaster, but otherwise it agrees so closely with the Public Record Office text that it may be concluded that what the lost Lyre cartulary contained was the summary of 1325, and not a transcript of the original charter. In view of the fact that the charter is one of the most important documents of the Anarchy, and also that it is of interest in connection with Lincoln castle, the Public Record Office text is printed below :

Concordia inter regem Stephanum 7 Rannulfum comitem Cestrie (marg.).

Carta Stephani regis Anglie per quam dedit 7 concessit Rannulfo comiti Cestrie castellum Lincoln' 7 ciuitatem donec idem rex fecerit ei terram suam Normannie 7 omnia castella sua habere Quo facto idem rex concessit firmare vnam de turribus suis de castro Lincoln' . de qua comes habebit dominium donec idem rex liberet ei castrum de Tichehilla 7 tunc remanebit eidem regi turris 7 ciuitas Lincoln' (Et dicto comiti remanebit turris sua . quam mater sua . firmauit cum constabulacione castelli Lincoln' 7 Lincolneshir' hereditario jure Et preter hoc idem rex dedit comiti predicto castrum de

---

[1] For the date see Dr J. H. Round's article in *E.H.R.* x, 87.
[2] Duchy of Lancaster, Miscell., portfolio 1, no. 36. These particulars are taken from Dr W. Farrer, *Early Lancashire Charters*, page 370, who prints the text of the charter (*ibid.*, pp. 367–8).
[3] *Baronage*, i, 39. The writer is indebted to the kindness of Mr J. D. Heaton-Armstrong, Chester Herald, for allowing him to search Glover's Collections in the College of Arms. Unfortunately, these MSS. do not contain anything about Stephen's charter.

Beluedeire cum omni honore eidem pertinente 7 totam terram
Willelmi de Albin' de quocunque eam tenuit 7 Graham cum soka .
7 si contingeret quod heredes . de Graham cum rege concordiam
fecissent . tamen remaneat comiti Rann*ulfo* honor predictus
hereditarie 7 idem rex dabit eis escambium suum Dedit eciam
idem rex hereditarie predicto comiti Nouum Castellum de Stafford-
shira . cum omnibus eidem pertinentibus et Roeleiam cum soka .
7 Torcheseia . cum pertinentibus 7 villam de Derby cum pertinentibus
7 Mammesfeld cum pertinentibus 7 Stanlegam cum pertinentibus
et Oswarbec wapentache cum pertinentibus Et totam terram Rogeri
de Bully cum toto honore de Blida sicut diuisum est Et totam
terram Rogeri Pictauis a Northampton' vsque in Scociam excepta
terra Rogeri de Monte Begonis in Lincolnshire Dedit eciam idem
rex eidem comiti hereditarie honorem de Lancastre cum pertinentibus
suis 7 totam terram deinter Ribliam 7 Mersam 7 terram quam
habuit in dominio in manerio de Grymesby Et terram quam comes
Gloece*strie* habuit in dominio in manerio de Grymesby cum
pertinentibus Et preterea pro amore dicto comiti Rannulf*o* . idem
rex reddidit Adelid' de Condia . totam terram suam sicut illa finiit
scilicet Horncastriam quando castrum illum [*sic*] prostratum fuerit .
Et idem rex reddidit ei totam aliam terram suam.

In his article on the Clifford family Dugdale speaks of Alice de
Condet as ' Lady of Horn Castle,' and, misinterpreting the *Stemma*,
he makes her the wife instead of the mother of Roger de Condet.[1]
Weir, amplifying Dugdale's statement, says that in the time of
Stephen, the manor of Horncastle was the demesne of Alice de
Cundi, which she probably held by inheritance from her father ;
and he pictures her as residing in her castle there, the strength of
which ' most probably consisted in a restoration of the walls of
the Roman fortress, which encircling some convenient and less
durable edifice, gave to the place of her residence the security of
a castle.'[2]   There is, however, nothing, apart from king Stephen's
charter to earl Rannulf, to indicate that the manor of Horncastle
passed out of the king's possession before Henry II gave it to
Gerbod d'Escaut,[3] or that the town contained a medieval castle
at all.   On the other hand, there is Stephen's charter to bishop
Alexander[4] to prove that Alice de Condet had the castle of Thorngate close to the wall of the city of Lincoln.   Now, seeing that
the existing text of the grant to earl Rannulf is no more than a

[1] *Baronage* i, 336.
[2] *Historical and Descriptive Sketches of the Town and Soke of Horncastle*, page 7.
[3] *Rotuli Hundredorum* i, 299.
[4] Above, page 61.

summary of the original charter, and seems in itself to be not free from error, it may be conjectured that the chancery clerks who, in 1325, summarized the muniments at Pontefract castle, substituted Horncastle for Thorngate castle. By that time Thorngate had long since been forgotten, while Horncastle was a familiar name. The practice of conjoining an initial *T* with an *h* which followed it may have contributed to the mistake.[1]

The charters printed above indicate that Alice was a person of considerable importance ; and the final clause of Stephen's grant suggests a close connection with earl Rannulf :

' For the love that the king bore to the said earl Rannulf, he has returned to Adelidis de Condia all her land, as she fined, namely, Horncastria when that castle has been demolished ; and the king has restored to her all her other land.'

The evidence is insufficient to prove Alice's parentage, but if it were permissible to hazard a guess that she was the daughter of earl Rannulf (le Meschin) by the countess Lucy, and sister of the earl Rannulf (des Gernons) of Stephen's charter, her personal consequence and her appearance in Stephen's charter, and possibly her interest in Skellingthorpe, might be accounted for. Adeliz, or Alice, daughter of earl Rannulf, had married Richard fitz Gilbert (of Clare), the eldest brother of Baldwin fitz Gilbert of Bourne. Richard was slain by the Welsh near Abergavenny, 15 April, 1136, Adeliz his wife being rescued by Miles of Gloucester.[2]

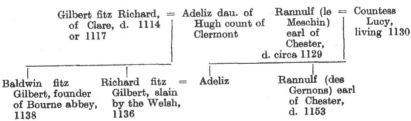

Robert de Condet

Robert de Condet, Alice's husband, in 1130, under the head of Kent and Sussex, rendered account of thirty marks and two destriers that the king might be brought into agreement with the bishop of Lincoln[3] ; and in the same year rendered account, in Lincoln-

[1] The *Th* of Thorngate is thus written in the Bardney Abbey cartulary, ff. 158d, 159.
[2] *Complete Peerage* (new ed.) iii, 243.
[3] *The Pipe Roll of Henry I*, page 67.

T

shire, of thirty marks for the relief of his father's land. Bishop Alexander at the same time rendered account of seventy marks for the service of Robert's land.[1] The lands held by Robert's father are not named in the rolls, but there can be no doubt that they included Wickhambreux which descended to Roger de Condet, from whom it passed, through the marriage of his daughter to Walter Clifford. In the thirteenth and fourteenth centuries a branch of the Condet family was settled at Cundishall in Sandwich, which was held of the lords of the manor of Wickhambreux by the service of a quarter of a knight's fee.[2] In Robert's inheritance there must also be reckoned some at least of the other lands mentioned in king Stephen's charter to bishop Alexander—Grimston, South Carlton, Thurlby, Eagle, and Skellingthorpe ; but the history of these estates gives no help in tracing Robert's ancestry. In 1086, Wickhambreux[3], and probably South Carlton[4], were held by the bishop of Bayeux ; Grimston[5] by the king ; Thurlby and Eagle by Odo the Arblaster[6] ; and Skellingthorpe by Baldwin the Fleming,[7] though it was claimed by the abbot of Westminster.

The ancestry of Robert de Condet is uncertain. Stapleton says that Peter de Condé married Emma Crispin, and that Robert was their descendant. Further, that Emma's sister, Hesilia, married William Malet[8], whose son, Robert Malet, was uncle to the countess Lucy.[9]

Roger de Condet

Roger de Condet, the son of Robert and Alice, was under age at the time of his father's death, *circa* 1141. In 1166 he held eight knights' fees of the bishop of Lincoln.[10] The size of this holding indicates that he was a person of importance, for of the other knights named in the bishop's charter of fees, only three had as many as six fees, while the holdings of the rest ranged from five fees down to half a fee. In addition to land in Lincolnshire, Nottinghamshire, and Kent, Roger held two of the bishop's fees in Milton

[1] *The Pipe Roll of Henry I*, page 111.
[2] *Book of Fees*, pp. 655, 683 ; *Feudal Aids* iii, 21, 23, 58, 59 ; Hasted, *Hist. of Kent* iii, 555 ; iv, 195, 261, 279, 394.
[3] *Domesday Book* i, 9, col. 2.
[4] *The Lincolnshire Domesday*, 4/1.
[5] *Domesday Book* i, 281, col. 2.
[6] *The Lincolnshire Domesday*, 48/14, 15.
[7] *Ibid.*, 65/4, 72/27.
[8] *Magni Rotuli Scaccarii Normaniæ* ii, p. cliii.
[9] Dugdale, *Baronage* i, 39.
[10] *Red Book* i, 375.

near Thame, co. Oxford,[1] half a knight's fee in Alderton in Wiltshire,[2] and perhaps land in Rutland.[3] He also held half a knight's
fee of Roger de Mowbray in 1166[4] ; and witnessed various charters
of Roger's, *circa* 1165,[5] and of his son, Nigel de Mowbray, *circa*
1180–1190.[6]

Roger de Cundi appears on the Pipe rolls of Michaelmas, 1167,
1168, and 1169, and on the last occasion he delivered twenty shillings
into the treasury, and was quit.[7] In 1191, under the head of
' Debts of Aaron the Jew ', in Lincolnshire and Yorkshire, Roger
owed fifteen pounds by charter ; and in the next year he rendered
account for the same sum, and for twenty marks by another charter,
and paid one mark into the treasury, leaving twenty-seven pounds
and one mark still due.[8] In 1193 he rendered account of twenty-
seven pounds and one mark, and paid one mark, leaving twenty-
seven pounds still due.[9] In 1194 and 1195 he still owed twenty-seven
pounds by two charters.[10]

Mr Salter attributes a gift by Roger de ' Cundi ' to Eynsham
abbey of four bovates in Milton by Thame[11] to a date before 1169,
on the ground that in the Pipe roll of that year William de Caisneto
is mentioned as holding nine fees of the bishop of Lincoln[12], and
he thinks that these fees must have been those of Roger which
William then held as guardian of Roger's heir. The evidence
given above, however, indicates that Roger was alive some years
later. The prominent place given to him among the witnesses to
the charters of the Mowbrays forbids the notion that it was his
nephew Roger who was the witness. Indeed the younger Roger
can scarcely have been old enough to appear in that capacity at
all. Mr. Salter's suggestion is based on the supposition that William

[1] Salter, *op. cit.*, i, 113–14.
[2] Above, page 245.
[3] Above, page 285.
[4] *Red Book* i, 420.
[5] *The Coucher Book of Selby* (Yorkshire Arch. and Top. Assoc., Record Series) ii,
281. The editor gives *circa* 1150 as the date of one of these charters, but this is too
early. See also *C.C.R.* ii, 441.
[6] Stenton, *Danelaw Charters*, pages 294–5.
[7] Pipe Roll Soc., xii, 73 ; xiii, 14 ; xv, 145.
[8] Pipe Roll Soc., N.S., ii, 17, 224.
[9] *Ibid.*, iii, 31.
[10] *Ibid.*, 96, 165. These entries, perhaps, do not prove that Roger was then alive,
because the names of Aaron's creditors often appear on the rolls long after they
were dead.
[11] Salter, *op. cit.*, i, 113–14.
[12] Pipe Roll Soc. xiii, 46.

Chesney was Roger's father-in-law, a mistake which is due to Dugdale's misinterpretation of the *Stemma*. Roger was dead in 1201, for in that year his son-in-law, Walter Clifford, answered for his fees.

In 1203, an assize came to recognize whether Roger de Cundi, uncle of Roger de Cundy, was seized in his demesne as of fee of three bovates and eight acres of meadow in Ketelbi and in Herdewic etc., which the brethren of the Temple hold, and they vouched to warrant William de Mobray, who was in the king's service.[1] Perhaps Roger the nephew was the son of the Robert de Cundi who witnessed Roger's gift to the church of Lincoln[2]. A John de Cundi held one twelfth of a knight's fee of Nigel de Mowbray, 1222–1228[3]. Early in the thirteenth century, Robert son of Hugh Bardolf granted to Barlings abbey one bovate in Magna Carlton (South Carlton) iuxta Lincoln[4], which was of the fee of Roger de Cundy, and which Robert the smith held, with the men belonging to it[5].

Agnes de Condet

Agnes de Condet, Roger's daughter and heiress, married Walter Clifford, the ancestor of the earls of Cumberland. In a list of the bishop of Lincoln's fees, in 1201, Walter de Clifford holds five fees, evidently as successor to Roger de Condet.[6] In another list, probably about 1206, he holds four and a half fees in Lincolnshire and Nottinghamshire,[7] and, in 1208–1212, he holds the two fees in Milton by Thame.[8] In 1235–6, Walter's son, another Walter Clifford, rendered account for half a fee in Alderton which was held by a feoffment granted before the death of Henry I.[9] An interesting entry in the *Book of Fees* indicates that the elder Walter had, in 1212, succeeded to Roger de Condet's land in Grimston.[10] The jurors say:

'Quod Grimeston' cum pertinenciis se defendit pro ij. carucatis terre que date fuerunt ecclesie Lincolnie in elemosinam, quando

[1] *Curia Regis Rolls* ii, 158. The index suggests that Herdewic is Hardwick (an extinct village) in Nettleton. Kettleby is near Brigg.
[2] Above, page 285.
[3] *Red Book* ii, 737.
[4] In 1242–3, Roger's grandson, Walter Clifford, held one knight's fee in Carlton Paynel (South Carlton) (*Book of Fees* ii, 1065, 1076).
[5] *Mon.* vii, 917.
[6] Rotuli de *Oblatis et Finibus*, page 153.
[7] *Red Book* ii, 515–16.
[8] *Book of Fees* i, 40.
[9] *Ibid.* i, 423.
[10] *Ibid.* i, p. 150.

ecclesia fundata fuit ante conquestum terre ; et Robertus Barduf' modo tenet eas de Waltero de Clifford' per servicium j. militis et Walterus in capite de episcopo et ecclesia ; et est senescallus episcopatus de feodo illo una cum reliquo feodo, quod similiter tenet de eisdem ; et tam antiquitus data fuit terra illa quod nescitur quis illam dedit.

In a plea concerning common of pasture in Grimestun and Welhag', *temp.* John, the abbot of Rufford asserted that the pastures belonged to the baronies of Robert de Cundy and Gilbert de Gant.[1]

Walter Clifford senior died 7 Henry III (A.D. 1222–3). The will of Agnes, his widow, which was made in her husband's lifetime, is printed below.[2] It will be observed that she makes a bequest to the church of Wickhambreux ; and that her husband had granted to her the issues of the manor of Caenby for a year after her death.

Testamentum Agnetis de Cundy uxoris Walteri de Cliffort.

Hoc est testamentum domine Agnetis de Clifford In nomine Patris et Filii et Spiritus Sancti Amen . Ego Agnes de Clifford in nomine sancti [*sic*] Trinitatis do, lego priori et conventui Sancte Trinitatis Cantuar'[3] centum solidatas terre in villa Wicham[4] una cum corpore meo per concessum et assensum domine mei Walteri de Clifford Et ad opus ecclesie sancti Augustini Cantuar'[5] quadraginta solidos . Et ad opus ecclesie sancti Gregorii viginti solidos . Et ad opus ecclesie sancti Sepulchri[6] viginti solidos . Et quinque hospitalibus Cant' duas marcas et dimidiam . Et singulis anachoritis Cantuar' duodecim solidos . Item heremite de Hoppa[7] unam marcam . Item tribus puellis maritandis triginta solidos . Item tria annualia pro anima mea ad alam ecclesie sancti Andree de Wicham faciendam et in eadem altari Omnium Sanctorum decem marcas . Item quinque tritennalia pro anima mea . Item ad fabricum [*sic*] [*folio 237d.*] ecclesie sancte Radigundis[8] viginti solidos . Item ad fabricum ecclesie de Holteg[9] . unam marcam . Item singulis ecclesiis parochialibus Cantuar' duodecim denarios . Item ad fabricum ecclesie sancti Edelberti de Herford[10] quadraginta solidos . Item

---

[1] *Abbreviatio Placitorum*, page 77.
[2] Brit. Mus., Lansdowne MS. 207A, ff. 237–238d. Nicholas Harris Nicolas, *Testamenta Vetusta* i, 45–7, prints a slightly different version, professedly from Lansdowne MS. 1402, but there is no such manuscript.
[3] Priory of the Holy Trinity, Canterbury.
[4] Wickhambreux.
[5] Abbey of Saint Augustine, Canterbury.
[6] Priory of Saint Gregory, and nunnery of Saint Sepulchre, Canterbury.
[7] Possibly Hope All Saints, co. Kent.
[8] Priory of Saint Radegund, near Dover.
[9] Probably Holdgate, Salop.
[10] Cathedral church of Hereford.

prioratui de Clifford[1] duas insulas et unicum tuniculum . Et ad fabr' ecclesie ejusdem loci quadraginta solidos . Item Elie capellano de Clifford decem solidos . Item ad fabricam ecclesie de Hagenby[2] quadraginta solidos et unam insulam . Item ad fabricam ecclesie de Wenloc[3] duas marcas . Item Basilie filie mee consulende viginti marcas . Item domine Cecilie quinque marcas . Terrico Flandrensi decem marcas . Item Radulfo dispensatori decem marcas . Item Willelmo filio Johannis decem marcas . Item Jacobo Normanno decem marcas . Nicholao clerico viginti solidos . Roberto vialatori viginti solidos . Hereberto Willelmo Ricardo garcionibus meis sexaginta solidos . Item Matilde domicelle mee decem marcas et unam robam skarket [sic], et unam gulecc'm[4] punctatam, et unum coopertorium cum linthiaminibus . Item Bartholomeo de Newlof viginti solidos . Galfrido cultario decem solidos . Giliberto de Chaury dimidiam marcam . Item Willelmo pistori dimidiam marcam . Item Ade Parker dimidiam marcam . Item Lamberto seruienti decem solidos [folio 238] . Domino Philippo canonico quinque solidos . Item duobus paruis pistoribus duos solidos . Item Hamoni preposito quinque solidos . Ricardo coco quinque solidos . Thome socio suo quinque solidos . Willelmo summetario domini duodecim denarios . Johanni Venatori duodecim denarios . Item palefridum et summum meum cum pertinenciis ecclesie sancte Trinitatis ubi jacebo . Item anachoritis sancti Andree de Wicham quamdiu vixerint annuatim duas summas bladi . Item Waltero aurifabro viginti solidos . Item Waltero de Nicholls viginti solidos . Item Waltero portario quinque solidos . Item matri[5] mee unum annulum aureum . Item Waltero filio meo unum annulum aureum . Item Rogero filio meo unum annulum aureum . Item Ricardo filio meo unum annulum aureum . Item Simoni filio meo unum annulum aureum . Item Ægidio filio meo unum annulum aureum . Item singulis filiabus meis unum annulum aureum . Item hospitali sancti Wolstani Wigorn'[6] unum culcetorem[7] de serico, et duo lintheamina et auriculare unum . Et ad hoc testamentum meum perficiendum dominus meus Walterus de Clifford mihi [folio 238d.] concessit omnes exitus manerii de Couenby per unum annum integrum post obitum meum . et wardam de le Graye quod emi a domino meo tam diu quousque hoc testamentum meum compleatur . Et etiam dimidiatum omnium mobilium per omnes terras suas . Et ego omnium que mea sunt aurum et argentum vasa et vestimenta ad hoc testamentum meum perficiendum vendenda constitui . Quicquid autem residuum fuerit per visum executorum meorum pro anima

---

[1] Clifford priory, co. Hereford.
[2] Probably Hagnaby abbey, co. Lincoln.
[3] Wenlock, co. Salop.
[4] Perhaps for gulettum, a red mantle.
[5] Agnes' mother, Basilia, was in living at Milton by Thame 3 Henry III [see Eyton, Antiquities of Shropshire v, 156–7).
[6] Hospital of Saint Wulstan without Worcester.
[7] Perhaps for calciternum, a couch made with cushions.

mea ubi melius fuerit distribuatur . Executores meos constituo dominum meum Walterum de Clifford dominum episcopum Herefordensem dominum priorem ecclesie Christi Cantuar'[1] dominum Henricum archidiaconum Cantuar' dominum Petrum de Hungria.

Item ad fabricam ecclesie sancti Martini de Doueria[2] viginti solidos.

In the later part of the twelfth century Beatrice de Cundi granted to Haverholme priory one bovate of land and one toft in Quarrington, with her body ; and her son, Alexander de Sancto Vedasto, who died before 1201, confirmed the gift.[3] Alexander also granted a bovate of 20 acres with a toft and a croft of three acres in Quarrington (probably the same land as above), with his mother's body when the priory received her as a sister.[4] A royal *inspeximus*, in 1337, adds, ' and three perches and a half of meadow.'[5] In 1166 Beatrice, who was then named Beatrice de Evdone (or Eaved'), held one knight's fee of the bishop of Lincoln,[6] which can be shown to have consisted in 1086 of the bishop of Lincoln's land in Quarrington, Laythorpe, and Evedon.[7] It may be presumed that Beatrice, who was evidently an heiress, married, first, Alexander's father, and afterwards a member of the Condet family. Possibly she may have been the wife of a brother of Roger de Condet.

It has seemed worth while to collect what may be known about the family of de Condet, for Roger was a baron of the bishop of Lincoln of a similar standing to Hamon Massey in the Chester fee or to Roger fitz Corbet under Roger de Montgomery. The fact that there was a castle in the fee of each of these men shews that it is easy to underestimate the position of the greater mesne tenants. Thorngate castle was close to the wall of the city of Lincoln, and Professor F. M. Stenton has suggested to the writer that a close parallel is to be found in Baynard's Castle, which answered on the west to the Tower of London on the east ; and that Henry of Winchester's Wolvesey Castle is another example of a private castle helping to grip a town, though not so close as the London instance.

[1] Cathedral church of Canterbury.
[2] Saint Martin's priory, Dover.
[3] *Haverholme Priory Charters*, nos. 39, 41 (printed in *Lincolnshire Notes and Queries* xvii, 21).
[4] *Ibid.*, no. 40.
[5] *C.C.R.* iv, 416.
[6] *Red Book* i, 375.
[7] *The Lincolnshire Domesday*, 7/48–50.

INDEX OF PERSONS AND PLACES

NOTE.—Since hereditary surnames are rarely found in the period covered by this volume, the plan here adopted is, either to index a person under his personal name, or to supply a reference from that name to the name under which he will be found.

Attention is called to the section of the Index headed *Son of*. In such a form as *Ailred son of Guthred*, references or cross-references are given under *Ailred*, *Guthred*, and *Son of*.

Clinton, Roger, bishop of Coventry, Lichfield, and Chester, 193; his charter, 116

Clopham. *See* Clapham

Clyua. *See* King's Cliffe

Coddington, Chodingtona, co. Nott., church of, 206

Codyngton'. *See* Cuddington

Coelestin II, pope, 247

Colegrim, 200

Coleman, John, knt, witn., 173

Colevill, William de, witn., 97

Colsuain, 199, 201, 207
    Picot son of. *See* Picot

Columban. *See* Son of

Columban, Geoffrey, witn., 286

Condet, Condeio, Condia, Cundeio, Cundet, Cundi, Cundy, Gundeio:
    family of, xvi, 282-95
    land of, in Kent and Lincs, 289
    ——, of Cundishall, 290
    Agnes de, dau. of Roger, wife of Walter de Clifford, 62, 283-4, 293
    ——, Basilia mother of, 283, 294, 294n
    ——, will of, 293-4
    Beatrice de, Beatrice of Evedon, 295
    ——, Alexander son of. *See* Vedasto, Sancto
    John de, 292
    Osbert de, 282-3
    Robert de, 282-5, 289-90
    ——, wife of. *See* Alice
    ——, junior, 285
    ——, *perhaps* son of Robert, junior, 292; his barony, 293
    Roger de, son of Robert and Alice, 61-2, 200, 207, 245, 282, 284-5, 290 (2)-2, 295; his fee, 292
    ——, nephew of Roger, 291-2

Conrad, cardinal-bishop of Sabina, witn., 248

Constanciensis. *See* Coutances

Coombe Keynes, Cumba, co. Dorset, church of, 242

Coringeham. *See* Corringham

Cornwall, Cornubiensis:
    earl of. *See* Plantaganet; Reginald Fitz-Roy
    master John of, witn., 256

Cornwell, co. Oxford, 83-4

Corringham, Coringeham, Coringham, co. Linc., 27-8, 105, 112, 206
    church of, 27-8, 105, 199, 205
    mandate dated at, 224-5
    preb. of Lincoln. *See* Brand
    wapentake of, 58-9

Coueneby. *See* Caenby

Counthorpe [in Castle Bytham], Cunthorp, co. Linc., 81-3

Coutances, Constanciensis [Manche, France], master Ralf of, witn., 256
    See also Walter bishop of Lincoln

Covenham St Bartholomew, co. Linc., Cawthorpe in, *q.v.*

Coventry, Lichfield, and Chester, bishop of, 185-6. *See* Clinton; Durdent; Limesey; Peche

Coxwold, Cucuwald, Cucwald, co. York, church and manor of, 19-20

Craucumb', Crawcumb, Godfrey de, witn., 166, 178-9; seneschal of Henry III, witn., 167, 177

Craumersa. *See* Crowmarsh Gifford

Crawcumb. *See* Craucumb'

Creeton, co. Linc., 81-3

Crevequer, Creuequer, Rainald de, witn., 56

Crochesby. *See* Croxby

Croilandia. *See* Croyland

Cropredy, Croper', Croperia, Croposia, co. Oxford, 83-4, 189, 191, 194, 203
    church of, 199, 207
    hundred of, 191
    Geoffrey of, 84

Crouch [in Banbury], Crouch Hill, Cruch', co. Oxford, 129-31

Crowmarsh Gifford, Craumersa, co. Oxford, siege of, charter dated at, 97-8

Croxby, Crochesby, co. Linc., 208

Croyland, Croilandia, Crulanda, co. Linc.:
    abbey, abbot of, 77
    ——, pension from, 203

Cruch'. *See* Crouch

Crulanda. *See* Croyland

Cucuwald. *See* Coxwold; Cuxwold

Cucwald. *See* Coxwold

Cuddington, Codyngton', co. Surrey, church of, 241

Cukewald. *See* Cuxwold

Cumba. *See* Coombe Keynes

Cumberland, earls of, 283

Cundishall [in Sandwich], co. Kent, 290

Cundy. *See* Condet

Cunthorp. *See* Counthorpe

Curcy, Curci:
    Matthew de, 118
    Robert de, witn., 8, 10

Curtenay, Curtenai:
    Reginald de, witn., 121
    Robert de, 161

Cuxwold, Cucuwald, Cukewald, co. Linc., 200, 207

Dalderby, John, bishop of Lincoln, xxx, xxxii-iii
    Laudum of, xxxii
    registrar of. *See* Schalby

Dammartin, Reginald, count of Boulogne, witn., 133, 136

Danelaw, the Northern, xv

Danish Army, the, men of, xvi

Darcy, de Aresci, Robert, fee of, 208

U

Darley, Derlega, Derleia, co. Derby, the king's church of, one of the churches of the Peak, 19, 48, 117
Darneford'. *See* Dornford
David, witn., 79 (2)
 abbot of Barlings, witn., 265
 archdeacon of Buckingham, 262
 land of prebend of, in Lincoln, 205–6
Davis, H. W. C., *Regesta*, quoted, 2–17
Decem Librarum, preb. of Lincoln, 55, *cp*. 61. *See* Sigillo, Baldric de
Deeping, co. Linc., lord of, 286
Derby, county of, xvi
 lieges of, 17, 29
 sheriff of. *See* Nottingham and Derby, counties
Derby, Derbeia, Derebia, co. Derby :
 archdeacon of, 186. *See also* Froger
 churches of, 206
 collegiate church of All Saints, a free royal chapel, granted *in prebendam*, 29, 92–3, 185, 199, 206
 earl of. *See* Ferrers
 town of, 288
Derebia. *See* Derby
Derlega, Derleia. *See* Darley
Devon, earl of. *See* Redvers
Dispenser, Dispensarius, Dispensator :
 Geoffrey, witn., 178–9
 Hugh, witn., 168, 170, 175–9
 Ralf, *q.v.*
Ditton, Long, Ditton', co. Surrey :
 church of, 242
 Talworth in, *q.v.*
Dodingtona. *See* Duddington
Donintuna. *See* Duddington
Donstanvilla. *See* Dunstanville
Dorand. *See* Durand
Dorcacastrensis. *See* Dorchester
Dorchester, Dorcacastrensis, Dorcacestra, Dorcacestria, Dorcestra, Dorchacestr', Dorchecestria, Dorkecestria, co. Oxford, 189, 191, 194, 196, 203
 abbey, abbot of. *See* Alvered
 ——, papal bull in favour of, 246–9
 ——, pension from, 203
 bishop of. *See* Wulfwig
 Brademera near, 247
 church of St Peter, formerly the cathedral church, granted by bishop Remigius, 247
 ——, chapels of, 247
 domus Dunningi near, 247
 episcopal houses in, 247
 hundred of, 191
 Queneford mill near, 247
 see of, transferred to Lincoln, xvi, 2, 3, 5, 6, 246–7
 Suiftelac meadow near, 247
Dornford [in Wootton], Darneford', co. Oxford, 83–4
Dorobernensis. *See* Canterbury

Douai [Nord, France], Peter of. *See* Peter
Dover, Douera, Doueria, Doura, co. Kent :
 archbishop of, witn., 7
 castle-guard of, 59, 268
 charter dated at, 68
 Dorobernensis. *See* Canterbury
 honour of, lieges of, 59
 priory of St Martin, 295
 See St Radegund
Drax, Dracae, co. York, W.R., charter dated at, 64
Drayton St Leonard, co. Oxford, Drætona, a chapel of Dorchester, 247
Dublin, Ireland, archbishop of. *See* Loundres
Duddington, Dodingtona, Donintuna, co. North'ton, church of, 199, 207
Dugdale, William, *Monasticon Anglicanum* quoted, *passim*
Dumping, Ketel, of Saltfleetby, xvi
Duneham. *See* Dunholme
Dunelmum. *See* Durham
Dunham. *See* Dunholme
Dunholme, Duneham, co. Linc. :
 church of, 198, 205
 Newport and Dunham, preb. of Lincoln, xxx. *See* Schalby
Dunningus. *See* Dorchester
Dunsby [near Bourne], Dunnesby, co. Linc., 166
Dunstanville, Donstanvilla, Dunestanvilla :
 Robert of, witn., 85, 87, 97, 99
 See Reginald Fitz-Roy
Durand, Dorand. *See* Son of
Durdent, Walter, bishop of Coventry, Lichfield, and Chester, 117
Durham, Dunelmum :
 bishop of. *See* Bek ; Flambard ; Poor ; Pudsey ; St Carileph
 cathedral church of, charters at, xxii, 148, 153, 160
 charter dated at, 59

E. :
 perhaps Erneis de Burun, sheriff of Yorkshire, 4, 17 ; witn., 3, 15
 See Eustace son of John
Eagle, Eicla, co. Linc., 61, 284, 290
 manor of, 57
Eakring, Eicring, co. Nott., 181
 land in, 285
Eaved'. *See* Evedon
Eboracum. *See* York
Eboroicensis. *See* Evreux
Edenestou. *See* Edwinstowe
Edmund. *See* Plantagenet ; Pontefract
Edward the Confessor, king of England, 11, 12, 17, 32, 48
 legates and letters of, 186

Longchamp, de Longocampo, William,
bishop of Ely, chancellor of
Richard I, witn., 125
Longespée :
William de, 1st earl of Salisbury,
140 ; witn., 139, 152, 159, 161
William [so called earl of Lincoln
and Salisbury], 282–4
——, wife of. *See* Clifford
Longo Campo, de. *See* Longchamp
Losinga :
Herbert, bishop of Thetford, witn.,
7, 10, 11
Robert, bishop of Hereford, 8
Lotheringus, Richard, witn., 81
Loundres, Henry de, archbishop of
Dublin, witn., 133–4, 136, 139
Louo, witn., 79
Louth, Luda, co. Linc. :
charter dated at, 81, 83
church of, [a preb. of Lincoln], 199,
205
fair at, 94, 103
manor of, 188, 190, 194, 196, 203
——, claimed by the archbishop of
York, 11–13
warren of, 68
Louth Park, co. Linc. :
abbey, abbot of. *See* Ralf
——, cellarer of. *See* Robert
——, pension from, 203
Lucebi. *See* Lusby
Luci :
Godfrey, bishop of Winchester,
witn., 125
Richard de, witn., 48–9, 51–2, 54–5,
58, 62–4, 66, 87, 93–4, 100, 105–6,
108 (2)–9, 115 (2), 117
Lucy, the countess, 78–9, 289
Luda. *See* Louth
Ludham, Godfrey de, archbishop of
York, 219–20
Luffa, Ralf, bishop of Chichester, witn.,
7, 8, 10
Lugdun'. *See* Lyons
Luke :
the chaplain, dean of St Martin
le Grand, London, witn., 169
See Turbervill
Lundonia. *See* London
Lusby, Lucebi, co. Linc. :
men of, 50
Imerus of, witn., 77
William clerk of, witn., 77
Luterel, Geoffrey, witn., 129, 142
Lyddington, Lidentona, co. Rutl., 113,
124–5, 188
church of, assigned in place of
preb. of Canwick, 207–8
park of, 174–5
bishop of Lincoln's woods of, 129–
30, 132
Lymberg. *See* Limber
Lyons, Lugdun' [Rhone, France], bull
dated at, 213–15, 225, 227

Lyre [Eure, France], abbey, cartulary
of, 287, 287n
Lyskes. *See* Licques

Mablethorpe, Malbertorp, co. Linc.,
Philip of, witn., canon, 255
Magneby, William de, 173
Major, Mr (17th cent.), 272
Malbertorp. *See* Mablethorpe
Malden, Meldon', co. Surrey, church of,
242
Malebissa :
Alexander, witn., 81
Geoffrey, clerk, witn., 78–9
Osbert, witn., 97
Malet, William, witn., 129
Maletot, Henry de, witn., 80
Malger, master, 120–1 ; clerk of bishop
Chesney, 250
Cp. Mauger
Malmesbury, Malmesbir', co. Wilts,
abbey, abbot of, witn., 152, 159 ;
See also Gregory
Malo Lacu, Peter de, witn., 152, 159
Maltby, co. York, W.R., Roche in, *q.v.*
Mamefelt. *See* Mansfield
Mamesfelda. *See* Mansfield
Maminot, Walchelin, witn., 97
Mammesfelt. *See* Mansfield
Manasser. *See* Bisset
Mandeville :
Geoffrey de, earl of Essex, witn., 2,
118
William de, earl of Essex, witn., 152,
159, 161
Mans, Le, Cenomannum, Cenomum
[Sarthe, France], charter dated
at, 73, 123
Mansfield, Mamefelt, Mamesfelda, Mam-
mesfelt, co. Nott., 288
church of, 17, 116, 199, 206
——, assigned to the deanery of
Lincoln, 219–20
manor of, 17, 116, 199
——, berewicks with chapels
adjoining, 17, 116, 199, 206
Mara, Peter de, witn., 75
Marcham, de. *See* Markham
Marescallus. *See* Marshall
Marisco, de. *See* Marsh
Markby, co. Linc., priory, prior and
convent of, xxx
Markham, de Marcham, Richard, 181
Marlesford, John de, clerk, notary public,
244
Marsh, de Marisco :
master Richard, chancellor of king
John, witn., 131, 133, 139
Robert, dean of Lincoln, 220
Marshall, Marescallus :
Gilbert, earl of Pembroke, witn.,
166
Henry, bishop of Exeter, witn., 123
J., witn., 131

X

Walton [in Grantham], Waltuna, co. Linc., 200, 207
  mill of, 200, 207
Waravill, Ralf de, 173
Warden, Chipping, Wardon, co. North'ton, market of, 168–70
Warden, Old, Guardona, co. Bedf., abbey, pension from, 203
Wareham, Warham, Alfred or Alured of, witn., 8–10
Warengford'. See Wallingford
Warenne, Warenna:
  earl of, or earl of Surrey:
    John, 6th earl, witn., lvi
    John, 7th earl, witn., lviii, lxi
    William, witn., 36, 52
    ——, 5th earl, 140; witn., 131, 133 (2), 136, 152, 159, 161, 177
  William of, witn., 123
Warewic'. See Warwick
Warham. See Wareham
Warin:
  son of Gerold, chamberlain of Henry II, witn., 72 (2), 87–9, 92–4, 96–7, 99, 101, 103–6, 113, 115, 142
  See Son of
Warkworth, Wauencurt, co. North'ton, manor of, 94–6
Warsop, co. Nott., warren in, 180–1
Wartona. See Wharton
Warwick, Warewic', earl of. See Beaumont; Newburgh
Watburn'. See Wooburn
Wateuilla, Watneuilla:
  Ralf de, 44
  Robert de, witn., 108
Wauencurt. See Warkworth
Wdecota. See Woodcote
Wdestoc. See Woodstock
Weburna. See Woburn
Welbourn [co. Linc.], Welburn, John of, treasurer of Lincoln, xliii, 127
Welingeham. See Willingham, South
Well (also called Stow), co. Linc., bishop's wapentake of, 5, 6, 13, 41, 99, 100, 129–30, 132
  barons, vavasors, and lords of, 99–100
  firma of, 53
  third penny of, 13, 105–6
  William of, 173
Welland, the river, xv
Welletona. See Welton by Lincoln
Wellingeham. See Willingham, South
Wellingore, Walingoure, Wallingoura, co. Linc.:
  church of, 2, 3, 5, 6, 56, 198, 205
  manor of, 2, 3, 5, 6, 91, 198
Wellow [in Grimsby], co. Linc., abbey:
  abbot of. See Thomas
  canon of. See Thomas
  pension from, 203
Wellow, co. Nott., 293

Wells, Welles, co. Somerset:
  bishop of. See Bath and Wells
  cathedral church of, 187
  papal bull in favour of, 187–8
  Hugh of, archdeacon of Wells, 128–9, 142
  Jocelin of, bishop of Bath and Glastonbury, 134 (2)–7; witn., 131, 139, 152, 159, 164, 168–9, 175, 179
  Simon of, bishop of Chichester, witn., 142
Wells, Hugh of, bishop of Lincoln, xx, 166; witn., 152, 159
  charters granted by, 171–4
  builder of palace at Lincoln, 274
  grants in favour of, 127–39, 143, 164, 167–70, 174–9
  licence to dispose of goods by will at death, 176–8
  papal bull addressed to, 234, 237
  pardon of debts of, 143
Welton by Lincoln, Welletona, co. Linc., manor of, preb. of Lincoln, xxx, 2, 3, 5, 6, 25, 56, 71–2 (2), 91, 106, 191, 198, 205
  Beckhall preb. of Lincoln, xxx. See also Schalby
Wem, co. Salop, query charter dated at, 39
Wenge, Gerard de, vicar of Castle Bytham and Holywell, 81–3
Wenlock, Wenloc, co. Salop, priory of, 294
Wentoniensis. See Winchester
Weodstocha. See Woodstock
Wercesworda, Werchesorda, Werchewerda. See Wirksworth
Werelwast, W. de, witn., 15
Werkeworda. See Wirksworth
Westbourne, Buneham, Burnham, co. Sussex, charter dated at, 34
Westgate. See Lincoln (3)
Westminster, Westmonasterium, co. Middx.:
  abbey, grant to, 4
  ——, abbot of, 193, 290; witn., 152, 159. See also Gilbert; Laurence
  charter dated at, lvi–viii (2)–lxi, 26, 30–2, 39, 64, 66, 71–2 (2), 75, 77, 93, 107, 111 (2)–12, 117–18, 120–2, 124–5, 140, 149, 152–3, 159, 162–9, 171, 174–5, 177–81, 184–5
  legate's council of, 240
Weybridge, co. Hunt., forest of, 139
Wharton [in Blyton], Wartona, co. Linc., 58–9, 191
Whitby, Wyteby, co. York, N.R., abbey, abbot of, witn., 152, 159
Whitchurch. See Albo Monasterio, de
Wicestra. See Winchester
Wicham. See Wickhambreux
Wickenden, Canon J. F., xl

Wickham [in Bodicote in Banbury], Wicham, Wicheam, Wicheham, Wykham, co. Oxford, 84–5, 99
　　manor of, 99
Wickhambreux, Wicham, co. Kent, 61–2, 284, 290
　　church of St Andrew of, 293
　　———　———, anchorite in, 294
　　manor of, 290
Widel'. *See* Woodlays
Wido. *See* Guido ; Guy
Wigan, co. Lanc., rector of. *See* Maunsell
Wigford. *See* Lincoln (3)
Wiggesle. *See* Wigsley
Wigoan', charter dated at, 110
Wigot :
　　son of Asger. *See* Skidbrooke
　　See Lincoln (5)
Wigsley, Wiggesle, co. Nott., 120
Wilchebi. *See* Willoughby, Silk
Wilgebia. *See* Willoughby, Silk
William I, king, xv, 25, 29–30, 32–3, 90–1
　　chancery of, 4
　　charters granted by, 1–4, 42
　　charters of, genuineness of, 4
　　grants by, 56
　　Maud wife of, 25, 29–30, 32–3
　　son of. *See* Robert count of Normandy
　　time of, referred to, 4, 16, 23 (2), 25, 54, 102, 106
　　transfers the see from Dorchester to Lincoln, xvi, 2, 3, 5, 6, 246–7
William II, king, 29–30, 32–3, 40
　　authority granted by, for constitution of the chapter of Lincoln, xvi, xvii, 7
　　chancellor of. *See* Bloet, Robert
　　charters granted by, lvi, 4–17
　　dapifer of. *See* Eudo ; Hamon
　　dispute about Lindsey settled by, xv, 11–12
　　sickness of, 16
　　time of, referred to, 23, 25–6, 54, 106, 116 (2)–17
William Fitz-Patrick, 2nd earl of Salisbury, witn., 123, 125
William Fitz-Robert. *See* Robert Fitz-Roy
William Fitz-Roy, earl of Gloucester, witn., 98
William son of Hacon [of Saleby], sheriff of Lincolnshire, 34
William :
　　abbot of Ramsey, witn., 65
　　archdeacon [*query* of Lincoln], witn., 80–1
　　the baker, 294
　　the canon, witn., 8
　　the chaplain, witn., 77
　　the clerk, witn., 257. *See also* Lusby
　　the deacon, witn., 286
　　the groom, 294

William—*cont.*
　　nepos of Martell. *See* Tanea
　　son of Adelm, 121
　　son of Bernard, 84–5
　　son of Fardain, of Lincoln, 190
　　master, son of Fulk, cl., witn., 145, 255
　　son of Godfrey, witn., 264
　　son of Hamon, witn., 85, 87–9, 103, 105 (2)–7, 113–14
　　son of John, 294 ; witn., 93, 119
　　son of Nigel, 84–5
　　son of Osbert, Philip son of, canon of Lincoln (*query* Thorngate preb.), 107, 118
　　son of Simon, 207
　　son of Warin, witn., 175
　　summetarius of Walter Clifford, senior, 294
　　See—

Alnwick	Magneby
Amundavill	Malet
Anderby	Mandeville
Aubigny	Marshall
Avallon	Martell
Ayreminne	Mauduit
Benniworth	Montibus, de
Blois	Mortimer
Bochart	Mowbray
Bramfeld	Papiloun
Braose	Percy
Brewer	Peverel
Briwerr'	Pont-de-
Broi	l'Arche
Buckden	Rabi
Burdet	Redvers
Cahaines	Roumare
Cantilupe	St Carileph
Chesney	St John
Clement	Sainte Mere
Colevill	l'Eglise
Ely	Sewelle
Eyneford'	Smith
Ferrers	Son of
Forz	Sutton
Gare	Tancarvilla
Harcourt	Turbe
Ipra	Turniant
Langton	Vere
Lanval	Wake
Longchamp	Warenne
Longespée	Well

Williams, John, bishop of Lincoln, 276
Willingham, Cherry, Willingham, co. Linc., land in, belonging preb. of Empingham, 205
Willingham, South, Welingeham, Wellingeham, Wollingham, co. Linc., 31, 102–3, 108
Willingthorpe. *See* Lincoln (3)
Willoughby, Silk, Wilchebi, Wilgebia, Willoughby iuxta Sleaford, co. Linc., 200, 202, 207
Wilton, Eustace of [canon of Lincoln], witn., 252, 254, 264

Y

INDEX OF COUNTIES AND COUNTRIES

GLOUCESTERSHIRE

HAMPSHIRE

HEREFORDSHIRE

HERTFORDSHIRE

HUNTINGDONSHIRE

KENT

LANCASHIRE

LEICESTERSHIRE

LINCOLNSHIRE

Deeping
Dunholme
Dunsby [near Bourne]
Eagle
Elkington, South
Elsham
Evedon
Faldingworth
Fenton [in Beckingham]
Fiskerton
Foss Dike, canal
Friesthorpe
Fulbeck
Gilby
Glentham
Gonerby
Goxhill
Grainsby
Grantham
Greetham
Greetwell
Grimsby, Great
Haceby
Hagnaby
Hainton
Halton
Hardwick [in Nettleton]
Hareby
Harrington
Hartsholme
Haverholme
Hibaldstow
Holme Spinney
Holton Beckering
Holywell
Horncastle
Hough on the Hill
Hougham
Hundon
Hykeham
Ingham
Keal
Kelsey
Kelsey, North
Kettleby
Kingerby

Kirkby Laythorpe
Kirkby cum Osgodby
Kirkstead
Kirton in Lindsey
Laythorpe
Limber
Lincoln
Lindsey
Linwood
Louth
Louth Park
Lusby
Mablethorpe
Markby
Marton
Melton Ross
Morton [in Swinderby]
Mumby
Nettleham
Nettleton
Newhouse
Newport
Newton on Trent
Normanby by Stow
Northorpe
Norton, Bishop
Norton Disney
Owersby
Owmby [in Searby]
Pilham
Pointon
Quarrington
Rauceby
Redbourne
Revesby
Riby
Ringstone
Rippingale
Ropsley
Saltfleetby
Scamblesby
Scawby
Scothorne
Searby
Sempringham
Sincil Dike, stream

Skellingthorpe
Skidbrooke
Skillington
Sleaford
Somercotes
Southorpe
Southrey
Spalding
Spridlington
Stamford
Steeping
Stoke, North and South
Stow St Mary
Stragglethorpe
Sturton by Stow
Sutton [in Beckingham]
Sutton le Marsh
Swallow
Swinderby
Tattershall
Thorngate
Thornholm
Thornton Curtis
Thorpe on the Hill
Thurlby [near Lincoln]
Timberland
Torksey
Tupholme
Uffington
Wainfleet
Walton
Welbourn
Well
Wellingore
Wellow
Welton by Lincoln
Westgate
Wharton
Wigford
Willingham, Cherry
Willingham, South
Willingthorpe
Willoughby, Silk
Winceby
Witham, the river

MIDDLESEX

Fulham

London

Westminster

NORFOLK

Matlask
Norwich

Plumstead [by Holt]
Raveningham

Thetford
Walsingham

NORTHAMPTONSHIRE

Appletree
Ashley
Aston le Walls
Duddington
Farthinghoe
Flore
Glinton
Gretton
Kilsby

King's Cliffe
Marston St Lawrence
Nassington
Newton, Wood
Northampton
Pattishall
Peterborough
Rockingham
Southwick

Stamford
Sutton, King's
Syresham
Tansor
Wakerley
Warden, Chipping
Warkworth
Wothorpe

WARWICKSHIRE

Kenilworth   Stoneleigh

WILTSHIRE

Alderton   Lacock   Salisbury
Chute   Malmesbury

WORCESTERSHIRE

Evesham   Pershore   Worcester

YORKSHIRE

Beverley   Kirkby Moorside   Roche
Coxwold   Maltby   Selby
Drax   Pontefract   Tickhill
Goldsborough   Richmond   Whitby
Helmsley   Rievaulx   York
Hovingham

WALES

Abergavenny, co. Mon.   Monmouth, co. Mon.   St David's, co. Pemb.

IRELAND
Dublin

FRANCE

Angers, Maine-et-Loire   Grainville, Seine-Inférieure
Arganchy, Calvados   Léon, Finisterre
Argentan, Orne   Licques, Pas-de-Calais
Arques, Seine-Inférieure   Lisieux, Calvados
Aubigny, Pas-de-Calais   Lyons, Rhone
Aumale, Seine-Inférieure   Lyre, Eure
Avallon, Yonne   Mans, Le, Sarthe
Avranches, Manche   Mortain, Manche
Bayeux, Calvados   Poitou
Boulogne, Pas-de-Calais   Pont-de-l'Arche, Eure
Caen, Calvados   Pontigny, Yonne
Caux, Seine-Inférieure   Rouen, Seine-Inférieure
Coutances, Manche   St-Fromond, Manche
Douai, Nord   Sées, Orne
Eu, Somme   Sens, Yonne
Evreux, Eure   Tinchebrai, Orne
Fécamp, Seine-Inférieure   Tours, Indre-et-Loire
Fiennes, Pas-de-Calais   Valoignes, Manche

ITALY

Anagni   Palestrina   Trastevere
Florence   Perugia   Tusculum
Lavagna   Rome   Viterbo
Ostia   Spoleto

MISCELLANEOUS

Ghent   Holy Land, the   Hungary

UNIDENTIFIED

. . . . . ide   Langley   Thorpe
Brudella   Langton   Wareham
Greneford   Leyburn'   Whitchurch
Hayles   Middleton   Wigoan'
Hedeham   Sutton'   Wilton
Hetherington   Tetford

INDEX OF SUBJECTS

NOTE—Magna Carta and the Forest Charters are not indexed herein.

Investiture, 4
 in bishopric with pastoral staff, 3,
  91
 in prebend, 55

Jew. *See* Aaron
Jurisdiction. *See* Lincoln (10)
Justice, royal. *See* counties of—
 Huntingdon   Nottingham
 Lincoln   Oxford
Justiciar, the king's, 50
 See Geoffrey Fitz-Peter ; Seagrave,
  Stephen of

King, the, acts as surety, 95, 97
Knights, military tenants :
 of bishop. *See* Lincoln (7)
 of dean and chapter. *See* Lincoln
  (9)

Laga, 47
Landgable, 86–7, 104, 270
Lateran Councils. *See* Rome
Latrocinium, 51
Legate. *See*—
 Blois,   Langton,
  Henry of   Stephen
 Gualo   Pandulph
     Theobald
Legate's Council. *See* Westminster
Letters patent, 133–4, 136, 143, 160–6,
  184–5
Lights in church, 82
Loga, 206

Maneriolum. See Lincoln (3), Wil-
 lingthorpe
Manor, pledged to Aaron the Jew, 129,
  132
Manor house, 281
Manors. *See*—
 Ashbourne   Huntingdon
 Banbury   Ingham
 Biggleswade   Kilsby
 Brampton   Kirkby
 Caenby and   Moorside
  Glentham   Kirton in
 Caistor   Lindsey
 Cawthorpe   Knighton
 Chesterfield   Leicester
 Coxwold   Leighton
 Eagle   Bromswold
 Elkington,   Louth
  South   Mansfield
 Friesthorpe   Marston St
 Grimsby, Great   Lawrence
 Holme   Nettleham
  Spinney   Norton,
 Horley   Bishop
 Horncastle   Orston
 Hovingham   Sleaford

Manors—*cont.*
 Spaldwick   Welton by
 Stow St Mary   Lincoln
 Thorngate   Wickham,
 Tixover   co. Oxf.
 Torksey   Wickhambreux
 Walton in   Willingthorpe
  Aylesbury   Winthorpe
 Warkworth   Wooburn
 Wellingore
Mansio, 12, 189, 191, 198, 200, 205–6
Mansura, mensura, 63, 121, 205–6, 208,
  285
Mantle, demand for a, released by
  Richard I, 123
Map, 246
Maresium, 285
Mariecorn, a render to cathedral of one
  thrave of corn from every plough,
  206, 208
Market-place. *See* Eynsham ; Sleaford
Markets, 76, 129–30, 132. *See*—
 Banbury   Stow St Mary
 Biggleswade   Thame
 Leighton   Warden,
  Buzzard   Chipping
 Sleaford
Marlpit, 151
Marriage of girls, bequest for, 293
Mayor. *See* Lincoln (3)
Medicus, 250, 253
Mills, 71, 140, 142, 151. *See*—
 Bedford   Oxford
 Dorchester   Tame
 Huntingdon   Thames
 Kirkby *cum*   Walton [in
  Osgodby   Grantham]
Missal, 82
Moneyer. *See* Guthred
Murdrum, 51, 72, 124

Names of men of native descent, xvi
Names, uncommon and early :
 Achi   Baldric
 Adelidis   Basilia
 Adelina   Basing
 Adelis   Berard
 Adelm   Berenger
 Aiax   Bochard
 Ailred   Brand
 Ailric   Clarembald
 Aimeric   Colegrim
 Alberic   Colsuain
 Aldulf   Conrad
 Almeric   Dumping
 Alured,   Durand
  Alvered   Elfred
 Anselm   Erneis
 Ansfrid   Fawkes
 Arneuin   Froger
 Arnoul   Gerbod
 Asger   Gladwin
 Aucer   Godiva
 Azo   Goisfrid

INDEX OF SUBJECTS

349

Names, uncommon and early—*cont.*

Gossumus	Pandulph
Gundulf	Picot
Guthred	Reinfrid
Haimo	Remigius
Hardinc	Romfara
Hubald	Rotrodus
Imarus	Saier, Seyer
Imerus	Severic
Ingelram	Sigefrid
Ingelram *or*	Siward
Þig	Suartebrand
Jordan	Tebert
Ketel	Terricus
Lanfranc	Theobald
Leofric	Theodoric
Leuiet	Thurstan
Leving	Turchil
Louo	Ulf
Malger]	Urse
Manasser	Walchelin
Martell	Waldric
Maruuen	Walkelin
Mauger	Waltheof
Oddo	Warin
Odo	Wigot
Osgot	Wulfstan
Osulf	Wulfwig

Notary public. *See* Marlesford, John

Oil, holy, 64–5
Ornaments of church, 82
Outlawry, 136

Palfrey, 294
Panis benedictus, 82
Pannagium, 147, 150
Parcage, *parcagium*, 86–7, 104, 270
Park:
  licence to make, 129–30, 132, 138.
  See—

Buckden	Spaldwick
Lyddington	Thame

Parmenus, 46
Parochia, diocese, 78–9, 188, 191, 206
Pastoral staff, gift of, by the king, 3, 4
Peace, the king's, 34, 57, 98, 108, 115, 148
Peasants, free, xvi. *See* Villeins
Peers, judgement by, 36
Pensions from religious houses, 203
Pentecostals, 258–9, 265
Pestilence, the Black Death, 125
Peter's pence, 264
Pledge, *uadium*, 36, 44–5, 61, 284
Plegius, fideiussor, the king intervenes as, 94–6
Plough-team, 160–1
Pope, the:
  form of peace sent to king John by, 134–5
  reservation of benefices by, 231
  papal curia, 246
  See Legate

Porter, 294
Prebend:
  division of, 231–3
  held by force. *See* Thame
  seisin of, 55
  to be conferred on men of English birth, 231–2
  See Investiture
Prebendal court. *See* Asgarby [by Spilsby]
Prebendam, gifts *in*, 14, 25–8, 30, 32, 39–40, 49, 51–4, 58, 61–3, 71–4, 76, 78–80, 93, 105–7, 112, 118, 142, 198, 206, 211–12, 262
Prebends. *See* Bedford; Lincoln (3); Lincoln (12)
Precept by the king's own mouth, 118–19
Privileged churches. *See* St Albans
Procurations, 82, 213–15, 225–7
Protection, the king's, 73, 133
Purgation, 210–11
Purprestura, 124, 146, 149

Recognition:
  by ancient men of the wapentake, 78–9
  by ancient men of the city of Lincoln, 110–11
  by good men of the county, 24
  by lawful men, 67–8, 100, 146, 150, 184
  by lawful men of the halimote and wapentake, 116
  by regarders of the forest, 150
Rector regis et regni. See Marshall, William
Reeve:
  the king's, 161, 176, 178
  See Hamon; John; Lincoln (3)
Religious houses. *See*—

Abbotsbury	Lacock
Abingdon	Leicester
Bardney	Licques
Barlings	Lincoln (3)
Battle	St Katherine
Belvoir	St Sepulchre
Bourne	Louth Park
Canterbury	Lyre
Cerne	Malmesbury
Chertsey	Markby
Cirencester	Merton
Clifford	Milton
Croyland	Missenden
Dorchester	Newhouse
Dover	Oseney
Elsham	Oxford, St
Evesham	Frideswide
Eynsham	Pershore
Gloucester	Peterborough
Hagnaby	Ramsey
Haverholme	Reading
Hyde	Revesby
Kirby Bellars	Rievaulx
Kirkstead	Roche

Printed and bound by CPI Group (UK) Ltd, Croydon, CR0 4YY

09/06/2025

14685698-0004